1983

LAW
and
BiOETHICS

PAULIST PRESS/New York, N.Y./Ramsey, N.J.

LAW and BIOETHICS

Texts with commentary on major U.S. court decisions

Edited by THOMAS A. SHANNON
and JO ANN MANFRA

DEDICATION

For our colleagues at WPI

Library of Congress
Catalog Card Number: 81-80876

ISBN: 0-8091-2353-3

Published by Paulist Press
545 Island Road, Ramsey, N.J. 07446

Printed and bound in the
United States of America

CONTENTS

V. NON-DISCLOSURE AND CONFIDENTIALITY

VI. ORGAN TRANSPLANTATION

VII. GENETICS

INTRODUCTION

Within the last few decades our society has witnessed developments in science and medicine resulting in technological interventions in human life never thought possible. Organs are shuttled almost routinely between different bodies with ever-increasing success. The recent birth of a child conceived *in vitro* suggests spectacular new possibilities with respect to the scientific control of human reproduction.

Scientific and medical advances, however, often outpace legal and ethical considerations of these processes. Dramatic new social and personal options become realities, but the long-range implications remain unknown. Traditional cultural values can be jeopardized, often unknowingly and frequently uncritically, by scientists boldly advancing the frontiers of medical knowledge.

In the present volume law and ethics are joined through a case law approach in considering questions raised by major scientific and medical developments. The selected cases appear to us to represent significant medico-legal decisions, defining specific rights and duties or having particularly far-reaching social consequences. Many are recent decisions; others are older and remain medico-legal "classics." All reflect a blend of legal principles, ethical theories, and personal or social values.

We have grouped the cases under rather traditional general headings with chapter introductions to each topic. In these introductions Dr. Shannon has written the commentary on the ethical dimensions of the cases, and is solely responsible for their contents, while Dr. Manfra is exclusively responsible for the commentary on the legal issues involved. From an ethical point of view some of the major themes are: identifying specific values and their functions within society, testing the relevance of these values for medical decision-making, and evaluating the possible consequences for society of specific policies based on these values. The law primarily speaks to the constitutionally protected rights of the individual and the legal standards and procedures necessary for asserting them. This gives rise to issues such as privacy, consent, disclosure, and competing interests.

We hope this casebook will serve as a valuable resource for those concerned with this increasingly perplexing dimension of modern American life.

I. ABORTION

1. THE ETHICAL ISSUES

At the heart of most discussions of the ethics of abortion is the complex question of under what circumstances, if any, it is morally permissible to kill a human being. Many traditions have stated that it is ethical directly to kill human beings in war, in self-defense, or as punishment for certain especially heinous crimes. Such instances involve a change in the victim's status from "innocent person" to "unjust aggressor," and some have postulated that abortion can be justified by describing the fetus as a type of "unjust aggressor." A second argument employs the concept of "indirect abortion." In other words, if the health needs of the mother so require it, treatment may be given that also, but indirectly and unintentionally, causes the death of the fetus. For example, Roman Catholic ethics have allowed a cancerous uterus to be removed, even though it contained a fetus. Yet a third attitude toward abortion derives from projections about a fetus's quality of life, typically based on either a disease or a predictably low social status. A fourth position attempts to remove the major ethical dilemma from the debate by defining abortion as a separation of the fetus from its mother. Thus while fetal death will often be the outcome of such a separation, it is neither a necessary element of the definition nor a consequence that the mother may demand. Many critics, of course, find none of these positions wholly palatable and base their arguments against abortion on the fetus's right to life.

An important ethical dimension of abortion involves the relation of second and third parties to a pregnant woman. What rights, if any, does the husband of a pregnant woman have with respect to an abortion decision? And what rights, if any, do parents have with respect to a minor daughter who desires an abortion? The court decisions, at present, suggest that the state cannot permit others to do what it itself cannot do—that is, stop an abortion during the first trimester. In so arguing, courts offer several value judgments about marriage and the family. For example, they assume that marriage partners or family members must be seen as autonomous individuals with rights that may come into conflict. Such a view stands in sharp contrast to the "organic" view of marriage and families. An acceptance of the organic model, which does not *a priori* exclude abortions, clearly would approach the problem in a different way. Neither model should, it is presumed, be given priority without justification. Especially is this true when a family is dealing with a minor child who is pregnant. The courts correctly note that such a situation may represent the final breakdown in parent-child relations.

3

The funding of abortions constitutes another series of issues. Federal and state subsidies through Medicare and Medicaid finance in part or in full a variety of health-care needs. Cancer and renal failure provide examples of diseases for which important funding has been allocated. Should unwanted pregnancy also merit a share of these health-care funds? A second question has to do with the seeming discrimination, on the federal level, involved in routinely providing monies for perinatal care, but making funding for abortions contingent on decisions of local legislators. Yet another aspect of the federal funding of abortion centers on the argument that abortion is cheaper than perinatal care and aid to dependent children. A fourth dimension suggests that a refusal to fund abortions discriminates against the poor because they typically cannot afford such treatment.

While recognizing that not each and every health-related problem can or ought to be subsidized, nonetheless reasonableness, fairness, and consistency need to be introduced into all deliberations about funding. It is unclear why some programs enjoy a privileged status and why others that primarily benefit the poor are the subject of almost continual attack. The evaluation of programs should not rest on the values of any small group of individuals. Legislative resolution of such social questions appears to be the most equitable way to make such key decisions. This allows for public debate, ensuring the presentation of a broad spectrum of values and positions.

2. THE LEGAL ISSUES

In *Roe* a woman's decision whether or not to terminate her pregnancy is protected through its inclusion in the right of personal privacy—one of those rights that are "fundamental" or "implicit" in the concept of ordered liberty"—that the United States Supreme Court, in what has been referred to as a substantive due process approach, located in the Due Process Clause of the Fourteenth Amendment of the federal Constitution.

Whenever the restriction of "fundamental rights" is the subject of constitutional adjudication, the Court may apply a higher or "strict standard of scrutiny," as it is termed. In short, if a state infringes upon a constitutionally protected fundamental right, it must assert a "compelling interest." In *Roe* the challenged Texas law making it a crime to procure or attempt to procure an abortion, except on medical advice for the purpose of saving the life of the mother, failed to show such state interest during the first trimester of pregnancy and is therefore deemed unconstitutional. According to the Court, the "abortion decision and its effectuation must be left to the medical judgment of the pregnant woman's attending physician" during the first trimester.

In subsequent cases the Court invalidates other types of restrictions on a woman's decision to terminate pregnancy. For example, in *Planned Parenthood* the Court views certain provisions in the Missouri abortion statute, such as spousal consent and *blanket* parental consent for minors during the first trimester, as "absolute obstacles" to a woman's freedom of choice, and therefore declares them unconstitutional. But provisions requiring a woman's written consent to an abortion during the first twelve weeks of pregnancy, as well as routine medical reporting and recordkeeping concerning abortions, are upheld as not unduly burdensome to a woman's decision to terminate pregnancy.

With the hindsight provided by *Beal* and *Maher,* the Court's position that any requirement respecting a lawful abortion is not unconstitutional, unless it unduly burdens the right to seek an abortion, is especially significant. Indeed, in *Maher* the Court illuminates its statement in *Roe* that "the right [of privacy] is not absolute and is subject to some limitations." It asserts unequivocally that "*Roe* did not declare an unqualified constitutional right to an abortion." Certainly *Roe* clearly asserts that at some point the state's interest in maternal health and prenatal life becomes dominant. During the second trimester, therefore, the state can "regulate the abortion procedure in ways that are reasonably related to maternal health." And in the third trimester the state can even "proscribe abortion except where it is necessary, in appropriate medical judgment, for the preservation of the life or health of the mother."

With *Maher* we know that—unless there is an unduly burdensome interference with a woman's freedom to decide whether or not to terminate her pregnancy—a state restriction can be sustained under the less demanding test of rationality even during the first trimester. In other words, the regulation need only be "rationally related" to a "constitutionally permissible" purpose rather than grounded in a "compelling state interest."

Thus in *Beal* and *Maher* the Court concludes, respectively, that neither Title XIX of the Social Security Act (that is, the statute establishing the Medicaid program) nor the United States Constitution requires states to pay for nontherapeutic abortions.

The issue of parental consent for minors desiring abortions is central in *Bellotti.* During the complex course of this litigation—explained in the case at hand—the Massachusetts Supreme Judicial Court had authoritatively interpreted that state's statute regulating a minor's access to abortions as requiring that every minor desiring an abortion, no matter how mature and capable of informed decision-making, must receive the consent of both parents or a Superior Court justice. On appeal the United States Supreme Court points out that, because of their vulnerability and need for parental attention, children's rights cannot be equated with those of adults. The state, therefore, "is entitled to adjust its legal system to account for" these special needs. But an abortion decision, says the Court, is of a "unique nature," and requires a state "to act with particular sensitivity when it legislates to foster parental involvement in this matter." Within this context, the justices conclude that if a state desires to require parental consent, then it must also provide an alternative procedure. This alternative must allow the pregnant minor to obtain an independent judgment that either she is mature and capable enough to make the abortion decision on her own or else that the abortion is in her best interests. (In the latter case, the judge may consider parental involvement in the decision.) Since the construed Massachusetts statute fell short of satisfying these standards, the Supreme Court affirms the District Court's finding that the statute is unconstitutional.*

In *Harris* the United States Supreme Court applies the "rationally related" standard to the so-called Hyde amendment to Medicaid coverage for "medically necessary" services for the poor, reversing the District Court's finding that the amended law—which disallows federal funds for abortions except where a pregnant woman's life is in danger or she is a victim of rape or incest—is unconstitutional. Reaffirming its ruling in *Roe* that a woman has a right to choose to have an abortion, the Court concludes that neither Medicaid law nor the Constitution requires state *or federal* governments to pay for such a procedure. In its decision, the majority reasons that "although the government may not place obstacles in the path of a woman's exercise of her freedom of choice, it need not remove those not of its own creation." And "indigency falls in the latter category," concludes the Court. Refusing to extend so-called suspect classification to include poor people, the Court only has to—and *does*—find that the amended law is "rationally related" to the "governmental objective of protecting potential life" rather than that it emanates from a "compelling state interest."

*After this reader had gone to press, the Massachusetts legislature on June 5, 1980 amended the state's parental consent statute to comport with *Bellotti* (1980 Mass. Adv. Legis. Serv.). And on March 23, 1981 the U.S. Supreme Court, in *H.L. v. Matheson*, 49 U.S.L.W. 4255, upheld a Utah statute requiring a doctor to notify a girl's parents prior to terminating her pregnancy, at least if the girl was an "immature" minor still dependent on her parents.

ROE V. WADE

Supreme Court of the United States, 1973.
410 U. S. 113, 93 S.Ct. 705, 35 L.Ed.2d 147.

MR. JUSTICE BLACKMUN delivered the opinion of the Court.

This Texas federal appeal and its Georgia companion, *Doe v. Bolton, post,* p. 179, present constitutional challenges to state criminal abortion legislation. The Texas statutes under attack here are typical of those that have been in effect in many States for approximately a century. The Georgia statutes, in contrast, have a modern cast and are a legislative product that, to an extent at least, obviously reflects the influences of recent attitudinal change, of advancing medical knowledge and techniques, and of new thinking about an old issue.

We forthwith acknowledge our awareness of the sensitive and emotional nature of the abortion controversy, of the vigorous opposing views, even among physicians, and of the deep and seemingly absolute convictions that the subject inspires. One's philosophy, one's experiences, one's exposure to the raw edges of human existence, one's religious training, one's attitudes toward life and family and their values, and the moral standards one establishes and seeks to observe, are all likely to influence and to color one's thinking and conclusions about abortion.

In addition, population growth, pollution, poverty, and racial overtones tend to complicate and not to simplify the problem.

Our task, of course, is to resolve the issue by constitutional measurement, free of emotion and of predilection. We seek earnestly to do this, and, because we do, we have inquired into, and in this opinion place some emphasis upon, medical and medical-legal history and what that history reveals about man's attitudes toward the abortion procedure over the centuries. We bear in mind, too, Mr. Justice Holmes' admonition in his now-vindicated dissent in *Lochner v. New York,* 198 U. S. 45, 76 (1905):

> "[The Constitution] is made for people of fundamentally differing views, and the accident of our finding certain opinions natural and familiar or novel and even shocking ought not to conclude our judgment upon the question whether statutes embodying them conflict with the Constitution of the United States."

I

The Texas statutes that concern us here are Arts. 1191–1194 and 1196 of the State's Penal Code.[1] These make it a crime to "procure an abortion," as therein defined, or to attempt one, except with respect to "an abortion procured or attempted by medical advice for the purpose of saving the life of the mother." Similar statutes are in existence in a majority of the States.[2]

Texas first enacted a criminal abortion statute in 1854. Texas Laws 1854, c. 49, § 1, set forth in 3 H. Gammel, Laws of Texas 1502 (1898). This was soon modified into language that has remained substantially unchanged to the present time. See Texas Penal Code of 1857, c. 7, Arts. 531–536; G. Paschal, Laws of Texas, Arts. 2192–2197 (1866); Texas Rev. Stat., c. 8, Arts. 536–541 (1879); Texas Rev. Crim. Stat., Arts. 1071–1076 (1911). The final article in each of these compilations provided the same exception, as does the present Article 1196, for an abortion by "medical advice for the purpose of saving the life of the mother."[3]

II

Jane Roe,[4] a single woman who was residing in Dallas County, Texas, instituted this federal action in March 1970 against the District Attorney of the county. She sought a declaratory judgment that the Texas criminal abortion statutes were unconstitutional on their face, and an injunction restraining the defendant from enforcing the statutes.

Roe alleged that she was unmarried and pregnant; that she wished to terminate her pregnancy by an abortion "performed by a competent, licensed physician, under safe, clinical conditions"; that she was unable to get a "legal" abortion in Texas because her life did not appear to be threatened by the continuation of her pregnancy; and that she could not afford to travel to another jurisdiction in order to secure a legal abortion under safe conditions. She claimed that the Texas statutes were unconstitutionally vague and that they abridged her right of personal privacy, protected by the First, Fourth, Fifth, Ninth, and Fourteenth Amendments. By an amendment to her complaint Roe purported to sue "on behalf of herself and all other women" similarly situated.

James Hubert Hallford, a licensed physician, sought and was granted leave to intervene in Roe's action. In his complaint he alleged that he had been arrested previously for violations of the Texas abortion statutes and that two such prosecutions were pending against him. He described conditions of patients who came to him seeking abortions, and he claimed that for many cases he, as a physician, was unable to determine whether they fell within or outside the exception recognized by Article 1196. He alleged that, as a consequence, the statutes were vague and uncertain, in violation of the Fourteenth Amendment, and that they violated his own and his patients' rights to privacy in the doctor-patient relationship and his own right to practice medicine, rights he claimed were guaranteed by the First, Fourth, Fifth, Ninth, and Fourteenth Amendments.

John and Mary Doe,[5] a married couple, filed a companion complaint to that of Roe. They also named the District Attorney as defendant, claimed like constitutional deprivations, and sought declaratory and injunctive relief. The Does alleged that they were a childless couple; that Mrs. Doe was suffering from a "neural-chemical" disorder; that her physician had "advised her to avoid pregnancy until such time as her condition has materially improved" (although a pregnancy at the present time would not present a "serious risk" to her life); that, pursuant to medical advice, she had discontinued use of birth control pills; and that if she should become pregnant, she would want to terminate the pregnancy by an abortion performed by a competent, licensed physician under safe, clinical conditions. By an amendment to their complaint, the Does purported to sue "on behalf of themselves and all couples similarly situated."

The two actions were consolidated and heard together by a duly convened three-judge district court. The suits thus presented the situations of the pregnant single woman, the childless couple, with the wife not pregnant, and the licensed practicing physician, all joining in the attack on the Texas criminal abortion statutes. Upon the filing of affidavits, motions were made for dismissal and for summary judgment. The court held that Roe and members of her class, and Dr. Hallford, had standing to sue and presented justiciable controversies, but that the Does had failed to allege facts sufficient to state a present controversy and did not have standing. It concluded that, with respect to the requests for a declaratory judgment, abstention was not warranted. On the merits, the District Court held that the "fundamental right of single women and married persons to choose whether to have children is protected by the Ninth Amendment, through the Fourteenth Amendment," and that the Texas criminal abortion statutes were void on their face because they were both unconstitutionally vague and constituted an overbroad infringement of the plaintiffs' Ninth Amendment rights. The court then held that abstention was warranted with respect to the requests for an injunction. It therefore dismissed the Does' complaint, declared the abortion statutes void, and dismissed the application for injunctive relief. 314 F. Supp. 1217, 1225 (ND Tex. 1970).

The plaintiffs Roe and Doe and the intervenor Hallford, pursuant to 28 U. S. C. § 1253, have appealed to this Court from that part of the District Court's judgment denying the injunction. The defendant District Attorney has purported to cross-appeal, pursuant to the same statute, from the court's grant of declaratory relief to Roe and Hallford. Both sides also have taken protective appeals to the United States Court of Appeals for the Fifth Circuit. That court ordered the appeals held in abeyance pending decision here. We postponed decision on jurisdiction to the hearing on the merits. 402 U. S. 941 (1971).

III

It might have been preferable if the defendant, pursuant to our Rule 20, had presented to us a petition for certiorari before judgment in the Court of Appeals with respect to the granting of the plaintiffs' prayer for declaratory relief. Our decisions in *Mitchell v. Donovan,* 398 U.S. 427 (1970), and *Gunn v. University Committee,* 399 U.S. 383 (1970), are to the effect that § 1253 does not authorize an appeal to this Court from the grant or denial of declaratory relief alone. We conclude, nevertheless, that those decisions do not foreclose our review of both the injunctive and the declaratory aspects of a case of this kind when it is properly here, as this one is, on appeal under § 1253 from specific denial of injunctive relief, and the arguments as to both aspects are necessarily identical. See *Carter v. Jury Comm'n,* 396 U.S. 320 (1970); *Florida Lime Growers v. Jacobsen,* 362 U.S. 73, 80–81 (1960).

It would be destructive of time and energy for all concerned were we to rule otherwise. Cf. *Doe v. Bolton, post,* p. 179.

IV

We are next confronted with issues of justiciability, standing, and abstention. Have Roe and the Does established that "personal stake in the outcome of the controversy," *Baker v. Carr,* 369 U.S. 186, 204 (1962), that insures that "the dispute sought to be adjudicated will be presented in an adversary context and in a form historically viewed as capable of judicial resolution," *Flast v. Cohen,* 392 U.S. 83, 101 (1968), and *Sierra Club v. Morton,* 405 U.S. 727, 732, (1972)? And what effect did the pendency of criminal abortion charges against Dr. Hallford in state court have upon the propriety of the federal court's granting relief to him as a plaintiff-intervenor?

A. *Jane Roe.* Despite the use of the pseudonym, no suggestion is made that Roe is a fictitious person. For purposes of her case, we accept as true, and as established, her existence; her pregnant state, as of the inception of her suit in March 1970 and as late as May 21 of that year when she filed an alias affidavit with the District Court; and her inability to obtain a legal abortion in Texas.

Viewing Roe's case as of the time of its filing and thereafter until as late as May, there can be little dispute that it then presented a case or controversy and that, wholly apart from the class aspects, she, as a pregnant single woman thwarted by the Texas criminal abortion laws, had standing to challenge those statutes. *Abele v. Markle,* 452 F. 2d 1121, 1125 (CA2 1971); *Crossen v. Breckenridge,* 446 F. 2d 883, 838–839 (CA6 1971); *Poe v. Menghini,* 339 F. Supp. 986, 990–991 (Kan. 1972). See *Truax v. Raich,* 239 U.S. 33 (1915). Indeed, we do not read the appellee's brief as really asserting anything to the contrary. The "logical nexus between the status asserted and the claim sought to be adjudicated," *Flast v. Cohen,* 392 U.S., at 102, and the necessary degree of contentiousness, *Golden v. Zwickler,* 394 U.S. 103 (1969), are both present.

The appellee notes, however, that the record does not disclose that Roe was pregnant at the time of the District Court hearing on May 22, 1970,[6] or on the following June 17 when the court's opinion and judgment were filed. And he suggests that Roe's case must now be moot because she and all other members of her class are no longer subject to any 1970 pregnancy.

The usual rule in federal cases is that an actual controversy must exist at stages of appellate or certiorari review, and not simply at the date the action is initiated. *United States v. Munsingwear, Inc.,* 340 U. S. 36 (1950); *Golden v. Zwickler, supra; SEC* v. *Medical Committee for Human Rights,* 404 U. S. 403 (1972).

But when, as here, pregnancy is a significant fact in the litigation, the normal 266-day human gestation period is so short that the pregnancy will come to term before the usual appellate process is complete. If that termination makes a case moot, pregnancy litigation seldom will survive much beyond the trial stage, and appellate review will be effectively denied. Our law should not be that rigid. Pregnancy often comes more than once to the same woman, and in the general population, if man is to survive, it will always be with us. Pregnancy provides a classic justification for a conclusion of nonmootness. It truly could be "capable of repetition, yet evading review." *Southern Pacific Terminal Co. v. ICC, 219 U. S. 498, 515* (1911). *See Moore v. Ogilvie,* 394 U. S. 814, 816 (1969); *Carroll v. Princess Anne,* 393 U. S. 175, 178–179 (1968); *United States v. W. T. Grant Co.,* 345 U. S. 629, 632–633 (1953).

We, therefore, agree with the District Court that Jane Roe had standing to undertake this litigation, that she presented a justiciable controversy, and that the termination of her 1970 pregnancy has not rendered her case moot.

B. *Dr. Hallford.* The doctor's position is different. He entered Roe's litigation as a plaintiff-intervenor, alleging in his complaint that he:

> "[I]n the past has been arrested for violating the Texas Abortion Laws and at the present time stands charged by indictment with violating said laws in the Criminal District Court of Dallas County, Texas to-wit: (1) The State of Texas vs. James H. Hallford, No. C-69-5307-IH, and (2) The State of Texas vs. James H. Hallford, No. C-69-2524-H. In both cases the defendant is charged with abortion. . . ."

In his application for leave to intervene, the doctor made like representations as to the abortion charges pending in the state court. These representations were also repeated in the affidavit he executed and filed in support of his motion for summary judgment.

Dr. Hallford is, therefore, in the position of seeking, in a federal court, declaratory and injunctive relief with respect to the same statutes under which he stands charged in criminal prosecutions simultaneously pending in state court. Although he stated that he has been arrested in the past for violating the State's abortion laws, he makes no allegation of any substantial and immediate threat to any federally protected right that cannot be asserted in his defense against the state prosecutions. Neither is there any allegation of harassment or bad-faith prosecution. In order to escape the rule articulated in the cases cited in the next paragraph of this opinion that, absent harassment and bad faith, a defendant in a pending state criminal case cannot affirmatively challenge in federal court the statutes under which the State is prosecuting him, Dr. Hallford seeks to distinguish his status as a present state defendant from his status as a "potential future defendant" and to assert only the latter for standing purposes here.

We see no merit in that distinction. Our decision in *Samuels* v. *Mackell,* 401 U. S. 66 (1971), compels the conclusion that the District Court erred when it granted declaratory relief to Dr. Hallford instead of refraining from so doing. The court, of course, was correct in refusing to grant injunctive relief to the doctor. The reasons supportive of that action, however, are those expressed in *Samuels* v. *Mackell, supra,* and in *Younger v. Harris,* 401 U. S. 37 (1971); *Boyle v. Landry,* 401 U. S. 77 (1971); *Perez v. Ledesma,* 401 U. S. 82 (1971); and *Byrne v. Karalexis,* 401 U. S. 216 (1971). See also *Dombrowski v. Pfister,* 380 U. S. 479 (1965). We note, in passing, that *Younger* and its companion cases were decided after the three-judge District Court decision in this case.

Dr. Hallford's complaint in intervention, therefore, is to be dismissed.[7] He is remitted to his defenses in the state criminal proceedings against him. We reverse the judgment of the District Court insofar as it granted Dr. Hallford relief and failed to dismiss his complaint in intervention.

C. *The Does.* In view of our ruling as to Roe's standing in her case, the issue of the Does' standing in their case has little significance. The claims they assert are essentially the same as those of Roe, and they attack the same statutes. Nevertheless, we briefly note the Does' posture.

Their pleadings present them as a childless married couple, the woman not being pregnant, who have no desire to have children at this time because of their having received medical advice that Mrs. Doe should avoid pregnancy, and for "other highly personal reasons." But they "fear . . . they may face the prospect of becoming parents." And if pregnancy ensues, they "would want to terminate" it by an abortion. They assert an inability to obtain an abortion legally in Texas and, consequently, the prospect of obtaining an illegal abortion there or of going outside Texas to some place where the procedure could be obtained legally and competently.

We thus have as plaintiffs a married couple who have, as their asserted immediate and present injury, only an alleged "detrimental effect upon [their] marital happiness" because they are forced to "the choice of refraining from normal sexual relations or of endangering Mary Doe's health through a possible pregnancy." Their claim is that sometime in the future Mrs. Doe might become pregnant because of possible failure of contraceptive measures, and at that time in the future she might want an abortion that might then be illegal under the Texas statutes.

This very phrasing of the Does' position reveals its speculative character. Their alleged injury rests on possible future contraceptive failure, possible future pregnancy, possible future impairment of health. Any one or more of these several possibilities may not take place and all may not combine. In the Does' estimation, these possibilities might have some real or imagined impact upon their marital happiness. But we are not prepared to say that the bare allegation of so indirect an injury is sufficient to present an actual case or controversy. *Younger v. Harris,* 401 U. S., at 41–42; *Golden v. Zwickler,* 394 U. S., at 109–110; *Abele v. Markle,* 452 F. 2d, at 1124–1125; *Crossen v. Breckenridge,* 446 F. 2d, at 839. The Does' claim falls far short of those resolved otherwise in the cases that the Does urge upon us, namely, *Investment Co. Institute v. Camp,* 401 U. S. 617 (1971); *Data Processing Service v. Camp,* 397 U. S. 150 (1970); and *Epperson v. Arkansas,* 393 U. S. 97 (1968). See also *Truax v. Raich,* 239 U. S. 33 (1915).

The Does therefore are not appropriate plaintiffs in this litigation. Their complaint was properly dismissed by the District Court, and we affirm that dismissal.

V

The principal thrust of appellant's attack on the Texas statutes is that they improperly invade a right, said to be possessed by the pregnant woman, to choose to terminate her pregnancy. Appellant would discover this right in the concept of personal "liberty" embodied in the Fourteenth Amendment's Due Process Clause; or in personal, marital, familial, and sexual privacy said to be protected by the Bill of Rights or its penumbras, see *Griswold* v. *Connecticut,* 381 U. S. 479 (1965); *Eisenstadt v. Baird,* 405 U. S. 438 (1972); *id.,* at 460 (WHITE, J., concurring in result); or among those rights reserved to the people by the Ninth Amendment, *Griswold v. Connecticut,* 381 U. S., at 486 (Goldberg, J., concurring). Before addressing this claim, we feel it desirable briefly to survey, in several aspects, the history of abortion, for such insight as that history may afford us, and then to examine the state · purposes and interests behind the criminal abortion laws.

VI

It perhaps is not generally appreciated that the restrictive criminal abortion laws in effect in a majority of States today are of relatively recent vintage. Those laws, generally proscribing abortion or its attempt at any time during pregnancy except when necessary to preserve the pregnant woman's life, are not of ancient or even of common-law origin. Instead, they derive from statutory changes effected, for the most part, in the latter half of the 19th century.

1. *Ancient attitudes.* These are not capable of precise determination. We are told that at the time of the Persian Empire abortifacients were known and that criminal abortions were severely punished.[8] We are also told, however, that abortion was practiced in Greek times as well as in the Roman Era,[9] and that "it was resorted to without scruple."[10] The Ephesian, Soranos, often described as the greatest of the ancient gynecologists, appears to have been generally opposed to Rome's prevailing free-abortion practices. He found it necessary to think first of the life of the mother, and he resorted to abortion when, upon this standard, he felt the procedure advisable.[11] Greek and Roman law afforded little protection to the unborn. If abortion was prosecuted in some places, it seems to have been based on a concept of a violation of the father's right to his offspring. Ancient religion did not bar abortion.[12]

2. *The Hippocratic Oath.* What then of the famous Oath that has stood so long as the ethical guide of the medical profession and that bears the name of the great Greek (460(?)–377(?) B. C.), who has been described as the Father of Medicine, the "wisest and the greatest practitioner of his art," and the "most important and most complete medical personality of antiquity," who dominated the medical schools of his time, and who typified the sum of the medical knowledge of the past?[13] The Oath varies somewhat according to the particular translation, but in any translation the content is clear: "I will give no deadly medicine to anyone if asked, nor suggest any such counsel; and in like manner I will not give to a woman a pessary to produce abortion,"[14] or "I will neither give a deadly drug to anybody if asked for it, nor will I make a suggestion to this effect. Similarly, I will not give to a woman an abortive remedy."[15]

Although the Oath is not mentioned in any of the principal briefs in this case or in *Doe v. Bolton, post,* p. 179, it represents the apex of the development of strict ethical concepts in medicine, and its influence endures to this day. Why did not the authority of Hippocrates dissuade abortion practice in his time and that of Rome? The late Dr. Edelstein provides us with a theory:[16] The Oath was not uncontested even in Hippocrates' day; only the Pythagorean school of philosophers frowned upon the related act of suicide. Most Greek thinkers, on the other hand, commended abortion, at least prior to viability. See Plato, *Republic*, V, 461; Aristotle, *Politics*, VII, 1335b 25. For the Pythagoreans, however, it was a matter of dogma. For them the embryo was animate from the moment of conception, and abortion meant destruction of a living being. The abortion clause of the Oath, therefore, "echoes Pythagorean doctrines," and "[i]n no other stratum of Greek opinion were such views held or proposed in the same spirit of uncompromising austerity."[17]

Dr. Edelstein then concludes that the Oath originated in a group representing only a small segment of Greek opinion and that it certainly was not accepted by all ancient physicians. He points out that medical writings down to Galen (A. D. 130–200) "give evidence of the violation of almost every one of its injunctions."[18] But with the end of antiquity a decided change took place. Resistance against suicide and against abortion became common. The Oath came to be popular. The emerging teachings of Christianity were in agreement with the Pythagorean ethics. The Oath "became the nucleus of all medical ethics" and "was applauded as the embodiment of truth." Thus, suggests Dr. Edelstein, it is "a Pythagorean manifesto and not the expression of an absolute standard of medical conduct."[19]

This, it seems to us, is a satisfactory and acceptable explanation of the Hippocratic Oath's apparent rigidity. It enables us to understand, in historical context, a long-accepted and revered statement of medical ethics.

3. *The common law.* It is undisputed that at common law, abortion performed *before* "quickening"—the first recognizable movement of the fetus *in utero,* appearing usually from the 16th to the 18th week of pregnancy[20]—was not an indictable offense.[21] The absence of a common-law crime for pre-quickening abortion appears to have developed from a confluence of earlier philosophical, theological, and civil and canon law concepts of when life begins. These disciplines variously approached the question in terms of the point at which the embryo or fetus became "formed" or recognizably human, or in terms of when a "person" came into being, that is, infused with a "soul" or "animated." A loose consensus evolved in early English law that these events occurred at some point between conception and live birth.[22] This was "mediate animation." Although Christian theology and the canon law came to fix the point of animation at 40 days for a male and 80 days for a female, a view that persisted until the 19th century, there was otherwise little agreement about the precise time of formation or animation. There was agreement, however, that prior to this point the fetus was to be regarded as part of the mother, and its destruction, therefore, was not homicide. Due to continued uncertainty about the precise time when animation occurred, to the lack of any empirical basis for the 40–80-day view, and perhaps to Aquinas' definition of movement as one of the two first principles of life, Bracton focused upon quickening as the critical point. The significance of quickening was echoed by later common-law scholars and found its way into the received common law in this country.

Whether abortion of a *quick* fetus was a felony at common law, or even a lesser crime, is still disputed. Bracton, writing early in the 13th century, thought it homicide.[23] But the later and predominant view, following the great common-law scholars, has been that it was, at most, a lesser offense. In a frequently cited passage, Coke took the position that abortion of a woman "quick with childe" is "a great misprision, and no murder."[24] Blackstone followed, saying that while abortion after quickening had once been considered manslaughter (though not murder), "modern law" took a less severe view.[25] A recent review of the common-law precedents argues, however, that these precedents contradict Coke and that even postquickening abortion was never established as a common-law crime.[26] This is of some importance because while most American courts ruled, in holding or dictum, that abortion of an unquickened fetus was not criminal under their received common law,[27] others followed Coke in stating that abortion of a quick fetus was a "misprision," a term they translated to mean "misdemeanor."[28] That their reliance on Coke on this aspect of the law was uncritical and, apparently in all the reported cases, dictum (due probably to the paucity of common-law prosecutions for postquickening abortion), makes it now appear doubtful that abortion was ever firmly established as a common-law crime even with respect to the destruction of a quick fetus.

4. *The English statutory law.* England's first criminal abortion statute, Lord Ellenborough's Act, 43 Geo. 3, c. 58, came in 1803. It made abortion of a quick fetus, § 1, a capital crime, but in § 2 it provided lesser penalties for the felony of abortion before quickening, and thus preserved the "quickening" distinction. This contrast was continued in the general revision of 1828, 9 Geo. 4, c. 31, § 13. It disappeared, however, together with the death penalty, in 1837, 7 Will. 4 & 1 Vict., c. 85, § 6, and did not reappear in the Offenses Against the Person Act of 1861, 24 & 25 Vict., c. 100, § 59, that formed the core of English anti-abortion law until the liberalizing reforms of 1967. In 1929, the Infant Life (Preservation) Act, 19 & 20 Geo. 5, c. 34, came into being. Its emphasis was upon the destruction of "the life of a child capable of being born alive." It made a willful act performed with the necessary intent a felony. It contained a proviso that one was not to be found guilty of the offense "unless it is proved that the act which caused the death of the child was not done in good faith for the purpose only of preserving the life of the mother."

A seemingly notable development in the English law was the case of *Rex v. Bourne,* [1939] 1 K. B. 687. This case apparently answered in the affirmative the question whether an abortion necessary to preserve the life of the pregnant woman was excepted from the criminal penalties of the 1861 Act. In his instructions to the jury, Judge Macnaghten referred to the 1929 Act, and observed that the Act related to "the case where a child is killed by a willful act at the time when it is being delivered in the ordinary course of nature." *Id.,* at 691. He concluded that the 1861 Act's use of the word "unlawfully," imported the same meaning expressed by the specific proviso in the 1929 Act, even though there was no mention of preserving the mother's life in the 1861 Act. He then construed the phrase "preserving the life of the mother" broadly, that is, "in a reasonable sense," to include a serious and permanent threat to the mother's *health,* and instructed the jury to acquit Dr. Bourne if it found he had acted in a good-faith belief that the abortion was necessary for this purpose. *Id.,* at 693–694. The jury did acquit.

Recently, Parliament enacted a new abortion law. This is the Abortion Act of 1967, 15 & 16 Eliz. 2, c. 87. The Act permits a licensed physician to perform an abortion where two other licensed physicians agree (a) "that the continuance of the pregnancy would involve risk to the life of the pregnant woman, or of injury to the physical or mental health of the pregnant woman or any existing children of her family, greater than if the pregnancy were terminated," or (b) "that there is a substantial risk that if the child were born it would suffer from such physical or mental abnormalities as to be seriously handicapped." The Act also provides that, in making this determination, "account may be taken of the pregnant woman's actual or reasonably foreseeable environment." It also permits a physician, without the concurrence of others, to terminate a pregnancy where he is of the good-faith opinion that the abortion "is immediately necessary to save the life or to prevent grave permanent injury to the physical or mental health of the pregnant woman."

5. *The American law.* In this country, the law in effect in all but a few States until mid-19th century was the pre-existing English common law. Connecticut, the first State to enact abortion legislation, adopted in 1821 that part of Lord Ellenborough's Act that related to a woman "quick with child."[29] The death penalty was not imposed. Abortion before quickening was made a crime in that State only in 1860.[30] In 1828, New York enacted legislation[31] that, in two respects, was to serve as a model for early anti-abortion statutes. First, while barring destruction of an unquickened fetus as well as a quick fetus, it made the former only a misdemeanor, but the latter second-degree manslaughter. Second, it incorporated a concept of therapeutic abortion by providing that an abortion was excused if it "shall have been necessary to preserve the life of such mother, or shall have been advised by two physicians to be necessary for such purpose." By 1840, when Texas had received the common law,[32] only eight American States had statutes dealing with abortion.[33] It was not until after the War Between the States that legislation began generally to replace the common law. Most of these initial statutes dealt severely with abortion after quickening but were lenient with it before quickening. Most punished attempts equally with completed abortions. While many statutes included the exception for an abortion thought by one or more physicians to be necessary to save the mother's life, that provision soon disappeared and the typical law required that the procedure actually be necessary for that purpose.

Gradually, in the middle and late 19th century the quickening distinction disappeared from statutory law of most States and the degree of the offense and the penalties were increased. By the end of the 1950's, a large majority of the jurisdictions banned abortion, however and whenever performed, unless done to save or preserve the life of the mother.[34] The exceptions, Alabama and the District of Columbia, permitted abortion to preserve the mother's health.[35] Three States permitted abortions that were not "unlawfully" performed or that were not "without lawful justification," leaving interpretation of those standards to the courts.[36] In the past several years, however, a trend toward liberalization of abortion statutes has resulted in adoption, by about one-third of the States, of less stringent laws, most of them patterned after the ALI Model Penal Code, § 230.3,[37] set forth as Appendix B to the opinion in *Doe v. Bolton, post,* p. 205.

It is thus apparent that at common law, at the time of the adoption of our Constitution, and throughout the major portion of the 19th century, abortion was viewed with less disfavor than under most American statutes currently in effect. Phrasing it another way, a woman enjoyed a substantially broader right to terminate a pregnancy than she does in most States today. At least with respect to the early stage of pregnancy, and very possibly without such a limitation, the opportunity to make this choice was present in this country well into the 19th century. Even later, the law continued for some time to treat less punitively an abortion procured in early pregnancy.

6. *The position of the American Medical Association.* The anti-abortion mood prevalent in this country in the late 19th century was shared by the medical profession. Indeed, the attitude of the profession may have played a significant role in the enactment of stringent criminal abortion legislation during that period.

An AMA Committee on Criminal Abortion was appointed in May 1857. It presented its report, 12 Trans. of the Am. Med. Assn. 73–78 (1859), to the Twelfth Annual Meeting. That report observed that the Committee had been appointed to investigate criminal abortion "with a view to its general suppression." It deplored abortion and its frequency and it listed three causes of "this general demoralization":

> "The first of these causes is a wide-spread popular ignorance of the true character of the crime—a belief, even among mothers themselves, that the foetus is not alive till after the period of quickening.
>
> "The second of the agents alluded to is the fact that the profession themselves are frequently supposed careless of foetal life. . . .
>
> "The third reason of the frightful extent of this crime is found in the grave defects of our laws, both common and statute, as regards the independent and actual existence of the child before birth, as a living being. These errors, which are sufficient in most instances to prevent conviction, are based, and only based, upon mistaken and exploded medical dogmas. With strange inconsistency, the law fully acknowledges the foetus in utero and its inherent rights, for civil purposes; while personally and as criminally affected, it fails to recognize it, and to its life as yet denies all protection." *Id.,* at 75–76.

The Committee then offered, and the Association adopted, resolutions protesting "against such unwarrantable destruction of human life," calling upon state legislatures to revise their abortion laws, and requesting the cooperation of state medical societies "in pressing the subject." *Id.,* at 28, 78.

In 1871 a long and vivid report was submitted by the Committee on Criminal Abortion. It ended with the observation, "We had to deal with human life. In a matter of less importance we could entertain no compromise. An honest judge on the bench would call things by their proper names. We could do no less." 22 Trans. of the Am. Med. Assn. 258 (1871). It proffered resolutions, adopted by the Association, *id.,* at 38–39, recommending, among other things, that it "be unlawful and unprofessional for any physician to induce abortion or premature labor, without the concurrent opinion of at least one respectable consulting physician, and then always with a view to the safety of the child—if that be possible," and calling "the attention of the clergy of all denominations to the perverted views of morality entertained by a large class of females—aye, and men also, on this important question."

Except for periodic condemnation of the criminal abortionist, no further formal AMA action took place until 1967. In that year, the Committee on Human Reproduction urged the adoption of a stated policy of opposition to induced abortion, except when there is "documented medical evidence" of a threat to the health or life of the mother, or that the child "may be born with incapacitating physical deformity or mental deficiency," or that a pregnancy "resulting from legally established statutory or forcible rape or incest may constitute a threat to the mental or physical health of the patient," two other physicians "chosen because of their recognized professional competence have examined the patient and have concurred in writing," and the procedure "is performed in a hospital accredited by the Joint Commission on Accreditation of Hospitals." The providing of medical information by physicians to state legislatures in their consideration of legislation regarding therapeutic abortion was "to be considered consistent with the principles of ethics of the American Medical Association." This recommendation was adopted by the House of Delegates. Proceedings of the AMA House of Delegates 40–51 (June 1967).

In 1970, after the introduction of a variety of proposed resolutions, and of a report from its Board of Trustees, a reference committee noted "polarization of the medical profession on this controversial issue"; division among those who had testified; a difference of opinion among AMA councils and committees; "the remarkable shift in testimony" in six months, felt to be influenced "by the rapid changes in state laws and by the judicial decisions which tend to make abortion more freely available;" and a feeling "that this trend will continue." On June 25, 1970, the House of Delegates adopted preambles and most of the resolutions proposed by the reference committee. The preambles emphasized "the best interests of the patient," "sound clinical judgment," and "informed patient consent," in contrast to "mere acquiescence to the patient's demand." The resolutions asserted that abortion is a medical procedure that should be performed by a licensed physician in an accredited hospital only after consultation with two other physicians and in conformity with state law, and that no party to the procedure should be required to violate personally held moral principles.[38] Proceedings of the AMA House of Delegates 220 (June 1970). The AMA Judicial Council rendered a complementary opinion.[39]

7. *The position of the American Public Health Association.* In October 1970, the Executive Board of the APHA adopted Standards for Abortion Services. These were five in number:

> "a. Rapid and simple abortion referral must be readily available through state and local public health departments, medical societies, or other nonprofit organizations.
>
> "b. An important function of counseling should be to simplify and expedite the provision of abortion services; it should not delay the obtaining of these services.
>
> "c. Psychiatric consultation should not be mandatory. As in the case of other specialized medical services, psychiatric consultation should be sought for definite indications and not on a routine basis.
>
> "d. A wide range of individuals from appropriately trained, sympa-

thetic volunteers to highly skilled physicians may qualify as abortion counselors.

"e. Contraception and/or sterilization should be discussed with each abortion patient." Recommended Standards for Abortion Services, 61 Am. J. Pub. Health 396 (1971).

Among factors pertinent to life and health risks associated with abortion were three that "are recognized as important":

"a. the skill of the physician,
"b. the environment in which the abortion is performed, and above all
"c. the duration of pregnancy, as determined by uterine size and confirmed by menstrual history." *Id.*, at 397.

It was said that "a well-equipped hospital" offers more protection "to cope with unforeseen difficulties than an office or clinic without such resources. . . . The factor of gestational age is of overriding importance." Thus, it was recommended that abortions in the second trimester and early abortions in the presence of existing medical complications be performed in hospitals as inpatient procedures. For pregnancies in the first trimester, abortion in the hopsital with or without overnight stay "is probably the safest practice." An abortion in an extramural facility, however, is an acceptable alternative "provided arrangements exist in advance to admit patients promptly if unforeseen complications develop." Standards for an abortion facility were listed. It was said that at present abortions should be performed by physicians or osteopaths who are licensed to practice and who have "adequate training." *Id.*, at 398.

8. *The position of the American Bar Association.* At its meeting in February 1972 the ABA House of Delegates approved, with 17 opposing votes, the Uniform Abortion Act that had been drafted and approved the preceding August by the Conference of Commissioners on Uniform State Laws. 58 A. B. A. J. 380 (1972). We set forth the Act in full in the margin.[40] The Conference has appended an enlightening Prefatory Note.[41]

VII

Three reasons have been advanced to explain historically the enactment of criminal abortion laws in the 19th century and to justify their continued existence.

It has been argued occasionally that these laws were the product of a Victorian social concern to discourage illicit sexual conduct. Texas, however, does not advance this justification in the present case, and it appears that no court or commentator has taken the argument seriously.[42] The appellants and *amici* contend, moreover, that this is not a proper state purpose at all and suggest that, if it were, the Texas statutes are overbroad in protecting it since the law fails to distinguish between married and unwed mothers.

A second reason is concerned with abortion as a medical procedure. When most criminal abortion laws were first enacted, the procedure was a hazardous one for the woman.[43] This was particularly true prior to the development of antisepsis. Antiseptic techniques, of course, were based on discoveries by Lister, Pasteur, and others first announced in 1867, but were not generally accepted and employed until about the turn of the century. Abortion mortality was high. Even after 1900, and perhaps until as late as the development of antibiotics in the 1940's, standard modern techniques such as dilation and curettage were not nearly so safe as they are today. Thus, it has been argued that a State's real concern in enacting a criminal abortion law was to protect the pregnant woman, that is, to restrain her from submitting to a procedure that placed her life in serious jeopardy.

Modern medical techniques have altered this situation. Appellants and various *amici* refer to medical data indicating that abortion in early pregnancy, that is, prior to the end of the first trimester, although not without its risk, is now relatively safe. Mortality rates for women undergoing early abortions, where the procedure is legal, appear to be as low as or lower than the rates for normal childbirth.[44] Consequently, any interest of the State in protecting the woman from an inherently hazardous procedure, except when it would be equally dangerous for her to forgo it, has largely disappeared. Of course, important state interests in the areas of health and medical standards do remain. The State has a legitimate interest in seeing to it that abortion, like any other medical procedure, is performed under circumstances that insure maximum safety for the patient. This interest obviously extends at least to the performing physician and his staff, to the facilities involved, to the availability of after-care, and to adequate provision for any complication or emergency that might arise. The prevalence of high mortality rates at illegal "abortion mills" strengthens, rather than weakens, the State's interest in regulating the conditions under which abortions are performed. Moreover, the risk to the woman increases as her pregnancy continues. Thus, the State retains a definite interest in protecting the woman's own health and safety when an abortion is proposed at a late stage of pregnancy.

The third reason is the State's interest—some phrase it in terms of duty—in protecting prenatal life. Some of the argument for this justification rests on the theory that a new human life is present from the moment of conception.[45] The State's interest and general obligation to protect life then extends, it is argued, to prenatal life. Only when the life of the pregnant mother herself is at stake, balanced against the life she carries within her, should the interest of the embryo or fetus not prevail. Logically, of course, a legitimate state interest in this area need not stand or fall on acceptance of the belief that life begins at conception or at some other point prior to live birth. In assessing the State's interest, recognition may be given to the less rigid claim that as long as at least *potential* life is involved, the State may assert interests beyond the protection of the pregnant woman alone.

Parties challenging state abortion laws have sharply disputed in some courts the contention that a purpose of these laws, when enacted, was to protect prenatal life.[46] Pointing to the absence of legislative history to support the contention, they claim that most state laws were designed solely to protect the woman. Because medical advances have lessened this concern, at least with respect to abortion in early pregnancy, they argue that with respect to such abortions, the laws can no longer be justified by any state interest. There is some scholarly support for this view of original purpose.[47] The few state courts called upon to interpret their laws in the late 19th and early 20th centuries did focus on the State's interest in protecting the woman's health rather than in preserving the embryo and fetus.[48] Proponents of this view point out that in many States, including Texas,[49] by statute or judicial interpretation, the pregnant woman herself could not be prosecuted for self-abortion or for cooperating in an abortion performed upon her by another.[50] They claim that adoption of the "quickening" distinction through received common law and state statutes tacitly recognizes the greater health hazards inherent in late abortion and impliedly repudiates the theory that life begins at conception.

It is with these interests, and the weight to be attached to them, that this case is concerned.

VIII

The Constitution does not explicitly mention any right of privacy. In a line of decisions, however, going back perhaps as far as *Union Pacific R. Co. v. Botsford,* 141 U. S. 250, 251 (1891), the Court has recognized that a right of personal privacy, or a guarantee of certain areas or zones of privacy, does exist under the Constitution. In varying contexts, the Court or individual Justices have, indeed, found at least the roots of that right in the First Amendment, *Stanley v. Georgia,* 394 U. S. 557, 564 (1969); in the Fourth and Fifth Amendments, *Terry v. Ohio,* 392 U. S. 1, 8-9 (1968), *Katz v. United States,* 389 U. S. 347, 350 (1967), *Boyd v. United States,* 116 U. S. 616 (1886), see *Olmstead v. United States,* 277 U. S. 438, 478 (1928) (Brandeis, J., dissenting); in the penumbras of the Bill of Rights, *Griswold v. Connecticut,* 381 U. S., at 484–485; in the Ninth Amendment, *id.,* at 486 (Goldberg, J., concurring); or in the concept of liberty guaranteed by the first section of the Fourteenth Amendment, see *Meyer v. Nebraska,* 262 U. S. 390, 399 (1923). These decisions make it clear that only personal rights that can be deemed "fundamental" or "implicit in the concept of ordered liberty," *Palko v. Connecticut,* 302 U. S. 319, 325 (1937), are included in this guarantee of personal privacy. They also make it clear that the right has some extension to activities relating to marriage, *Loving v. Virginia,* 388 U. S. 1, 12 (1967); procreation, *Skinner v. Oklahoma,* 316 U. S. 535, 541–542 (1942); contraception, *Eisenstadt v. Baird,* 405 U. S., at 453–454; *id.,* at 460, 463–465 (WHITE, J., concurring in result); family relationships, *Prince v. Massachusetts,* 321 U. S. 158, 166 (1944); and child rearing and education, *Pierce v. Society of Sisters,* 268 U. S. 510, 535 (1925), *Meyer v. Nebraska, supra.*

This right of privacy, whether it be founded in the Fourteenth Amendment's concept of personal liberty and restrictions upon state action, as we feel it is, or, as the District Court determined, in the Ninth Amendment's reservation of rights to the people, is broad enough to encompass a woman's decision whether or not to terminate her pregnancy. The detriment that the State would impose upon the pregnant woman by denying this choice altogether is apparent. Specific and direct harm medically diagnosable even in early pregnancy may be involved. Maternity, or additional offspring, may force upon the woman a distressful life and future. Psychological harm may be imminent. Mental and physical health may be taxed by child care. There is also the distress, for all concerned, associated with the unwanted child, and there is the problem of bringing a child into a family already unable, psychologically and otherwise, to care for it. In other cases, as in this one, the additional difficulties and continuing stigma of unwed motherhood may be involved. All these are factors the woman and her responsible physician necessarily will consider in consultation.

On the basis of elements such as these, appellant and some *amici* argue that the woman's right is absolute and that she is entitled to terminate her pregnancy at whatever time, in whatever way, and for whatever reason she alone chooses. With this we do not agree. Appellant's arguments that Texas either has no valid interest at all in regulating the abortion decision, or no interest strong enough to support any limitation upon the woman's sole determination, are unpersuasive. The Court's decisions recognizing a right of privacy also acknowledge that some state regulation in areas protected by that right is appropriate. As noted above, a State may properly assert important interests in safeguarding health, in maintaining medical standards, and in protecting potential life. At some point in pregnancy, these respective interests become sufficiently compelling to sustain regulation of the factors that govern the abortion decision. The privacy right involved, therefore, cannot be said to be absolute. In fact, it is not clear to us that the claim asserted by some *amici* that one has an unlimited right to do with one's body as one pleases bears a close relationship to the right of privacy previously articulated in the Court's decisions. The Court has refused to recognize an unlimited right of this kind in the past. *Jacobson v. Massachusetts,* 197 U. S. 11 (1905) (vaccination); *Buck v. Bell,* 274 U. S. 200 (1927) (sterilization).

We, therefore, conclude that the right of personal privacy includes the abortion decision, but that this right is not unqualified and must be considered against important state interests in regulation.

We note that those federal and state courts that have recently considered abortion law challenges have reached the same conclusion. A majority, in addition to the District Court in the present case, have held state laws unconstitutional, at least in part, because of vagueness or because of overbreadth and abridgment of rights. *Abele v. Markle,* 342 F. Supp. 800 (Conn. 1972), appeal docketed, No. 72–56; *Abele v. Markle,* 351 F. Supp. 224 (Conn. 1972), appeal docketed, No. 72–730; *Doe v. Bolton,* 319 F. Supp. 1048 (ND Ga. 1970), appeal decided today, *post,* p. 179; *Doe v. Scott,* 321 F. Supp. 1385 (ND Ill. 1971), appeal docketed, No. 70–105; *Poe v. Menghini,* 339 F. Supp. 986 (Kan. 1972); *YWCA v. Kugler,* 342 F. Supp. 1048 (NJ 1972); *Babbitz v. McCann,* 310 F. Supp. 293 (ED Wis. 1970), appeal dismissed, 400 U. S. 1 (1970); *People v. Belous,* 71 Cal. 2d 954, 458 P. 2d 194 (1969), cert. denied, 397 U. S. 915 (1970); *State v. Barquet,* 262 So. 2d 431 (Fla. 1972).

Others have sustained state statutes. *Crossen v. Attorney General,* 344 F. Supp. 587 (ED Ky. 1972), appeal docketed, No. 72–256; *Rosen v. Louisiana State Board of Medical Examiners,* 318 F. Supp. 1217 (ED La. 1970), appeal docketed, No. 70–42; *Corkey v. Edwards,* 322 F. Supp. 1248 (WDNC 1971), appeal docketed, No. 71–92; *Steinberg v. Brown,* 321 F. Supp. 741 (ND Ohio 1970); *Doe v. Rampton* (Utah 1971), appeal docketed, No. 71–5666; *Cheaney v. State,* _____ Ind. _____, 285 N. E. 2d 265 (1972); *Spears v. State,* 257 So. 2d 876 (Miss. 1972);

State v. Munson, 86 S. D. 663, 201 N. W. 2d 123 (1972), appeal docketed, No. 72–631.

Although the results are divided, most of these courts have agreed that the right of privacy, however based, is broad enough to cover the abortion decision; that the right, nonetheless, is not absolute and is subject to some limitations; and that at some point the state interests as to protection of health, medical standards, and prenatal life, become dominant. We agree with this approach.

Where certain "fundamental rights" are involved, the Court has held that regulation limiting these rights may be justified only by a "compelling state interest," *Kramer v. Union Free School District,* 395 U. S. 621, 627 (1969); *Shapiro v. Thompson,* 394 U. S. 618, 634 (1969), *Sherbert v. Verner,* 374 U. S. 398, 406 (1963), and that legislative enactments must be narrowly drawn to express only the legitimate state interests at stake. *Griswold* v. *Connecticut,* 381 U. S., at 485; *Aptheker* v. *Secretary of State,* 378 U. S. 500, 508 (1964); *Cantwell v. Connecticut,* 310 U. S. 296, 307–308 (1940); see *Eisenstadt v. Baird,* 405 U. S., at 460, 463-464 (WHITE, J., concurring in result).

In the recent abortion cases, cited above, courts have recognized these principles. Those striking down state laws have generally scrutinized the State's interests in protecting health and potential life, and have concluded that neither interest justified broad limitations on the reasons for which a physician and his pregnant patient might decide that she should have an abortion in the early stages of pregnancy. Courts sustaining state laws have held that the State's determinations to protect health or prenatal life are dominant and constitutionally justifiable.

IX

The District Court held that the appellee failed to meet his burden of demonstrating that the Texas statute's infringement upon Roe's rights was necessary to support a compelling state interest, and that, although the appellee presented "several compelling justifications for state presence in the area of abortions," the statutes outstripped these justifications and swept "far beyond any areas of compelling state interest." 314 F. Supp., at 1222–1223. Appellant and appellee both contest that holding. Appellant, as has been indicated, claims an absolute right that bars any state imposition of criminal penalties in the area. Appellee argues that the State's determination to recognize and protect prenatal life from and after conception constitutes a compelling state interst. As noted above, we do not agree fully with either formulation.

A. The appellee and certain *amici* argue that the fetus is a "person" within the language and meaning of the Fourteenth Amendment. In support of this, they outline at length and in detail the well-known facts of fetal development. If this suggestion of personhood is established, the appellant's case, of course, collapses, for the fetus' right to life would then be guaranteed specifically by the Amendment. The appellant conceded as much on reargument.[51] On the other hand, the appellee conceded on reargument[52] that no case could be cited that holds that a fetus is a person within the meaning of the Fourteenth Amendment.

The Constitution does not define "person" in so many words. Section 1 of the

Fourteenth Amendment contains three references to "person." The first, in defining "citizens," speaks of "persons born or naturalized in the United States." The word also appears both in the Due Process Clause and in the Equal Protection Clause. "Person" is used in other places in the Constitution: in the listing of qualifications for Representatives and Senators, Art. I, § 2, cl. 2, and § 3, cl. 3; in the Apportionment Clause, Art. I, § 2, cl. 3;[53] in the Migration and Importation provision, Art. I, § 9, cl. 1; in the Emolument Clause, Art. I, § 9, cl. 8; in the Electors provisions, Art II, § 1, cl. 2, and the superseded cl. 3; in the provision outlining qualifications for the office of President, Art. II, § 1, cl. 5; in the Extradition provisions, Art. IV, § 2, cl. 2, and the superseded Fugitive Slave Clause 3; and in the Fifth, Twelfth, and Twenty-second Amendments, as well as in §§ 2 and 3 of the Fourteenth Amendment. But in nearly all these instances, the use of the word is such that it has application only postnatally. None indicates, with any assurance, that it has any possible pre-natal application.[54]

All this, together with our observation, *supra,* that throughout the major portion of the 19th century prevailing legal abortion practices were far freer than they are today, persuades us that the word "person," as used in the Fourteenth Amendment, does not include the unborn.[55] This is in accord with the results reached in those few cases where the issue has been squarely presented. *McGarvey v. Magee-Women's Hospital,* 340 F. Supp. 751 (WD Pa. 1972); *Byrn v. New York City Health & Hospitals Corp.,* 31 N. Y. 2d 194, 286 N. E. 2d 887 (1972), appeal docketed, No. 72-434; *Abele v. Markle,* 351 F. Supp. 224 (Conn. 1972), appeal docketed, No. 72-730. Cf. *Cheaney* v. *State,* _____ Ind., at _____, 285 N. E. 2d, at 270; *Montana v. Rogers,* 278 F. 2d 68, 72 (CA7 1960), aff'd *sub nom. Montana v. Kennedy,* 366 U. S. 308 (1961); *Keeler v. Superior Court,* 2 Cal. 3d 619, 470 P. 2d 617 (1970); *State v. Dickinson,* 28 Ohio St. 2d 65, 275 N. E. 2d 599 (1971). Indeed, our decision in *United States v. Vuitch,* 402 U. S. 62 (1971), inferentially is to the same effect, for we there would not have indulged in statutory interpretation favorable to abortion in specified circumstances if the necessary consequence was the termination of life entitled to Fourteenth Amendment protection.

This conclusion, however, does not of itself fully answer the contentions raised by Texas, and we pass on to other considerations.

B. The pregnant woman cannot be isolated in her privacy. She carries an embryo and, later, a fetus, if one accepts the medical definitions of the developing young in the human uterus. See Dorland's Illustrated Medical Dictionary 478–479, 547 (24th ed. 1965). The situation therefore is inherently different from marital intimacy, or bedroom possession of obscene material, or marriage, or procreation, or education, with which *Eisenstadt* and *Griswold, Stanley, Loving, Skinner,* and *Pierce* and *Meyer* were respectively concerned. As we have intimated above, it is reasonable and appropriate for a State to decide that at some point in time another interest, that of health of the mother or that of potential human life, becomes significantly involved. The woman's privacy is no longer sole and any right of privacy she possesses must be measured accordingly.

Texas urges that, apart from the Fourteenth Amendment, life begins at conception and is present throughout pregnancy, and that, therefore, the State has a compelling interest in protecting that life from and after conception. We need not resolve the difficult question of when life begins. When those trained in the respective disciplines of medicine, philosophy, and theology are unable to arrive at any consensus, the judiciary, at this point in the development of man's knowledge, is not in a position to speculate as to the answer.

It should be sufficient to note briefly the wide divergence of thinking on this most sensitive and difficult question. There has always been strong support for the view that life does not begin until live birth. This was the belief of the Stoics.[56] It appears to be the predominant, though not the unanimous, attitude of the Jewish faith.[57] It may be taken to represent also the position of a large segment of the Protestant community, insofar as that can be ascertained; organized groups that have taken a formal position on the abortion issue have generally regarded abortion as a matter for the conscience of the individual and her family.[58] As we have noted, the common law found greater significance in quickening. Physicians and their scientific colleagues have regarded that event with less interest and have tended to focus either upon conception, upon live birth, or upon the interim point at which the fetus becomes "viable," that is, potentially able to live outside the mother's womb, albeit with artificial aid.[59] Viability is usually placed at about seven months (28 weeks) but may occur earlier, even at 24 weeks.[60] The Aristotelian theory of "mediate animation," that held sway throughout the Middle Ages and the Renaissance in Europe, continued to be official Roman Catholic dogma until the 19th century, despite opposition to this "ensoulment" theory from those in the Church who would recognize the existence of life from the moment of conception.[61] The latter is now, of course, the official belief of the Catholic Church. As one brief *amicus* discloses, this is a view strongly held by many non-Catholics as well, and by many physicians. Substantial problems for precise definition of this view are posed, however, by new embryological data that purport to indicate that conception is a "process" over time, rather than an event, and by new medical techniques such as menstrual extraction, the "morning-after" pill, implantation of embryos, artificial insemination, and even artificial wombs.[62]

In areas other than criminal abortion, the law has been reluctant to endorse any theory that life, as we recognize it, begins before live birth or to accord legal rights to the unborn except in narrowly defined situations and except when the rights are contingent upon live birth. For example, the traditional rule of tort law denied recovery for prenatal injuries even though the child was born alive.[63] That rule has been changed in almost every jurisdiction. In most States, recovery is said to be permitted only if the fetus was viable, or at least quick, when the injuries were sustained, though few courts have squarely so held.[64] In a recent development, generally opposed by the commentators, some States permit the parents of a stillborn child to maintain an action for wrongful death because of prenatal injuries.[65] Such an action, however, would appear to be one to vindicate the parents' interest and is thus consistent with the view that the fetus, at most, represents only the potentiality of life. Similarly, unborn children have been recognized as acquiring rights or interests by way of inheritance or other devolution of property, and have been represented by guardians *ad litem*.[66] Perfection of the interests involved, again, has generally been contingent upon live birth. In short, the unborn have never been recognized in the law as persons in the whole sense.

X

In view of all this, we do not agree that, by adopting one theory of life, Texas may override the rights of the pregnant woman that are at stake. We repeat, however, that the State does have an important and legitimate interest in preserving and protecting the health of the pregnant woman, whether she be a resident of the State or a nonresident who seeks medical consultation and treatment there, and that it has still *another* important and legitimate interest in protecting the potentiality of human life. These interests are separate and distinct. Each grows in substantiality as the woman approaches term and, at a point during pregnancy, each becomes "compelling."

With respect to the State's important and legitimate interest in the health of the mother, the "compelling" point, in the light of present medical knowledge, is at approximately the end of the first trimester. This is so because of the now-established medical fact, referred to above at 149, that until the end of the first trimester mortality in abortion may be less than mortality in normal childbirth. It follows that, from and after this point, a State may regulate the abortion procedure to the extent that the regulation reasonably relates to the preservation and protection of maternal health. Examples of permissible state regulation in this area are requirements as to the qualifications of the person who is to perform the abortion; as to the licensure of that person; as to the facility in which the procedure is to be performed, that is, whether it must be a hospital or may be a clinic or some other place of less-than-hospital status; as to the licensing of the facility; and the like.

This means, on the other hand, that, for the period of pregnancy prior to this "compelling" point, the attending physician, in consultation with his patient, is free to determine, without regulation by the State, that, in his medical judgment, the patient's pregnancy should be terminated. If that decision is reached, the judgment may be effectuated by an abortion free of interference by the State.

With respect to the State's important and legitimate interest in potential life, the "compelling" point is at viability. This is so because the fetus then presumably has the capability of meaningful life outside the mother's womb. State regulation protective of fetal life after viability thus has both logical and biological justifications. If the State is interested in protecting fetal life after viability, it may go so far as to proscribe abortion during that period, except when it is necessary to preserve the life or health of the mother.

Measured against these standards, Art. 1196 of the Texas Penal Code, in restricting legal abortions to those "procured or attempted by medical advice for the purpose of saving the life of the mother," sweeps too broadly. The statute makes no distinction between abortions performed early in pregnancy and those performed later, and it limits to a single reason, "saving" the mother's life, the legal justification for the procedure. The statute, therefore, cannot survive the constitutional attack made upon it here.

This conclusion makes it unnecessary for us to consider the additional challenge to the Texas statute asserted on grounds of vagueness. See *United States v. Vuitch,* 402 U. S., at 67–72.

XI

To summarize and to repeat:

1. A state criminal abortion statute of the current Texas type, that excepts from criminality only a *lifesaving* procedure on behalf of the mother, without regard to pregnancy stage and without recognition of the other interests involved, is violative of the Due Process Clause of the Fourteenth Amendment.

(a) For the stage prior to approximately the end of the first trimester, the abortion decision and its effectuation must be left to the medical judgment of the pregnant woman's attending physician.

(b) For the stage subsequent to approximately the end of the first trimester, the State, in promoting its interest in the health of the mother, may, if it chooses, regulate the abortion procedure in ways that are reasonably related to maternal health.

(c) For the stage subsequent to viability, the State in promoting its interest in the potentiality of human life may, if it chooses, regulate, and even proscribe, abortion except where it is necessary, in appropriate medical judgment, for the preservation of the life or health of the mother.

2. The state may define the term "physician," as it has been employed in the preceding paragraphs of this Part XI of this opinion, to mean only a physician currently licensed by the State, and may proscribe any abortion by a person who is not a physician as so defined.

In *Doe v. Bolton, post,* p. 179, procedural requirements contained in one of the modern abortion statutes are considered. That opinion and this one, of course, are to be read together.[67]

This holding, we feel, is consistent with the relative weights of the respective interests involved, with the lessons and examples of medical and legal history, with the lenity of the common law, and with the demands of the profound problems of the present day. The decision leaves the State free to place increasing restrictions on abortion as the period of pregnancy lengthens, so long as those restrictions are tailored to the recognized state interests. The decision vindicates the right of the physician to administer medical treatment according to his professional judgment up to the points where important state interests provide compelling justifications for intervention. Up to those points, the abortion decision in all its aspects is inherently, and primarily, a medical decision, and basic responsibility for it must rest with the physician. If an individual practitioner abuses the privilege of exercising proper medical judgment, the usual remedies, judicial and intra-professional, are available.

XII

Our conclusion that Art. 1196 is unconstitional means, of course, that the Texas abortion statutes, as a unit, must fall. The exception of Art. 1196 cannot be struck down separately, for then the State would be left with a statute proscribing all abortion procedures no matter how medically urgent the case.

Although the District Court granted appellant Roe declaratory relief, it stopped short of issuing an injunction against enforcement of the Texas statutes. The Court has recognized that different considerations enter into a federal court's decision as to declaratory relief, on the one hand, and injunctive relief, on the other. *Zwickler v. Koota,* 389 U. S. 241, 252–255 (1967); *Dombrowski v. Pfister,* 380 U. S. 479 (1965). We are not dealing with a statute that, on its face, appears to abridge free expression, an area of particular concern under *Dombrowski* and refined in *Younger v. Harris,* 401 U. S., at 50.

We find it unnecessary to decide whether the District Court erred in withholding injunctive relief, for we assume the Texas prosecutorial authorities will give full credence to this decision that the present criminal abortion statutes of that State are unconstitutional.

The judgment of the District Court as to intervenor Hallford is reversed, and Dr. Hallford's complaint in intervention is dismissed. In all other respects, the judgment of the District Court is affirmed. Costs are allowed to the appellee.

It is so ordered.

MR. JUSTICE STEWART, concurring.

In 1963, this Court, in *Ferguson v. Skrupa,* 372 U. S. 726, purported to sound the death knell for the doctrine of substantive due process, a doctrine under which many state laws had in the past been held to violate the Fourteenth Amendment. As Mr. Justice Black's opinion for the Court in *Skrupa* put it: "We have returned to the original constitutional proposition that courts do not substitute their social and economic beliefs for the judgment of legislative bodies, who are elected to pass laws." *Id.,* at 730.[68]

Barely two years later, in *Griswold v. Connecticut,* 381 U. S. 479, the Court held a Connecticut birth control law unconstitutional. In view of what had been so recently said in *Skrupa,* the Court's opinion in *Griswold* understandably did its best to avoid reliance on the Due Process Clause of the Fourteenth Amendment as the ground for decision. Yet, the Connecticut law did not violate any provision of the Bill of Rights, nor any other specific provision of the Constitution.[69] So it was clear to me then, and it is equally clear to me now, that the *Griswold* decision can be rationally understood only as a holding that the Connecticut statute substantively invaded the "liberty" that is protected by the Due Process Clause of the Fourteenth Amendment.[70] As so understood, *Griswold* stands as one in a long line of pre-*Skrupa* cases decided under the doctrine of substantive due process, and I now accept it as such.

"In a Constitution for a free people, there can be no doubt that the meaning of 'liberty' must be broad indeed." *Board of Regents v. Roth,* 408 U. S. 564, 572. The Constitution nowhere mentions a specific right of personal choice in matters of marriage and family life, but the "liberty" protected by the Due Process Clause of the Fourteenth Amendment covers more than those freedoms explicitly named in the Bill of Rights. See *Schware v. Board of Bar Examiners,* 353 U. S. 232, 238–239; *Pierce v. Society of Sisters,* 268 U. S. 510, 534–535; *Meyer v. Nebraska,* 262 U. S. 390, 399–400. Cf. *Shapiro v. Thompson,* 394 U. S. 618, 629–630; *United States v. Guest,* 383 U. S. 745, 757–758; *Carrington v. Rash,* 380 U. S. 89, 96; *Aptheker v. Secretary of State,* 378 U. S. 500, 505; *Kent v. Dulles,* 357 U. S. 116, 127; *Bolling v. Sharpe,* 347 U. S. 497, 499–500; *Truax v. Raich,* 239 U. S. 33, 41.

As Mr. Justice Harlan once wrote: "[T]he full scope of the liberty guaranteed by the Due Process Clause cannot be found in or limited by the precise terms of the specific guarantees elsewhere provided in the Constitution. This 'liberty' is not a series of isolated points picked out in terms of the taking of property; the freedom of speech, press, and religion; the right to keep and bear arms; the freedom from unreasonable searches and seizures; and so on. It is a rational continuum which, broadly speaking, includes a freedom from all substantial arbitrary impositions and purposeless restraints . . . and which also recognizes, what a reasonable and sensitive judgment must, that certain interests require particularly careful scrutiny of the state needs asserted to justify their abridgment." *Poe v. Ullman,* 367 U. S. 497, 543 (opinion dissenting from dismissal of appeal) (citations omitted). In the words of Mr. Justice Frankfurter, "Great concepts like . . . 'liberty' . . . were purposely left to gather meaning from experience. For they relate to the whole domain of social and economic fact, and the statesmen who founded this Nation knew too well that only a stagnant society remains unchanged." *National Mutual Ins. Co. v. Tidewater Transfer Co.,* 337 U. S. 582, 646 (dissenting opinion).

Several decisions of this Court make clear that freedom of personal choice in matters of marriage and family life is one of the liberties protected by the Due Process Clause of the Fourteenth Amendment. *Loving v. Virginia,* 388 U. S. 1, 12; *Griswold v. Connecticut, supra; Pierce v. Society of Sisters, supra; Meyer v. Nebraska, supra.* See also *Prince v. Massachusetts,* 321 U. S. 158, 166; *Skinner v. Oklahoma,* 316 U. S. 535, 541. As recently as last Term, in *Eisenstadt v. Baird,* 405 U. S. 438, 453, we recognized "the right of the *individual,* married or single, to be free from unwarranted governmental intrusion into matters so fundamentally affecting a person as the decision whether to bear or beget a child." That right necessarily includes the right of a woman to decide whether or not to terminate her pregnancy. "Certainly the interests of a woman in giving of her physical and emotional self during pregnancy and the interests that will be affected throughout her life by the birth and raising of a child are of a far greater degree of significance and personal intimacy than the right to send a child to private school protected in *Pierce v. Society of Sisters,* 268 U. S. 510 (1925), or the right to teach a foreign language protected in *Meyer v. Nebraska,* 262 U. S. 390 (1923)." *Abele v. Markle,* 351 F. Supp. 224, 227 (Conn. 1972).

Clearly, therefore, the Court today is correct in holding that the right asserted by Jane Roe is embraced within the personal liberty protected by the Due Process Clause of the Fourteenth Amendment.

It is evident that the Texas abortion statute infringes that right directly. Indeed, it is difficult to imagine a more complete abridgment of a constitutional freedom than that worked by the inflexible criminal statute now in force in Texas. The question then becomes whether the state interests advanced to justify this abridgment can survive the "particularly careful scrutiny" that the Fourteenth Amendment here requires.

The asserted state interests are protection of the health and safety of the pregnant woman, and protection of the potential future human life within her. These are legitimate objectives, amply sufficient to permit a State to regulate abortions as it does other surgical procedures, and perhaps sufficient to permit a State to regulate abortions more stringently or even to prohibit them in the late stages of pregnancy. But such legislation is not before us, and I think the Court today has thoroughly demonstrated that these state interests cannot constitutionally support the broad abridgment of personal liberty worked by the existing Texas law. Accordingly, I join the Court's opinion holding that that law is invalid under the Due Process Clause of the Fourteenth Amendment.

MR. JUSTICE REHNQUIST, dissenting.

The Court's opinion brings to the decision of this troubling question both extensive historical fact and a wealth of legal scholarship. While the opinion thus commands my respect, I find myself nonetheless in fundamental disagreement with those parts of it that invalidate the Texas statute in question, and therefore dissent.

I

The Court's opinion decides that a State may impose virtually no restriction on the performance of abortions during the first trimester of pregnancy. Our previous decisions indicate that a necessary predicate for such an opinion is a plaintiff who was in her first trimester of pregnancy at some time during the pendency of her lawsuit. While a party may vindicate his own constitutional rights, he may not seek vindication for the rights of others. *Moose Lodge v. Irvis,* 407 U. S. 163 (1972); *Sierra Club v. Morton,* 405 U. S. 727 (1972). The Court's statement of facts in this case makes clear, however, that the record in no way indicates the presence of such a plaintiff. We know only that plaintiff Roe at the time of filing her complaint was a pregnant woman; for aught that appears in this record, she may have been in her *last* trimester of pregnancy as of the date the complaint was filed.

Nothing in the Court's opinion indicates that Texas might not constitutionally apply its proscription of abortion as written to a woman in that stage of pregnancy. Nonetheless, the Court uses her complaint against the Texas statute as a fulcrum for deciding that States may impose virtually no restrictions on medical abortions performed during the *first* trimester of pregnancy. In deciding such a hypothetical lawsuit, the Court departs from the longstanding admonition that it should never "formulate a rule of constitutional law broader than is required by the precise facts to which it is to be applied." *Liverpool, New York & Philadelphia S. S. Co. v. Commissioners of Emigration,* 113 U. S. 33, 39 (1885). See also *Ashwander v. TVA,* 297 U. S. 288, 345 (1936) (Brandeis, J., concurring).

II

Even if there were a plaintiff in this case capable of litigating the issue which the Court decides, I would reach a conclusion opposite to that reached by the Court. I have difficulty in concluding, as the Court does, that the right of "privacy" is involved in this case. Texas, by the statute here challenged, bars the performance of a medical abortion by a licensed physician on a plaintiff such as Roe. A transaction resulting in an operation such as this is not "private" in the ordinary usage of that word. Nor is the "privacy" that the Court finds here even a distant relative of the freedom from searches and seizures protected by the Fourth Amendment to the Constitution, which the Court has referred to as embodying a right to privacy. *Katz v. United States,* 389 U. S. 347 (1967).

If the Court means by the term "privacy" no more than that the claim of a person to be free from unwanted state regulation of consensual transactions may be a form of "liberty" protected by the Fourteenth Amendment, there is no doubt that similar claims have been upheld in our earlier decisions on the basis of that liberty. I agree with the statement of MR. JUSTICE STEWART in his concurring opinion that the "liberty," against deprivation of which without due process the Fourteenth Amendment protects, embraces more than the rights found in the Bill of Rights. But that liberty is not guaranteed absolutely against deprivation, only against deprivation without due process of law. The test traditionally applied in the area of social and economic legislation is whether or not a law such as that challenged has a rational relation to a valid state objective. *Williamson v. Lee Optical Co.,* 348 U. S. 483, 491 (1955). The Due Process Clause of the Fourteenth Amendment undoubtedly does place a limit, albeit a broad one, on legislative power to enact laws such as this. If the Texas statute were to prohibit an abortion even where the mother's life is in jeopardy, I have little doubt that such a statute would lack a rational relation to a valid state objective under the test stated in *Williamson, supra.* But the Court's sweeping invalidation of any restrictions on abortion during the first trimester is impossible to justify under that standard, and the conscious weighing of competing factors that the Court's opinion apparently substitutes for the established test is far more appropriate to a legislative judgment than to a judicial one.

The Court eschews the history of the Fourteenth Amendment in its reliance on the "compelling state interest" test. See *Weber v. Aetna Casualty & Surety Co.,* 406 U. S. 164, 179 (1972) (dissenting opinion). But the Court adds a new wrinkle to this test by transposing it from the legal considerations associated with the Equal Protection Clause of the Fourteenth Amendment to this case arising under the Due Process Clause of the Fourteenth Amendment. Unless I misapprehend the consequences of this transplanting of the "compelling state interest test," the Court's opinion will accomplish the seemingly impossible feat of leaving this area of the law more confused than it found it.

While the Court's opinion quotes from the dissent of Mr. Justice Holmes in *Lochner v. New York,* 198 U. S. 45, 74 (1905), the result it reaches is more closely attuned to the majority opinion of Mr. Justice Peckham in that case. As in *Lochner* and similar cases applying substantive due process standards to economic and social welfare legislation, the adoption of the compelling state interest standard will inevitably require this Court to examine the legislative policies and pass on the wisdom of these policies in the very process of deciding whether a particular state interest put forward may or may not be "compelling." The decision here to break pregnancy into three distinct terms and to outline the permissible restrictions the State may impose in each one, for example, partakes more of judicial legislation than it does of a determination of the intent of the drafters of the Fourteenth Amendment.

The fact that a majority of the States reflecting, after all, the majority sentiment in those States, have had restrictions on abortions for at least a century is a strong indication, it seems to me, that the asserted right to an abortion is not "so rooted in the traditions and conscience of our people as to be ranked as fundamental," *Snyder v. Massachusetts,* 291 U. S. 97,105 (1934). Even today, when society's views on abortion are changing, the very existence of the debate is evidence that the "right" to an abortion is not so universally accepted as the appellant would have us believe.

To reach its result, the Court necessarily has had to find within the scope of the Fourteenth Amendment a right that was apparently completely unknown to the drafters of the Amendment. As early as 1821, the first state law dealing directly with abortion was enacted by the Connecticut Legislature. Conn. Stat., Tit. 22, §§ 14, 16. By the time of the adoption of the Fourteenth Amendment in 1868, there were at least 36 laws enacted by state or territorial legislatures limiting abortion.[71] While many States have amended or updated their laws, 21 of the laws on the books in 1868 remain in effect today.[72] Indeed, the Texas statute struck down today was, as the majority notes, first enacted in 1857 and "has remained substantially unchanged to the present time." *Ante,* at 119.

There apparently was no question concerning the validity of this provision or of any of the other state statutes when the Fourteenth Amendment was adopted. The only conclusion possible from this history is that the drafters did not intend to have the Fourteenth Amendment withdraw from the States the power to legislate with respect to this matter.

III

Even if one were to agree that the case that the Court decides were here, and that the enunciation of the substantive constitutional law in the Court's opinion were proper, the actual disposition of the case by the Court is still difficult to justify. The Texas statute is struck down *in toto,* even though the Court apparently concedes that at later periods of pregnancy Texas might impose these selfsame statutory limitations on abortion. My understanding of past practice is that a statute found to be invalid as applied to a particular plaintiff, but not unconstitutional as a whole, is not simply "struck down" but is, instead, declared unconstitutional as applied to the fact situation before the Court. *Yick Wo v. Hopkins,* 118 U. S. 356 (1886); *Street v. New York,* 394 U. S. 576 (1969).

For all of the foregoing reasons, I respectfully dissent.

NOTES

1. "Article 1191. Abortion

"If any person shall designedly administer to a pregnant woman or knowingly procure to be administered with her consent any drug or medicine, or shall use towards her any violence or means whatever externally or internally applied, and thereby procure an abortion, he shall be confined in the penitentiary not less than two nor more than five years; if it be done without her consent, the punishment shall be doubled. By 'abortion' is meant that the life of the fetus or embryo shall be destroyed in the woman's womb or that a premature birth thereof be caused.

"Art. 1192. Furnishing the means

"Whoever furnishes the means for procuring an abortion knowing the purpose intended is guilty as an accomplice.

"Art. 1193. Attempt at abortion

"If the means used shall fail to produce an abortion, the offender is nevertheless guilty of an attempt to produce abortion, provided it be shown that such means were calculated to produce that result, and shall be fined not less than one hundred nor more than one thousand dollars.

"Art. 1194. Murder in producing abortion

"If the death of the mother is occasioned by an abortion so produced or by an attempt to effect the same it is murder."

"Art. 1196. By medical advice

"Nothing in this chapter applies to an abortion procured or attempted by medical advice for the purpose of saving the life of the mother."

The foregoing Articles, together with Art. 1195, compose Chapter 9 of Title 15 of the Penal Code. Article 1195, not attacked here, reads:

"Art. 1195. Destroying unborn child

"Whoever shall during parturition of the mother destroy the vitality or life in a child in a state of being born and before actual birth, which child would otherwise have been born alive, shall be confined in the penitentiary for life or for not less than five years."

2. Ariz. Rev. Stat. Ann. § 13–211 (1956); Conn. Pub. Act No. 1 (May 1972 special session) (in 4 Conn. Leg. Serv. 677 (1972)), and Conn. Gen. Stat. Rev. §§ 53-29, 53-30 (1968) (or unborn child); Idaho Code § 18-601 (1948); Ill. Rev. Stat., c. 38, § 23-1 (1971); Ind. Code § 35-1-58-1 (1971); Iowa Code § 701.1 (1971); Ky. Rev. Stat. § 436.020 (1962); La. Rev. Stat. § 37:1285 (6) (1964) (loss of medical license) (but see § 14:87 (Supp. 1972) containing no exception for the life of the mother under the criminal statute); Me. Rev. Stat. Ann., Tit. 17, § 51 (1964); Mass. Gen. Laws Ann., c. 272, § 19 (1970) (using the term "unlawfully," construed to exclude an abortion to save the mother's life), *Kudish* v. *Bd. of Registration,* 356 Mass. 98, 248 N. E. 2d 264 (1969); Mich. Comp. Laws § 750.14 (1948); Minn. Stat. § 617.18 (1971); Mo. Rev. Stat. § 559.100 (1969); Mont. Rev. Codes Ann. § 94-401 (1969); Neb. Rev. Stat. § 28-405 (1964); Nev. Rev. Stat. § 200.220 (1967); N. H. Rev. Stat. Ann. § 585:13 (1955); N.J. Stat. Ann. § 2A:87-1 (1969) ("without lawful justification"); N. D. Cent. Code §§ 12-25-01, 12-25-02 (1960); Ohio Rev. Code Ann. § 2901.16 (1953); Okla. Stat. Ann., Tit. 21, § 861 (1972–1973 Supp.); Pa. Stat. Ann., Tit. 18, §§ 4718, 4719 (1963) ("unlawful"); R. I. Gen. Laws Ann. § 11-3-1 (1969); S. D. Comp. Laws Ann. § 22-17-1 (1967); Tenn. Code Ann. §§ 39-301, 39-302 (1956); Utah Code Ann. §§76-2-1, 76-2-2 (1953); Vt. Stat. Ann., Tit. 13, § 101 (1958); W. Va. Code Ann. § 61-2-8 (1966); Wis. Stat. § 940.04 (1969); Wyo. Stat. Ann. §§ 6-77, 6-78 (1957).

3. Long ago, a suggestion was made that the Texas statutes were unconstitutionally vague because of definitional deficiencies. The Texas Court of Criminal Appeals disposed of that suggestion peremptorily, saying only,

"It is also insisted in the motion in arrest of judgment that the statute is unconstitutional and void in that it does not sufficiently define or describe the offense of abortion. We do not concur in respect to this question." *Jackson* v. *State,* 55 Tex. Cr. R. 79, 89, 115 S. W. 262, 268 (1908).

The same court recently has held again that the State's abortion statutes are not unconstitutionally vague or overbroad. *Thompson* v. *State* (Ct. Crim. App. Tex. 1971), appeal docketed, No. 71-1200. The court held that "the State of Texas has a compelling interest to protect fetal life"; that Art. 1191 "is designed to protect fetal life"; that the Texas homicide statutes, particularly Art. 1205 of the Penal Code, are intended to protect a person "in existence by actual birth" and thereby implicitly recognize other human life that is not "in existence by actual birth"; that the definition of human life is for the legislature and not the courts; that Art. 1196 "is more definite than the District of Columbia statute upheld in [*United States* v.] *Vuitch*" (402 U. S. 62); and that the Texas statute "is not vague and indefinite or overbroad." A physician's abortion conviction was affirmed.

In *Thompson,* n. 2, the court observed that any issue as to the burden of proof under the exemption of Art. 1196 "is not before us." But see *Veevers* v. *State,* 172 Tex. Cr. R. 162, 168–169, 354 S. W. 2d 161, 166–167 (1962). Cf. *United States* v. *Vuitch,* 402 U. S. 62, 69–71 (1971).

    4. The name is a pseudonym.

    5. These names are pseudonyms.

    6. The appellee twice states in his brief that the hearing before the District Court was held on July 22, 1970. Brief for Appellee 13. The docket entries, App. 2, and the transcript, App. 76, reveal this to be an error. The July date appears to be the time of the reporter's transcription. See App. 77.

    7. We need not consider what different result, if any, would follow if Dr. Hallford's intervention were on behalf of a class. His complaint in intervention does not purport to assert a class suit and makes no reference to any class apart from an allegation that he "and others similarly situated" must necessarily guess at the meaning of Art. 1196. His application for leave to intervene goes somewhat further, for it asserts that plaintiff Roe does not adequately protect the interest of the doctor "and the class of people who are physicians . . . [and] the class of people who are . . . patients. . . ." The leave application, however, is not the complaint. Despite the District Court's statement to the contrary, 314 F.Supp., at 1225, we fail to perceive the essentials of a class suit in the Hallford complaint.

    8. A. Castiglioni, A History of Medicine 84 (2d ed. 1947), E. Krumbhaar, translator and editor (hereinafter Castiglioni).

    9. J. Ricci, The Genealogy of Gynaecology 52, 84, 113, 149 (2d ed. 1950) (hereinafter Ricci); L. Lader, Abortion 75–77 (1966) (hereinafter Lader); K. Niswander, Medical Abortion Practices in the United States, in Abortion and the Law 37, 38–40 (D. Smith ed. 1967); G. Williams, The Sanctity of Life and the Criminal Law 148 (1957) (hereinafter Williams); J. Noonan, An Almost Absolute Value in History, in The Morality of Abortion 1, 3–7 (J. Noonan ed. 1970) (hereinafter Noonan); Quay, Justifiable Abortion—Medical and Legal Foundations (pt. 2), 49 Geo. L. J. 395, 406–422 (1961) (hereinafter Quay).

    10. L. Edelstein, The Hippocratic Oath 10 (1943) (hereinafter Edelstein). But see Castiglioni 227.

    11. Edelstein 12; Ricci 113–114, 118–119; Noonan 5.

    12. Edelstein 13–14.

    13. Castiglioni 148.

    14. *Id.,* at 154.

    15. Edelstein 3.

    16. *Id.,* at 12, 15–18.

    17. *Id.,* at 18; Lader 76.

    18. Edelstein 63.

    19. *Id.,* at 64.

    20. Dorland's Illustrated Medical Dictionary 1261 (24th ed. 1965).

    21. E. Coke, Institutes III *50; 1 W. Hawkins, Pleas of the Crown. c. 31 § 16 (4th ed. 1762); 1 W. Blackstone, Commentaries *129–130; M. Hale, Pleas of the Crown 433 (1st Amer. ed. 1847). For discussions of the role of the quickening concept in English common law, see Lader 78; Noonan 223–226; Means, The Law of New York Concerning Abortion and the Status of the Foetus, 1664–1968: A Case of Cessation of Constitutionality (pt. 1), 14 N. Y. L. F. 411, 418–428 (1968) (hereinafter Means I); Stern, Abortion: Reform and the Law, 59 J. Crim. L. C. & P. S. 84 (1968) (hereinafter Stern); Quay 430–432; Williams 152.

22. Early philosophers believed that the embryo or fetus did not become formed and begin to live until at least 40 days after conception for a male, and 80 to 90 days for a female. See, for example, Aristotle, Hist. Anim. 7.3.583b; Gen. Anim. 2.3.736, 2.5.741; Hippocrates, Lib. de Nat. Puer., No. 10. Aristotle's thinking derived from his three-stage theory of life: vegetable, animal, rational. The vegetable stage was reached at conception, the animal at "animation," and the rational soon after live birth. This theory, together with the 40/80 day view, came to be accepted by early Christian thinkers.

The theological debate was reflected in the writings of St. Augustine, who made a distinction between *embryo inanimatus,* not yet endowed with a soul, and *embryo animatus.* He may have drawn upon Exodus 21:22. At one point, however, he expressed the view that human powers cannot determine the point during fetal development at which the critical change occurs. See Augustine, De Origine Animae 4.4 (Pub. Law 44.527). See also W. Reany, The Creation of the Human Soul, c.2 and 83–86 (1932); Huser, The Crime of Abortion in Canon Law 15 (Catholic Univ. of America, Canon Law Studies No. 162, Washington, D. C., 1942).

Galen, in three treatises related to embryology, accepted the thinking of Aristotle and his followers. Quay 426–427. Later, Augustine on abortion was incorporated by Gratian into the Decretum, published about 1140. Decretum Magistri Gratiani 2.32.2.7 to 2.32.2.10, in 1 Corpus Juris Canonici 1122, 1123 (A. Friedburg, 2d ed. 1879). This Decretal and the Decretals that followed were recognized as the definitive body of canon law until the new Code of 1917.

For discussions of the canon-law treatment, see Means I, pp. 411–412; Noonan 20–26; Quay 426–430; see also J. Noonan, Contraception: A History of Its Treatment by the Catholic Theologians and Canonists 18–29 (1965).

23. Bracton took the position that abortion by blow or poison was homicide "if the foetus be already formed and animated, and particularly if it be animated." 2 H. Bracton, De Legibus et Consuetudinibus Angliae 279 (T. Twiss ed. 1879), or, as a later translation puts it, "if the foetus is already formed or quickened, especially if it is quickened," 2 H. Bracton, On the Laws and Customs of England 341 (S. Thorne ed. 1968). See Quay 431; see also 2 Fleta 60–61 (Book 1, c. 23) (Selden Society ed. 1955).

24. E. Coke, Institutes III *50.

25. 1 W. Blackstone, Commentaries *129–130.

26. Means, The Phoenix of Abortional Freedom: Is a Penumbral or Ninth-Amendment Right About to Arise from the Nineteenth-Century Legislative Ashes of a Fourteenth-Century Common-Law Liberty?, 17 N. Y. L. F. 335 (1971) (hereinafter Means II). The author examines the two principal precedents cited marginally by Coke, both contrary to his dictum, and traces the treatment of these and other cases by earlier commentators. He concludes that Coke, who himself participated as an advocate in an abortion case in 1601, may have intentionally misstated the law. The author even suggests a reason: Coke's strong feelings against abortion, coupled with his determination to assert common-law (secular) jurisdiction to assess penalties for an offense that traditionally had been an exclusively ecclesiastical or canon-law crime. See also Lader 78–79, who notes that some scholars doubt that the common law ever was applied to abortion; that the English ecclesiastical courts seem to have lost interest in the problem after 1527; and that the preamble to the English legislation of 1803, 43 Geo. 3, c. 58, § 1, referred to in the text, *infra,* at 136, states that "no adequate means have been hitherto provided for the prevention and punishment of such offenses."

27. *Commonwealth v. Bangs,* 9 Mass. 387, 388 (1812); *Commonwealth* v. *Parker,* 50 Mass. (9 Metc.) 263, 265–266 (1845); *State v. Cooper,* 22 N. J. L. 52, 58 (1849); *Abrams v. Foshee,* 3 Iowa 274, 278–280 (1856); *Smith v. Gaffard,* 31 Ala. 45, 51 (1857); *Mitchell v. Commonwealth,* 78 Ky. 204, 210 (1879); *Eggart v. State,* 40 Fla. 527, 532, 25 So. 144, 145 (1898); *State v. Alcorn,* 7 Idaho 599, 606, 64 P. 1014, 1016 (1901); *Edwards v. State,* 79 Neb. 251, 252, 112 N. W. 611, 612 (1907); *Gray v. State,* 77 Tex. Cr. R. 221, 224, 178 S. W. 337, 338 (1915); *Miller v. Bennett,* 190 Va. 162, 169, 56 S. E. 2d 217, 221 (1949). Contra, *Mills v. Commonwealth,* 13 Pa. 631, 633 (1850); *State v. Slagle,* 83 N. C. 630, 632 (1880).

28. See *Smith v. State,* 33 Me. 48, 55 (1851); *Evans v. People,* 49 N. Y. 86, 88 (1872); *Lamb* v. *State,* 67 Md. 524, 533, 10 A. 208 (1887).

29. Conn. Stat., Tit. 20, § 14 (1821).

30. Conn. Pub. Acts, c. 71, § 1 (1860).

31. N. Y. Rev. Stat., pt. 4, c. 1, Tit. 2, Art. 1, § 9, p. 661, and Tit. 6, § 21, p. 694 (1829).

32. Act of Jan. 20, 1840, § 1, set forth in 2 H. Gammel, Laws of Texas 177–178 (1898); see *Grigsby v. Reib,* 105 Tex. 597, 600, 153 S. W. 1124, 1125 (1913).

33. The early statutes are discussed in Quay 435–438. See also Lader 85–88; Stern 85–86; and Means II 375–376.

34. Criminal abortion statutes in effect in the States as of 1961, together with historical statutory development and important judicial interpretations of the state statutes, are cited and quoted in Quay 447–520. See Comment, A Survey of the Present Statutory and Case Law on Abortion: The Contradictions and the Problems, 1972 U. Ill. L. F. 177, 179, classifying the abortion statutes and listing 25 States as permitting abortion only if necessary to save or preserve the mother's life.

35. Ala. Code, Tit. 14, § 9 (1958); D. C. Code Ann. § 22–201 (1967).

36. Mass. Gen. Laws Ann., c. 272, § 19 (1970); N. J. Stat. Ann. § 2A:87–1 (1969); Pa. Stat. Ann., Tit. 18, §§ 4718, 4719 (1963).

37. Fourteen States have adopted some form of the ALI statute. See Ark. Stat. Ann. §§ 41–303 to 41–310 (Supp. 1971); Calif. Health & Safety Code §§ 25950–25955.5 (Supp. 1972); Colo. Rev. Stat. Ann. §§ 40-2-50 to 40-2-53 (Cum. Supp. 1967); Del. Code Ann., Tit. 24, §§ 1790–1793 (Supp. 1972); Florida Law of Apr. 13, 1972, c. 72–196, 1972 Fla. Sess. Law Serv., pp. 380–382; Ga. Code §§ 26–1201 to 26–1203 (1972); Kan. Stat. Ann. § 21–3407 (Supp. 1971); Md. Ann. Code, Art. 43, §§ 137–139 (1971); Miss. Code Ann. § 2223 (Supp. 1972); N. M. Stat. Ann. §§ 40A-5-1 to 40A-5-3 (1972); N. C. Gen. Stat. § 14–45.1 (Supp. 1971); Ore. Rev. Stat. §§ 435.405 to 435.495 (1971); S. C. Code Ann. §§ 16–82 to 16–89 (1962 and Supp. 1971); Va. Code Ann. §§ 18.1–62 to 18.1–62.3 (Supp. 1972). Mr. Justice Clark described some of these States as having "led the way." Religion, Morality, and Abortion: A Constitutional Appraisal, 2 Loyola U. (L. A.) L. Rev. 1, 11 (1969).

By the end of 1970, four other States had repealed criminal penalties for abortions performed in early pregnancy by a licensed physician, subject to stated procedural and health requirements. Alaska Stat. § 11.15.060 (1970); Haw. Rev. Stat. § 453–16 (Supp. 1971); N. Y. Penal Code § 125.05, subd. 3 (Supp. 1972–1973); Wash. Rev. Code §§ 9.02.060 to 9.02.080 (Supp. 1972). The precise status of criminal abortion laws in some States is made unclear by recent decisions in state and federal courts striking down existing state laws, in whole or in part.

38. "Whereas, Abortion, like any other medical procedure, should not be performed when contrary to the best interests of the patient since good medical practice requires due consideration for the patient's welfare and not mere acquiescence to the patient's demand; and

"Whereas, The standards of sound clinical judgment, which, together with informed patient consent should be determinative according to the merits of each individual case; therefore be it

"*RESOLVED,* That abortion is a medical procedure and should be performed only by a duly licensed physician and surgeon in an accredited hospital acting only after consultation with two other physicians chosen because of their professional competency and in conformance with standards of good medical practice and the Medical Practice Act of his State; and be it further

"*RESOLVED,* That no physician or other professional personnel shall be compelled to perform any act which violates his good medical judgment. Neither physician, hospital, nor hospital personnel shall be required to perform any act violative of personally-held moral principles. In these circumstances good medical practice requires only that the physician or other professional personnel withdraw from the case so long as the withdrawal is consistent with good medical practice." Proceedings of the AMA House of Delegates 220 (June 1970).

39. "The Principles of Medical Ethics of the AMA do not prohibit a physician from performing an abortion that is performed in accordance with good medical practice and under circumstances that do not violate the laws of the community in which he practices.

"In the matter of abortions, as of any other medical procedure, the Judicial Council becomes involved whenever there is alleged violation of the Principles of Medical Ethics as established by the House of Delegates."

40.   "UNIFORM ABORTION ACT

"SECTION 1. [Abortion Defined; When Authorized.]

"(a) 'Abortion' means the termination of human pregnancy with an intention other than to produce a live birth or to remove a dead fetus.

"(b) An abortion may be performed in this state only if it is performed:

"(1) by a physician licensed to practice medicine [or osteopathy] in this state or by a physician practicing medicine [or osteopathy] in the employ of the government of the United States or of this state, [and the abortion is performed [in the physician's office or in a medical clinic, or] in a hospital approved by the [Department of Health] or operated by the United States, this state, or any department, agency, or political subdivision of either; or by a female upon herself upon the advice of the physician; and

"(2) within [20] weeks after the commencement of the pregnancy [or after [20] weeks only if the physician has reasonable cause to believe (i) there is a substantial risk that continuance of the pregnancy would endanger the life of the mother or would gravely impair the physical or mental health of the mother, (ii) that the child would be born with grave physical or mental defect, or (iii) that the pregnancy resulted from rape or incest, or illicit intercourse with a girl under the age of 16 years].

"SECTION 2. [Penalty.] Any person who performs or procures an abortion other than authorized by this Act is guilty of a [felony] and, upon conviction thereof, may be sentenced to pay a fine not exceeding [$1,000] or to imprisonment [in the state penitentiary] not exceeding [5 years], or both.

"SECTION 3. [Uniformity of Interpretation.] This Act shall be construed to effectuate its general purpose to make uniform the law with respect to the subject of this Act among those states which enact it.

"SECTION 4. [Short Title.] This Act may be cited as the Uniform Abortion Act.

"SECTION 5. [Severability.] If any provision of this Act or the application thereof to any person or circumstance is being invalid, the invalidity does not affect other provisions or applications of this Act which can be given effect without the invalid provision or application, and to this end the provisions of this Act are severable.

"SECTION 6. [Repeal.] The following acts and parts of acts are repealed:

"(1)

"(2)

"(3)

"SECTION 7. [Time of Taking Effect.] This Act shall take effect _____."

41. "This Act is based largely upon the New York abortion act following a review of the more recent laws on abortion in several states and upon recognition of a more liberal trend in laws on this subject. Recognition was given also to the several decisions in state and federal courts which show a further trend toward liberalization of abortion laws, especially during the first trimester of pregnancy.

"Recognizing that a number of problems appeared in New York, a shorter time period for 'unlimited' abortions was advisable. The time period was bracketed to permit the various states to insert a figure more in keeping with the different conditions that might exist among the states. Likewise, the language limiting the place or places in which abortions may be performed was also bracketed to account for different conditions among the states. In addition, limitations on abortions after the initial 'unlimited' period were placed in brackets so that individual states may adopt all or any of these reasons, or place further restrictions upon abortions after the initial period.

"This Act does not contain any provision relating to medical review committees or prohibitions against sanctions imposed upon medical personnel refusing to participate in abortions because of religious or other similar reasons, or the like. Such provisions, while related, do not directly pertain to when, where, or by whom abortions may be performed; however, the Act is not drafted to exclude such a provision by a state wishing to enact the same."

42. See, for example, YWCA v. Kugler, 342 F. Supp. 1048, 1074 (N. J. 1972); Abele v.

Markle, 342 F. Supp. 800, 805–806 (Conn. 1972) (Newman, J., concurring in result), appeal docketed, No. 72–56; *Walsingham v. State,* 250 So. 2d 857, 863 (Ervin, J., concurring) (Fla. 1971); *State v. Gedicke,* 43 N. J. L. 86, 90 (1881); Means II 381–382.

43. See C. Haagensen & W. Lloyd, A Hundred Years of Medicine 19 (1943).

44. Potts, Postconceptive Control of Fertility, 8 Int'l J. of G. & O. 957, 967 (1970) (England and Wales); Abortion Mortality, 20 Morbidity and Mortality 208, 209 (June 12, 1971) (U. S. Dept. of HEW, Public Health Service) (New York City); Tietze, United States; Therapeutic Abortions, 1963–1968, 59 Studies in Family Planning 5, 7 (1970); Tietze, Mortality with Contraception and Induced Abortion, 45 Studies in Family Planning 6 (1969) (Japan, Czechoslovakia, Hungary); Tietze & Lehfeldt, Legal Abortion in Eastern Europe, 175 J. A. M. A. 1149, 1152 (April 1961). Other sources are discussed in Lader 17–23.

45. See Brief of *Amicus* National Right to Life Committee; R. Drinan, The Inviolability of the Right to Be Born, in Abortion and the Law 107 (D. Smith ed. 1967); Louisell, Abortion, The Practice of Medicine and the Due Process of Law, 16 U. C. L. A. L. Rev. 233 (1969); Noonan 1.

46. See, *e.g., Abele v. Markle,* 342 F. Supp. 800 (Conn. 1972), appeal docketed, No. 72–56.

47. See discussions in Means I and Means II.

48. See, *e.g., State v. Murphy,* 27 N. J. L. 112, 114 (1858).

49. *Watson v. State,* 9 Tex. App. 237, 244–245 (1880); *Moore v. State,* 37 Tex. Cr. R. 552, 561, 40 S. W. 287, 290 (1897); *Shaw v. State,* 73 Tex. Cr. R. 337, 339, 165 S. W. 930, 931 (1914); *Fondren v. State,* 74 Tex. Cr. R. 552, 557, 169 S. W. 411, 414 (1914); *Gray v. State,* 77 Tex. Cr. R. 221, 229, 178 S. W. 337, 341 (1915). There is no immunity in Texas for the father who is not married to the mother. *Hammett v. State,* 84 Tex. Cr. R. 635, 209 S. W. 661 (1919); *Thompson v. State* (Ct. Crim. App. Tex. 1971), appeal docketed, No. 71–1200.

50. See *Smith v. State,* 33 Me., at 55; *In re Vince,* 2 N. J. 443, 450, 67 A. 2d 141, 144 (1949). A short discussion of the modern law on this issue is contained in the Comment to the ALI's Model Penal Code § 207.11, at 158 and nn. 35–37 (Tent. Draft No. 9, 1959).

51. Tr. of Oral Rearg. 20–21.

52. Tr. of Oral Rearg. 24.

53. We are not aware that in the taking of any census under this clause, a fetus has ever been counted.

54. When Texas urges that a fetus is entitled to Fourteenth Amendment protection as a person, it faces a dilemma. Neither in Texas nor in any other State are all abortions prohibited. Despite broad proscription, an exception always exists. The exception contained in Art. 1196, for an abortion procured or attempted by medical advice for the purpose of saving the life of the mother, is typical. But if the fetus is a person who is not to be deprived of life without due process of law, and if the mother's condition is the sole determinant, does not the Texas exception appear to be out of line with the Amendment's command?

There are other inconsistencies between Fourteenth Amendment status and the typical abortion statute. It has already been pointed out, n. 49, *supra,* that in Texas the woman is not a principal or an accomplice with respect to an abortion upon her. If the fetus is a person, why is the woman not a principal or an accomplice? Further, the penalty for criminal abortion specified by Art. 1195 is significantly less than the maximum penalty for murder prescribed by Art. 1257 of the Texas Penal Code. If the fetus is a person, may the penalties be different?

55. Cf. the Wisconsin abortion statute, defining "unborn child" to mean "a human being from the time of conception until it is born alive," Wis. Stat. § 940.04 (6) (1969), and the new Connecticut statute, Pub. Act. No. 1 (May 1972 special session), declaring it to be the public policy of the State and the legislative intent "to protect and preserve human life from the moment of conception."

56. Edelstein 16.

57. Lader 97–99; D. Feldman, Birth Control in Jewish Law 251–294 (1968). For a stricter view, see I. Jakobovits, Jewish Views on Abortion, in Abortion and the Law 124 (D. Smith ed. 1967).

58. Amicus Brief for the American Ethical Union et al. For the position of the National Council of Churches and of other denominations, see Lader 99–101.

59. L. Hellman & J. Pritchard, Williams Obstetrics 493 (14th ed. 1971); Dorland's Illustrated Medical Dictionary 1689 (24th ed. 1965).

60. Hellman & Pritchard, *supra,* n. 59, at 493.

61. For discussions of the development of the Roman Catholic position, see D. Callahan, Abortion: Law, Choice, and Morality 409–447 (1970); Noonan 1.

62. See Brodie, The New Biology and the Prenatal Child, 9 J. Family L. 391, 397 (1970); Gorney, The New Biology and the Future of Man, 15 U. C. L. A. L. Rev. 273 (1968); Note, Criminal Law—Abortion—The "Morning-After Pill" and Other Pre-Implantation Birth-Control Methods and the Law, 46 Ore. L. Rev. 211 (1967); G. Taylor, The Biological Time Bomb 32 (1968); A. Rosenfeld, The Second Genesis 138–139 (1969); Smith, Through a Test Tube Darkly: Artificial Insemination and the Law, 67 Mich. L. Rev. 127 (1968); Note, Artificial Insemination and the Law, 1968 U. Ill. L. F. 203.

63. W. Prosser, The Law of Torts 335–338 (4th ed. 1971); 2 F. Harper & F. James, The Law of Torts 1028–1031 (1956); Note, 63 Harv. L. Rev. 173 (1949).

64. See cases cited in Prosser, *supra,* n. 63, at 336–338; Annotation, Action for Death of Unborn Child, 15 A. L. R. 3d 992 (1967).

65. Prosser, *supra,* n. 63, at 338; Note, The Law and the Unborn Child: The Legal and Logical Inconsistencies, 46 Notre Dame Law. 349, 354–360 (1971).

66. Louisell, Abortion, The Practice of Medicine and the Due Process of Law, 16 U. C. L. A. L. Rev. 233, 235–238 (1969); Note, 56 Iowa L. Rev. 994, 999–1000 (1971); Note, The Law and the Unborn Child, 46 Notre Dame Law. 349, 351–354 (1971).

67. Neither in this opinion nor in *Doe v. Bolton, post,* p. 179, do we discuss the father's rights, if any exist in the constitutional context, in the abortion decision. No paternal right has been asserted in either of the cases, and the Texas and the Georgia statutes on their face take no cognizance of the father. We are aware that some statutes recognize the father under certain circumstances. North Carolina, for example, N. C. Gen. Stat. § 14–45.1 (Supp. 1971), requires written permission for the abortion from the husband when the woman is a married minor, that is, when she is less than 18 years of age, 41 N. C. A. G. 489 (1971); if the woman is an unmarried minor, written permission from the parents is required. We need not now decide whether provisions of this kind are constitutional.

68. Only Mr. Justice Harlan failed to join the Court's opinion, 372 U. S., at 733.

69. There is no constitutional right of privacy, as such. "[The Fourth] Amendment protects individual privacy against certain kinds of governmental intrusion, but its protections go further, and often have nothing to do with privacy at all. Other provisions of the Constitution protect personal privacy from other forms of governmental invasion. But the protection of a person's *general* right to privacy—his right to be let alone by other people—is, like the protection of his property and of his very life, left largely to the law of the individual States." *Katz v. United States,* 389 U. S. 347, 350–351 (footnotes omitted).

70. This was also clear to Mr. Justice Black, 381 U. S., at 507 (dissenting opinion); to Mr. Justice Harlan, 381 U. S., at 499 (opinion concurring in the judgment); and to Mr. Justice White, 381 U. S., at 502 (opinion concurring in the judgment). See also Mr. Justice Harlan's thorough and thoughtful opinion dissenting from dismissal of the appeal in *Poe v. Ullman,* 367 U. S. 497, 522.

71. Jurisdictions having enacted abortion laws prior to the adoption of the Fourteenth Amendment in 1868:

    1. Alabama—Ala. Acts, c. 6, § 2 (1840).

    2. Arizona—Howell Code, c. 10, § 45 (1865).

    3. Arkansas—Ark. Rev. Stat., c. 44, div. III, Art. II, § 6 (1838).

    4. California—Cal. Sess. Laws, c. 99, § 45, p. 233 (1849–1850).

    5. Colorado (Terr.)—Colo. Gen. Laws of Terr. of Colo., 1st Sess., § 42, pp. 296–297 (1861).

    6. Connecticut—Conn. Stat., Tit. 20, §§ 14, 16 (1821). By 1868, this statute had been replaced by another abortion law. Conn. Pub. Acts, c. 71, §§ 1, 2, p. 65 (1860).

7. Florida—Fla. Acts 1st Sess., c. 1637, subc. 3, §§ 10, 11, subc. 8, §§ 9, 10, 11 (1868), as amended, now Fla. Stat. Ann. §§ 782.09, 782.10, 797.01, 797.02, 782.16 (1965).

8. Georgia—Ga. Pen. Code, 4th Div., § 20 (1833).

9. Kingdom of Hawaii—Hawaii Pen. Code, c. 12, §§ 1, 2, 3 (1850).

10. Idaho (Terr.)—Idaho (Terr.) Laws, Crimes and Punishments §§ 33, 34, 42, pp. 441, 443 (1863).

11. Illinois—Ill. Rev. Criminal Code §§ 40, 41, 46, pp. 130, 131 (1827). By 1868, this statute had been replaced by a subsequent enactment. Ill. Pub. Laws §§ 1, 2, 3, p. 89 (1867).

12. Indiana—Ind. Rev. Stat. §§ 1, 3, p. 224 (1838). By 1868 this statute had been superseded by a subsequent enactment. Ind. Laws, c. LXXXI, § 2 (1859).

13. Iowa (Terr.)—Iowa (Terr.) Stat., 1st Legis., 1st Sess., § 18, p. 145 (1838). By 1868, this statute had been superseded by a subsequent enactment. Iowa (Terr.) Rev. Stat., c. 49, §§ 10, 13 (1843).

14. Kansas (Terr.)—Kan. (Terr.) Stat., c. 48, §§ 9, 10, 39 (1855). By 1868, this statute had been superseded by a subsequent enactment. Kan. (Terr.) Laws, c. 28, §§ 9, 10, 37 (1859).

15. Louisiana—La. Rev. Stat., Crimes and Offenses § 24, p. 138 (1856).

16. Maine—Me. Rev. Stat., c. 160, §§ 11, 12, 13, 14 (1840).

17. Maryland—Md. Laws, c. 179, § 2, p. 315 (1868).

18. Massachusetts—Mass. Acts & Resolves, c. 27 (1845).

19. Michigan—Mich. Rev. Stat., c. 153, §§ 32, 33, 34, p. 662 (1846).

20. Minnesota (Terr.)—Minn. (Terr.) Rev. Stat., c. 100, §§ 10, 11, p. 493 (1851).

21. Mississippi—Miss. Code, c. 64, §§ 8, 9, p. 958 (1848).

22. Missouri—Mo. Rev. Stat., Art. II, §§ 9, 10, 36, pp. 168, 172 (1835).

23. Montana (Terr.)—Mont. (Terr.) Laws, Criminal Practice Acts § 41, p. 184 (1864).

24. Nevada (Terr.)—Nev. (Terr.) Laws, c. 28, § 42, p. 63 (1861).

25. New Hampshire—N. H. Laws, c. 743, § 1, p. 708 (1848).

26. New Jersey—N. J. Laws, p. 266 (1849).

27. New York—N. Y. Rev. Stat., pt. 4, c. 1, Tit. 2, §§ 8, 9, pp. 12–13 (1828). By 1868, this statute had been superseded. N. Y. Laws, c. 260, §§ 1–6, pp. 285–286 (1845); N. Y. Laws, c. 22, § 1, p. 19 (1846).

28. Ohio—Ohio Gen. Stat. §§ 111 (1), 112 (2), p. 252 (1841).

29. Oregon—Ore. Gen. Laws, Crim. Code, c. 43, § 509, p. 528 (1845–1864).

30. Pennsylvania—Pa. Laws No. 374, §§ 87, 88, 89 (1860).

31. Texas—Tex. Gen. Stat. Dig., c. VII, Arts. 531–536, p. 524 (Oldham & White 1859).

32. Vermont—Vt. Acts No. 33, § 1 (1846). By 1868, this statute had been amended. Vt. Acts No. 57, §§ 1, 3 (1867).

33. Virginia—Va. Acts, Tit. II, c. 3, § 9, p. 96 (1848).

34. Washington (Terr.)—Wash. (Terr.) Stats., c. II, §§ 37, 38, p. 81 (1854).

35. West Virginia—See Va. Acts., Tit. II, c. 3, § 9, p. 96 (1848); W. Va. Const., Art. XI, par. 8 (1863).

36. Wisconsin—Wis. Rev. Stat., c. 133, §§ 10, 11 (1849). By 1868, this statute had been superseded. Wis. Rev. Stat., c. 164, §§ 10, 11; c. 169, §§ 58, 59 (1858).

72. Abortion laws in effect in 1868 and still applicable as of August 1970:

1. Arizona (1865).

2. Connecticut (1860).

3. Florida (1868).

4. Idaho (1863).

5. Indiana (1838).

6. Iowa (1843).

7. Maine (1840).

8. Massachusetts (1845).

9. Michigan (1846).

10. Minnesota (1851).
11. Missouri (1835).
12. Montana (1864).
13. Nevada (1861).
14. New Hampshire (1848).
15. New Jersey (1849).
16. Ohio (1841).
17. Pennsylvania (1860).
18. Texas (1859).
19. Vermont (1867).
20. West Virginia (1863).
21. Wisconsin (1858).

PLANNED PARENTHOOD OF CENTRAL MISSOURI v. DANFORTH

Supreme Court of the United States, 1976.
428 U.S. 52, 96 S.Ct. 2831, 49 L.Ed.2d 788.

MR. JUSTICE BLACKMUN delivered the opinion of the Court.

This case is a logical and anticipated corollary to *Roe v. Wade,* 410 U. S. 113, 93 S.Ct. 705, 35 L.Ed.2d 147 (1973), and *Doe v. Bolton,* 410 U. S. 179, 93 S.Ct. 739, 35 L.Ed.2d 201 (1973), for it raises issues secondary to those that were then before the Court. Indeed, some of the questions now presented were forecast and reserved in *Roe* and *Doe.* 410 U. S., at 165 n. 67, 93 S.Ct., at 733.

I

After the decisions in *Roe* and *Doe,* this Court remanded for reconsideration a pending Missouri federal case in which the State's then existing abortion legislation, Mo.Rev.Stat. §§ 559.100, 542.380, and 563.300 (1969), was under constitutional challenge. *Rodgers v. Danforth,* 410 U. S. 949, 93 S.Ct. 1410, 35 L.Ed.2d 682 (1973). A three-judge federal court for the Western District of Missouri, in an unreported decision, thereafter declared the challenged Missouri statutes unconstitutional and granted injunctive relief. On appeal here, that judgment was summarily affirmed. *Danforth v. Rodgers,* 414 U. S. 1035, 94 S.Ct. 534, 38 L.Ed.2d 327 (1973).

In June 1974, somewhat more than a year after *Roe* and *Doe* had been decided, Missouri's 77th General Assembly, in its Second Regular Session, enacted House Committee Substitute for House Bill No. 1211 (hereinafter referred to as the "Act"). The legislation was approved by the Governor on June 14, 1974, and became effective immediately by reason of an emergency clause contained in § A of the statute. The Act is set forth in full as the Appendix to this opinion. It imposes a structure for the control and regulation of abortions in Missouri during all stages of pregnancy.

II

Three days after the Act became effective, the present litigation was instituted in the United States District Court for the Eastern District of Missouri. The plaintiffs are Planned Parenthood of Central Missouri, a not-for-profit Missouri corporation which maintains a facility in Columbia, Mo., for the performance of abortions; David Hall, M.D.; and Michael Freiman, M.D. Doctor Hall is a resident of Columbia, is licensed as a physician in Missouri, is chairman of the Department and Professor of Obstetrics and Gynecology at the University of Missouri Medical School at Columbia, and supervises abortions at the Planned Parenthood facility. He was described by the three-judge court in the 1973 case as one of four plaintiffs who were "eminent, Missouri-licensed obstetricians and gynecologists." No. 73–426, *Danforth v. Rodgers,* Juris. Statement A7. Doctor Freiman is a resident of St. Louis, is licensed as a physician in Missouri, is an instructor of Clinical Obstetrics and Gynecology at Washington University Medical School, and performs abortions at two St. Louis hospitals and at a clinic in that city.

The named defendants are the Attorney General of Missouri and the Circuit Attorney of the city of St. Louis "in his representative capacity" and "as the representative of the class of all similar Prosecuting Attorneys of the various counties of the State of Missouri." Complaint 10.

The plaintiffs brought the action on their own behalf and, purportedly, "on behalf of the entire class consisting of duly licensed physicians and surgeons presently performing or desiring to perform the termination of pregnancies and on behalf of the entire class consisting of their patients desiring the termination of pregnancy, all within the State of Missouri." *Id.,* at 9. Plaintiffs sought declaratory relief and also sought to enjoin enforcement of the Act on the ground, among others, that certain of its provisions deprived them and their patients of various constitutional rights: "the right to privacy in the physician-patient relationship"; the physicians' "right to practice medicine according to the highest standards of medical practice"; the female patients' right to determine whether to bear children; the patients' "right to life due to the inherent risk involved in childbirth" or in medical procedures alternative to abortion; the physicians' "right to give and plaintiffs' patients' right to receive safe and adequate medical advice and treatment, pertaining to the decision of whether to carry a given pregnancy to term and method of termination"; the patients' right under the Eighth Amendment to be free from cruel and unusual punishment "by forcing and coercing them to bear each pregnancy they conceive"; and, by being placed "in the position of decision making beset with . . . inherent possibilities of bias and conflict of interest," the physician's right to due process of law guaranteed by the Fourteenth Amendment. *Id.,* at 10–11.

The particular provisions of the Act that remained under specific challenge at the end of trial were § 2(2), defining the term "viability"; § 3(2), requiring from the woman, prior to submitting to abortion during the first 12 weeks of pregnancy, a certification in writing that she consents to the procedure and "that her consent is informed and freely given and is not the result of coercion"; § 3(3), requiring, for the same period, "the written consent of the woman's spouse, unless the abortion is certified by a licensed physician to be necessary in order to preserve the life of the mother"; § 3(4), requiring, for the same period, "the written consent of one parent or person in loco parentis of the woman if the woman is unmarried and under the age of eighteen years, unless the abortion is certified by a licensed physician as necessary in order to preserve the life of the mother"; § 6(1), requiring the physician to exercise professional care "to preserve the life and health of the fetus" and, failing such, deeming him guilty of manslaughter and making him liable in an action for damages; § 7, declaring an infant, who survives "an attempted abortion which was not performed to save the life or health of the mother," to be "an abandoned ward of the state under the jurisdiction of the juvenile court," and depriving the mother, and also the father if he consented to the abortion, of parental rights; § 9, the legislative finding that method of abortion known as saline amniocentesis "is deleterious to maternal health," and prohibiting that method after the first 12 weeks of pregnancy; and §§ 10 and 11, imposing reporting and maintenance of record requirements for health facilities and for physicians who perform abortions.

The case was presented to a three-judge District Court convened pursuant to the provisions of 28 U. S. C. §§ 2281 and 2284. 392 F.Supp. 1362 (1975). The court ruled that the two physician-plaintiffs had standing inasmuch as § 6(1) provides that the physician who fails to exercise the prescribed standard of professional care due the fetus in the abortion procedure shall be guilty of manslaughter, and § 14 provides that any person who performs or aids in the performance of an abortion contrary to the provisions of the Act shall be guilty of a misdemeanor. *Id.,* at 1366–1367. Due to this "obvious standing" of the two physicians, *id.,* at 1367, the court deemed it unnecessary to determine whether Planned Parenthood also had standing.

On the issues as to the constitutionality of the several challenged sections of the Act, the District Court, largely by a divided vote, ruled that all except the first sentence of § 6(1) withstood the attack. That sentence was held to be constitutionally impermissible because it imposed upon the physician the duty to exercise at all stages of pregnancy "that degree of professional skill, care and diligence to preserve the life and health of the fetus" that "would be required . . . to preserve the life and health of any fetus intended to be born." Inasmuch as this failed to exclude the stage of pregnancy prior to viability, the provision was "unconstitutionally overbroad." *Id.,* at 1371.

One judge concurred in part and dissented in part. *Id.,* at 1374. He agreed with the majority as to the constitutionality of §§ 2(2), 3(2), 10, and 11, respectively relating to the definition of "viability," the woman's prior written consent, maintenance of records, and retention of records. He also agreed with the majority that § 6(1) was unconstitutionally overbroad. He dissented from the majority opinion upholding the constitutionality of §§ 3(3), 3(4), 7, and 9, relating, respectively, to spousal consent, parental consent, the termination of parental rights, and the proscription of saline amniocentesis.

In No. 74–1151, the plaintiffs appeal from that part of the District Court's judgment upholding sections of the Act as constitutional and denying injunctive relief against their application and enforcement. In No. 74–1419, the defendant Attorney General cross-appeals from that part of the judgment holding § 6(1) unconstitutional and enjoining enforcement thereof. We granted the plaintiffs' application for stay of enforcement of the Act pending appeal. 420 U. S. 918, 95 S.Ct. 1111, 43 L.Ed.2d 389 (1975). Probable jurisdiction of both appeals thereafter was noted. 423 U. S. 819, 96 S.Ct. 31, 46 L.Ed.2d 36 (1975).

For convenience, we shall usually refer to the plaintiffs as "appellants" and to both named defendants as "appellees."

III

In *Roe v. Wade* the Court concluded that the "right of privacy, whether it be founded in the Fourteenth Amendment's concept of personal liberty and restrictions upon state action, as we feel it is, or, as the District Court determined, in the Ninth Amendment's reservation of rights to the people, is broad enough to encompass a woman's decision whether or not to terminate her pregnancy." 410 U. S., at 153, 93 S.Ct., at 727. It emphatically rejected, however, the proffered argument "that the woman's right is absolute and that she is entitled to terminate her pregnancy at whatever time, in whatever way, and for whatever reason she alone chooses." *Ibid.* Instead, this right "must be considered against important state interests in regulation." *Id.,* at 154, 93 S.Ct. at 727.

The Court went on to say that the "pregnant woman cannot be isolated in her privacy," for she "carries an embryo and, later, a fetus." *Id.,* at 159, 93 S.Ct., at 730. It was therefore "reasonable and appropriate for a State to decide that at some point in time another interest, that of health of the mother or that of potential human life, becomes significantly involved. The woman's privacy is no longer sole and any right of privacy she possesses must be measured accordingly." *Ibid.* The Court stressed the measure of the State's interest in "the light of present medical knowledge." *Id.,* at 163, 93 S.Ct., at 731. It concluded that the permissibility of State regulation was to be viewed in three stages: "For the stage prior to approximately the end of the first trimester, the abortion decision and its effectuation must be left to the medical judgment of the pregnant woman's attending physician," without interference from the State. *Id.,* at 164, 93 S.Ct., at 732. The participation by the attending physician in the abortion decision, and his responsibility in that decision, thus, were emphasized. After the first stage, as so described, the State may, if it chooses, reasonably regulate the abortion procedure to preserve and protect maternal health. *Ibid.* Finally, for the stage subsequent to viability, a point purposefully left flexible for professional determination, and dependent upon developing medical skill and technical ability,[1] the State may regulate an abortion to protect the life of the fetus and even may proscribe abortion except where it is necessary, in appropriate medical judgment, for the preservation of the life or health of the mother. *Id.,* at 163–165, 93 S.Ct., at 731–733.

IV

[1] With the exception specified in n. 2, *infra,* we agree with the District Court that the physician-appellants clearly have standing. This was established in *Doe v. Bolton,* 410 U. S., at 188, 93 S.Ct., at 745. Like the Georgia statutes challenged in that case, "[t]he physician is the one against whom [the Missouri Act] directly operate[s] in the event he procures an abortion that does not meet the statutory exceptions and conditions. The physician-appellants, therefore, assert a sufficiently direct threat of personal detriment. They should not be required to await and undergo a criminal prosecution as the sole means of seeking relief."[2] *Ibid.*

Our primary task, then, is to consider each of the challenged provisions of the new Missouri abortion statute in the particular light of the opinions and decisions in *Roe* and in *Doe*. To this we now turn, with the assistance of helpful briefs from both sides and from some of the *amici*.

A

[2] *The definition of viability.* Section 2(2) of the Act defines "viability" as "that stage of fetal development when the life of the unborn child may be continued indefinitely outside the womb by natural or artificial life-supportive systems." Appellants claim that this definition violates and conflicts with the discussion of viability in our opinion in *Roe*. 410 U. S., at 160, 163, 93 S.Ct., at 730, 731. In particular, appellants object to the failure of the definition to contain any reference to a gestational time period, to its failure to incorporate and reflect the three stages of pregnancy, to the presence of the word "indefinitely," and to the extra burden of regulation imposed. It is suggested that the definition expands the Court's definition of viability, as expressed in *Roe,* and amounts to a legislative determination of what is properly a matter for medical judgment. It is said that the "mere possibility of momentary survival is not the medical standard of viability." Brief for Appellants 67.

In *Roe,* we used the term "viable," properly we thought, to signify the point at which the fetus is "potentially able to live outside the mother's womb, albeit with artificial aid," and presumably capable of "meaningful life outside the mother's womb," 410 U. S., at 160, 163, 93 S.Ct. at 730, 732. We noted that this point "is usually placed" at about seven months or 28 weeks, but may occur earlier. *Id.,* at 160, 93 S.Ct., at 730.

We agree with the District Court and conclude that the definition of viability in the Act does not conflict with what was said and held in *Roe*. In fact, we believe that § 2(2), even when read in conjunction with § 5 (proscribing an abortion "not necessary to preserve the life or health of the mother . . . unless the attending physician first certifies with reasonable medical certainty that the fetus is not viable"), the constitutionality of which is not explicitly challenged here, reflects an attempt on the part of the Missouri General Assembly to comply with our observations and discussion in *Roe* relating to viability. Appellant Hall, in his deposition, had no particular difficulty with the statutory definition.[3] As noted above, we recognized in *Roe* that viability was a matter of medical judgment, skill, and technical ability, and we preserved the flexibility of the term. Section 2(2) does the same. Indeed, one might argue, as the appellees do, that the presence of the statute's words "continued indefinitely" favor, rather than disfavor, the appellants, for, arguably, the point when life can be "continued indefinitely outside the womb" may well occur later in pregnancy than the point where the fetus is "potentially able to live outside the mother's womb." *Roe v. Wade,* 410 U. S., at 160, 93 S.Ct., at 730.

In any event, we agree with the District Court that it is not the proper function of the legislature or the courts to place viability, which essentially is a medical concept, at a specific point in the gestation period. The time when viability is achieved may vary with each pregnancy, and the determination of whether a particular fetus is viable is, and must be, a matter for the judgment of the responsible attending physician. The definition of viability in § 2(2) merely reflects this fact.

The appellees do not contend otherwise, for they insist that the determination of viability rests with the physician in the exercise of his professional judgment.[4]

We thus do not accept appellants' contention that a specified number of weeks in pregnancy must be fixed by statute as the point of viability. See *Wolfe v. Schroering*, 388 F.Supp. 631, 637 (W.D.Ky.1974); *Hodgson v. Anderson*, 378 F.Supp. 1008, 1016 (Minn.1974), dism'd for want of jurisdiction *sub nom., Spannaus v. Hodgson*, 420 U. S. 903, 95 S.Ct. 819, 42 L.Ed.2d 832 (1975).[5]

We conclude that the definition in § 2(2) of the Act does not circumvent the limitations on state regulation outlined in *Roe*. We therefore hold that the Act's definition of "viability" comports with *Roe* and withstands the constitutional attack made upon it in this litigation.

B

[3] *The woman's consent.* Under § 3(2) of the Act, a woman, prior to submitting to an abortion during the first 12 weeks of pregnancy, must certify in writing her consent to the procedure and "that her consent is informed and freely given and is not the result of coercion." Appellants argue that this requirement is violative of *Roe v. Wade*, 410 U. S., at 164–165, 93 S.Ct., at 732–733, by imposing an extra layer and burden of regulation on the abortion decision. See *Doe v. Bolton*, 410 U. S., at 195–200, 93 S.Ct., at 749–751. Appellants also claim that the provision is overbroad and vague.

The District Court's majority relied on the propositions that the decision to terminate a pregnancy, of course, "is often a stressful one," and that the consent requirement of § 3(2) "insures that the pregnant woman retains control over the discretions of her consulting physician." 392 F.Supp., at 1368, 1369. The majority also felt that the consent requirement "does not single out the abortion procedure, but merely includes it within the category of medical operations for which consent is required."[6] *Id.,* at 1369. The third judge joined the majority in upholding § 3(2), but added that the written consent requirement was "not burdensome or chilling" and manifested "a legitimate interest of the state that this important decision has in fact been made by the person constitutionally empowered to do so." 392 F.Supp., at 1374. He went on to observe that the requirement "in no way interposes the state or third parties in the decision-making process." *Id.,* at 1375.

We do not disagree with the result reached by the District Court as to § 3(2). It is true that *Doe* and *Roe* clearly establish the State may not restrict the decision of the patient and her physician regarding abortion during the first stage of pregnancy. Despite the fact that apparently no other Missouri statute, with the exceptions referred to in n. 6, *supra,* requires a patient's prior written consent to a surgical procedure,[7] the imposition by § 3(2) of such a requirement for termination of pregnancy even during the first stage, in our view, is not in itself an unconstitutional requirement. The decision to abort, indeed, is an important, and often a stressful one, and it is desirable and imperative that it be made with full knowledge of its nature and consequences. The woman is the one primarily concerned, and her awareness of the decision and its significance may be assured, constitutionally, by the State to the extent of requiring her prior written consent.

We could not say that a requirement imposed by the State that a prior written consent for any surgery would be unconstitutional. As a consequence, we see no constitutional defect in requiring it only for some types of surgery as, for example, an intracardiac procedure, or where the surgical risk is elevated above a specified mortality level, or, for that matter, for abortions.[8]

C

[4] *The spouse's consent.* Section 3(3) requires the prior written consent of the spouse of the woman seeking an abortion during the first 12 weeks of pregnancy, unless "the abortion is certified by a licensed physician to be necessary in order to preserve the life of the mother."[9]

The appellees defend § 3(3) on the ground that it was enacted in the light of the General Assembly's "perception of marriage as an institution," Brief for Appellees 34, and that any major change in family status is a decision to be made jointly by the marriage partners. Reference is made to an abortion's possible effect on the woman's childbearing potential. It is said that marriage always has entailed some legislatively imposed limitations: reference is made to adultery and bigamy as criminal offenses; to Missouri's general requirement, Mo.Rev. Stat. § 453.030.3 (1969), that for an adoption of a child born in wedlock the consent of both parents is necessary; to similar joint consent requirements imposed by a number of States with respect to artificial insemination and the legitimacy of children so conceived; to the laws of two States requiring spousal consent for voluntary sterilization; and to the long-established requirement of spousal consent for the effective disposition of an interest in real property. It is argued that "[r]ecognizing that the consent of both parties is generally necessary . . . to begin a family, the legislature has determined that a change in the family structure set in motion by mutual consent should be terminated only by mutual consent," Brief for Appellees 38, and that what the legislature did was to exercise its inherent policy-making power "for what was believed to be in the best interests of all people of Missouri." *Id.,* at 40.

The appellants on the other hand, contend that § 3(3) obviously is designed to afford the husband the right unilaterally to prevent or veto an abortion, whether or not he is the father of the fetus, and that this not only violates *Roe* and *Doe* but is also in conflict with other decided cases. See, *e.g., Poe v. Gerstein,* 517 F.2d 787, 794–796 (CA5 1975), Juris. Statement pending, No. 75–713; *Wolfe v. Schroering,* 388 F. Supp., at 636–637; *Doe v. Rampton,* 366 F.Supp. 189, 193 (Utah 1973). They also refer to the situation where the husband's consent cannot be obtained because he cannot be located. And they assert that § 3(3) is vague and overbroad.

In *Roe* and *Doe* we specifically reserved decision on the question whether a requirement for consent by the father of the fetus, by the spouse, or by the parents, or a parent, of an unmarried minor, may be constitutionally imposed. 410 U. S., at 165 n. 67, 93 S.Ct., at 733. We now hold that the State may not constitutionally require the consent of the spouse, as is specified under § 3(3) of the Missouri Act, as a condition for abortion during the first 12 weeks of pregnancy. We thus agree with the dissenting judge in the present case, and with the courts whose decisions are cited above, that the State cannot "delegate to a spouse a veto power which the state itself is absolutely and totally prohibited from exercising during the first trimester of pregnancy." 392 F.Supp., at 1375. Clearly, since the State cannot regulate or proscribe abortion during the first stage, when the physician and his patient make that decision, the State cannot delegate authority to any particular person, even the spouse, to prevent abortion during that same period.

We are not unaware of the deep and proper concern and interest that a devoted and protective husband has in his wife's pregnancy and in the growth and development of the fetus she is carrying. Neither has this Court failed to appreciate the importance of the marital relationship in our society. See, *e.g., Griswold v. Connecticut,* 381 U. S. 479, 486, 85 S.Ct. 1678, 1682, 14 L.Ed.2d 510 (1965); *Maynard v. Hill,* 125 U. S. 190, 211, 8 S.Ct. 723, 729, 31 L.Ed. 654 (1888).[10] Moreover, we recognize that the decision whether to undergo or to forego an abortion may have profound effects on the future of any marriage, effects that are both physical and mental, and possibly deleterious. Notwithstanding these factors, we cannot hold that the State has the constitutional authority to give the spouse unilaterally the ability to prohibit the wife from terminating her pregnancy, when the State itself lacks that right. See *Eisenstadt v. Baird,* 405 U. S. 438, 453, 92 S.Ct. 1029, 1038, 31 L.Ed.2d 349 (1972).[11]

It seems manifest that, ideally, the decision to terminate a pregnancy should be one concurred in by both the wife and her husband. No marriage may be viewed as harmonious or successful if the marriage partners are fundamentally divided on so important and vital an issue. But it is difficult to believe that the goal of fostering mutuality and trust in a marriage, and of strengthening the marital relationship and the marriage institution, will be achieved by giving the husband a veto power exercisable for any reason whatsoever or for no reason at all. Even if the State had the ability to delegate to the husband a power it itself could not exercise, it is not at all likely that such action would further, as the District Court majority phrased it, the "interest of the state in protecting the mutuality of decisions vital to the marriage relationship." 392 F.Supp., at 1370.

We recognize, of course, that when a woman, with the approval of her physician but without the approval of her husband, decides to terminate her pregnancy, it could be said that she is acting unilaterally. The obvious fact is that when the wife and the husband disagree on this decision, the view of only one of the two marriage partners can prevail. Since it is the woman who physically bears the child and who is the more directly and immediately affected by the pregnancy, as between the two, the balance weighs in her favor. Cf. *Roe v. Wade,* 410 U. S., at 153, 93 S.Ct., at 726.

We conclude that § 3(3) of the Missouri Act is inconsistent with the standards enunciated in *Roe v. Wade,* 410 U. S., at 164–165, 93 S.Ct., at 732-733, and is unconstitutional. It is therefore unnecessary for us to consider the appellant's additional challenges to § 3(3) based on vagueness and overbreadth.

D

[5] *Parental consent.* Section 3(4) requires, with respect to the first 12 weeks of pregnancy, where the woman is unmarried and under the age of 18 years, the

written consent of a parent or person *in loco parentis* unless, again, "the abortion is certified by a licensed physician as necessary in order to preserve the life of the mother." It is to be observed that only one parent need consent.

The appellees defend the statute in several ways. They point out that the law properly may subject minors to more stringent limitations than are permissible with respect to adults, and they cite, among other cases, *Prince v. Massachusetts,* 321 U. S. 158, 64 S.Ct. 438, 88 L.Ed. 645 (1944), and *McKeiver v. Pennsylvania,* 403 U. S. 528, 91 S.Ct. 1976, 29 L.Ed.2d 647 (1971). Missouri law, it is said, "is replete with provisions reflecting the interest of the state in assuring the welfare of minors," citing statutes relating to a guardian *ad litem* for a court proceeding, to the care of delinquent and neglected children, to child labor, and to compulsory education. Brief for Appellees 42. Certain decisions are considered by the State to be outside the scope of a minor's ability to act in his own best interest or in the interest of the public, citing statutes proscribing the sale of firearms and deadly weapons to minors without parental consent, and other statutes relating to minors' exposure to certain types of literature, the purchase by pawnbrokers of property from minors, and the sale of cigarettes and alcoholic beverages to minors. It is pointed out that the record contains testimony to the effect that children of tender years (even ages 10 and 11) have sought abortions. Thus, a State's permitting a child to obtain an abortion without the counsel of an adult "who has responsibility or concern for the child would constitute an irresponsible abdication of the State's duty to protect the welfare of minors." *Id.,* at 44. Parental discretion, too, has been protected from unwarranted or unreasonable interference from the State, citing *Meyer v. Nebraska,* 262 U. S. 390, 43 S.Ct. 625, 67 L.Ed. 1042 (1923); *Pierce v. Society of Sisters,* 268 U. S. 510, 45 S.Ct. 571, 69, L.Ed. 1070 (1925); *Wisconsin v. Yoder,* 406 U. S. 205, 92 S.Ct. 1526, 32 L.Ed.2d 15 (1972). Finally, it is said that § 3(4) imposes no additional burden on the physician because even prior to the passage of the Act the physician would require parental consent before performing an abortion on a minor.

The appellants, in their turn, emphasize that no other Missouri statute specifically requires the additional consent of a minor's parent for medical or surgical treatment, and that in Missouri a minor legally may consent to medical services for pregnancy (excluding abortion), venereal disease, and drug abuse. Mo.Laws 1971, p. 425–426, H.B.No.73, §§ 1–3. The result of § 3(4), it is said, "is the ultimate supremacy of the parents' desires over those of the minor child, the pregnant patient." Brief for Appellants 93. It is noted that in Missouri a woman under the age of 18 who marries with parental consent does not require parental consent to abort, and yet her contemporary who has chosen not to marry must obtain parental approval.

The District Court majority recognized that, in contrast to § 3(3), the State's interest in protecting the mutuality of a marriage relationship is not present with respect to § 3(4). It found "a compelling basis," however, in the State's interest "in safeguarding the authority of the family relationship." 392 F.Supp., at 1370. The dissenting judge observed that one could not seriously argue that a minor must submit to an abortion if her parents insist, and he could not see "why she would not be entitled to the same right of self-determination now explicitly accorded to adult women, provided she is sufficiently mature to understand the procedure and to make an intelligent assessment of her circumstances with the advice of her physician." *Id.,* at 1376.

Of course, much of what has been said above, with respect to § 3(3), applies with equal force to § 3(4). Other courts that have considered the parental consent issue in the light of *Roe* and *Doe,* have concluded that a statute like § 3(4) does not withstand constitutional scrutiny. See, *e.g., Poe v. Gerstein,* 517 F.2d, at 792; *Wolfe v. Schroering,* 388 F.Supp., at 636–637; *Doe v. Rampton,* 366 F.Supp., at 193, 199; *State v. Koome,* 84 Wash.2d 901, 530 P.2d 260 (1975).

We agree with appellants and with the courts whose decisions have just been cited that the State may not impose a *blanket provision,* such as § 3(4), requiring the consent of a parent or person *in loco parentis* as a condition for abortion of an unmarried minor during the first 12 weeks of her pregnancy. Just as with the requirement of consent from the spouse, so here, the State does not have the constitutional authority to give a third party an absolute, and possibly arbitrary, veto over the decision of the physician and his patient to terminate the patient's pregnancy, regardless of the reason for withholding the consent.

[6] Constitutional rights do not mature and come into being magically only when one attains the state-defined age of majority. Minors, as well as adults, are protected by the Constitution and possess constitutional rights. See, *e.g., Breed v. Jones,* 421 U. S. 519, 95 S.Ct. 1779, 44 L.Ed.2d 346 (1975); *Goss v. Lopez,* 419 U. S. 565, 95 S.Ct. 729, 42 L.Ed.2d 725 (1975); *Tinker v. Des Moines School District,* 393 U. S. 503, 89 S.Ct. 733, 21 L.Ed.2d 731 (1969); *In re Gault,* 387 U. S. 1, 87 S.Ct. 1428, 18 L.Ed.2d 527 (1967). The Court indeed, however, long has recognized that the State has somewhat broader authority to regulate the activities of children than of adults. *Prince v. Massachusetts,* 321 U. S., at 170, 64 S.Ct., at 444; *Ginsberg v. New York,* 390 U. S. 629, 88 S.Ct. 1274, 20 L.Ed.2d 195 (1968). It remains, then, to examine whether there is any significant state interest in conditioning an abortion on the consent of a parent or person *in loco parentis* that is not present in the case of an adult.

One suggested interest is the safeguarding of the family unit and of parental authority. 392 F.Supp., at 1370. It is difficult, however, to conclude that providing a parent with absolute power to overrule a determination, made by the physician and his minor patient, to terminate the patient's pregnancy will serve to strengthen the family unit. Neither is it likely that such veto power will enhance parental authority or control where the minor and the nonconsenting parent are so fundamentally in conflict and the very existence of the pregnancy already has fractured the family structure. Any independent interest the parent may have in the termination of the minor daughter's pregnancy is no more weighty than the right of privacy of the competent minor mature enough to have become pregnant.

We emphasize that our holding that § 3(4) is invalid does not suggest that every minor, regardless of age or maturity, may give effective consent for termination of her pregnancy. See *Bellotti v. Baird, post.* The fault with § 3(4) is that it imposes a special consent provision, exercisable by a person other than the woman and her physician, as a prerequisite to a minor's termination of her pregnancy and does so without a sufficient justification for the restriction. It violates the strictures of *Roe* and *Doe*.

E

[7] *Saline amniocentesis.* Section 9 of the statute prohibits the use of saline amniocentesis, as a method or technique of abortion, after the first 12 weeks of pregnancy. It describes the method as one whereby the amniotic fluid is withdrawn and "a saline or other fluid" is inserted into the amniotic sac. The statute imposes this proscription on the ground that the technique "is deleterious to maternal health," and places it in the form of a legislative finding. Appellants challenge this provision on the ground that it operates to preclude virtually all abortions after the first trimester. This is so, it is claimed, because a substantial percentage, in the neighborhood of 70% according to the testimony, of all abortions performed in the United States after the first trimester are effected through the procedure of saline amniocentesis. Appellants stress the fact that the alternative methods of hysterotomy and hysterectomy are significantly more dangerous and critical for the woman than the saline technique; they also point out that the mortality rate for normal childbirth exceeds that where saline amniocentesis is employed. Finally, appellants note that the perhaps safer alternative of prostaglandin installation, suggested and strongly relied upon by the appellees, at least at the time of the trial, is not yet widely used in this country.

We held in *Roe* that after the first stage, "the State, in promoting its interest in the health of the mother, may, if it chooses, regulate the abortion procedure in ways that are reasonably related to maternal health." 410 U. S., at 164, 93 S.Ct., at 732. The question with respect to § 9 therefore is whether the flat prohibition of saline amniocentesis is a restriction which "reasonably relates to the preservation and protection of maternal health." *Id.,* at 163, 93 S.Ct., at 732. The appellees urge that what the Missouri General Assembly has done here is consistent with that guideline and is buttressed by substantial supporting medical evidence in the record to which this Court should defer.

The District Court's majority determined, on the basis of the evidence before it, that the maternal mortality rate in childbirth does, indeed, exceed the mortality rate where saline amniocentesis is used. Therefore, the majority acknowledged, § 9 could be upheld only if there were safe alternative methods of inducing abortion after the first 12 weeks. 392 F.Supp., at 1373. Referring to such methods as hysterotomy, hysterectomy, "mechanical means of inducing abortion," and prostaglandin injection, the majority said that at least the latter two techniques were safer than saline. Consequently, the majority concluded, the restriction in § 9 could be upheld as reasonably related to maternal health.

We feel that the majority, in reaching its conclusion, failed to appreciate and to consider several significant facts. First, it did not recognize the prevalence, as the record conclusively demonstrates, of the use of saline amniocentesis as an accepted medical procedure in this country; the procedure, as noted above, is employed in a substantial majority (the testimony from both sides ranges from 68% to 80%) of all post-first trimester abortions. Second, it failed to recognize that at the time of trial, there were severe limitations on the availability of the prostaglandin technique, which, although promising, was used only on an experimental basis until less than two years before. See *Wolfe v. Schroering,* 388 F.Supp., at 637, where it was said that at that time (1974), "there are no physicians in Kentucky competent in the technique of prostaglandin amnio infusion." And the State offered no evidence that prostaglandin abortions were available in Missouri.[12] Third, the statute's reference to the insertion of "a saline or other fluid" appears to include within its proscription the intra-amniotic injection of prostaglandin itself and other methods that may be developed in the future and that may prove highly effective and completely safe. Finally, the majority did not consider the anomaly inherent in § 9 when it proscribes the use of saline but does not prohibit techniques that are many times more likely to result in maternal death. See 393 F.Supp., at 1378 n. 8 (dissenting opinion).

These unappreciated or overlooked factors place the State's decision to bar use of the saline method in a completely different light. The State, through § 9, would prohibit the use of a method which the record shows is the one most commonly used nationally by physicians after the first trimester and which is safer, with respect to maternal mortality, than even continuation of the pregnancy until normal childbirth. Moreover, as a practical matter, it forces a woman and her physician to terminate her pregnancy by methods more dangerous to her health than the method outlawed.

As so viewed, particularly in the light of the present unavailability—as demonstrated by the record—of the prostaglandin technique, the outright legislative proscription of saline fails as a reasonable regulation for the protection of maternal health. It comes into focus, instead, as an unreasonable or arbitrary regulation designed to inhibit, and having the effect of inhibiting, the vast majority of abortions after the first 12 weeks. As such, it does not withstand constitutional challenge. See *Wolfe v. Schroering,* 388 F.Supp., at 637.

F

[8] *Recordkeeping.* Sections 10 and 11 of the Act impose recordkeeping requirements for health facilities and physicians concerned with abortions irrespective of the pregnancy stage. Under § 10, each such facility and physician is to be supplied with forms "the purpose and function of which shall be the preservation of maternal health and life by adding to the sum of medical knowledge through the compilation of relevant maternal health and life data and to monitor all abortions performed to assure that they are done only under and in accordance with the provisions of the law." The statute states that the information on the forms "shall be confidential and shall be used only for statistical purposes." The "records, however, may be inspected and health data acquired by local, state, or national public

health officers." Under § 11 the records are to be kept for seven years in the permanent files of the health facility where the abortion was performed.

Appellants object to these reporting and recordkeeping provisions on the ground that they, too, impose an extra layer and burden of regulation, and that they apply throughout all stages of pregnancy. All the judges of the District Court panel, however, viewed these provisions as statistical requirements "essential to the advancement of medical knowledge," and as nothing that would "restrict either the abortion decision itself or the exercise of medical judgment in performing an abortion." 392 F.Supp. at 1374.

One may concede that there are important and perhaps conflicting interests affected by recordkeeping requirements. On the one hand, maintenance of records indeed may be helpful in developing information pertinent to the preservation of maternal health. On the other hand, as we stated in *Roe,* during the first stage of pregnancy the State may impose no restrictions or regulations governing the medical judgment of the pregnant woman's attending physician with respect to the termination of her pregnancy. 410 U. S., at 163, 164, 93 S.Ct., at 731, 732. Furthermore, it is readily apparent that one reason for the recordkeeping requirement, namely, to assure that all abortions in Missouri are performed in accordance with the Act, fades somewhat into insignificance in view of our holding above as to spousal and parental consent requirements.

[9] Recordkeeping and reporting requirements that are reasonably directed to the preservation of maternal health and that properly respect a patient's confidentiality and privacy are permissible. This surely is so for the period after the first stage of pregnancy, for then the State may enact substantive as well as recordkeeping regulations that are reasonable means of protecting maternal health. As to the first stage, one may argue forcefully, as the appellants do, that the State should not be able to impose any recordkeeping requirements that significantly differ from those imposed with respect to other, and comparable, medical or surgical procedures. We conclude, however, that the provisions of §§ 10 and 11, while perhaps approaching permissible limits, are not constitutionally offensive in themselves. Recordkeeping of this kind, if not abused or overdone, can be useful to the State's interest in protecting the health of its female citizens, and may be a resource that is relevant to decisions involving medical experience and judgment.[13] The added requirements for confidentiality, with the sole exception for public health officers, and for retention for seven years, a period not unreasonable in length, assist and persuade us in our determination of the constitutional limits. As so regarded, we see no legally significant impact or consequence on the abortion decision or on the physician-patient relationship. We naturally assume, furthermore, that these recordkeeping and record-maintaining provisions will be interpreted and enforced by Missouri's Division of Health in the light of our decision with respect to the Act's other provisions, and that, of course, they will not be utilized in such a way as to accomplish, through the sheer burden of recordkeeping detail, what we have held to be an otherwise unconstitutional restriction. Obviously, the State may not require execution of spousal and parental consent forms that have been invalidated today.

G

[10] *Standard of care.* Appellee Danforth in No. 74-1419 appeals from the unanimous decision of the District Court that § 6(1) of the Act is unconstitutional. That section provides:

> "No person who performs or induces an abortion shall fail to exercise that degree of professional skill, care and diligence to preserve the life and health of the fetus which such person would be required to exercise in order to preserve the life and health of any fetus intended to be born and not aborted. Any physician or person assisting in the abortion who shall fail to take such measures to encourage or to sustain the life of the child, and the death of the child results, shall be deemed guilty of manslaughter. . . . Further, such physician or other person shall be liable in an action for damages."

The District Court held that the first sentence was unconstitutionally overbroad because it failed to exclude from its reach the stage of pregnancy prior to viability. 392 F.Supp., at 1371.

The Attorney General argues that the District Court's interpretation is erroneous and unnecessary. He claims that the first sentence of § 6(1) establishes only the general standard of care that applies to the person who performs the abortion, and that the second sentence describes the circumstances when that standard of care applies, namely, when a live child results from the procedure. Thus, the first sentence, it is said, despite its reference to the fetus, has no application until a live birth results.

The appellants, of course, agree with the District Court. They take the position that § 6(1) imposes its standard of care upon the person performing the abortion even though the procedure takes place before viability. They argue that the statute on its face effectively precludes abortion and was meant to do just that.

[11] We see nothing that requires federal court abstention on this issue. *Wisconsin v. Constantineau,* 400 U. S. 433, 437–439, 91 S.Ct. 507, 510–511, 27 L.Ed.2d 515 (1971); *Kusper v. Pontikes,* 414 U. S. 51, 54–55, 94 S.Ct. 303, 306–307, 38 L.Ed.2d 260 (1973). And, like the three judges of the District Court, we are unable to accept the appellee's sophisticated interpretation of the statute. Section 6(1) requires the physician to exercise the prescribed skill, care, and diligence to preserve the life and health of the fetus. It does not specify that such care need be taken only after the stage of viability has been reached. As the provision now reads, it impermissibly requires the physician to preserve the life and health of the fetus, whatever the stage of pregnancy. The fact that the second sentence of § 6(1) refers to a criminal penalty where the physician fails "to take such measures to encourage or to sustain the life of the *child,* and the death of the *child* results" (emphasis supplied), simply does not modify the duty imposed by the previous sentence or limit that duty to pregnancies that have reached the stage of viability.

The appellees finally argue that if the first sentence of § 6(1) does not survive constitutional attack, the second sentence does, and, under the Act's severability provision, § B, is severable from the first. The District Court's ruling of unconstitutionality, 392 F.Supp., at 1371, made specific reference to the first sentence but its conclusion of law and its judgment invalidated all of § 6(1). *Id.,* at 1374; Juris. Statement, No. 74-1419, A-34. Appellee Danforth's motion to alter or amend the judgment, so far as the second sentence of § 6(1) was concerned, was denied by the District Court. *Id.,* at A–39.

We conclude, as did the District Court, that § 6(1) must stand or fall as a unit. Its provisions are inextricably bound together. And a physician's or other person's criminal failure to protect a live-born infant surely will be subject to prosecution in Missouri under the State's criminal statutes.

The judgment of the District Court is affirmed in part and reversed in part and the case is remanded for further proceedings consistent with this opinion.

It is so ordered.

Appendix
H. C. S. House Bill No. 1211

AN ACT relating to abortion with penalty provisions and emergency clause.

Be it enacted by the General Assembly of the State of Missouri, as follows:

SECTION 1. It is the intention of the general assembly of the state of Missouri to reasonably regulate abortion in conformance with the decisions of the supreme court of the United States.

SECTION 2. Unless the language or context clearly indicates a different meaning is intended, the following words or phrases for the purpose of this act shall be given the meaning ascribed to them:

(1) "Abortion," the intentional destruction of the life of an embryo or fetus in his or her mother's womb or the intentional termination of the pregnancy of a mother with an intention other than to increase the probability of a live birth or to remove a dead or dying unborn child;

(2) "Viability," that stage of fetal development when the life of the unborn child may be continued indefinitely outside the womb by natural or artificial life-supportive systems;

(3) "Physician," any person licensed to practice medicine in this state by the state board of registration of the healing arts.

SECTION 3. No abortion shall be performed prior to the end of the first twelve weeks of pregnancy except:

(1) By a duly licensed, consenting physician in the exercise of his best clinical medical judgment.

(2) After the woman, prior to submitting to the abortion, certifies in writing her consent to the abortion and that her consent is informed and freely given and is not the result of coercion.

(3) With the written consent of the woman's spouse, unless the abortion is certified by a licensed physician to be necessary in order to preserve the life of the mother.

(4) With the written consent of one parent or person in loco parentis of the woman if the woman is unmarried and under the age of eighteen years, unless the abortion is certified by a licensed physician as necessary in order to preserve the life of the mother.

SECTION 4. No abortion performed subsequent to the first twelve weeks of pregnancy shall be performed except where the provisions of section 3 of this act are satisfied and in a hospital.

SECTION 5. No abortion not necessary to preserve the life or health of the mother shall be performed unless the attending physician first certifies with reasonable medical certainty that the fetus is not viable.

SECTION 6. (1) No person who performs or induces an abortion shall fail to exercise that degree of professional skill, care and diligence to preserve the life and health of the fetus which such person would be required to exercise in order to preserve the life and health of any fetus intended to be born and not aborted. Any physician or person assisting in the abortion who shall fail to take such measures to encourage or to sustain the life of the child, and the death of the child results, shall be deemed guilty of manslaughter and upon conviction shall be punished as provided in Section 559.140, RSMo. Further, such physician or other person shall be liable in an action for damages as provided in Section 537.080, RSMo.

(2) Whoever, with intent to do so, shall take the life of a premature infant aborted alive, shall be guilty of murder of the second degree.

(3) No person shall use any fetus or premature infant aborted alive for any type of scientific, research, laboratory or other kind of experimentation either prior to or subsequent to any abortion procedure except as necessary to protect or preserve the life and health of such premature infant aborted alive.

SECTION 7. In every case where a live-born infant results from an attempted abortion which was not performed to save the life or health of the mother, such infant shall be an abandoned ward of the state under the jurisdiction of the juvenile court wherein the abortion occurred, and the mother and father, if he consented to the abortion, of such infant shall have no parental rights or obligations whatsoever relating to such infant, as if the parental rights had been terminated pursuant to section 211.411, RSMo. The attending physician shall forthwith notify said juvenile court of the existence of such live-born infant.

SECTION 8. Any woman seeking an abortion in the state of Missouri shall be verbally informed of the provisions of section 7 of this act by the attending physician and the woman shall certify in writing that she has been so informed.

SECTION 9. The general assembly finds that the method or technique of abortion known as saline amniocentesis whereby the amniotic fluid is withdrawn and a saline or other fluid is inserted into the amniotic sac for the purpose of killing the fetus and artificially inducing labor is deleterious to maternal health and is hereby prohibited after the first twelve weeks of pregnancy.

SECTION 10. (1) Every health facility and physician shall be supplied with forms promulgated by the division of health, the purpose and function of which shall be the preservation of maternal health and life by adding to the sum of medical knowledge through the compilation of relevant maternal health and life data and to monitor all abortions performed to assure that they are done only under and in accordance with the provisions of the law.

(2) The forms shall be provided by the state division of health.

(3) All information obtained by physician, hospital, clinic or other health facility from a patient for the purpose of preparing reports to the division of health under this section or reports received by the division of health shall be confidential and shall be used only for statistical purposes. Such records, however, may be inspected and health data acquired by local, state, or national public health officers.

SECTION 11. All medical records and other documents required to be kept shall be maintained in the permanent files of the health facility in which the abortion was performed for a period of seven years.

SECTION 12. Any practitioner of medicine, surgery, or nursing, or other health personnel who shall willfully and knowingly do or assist any actions made unlawful by this act shall be subject to having his license, application for license, or authority to practice his profession as a physician, surgeon, or nurse in the state of Missouri rejected or revoked by the appropriate state licensing board.

SECTION 13. Any physician or other person who fails to maintain the confidentiality of any records or reports required under this act is guilty of a misdemeanor and, upon conviction, shall be punished as provided by law.

SECTION 14. Any person who contrary to the provisions of this act knowingly performs or aids in the performance of any abortion or knowingly fails to perform any action required by this act shall be guilty of a misdemeanor and, upon conviction, shall be punished as provided by law.

SECTION 15. Any person who is not a licensed physician as defined in section 2 of this act who performs or attempts to perform an abortion on another as defined in subdivision (1) of section 2 of this act, is guilty of a felony, and upon conviction, shall be imprisoned by the department of corrections for a term of not less than two years nor more than seventeen years.

SECTION 16. Nothing in this act shall be construed to exempt any person, firm, or corporation from civil liability for medical malpractice for negligent acts or certification under this act.

SECTION A. Because of the necessity for immediate state action to regulate abortions to protect the lives and health of citizens of this state, this act is deemed necessary for the immediate preservation of the public health, welfare, peace and safety, and is hereby declared to be an emergency act within the meaning of the constitution, and this act shall be in full force and effect upon its passage and approval.

SECTION B. If any provision of this Act or the application thereof to any person or circumstance shall be held invalid, such invalidity does not affect the provisions or application of this Act which can be given effect without the invalid provision or application, and to this end the provisions of this Act are declared to be severable.

Approved June 14, 1974
Effective June 14, 1974

MR. JUSTICE STEWART with whom MR. JUSTICE POWELL joins, concurring.

While joining the Court's opinion, I write separately to indicate my understanding of some of the constitutional issues raised by this case.

With respect to the definition of viability in § 2(2) of the Act, it seems to me that the critical consideration is that the statutory definition has almost no operative significance. The State has merely required physicians performing abortions to *certify* that the fetus to be aborted is not viable. While the physician may be punished for failing to issue a certification, he may not be punished for erroneously concluding that the fetus is not viable. There is thus little chance that a physician's professional decision to perform an abortion will be "chilled."

I agree with the Court that the patient consent provision in § 3(2) is constitutional. While § 3(2) obviously regulates the abortion decision during all stages of pregnancy, including the first trimester, I do not believe it conflicts with the statement in *Roe v. Wade,* 410 U. S., at 163, 93 S.Ct., at 731, that "for the period of pregnancy prior to [approximately the end of the first trimester] the attending physician, in consultation with his patient, is free to determine without regulation by the State, that, in his medical judgment, the patient's pregnancy should be terminated. If that decision is reached, the judgment may be effectuated by an abortion free of interference by the State." 410 U. S., at 163, 93 S.Ct., at 732. That statement was made in the context of invalidating a state law aimed at thwarting a woman's decision to have an abortion. It was not intended to preclude the State from enacting a provision aimed at ensuring that the abortion decision is made in a knowing, intelligent, and voluntary fashion.

As to the provision of the law that requires a husband's consent to an abortion, § 3(3), the primary issue that it raises is whether the State may constitutionally recognize and give effect to a right on his part to participate in the decision to abort a jointly conceived child. This seems to me a rather more difficult problem than the Court acknowledges. Previous decisions have recognized that a man's right to father children and enjoy the association of his offspring is a constitutionally protected freedom. See *Stanley v. Illinois,* 405 U. S. 645, 92 S.Ct. 1208, 31 L.Ed.2d 551; *Skinner v. Oklahoma,* 316 U. S. 535, 62 S.Ct. 1110, 86 L.Ed. 1655. But the Court has recognized as well that the Constitution protects "a *woman's* decision whether or not to terminate her pregnancy." 410 U. S., at 153, 93 S.Ct. at 727 (emphasis added). In assessing the constitutional validity of § 3(3) we are called upon to choose between these competing rights. I agree with the Court that since "it is the woman who physically bears the child and who is the more directly and immediately affected by the pregnancy . . . the balance weighs in her favor." *Ante,* at 2842.

With respect to the state law's requirement of parental consent, § 3(4), I think it clear that its primary constitutional deficiency lies in its imposition of an abso-

lute limitation on the minor's right to obtain an abortion. The Court's opinion today in *Bellotti v. Baird,* _____ U. S. _____, _____, 96 S. Ct. 2857,
_____, 48 L.Ed.2d _____, suggests that a materially different constitu-
tional issue would be presented under a provision requiring parental consent or
consultation in most cases but providing for prompt (i) judicial resolution of any
disagreement between the parent and the minor, or (ii) judicial determination that
the minor is mature enough to give an informed consent without parental concurrence or that abortion in any event is in the minor's best interest. Such a provision
would not impose parental approval as an absolute condition upon the minor's
right but would assure in most instances consultation between the parent and
child.[14]

There can be little doubt that the State furthers a constitutionally permissible
end by encouraging an unmarried pregnant minor to seek the help and advice of
her parents in making the very important decision whether or not to bear a child.
That is a grave decision, and a girl of tender years, under emotional stress, may be
ill-equipped to make it without mature advice and emotional support. It seems unlikely that she will obtain adequate counsel and support from the attending physician at an abortion clinic, where abortions for pregnant minors frequently take
place.[15]

As to the constitutional validity of § 9 of the Act, prohibiting the use of the
saline amniocentesis procedure, I agree fully with the views expressed by Mr. Justice STEVENS.

MR. JUSTICE WHITE, with whom THE CHIEF JUSTICE and MR. JUSTICE REHN-
QUIST join, concurring in the judgment in part and dissenting in part.

In *Roe v. Wade,* 410 U. S. 113, 93 S.Ct. 705, 35 L.Ed.2d 147, this Court recognized a right to an abortion free from state prohibition. The task of policing this
limitation on state police power is and will be a difficult and continuing venture in
substantive due process. However, even accepting *Roe v. Wade,* there is nothing in
the opinion in that case and nothing articulated in the Court's opinion in this case
which justifies the invalidation of four provisions of House Committee Substitute
for House Bill No. 1211 (hereafter referred to as the "Act") enacted by the Missouri Seventy-Seventh General Assembly in 1974 in response to *Roe v. Wade.* Accordingly, I dissent, in part.

I

Roe v. Wade, 410 U. S. 113, 163, 93 S.Ct. 705, 731, 35 L.Ed.2d 147, holds that
until a fetus becomes viable, the interest of the State in the life or potential life it
represents is outweighed by the interest of the mother in choosing "whether or not
to terminate her pregnancy." *Id.,* at 153, 93 S.Ct., at 727. Section 3(3) of the Act
provides that a married woman may not obtain an abortion without her husband's
consent. The Court strikes down this statute in one sentence. It says that "since the
State cannot . . . proscribe abortion . . . the State cannot delegate authority to any
particular person, even the spouse, to prevent abortion. . . ." *Ante,* at 2841. But the

State is not—under § 3(3)—delegating to the husband the power to vindicate the *State's* interest in the future life of the fetus. It is instead recognizing that the husband has an interest of his own in the life of the fetus which should not be extinguished by the unilateral decision of the wife.[16] It by no means follows, from the fact that the mother's interest in deciding "whether or not to terminate her pregnancy" outweighs the *State*'s interest in the potential life of the fetus, that the husband's interest is also outweighed and may not be protected by the State. A father's interest in having a child—perhaps his only child—may be unmatched by any other interest in his life. See *Stanley v. Illinois,* 405 U. S. 645, 651, 92 S.Ct. 1208, 1212, 31 L.Ed.2d 551, and cases there cited. It is truly surprising that the majority finds in the United States Constitution, as it must in order to justify the result it reaches, a rule that the State must assign a greater value to a mother's decision to cut off a potential human life by abortion than to a father's decision to let it mature into a live child. Such a rule cannot be found there, nor can it be found in *Roe v. Wade, supra.* These are matters which a State should be able to decide free from the suffocating power of the federal judge, purporting to act in the name of the Constitution.

In describing the nature of a mother's interest in terminating a pregnancy, the Court in *Roe v. Wade* mentioned only the post-birth burdens of rearing a child, *id.,* at p. 153, 93 S.Ct., at 726, and rejected a rule based on her interest in controlling her own body during pregnancy. *Id.,* at 154, 93 S.Ct., at 727. Missouri has a law which prevents a woman from putting a child up for adoption over her husband's objection, § 453.030 R.S.Mo.1969. This law represents a judgment by the State that the mother's interest in avoiding the burdens of child rearing do not outweigh or snuff out the father's interest in participating in bringing up his own child. That law is plainly valid, but no more so than § 3(3) of the Act now before us, resting as it does on precisely the same judgment.

II

Section 3(4) requires that an unmarried woman under 18 years of age obtain the consent of a parent or a person *in loco parentis* as a condition to an abortion. Once again the Court strikes the provision down in a sentence. It states: "Just as with the requirement of consent from the spouse, so here, the State does not have the constitutional authority to give a third party an absolute, and possibly arbitrary, veto over the decision of the physician and his patient to terminate the patient's pregnancy. . . ." *Id.,* at 2843. The Court rejects the notions that the *State* has an interest in strengthening the family unit or that the *parent* has an "independent interest" in the abortion decision, sufficient to justify the statute and apparently concludes that the statute is therefore unconstitutional. But the purpose of the parental consent requirement is not merely to vindicate any interest of the parent or of the State. The purpose of the requirement is to vindicate the very right created in *Roe v. Wade, supra*—the right of the pregnant woman to decide "whether or not to terminate her pregnancy." *Id.,* at 153, 93 S.Ct., at 727 (emphasis added). The abortion decision is unquestionably important and has irrevocable consequences whichever way it is made. Missouri is entitled to protect the minor unmarried woman from making the decision in a way which is not in her own best interests, and it seeks to achieve this goal by requiring parental consultation and consent. This is the traditional way by which States have sought to protect children from their own immature and improvident decisions;[17] and there is absolutely no reason expressed by the majority why the State may not utilize that method here.

III

Section 9 of the Act prohibits abortion by the method known as saline amniocentesis—a method used at the time the Act was passed for 70% of abortions performed after the first trimester. Legislative history reveals that the Missouri Legislature viewed saline amniocentesis as far less safe a method of abortion than the so-called prostaglandin method. The court below took evidence on the question and summarized it as follows:

> "The record of trial discloses that use of the saline method exposes a woman to the danger of severe complications, regardless of the skill of the physician or the precaution taken. Saline may cause one or more of the following conditions: Disseminated intravascular coagulation or 'consumptive coagulapathy' (disruption of the blood clotting mechanism [Dr. Warren, Tr. 57–58; Dr. Klaus, Tr. 269–270; Dr. Anderson, Tr. 307; Defendants' Exhibits H & M]), which may result in severe bleeding and possibly death (Dr. Warren, Tr. 58); hypernatremia (increase in blood sodium level), which may lead to convulsions and death (Dr. Klaus, Tr. 268); and water intoxication (accumulated water in the body tissue which may occur when oxygen is used in conjunction with the injection of saline), resulting in damage to the central nervous system or death (Dr. Warren, Tr. 76; Dr. Klaus, Tr. 270–271; Dr. Anderson, Tr. 310; Defendants' Exhibit L). There is also evidence that saline amniocentesis causes massive tissue destruction to the inside of the uterus (Dr. Anderson, Tr. 308)."

The District Court also cited considerable evidence establishing that the prostaglandin method is safer. In fact, the Chief of Obstetrics at Yale University, Dr. Anderson, suggested that "physicians should be liable for malpractice if they chose saline over prostaglandin after having been given all the facts on both methods." The Court nevertheless reverses the decision of the District Court sustaining § 9 against constitutional challenge. It does so apparently because saline amniocentesis was widely used before the Act was passed; because the prostaglandin method was seldom used and was not generally available; and because other abortion techniques more dangerous than saline amniocentesis were not banned. At bottom the majority's holding—as well as the concurrence—rests on its *factual* finding that the prostaglandin method is unavailable to the women of Missouri. It therefore concludes that the ban on the saline method is "an unreasonable or arbitrary regulation designed to inhibit, and having the effect of inhibiting, the vast majority of abortions after the first 12 weeks," *ante,* at 2845. This factual finding was not made either by the majority or by the dissenting judge below. Appellants have not argued that the record below supports such a finding. In fact the record below does not support such a finding. There is *no* evidence in the record that women in Missouri will be unable to obtain abortions by the prostaglandin method. What evidence there is in the record on this question supports the contrary conclusion.[18] The record discloses that the prostaglandin method of abortion was the country's second most common method of abortion during the second trimester, Trial Transcript, at 42, 89–90; that although the prostaglandin method had previously been available only on an experimental basis, it was, at the time of trial available in "small hospitals all over the country," Trial Transcript, at 342; that in another year or so the prostaglandin method would become—even in the absence of legislation on the subject—the most prevalent method. Anderson deposition, at 47. Moreover, one doctor quite sensibly testified that if the saline method were banned, hospitals would quickly switch to the prostaglandin method.

The majority relies on the testimony of one doctor that—as already noted—prostaglandin had been available on an experimental basis only until January 1, 1974; and that its manufacturer, the Upjohn Company, restricted its sales to large medical centers for the following six months, after which sales were to be unrestricted. Trial Transcript, 334, 335. In what manner this evidence supports the proposition that prostaglandin is unavailable to the women of Missouri escapes me. The statute involved in this case was passed on June 14, 1974; evidence was taken in July 1974; the District Court's decree sustaining the ban on the saline method which this Court overturns was entered in January 1975; and this Court declares the statute unconstitutional in July of 1976. There is simply no evidence in the record that prostaglandin was or is unavailable at any time relevant to this case. Without such evidence and without any factual finding by the court below this Court cannot properly strike down a statute passed by one of the States. Of course, there is no burden on a State to establish the constitutionality of one of its laws. Absent proof of a fact essential to its unconstitutionality, the statute remains in effect.

The only other basis for its factual finding which the majority offers is a citation to *another* case—*Wolfe v. Schroering,* 388 F.Supp. 631, 637 (WDKy.1974)—in which a different court concluded that the record in its case showed the prostaglandin method to be unavailable in another State—Kentucky—at another time—two years ago. This case must be decided on its own record. I am not yet prepared to accept the notion that normal rules of law, procedure, and constitutional adjudication suddenly become irrelevant solely because a case touches on the subject of abortion. The majority's finding of fact that women in Missouri will be unable to obtain abortions after the first trimester if the saline method is banned is wholly unjustifiable.

In any event, the point of § 9 is to change the practice under which most abortions were performed under the saline amniocentesis method and to make the safer prostaglandin method generally available. It promises to achieve that result, if it remains operative, and the evidence discloses that the result is a desirable one or at least that the legislature could have so viewed it. That should end our inquiry, unless we purport to be not only the country's continuous constitutional convention but also its *ex officio* medical board with powers to approve or disapprove medical and operative practices and standards throughout the United States.

IV

Section 6(1) of the Act provides:

"No person who performs or induces an abortion shall fail to exercise that degree of professional skill, care and diligence to preserve the life and health of the fetus which such person would be required to exercise in order to preserve the life and health of any fetus intended to be born and not aborted. Any physician or person assisting in the abortion who shall fail to take such measures to encourage or to sustain the life of the child, and the death of the child results, shall be deemed guilty of manslaughter. . . . Further, such physician or other person shall be liable in an action for damages."

If this section is read in any way other than through a microscope, it is plainly intended to require that, where a "fetus . . . [may have] the capability of meaningful life outside the mother's womb," *Roe v. Wade, supra,* at 163, 93 S.Ct., at 732, the abortion be handled in a way which is designed to preserve that life notwithstanding the mother's desire to terminate it. Indeed, even looked at through a microscope the statute seems to go no further. It requires a physician to exercise "*that* degree of professional skill . . . to preserve the life and health of the fetus," which he would be required to exercise if the mother wanted a live child. Plainly, if the pregnancy is to be terminated at a time when there is no chance of life outside the womb, a physician would not be required to exercise any care or skill to preserve the life of the fetus during abortion no matter what the mother's desires. The statute would appear then to operate only in the gray area after the fetus *might* be viable but while the physician is still able to certify "with reasonable medical certainty that the fetus is not viable." See § 5 of the Act which flatly prohibits abortions absent such a certification. Since the State has a compelling interest, sufficient to outweigh the mother's desire to kill the fetus, when the "fetus . . . has the capability of meaningful life outside the mother's womb," *Roe v. Wade, supra,* at 163, 93 S.Ct. at 732, the statute is constitutional.

Incredibly, the Court reads the statute instead to require "the physician to preserve the life and health of the fetus, whatever the stage of pregnancy," *ante,* at 2847, thereby attributing to the Missouri Legislature the strange intention of passing a statute with absolutely no chance of surviving constitutional challenge under *Roe v. Wade, supra.*

The Court compounds its error by also striking down as unseverable the wholly unobjectionable requirement in the second sentence of § 6(1) that where an abortion produces a live child, steps must be taken to sustain its life. It explains its result in two sentences:

"We conclude, as did the District Court, that § 6(1) must stand or fall as a unit. Its provisions are inextricably bound together."

The question whether a constitutional provision of state law is severable from an unconstitutional provision is *entirely* a question of the intent of the state legislature. There is not the slightest reason to suppose that the Missouri Legislature would not require proper care for live babies just because it cannot require physicians performing abortions to take care to preserve the life of fetuses. The Attorney General of Missouri has argued here that the *only* intent of § 6(1) was to require physicians to support a live baby which resulted from an abortion.

At worst, § 6(1) is ambiguous on both points and the District Court should be directed to abstain until a construction may be had from the state courts. Under no circumstances should § 6(1) be declared unconstitutional at this point.[19]

V

I join the judgment of the Court insofar as it upholds the other portions of the Act against constitutional challenge.

MR. JUSTICE STEVENS, concurring in part and dissenting in part.

With the exception of Parts IV–D and IV–E, I join the Court's opinion.

In *Roe v. Wade,* 410 U. S. 113, 93 S.Ct. 705, 35 L.Ed.2d 147, the Court held that a woman's right to decide whether to abort a pregnancy is entitled to constitutional protection. That decision, which is now part of our law, answers the question discussed in Part IV–E of the Court's opinion, but merely poses the question decided in Part IV–D.

If two abortion procedures had been equally accessible to Missouri women, in my judgment the United States Constitution would not prevent the state legislature from outlawing the one it found to be the less safe even though its conclusion might not reflect a unanimous consensus of informed medical opinion. However, the record indicates that when the Missouri statute was enacted, a prohibition of the *saline amniocentesis* procedure was almost tantamount to a prohibition of any abortion in the State after the first 12 weeks of pregnancy. Such a prohibition is inconsistent with the essential holding of *Roe v. Wade* and therefore cannot stand.

In my opinion, however, the parental consent requirement is consistent with the holding in *Roe.* The State's interest in the welfare of its young citizens justifies a variety of protective measures. Because he may not foresee the consequences of his decision, a minor may not make an enforceable bargain. He may not lawfully work or travel where he pleases, or even attend exhibitions of constitutionally protected adult motion pictures. Persons below a certain age may not marry without parental consent. Indeed, such consent is essential even when the young woman is already pregnant. The State's interest in protecting a young person from harm justifies the imposition of restraints on his or her freedom even though comparable restraints on adults would be constitutionally impermissible. Therefore, the holding in *Roe v. Wade* that the abortion decision is entitled to constitutional protection merely emphasizes the importance of the decision; it does not lead to the conclusion that the state legislature has no power to enact legislation for the purpose of protecting a young pregnant woman from the consequences of an incorrect decision.

The abortion decision is, of course, more important than the decision to attend or to avoid an adult motion picture, or the decision to work long hours in a factory. It is not necessarily any more important than the decision to run away from home or the decision to marry. But even if it is the most important kind of a decision a young person may ever make, that assumption merely enhances the quality of the State's interest in maximizing the probability that the decision be made correctly and with full understanding of the consequences of either alternative.

The Court recognizes that the State may insist that the decision not be made without the benefit of medical advice. But since the most significant consequences of the decision are not medical in character, it would seem to me that the State may, with equal legitimacy, insist that the decision be made only after other appropriate counsel has been had as well. Whatever choice a pregnant young woman makes—to marry, to abort, to bear her child out of wedlock—the consequences of her decision may have a profound impact on her entire future life. A legislative determination that such a choice will be made more wisely in most cases if the advice and moral support of a parent play a part in the decisionmaking process is surely not irrational. Moreover, it is perfectly clear that the parental consent requirement will necessarily involve a parent in the decisional process.

If there is no parental consent requirement, many minors will submit to the abortion procedure without ever informing their parents. An assumption that the parental reaction will be hostile, disparaging or violent no doubt persuades many children simply to bypass parental counsel which would in fact be loving, supportive and, indeed for some indispensable. It is unrealistic, in my judgment, to assume that every parent-child relationship is either (a) so perfect that communication and accord will take place routinely or (b) so imperfect that the absence of communication reflects the child's correct prediction that the parent will exercise his or her veto arbitrarily to further a selfish interest rather than the child's interest. A state legislature may conclude that most parents will be primarily interested in the welfare of their children, and further, that the imposition of a parental consent requirement is an appropriate method of giving the parents an opportunity to foster that welfare by helping a pregnant distressed child to make and to implement a correct decision.

The State's interest is not dependent on an estimate of the impact the parental consent requirement may have on the total number of abortions that may take place. I assume that parents will sometimes prevent abortions which might better be performed; other parents may advise abortions that should not be performed. Similarly, even doctors are not omniscient; specialists in performing abortions may incorrectly conclude that the immediate advantages of the procedure outweigh the disadvantages which a parent could evaluate in better perspective. In each individual case factors much more profound than a mere medical judgment may weigh heavily in the scales. The overriding consideration is that the right to make the choice be exercised as wisely as possible.

The Court assumes that parental consent is an appropriate requirement if the minor is not capable of understanding the procedure and of appreciating its consequences and those of available alternatives. This assumption is, of course, correct and consistent with the predicate which underlies all State legislation seeking to protect minors from the consequences of decisions they are not yet prepared to make. In all such situations chronological age has been the basis for imposition of a restraint on the minor's freedom of choice even though it is perfectly obvious that such a yardstick is imprecise and perhaps even unjust in particular cases. The Court seems to assume that the capacity to conceive a child and the judgment of the physician are the only constitutionally permissible yardsticks for determining whether a young woman can independently make the abortion decision. I doubt the accuracy of the Court's empirical judgment. Even if it were correct, however, as a matter of constitutional law I think a State has power to conclude otherwise and to select a chronological age as its standard.

In short, the State's interest in the welfare of its young citizens is sufficient, in my judgment, to support the parental consent requirement.

NOTES

1. "Viability is usually placed at about seven months (28 weeks) but may occur earlier, even at 24 weeks." *Roe v. Wade,* 410 U. S. 113, 160, 93 S.Ct. 705, 730, 35 L.Ed.2d 147 (1973).

2. This is not so, however, with respect to § 7 of the Act pertaining to state wardship of a live born infant. Section 7 applies "where a live born infant results from an attempted abortion which was not performed to save the life or health of the mother." It then provides that the infant "shall be an abandoned ward of the state" and that the mother—and the father, too, if he consented to the abortion—"shall have no parental rights or obligations whatsoever relating to such infant."

The physician-appellants do not contend that this section of the Act imposes any obligation on them or that its operation otherwise injures them in fact. They do not claim any interest in the question of who receives custody that is "sufficiently concrete" to satisfy the "case or controversy" requirement of a federal court's Art. III jurisdiction. *Singleton v. Wulff,* _____ U. S. _____ at _____, 96 S.Ct. 2868 at 2873, 48 L.Ed. _____. Accordingly, the physician-appellants do not have standing to challenge § 7 of the Act.

The District Court did not decide whether Planned Parenthood has standing to challenge the Act, or any portion of it, because of its view that the physician-appellants have standing to challenge the entire Act. 392 F.Supp. 1362, 1366–1367 (E.D.Mo.1975). We decline to consider here the standing of Planned Parenthood to attack § 7. That question appropriately may be left to the District Court for reconsideration on remand. As a consequence, we do not decide the issue of § 7's constitutionality.

3. "[A]lthough I agree with the definition of 'viability,' I think it must be understood that viability is a very difficult state to assess." Transcript 369.

4. "The determination of when the fetus is viable rests, as it should, with the physician, in the exercise of his medical judgment, on a case-by-case basis." Brief for Appellees 26. "Because viability may vary from patient to patient and with advancements in medical technology, it is essential that physicians make the determination in the exercise of their medical judgment." *Id.,* at 28. "Defendant agrees that 'viability' will vary, that it is a difficult state to assess . . . and that it must be left to the physician's judgment." *Id.,* at 29.

5. The Minnesota statute under attack in *Hodgson* provided that a fetus "shall be considered potentially 'viable' " during the second half of its gestation period. Noting that the defendants had presented no evidence of viability at 20 weeks, the three-judge District Court held that that definition of viability was "unreasonable and cannot stand." 378 F.Supp., at 1016.

6. Apparently, however, the only other Missouri statutes concerned with consent for general medical or surgical care relate to persons committed to the Missouri state chest hospital, Mo. Rev.Stat. § 199.240 (1969), or to mental or correctional institutions, *Id.,* § 105.700.

7. There is some testimony in the record to the effect that taking from the patient a prior written consent to surgery is the custom. That may be so in some areas of Missouri, but we definitely refrain from characterizing it extremely as "the universal practice of the medical profession," as the appellees do. Brief for Appellees 32.

8. The appellants' vagueness argument centers on the word "informed." One might well wonder, offhand, just what "informed consent" of a patient is. The three Missouri federal judges who comprised the three-judge District Court, however, were not concerned, and we are content to accept, as the meaning, the giving of information to the patient as to just what would be done and as to its consequences. To ascribe more meaning than this might well confine the attending physician in an undesired and uncomfortable straitjacket in the practice of his profession.

9. It is of some interest to note that the condition does not relate as most statutory conditions in this area do, to the preservation of the life or *health* of the mother.

10. "We deal with a right of privacy older than the Bill of Rights—older than our political parties, older than our school system. Marriage is a coming together for better or for worse, hopefully enduring, and *intimate to the degree of being sacred.* It is an association that promotes a way of life, not causes; a harmony in living, not political faiths; a bilateral loyalty, not commercial or social projects. Yet it is an association for as noble a purpose as any involved in our prior decisions." *Griswold v. Connecticut,* 381 U. S. 479, 486, 85 S.Ct. 1678, 1682, 14 L.Ed.2d 510 (1965).

11. As the Court recognized in *Eisenstadt v. Baird,* "the marital couple is not an independent entity with a mind and heart of its own, but an association of two individuals each with a separate intellectual and emotional makeup. If the right of privacy means anything, it is the right of the *individual,* married or single, to be free from unwarranted governmental intrusion into matters so fundamentally affecting a person as the decision whether to bear or beget a child." 405 U. S., at 453, 92 S.Ct., at 1038 (emphasis in original). The dissenting opinion of our Brother WHITE appears to overlook the implications of this statement upon the issue whether § 3(3) is constitutional. This section does much more than insure that the husband participate in the decision whether his wife should have an abortion. The State, instead, has determined that the husband's interest in continuing the pregnancy of his wife always outweighs any interest on her part in terminating it irrespective of the condition of their marriage. The State, accordingly, has granted him the right to prevent unilaterally, and for whatever reason, the effectuation of his wife's and her physician's decision to terminate her pregnancy. This state determination not only may discourage the consultation that might normally be expected to precede a major decision affecting the marital couple but also, and more importantly, the State has interposed an absolute obstacle to a woman's decision that *Roe* held to be constitutionally protected from such interference.

12. In response to Mr. Justice WHITE's criticism that the prostaglandin method of inducing abortion was available in Missouri, either at the time the Act was passed or at the time of trial, we make the following observations. First, there is no evidence in the record to which our Brother has pointed that demonstrates that the prostaglandin method was or is available in Missouri. Second, the evidence presented to the District Court does not support such a view. Until January 1974 prostaglandin was used only on an experimental basis in a few medical centers. And, at the time the Missouri General Assembly proscribed saline, the sole distributor of prostaglandin "restricted sales to around twenty medical centers from coast to coast." Brief for Appellee Danforth 68.

It is clear, therefore, that at the time the Missouri General Assembly passed the Act, prostaglandin was not available, in any meaningful sense of that term. Because of this undisputed fact, it was incumbent upon the State to show that at the time of trial in 1974 prostaglandin was available. It failed to do so. Indeed, the State's expert witness, on whose testimony the dissenting opinion relies, does not fill this void. He was able to state only that prostaglandin was used in a limited way until shortly before trial and that he "would think" that it was more readily available at the time of trial. R. 335. Such an experimental and limited use of prostaglandin throughout the country does not make it available or accessible to concerned persons in Missouri.

13. We note that in Missouri physicians must participate in the reporting of births and

deaths. Mo.Rev.Stat. §§ 193.100 and 193.140 (1969), and communicable diseases, §§ 192.020 and 192.040, and that their use of controlled substances is rigidly monitored by the State, Mo.Rev.Stat. c. 195.

14. For some of the considerations that support the State's interest in encouraging parental consent, see the opinion of Mr. Justice STEVENS, concurring in part and dissenting in part. *Post,* at 2856–2857.

15. The mode of operation of one such clinic is revealed by the record in *Bellotti v. Baird, supra,* and accurately described in the Brief for the Appellants in that case.

"The counseling . . . occurs entirely on the day the abortion is to be performed . . . It lasts for two hours and takes place in groups that include both minors and adults who are strangers to one another. . . . The physician takes no part in this counseling process. . . . Counseling is typically limited to a description of abortion procedures, possible complications, and birth control techniques. . . .

"The abortion itself takes five to seven minutes. . . . The physician has no prior contact with the minor, and on the days that abortions are being performed at the [clinic], the physician, . . . may be performing abortions on many other adults and minors. . . . On busy days patients are scheduled in separate groups, consisting usually of five patients. . . . After the abortion [the physician] spends a brief period with the minor and others in the group in the recovery room. . . ." *Id.,* at 43–44.

16. There are countless situations in which the State prohibits conduct only when it is objected to by a private person most closely affected by it. Thus a State cannot forbid anyone to enter on private property with the owner's consent, but it may enact and enforce trespass laws against unauthorized entrances. It cannot forbid transfer of property held in tenancy by the entireties but it may require consent by both husband and wife to such a transfer. These situations plainly do not involve delegations of legislative power to private parties; and neither does the requirement in § 3(3) that a woman not deprive her husband of his future child without his consent.

17. As Mr. Justice STEVENS states in his dissenting opinion:

"The State's interest in the welfare of its young citizens justifies a variety of protective measures. Because he may not foresee the consequences of his decision, a minor may not make an enforceable bargain. He may not lawfully work or travel where he pleases, or even attend exhibitions of constitutionally protected adult motion pictures. Persons below a certain age may not marry without parental consent. Indeed, such consent is essential even when the young woman is already pregnant."

18. The absence of more evidence on the subject in the record seems to be a result of the fact that the claim that the prostaglandin method is unavailable was not part of their litigating strategy below.

19. The majority's construction of state law is, of course, not binding on the Missouri courts. If they should disagree with the majority's reading of state law on one or both of the points treated by the majority, the State could validly enforce the relevant parts of the statute—at least against all those people not parties to this case. Cf. *Dombrowski v. Pfister,* 380 U. S. 479, 492, 85 S.Ct. 1116, 1124, 14 L.Ed.2d 22.

BEAL V. DOE

Supreme Court of the United States, 1977.
432 U. S. 438, 97 S.Ct. 2366, 53 L.Ed.2d 464.

MR. JUSTICE POWELL delivered the opinion of the Court.

The issue in this case is whether Title XIX of the Social Security Act, as added, 79 Stat. 343, and amended, 42 U. S. C. § 1396 *et seq.* (1970 ed. and Supp. V), requires States that participate in the Medical Assistance (Medicaid) program to fund the cost of nontherapeutic abortions.

I

Title XIX establishes the Medicaid program under which participating States may provide federally funded medical assistance to needy persons.[1] The statute requires participating States to provide qualified individuals with financial assistance in five general categories of medical treatment.[2] 42 U. S. C. §§ 1396a (a) (13) (B) (1970 ed. Supp. V), 1396d (a) (1)–(5) (1970 ed. and Supp. V). Although Title XIX does not require States to provide funding for all medical treatment falling within the five general categories, it does require that state Medicaid plans establish "reasonable standards . . . for determining . . . the extent of medical assistance under the plan which . . . are consistent with the objectives of [Title XIX]." 42 U. S. C. § 1396a (a) (17) (1970 ed., Supp. V).

Respondents, who are eligible for medical assistance under Pennsylvania's federally approved Medicaid plan, were denied financial assistance for desired abortions pursuant to Pennsylvania regulations limiting such assistance to those abortions that are certified by physicians as medically necessary.[3] When respondents' applications for Medicaid assistance were denied because of their failure to furnish the required certificates, they filed this action in United States District Court for the Western District of Pennsylvania seeking declaratory and injunctive relief. Their complaint alleged that Pennsylvania's requirement of a certificate of medical necessity contravened relevant provisions of Title XIX and denied them equal protection of the laws in violation of the Fourteenth Amendment.

A three-judge District Court was convened pursuant to 28 U. S. C. § 2281. After resolving the statutory issue against respondents, the District Court held that Pennsylvania's medical-necessity restriction denied respondents equal protection of the laws. *Doe v. Wohlgemuth,* 376 F. Supp. 173 (1974).[4] Accordingly, the court granted a declaratory judgment that the Pennsylvania requirement was unconstitutional as applied during the first trimester. The United States Court of Appeals for the Third Circuit, sitting en banc, reversed on the statutory issue, holding that Ti-tle XIX prohibits participating States from requiring a physician's certificate of medical necessity as a condition for funding during both the first and second tri-mesters of pregnancy.[5] 523 F.2d 611 (1975). The Court of Appeals therefore did not reach the constitutional issue.[6]

We granted certiorari to resolve a conflict among the federal courts as to the requirements of Title XIX.[7] 428 U. S. 909 (1976).

II

The only question before us is one of statutory construction: whether Title XIX requires Pennsylvania to fund under its Medicaid program the cost of *all* abortions that are permissible under state law. "The starting point in every case involving construction of a statute is the language itself." *Blue Chip Stamps v. Manor Drug Stores,* 421 U. S. 723, 756 (1975) (POWELL, J., concurring). Title XIX makes no reference to abortions, or, for that matter, to any other particular medi-cal procedure. Instead, the statute is cast in terms that require participating States to provide financial assistance with respect to five broad categories of medical treatment. See n. 2, *supra.* But nothing in the statute suggests that participating States are required to fund every medical procedure that falls within the delineated categories of medical care. Indeed, the statute expressly provides:

> "A State plan for medical assistance must . . . include reasonable standards . . . for determining eligibility for and the extent of medical assistance under the plan which . . . are consistent with the objectives of this [Title]. . . ." 42 U. S. C. § 1396a (a) (17) (1970 ed., Supp. V).

This language confers broad discretion on the States to adopt standards for deter-mining the extent of medical assistance, requiring only that such standards be "rea-sonable" and "consistent with the objectives" of the Act.[8]

Pennsylvania's regulation comports fully with Title XIX's broadly stated pri-mary objective to enable each State, as far as practicable, to furnish medical assis-tance to individuals whose income and resources are insufficient to meet the costs of necessary medical services. See 42 U. S. C. §§ 1396, 1396a (10) (C) (1970 ed., Supp. V). Although serious statutory questions might be presented if a state Medi-caid plan excluded necessary medical treatment from its coverage, it is hardly in-consistent with the objectives of the Act for a State to refuse to fund *unnecessary—* though perhaps desirable—medical services.

The thrust of respondents' argument is that the exclusion of nontherapeutic abortions from Medicaid coverage is unreasonable on both economic and health grounds.[9] The economic argument is grounded on the view that abortion is gener-ally a less expensive medical procedure than childbirth. Since a pregnant woman normally will either have an abortion or carry her child full term, a State that elects not to fund nontherapeutic abortions will eventually be confronted with the greater expenses associated with childbirth. The corresponding health argument is based on the view that an early abortion poses less of a risk to the woman's health than childbirth. Consequently, respondents argue, the economic and health considerations that ordinarily support the reasonableness of state limitations on financing of unnecessary medical services are not applicable to pregnancy.

Accepting respondents' assumptions as accurate, we do not agree that the exclusion of nontherapeutic abortions from Medicaid coverage is unreasonable under Title XIX. As we acknowledged in *Roe v. Wade,* 410 U. S. 113 (1973), the State has a valid and important interest in encouraging childbirth. We expressly recognized in *Roe* the "important and legitimate interest [of the State] . . . in protecting the potentiality of human life." *Id.,* at 162. That interest alone does not, at least until approximately the third trimester, become sufficiently compelling to justify unduly burdensome state interference with the woman's constitutionally protected privacy interest. But it is a significant state interest existing throughout the course of the woman's pregnancy. Respondents point to nothing in either the language or the legislative history of Title XIX that suggests that it is unreasonable for a participating State to further this unquestionably strong and legitimate interest in encouraging normal childbirth.[10] Absent such a showing, we will not presume that Congress intended to condition a State's participation in the Medicaid program on its willingness to undercut this important interest by subsidizing the costs of nontherapeutic abortions.[11]

Our interpretation of the statute is reinforced by two other relevant considerations. First, when Congress passed Title XIX in 1965, nontherapeutic abortions were unlawful in most States.[12] In view of the then-prevailing state law, the contention that Congress intended to require—rather than permit—participating States to fund nontherapeutic abortions requires far more convincing proof than respondents have offered. Second, the Department of Health, Education, and Welfare, the agency charged with the administration of this complicated statute,[13] takes the position that Title XIX allows—but does not mandate—funding for such abortions. "[W]e must be mindful that 'the construction of a statute by those charged with its execution should be followed unless there are compelling indications that it is wrong. . . .' " *New York Dept. of Soc. Services v. Dublino,* 413 U. S. 405, 421 (1973), quoting *Red Lion Broadcasting Co. v. FCC,* 395 U. S. 367, 381 (1969). Here, such indications are completely absent.

We therefore hold that Pennsylvania's refusal to extend Medicaid coverage to nontherapeutic abortions is not inconsistent with Title XIX.[14] We make clear, however, that the federal statute leaves a State free to provide such coverage if it so desires.[15]

III

There is one feature of the Pennsylvania Medicaid program, not addressed by the Court of Appeals, that may conflict with Title XIX. Under the Pennsylvania program, financial assistance is not provided for medically necessary abortions unless two physicians in addition to the attending physician have examined the patient and have concurred in writing that the abortion is medically necessary. See n. 3, *supra.* On this record, we are unable to determine the precise role played by these two additional physicians, and consequently we are unable to ascertain whether this requirement interferes with the attending physician's medical judgment in a manner not contemplated by the Congress. The judgment of the Court of Appeals is therefore reversed, and the case is remanded for consideration of this requirement.

It is so ordered.

MR. JUSTICE BRENNAN, with whom MR. JUSTICE MARSHALL and MR. JUSTICE BLACKMUN join, dissenting.

The Court holds that the "necessary medical services" which Pennsylvania must fund for individuals eligible for Medicaid do not include services connected with elective abortions. I dissent.

Though the question presented by this case is one of statutory interpretation, a difficult constitutional question would be raised where Title XIX of the Social Security Act, as amended, 42 U. S. C. 1396 *et seq.* (1970 ed. and Supp. V), is read not to require funding of elective abortions. *Maher v. Roe, post,* p. 464; *Doe v. Bolton,* 410 U.S. 179 (1973); *Roe v. Wade,* 410 U. S. 113 (1973). Since the Court should "first ascertain whether a construction of the statute is fairly possible by which the [constitutional] question may be avoided," *Ashwander v. TWA,* 297 U. S. 288, 341, 348 (1936) (Brandeis, J., concurring); see *Westby v. Doe,* 420 U. S. 968 (1975), Title XIX, in my view, read fairly in light of the principle of avoidance of unnecessary constitutional decisions, requires agreement with the Court of Appeals that the legislative history of Title XIX and our abortion cases compel the conclusion that elective abortions constitute medically necessary treatment for the condition of pregnancy. I would therefore find that Title XIX requires that Pennsylvania pay the costs of elective abortions for women who are eligible participants in the Medicaid program.

Pregnancy is unquestionably a condition requiring medical services. See *Roe v. Norton,* 380 F. Supp. 726, 729 (1974); *Klein v. Nassau County Medical Center,* 347 F. Supp. 496, 500 (1972), vacated for further consideration in light of *Roe v. Wade* and *Doe v. Bolton,* 412 U. S. 925 (1973). Treatment for the condition may involve medical procedures for its termination, or medical procedures to bring the pregnancy to term, resulting in a live birth. "[A]bortion and childbirth, when stripped of the sensitive moral arguments surrounding the abortion controversy, are simply two alternative medical methods of dealing with pregnancy . . ." *Roe v. Norton,* 408 F. Supp. 660, 663 n. 3 (1975). The Medicaid statutes leave the decision as to choice among pregnancy procedures exclusively with the doctor and his patient, and make no provision whatever for intervention by the State in that decision. Section 1396a (a) (19) expressly imposes the obligation upon participating States to incorporate safeguards in their programs that assure medical "care and services will be provided, in a manner consistent with . . . the best interests of the recipients." And, significantly, the Senate Finance Committee Report on the Medicaid bill expressly stated that the "physician is to be the key figure in determining utilization of health services." S. Rep. No. 404, 89th Cong., 1st Sess., 46 (1965). Thus the very heart of the congressional scheme is that the physician and patient should have complete freedom to choose those medical procedures for a given condition which are best suited to the needs of the patient.

The Court's original abortion decisions dovetail precisely with the congressional purpose under Medicaid to avoid interference with the decision of the woman and her physician. *Roe v. Wade, supra,* at 163, held that "[t]he attending physician, in consultation with his patient, is free to determine, without regulation by the State, that, in his medical judgment, the patient's pregnancy should be terminated." And *Doe v. Bolton, supra,* at 192, held that "the medical judgment may be exercised in the light of all factors—physical, emotional, psychological, familial, and the woman's age—relevant to the well-being of the patient. All these factors may relate to health. This allows the attending physician the room he needs to make his best medical judgment. And it is room that operates for the benefit, not the disadvantage, of the pregnant woman."[16] Once medical treatment of some sort is necessary, Title XIX does not dictate what that treatment should be. In the face of Title XIX's emphasis upon the joint autonomy of the physician and his patient in the decision of how to treat the condition of pregnancy, it is beyond comprehension how treatment for therapeutic abortions and live births constitutes "necessary medical services" under Title XIX, but that for elective abortions does not.

If Pennsylvania is not obligated to fund medical services rendered in performing elective abortions because they are not "necessary" within the meaning of 42 U. S. C. § 1396 (1970 ed., Supp. V), it must follow that Pennsylvania also would not violate the statute if it refused to fund medical services for "therapeutic" abortions or live births. For if the availability of therapeutic abortions and live births makes elective abortions "unnecessary," the converse must also be true. This highlights the violence done the congressional mandate by today's decision. If the State must pay the costs of therapeutic abortions and of live births as constituting medically necessary responses to the condition of pregnancy, it must, under the command of § 1396, also pay the costs of elective abortions; the procedures in each case constitute necessary medical treatment for the condition of pregnancy.

The 1972 family-planning amendment to the Act, 42 U. S. C. § 1396d (a)(4)(C) (1970 ed., Supp. V), buttresses my conclusion that the Court's construction frustrates the objectives of the Medicaid program. Section 1396 (2) states that an explicit purpose of Medicaid is to assist eligible indigent recipients to "attain or retain capability for independence or self-care." The 1972 amendment furthered this objective by assisting those who "desire to control family size in order to enhance their capacity and ability to seek employment and better meet family needs." S. Rep. No. 92–1230, p. 297 (1972). Though far less than an ideal family-planning mechanism, elective abortions are one method for limiting family size and avoiding the financial and emotional problems that are the daily lot of the impoverished. See Special Subcommittee on Human Resources of the Senate Committee on Labor and Public Welfare, 92d Cong., 1st Sess., Report of the Secretary of Health, Education, and Welfare Submitting Five-Year Plan for Family Planning Services and Population Research Programs 319 (Comm. Print 1971).

It is no answer that abortions were illegal in 1965 when Medicaid was enacted, and in 1972 when the family-planning amendment was adopted. Medicaid deals with general categories of medical services, not with specific procedures, and nothing in the statute even suggests that Medicaid is designed to assist in payment for only those medical services that were legally permissible in 1965 and 1972. I fully agree with the Court of Appeals statement:

> "It is impossible to believe that in enacting Title XIX Congress intended to freeze the medical services available to recipients at those which were legal in 1965. Congress surely intended Medicaid to pay for drugs not legally marketable under the FDA's regulations in 1965 which are subsequently found to be marketable. We can see no reason why the same analysis should not apply to the Supreme Court's legalization of elective abortion in 1973." 523 F. 2d 611, 622–623 (1975).

Nor is the administrative interpretation of the Department of Health, Education, and Welfare that funding of elective abortions is permissible but not mandatory dispositive of the construction of "necessary medical services." The principle of according weight to agency interpretation is inapplicable when a departmental interpretation, as here, is patently inconsistent with the controlling statute. *Townsend v. Swank,* 404 U. S. 282, 286 (1971).

Finally, there is certainly no affirmative policy justification of the State that aids the Court's construction of "necessary medical services" as not including medical services rendered in performing elective abortions. The State cannot contend that it protects its fiscal interests in not funding elective abortions when it incurs far greater expense in paying for the more costly medical services performed in carrying pregnancies to term, and, after birth, paying the increased welfare bill incurred to support the mother and child. Nor can the State contend that it protects the mother's health by discouraging an abortion, for not only may Pennsylvania's exclusion force the pregnant woman to use of measures dangerous to her life and health but, as *Roe v. Wade,* 410 U.S., at 149, concluded, elective abortions by competent licensed physicians are now "relatively safe" and the risks to women undergoing abortions by such means "appear to be as low as or lower than . . . for normal childbirth."

The Court's construction can only result as a practical matter in forcing penniless pregnant women to have children they would not have borne if the State had not weighted the scales to make their choice to have abortions substantially more onerous. Indeed, as the Court said only last Term: "For a doctor who cannot afford to work for nothing, and a woman who cannot afford to pay him, the State's refusal to fund an abortion is as effective an 'interdiction' of it as would ever be necessary." *Singleton v. Wulff,* 428 U. S. 106, 118–119, n. 7 (1976). The Court's construction thus makes a mockery of the congressional mandate that States provide "care and services . . . in a manner consistent with . . . the best interests of the recipients." We should respect the congressional plan by construing § 1396 as requiring States to pay the costs of the "necessary medical services" rendered in performing elective abortions, chosen by physicians and their women patients who participate in Medicaid as the appropriate treatment for their pregnancies.

The Court does not address the question whether the provision requiring the concurrence in writing of two physicians in addition to the attending physician conflicts with Title XIX. I would hold that the provision is invalid as clearly in conflict with Title XIX under my view of the paramount role played by the attending physician in the abortion decision, and in any event is constitutionally invalid under *Doe v. Bolton,* 410 U.S., at 198–200.

I would affirm the judgment of the Court of Appeals.

MR. JUSTICE MARSHALL, dissenting.[17]

It is all too obvious that the governmental actions in these cases, ostensibly taken to "encourage" women to carry pregnancies to term, are in reality intended to impose a moral viewpoint that no State may constitutionally enforce. *Roe v. Wade,* 410 U.S. 113 (1973); *Doe v. Bolton,* 410 U. S. 179 (1973). Since efforts to overturn those decisions have been unsuccessful, the opponents of abortion have attempted every imaginable means to circumvent the commands of the Constitution and impose their moral choices upon the rest of society. See. *e.g., Planned Parenthood of Missouri v. Danforth,* 428 U. S. 52 (1976); *Singleton v. Wulff,* 428 U. S. 106 (1976); *Bellotti v. Baird,* 428 U. S. 132 (1976). The present cases involve the most vicious attacks yet devised. The impact of the regulations here falls tragically upon those among us least able to help or defend themselves. As the Court well knows, these regulations inevitably will have the practical effect of preventing nearly all poor women from obtaining safe and legal abortions.[18]

The enactments challenged here brutally coerce poor women to bear children whom society will scorn for every day of their lives. Many thousands of unwanted minority and mixed-race children now spend blighted lives in foster homes, orphanages, and "reform" schools: Cf. *Smith v. Organization of Foster Families,* 431 U. S. 816 (1977). Many children of the poor, sadly, will attend second-rate segregated schools. Cf. *Milliken v. Bradley,* 418 U. S. 717 (1974). And opposition remains strong against increasing Aid to Families With Dependent Children benefits for impoverished mothers and children, so that there is little chance for the children to grow up in a decent environment. Cf. *Dandridge v. Williams,* 397 U. S. 471 (1970). I am appalled at the ethical bankruptcy of those who preach a "right to life" that means, under present social policies, a bare existence in utter misery for so many poor women and their children.

I

The Court's insensitivity to the human dimension of these decisions is particularly obvious in its cursory discussion of appellees' equal protection claims in *Maher v. Roe.* That case points up once again the need for this Court to repudiate its outdated and intellectually disingenuous "two-tier" equal protection analysis. See generally *Massachusetts Bd. of Retirement v. Murgia,* 427 U. S. 307, 317 (1976) (MARSHALL, J., dissenting). As I have suggested before, this "model's two fixed modes of analysis, strict scrutiny and mere rationality, simply do not describe the inquiry the Court has undertaken—or should undertake—in equal protection cases." *Id.,* at 318. In the present case, in its evident desire to avoid strict scrutiny—or indeed any meaningful scrutiny—of the challenged legislation, which would almost surely result in its invalidation, see *id.,* at 319, the Court pulls from thin air a distinction between laws that absolutely prevent exercise of the fundamental right to abortion and those that "merely" make its exercise difficult for some people. See *Maher v. Roe, post,* at 471-474. MR. JUSTICE BRENNAN demonstrates that our cases support no such distinction, *post,* at 485-489, and I have argued above that the challenged regulations are little different from a total prohibition from the viewpoint of the poor. But the Court's legal legerdemain has produced the desired result: A fundamental right is no longer at stake and mere rationality becomes the appropriate mode of analysis. To no one's surprise, application of that test—combined with misreading of *Roe v. Wade* to generate a "strong" state interest in "potential life" during the first trimester of pregnancy, see *infra,* at 460; *Maher v. Roe, post,* at 489–490 (BRENNAN, J., dissenting); *post,* at 462 (BLACKMUN, J., dissenting)—"leaves little doubt about the outcome; the challenged legislation is [as] always upheld." *Massachusetts Bd. of Retirement v. Murgia, supra,* at 319. And once again, "relevant factors [are] misapplied or ignored," 427 U. S., at 321, while the Court "forgo[es] all judicial protection against discriminatory legislation bearing upon" a right "vital to the flourishing of a free society" and a class "unfairly burdened by invidious discrimination unrelated to the individual worth of [its] members." *Id.,* at 320.

As I have argued before, an equal protection analysis far more in keeping with the actions rather than the words of the Court, see *id.,* at 320–321, carefully weighs three factors—"the importance of the governmental benefits denied, the character of the class, and the asserted state interests," *id.,* at 322. Application of this standard would invalidate the challenged regulations.

The governmental benefits at issue here, while perhaps not representing large amounts of money for any individual, are nevertheless of absolutely vital importance in the lives of the recipients. The right of every woman to choose whether to bear a child is, as *Roe v. Wade* held, of fundamental importance. An unwanted child may be disruptive and destructive of the life of any woman, but the impact is felt most by those too poor to ameliorate those effects. If funds for an abortion are unavailable, a poor woman may feel that she is forced to obtain an illegal abortion that poses a serious threat to her health and even her life. See n. 1, *supra.* If she refuses to take this risk, and undergoes the pain and danger of state-financed pregnancy and childbirth, she may well give up all chance of escaping the cycle of poverty. Absent day-care facilities, she will be forced into full-time child care for years to come; she will be unable to work so that her family can break out of the welfare system or the lowest income brackets. If she already has children, another infant to feed and clothe may well stretch the budget past the breaking point. All chance to control the direction of her own life will have been lost.

I have already adverted to some of the characteristics of the class burdened by these regulations. While poverty alone does not entitle a class to claim government benefits, it is surely a relevant factor in the present inquiry. See *San Antonio School Dist. v. Rodriguez,* 411 U. S. 1, 70, 117–124 (1973) (MARSHALL, J., dissenting). Indeed, it was in the *San Antonio* case that MR. JUSTICE POWELL for the Court stated a test for analyzing discrimination on the basis of wealth that would, if fairly applied here, strike down the regulations. The Court there held that a wealth dis-

crimination claim is made out by persons who share "two distinguishing characteristics: because of their impecunity they [are] completely unable to pay for some
desired benefit, and as a consequence, they sustai[n] an absolute deprivation of a
meaningful opportunity to enjoy that benefit." *Id.,* at 20. Medicaid recipients are,
almost by definition, "completely unable to pay for" abortions, and are thereby
completely denied "a meaningful opportunity" to obtain them.[19]

It is no less disturbing that the effect of the challenged regulations will fall
with great disparity upon women of minority races. Nonwhite women now obtain
abortions at nearly twice the rate of whites,[20] and it appears that almost 40 percent
of minority women—more than five times the proportion of whites—are dependent
upon Medicaid for their health care.[21] Even if this strongly disparate racial impact
does not alone violate the Equal Protection Clause, see *Washington v. Davis,* 426
U. S. 229 (1976); *Jefferson v. Hackney,* 406 U. S. 535 (1972), "at some point a
showing that state action has a devastating impact on the lives of minority racial
groups must be relevant." *Id.,* at 558, 575–576 (MARSHALL, J., dissenting).

Against the brutal effect that the challenged laws will have must be weighed
the asserted state interest. The Court describes this as a "strong interest in protecting the potential life of the fetus." *Maher v. Roe, post,* at 478. Yet in *Doe v. Bolton,
supra,* the Court expressly held that any state interest during the first trimester of
pregnancy, when 86 percent of all abortions occur, CDC Surveillance 3, was wholly insufficient to justify state interference with the right to abortion. 410 U. S. at
192–200.[22] If a State's interest in potential human life before the point of viability is
insufficient to justify requiring several physicians' concurrence for an abortion,
ibid., I cannot comprehend how it magically becomes adequate to allow the present
infringement on rights of disfavored classes. If there is any state interest in potential life before the point of viability, it certainly does not outweigh the deprivation
or serious discouragement of a vital constitutional right of especial importance to
poor and minority women.[23]

Thus, taking account of all relevant factors under the flexible standard of
equal protection review, I would hold the Connecticut and Pennsylvania Medicaid
regulations and the St. Louis public hospital policy violative of the Fourteenth
Amendment.

II

When this Court decided *Roe v. Wade* and *Doe v. Bolton,* it properly embarked on a course of constitutional adjudication no less controversial than that
begun by *Brown v. Board of Education,* 347 U. S. 483 (1954). The abortion decisions are sound law and undoubtedly good policy. They have never been questioned by the Court, and we are told that today's cases "signa[l] no retreat from
Roe or the cases applying it." *Maher v. Roe, post,* at 475. The logic of those cases
inexorably requires invalidation of the present enactments. Yet I fear that the
Court's decisions will be an invitation to public officials, already under extraordinary pressure from well-financed and carefully orchestrated lobbying campaigns,
to approve more such restrictions. The effect will be to relegate millions of people

to lives of poverty and despair. When elected leaders cower before public pressure, this Court, more than ever, must not shirk its duty to enforce the Constitution for the benefit of the poor and powerless.

MR. JUSTICE BLACKMUN, with whom MR. JUSTICE BRENNAN and MR. JUSTICE MARSHALL join, dissenting.[24]

The Court today, by its decisions in these cases, allows the States, and such municipalities as choose to do so, to accomplish indirectly what the Court in *Roe v. Wade,* 410 U. S. 113 (1973), and *Doe v. Bolton,* 410 U. S. 179 (1973)—by a substantial majority and with some emphasis, I had thought—said they could not do directly. The Court concedes the existence of a constitutional right but denies the realization and enjoyment of that right on the ground that existence and realization are separate and distinct. For the individual woman concerned, indigent and financially helpless, as the Court's opinions in the three cases concede her to be, the result is punitive and tragic. Implicit in the Court's holdings is the condescension that she may go elsewhere for her abortion. I find that disingenuous and alarming, almost reminiscent of: "Let them eat cake."

The result the Court reaches is particularly distressing in *Poelker v. Doe, post,* p. 519, where a presumed majority, in electing as mayor one whom the record shows campaigned on the issue of closing public hospitals to nontherapeutic abortions, punitively impresses upon a needy minority its own concepts of the socially desirable, the publicly acceptable, and the morally sound, with a touch of the devil-take-the-hindmost. This is not the kind of thing for which our Constitution stands.

The Court's financial argument, of course, is specious. To be sure, welfare funds are limited and welfare must be spread perhaps as best meets the community's concept of its needs. But the cost of a nontherapeutic abortion is far less than the cost of maternity care and delivery, and holds no comparison whatsoever with the welfare costs that will burden the State for the new indigents and their support in the long, long years ahead.

Neither is it an acceptable answer, as the Court well knows, to say that the Congress and the States are free to authorize the use of funds for nontherapeutic abortions. Why should any politician incur the demonstrated wrath and noise of the abortion opponents when mere silence and nonactivity accomplish the results the opponents want?

There is another world "out there," the existence of which the Court, I suspect, either chooses to ignore or fears to recognize. And so the cancer of poverty will continue to grow. This is a sad day for those who regard the Constitution as a force that would serve justice to all evenhandedly and, in so doing would better the lot of the poorest among us.

NOTES

1. Title XIX establishes two groups of needy persons: (1) the "categorically" needy, which includes needy persons with dependent children and the aged, blind, and disabled, 42

U. S. C. § 1396a (a) (10) (A) (1970 ed., Supp. V); and (2) the "medically" needy, which includes other needy persons, § 1396a (10)(C) (1970 ed., Supp. V). Participating States are not required to extend Medicaid coverage to the "medically" needy, but Pennsylvania has chosen to do so.

2. The general categories of medical treatment enumerated are:

"(1) inpatient hospital services (other than services in an institution for tuberculosis or mental diseases);

"(2) outpatient hospital services;

"(3) other laboratory and X-ray services;

"(4) (A) skilled nursing facility services (other than services in an institution for tuberculosis or mental diseases) for individuals 21 years of age or older; (B) effective July 1, 1969, such early and periodic screening and diagnosis of individuals who are eligible under the plan and are under the age of 21 to ascertain their physical or mental defects, and such health care, treatment, and other measures to correct or ameliorate defects and chronic conditions discovered thereby, as may be provided in regulations of the Secretary; and (C) family planning services and supplies furnished (directly or under arrangements with others) to individuals of child-bearing age (including minors who can be considered to be sexually active) who are eligible under the State plan and who desire such services and supplies;

"(5) physicians' services furnished by a physician (as defined in section 1395x (r) (1) of this title), whether furnished in the office, the patient's home, a hospital, or a skilled nursing facility, or elsewhere." 42 U. S. C. § 1396d (a) (1970 ed. and Supp. V).

Participating States that elect to extend coverage to the "medically" needy, see n. 1, *supra,* have the option of providing somewhat different categories of medical services to those individuals. 42 U. S. C. § 1396a (a) (13) (C) (ii) (1970 ed., Supp. V).

3. An abortion is deemed medically necessary under the Pennsylvania Medicaid program if:

"(1) There is documented medical evidence that continuance of the pregnancy may threaten the health of the mother;

"(2) There is documented medical evidence that an infant may be born with incapacitating physical deformity or mental deficiency; or

"(3) There is documented medical evidence that continuance of a pregnancy resulting from legally established statutory or forcible rape or incest, may constitute a threat to the mental or physical health of a patient; and

"(4) Two other physicians chosen because of their recognized professional competency have examined the patient and have concurred in writing; and

"(5) The procedure is performed in a hospital accredited by the Joint Commission on Accreditation of Hospitals." Brief for Petitioners 4, citing 3 Pennsylvania Bulletin 2207, 2209 (Sept. 29, 1973).

In *Doe v. Bolton,* 410 U. S. 179, 192 (1973), this Court indicated that "[w]hether 'an abortion is necessary' is a professional judgment that . . . may be exercised in the light of all factors—physical, emotional, psychological, familial, and the woman's age—relevant to the well-being of the patient. All these factors may relate to health. This allows the attending physician the room he needs to make his best medical judgment." We were informed during oral argument that the Pennsylvania definition of medical necessity is broad enough to encompass the factors specified in *Bolton.* Tr. of Oral Arg. 7–8.

The dissent of Mr. JUSTICE BRENNAN emphasizes the "key" role of the physician within the Medicaid program, noting that "[t]he Medicaid statutes leave the decision as to the choice among pregnancy procedures exclusively with the doctor and his patient. . . ." *Post,* at 449–450. This is precisely what Pennsylvania has done. Its regulations provide for the funding of abortions upon certification of medical necessity, a determination that the physician is authorized to make on the basis of all relevant factors.

4. The District Court was of the view that the regulation creates "an unlawful distinction between indigent women who choose to carry their pregnancies to birth, and indigent women who choose to terminate their pregnancies by abortion." 376 F. Supp., at 191. In *Maher v. Roe, post,* p. 464, we today conclude that the Equal Protection Clause of the Fourteenth Amendment does not prevent a State from making the policy choice to fund costs inci-

dent to childbirth without providing similar funding for costs incident to nontherapeutic abortion.

5. Petitioners appealed the District Court's declaratory judgment to the Court of Appeals. Respondents cross-appealed from the denial of declaratory relief with respect to the second and third trimesters of pregnancy. Since respondents did not seek review of the District Court's denial of injunctive relief, the Court of Appeals had jurisdiction over the appeals. *Gerstein v. Coe,* 417 U. S. 279 (1974).

6. As a result of the decision of the Court of Appeals, petitioners issued a Temporary Revised Policy on September 25, 1975. This interim policy allows financial assistance for abortions without regard to medical necessity. Brief for Petitioners 3 n. 3.

7. Two other Courts of Appeals have concluded that the federal statute does not require participating States to fund the cost of nontherapeutic abortions. *Roe v. Norton,* 522 F. 2d 928 (CA2 1975); *Roe v. Ferguson,* 515 F. 2d 279 (CA 6 1975). See also, *e.g., Doe v. Westby,* 402 F. Supp. 140 (WDSD 1975) (three-judge court) (Title XIX requires funding of nontherapeutic abortions), appeal docketed, No. 75–813; *Doe v. Stewart,* Civ. No. 74–3197 (ED La., Jan. 26, 1976) (three-judge court) (Title XIX does not require funding of nontherapeutic abortions), appeal docketed, No. 75-6721.

8. Respondents concede that Title XIX "indicates that the states will have wide discretion in determining the extent of services to be provided." Brief for Respondents 9.

9. Respondents also contend that Pennsylvania's restriction on coverage is unreasonable within the meaning of Title XIX in that it interferes with the physician's professional judgment concerning appropriate treatment. With one possible exception addressed in Part III, *infra,* the Pennsylvania program does not interfere with the physician's medical judgment concerning his patient's needs. If a physician certifies that an abortion is medically necessary, see n. 3, *supra,* the medical expenses are covered under the Pennsylvania Medicaid program. If, however, the physician concludes that the abortion is not medically necessary, but indicates a willingness to perform the abortion at the patient's request, the expenses are not covered. The decision whether to fund the costs of the abortion thus depends solely on the physician's determination of medical necessity. Respondents point to nothing in the Pennsylvania Medicaid plan that indicates state interference with the physician's initial determination.

10. Respondents rely heavily on the fact that in amending Title XIX in 1972 to include "family planning services" within the five broad categories of required medical treatment, see n. 2, *supra,* Congress did not expressly *exclude* abortions as a covered service. Since Congress had expressly excluded abortions as a method of family planning services in prior legislation, see 42 U. S. C. § 300a–6, respondents conclude that the failure of Congress to exclude coverage of abortions in the 1972 amendments to Title XIX "strongly indicates" an intention to *require* coverage of abortions. This line of reasoning is flawed. The failure to exclude abortions from coverage indicates only that Congress intended to allow such coverage, not that such coverage is mandatory for nontherapeutic abortions.

11. The Court of Appeals concluded that Pennsylvania's regulation also violated the equality provisions of Title XIX requiring that an individual's medical assistance "shall not be less in amount, duration, or scope than the medical assistance made available to any other such individual." 42 U. S. C. § 1396a (a) (10) (B) (1970 ed., Supp. V). See § 1396a (a) (10) (C) (1970 ed., Supp. V). According to the Court of Appeals, the Pennsylvania regulation "force[s] pregnant women to use the least voluntary method of treatment, while not imposing a similar requirement on other persons who qualify for aid." 523 F. 2d 611, 619 (1975). We find the Pennsylvania regulation to be entirely consistent with the equality provisions of Title XIX. Pennsylvania has simply decided that there is reasonable justification for excluding from Medicaid coverage a particular medically unnecessary procedure—nontherapeutic abortions.

12. At the time of our 1973 decision in *Roe,* some eight years after the enactment of Title XIX, at least 30 States had statutory prohibitions against nontherapeutic abortions. 410 U. S. 113, 118 n. 2 (1973).

13. Federal funds are made available only to those States whose Medicaid plans have been approved by the Secretary of HEW. 42 U. S. C. § 1396 (1970 ed., Supp. V).

14. Congress by statute has expressly prohibited the use during fiscal year 1977 of federal Medicaid funds for abortions except when the life of the mother would be endangered if the fetus were carried to term. Departments of Labor and Health, Education, and Welfare Appropriation Act, 1977, § 209, Pub. L. 94–439, 90 Stat. 1434.

15. Our dissenting Brothers, in this case and in *Maher v. Roe, post,* p. 482, express in vivid terms their anguish over the perceived impact of today's decisions on indigent pregnant women who prefer abortion to carrying a fetus to childbirth. We think our Brothers misconceive the issues before us, as well as the role of the judiciary.

In these cases we have held merely that (i) the provisions of the Social Security Act do not *require* a State, as a condition of participation, to include the funding of elective abortions in its Medicaid program; and (ii) the Equal Protection Clause does not require a State that elects to fund expenses incident to childbirth also to provide funding for elective abortions. But we leave entirely free both the Federal Government and the States, through the normal processes of democracy, to provide the desired funding. The issues present policy decisions of the widest concern. They should be resolved by the representatives of the people, not by this Court.

16. The Court states, *ante,* at 442 n. 3, that Pennsylvania has left the abortion decision to the patient and her physician in the manner prescribed in *Doe v. Bolton.* Pennsylvania indeed does allow the attending physician to provide a certificate of medical necessity "on the basis of all relevant factors," *ante,* at 442 n. 3, but Pennsylvania's concept of relevance does not extend far enough to permit doctors freely to provide certificates of medical necessity for all elective abortions. At oral argument, counsel for petitioners carefully stated the State's position as follows:

"[L]et me make perfectly clear my concession. That is, that a physician, in examining a patient, may take psychological, physical, emotional, familial considerations into mind and in the light of those considerations, may determine if those factors affect the health of the mother to such an extent as he would deem an abortion necessary.

"I think the key in the *Bolton* language, and the key in the *Vuitch* language [402 U. S. 62] is the fact that the physician, using all of these facts—and there are probably more that he should use—must determine if the woman's health—that is, her physicial or psychological health—is jeopardized by the condition of pregnancy.

"That is not to say, obviously, as I believe the Plaintiffs are asserting, that the fact that the family is going to increase makes an abortion medically necessary." Tr. of Oral Arg. 8.

Petitioners' "concession" only goes so far as to permit an attending physician to consider an abortion as it relates to a woman's health. *Bolton* recognized that the factors considered by a physician "*may* relate to health," but in the very same paragraph made clear that those factors were more broadly directed to the "well-being" of the woman. 410 U. S., at 192 (emphasis added). While the right to privacy does implicate health considerations, the constitutional right recognized and protected by the Court's abortion decisions is the "right of the *individual,* married or single, to be free from unwarranted governmental intrusion into matters so fundamentally affecting a person as the decision whether to bear or beget a child." *Eisenstadt v. Baird,* 405 U. S. 438, 453 (1972).

17. [This opinion applies also to No. 75–1440, *Maher, Commissioner of Social Services of Connecticut v. Roe et al., post,* p. 464, and No. 75–442, *Poelker, Mayor of St. Louis, et al. v. Doe, post,* p. 519.]

18. Although an abortion performed during the first trimester of pregnancy is a relatively inexpensive surgical procedure, usually costing under $200, even this modest sum is far beyond the means of most Medicaid recipients. And "if one does not have it and is unable to get it the fee might as well be" one hundred times as great. *Smith v. Bennett,* 365 U. S. 708, 712 (1961).

Even before today's decisions, a major reason that perhaps as much as one-third of the annual need for an estimated 1.8 million abortions went unmet was the fact that 8 out of 10 American counties did not have a single abortion provider. Sullivan, Tietze, & Dryfoos, Legal Abortion in the United States, 1975–1976, 9 Family Planning Perspectives 116–117, 121, 129 (1977). In 1975, 83,000 women had to travel from their home States to obtain abortions (there were 100 abortions performed in West Virginia and 310 in Mississippi), and about 300,000 more, or a total of nearly 40% of abortion patients, had to seek help outside their home counties. *Id.,* at 116, 121, 124. In addition, only 18% of the public hospitals in the Nation performed even a single abortion in 1975 and in 10 States not one public hospital provided abortion services. *Id.,* at 121, 128.

Given the political realities, it seems inevitable that the number and geographical distribution of abortion providers will diminish as a result of today's decisions. It is regrettable but likely that fewer public hospitals will provide the service and if Medicaid payments are unavailable, other hospitals, clinics, and physicians will be unable to do so. Since most Medicaid and public hospital patients probably do not have the money, the time, or the familiarity with the medical delivery system to travel to distant States or cities where abortions are available, today's decisions will put safe and legal abortions beyond their reach. The inevitable human tragedy that will result is reflected in a Government report:

"[F]or some women, the lack of public funding for legal abortion acted as a deterrent to their obtaining the safer procedures. The following case history [of a death which occurred during 1975] exemplifies such a situation:

". . . A 41-year-old married woman with a history of 6 previous pregnancies, 5 living children, and 1 previous abortion sought an illegal abortion from a local dietician. Her stated reason for seeking an illegal procedure was financial, since Medicaid in her state of residence would not pay for her abortion. The illegal procedure cost $30, compared with an estimated $150 for a legal procedure. . . . Allegedly the operation was performed by inserting a metal rod to dilate the cervix. . . . [The woman died of cardiac arrest after two weeks of intensive hospital care and two operations.]" U. S. Dept. of Health, Education, and Welfare, Center for Disease Control, Abortion Surveillance, 1975; p. 9 (1977) (hereafter CDC Surveillance).

19. If public funds and facilities for abortions are sharply reduced, private charities, hospitals, clinics, and doctors willing to perform abortions for far less than the prevailing fee will, I trust, accommodate some of the need. But since abortion services are inadequately available even now, see n. 1, *supra,* such private generosity is unlikely to give many poor women "a meaningful opportunity" to obtain abortions.

20. Blacks and other nonwhite groups are heavily overrepresented among both abortion patients and Medicaid recipients. In 1975, about 13.1% of the population was nonwhite, Statistical Abstract of the United States, 1976, p. 25, yet 31% of women obtaining abortions were of a minority race. CDC Surveillance 2 and 24, Table 8. Furthermore, nonwhites secured abortions at the rate of 476 per 1,000 births, while the corresponding figure for whites was only 277. *Id.,* at 2, and Tables 8, 9. Abortion is thus a family-planning method of considerably more significance for minority groups than for whites.

21. Although complete statistics are unavailable (three States, Puerto Rico and the Virgin Islands having furnished no racial breakdown, and eight States giving incomplete data), nonwhites accounted for some 43.4% of Medicaid recipients during fiscal year 1974 in jurisdictions reporting. U.S. Dept. of HEW, National Center for Social Statistics, Medicaid Recipient Characteristics and Units of Selected Medical Services, Fiscal Year 1974, p. 2 (Feb. 1977). Extrapolating this percentage to cover the entire Medicaid caseload of over 17.6 million, minority racial groups would account for 7,656,000 recipients. Assuming comparability of the HEW and census figures, this amounts to 27.4% of the Nation's nonwhite population. See Statistical Abstract, *supra,* n. 3, at 25. Since there are 1.8 female Medicaid recipients for every male, see Medicaid Recipient Characteristics, *supra,* the proportion of nonwhite women who must rely upon Medicaid is probably far higher, about 38.5%. The comparable figure for white women appears to be about 7%.

22. Requirements that the abortion be performed by a physician exercising his best clinical judgment, and in a facility meeting narrowly tailored health standards, are allowable. *Doe v. Bolton,* 410 U. S., at 192–200.

23. Application of the flexible equal protection standard would allow the Court to strike down the regulations in these cases without calling into question laws funding public education or English language teaching in public schools. See *Maher v. Roe, post,* at 476–477. By permitting a court to weigh all relevant factors, the flexible standard does not logically

require acceptance of any equal protection claim that is "identical in principle" under the traditional approach to those advanced here. See *Maher, post,* at 477.

24. [This opinion applies also to No. 75–1440, *Maher, Commissioner of Social Services of Connecticut v. Roe et al., post,* p. 464, and No. 75–442, *Poelker, Mayor of St. Louis, et al. v. Doe, post,* p. 519.]

MAHER V. ROE

Supreme Court of the United States, 1977.
432 U.S. 464, 97 S.Ct. 2376, 53 L.Ed.2d 484.

MR. JUSTICE POWELL delivered the opinion of the Court.

In *Beal v. Doe, ante,* p. 438, we hold today that Title XIX of the Social Security Act does not require the funding of nontherapeutic abortions as a condition of participation in the joint federal-state Medicaid program established by that statute. In this case, as a result of our decision in *Beal,* we must decide whether the Constitution requires a participating State to pay for nontherapeutic abortions when it pays for childbirth.

I

A regulation of the Connecticut Welfare Department limits state Medicaid benefits for first trimester abortions[1] to those that are "medically necessary," a term defined to include psychiatric necessity. Connecticut Welfare Department, Public Assistance Program Manual, Vol. 3, c. III, § 275 (1975).[2] Connecticut enforces this limitation through a system of prior authorization from its Department of Social Services. In order to obtain authorization for a first trimester abortion, the hospital or clinic where the abortion is to be performed must submit, among other things, a certificate from the patient's attending physician stating that the abortion is medically necessary.

This attack on the validity of the Connecticut regulation was brought against appellant Maher, the Commissioner of Social Services, by appellees Poe and Roe, two indigent women who were unable to obtain a physician's certificate of medical necessity.[3] In a complaint filed in the United States District Court for the District of Connecticut, they challenged the regulation both as inconsistent with the requirements of Title XIX of the Social Security Act, as added, 79 Stat. 343, as amended, 42 U. S. C. § 1396 *et seq.* (1970 ed. and Supp. V), and as violative of their constitutional rights, including the Fourteenth Amendment's guarantees of due process and equal protection. Connecticut originally defended its regulation on the theory that Title XIX of the Social Security Act prohibited the funding of abortions that were not medically necessary. After certifying a class of women unable to obtain Medicaid assistance for abortions because of the regulation, the District Court held that the Social Security Act not only allowed state funding of nontherapeutic abortions but also required it. *Roe v. Norton,* 380 F. Supp. 726 (1974). On appeal, the Court of Appeals for the Second Circuit read the Social Security Act to allow, but not to require, state funding of such abortions. 522 F. 2d 928 (1975). Upon remand for consideration of the constitutional issues raised in the complaint, a three-judge District Court was convened. That court invalidated the Connecticut regulation. 408 F. Supp. 660 (1975).

Although it found no independent constitutional right to a state-financed abortion, the District Court held that the Equal Protection Clause forbids the exclusion of nontherapeutic abortions from a state welfare program that generally subsidizes the medical expenses incident to pregnancy and childbirth. The court found implicit in *Roe v. Wade,* 410 U. S. 113 (1973), and *Doe v. Bolton,* 410 U. S. 179 (1973), the view that "abortion and childbirth, when stripped of the sensitive moral arguments surrounding the abortion controversy, are simply two alternative medical methods of dealing with pregnancy. . . ." 408 F. Supp., at 663 n. 3. Relying also on *Shapiro v. Thompson,* 394 U. S. 618 (1969), and *Memorial Hospital v. Maricopa County,* 415 U. S. 250 (1974), the court held that the Connecticut program "weights the choice of the pregnant mother against choosing to exercise her constitutionally protected right" to a nontherapeutic abortion and "thus infringes upon a fundamental interest." 408 F. Supp., at 663–664. The court found no state interest to justify this infringement. The State's fiscal interest was held to be "wholly chimerical because abortion is the least expensive medical response to a pregnancy." *Id.,* at 664 (footnote omitted). And any moral objection to abortion was deemed constitutionally irrelevant:

> "The state may not justify its refusal to pay for one type of expense arising from pregnancy on the basis that it morally opposes such an expenditure of money. To sanction such a justification would be to permit discrimination against those seeking to exercise a constitutional right on the basis that the state simply does not approve of the exercise of that right." *Ibid.*

The District Court enjoined the State from requiring the certificate of medical necessity for Medicaid-funded abortions.[4] The court also struck down the related requirements of prior written request by the pregnant woman and prior authorization by the Department of Social Services, holding that the State could not impose any requirements on Medicaid payments for abortions that are not "equally applicable to medicaid payments for childbirth, if such conditions or requirements tend to discourage a woman from choosing an abortion or to delay the occurrence of an abortion that she has asked her physician to perform." *Id.,* at 665. We noted probable jurisdiction to consider the constitutionality of the Connecticut regulation. 428 U. S. 908 (1976).

II

The Consititution imposes no obligation on the States to pay the pregnancy-related medical expenses of indigent women, or indeed to pay any of the medical expenses of indigents.[5] But when a State decides to alleviate some of the hardships of poverty by providing medical care, the manner in which it dispenses benefits is subject to constitutional limitations. Appellees' claim is that Connecticut must accord equal treatment to both abortion and childbirth, and may not evidence a policy preference by funding only the medical expenses incident to childbirth. This challenge to the classifications established by the Connecticut regulation presents a question arising under the Equal Protection Clause of the Fourteenth Amendment. The basic framework of analysis of such a claim is well settled:

> "We must decide, first, whether [state legislation] operates to the disadvantage of some suspect class or impinges upon a fundamental right explicitly or implicitly protected by the Constitution, thereby requiring strict judicial scrutiny.... If not, the [legislative] scheme must still be examined to determine whether it rationally furthers some legitimate, articulated state purpose and therefore does not constitute an invidious discrimination...." *San Antonio School Dist. v. Rodriguez,* 411 U. S. 1, 17 (1973).

Accord, *Massachusetts Bd. of Retirement v. Murgia,* 427 U. S. 307, 312, 314 (1976). Applying this analysis here, we think the District Court erred in holding that the Connecticut regulation violated the Equal Protection Clause of the Fourteenth Amendment.

A

This case involves no discrimination against a suspect class. An indigent woman desiring an abortion does not come within the limited category of disadvantaged classes so recognized by our cases. Nor does the fact that the impact of the regulation falls upon those who cannot pay lead to a different conclusion. In a sense, every denial of welfare to an indigent creates a wealth classification as compared to nonindigents who are able to pay for the desired goods or services. But this Court has never held that financial need alone identifies a suspect class for purposes of equal protection analysis. See *Rodriguez, supra,* at 29; *Dandridge v. Williams,* 397 U. S. 471 (1970).[6] Accordingly, the central question in this case is whether the regulation "impinges upon a fundamental right explicitly or implicitly protected by the Constitution." The District Court read our decisions in *Roe v. Wade,* 410 U. S. 113 (1973), and the subsequent cases applying it, as establishing a fundamental right to abortion and therefore concluded that nothing less than a compelling state interest would justify Connecticut's different treatment of abortion and childbirth. We think the District Court misconceived the nature and scope of the fundamental right recognized in *Roe.*

B

At issue in *Roe* was the constitutionality of a Texas law making it a crime to procure or attempt to procure an abortion, except on medical advice for the purpose of saving the life of the mother. Drawing on a group of disparate cases restricting governmental intrusion, physical coercion, and criminal prohibition of certain activities, we concluded that the Fourteenth Amendment's concept of personal liberty affords constitutional protection against state interference with certain aspects of an individual's personal "privacy," including a woman's decision to terminate her pregnancy.[7] *Id.,* at 153.

The Texas statute imposed severe criminal sanctions on the physicians and other medical personnel who performed abortions, thus drastically limiting the availability and safety of the desired service. As MR. JUSTICE STEWART observed, "it is difficult to imagine a more complete abridgment of a constitutional freedom. . . ." *Id.,* at 170 (concurring opinion.) We held that only a compelling state interest would justify such a sweeping restriction on a constitutionally protected interest, and we found no such state interest during the first trimester. Even when judged against this demanding standard, however, the State's dual interest in the health of the pregnant woman and the potential life of the fetus were deemed sufficient to justify substantial regulation of abortions in the second and third trimesters. "These interests are separate and distinct. Each grows in substantiality as the woman approaches term and, at a point during pregnancy, each becomes 'compelling.' " *Id.,* at 162–163. In the second trimester, the State's interest in the health of the pregnant woman justifies state regulation reasonably related to that concern. *Id.,* at 163. At viability, usually in the third trimester, the State's interest in the potential life of the fetus justifies prohibition with criminal penalties, except where the life or health of the mother is threatened. *Id.,* at 163–164.

The Texas law in *Roe* was a stark example of impermissible interference with the pregnant woman's decision to terminate her pregnancy. In subsequent cases, we have invalidated other types of restrictions, different in form but similar in effect, on the woman's freedom of choice. Thus, in *Planned Parenthood of Central Missouri v. Danforth,* 428 U. S. 52, 70–71, n. 11 (1976), we held that Missouri's requirement of spousal consent was unconstitutional because it "granted [the husband] the right to prevent unilaterally, and for whatever reason, the effectuation of his wife's and her physician's decision to terminate her pregnancy." Missouri had interposed an "*absolute obstacle* to a woman's decision that *Roe* held to be constitutionally protected from such interference." (Emphasis added.) Although a state-created obstacle need not be absolute to be impermissible, see *Doe v. Bolton,* 410 U. S. 179 (1973), *Carey v. Population Services International,* 431 U. S. 678 (1977), we have held that a requirement for a lawful abortion "is not unconstitutional unless it unduly burdens the right to seek an abortion." *Bellotti v. Baird,* 428 U. S. 132, 147 (1976). We recognized in *Bellotti* that "not all distinction between abortion and other procedures is forbidden" and that "[t]he constitutionality of such distinction will depend upon its degree and the justification for it." *Id.,* at 149–150. We therefore declined to rule on the constitutionality of a Massachusetts statute regulating a minor's access to an abortion until the state courts had had an opportunity to determine whether the statute authorized a parental veto over the minor's decision or the less burdensome requirement of parental consultation.

These cases recognize a constitutionally protected interest "in making certain kinds of important decisions" free from governmental compulsion. *Whalen v. Roe,* 429 U. S. 589, 599–600, and nn. 24 and 26 (1977). As *Whalen* makes clear, the right in *Roe v. Wade* can be understood only by considering both the woman's interest and the nature of the State's interference with it. *Roe* did not declare an unqualified "constitutional right to an abortion," as the District Court seemed to think. Rather, the right protects the woman from unduly burdensome interference with her freedom to decide whether to terminate her pregnancy. It implies no limitation on the authority of a State to make a value judgment favoring childbirth over abortion, and to implement that judgment by the allocation of public funds.

The Connecticut regulation before us is different in kind from the laws invalidated in our previous abortion decisions. The Connecticut regulation places no obstacles—absolute or otherwise—in the pregnant woman's path to an abortion. An indigent woman who desires an abortion suffers no disadvantage as a consequence of Connecticut's decision to fund childbirth; she continues as before to be dependent on private sources for the service she desires. The State may have made childbirth a more attractive alternative, thereby influencing the woman's decision, but it has imposed no restriction on access to abortions that was not already there. The indigency that may make it difficult—and in some cases, perhaps, impossible—for some women to have abortions is neither created nor in any way affected by the Connecticut regulation. We conclude that the Connecticut regulation does not impinge upon the fundamental right recognized in *Roe*.[8]

C

Our conclusion signals no retreat from *Roe* or the cases applying it. There is a basic difference between direct state interference with a protected activity and state encouragement of an alternative activity consonant with legislative policy.[9] Constitutional concerns are greatest when the State attempts to impose its will by force of law; the State's power to encourage actions deemed to be in the public interest is necessarily far broader.

This distinction is implicit in two cases cited in *Roe* in support of the pregnant woman's right under the Fourteenth Amendment. *Meyer v. Nebraska,* 262 U. S. 390 (1923), involved a Nebraska law making it criminal to teach foreign languages to children who had not passed the eighth grade. *Id.,* at 396–397. Nebraska's imposition of a criminal sanction on the providers of desired services makes *Meyer* closely analogous to *Roe.* In sustaining the constitutional challenge brought by a teacher convicted under the law, the Court held that the teacher's "right thus to teach and the right of parents to engage him so to instruct their children" were "within the liberty of the Amendment." 262 U. S., at 400. In *Pierce v. Society of Sisters,* 268 U. S. 510 (1925), the Court relied on *Meyer* to invalidate an Oregon criminal law requiring the parent or guardian of a child to send him to a public school, thus precluding the choice of a private school. Reasoning that the Fourteenth Amendment's concept of liberty "excludes any general power of the State to standardize its children by forcing them to accept instruction from public teachers only," the Court held that the law "unreasonably interfere[d] with the liberty of parents and guardians to direct the upbringing and education of children under their control." 268 U. S., at 534–535.

Both cases invalidated substantial restrictions on constitutionally protected liberty interests: in *Meyer,* the parent's right to have his child taught a particular foreign language; in *Pierce,* the parent's right to choose private rather than public school education. But neither case denied to a State the policy choice of encouraging the preferred course of action. Indeed, in *Meyer* the Court was careful to state that the power of the State "to prescribe a curriculum" that included English and excluded German in its free public schools "is not questioned." 262 U. S., at 402. Similarly, *Pierce* casts no shadow over a State's power to favor public education by funding it—a policy choice pursued in some States for more than a century. See *Brown v. Board of Education,* 347 U. S. 483, 489 n. 4 (1954). Indeed, in *Norwood v. Harrision,* 413 U. S. 455, 462 (1973), we explicitly rejected the argument that *Pierce* established a "right of private or parochial schools to share with public schools in state largesse," noting that "[i]t is one thing to say that a State may not prohibit the maintenance of private schools and quite another to say that such schools must, as a matter of equal protection, receive state aid." Yet, were we to accept appellees' argument, an indigent parent could challenge the state policy of favoring public rather than private schools, or of preferring instruction in English rather than German, on grounds identical in principle to those advanced here. We think it abundantly clear that a State is not required to show a compelling interest for its policy choice to favor normal childbirth any more than a State must so justify its election to fund public but not private education.[10]

D

The question remains whether Connecticut's regulation can be sustained under the less demanding test of rationality that applies in the absence of a suspect classification or the impingement of a fundamental right. This test requires that the distinction drawn between childbirth and nontherapeutic abortion by the regulation be "rationally related" to a "constitutionally permissible" purpose. *Lindsey v. Normet,* 405 U. S. 56, 74 (1972); *Massachusetts Bd. of Retirement v. Murgia,* 427 U. S., at 314. We hold that the Connecticut funding scheme satisfies this standard.

Roe itself explicitly acknowledged the State's strong interest in protecting the potential life of the fetus. That interest exists throughout the pregnancy, "grow-[ing] in substantiality as the woman approaches term." 410 U. S., at 162–163. Because the pregnant woman carries a potential human being, she "cannot be isolated in her privacy. . . . [Her] privacy is no longer sole and any right of privacy she possesses must be measured accordingly." *Id.,* at 159. The State unquestionably has a "strong and legitimate interest in encouraging normal childbirth," *Beal v. Doe, ante,* at 446, an interest honored over the centuries.[11] Nor can there be any question that the Connecticut regulation rationally furthers that interest. The medical costs associated with childbirth are substantial, and have increased significantly in recent years. As recognized by the District Court in this case, such costs are significantly greater than those normally associated with elective abortions during the first trimester. The subsidizing of costs incident to childbirth is a rational means of encouraging childbirth.

We certainly are not unsympathetic to the plight of an indigent woman who desires an abortion, but "the Constitution does not provide judicial remedies for every social and economic ill," *Lindsey v. Normet, supra,* at 74. Our cases uniformly have accorded the States a wider latitude in choosing among competing demands for limited public funds.[12] In *Dandridge v. Williams,* 397 U. S., at 485, despite recognition that laws and regulations allocating welfare funds involve "the most basic economic needs of impoverished human beings," we held that classifications survive equal protection challenge when a "reasonable basis" for the classification is shown. As the preceding discussion makes clear, the state interest in encouraging normal childbirth exceeds this minimal level.

The decision whether to expend state funds for nontherapeutic abortion is fraught with judgments of policy and value over which opinions are sharply divided. Our conclusion that the Connecticut regulation is constitutional is not based on a weighing of its wisdom or social desirability, for this Court does not strike down state laws "because they may be unwise, improvident, or out of harmony with a particular school of thought." *Williamson v. Lee Optical Co.,* 348 U. S. 483, 488 (1955), quoted in *Dandridge v. Williams, supra,* at 484. Indeed, when an issue involves policy choices as sensitive as those implicated by public funding of nontherapeutic abortions, the appropriate forum for their resolution in a democracy is the legislature. We should not forget that "legislatures are ultimate guardians of the liberties and welfare of the people in quite as great a degree as the courts." *Missouri, K. & T. R. Co. v. May,* 194 U. S. 267, 270 (1904) (Holmes, J.).[13]

In conclusion, we emphasize that our decision today does not proscribe government funding of nontherapeutic abortions. It is open to Congress to require provision of Medicaid benefits for such abortions as a condition of state participation in the Medicaid program. Also, under Title XIX as construed in *Beal v. Doe, ante,* p. 438, Connecticut is free—through normal democratic processes—to decide that such benefits should be provided. We hold only that the Constitution does not require a judicially imposed resolution of these difficult issues.

III

The District Court also invalidated Connecticut's requirements of prior written request by the pregnant woman and prior authorization by the Department of Social Services. Our analysis above rejects the basic premise that prompted invalidation of these procedural requirements. It is not unreasonable for a State to insist upon a prior showing of medical necessity to insure that its money is being spent only for authorized purposes. The simple answer to the argument that similar requirements are not imposed for other medical procedures is that such procedures do not involve the termination of a potential human life. In *Planned Parenthood of Central Missouri v. Danforth,* 428 U. S. 52 (1976), we held that the woman's written consent to an abortion was not an impermissible burden under *Roe.* We think that decision is controlling on the similar issue here.

The judgment of the District Court is reversed, and the case is remanded for further proceedings consistent with this opinion.

It is so ordered.

MR. CHIEF JUSTICE BURGER, concurring.

I join the Court's opinion. Like the Court, I do not read any decision of this Court as requiring a State to finance a nontherapeutic abortion. The Court's holdings in *Roe v. Wade,* 410 U. S. 113 (1973), and *Doe v. Bolton,* 410 U. S. 179 (1973), simply require that a State not create an absolute barrier to a woman's decision to have an abortion. These precedents do not suggest that the State is constitutionally required to assist her in procuring it.

From time to time, every state legislature determines that, as a matter of sound public policy, the government ought to provide certain health and social services to its citizens. Encouragement of childbirth and child care is not a novel undertaking in this regard. Various governments, both in this country and in others, have made such a determination for centuries. In recent times, they have similarly provided educational services. The decision to provide any one of these services— or not to provide them—is not required by the Federal Constitution. Nor does the providing of a particular service require, as a matter of federal constitutional law, the provision of another.

Here, the State of Connecticut has determined that it will finance certain childbirth expenses. That legislative determination places no state-created barrier to a woman's choice to procure an abortion, and it does not require the State to provide it. Accordingly, I concur in the judgment.

MR. JUSTICE BRENNAN, with whom MR. JUSTICE MARSHALL and MR. JUSTICE BLACKMUN join, dissenting.

The District Court held:

> "When Connecticut refuses to fund elective abortions while funding therapeutic abortions and prenatal and postnatal care, it weighs the choice of the pregnant mother against choosing to exercise her constitutionally protected right to an elective abortion. . . . Her choice is affected not simply by the absence of payment for the abortion, but by the availability of public funds for childbirth if she chooses not to have the abortion. When the state thus infringes upon a fundamental interest, it must assert a compelling state interest." *Roe v. Norton,* 408 F. Supp. 660, 663–664 (1975).

This Court reverses on the ground that "the District Court misconceived the nature and scope of the fundamental right recognized in *Roe* [*v. Wade,* 410 U. S. 113 (1973)]," *ante,* at 471, and therefore that Connecticut was not required to meet the "compelling interest" test to justify its discrimination against elective abortion but only "the less demanding test of rationality that applies in the absence of . . . the impingement of a fundamental right," *ante,* at 477, 478. This holding, the Court insists, "places no obstacles—absolute or otherwise—in the pregnant woman's path to an abortion"; she is still at liberty to finance the abortion from "private sources." *Ante,* at 474. True, "the State may [by funding childbirth] have made childbirth a more attractive alternative, thereby influencing the woman's decision, but it has imposed no restriction on access to abortions that was not already there." *Ibid.* True, also, indigency "may make it difficult—and in some cases, perhaps impossible—for some women to have abortions," but that regrettable consequence "is neither created nor in any way affected by the Connecticut regulation."*Ibid.*

But a distressing insensitivity to the plight of impoverished pregnant women is inherent in the Court's analysis. The stark reality for too many, not just "some," indigent pregnant women is that indigency makes access to competent licensed physicians not merely "difficult" but "impossible." As a practical matter, many indigent women will feel they have no choice but to carry their pregnancies to term because the State will pay for the associated medical services, even though they would have chosen to have abortions if the State had also provided funds for that procedure, or indeed if the State had provided funds for neither procedure. This disparity in funding by the State clearly operates to coerce indigent pregnant women to bear children they would not otherwise choose to have, and just as clearly, this coercion can only operate upon the poor, who are uniquely the victims of this form of financial pressure. Mr. Justice Frankfurter's words are apt:

> "To sanction such a ruthless consequence, inevitably resulting from a money hurdle erected by the State, would justify a latter-day Anatole France to add one more item to his ironic comments on the 'majestic equality' of the law. 'The law, in its majestic equality, forbids the rich as well as the poor to sleep under bridges, to beg in the streets, and to steal bread'. . . ." *Griffin v. Illinois,* 351 U. S. 12, 23 (1956) (concurring opinion).

None can take seriously the Court's assurance that its "conclusion signals no retreat from *Roe* [*v. Wade*] or the cases applying it," *ante,* at 475. That statement must occasion great surprise among the Courts of Appeals and District Courts that, relying upon *Roe v. Wade* and *Doe v. Bolton,* 410 U. S. 179 (1973), have held that States are constitutionally required to fund elective abortions if they fund pregnancies carried to term. See *Doe v. Rose,* 499 F. 2d 1112 (CA10 1974); *Wulff v. Singleton,* 508 F. 2d 1211 (CA8 1974), rev'd and remanded on other grounds, 428 U. S. 106 (1976); *Doe v. Westby,* 383 F. Supp. 1143 (WDSD 1974), vacated and remanded in light of *Hagans v. Lavine,* 415 U. S. 528 (1974), 420 U. S. 968, on remand, 402 F. Supp. 140 (WDSD 1975); *Doe v. Wohlgemuth,* 376 F. Supp. 173 (WD Pa. 1974), aff'd on statutory grounds *sub nom. Doe v. Beal,* 523 F. 2d 611 (CA3 1975), rev'd, *ante,* p. 438; *Doe v. Rampton,* 366 F. Supp. 189 (Utah 1973); *Klein v. Nassau County Medical Center,* 347 F. Supp. 496 (EDNY 1972); vacated and remanded (in light of *Roe v. Wade* and *Doe v. Bolton,* 412 U. S. 925 (1973), on remand, 409 F. Supp. 731 (EDNY 1976). Indeed, it cannot be gainsaid that today's decision seriously erodes the principles that *Roe* and *Doe* announced to guide the determination of what constitutes an unconstitutional infringement of the fundamental right of pregnant women to be free to decide whether to have an abortion.

The Court's premise is that only an equal protection claim is presented here. Claims of interference with enjoyment of fundamental rights have, however, occupied a rather protean position in our constitutional jurisprudence. Whether or not the Court's analysis may reasonably proceed under the Equal Protection Clause, the Court plainly errs in ignoring, as it does, the unanswerable argument of appellees, and the holding of the District Court, that the regulation unconstitutionally impinges upon their claim of privacy derived from the Due Process Clause.

Roe v. Wade and cases following it hold that an area of privacy invulnerable to the State's intrusion surrounds the decision of a pregnant woman whether or not to carry her pregnancy to term. The Connecticut scheme clearly infringes upon that area of privacy by bringing financial pressures on indigent women that force them to bear children they would not otherwise have. That is an obvious impairment of the fundamental right established by *Roe v. Wade.* Yet the Court concludes that "the Connecticut regulation does not impinge upon [that] fundamental right." *Ante,* at 474. This conclusion is based on a perceived distinction, on the one hand, between the imposition of criminal penalties for the procurement of an abortion present in *Roe v. Wade* and *Doe v. Bolton* and the absolute prohibition present in *Planned Parenthood of Central Missouri v. Danforth,* 428 U. S. 52 (1976), and, on the other, the assertedly lesser inhibition imposed by the Connecticut scheme. *Ante,* at 472–474.

The last time our Brother POWELL espoused the concept in an abortion case that "[t]here is a basic difference between direct state interference with a protected activity and state encouragement of an alternative activity consonant with legislative policy," *ante,* at 475, the Court refused to adopt it. *Singleton v. Wulff,* 428 U. S. 106, 122 (1976). This was made explicit in Part II of our Brother BLACKMUN'S opinion for four of us and is implicit in our Brother STEVENS' essential agreement with the analysis of Part II-B. *Id.,* at 121–122 (concurring in part). Part II-B stated:

> "MR. JUSTICE POWELL would so limit *Doe* and the other cases cited, explaining them as cases in which the State 'directly interfered with the abortion decision' and 'directly interdicted the normal functioning of the physician-patient relationship by criminalizing certain procedures,' [428 U. S.,] at 128. There is no support in the language of the cited cases for this distinction.... Moreover, a 'direct interference' or 'interdiction' test does not appear to be supported by precedent.... For a doctor who cannot afford to work for nothing, and a woman who cannot afford to pay him, the State's refusal to fund an abortion is as effective an 'interdiction' of it as would ever be necessary. Furthermore, since the right ... is not simply the right to have an abortion, but the right to have abortions nondiscriminatorily funded, the denial of such funding is as complete an 'interdiction' of the exercise of the right as could ever exist." *Id.,* at 118 n. 7.

We have also rejected this approach in other abortion cases. *Doe v. Bolton,* the companion to *Roe v. Wade,* in addition to striking down the Georgia criminal prohibition against elective abortions, struck down the procedural requirements of certification of hospitals, of approval by a hospital committee, and of concurrence in the abortion decision by two doctors other than the woman's own doctor. None of these requirements operated as an absolute bar to elective abortions in the manner of the criminal prohibitions present in the other aspect of the case or in *Roe,* but this was not sufficient to save them from unconstitutionality. In *Planned Parent-*

hood, supra, we struck down a requirement for spousal consent to an elective abortion which the Court characterizes today simply as an "absolute obstacle" to a woman's obtaining an abortion. *Ante,* at 473. But the obstacle was "absolute" only in the limited sense that a woman who was unable to persuade her spouse to agree to an elective abortion was prevented from obtaining one. Any woman whose husband agreed, or could be persuaded to agree, was free to obtain an abortion, and the State never imposed directly any prohibition of its own. This requirement was qualitatively different from the criminal statutes that the Court today says are comparable, but we nevertheless found it unconstitutional.

Most recently, also in a privacy case, the Court squarely reaffirmed that the right of privacy was fundamental, and that an infringement upon that right must be justified by a compelling state interest. *Carey v. Population Services International,* 431 U. S. 678 (1977). That case struck down in its entirety a New York law forbidding the sale of contraceptives to minors under 16 years old, limiting persons who could sell contraceptives to pharmacists, and forbidding advertisement and display of contraceptives. There was no New York law forbidding *use* of contraceptives by anyone, including minors under 16, and therefore no "absolute" prohibition against the exercise of the fundamental right. Nevertheless the statute was declared unconstitutional as a burden on the right to privacy. In words that apply fully to Connecticut's statute, and that could hardly be more explicit, *Carey* stated: " 'Compelling' is of course the key word; where a decision as fundamental as that whether to bear or beget a child is involved, regulations imposing a burden on it may be justifed only by compelling state interests, and must be narrowly drawn to express only those interests." *Id.,* at 686. *Carey* relied specifically upon *Roe, Doe,* and *Planned Parenthood,* and interpreted them in a way flatly inconsistent with the Court's interpretation today: "The significance of these cases is that they establish that the same test must be applied to state regulations that burden an individual's right to decide to prevent conception or terminate pregnancy by substantially limiting access to the means of effectuating that decision as is applied to state statutes that prohibit the decision entirely." 431 U. S., at 688.

Finally, cases involving other fundamental rights also make clear that the Court's concept of what constitutes an impermissible infringement upon the fundamental right of a pregnant woman to choose to have an abortion makes new law. We have repeatedly found that infringements of fundamental rights are not limited to outright denials of those rights. First Amendment decisions have consistently held in a wide variety of contexts that the compelling-state-interest test is applicable not only to outright denials but also to restraints that make exercise of those rights more difficult. See, *e.g., Sherbert v. Verner,* 374 U. S. 398 (1963) (free exercise of religion); *NAACP v. Button,* 371 U. S. 415 (1963) (freedom of expression and association), *Linmark Associates v. Township of Willingboro,* 431 U. S. 85 (1977) (freedom of expression). The compelling-state-interest test has been applied in voting cases, even where only relatively small infringements upon voting power, such as dilution of voting strength caused by malapportionment, have been involved. See, *e.g., Reynolds v. Sims,* 377 U. S. 533, 562, 566 (1964), *Chapman v. Meier,* 420 U. S. 1 (1975), *Connor v. Finch,* 431 U. S. 407 (1977). Similarly, cases involving the right to travel have consistently held that statutes penalizing the fundamental right to travel must pass muster under the compelling-state-interest test, irrespective of whether the statutes actually deter travel. *Memorial Hospital v. Maricopa County,* 415 U. S. 250, 257–258 (1974); *Dunn v. Blumstein,* 405 U. S. 330, 339–341 (1972); *Shapiro v. Thompson,* 394 U. S. 618 (1969). And indigents asserting a fundamental right of access to the courts have been excused payment of entry costs without being required first to show that their indigency was an absolute bar to access. *Griffin v. Illinois,* 351 U. S. 12 (1956); *Douglas v. California,* 372 U. S. 353 (1963), *Boddie v. Connecticut,* 401 U. S. 371 (1971).

Until today, I had not thought the nature of the fundamental right established in *Roe* was open to question, let alone susceptible of the interpretation advanced by the Court. The fact that the Connecticut scheme may not operate as an absolute bar preventing all indigent women from having abortions is not critical. What is critical is that the State has inhibited their fundamental right to make that choice free from state interference.

Nor does the manner in which Connecticut has burdened the right freely to choose to have an abortion save its Medicaid program. The Connecticut scheme cannot be distinguished from other grants and withholdings of financial benefits that we have held unconstitutionally burdened a fundamental right. *Sherbert v. Verner, supra,* struck down a South Carolina statute that denied unemployment compensation to a woman who for religious reasons could not work on Saturday, but that would have provided such compensation if her unemployment had stemmed from a number of other nonreligious causes. Even though there was no proof of indigency in that case, *Sherbert* held that "the pressure upon her to forgo [her religious] practice [was] unmistakable," 374 U. S., at 404, and therefore held that the effect was the same as a fine imposed for Saturday worship. Here, though the burden is upon the right to privacy derived from the Due Process Clause and not upon freedom of religion under the Free Exercise Clause of the First Amendment, the governing principle is the same, for Connecticut grants and withholds financial benefits in a manner that discourages significantly the exercise of a fundamental constitutional right. Indeed, the case for application of the principle actually is stronger than in *Verner* since appellees are all indigents and therefore even more vulnerable to the financial pressures imposed by the Connecticut regulations.

Bellotti v. Baird, 428 U. S. 132, 147 (1976), held, and the Court today agrees, *ante,* at 473, that a state requirement is unconstitutional if it "unduly burdens the right to seek an abortion." Connecticut has "unduly" burdened the fundamental right of pregnant women to be free to choose to have an abortion because the State has advanced no compelling state interest to justify its interference in that choice.

Although appellant does not argue it as justification, the Court concludes that the State's interest "in protecting the potential life of the fetus" suffices, *ante,* at 478.[14] Since only the first trimester of pregnancy is involved in this case, that justification is totally foreclosed if the Court is not overruling the holding of *Roe v. Wade* that "[w]ith respect to the State's important and legitimate interest in potential life, the 'compelling' point is at viability," occurring at about the end of the second trimester. 410 U. S., at 163. The appellant also argues a further justification not relied upon by the Court, namely, that the State needs "to control the amount of its limited public funds which will be allocated to its public welfare budget."

Brief for Appellant 22. The District Court correctly held, however, that the asserted interest was "wholly chimerical" because the "state's assertion that it saves money when it declines to pay the cost of a welfare mother's abortion is simply contrary to undisputed facts." 408 F. Supp., at 664.

Finally, the reasons that render the Connecticut regulation unconstitutional also render invalid, in my view, the requirement of a prior written certification by the woman's attending physician that the abortion is "medically necessary," and the requirement that the hospital submit a Request for Authorization of Professional Services including a "statement indicating the medical need for the abortion." Brief for Appellees 2–3. For the same reasons, I would also strike down the requirement for prior authorization of payment by the Connecticut Department of Social Services.

NOTES

1. The procedures governing abortions beyond the first trimester are not challenged here.

2. Section 275 provides in relevant part:
"The Department makes payment for abortion services under the Medical Assistance (Title XIX) Program when the following conditions are met:
"1. In the opinion of the attending physician the abortion is medically necessary. The term 'Medically Necessary' includes psychiatric necessity.
"2. The abortion is to be performed in an accredited hospital or licensed clinic when the patient is in the first trimester of pregnancy. . . .
"3. The written request for the abortion is submitted by the patient, and in the case of a minor, from the parent or guardian.
"4. Prior authorization for the abortion is secured from the Chief of Medical Services, Division of Health Services, Department of Social Services."
See n. 4, *infra.*

3. At the time this action was filed, Mary Poe, a 16-year-old high school junior, had already obtained an abortion at a Connecticut hospital. Apparently because of Poe's inability to obtain a certificate of medical necessity, the hospital was denied reimbursement by the Department of Social Services. As a result, Poe was being pressed to pay the hospital bill of $244. Susan Roe, an unwed mother of three children, was unable to obtain an abortion because of her physician's refusal to certify that the procedure was medically necessary. By consent, a temporary restraining order was entered by the District Court enjoining the Connecticut officials from refusing to pay for Roe's abortion. After the remand from the Court of Appeals, the District Court issued temporary restraining orders covering three additional women. *Roe v. Norton,* 408 F. Supp. 660, 663 (1975).

4. The District Court's judgment and order, entered on January 16, 1976, were not stayed. On January 26, 1976, the Department of Social Services revised § 275 to allow reimbursement for nontherapeutic abortions without prior authorization or consent. The fact that this revision was made retroactive to January 16, 1976, suggests that the revision was made only for the purpose of interim compliance with the District Court's judgment and order, which were entered the same date. No suggestion of mootness has been made by any of the parties, and this appeal was taken and submitted on the theory that Connecticut desires to reinstate the invalidated regulation. Under these circumstances, the subsequent revision of the regulation does not render the case moot. In any event, there would remain the denial of reimbursement to Mary Poe, and similarly situated members of the class, under the prerevision regulation. See 380 F. Supp., at 730 n. 3. The State has asserted no Eleventh Amendment defense to this relief sought by Poe and those whom she represents.

5. *Boddie v. Connecticut,* 401 U. S. 371 (1971), cited by appellees, is not to the contrary. There the Court invalidated under the Due Process Clause "certain state procedures

for the commencement of litigation, including requirements for payment of court fees and costs for service of process," restricting the ability of indigent persons to bring an action for divorce. *Id.,* at 372. The Court held:

"[G]iven the basic position of the marriage relationship in this society's hierarchy of values and the concomitant state monopolization of the means for legally dissolving this relationship, due process does prohibit a State from denying, solely because of inability to pay, access to its courts to individuals who seek judicial dissolution of their marriages." *Id.,* at 374. Because Connecticut has made no attempt to monopolize the means for terminating pregnancies through abortion the present case is easily distinguished from *Boddie.* See also *United States v. Kras,* 409 U. S. 434 (1973); *Ortwein v. Schwab,* 410 U. S. 656 (1973).

6. In cases such as *Griffin v. Illinois,* 351 U. S. 12 (1956) and *Douglas v. California,* 372 U. S. 353 (1963), the Court held that the Equal Protection Clause requires States that allow appellate review of criminal convictions to provide indigent defendants with trial transcripts and appellate counsel. These cases are grounded in the criminal justice system, a governmental monopoly in which participation is compelled. Cf. n. 5, *supra.* Our subsequent decisions have made it clear that the principles underlying *Griffin* and *Douglas* do not extend to legislative classifications generally.

7. A woman has at least an equal right to choose to carry her fetus to term as to choose to abort it. Indeed, the right of procreation without state interference has long been recognized as "one of the basic civil rights of man . . . fundamental to the very existence and survival of the race." *Skinner v. Oklahoma,* 316 U. S. 535, 541 (1942).

8. Appellees rely on *Shapiro v. Thompson,* 394 U. S. 618 (1969), and *Memorial Hospital v. Maricopa County,* 415 U. S. 250 (1974). In those cases durational residence requirements for the receipt of public benefits were found to be unconstitutional because they "penalized" the exercise of the constitutional right to travel interstate.

Appellees' reliance on the penalty analysis of *Shapiro* and *Maricopa County* is misplaced. In our view there is only a semantic difference between appellees' assertion that the Connecticut law unduly interferes with a woman's right to terminate her pregnancy and their assertion that it penalizes the exercise of that right. Penalties are most familiar to the criminal law, where criminal sanctions are imposed as a consequence of proscribed conduct. *Shapiro* and *Maricopa County* recognized that denial of welfare to one who had recently exercised the right to travel across state lines was sufficiently analogous to a criminal fine to justify strict judicial scrutiny.

If Connecticut denied general welfare benefits to all women who had obtained abortions and who were otherwise entitled to the benefits, we would have a close analogy to the facts in *Shapiro,* and strict scrutiny might be appropriate under either the penalty analysis or the analysis we have applied in our previous abortion decisions. But the claim here is that the State "penalizes" the woman's decision to have an abortion by refusing to pay for it. *Shapiro* and *Maricopa County* did not hold that States would penalize the right to travel interstate by refusing to pay the bus fares of the indigent travelers. We find no support in the right-to-travel cases for the view that Connecticut must show a compelling interest for its decision not to fund elective abortions.

Sherbert v. Verner, 374 U. S. 398 (1963), similarly is inapplicable here. In addition, that case was decided in the significantly different context of a constitutionally imposed "governmental obligation of neutrality" originating in the Establishment and Freedom of Religion Clauses of the First Amendment. *Id.,* at 409.

9. In *Buckley v. Valeo,* 424 U. S. 1 (1976), we drew this distinction in sustaining the public financing of the Federal Election Campaign Act of 1971. The Act provided public funds to some candidates but not to others. We rejected an asserted analogy to cases such as *American Party of Texas v. White,* 415 U. S. 767 (1974), which involved restrictions on access to the electoral process:

"These cases, however, dealt primarily with state laws requiring a candidate to satisfy certain requirements in order to have his name appear on the ballot. These were, of course, *direct burdens* not only on the candidate's ability to run for office but also on the voter's ability to voice preferences regarding representative government and contemporary issues. In contrast, the denial of public financing to some Presidential candidates is not restrictive of voters' rights and less restrictive of candidates'. Subtitle H does not prevent any candidate from getting on the ballot or any voter from casting a vote for the candidate of his choice; *the inability, if any, of minority party candidates to wage effective campaigns will derive not from lack of public funding but from their inability to raise private contributions.* Any disadvantage suffered by operation of the eligibility formula under Subtitle H is thus limited to the claimed denial of the enhancement of opportunity to communicate with the electorate that the formulae afford eligible candidates." 424 U. S., at 94–95 (emphasis added; footnote omitted).

10. In his dissenting opinion, MR. JUSTICE BRENNAN rejects the distinction between direct state interference with a protected activity and state encouragement of an alternative activity and argues that our previous abortion decisions are inconsistent with today's decision. But as stated above, all of those decisions involved laws that placed substantial state-created obstacles in the pregnant woman's path to an abortion. Our recent decision in *Carey v. Population Services International,* 431 U. S. 678 (1977), differs only in that it involved state-created restrictions on access to contraceptives, rather than abortions. MR. JUSTICE BRENNAN simply asserts that the Connecticut regulation "is an obvious impairment of the fundamental right established by *Roe v. Wade.*" *Post,* at 484–485. The only suggested source for this purportedly "obvious" conclusion is a quotation from *Singleton v. Wulff,* 428 U. S. 106 (1976). Yet, as MR. JUSTICE BLACKMUN was careful to note at the beginning of his opinion in *Singleton,* that case presented "issues [of standing] not going to the merits of this dispute." *Id.,* at 108. Significantly, MR. JUSTICE BRENNAN makes no effort to distinguish or explain the much more analogous authority of *Norwood v. Harrison,* 413 U. S. 455 (1973).

11. In addition to the direct interest in protecting the fetus, a State may have legitimate demographic concerns about its rate of population growth. Such concerns are basic to the future of the State and in some circumstances could constitute a substantial reason for departure from a position of neutrality between abortion and childbirth.

12. See generally Wilkinson, The Supreme Court, The Equal Protection Clause, and The Three Faces of Constitutional Equality, 61 Va. L. Rev. 945, 998–1017 (1975).

13. Much of the rhetoric of the three dissenting opinions would be equally applicable if Connecticut had elected not to fund either abortions or childbirth. Yet none of the dissents goes so far as to argue that the Constitution *requires* such assistance for all indigent pregnant women.

14. The Court also suggests, *ante,* at 478 n. 11, that a "State may have legitimate demographic concerns about its rate of population growth" which might justify a choice to favor live births over abortions. While it is conceivable that under some circumstances this might be an appropriate factor to be considered as part of a State's "compelling" interest, no one contends that this is the case here, or indeed that Connecticut has any demographic concerns at all about the rate of its population growth.

BELLOTTI V. BAIRD

Supreme Court of the United States, 1979.
443 U.S. 622, 99 S.Ct. 3035, 61 L.Ed.2d 797.

MR. JUSTICE POWELL announced the judgment of the Court and delivered an opinion in which THE CHIEF JUSTICE, MR. JUSTICE STEWART, and MR. JUSTICE REHNQUIST joined.

These appeals present a challenge to the constitutionality of a state statute regulating the access of minors to abortions. They require us to continue the inquiry we began in *Planned Parenthood v. Danforth,* 428 U.S. 52, 96 S.Ct. 2831, 49 L. Ed.2d 788 (1976), and *Bellotti v. Baird,* 428 U.S. 132, 96 S.Ct. 2857, 49 L.Ed.2d 844 (1976)

I

A

On August 2, 1974, the legislature of the Commonwealth of Massachusetts passed, over the Governor's veto, an act pertaining to abortions performed within the State. 1974 Mass. Acts, ch. 706. According to its title, the statute was intended to regulate abortions "within present constitutional limits." Shortly before the act was to go into effect, the class action from which these appeals arise was commenced in the District Court[1] to enjoin, as unconstitutional, the provision of the act now codified as Mass.Gen.Laws Ann., ch. 112, § 12S (West).[2]

Section 12S provides in part:

"If the mother is less than eighteen years of age and has not married, the consent of both the mother and her parents [to an abortion to be performed on the mother] is required. If one or both of the mother's parents refuse such consent, consent may be obtained by order of a judge of the superior court for good cause shown, after such hearing as he deems necessary. Such a hearing will not require the appointment of a guardian for the mother. If one of the parents has died or has deserted his or her family, consent by the remaining parent is sufficient. If both parents have died or have deserted their family, consent of the mother's guardian or other person having duties similar to a guardian, or any person who had assumed the care and custody of the mother is sufficient. The commissioner of public health shall prescribe a written form for such consent. Such form shall be signed by the proper person or persons and given to the physician performing the abortion who shall maintain it in his permanent files."

Physicians performing abortions in the absence of the consent required by § 12S are subject to injunctions and criminal penalties. See Mass.Gen.Laws Ann., ch. 112, §§ 12Q, 12T and 12U (West).

A three-judge District Court was convened to hear the case pursuant to 28 U.S.C. § 2281 (1970 ed.), repealed by Pub.L. 94–381, § 1, 90 Stat. 1119 (1976).[3] Plaintiffs in the suit, appellees in both the cases before us now, were William Baird; Parents Aid Society, Inc. (Parents Aid), of which Baird is founder and director; Gerald Zupnick, M. D., who regularly performs abortions at the Parents Aid clinic; and an unmarried minor, identified by the pseudonym "Mary Moe," who, at the commencement of the suit, was pregnant, residing at home with her parents, and desirous of obtaining an abortion without informing them.[4]

Mary Moe was permitted to represent the "class of unmarried minors in Massachusetts who have adequate capacity to give a valid and informed consent [to abortion], and who do not wish to involve their parents." *Baird v. Bellotti,* 393 F. Supp. 847, 850 (Mass.1975). Initially there was some confusion whether the rights of minors who wish abortions without parental involvement but who lack "adequate capacity" to give such consent also could be adjudicated in the suit. The District Court ultimately determined that Dr. Zupnick was entitled to assert the rights of these minors. See *Baird v. Bellotti,* 450 F. Supp. 997, 1001, and n. 6 (Mass.1978).[5]

Planned Parenthood League of Massachusetts and Crittenton Hastings House & Clinic, both organizations that provide counseling to pregnant adolescents, and Phillip Stubblefield, M. D., (intervenors)[6] appeared as *amicus curiae* on behalf of the plantiffs. The District Court "accepted [this group] in a status something more than *amici* because of reservations about the adequacy of plaintiff's representation [of the plaintiff classes in the suit]." *Baird v. Bellotti,* 450 F.Supp., at 999 n. 3.

Defendants in the suit, appellants here in No. 78–329, were the Attorney General of Massachusetts and the district attorneys of all counties in the State. Jane Hunerwadel was permitted to intervene as a defendant and representative of the class of Massachusetts parents having unmarried minor daughters who then were, or might become, pregnant. She and the class she represents are appellants in No. 78–330.[7]

Following three days of testimony, the District Court issued an opinion invalidating § 12S. *Baird v. Bellotti,* 393 F.Supp. 847 (1975) (*Baird I*). The court rejected appellees' argument that all minors capable of becoming pregnant also are capable of giving informed consent to an abortion, or that it always is in the best interests of a minor who desires an abortion to have one. See *id.,* at 854. But the court was convinced that "a substantial number of females under the age of 18 are capable of forming a valid consent," *id.,* at 855, and "that a significant number of [these] are unwilling to tell their parents." *Id.,* at 853.

In its analysis of the relevant constitutional principles, the court stated that "there can be no doubt but that a female's constitutional right to an abortion in the first trimester does not depend upon her calendar age." *Id.,* at 855–856. The court

found no justification for the parental consent limitation placed on that right by §
12S, since it concluded that the statute was "cast not in terms of protecting the
minor, . . . but in recognizing independent rights of parents." *Id.,* at 856. The "independent" parental rights protected by § 12S, as the court understood them, were
wholly distinct from the best interests of the minor.[8]

B

Appellants sought review in this Court, and we noted probable jurisdiction.
Bellotti v. Baird, 423 U.S. 982, 96 S.Ct. 390, 46 L.Ed.2d 301 (1975). After briefing
and oral argument, it became apparent that § 12S was susceptible of a construction
that "would avoid or substantially modify the federal constitutional challenge to
the statute." *Bellotti v. Baird,* 428 U.S. 132, 148, 96 S.Ct. 2857, 2866, 49 L.Ed.2d
844 (1976) *(Bellotti I).* We therefore vacated the judgment of the District Court,
concluding that it should have abstained and certified to the Supreme Judicial
Court of Massachusetts appropriate questions concerning the meaning of § 12S.
pursuant to existing procedure in that State. See Mass. Rules of Court, Sup.Jud.Ct.
Rule 3:21 (1978).

On remand, the District Court certified nine questions to the Supreme Judicial
Court.[9] These were answered in an opinion styled *Baird v. Attorney General,* 371
Mass. 741, 360 N.E.2d 288 (1977) (Attorney General). Among the more important
aspects of § 12S, as authoritatively construed by the Supreme Judicial Court, are
the following:

1. In deciding whether to grant consent to their daughter's abortion, parents
are required by § 12S to consider exclusively what will serve her best interests. See
id., at _____, 360 N.E.2d, at 292–293.

2. The provision in § 12S that judicial consent for an abortion shall be granted, parental objections notwithstanding, "for good cause-shown" means that such
consent shall be granted if found to be in the minor's best interests. The judge
"must disregard all parental objections, and other considerations, which are not
based exclusively" on that standard. *Id.,* at_____, 360 N.E.2d, at 293.

3. Even if the judge in a § 12S proceeding finds "that the minor is capable of
making, and has made, an informed and reasonable decision to have an abortion,"
he is entitled to withhold consent "in circumstances where he determines that the
best interests of the minor will not be served by an abortion." *Ibid.*

4. As a general rule, a minor who desires an abortion may not obtain judicial
consent without first seeking both parents' consent. Exceptions to the rule exist
when a parent is not available or when the need for the abortion constitutes "an
emergency requiring immediate action."[10] *Id.,* at 294. Unless a parent is not available, he must be notified of any judicial proceedings brought under § 12S. *Id.,*
at_____, 360 N.E.2d, at 297.

5. The resolution of § 12S cases and any appeals that follow can be expected
to be prompt. The name of the minor and her parents may be held in confidence. If
need be, the Supreme Judicial Court and the Superior Courts can promulgate rules
or issue orders to ensure that such proceedings are handled expeditiously. *Id.,*
at_____, 360 N.E.2d, at 297–298.

6. Mass.Gen.Laws Ann. ch. 112, § 12F, which provides, *inter alia,* that certain classes of minors may consent to most kinds of medical care without parental approval, does not apply to abortions, except as to minors who are married, widowed, or divorced. See *id.,* at_____, 360 N.E.2d, at 298–300. Nor does the State's common law "mature minor rule" create an exception to § 12S. *Id.,* at_____, 360 N.E.2d, at 294. See n. 27, *infra.*

C

Following the judgment of the Supreme Judicial Court, appellees returned to the District Court and obtained a stay of the enforcement of § 12S until its constitutionality could be determined. *Baird v. Bellotti,* 428 F.Supp. 854 (1977) *(Baird II).* After permitting discovery by both sides, holding a pretrial conference, and conducting further hearings, the District Court again declared § 12S unconstitutional and enjoined its enforcement. *Baird v. Bellotti,* 450 F.Supp. 997 (Mass.1978) *(Baird III).* The court identified three particular aspects of the statute which, in its view, rendered it unconstitutional.

First, as construed by the Supreme Judicial Court, § 12S requires parental notice in virtually every case where the parent is available. The court believed that the evidence warranted a finding "that many, perhaps a large majority of 17-year-olds are capable of informed consent, as are a not insubstantial number of 16-year-olds, and some even younger." *Id.,* at 1001. In addition, the court concluded that it would not be in the best interests of some "immature" minors—those incapable of giving informed consent—even to inform their parents of their intended abortions. Although the court declined to decide whether the burden of requiring a minor to take her parents to court was, per se, an impermissible burden on her right to seek an abortion, it concluded that Massachusetts could not constitutionally insist that parental permission be sought or notice given "in those cases where a court, if given free rein, would find that it was to the minor's best interests that one or both of her parents not be informed. . . ." *Id.,* at 1002.

Second, the District Court held that § 12S was defective in permitting a judge to veto the abortion decision of a minor found to be capable of giving informed consent. The court reasoned that upon a finding of maturity and informed consent, the State no longer was entitled to impose legal restrictions upon this decision. *Id.,* at 1003. Given such a finding, the court could see "no reasonable basis" for distinguishing between a minor and an adult, and it therefore concluded that § 12S was not only "an undue burden in the due process sense, [but] a discriminatory denial of equal protection [as well]." *Id.,* at 1004.

Finally, the court decided that § 12S suffered from what it termed "formal overbreadth," *ibid.,* because the statute failed explicitly to inform parents that they must consider only the minor's best interests in deciding whether to grant consent. The court believed that, despite the Supreme Judicial Court's construction of § 12S, parents naturally would infer from the statute that they were entitled to withhold consent for other, impermissible reasons. This was thought to create a "chilling effect" by enhancing the possibility that parental consent would be denied wrongfully and that the minor would have to proceed in court.

Having identified these flaws in § 12S, the District Court considered whether it should engage in "judicial repair." *Id.,* at 1005. It declined either to sever the statute or to give it a construction different from that set out by the Supreme Judicial Court, as that tribunal arguably had invited it to do. See *Attorney General, supra,* at_____, 360 N.E.2d, at 292. The District Court therefore adhered to its previous position, declaring § 12S unconstitutional and permanently enjoining its enforcement.[11] Appellants sought review in this Court a second time, and we again noted probable jurisdiction._____U.S._____, 99 S.Ct. 307, 58 L.Ed.2d 317 (1978).

II

[1,2] A child, merely on account of his minority, is not beyond the protection of the Constitution. As the Court said in *In re Gault,* 387 U.S. 1, 13, 87 S.Ct. 1428, 1436, 18 L.Ed.2d 527 (1967), "whatever may be their precise impact, neither the Fourteenth Amendment nor the Bill of Rights is for adults alone."[12] This observation, of course, is but the beginning of the analysis. The Court long has recognized that the status of minors under the law is unique in many respects. As Mr. Justice Frankfurter aptly put it, "[c]hildren have a very special place in life which law should reflect. Legal theories and their phrasing in other cases readily lead to fallacious reasoning if uncritically transferred to determination of a State's duty towards children." *May v. Anderson,* 345 U.S. 528, 536, 73 S.Ct. 840, 844, 97 L.Ed. 1221 (1953) (concurring opinion). The unique role in our society of the family, the institution by which "we inculcate and pass down many of our most cherished values, moral and cultural," *Moore v. City of East Cleveland,* 431 U.S. 494, 503–504, 97 S.Ct. 1932, 1938, 52 L.Ed.2d 531 (1977) (plurality opinion), requires that constitutional principles be applied with sensitivity and flexibility to the special needs of parents and children. We have recognized three reasons justifying the conclusion that the constitutional rights of children cannot be equated with those of adults: the peculiar vulnerability of children; their inability to make critical decisions in an informed, mature manner; and the importance of the parental role in child-rearing.

A

The Court's concern for the vulnerability of children is demonstrated in its decisions dealing with minors' claims to constitutional protection against deprivations of liberty or property interests by the State. With respect to many of these claims, we have concluded that the child's right is virtually coextensive with that of an adult. For example, the Court has held that the Fourteenth Amendment's guarantee against the deprivation of liberty without due process of law is applicable to children in juvenile delinquency proceedings. In *re Gault,* 387 U.S. 1, 87 S.Ct. 1428, 18 L.Ed.2d 527 (1967). In particular, minors involved in such proceedings are entitled to adequate notice, the assistance of counsel, and the opportunity to confront their accusers. They can be found guilty only upon proof beyond a reasonable doubt, and they may assert the privilege against compulsory self-incrimination. *In re Winship,* 397 U.S. 358, 90 S.Ct. 1068, 25 L.Ed.2d 368 (1970); *In re Gault, supra.* See also *Ingraham v. Wright,* 430 U.S. 651, 674, 97 S.Ct. 1401, 1414, 51 L.Ed.2d 711 (1977) (corporal punishment of school children implicates constitutionally protected liberty interest); cf. *Breed v. Jones,* 421 U.S. 519, 95 S.Ct. 1779, 44 L.Ed.2d 346 (1975) (Double Jeopardy Clause prohibits prosecuting juvenile as an adult after an adjudicatory finding in junvenile court that he had violated a criminal statute). Similarly, in *Goss v. Lopez,* 419 U.S. 565, 95, S.Ct. 729, 42 L.Ed.2d 725 (1975), the Court held that children may not be deprived of certain property interests without due process.

[3] These rulings have not been made on the uncritical assumption that the constitutional rights of children are indistinguishable from those of adults. Indeed, our acceptance of juvenile courts distinct from the adult criminal justice system assumes that juvenile offenders constitutionally may be treated differently from adults. In order to preserve this separate avenue for dealing with minors, the Court has said that hearings in juvenile delinquency cases need not necessarily "conform with all the requirements of a criminal trial or even of the usual administrative hearing." *In re Gault, supra,* 387 U.S., at 30, 87 S.Ct., at 1445, quoting *Kent v. United States,* 383 U.S. 541, 562, 86 S.Ct. 1045, 1057, 16 L.Ed.2d 84 (1966). Thus, juveniles are not constitutionally entitled to trial by jury in delinquency adjudications. *McKeiver v. Pennsylvania,* 403 U.S. 528, 91 S.Ct. 1976, 29 L.Ed.2d 647 (1978). Viewed together, our cases show that although children generally are protected by the same constitutional guarantees against governmental deprivations as are adults, the State is entitled to adjust its legal system to account for children's vulnerability and their needs for "concern, . . . sympathy, and . . . paternal attention." *Id.,* at 550, 91 S.Ct., at 1989 (plurality opinion).

B

Second, the Court has held that the States validly may limit the freedom of children to choose for themselves in the making of important, affirmative choices with potentially serious consequences. These rulings have been grounded in the recognition that, during the formative years of childhood and adolescence, minors often lack the experience, perspective, and judgment to recognize and avoid choices that could be detrimental to them.[13]

Ginsberg v. New York, 390 U.S. 629, 88 S.Ct. 1274, 20 L.Ed.2d 195 (1968), illustrates well the Court's concern over the inability of children to make mature choices, as the First Amendment rights involved are clear examples of constitutionally protected freedoms of choice. At issue was a criminal conviction for selling sexually oriented magazines to a minor under the age of 17 in violation of a New York state law. It was conceded that the conviction could not have stood under the First Amendment if based upon a sale of the same material to an adult. *Id.,* at 634, 88 S.Ct.1277. Notwithstanding the importance the Court always has attached to First Amendment rights, it concluded that "even where there is an invasion of protected freedoms 'the power of the state to control the conduct of children reaches beyond the scope of its authority over adults . . . ,' " *id.,* at 638, 88 S.Ct., at 1280, quoting *Prince v. Massachuseets,* 321 U.S. 158, 170, 64 S.Ct. 438, 444, 88 L.Ed. 645 (1944).[14] The Court was convinced that the New York Legislature rationally could conclude that the sale to children of the magazines in question presented a danger against which they should be guarded. *Ginsberg, supra,* 390 U.S., at 641, 88 S.Ct., at 1281. It therefore rejected the argument that the New York law violated the constitutional rights of minors.[15]

C

Third, the guiding role of parents in the upbringing of their children justifies limitations on the freedoms of minors. The State commonly protects its youth from adverse governmental action and from their own immaturity by requiring parental consent to or involvement in important decisions by minors.[16] But an additional and more important justification for state deference to parental control over children is that "[t]he child is not the mere creature of the state; those who nurture him and direct his destiny have the right, coupled with the high duty, to recognize and prepare him for additional obligations." *Pierce v. Society of Sisters,* 268 U.S. 510, 535, 45 S.Ct. 571, 573, 69 L.Ed. 1070 (1925). "The duty to prepare the child for 'additional obligations' . . . must be read to include the inculcation of moral standards, religious beliefs, and elements of good citizenship." *Wisconsin v. Yoder,* 406 U.S. 205, 233, 92 S.Ct. 1526, 1542, 32 L.Ed.2d 15 (1972). This affirmative process of teaching, guiding, and inspiring by precept and example is essential to the growth of young people into mature, socially responsible citizens.

We have believed in this country that this process, in large part, is beyond the competence of impersonal political institutions. Indeed, affirmative sponsorship of particular ethical, religious, or political beliefs is something we expect the State *not* to attempt in a society constitutionally committed to the ideal of individual liberty and freedom of choice. Thus, "[i]t is cardinal with us that the custody, care and nurture of the child reside first in the parents, whose primary function and freedom include *preparation for obligations the state can neither supply nor hinder."* Prince v. Massachusetts, supra, 321 U.S., at 166, 64 S.Ct., at 442 (emphasis added).

Unquestionably, there are many competing theories about the most effective way for parents to fulfill their central role in assisting their children on the way to responsible adulthood. While we do not pretend any special wisdom on this subject, we cannot ignore that central to many of these theories, and deeply rooted in our nation's history and tradition, is the belief that the parental role implies a substantial measure of authority over one's children. Indeed, "constitutional interpretation has consistently recognized that the parents' claim to authority in their own household to direct the rearing of their children is basic in the structure of our society." *Ginsberg v. New York, supra,* 390 U.S., at 639, 88 S.Ct., at 1280.

Properly understood, then, the tradition of parental authority is not inconsistent with our tradition of individual liberty; rather, the former is one of the basic presuppositions of the latter. Legal restrictions on minors, especially those supportive of the parental role, may be important to the child's chances for the full growth and maturity that make eventual participation in a free society meaningful and rewarding.[17] Under the Constitution, the State can "properly conclude that parents and others, teachers for example, who have [the] primary responsibility for children's well-being are entitled to the support of laws designed to aid discharge of that responsibility." *Ginsberg v. New York, supra,* at 639, 88 S.Ct., at 1280.[18]

III

With these principles in mind, we consider the specific constitutional questions presented by these appeals. In § 12S Massachusetts has attempted to reconcile the constitutional right of a woman, in consultation with her physician, to choose to terminate her pregnancy as established by *Roe v. Wade,* 410 U.S. 113, 93 S.Ct. 705, 35 L.Ed.2d 147 (1973) and *Doe v. Bolton,* 410 U.S. 179, 93, S.Ct. 739, 35 L.Ed.2d 201 (1973), with the special interest of the State in encouraging an unmarried pregnant minor to seek the advice of her parents in making the important decision whether or not to bear a child. As noted above, § 12S was before us in *Bellotti I,* 428 U.S. 132, 96 S.Ct 2857, 49 L.Ed.2d 844 (1976), where we remanded the case for interpretation of its provisions by the Supreme Judicial Court of Massachusetts. We previously had held in *Planned Parenthood v. Danforth,* 428 U.S. 52, 96 S.Ct. 2831, 49 L.Ed. 2d 788 (1976), that a State could not lawfully authorize an absolute parental veto over the decision of a minor to terminate her pregnancy. *Id.,* at 74, 96 S.Ct., at 2843. In *Bellotti, supra,* we recognized that § 12S could be read as "fundamentally different from a statute that creates a 'parental veto,' " *id.,* at 145, 96 S.Ct., at 2865, thus "avoid[ing] or substantially modify[ing] the federal constitutional challenge to the statute." *Id.,* at 148, 96 S.Ct., at 2866. The question before us—in light of what we have said in the prior cases—is whether § 12S, as authoritatively interpreted by the Supreme Judicial Court, provides for parental notice and consent in a manner that does not unduly burden the right to seek an abortion. See *id.,* at 147, 96 S.Ct., at 2866.

[4] Appellees and intervenors contend that even as interpreted by the Supreme Judicial Court of Massachusetts § 12S does unduly burden this right. They suggest, for example, that the mere requirement of parental notice constitutes such a burden. As stated in Part II above, however, parental notice and consent are qualifications that typically may be imposed by the State on a minor's right to make important decisions. As immature minors often lack the ability to make fully informed choices that take account of both immediate and long-range consequences, a State reasonably may determine that parental consultation often is desirable and in the best interest of the minor.[19] It may further determine, as a general proposition, that such consultation is particularly desirable with respect to the abortion decision—one that for some people raises profound moral and religious concerns.[20] As Mr. Justice STEWART wrote in concurrence in *Planned Parenthood v. Danforth,* 428 U. S., at 91, 96 S.Ct., at 2851:

> "There can be little doubt that the State furthers a constitutionally permissible end by encouraging an unmarried pregnant minor to seek the help and advice of her parents in making the very important decision whether or

not to bear a child. That is a grave decision, and a girl of tender years, under emotional stress, may be ill-equipped to make it without mature advice
and emotional support. It seems unlikely that she will obtain counsel and
support from the attending physician at an abortion clinic, where abortions
for pregnant minors frequently take place." (Footnote omitted.)[21]

But we are concerned here with a constitutional right to seek an abortion. The
abortion decision differs in important ways from other decisions that may be made
during minority. The need to preserve the constitutional right and the unique nature of the abortion decision, especially when made by a minor, require a State to
act with particular sensitivity when it legislates to foster parental involvement in
this matter.

A

The pregnant minor's options are much different from those facing a minor in
other situations, such as deciding whether to marry. A minor not permitted to
marry before the age of majority is required simply to postpone her decision. She
and her intended spouse may preserve the opportunity for later marriage should
they continue to desire it. A pregnant adolescent, however, cannot preserve for
long the possibility of aborting, which effectively expires in a matter of weeks from
the onset of pregnancy.

Moreover, the potentially severe detriment facing a pregnant woman, see *Roe
v. Wade,* 410 U. S., at 153, S.Ct., at 726, is not mitigated by her minority. Indeed,
considering her probable education, employment skills, financial resources, and
emotional maturity, unwanted motherhood may be exceptionally burdensome for a
minor. In addition, the fact of having a child brings with it adult legal responsibility, for parenthood, like attainment of the age of majority, is one of the traditional
criteria for the termination of the legal disabilities of minority. In sum, there are
few situations in which denying a minor the right to make an important decision
will have consequences so grave and indelible.

Yet, an abortion may not be the best choice for the minor. The circumstances
in which this issue arises will vary widely. In a given case, alternatives to abortion,
such as marriage to the father of the child, arranging for its adoption, or assuming
the responsibilities of motherhood with the assured support of family, may be feasible and relevant to the minor's best interests. Nonetheless, the abortion decision is
one that simply cannot be postponed, or it will be made by default with far-reaching consequences.

[5,6] For these reasons, as we held in *Planned Parenthood v. Danforth, supra,*
428 U. S., at 74, 96 S.Ct., at 2843, "the State may not impose a blanket provision
. . . requiring the consent of a parent or person *in loco parentis* as a condition for
abortion of an unmarried minor during the first 12 weeks of her pregnancy." Although, as stated in Part II, *supra,* such deference to parents may be permissible
with respect to other choices facing a minor, the unique nature and consequences
of the abortion decision make it inappropriate "to give a third party an absolute,

and possibly arbitrary, veto over the decision of the physician and his patient to terminate the patient's pregnancy, regardless of the reason for withholding consent." *Ibid.* We therefore conclude that if the State decides to require a pregnant minor to obtain one or both parents' consent to an abortion, it also must provide an alternative procedure[22] whereby authorization for the abortion can be obtained.

A pregnant minor is entitled in such a proceeding to show either: (1) that she is mature enough and well enough informed to make her abortion decision, in consultation with her physician, independently of her parents' wishes;[23] or (2) that even if she is not able to make this decision independently, the desired abortion would be in her best interests. The proceeding in which this showing is made must assure that a resolution of the issue, and any appeals that may follow, will be completed with anonymity and sufficient expedition to provide an effective opportunity for an abortion to be obtained. In sum, the procedure must ensure that the provision requiring parental consent does not in fact amount to the "absolute, and possibly arbitrary, veto" that was found impermissible in *Danforth. Ibid.*

B

[7,8] It is against these requirements that § 12S must be tested. We observe initially that as authoritatively construed by the highest court of the State, the statute satisfies some of the concerns that require special treatment of a minor's abortion decison. It provides that if parental consent is refused, authorization may be "obtained by order of a judge of the superior court for good cause shown, after such hearing as he deems necessary." A superior court judge presiding over a § 12S proceeding must disregard all parental objections, and other considerations, which are not based exclusively on what would serve the minor's best interests."[24] *Attorney General* 371 Mass., at_____, 360 N.E.2d, at 293. The Supreme Judicial Court also stated that "[p]rompt resolution of a [§ 12S] proceeding may be expected. . . . The proceeding need not be brought in the minor's name and steps may be taken, by impoundment or otherwise, to preserve confidentiality as to the minor and her parents. . . . [W]e believe that an early hearing and decision on appeal from a judgment of a Superior Court judge may also be achieved." *Id., at*_____, 360 N.E.2d, at 298. The court added that if these expectations were not met, either the Superior Court, in the exercise of its rulemaking power, or the Supreme Judicial Court would be willing to eliminate any undue burdens by rule or order. *Ibid.*[25]

Despite these safeguards, which avoid much of what was objectionable in the statute successfully challenged in *Danforth* § 12S falls short of constitutional standards in certain respects. We now consider these.

(1)

Among the questions certified to the Supreme Judicial Court was whether § 12S permits any minors—mature or immature—to obtain judicial consent to an abortion without any parental consultation whatsoever. See n. 9, *supra.* The state court answered that, in general, they may not. "[T]he consent required by [§ 12S must] be obtained for every nonemergency abortion where the mother is less than eighteen years of age and unmarried." *Attorney General, supra,* at_____, 360 N.E.2d, at 294. The text of § 12S itself states an exception to this rule, making consent unnecessary from any parent who has "died or has deserted his or her family."[26] The Supreme Judicial Court construed the statute as containing an additional exception: Consent need not be obtained "where no parent (or statutory substitute) is available." *Ibid.* The court also ruled that an available parent must be given notice of any judicial proceedings brought by a minor to obtain consent for an abortion.[27] *Id.,* at_____, 360 N.E.2d, at 297.

[9] We think that, construed in this manner, § 12S would impose an undue burden upon the exercise by minors of the right to seek an abortion. As the District Court recognized, "there are parents who would obstruct, and perhaps altogether prevent, the minor's right to go to court." *Baird III, supra,* at 1001. There is no reason to believe that this would be so in the majority of cases where consent is withheld. But many parents hold strong views on the subject of abortion, and young pregnant minors, especially those living at home, are particularly vulnerable to their parents' efforts to obstruct both an abortion and their access to court. It would be unrealistic, therefore, to assume that the mere existence of a legal right to seek relief in superior court provides an effective avenue of relief for some of those who need it the most.

[10] We conclude, therefore, that under state regulation such as that undertaken by Massachusetts, every minor must have the opportunity—if she so desires—to go directly to a court without first consulting or notifying her parents. If she satisfies the court that she is mature and well-informed enough to make intelligently the abortion decision on her own, the court must authorize her to act without parental consultation or consent. If she fails to satisfy the court that she is competent to make this decision independently, she must be permitted to show that an abortion nevertheless would be in her best interest. If the court is persuaded that it is, the court must authorize the abortion. If, however, the court is not persuaded by the minor that she is mature or that the abortion would be in her best interest, it may decline to sanction the operation.

[11] There is, however, an important state interest in encouraging a family rather than a judicial resolution of a minor's abortion decision. Also, as we have observed above, parents naturally take an interest in the welfare of their children— an interest that is particularly strong where a normal family relationship exists and where the child is living with one or both parents. These factors properly may be taken into account by a court called upon to determine whether an abortion in fact is in a minor's best interests. If, all things considered, the court determines that an abortion is in the minor's best interests, she is entitled to court authorization without any parental involvement. On the other hand, the court may deny the abortion request of an immature minor in the absence of parental consultation if it concludes that her best interests would be served thereby, or the court may in such a case defer decision until there is parental consultation in which the court may participate. But this is the full extent to which parental involvement may be required.[28] For the reasons stated above, the constitutional right to seek an abortion may not be unduly burdened by state-imposed conditions upon initial access to court.

(2)

Section 12S requires that both parents consent to a minor's abortion. The District Court found it to be "custom" to perform other medical and surgical procedures on minors with the consent of only one parent, and it concluded that "nothing about abortions . . . requires the minor's interest to be treated differently." *Baird I, supra,* at 852. See *Baird III, supra,* at 1004 n. 9.

[12,13] We are not persuaded that, as a general rule, the requirement of obtaining both parents' consent unconstitutionally burdens a minor's right to seek an abortion. The abortion decision has implications far broader than those associated with most other kinds of medical treatment. At least when the parents are together and the pregnant minor is living at home, both the father and mother have an interest—one normally supportive—in helping to determine the course that is in the best interest of a daughter. Consent and involvement by parents in important decisions by minors long have been recognized as protective of their immaturity. In the case of the abortion decision, for reasons we have stated, the focus of the parents' inquiry should be the best interests of their daughter. As every pregnant minor is entitled in the first instance to go directly to the court for a judicial determination without prior parental notice, consultation or consent, the general rule with respect to parental consent does not unduly burden the constitutional right. Moreover, where the pregnant minor goes to her parents and consent is denied. she still must have recourse to a prompt judicial determination of her maturity or best interests.[29]

(3)

Another of the questions certified by the District Court to the Supreme Judicial Court was the following: "If the superior court finds that the minor is capable [of making], and has, in fact, made and adhered to, an informed and reasonable decision to have an abortion, may the court refuse its consent on a finding that a parent's, or its own, contrary decision is a better one?" *Attorney General, supra,* 371 Mass., at_____, 360 N.E.2d, at 293 n. 5. To this the state court answered:

> "[W]e do not view the judge's role as limited to a determination that the minor is capable of making, and has made, an informed and reasonable decision to have an abortion. Certainly the judge must make a determination of those circumstances, but, if the statutory role of the judge to determine the best interests of the minor is to be carried out, he must make a finding on the basis of all relevant views presented to him. We suspect that the judge will give great weight to the minor's determination, if informed and reasonable, but in circumstances where he determines that the best interests of the minor will not be served by an abortion, the judge's determination should prevail, assuming that his conclusion is supported by the evidence and adequate findings of fact." *Id.,* at_____, 360 N.E.2d, at 293.

The Supreme Judicial Court's statement reflects the general rule that a State may require a minor to wait until the age of majority before being permitted to exercise legal rights independently. See n. 23, *supra*. But we are concerned here with the exercise of a constitutional right of unique character. See pp. 3047–3048, *supra*. As stated above, if the minor satisfies a court that she has attained sufficient maturity to make a fully informed decision, she then is entitled to make her abortion decision independently. We therefore agree with the District Court that § 12S cannot constitutionally permit judicial disregard of the abortion decision of a minor who has been determined to be mature and fully competent to assess the implications of the choice she has made.[30]

IV

[14,15] Although it satisfies constitutional standards in large part, § 12S falls short of them in two respects: First, it permits judicial authorization for an abortion to be withheld from a minor who is found by the superior court to be mature and fully competent to make this decision independently. Second, it requires parental consultation or notification in every instance, without affording the pregnant minor an opportunity to receive an independent judicial determination that she is mature enough to consent or that an abortion would be in her best interests.[31] Accordingly, we affirm the judgment of the District Court insofar as it invalidates this statute and enjoins its enforcement.[32]

Affirmed.

MR. JUSTICE REHNQUIST, concurring.

I join the opinion of Mr. Justice POWELL and in the judgment of the Court. At such time as this Court is willing to reconsider its earlier decision in *Planned Parenthood of Missouri v. Danforth*, 428 U. S. 52, 96 S.Ct. 2831, 49 L.Ed.2d 788 (1976), in which I joined the dissenting opinion of Mr. Justice WHITE, I shall be more than willing to participate in that task. But unless and until that time comes, literally thousands of judges cannot be left with nothing more than the guidance offered by a truly fragmented holding of this Court.

MR. JUSTICE STEVENS, with whom MR. JUSTICE BRENNAN, MR. JUSTICE MARSHALL, and MR. JUSTICE BLACKMUN join, concurring in the judgment.

In *Roe v. Wade,* 410 U. S. 113, 93 S.Ct. 705, 35 L.Ed.2d 147, the Court held that a woman's right to decide whether to terminate a pregnancy is entitled to constitutional protection. In *Planned Parenthood of Missouri v. Danforth,* 428 U. S. 52, 72–75, 96 S.Ct. 2831, 2842–2843, 49 L.Ed.2d 788, the Court held that a pregnant minor's right to make the abortion decision may not be conditioned on the consent of one parent. I am persuaded that these decisions require affirmance of the District Court's holding that the Massachusetts statute is unconstitutional.

The Massachusetts statute is, on its face, simple and straightforward. It provides that every woman under 18 who has not married must secure the consent of both her parents before receiving an abortion. "If one or both of the mother's parents refuse such consent, consent may be obtained by order of a judge of the Superior Court for good cause shown." Mass.Gen.Laws Ann., ch. 112, § 12S (West).

Whatever confusion or uncertainty might have existed as to how this statute was to operate, see *Bellotti v. Baird,* 428 U. S. 132, 96 S.Ct. 2857, 49 L.Ed.2d 844, has been eliminated by the authoritative construction of its provisions by the Massachusetts Supreme Judicial Court. See *Baird v. Attorney General,* 371 Mass. 741, 360 N.E.2d 288 (1977). The statute was construed to require that every minor who wishes an abortion must first seek the consent of both parents, unless a parent is not available or unless the need for the abortion constitutes "an emergency requiring immediate action." *Id.,* at_____, 360 N.E.2d, at 294. Both parents, so long as they are available, must also receive notice of judicial proceedings brought under the statute by the minor. In those proceedings, the task of the judge is to determine whether the best interests of the minor will be served by an abortion. The decision is his to make, even if he finds "that the minor is capable of making, and has made, an informed and reasonable decision to have an abortion." *Id.,* at_____, 360 N.E.2d, at 293. Thus, no minor in Massachusetts, no matter how mature and capable of informed decisionmaking, may receive an abortion without the consent of either both her parents or a Superior Court Judge. In every instance, the minor's decision to secure an abortion is subject to an absolute third-party veto.[33]

In *Planned Parenthood of Missouri v. Danforth, supra,* this Court invalidated statutory provisions requiring the consent of the husband of a married woman and of one parent of a pregnant minor to an abortion. As to the spousal consent, the Court concluded that "we cannot hold that the State has the constitutional authority to give the spouse unilaterally the ability to prohibit the wife from terminating her pregnancy, when the State itself lacks that right." 428 U. S., at 70, 96 S.Ct. at 2841. And as to the parental consent, the Court held that "[j]ust as with the requirement of consent from the spouse, so here, the State does not have the constitutional authority to give a third party an absolute, and possibly arbitrary, veto over the decision of the physician and his patient to terminate the patient's pregnancy, regardless of the reason for withholding the consent." *Id.,* at 74, 96 S.Ct., at 2843. These holdings, I think, equally apply to the Massachusetts statute. The differences between the two statutes are few. Unlike the Missouri statute, Massachusetts requires the consent of both of the woman's parents. It does, of course, provide an alternative in the form of a suit initiated by the woman in Superior Court. But in that proceeding, the judge is afforded an absolute veto over the minor's decisions, based on his judgment of her best interests. In Massachusetts, then, as in Missouri, the State has imposed an "absolute limitation on the minor's right to obtain an abortion," *id.,* at 90, 96 S.Ct., at 2851 (STEWART, J., concurring), applicable to every pregnant minor in the State who has not married.

The provision of an absolute veto to a judge—or, potentially, to an appointed administrator[34]—is to me particularly troubling. The constitutional right to make the abortion decision affords protection to both of the privacy interests recognized in this Court's cases: "One is the individual's interest in avoiding disclosure of personal matters, and another is the interest in independence in making certain kinds of important decisions." *Whalen v. Roe,* 429 U. S. 589, 599–600, 97 S.Ct. 869, 876, 51 L.Ed.2d 64. It is inherent in the right to make the abortion decision that the right may be exercised without public scrutiny and in defiance of the contrary opinion of the sovereign or other third parties. In Massachusetts, however, every minor who cannot secure the consent of both her parents—which under *Danforth* cannot be an absolute prerequisite to an abortion—is required to secure the consent of the sovereign. As a practical matter, I would suppose that the need to commence judicial proceedings in order to obtain a legal abortion would impose a burden at least as great as, and probably greater than, that imposed on the minor child by the need to obtain the consent of a parent.[35] Moreover, once this burden is met, the only standard provided for the judge's decision is the best interest of the minor. That standard provides little real guidance to the judge, and his decision must necessarily reflect personal and societal values and mores whose enforcement upon the minor—particularly when contrary to her own informed and reasonable decision—is fundamentally at odds with privacy interests underlying the constitutional protection afforded to her decision.

In short, it seems to me that this case is governed by *Danforth;* to the extent this statute differs from that in *Danforth,* it is potentially even more restrictive of the constitutional right to decide whether or not to terminate a pregnancy. Because the statute has been once authoritatively construed by the Massachusetts Supreme Judicial Court, and because it is clear that the statute as written and construed is not constitutional, I agree with Mr. Justice POWELL that the District Court's judgment should be affirmed. Because his opinion goes further, however, and addresses the constitutionality of an abortion statute that Massachusetts has not enacted, I decline to join his opinion.[36]

MR. JUSTICE WHITE, dissenting.

I was in dissent in *Planned Parenthood of Missouri v. Danforth,* 428 U. S. 52, 94–95, 96 S.Ct. 2831, 2853, 49 L.Ed.2d 788 (1976), on the issue of the validity of requiring the consent of a parent when an unmarried woman under 18 years of age seeks an abortion. I continue to have the views I expressed there and also agree with much of what Mr. Justice STEVENS said in dissent in that case. *Id.,* at 101–105, 96 S.Ct. at 2855–2857. I would not, therefore, strike down this Massachusetts law.

But even if a parental consent requirement of the kind involved in *Danforth* must be deemed invalid, that does not condemn the Massachusetts law, which, when the parents object, authorizes a judge to permit an abortion if he concludes that an abortion is in the best interests of the child. Going beyond *Danforth,* the Court now holds it unconstitutional for a State to require that in all cases parents receive notice that their daughter seeks an abortion and, if they object to the abortion, an opportunity to participate in a hearing that will determine whether it is in the "best interests" of the child to undergo the surgery. Until now, I would have thought inconceivable a holding that the United States Constitution forbids even notice to parents when their minor child who seeks surgery objects to such notice and is able to convince a judge that the parents should be denied participation in the decision.

With all due respect, I dissent.

NOTES

1. The court promptly issued a restraining order which remained in effect until its decision on the merits. Subsequent stays of enforcement were issued during the complex course of this litigation, with the result that Mass. Gen. Laws Ann., ch. 112, § 12S (West), never has been enforced by Massachusetts.

2. As originally enacted, § 12S was designated as § 12P of chapter 112. In 1977, the provision was renumbered as § 12S, and the numbering of subdivisions within the section was eliminated. No changes of substance were made. We shall refer to the section as § 12S throughout this opinion.

3. The proceedings before the court and the substance of its opinion are described in detail in *Bellotti v. Baird,* 428 U. S. 132, 136–143, 96 S.Ct. 2857, 2861–2864, 49 L.Ed.2d 844 (1976).

4. Three other minors in similar circumstances were named in the complaint, but the complaint was dismissed as to them for want of proof of standing. That decision has not been challenged on appeal.

5. Appellants argue that these "immature" minors never were before the District Court and that the court's remedy should have been tailored to grant relief only to the class of "mature" minors. It is apparent from the District Court's opinions, however, that it considered the constitutionality of § 12S as applied to all pregnant minors who might be affected by it. We accept that the rights of this entire category of minors properly were subject to adjudication.

6. In 1978, the District Court permitted postjudgment intervention by these parties, who now appear jointly before this Court as intervenor-appellees.

7. As their positions are closely aligned, if not identical, appellants in Nos. 78–329 and 78–330 are hereinafter referred to collectively as appellants.

8. One member of the three-judge court dissented, arguing that the decision of the majority to allow Mary Moe to proceed in the case without notice to her parents denied them their parental rights without due process of law, and that § 12S was consistent with the decisions of this Court recognizing the propriety of parental control over the conduct of children. See 393 F.Supp., at 857–865.

9. The nine questions certified by the District Court, with footnotes omitted, are as follows:

"1. What standards, if any, does the statute establish for a parent to apply when considering whether or not to grant consent?

"a) Is the parent to consider 'exclusively . . . what will serve the child's best interests'?

"b) If the parent is not limited to considering exclusively the minor's best interests, can the parent take into consideration the 'long-term consequences to the family and her parents' marriage relationship'?

"c) Other?

"2. What standard or standards is the superior court to apply?

"a) Is the superior court to disregard all parental objections that are not based exclusively on what would serve the minor's best interests?

"b) If the superior court finds that the minor is capable, and has, in fact, made and adhered to, an informed and reasonable decision to have an abortion, may the court refuse its consent based on a finding that a parent's, or its own, contrary decision is a better one?

"c) Other?

"3. Does the Massachusetts law permit a minor (a) 'capable of giving informed consent,' or (b) 'incapable of giving informed consent,' 'to obtain [a court] order without parental consultation'?

"4. If the court answers any of question 3 in the affirmative, may the superior court, for good cause shown, enter an order authorizing an abortion, (a), without prior notification to the parents, and (b), without subsequent notification?

"5. Will the Supreme Judicial Court prescribe a set of procedures to implement c. 112, [§ 12S] which will expedite the application, hearing, and decision phases of the superior court proceeding provided thereunder? Appeal?

"6. To what degree do the standards and procedures set forth in c. 112 § 12F (Stat.1975, c. 564), authorizing minors to give consent to medical and dental care in specified circumstances, parallel the grounds and procedures for showing good cause under c. 112, [§ 12S]?

"7. May a minor, upon a showing of indigency, have court-appointed counsel?

"8. Is it a defense to his criminal prosecution if a physician performs an abortion solely with the minor's own, valid, consent, that he reasonably, and in good faith, though erroneously, believed that she was eighteen or more years old or had been married?

"9. Will the Court make any other comments about the statute which, in its opinion, might assist us in determining whether it infringes the United States Constitution?"

10. Section 12S itself dispenses with the need for the consent of any parent who "has died or has deserted his or her family."

11. The dissenting judge agreed that the State could not permit a judge to override the decision of a minor found to be mature and capable of giving informed consent to an abortion. He disagreed with the remainder of the court's conclusions: the best-interests limitation on the withholding of parental consent in the Supreme Judicial Court's opinion, he argued, must be treated as if part of the statutory language itself; and he read the evidentiary record as proving that only rarely would a pregnant minor's interests be disserved by consulting with her parents about a desired abortion. He also noted the value to a judge in a § 12S proceeding of having the parents before him as a source of evidence as to the minor's maturity and what course would serve her best interests. See *Baird III, supra,* at 1006–1020.

12. Similarly, the Court said in *Planned Parenthood of Central Missouri v. Danforth,* 428 U. S. 52, 74, 96 S.Ct. 2831, 2843, 49 L.Ed.2d 788 (1976):

"Constitutional rights do not mature and come into being magically only when one attains the state-defined age of majority. Minors, as well as adults, are protected by the Constitution and possess constitutional rights."

13. As Mr. Justice STEWART wrote of the exercise by minors of the First Amendment rights that "secur[e] . . . the liberty of each man to decide for himself what he will read and to what he will listen," *Ginsberg v. New York,* 390 U. S. 629, 649, 88 S.Ct. 1274, 1285, 20 L.Ed.2d 195 (1968) (STEWART, J., concurring in the result):

"[A]t least in some precisely delineated areas, a child—like someone in a captive audience—is not possessed of that full capacity for individual choice which is the presupposition of First Amendment guarantees. It is only upon such a premise, I should suppose, that a State may deprive children of other rights—the right to marry, for example, or the right to vote—deprivations that would be constitutionally intolerable for adults." *Id.,* at 649–650, 88 S.Ct., at 1286 (footnotes omitted).

14. In *Prince* an adult had permitted a child in her custody to sell religious literature on a public street in violation of a state child-labor statute. The child had been permitted to engage in this activity upon her own sincere request. 321 U. S., at 162, 64 S.Ct., at 440. In upholding the adult's conviction under the statute, we found that "the interests of society to protect the welfare of children" and to give them "opportunities for growth into free and independent well-developed men and citizens," *id.,* at 165, 64 S.Ct., at 442, permitted the State

to enforce its statute, which "[c]oncededly . . . would be invalid," *id.,* at 167, 64 S.Ct., at 442, if made applicable to adults.

15. Although the State has considerable latitude in enacting laws affecting minors on the basis of their lesser capacity for mature, affirmative choice, *Tinker v. Des Moines Independent Community School District,* 393 U. S. 503, 89 S.Ct. 733, 21 L.Ed.2d 731 (1969), illustrates that it may not arbitrarily deprive them of their freedom of action altogether. The Court held in *Tinker* that a school child's First Amendment freedom of expression entitled him, contrary to school policy, to attend school wearing a black armband as a silent protest against American involvement in the hostilities in Viet Nam. The Court acknowledged that the State was permitted to prohibit conduct otherwise shielded by the Constitution that "for any reason—whether it stems from time, place, or type of behavior—materially disrupts classwork or involves substantial disorder or invasion of the rights of others." *Id.,* at 513, 89 S.Ct., at 740. It upheld the First Amendment right of the schoolchildren in that case, however, not only because it found no evidence in the record that their wearing of black armbands threatened any substantial interference with the proper objectives of the school district, but also because it appeared that the challenged policy was intended primarily to stifle any debate whatsoever—even nondisruptive discussions—on important political and moral issues. See *id.,* at 510, 89 S.Ct., at 738.

16. See, *e.g.,* Mass.Gen.Laws Ann., ch. 207, §§ 7, 24, 25, 33, 33A (West 1958 & Supp. 1979) (parental consent required for marriage of person under 18); Mass.Gen.Laws Ann., ch. 119, § 55A (West Supp. 1979) (waiver of counsel by minor in juvenile delinquency proceedings must be made through parent or guardian).

17. See Hafen, Children's Liberation and the New Egalitarianism: Some Reservations About Abandoning Children to Their "Rights," 1976 B.Y.U.L. Rev. 605.

18. The Court's opinions discussed in the text above—*Pierce, Yoder, Prince,* and *Ginsberg*—all have contributed to a line of decisions suggesting the existence of a constitutional parental right against undue, adverse interference by the State. See also *Smith v. Organization of Foster Families,* 431 U. S. 816, 842–844, 97 S.Ct. 2094, 2109, 53 L.Ed.2d 14 (1977); *Carey v. Population Services,* 431 U. S. 678, 708, 97 S.Ct. 2010, 2028, 52 L.Ed.2d 675 (1977) (opinion of Mr. Justice POWELL); *Moore v. City of East Cleveland,* 431 U. S. 494, 97 S.Ct. 1932, 52 L.Ed.2d 531 (1977) (plurality opinion); *Stanley v. Illinois,* 405 U. S. 645, 651, 92 S.Ct. 1208, 1212, 31 L.Ed.2d 551 (1972); *Meyer v. Nebraska,* 262 U. S. 390, 399, 43 S.Ct. 625, 67 L.Ed. 1042 (1923). *Cf. Parham v. J. R.,*_____ U. S._____, 99 S.Ct. 2493, 60 L.Ed.2d_____(1979); *id.,* at_____, 99 S.Ct., at 2513 (opinion of Mr. Justice STEWART, concurring in the result).

19. In *Planned Parenthood v. Danforth,* 428 U. S., at 75, 96 S.Ct., at 2844, "[W]e emphasize[d] that our holding [did] not suggest that every minor, regardless of age or maturity, may give effective consent for termination of her pregnancy."

20. The expert testimony at the hearings in the District Court uniformly was to the effect that parental involvement in a minor's abortion decision, if compassionate and supportive, was highly desirable. The findings of the court reflect this consensus. See *Baird I,* 393 F. Supp., at 853.

21. Mr. Justice STEWART's concurring opinion in *Danforth* underscored the need for parental involvement in minors' abortion decisions by describing the procedures followed at the clinic operated by the Parents Aid Society and Dr. Gerald Zupnick:

> "The counseling . . . occurs entirely on the day the abortion is to be performed. . . . It lasts for two hours and takes place in groups that include both minors and adults who are strangers to one another. . . . The physician takes no part in this counseling process. . . . Counseling is typically limited to a description of abortion procedures, possible complications, and birth control techniques. . . .
>
> "The abortion itself takes five to seven minutes. . . . The physician has no prior contact with the minor, and on the days that abortions are being performed at the [clinic], the physician, . . . may be performing abortions on many other adults and minors. . . . On busy days patients are scheduled in separate groups, consisting usually of

five patients. . . . After the abortion [the physician] spends a brief period with the minor and others in the group in the recovery room. . . ." 428 U. S., at 91–92, n. 2, 96 S.Ct., at 2851 n. 2, quoting Brief for Appellants in *Bellotti I, supra.*

In *Roe v. Wade,* 410 U. S. 113, 93 S.Ct. 705, 35 L.Ed.2d 147 (1973), and *Doe v. Bolton, id.,* 410 U. S., at 179, 93 S.Ct., at 739, we emphasized the importance of the role of the attending physician. Those cases involved adult women presumably capable of selecting and obtaining a competent physician. In this case, however, we are concerned only with minors who, according to the record, may range in age from children of 12 years to 17-year-old teenagers. Even the latter are less likely than adults to know or be able to recognize ethical, qualified physicians, or to have the means to engage such professionals. Many minors who bypass their parents probably will resort to an abortion clinic, without being able to distinguish the competent and ethical from those that are incompetent or unethical.

22. As § 12S provides for involvement of the state superior court in minors' abortion decisions, we discuss the alternative procedure described in the text in terms of judicial proceedings. We do not suggest, however, that a State choosing to require parental consent could not delegate the alternative procedure to a juvenile court or an administrative agency or officer. Indeed, much can be said for employing procedures and a forum less formal than those associated with a court of general jurisdiction.

23. The nature of both the State's interest in fostering parental authority and the problem of determining "maturity" makes clear why the State generally may resort to objective, though inevitably arbitrary, criteria such as age limits, marital status, or membership in the armed forces for lifting some or all of the legal disabilities of minority. Not only is it difficult to define, let alone determine, maturity, but the fact that a minor may be very much an adult in some respects does not mean that his need and opportunity for growth under parental guidance and discipline have ended. As discussed in the text, however, the peculiar nature of the abortion decision requires the opportunity for case-by-case evaluations of the maturity of pregnant minors.

24. The Supreme Judicial Court held that § 12S imposed this standard on the Superior Court in large part because it construed the statute as containing the same restriction on parents. See pp. 3041–3042, *supra.* The court concluded that the judge should not be entitled "to exercise his authority on a standard broader than that to which a parent must adhere." *Attorney General, supra,* at_____, 360 N.E.2d, at 293.

Intervenors argue that, assuming state-supported parental involvement in the minor's abortion decision is permissible, the State may not endorse the withholding of parental consent for any reason not believed to be in the minor's best interests. They agree with the District Court that, even though § 12S was construed by the highest state court to impose this restriction, the statute is flawed because the restriction is not apparent on its face. Intervenors thus concur in the District Court's assumption that the statute will encourage parents to withhold consent for impermissible reasons. See *Baird III,* 450 F.Supp., at 1004–1005; *Baird II,* 428 F. Supp., at 855–856.

There is no basis for this assertion. As a general rule, the interpretation of a state statute by the State's highest court "is as though written into the ordinance itself," *Poulos v. New Hampshire,* 345 U. S. 395, 402, 73 S.Ct. 760, 765, 97 L.Ed. 1105 (1953), and we are obliged to view the restriction on the parental consent requirement "as if [§ 12S] had been so amended by the [Massachusetts] legislature." *Winters v. New York,* 333 U. S. 507, 514, 68 S.Ct. 665, 669, 92 L.Ed. 840 (1948).

25. Intervenors take issue with the Supreme Judicial Court's assurances that judicial proceedings will provide the necessary confidentiality, lack of procedural burden, and speed of resolution. In the absence of any evidence as to the operation of judicial proceedings under § 12S—and there is none, since appellees successfully sought to enjoin Massachusetts from putting it into effect—we must assume that the Supreme Judicial Court's judgment is correct.

26. The statute also provides that "[i]f both parents have died or have deserted their family, consent of the mother's guardian or other person having duties similar to a guardian, or any person who has assumed the care and custody of the mother is sufficient."

27. This reading of the statute requires parental consultation and consent more strictly than appellants themselves previously believed was necessary. In their first argument before this Court, and again before the Supreme Judicial Court, appellants argued that § 12S was not intended to abrogate Massachusetts' common-law "mature minor" rule as it applies to abortions. See 428 U. S., at 144, 96 S.Ct., at 2864. They also suggested that, under some circumstances, § 12S might permit even immature minors to obtain judicial approval for an abortion without any parental consultation. See 428 U. S., at 145, 96 S.Ct., at 2865; *Attorney General, supra,* 371 Mass., at_____, 360 N.E.2d, at 294. The Supreme Judicial Court sketched the outlines of the mature minor rule that would apply in the absence of § 12S: "The mature minor rule calls for an analysis of the nature of the operation, its likely benefit, and the capacity of the particular minor to understand fully what the medical procedure involves. . . . Judicial intervention is not required. If judicial approval is obtained, however, the doctor is protected from a subsequent claim that the circumstances did not warrant his reliance on the mature minor rule, and, of course, the minor patient is afforded advance protection against a misapplication of the rule. *Attorney General, supra,* at_____, 360 N.E.2d, at 295. "We conclude that, apart from statutory limitations which are constitutional, where the best interests of a minor will be served by not notifying his or her parents of intended medical treatment and where the minor is capable of giving informed consent to that treatment, the mature minor rule applies in this Commonwealth." *Id.,* at_____, 360 N.E.2d, at 296. The Supreme Judicial Court held that the common-law mature minor rule was inapplicable to abortions because it had been legislatively superseded by § 12S.

28. Of course, if the minor consults with her parents voluntarily and they withhold consent, she is free to seek judicial authorization for the abortion immediately.

29. There will be cases where the pregnant minor has received approval of the abortion decision by one parent. In that event, the parent can support the daughter's request for a prompt judicial determination, and the parent's support should be given great, if not dispositive, weight.

30. Appellees and intervenors have argued that § 12S violates the Equal Protection Clause of the Fourteenth Amendment. As we have concluded that the statute is constitutionally infirm for other reasons, there is no need to consider this question.

31. Section 12S evidently applies to all nonemergency abortions performed on minors, without regard to the period in pregnancy during which the procedure occurs. As the court below recognized, most abortions are performed during the early stages of pregnancy, before the end of the first trimester. See *Baird III, supra,* at 1001; see *Baird I, supra,* at 853. This coincides approximately with the previability period during which a pregnant woman's right to decide, in consultation with her physician, to have an abortion is most immune to state intervention. See *Roe v. Wade,* 410 U. S. 113, 164–165, 93 S.Ct. 705, 732, 35 L.Ed.2d 147 (1973).

The propriety of parental involvement in a minor's abortion decision does not diminish as the pregnancy progresses and legitimate concerns for the pregnant minor's health increase. Furthermore, the opportunity for direct access to court which we have described is adequate to safeguard throughout pregnancy the constitutionally protected interests of a minor in the abortion decision. Thus, although a significant number of abortions within the scope of § 12S might be performed during the later stages of pregnancy, we do not believe a different analysis of the statute is required for them.

32. The opinion of Mr. Justice STEVENS, concurring in the judgment, joined by three Members of the Court, characterizes this opinion as "advisory" and the questions it addresses as "hypothetical." Apparently this is criticism of our attempt to provide some guidance as to how a State constitutionally may provide for adult involvement—either by parents or a state official such as a judge—in the abortion decisions of minors. In view of the importance of the issue raised, and the protracted litigation to which these parties already have been subjected, we think it would be irresponsible simply to invalidate § 12S without stating our views as to the controlling principles.

The statute before us today is the same one that was here in *Bellotti I, supra.* The issues it presents were not then deemed "hypothetical." In a unanimous opinion, we remanded the case with directions that appropriate questions be certified to the Supreme Judicial Court of

Massachusetts "concerning the meaning of [§ 12S] and the procedure it imposes." *Id.,* 428 U. S., at 151, 96 S.Ct., at 2868. We directed that this be done because, as stated in the opinion, we thought the construction of § 12S urged by appellants would "avoid or substantially modify the federal constitutional challenge to the statute." *Id.,* at 148, 96 S.Ct., at 2866. The central feature of § 12S was its provision that a state court judge could make the ultimate decision, when necessary, as to the exercise by a minor of the right to an abortion. See *id.,* at 145, 96 S.Ct., at 2865. We held that this "would be fundamentally different from a statute that creates a 'parental veto' [of the kind rejected in *Danforth*]." *Ibid.* (footnote omitted). Thus, all Members of the Court agreed that providing for decisionmaking authority in a judge was not the kind of veto power held invalid in *Danforth.* The basic issues that were before us in *Bellotti I* remain in the case, sharpened by the construction of § 12S by the Supreme Judicial Court.

33. By affording such a veto, the Massachusetts statute does far more than simply provide for notice to the parents. See *post,* at 3055 (WHITE, J., dissenting). Neither *Danforth* nor this case determines the constitutionality of a statute which does no more than require notice to the parents, without affording them or any other third party an absolute veto.

34. See *ante,* at 3048, n. 22.

35. A minor may secure the assistance of counsel in filing and prosecuting her suit, but that is not guaranteed. The Massachusetts Supreme Judicial Court in response to the question whether a minor, upon a showing of indigency, may have court-appointed counsel, "construe[d] the statutes of the Commonwealth to authorize the appointment of counsel or a guardian ad litem for an indigent minor at public expense, if necessary, if the judge, in *his discretion,* concludes that the best interests of the minor would be served by such an appointment." *Baird v. Attorney General, supra,* 371 Mass., at_____, 360 N.E.2d, at 301 (emphasis added).

36. Until and unless Massachusetts or another State enacts a less restrictive statutory scheme, this Court has no occasion to render an advisory opinion on the constitutionality of such a scheme. A real statute—rather than a mere outline of a possible statute—and a real case or controversy may well present questions that appear quite different from the hypothetical questions Mr. Justice POWELL has elected to address. Indeed, there is a certain irony in his suggestion that a statute that is intended to vindicate "the special interests of the State in encouraging an unmarried pregnant minor to seek the advice of her parents in making the important decision whether or not to bear a child," see *ante,* at 3046, need not require notice to the parents of the minor's intended decision. That irony makes me wonder whether any legislature concerned with parental consultation would, in the absence of today's advisory opinion, have enacted a statute comparable to the one my Brethren have discussed.

HARRIS V. MCRAE

Supreme Court of the United States, 1980.
448 U.S. 297, 100 S.Ct. 2671, 62 L.Ed.2d 750.

MR. JUSTICE STEWART delivered the opinion of the Court.

This case presents statutory and constitutional questions concerning the public funding of abortions under Title XIX of the Social Security Act, commonly known as the "Medicaid" Act, and recent annual appropriations acts containing the so-called "Hyde Amendment." The statutory question is whether Title XIX requires a State that participates in the Medicaid program to fund the cost of medically necessary abortions for which federal reimbursement is unavailable under the Hyde Amendment. The constitutional question, which arises only if Title XIX imposes no such requirement, is whether the Hyde Amendment, by denying public funding for certain medically necessary abortions, contravenes the liberty or equal protection guarantees of the Due Process Clause of the Fifth Amendment, or either of the Religion Clauses of the First Amendment.

I

The Medicaid program was created in 1965, when Congress added Title XIX to the Social Security Act, 79 Stat. 343, as amended, 42 U.S.C. § 1396 et seq. (1976 ed. and Supp. II), for the purpose of providing federal financial assistance to States that choose to reimburse certain costs of medical treatment for needy persons. Although participation in the Medicaid program is entirely optional, once a State elects to participate, it must comply with the requirements of Title XIX.

One such requirement is that a participating State agree to provide financial assistance to the "categorically needy"[1] with respect to five general areas of medical treatment: (1) inpatient hospital services, (2) outpatient hospital services, (3) other laboratory and X-ray services, (4) skilled nursing facilities services, periodic screening and diagnosis of children, and family planning services, and (5) services of physicians. 42 U. S. C. §§ 1396a(a)(13)(B), 1396d(a))1)(5). Although a participating State need not "provide funding for all medical treatment falling within the five general categories, [Title XIX] does require that [a] state Medicaid plan[ ] establish 'reasonable standards . . . for determining . . . the extent of medical assistance under the plan which . . . are consistent with the objectives of [Title XIX].' 42 U. S. C. § 1396a(a)(17)." *Beal v. Doe*, 432 U. S. 438, 441, 97 S.Ct. 2366, 2369, 53 L.Ed.2d 464.

Since September 1976, Congress has prohibited—either by an amendment to the annual appropriations bill for the Department of Health, Education, and Welfare[2] or by a joint resolution—the use of any federal funds to reimburse the cost of abortions under the Medicaid program except under certain specified circumstances. This funding restriction is commonly known as the "Hyde Amendment," after its original congressional sponsor, Representative Hyde. The current version of the Hyde Amendment, applicable for fiscal year 1980, provides:

> "[N]one of the funds provided by this joint resolution shall be used to perform abortions except where the life of the mother would be endangered if the fetus were carried to term; or except for such medical procedures necessary for the victims of rape or incest when such rape or incest has been reported promptly to a law enforcement agency or public health service." Pub.L.No.96–123, § 109, 93 Stat. 926. See also Pub.L.No.96–86, § 118, 93 Stat. 662.

This version of the Hyde Amendment is broader than that applicable for fiscal year 1977, which did not include the "rape or incest" exception, Pub.L.No.94–439, § 209, 90 Stat. 1434, but narrower than that applicable for most of fiscal year 1978,[3] and all of fiscal year 1979, which had an additional exception for "instances where severe and long-lasting physical health damage to the mother would result if the pregnancy were carried to term when so determined by two physicians," Pub.L.No.95–205, § 101, 91 Stat. 1460; Pub.L.No.95–480, § 210, 92 Stat. 1586.[4]

On September 30, 1976, the day on which Congress enacted the initial version of the Hyde Amendment, these consolidated cases were filed in the District Court for the Eastern District of New York. The plaintiffs—Cora McRae, a New York Medicaid recipient then in the first trimester of a pregnancy that she wished to terminate, the New York City Health and Hospitals Corp., a public benefit corporation that operates 16 hospitals, 12 of which provide abortion services, and others—sought to enjoin the enforcement of the funding restriction on abortions. They alleged that the Hyde Amendment violated the First, Fourth, Fifth, and Ninth Amendments of the Constitution insofar as it limited the funding of abortions to those necessary to save the life of the mother, while permitting the funding of costs associated with childbirth. Although the sole named defendant was the Secretary of Health, Education, and Welfare, the District Court permitted Senators James L. Buckley and Jesse A. Helms and Representative Henry J. Hyde to intervene as defendants.[5]

After a hearing, the District Court entered a preliminary injunction prohibiting the Secretary from enforcing the Hyde Amendment and requiring him to continue to provide federal reimbursement for abortions under the standards applicable before the funding restriction had been enacted. *McRae v. Mathews,* 421 F.Supp. 533. Although stating that it had not expressly held that the funding restriction was unconstitutional, since the preliminary injunction was not its final judgment, the District Court noted that such a holding was "implicit" in its decision granting the injunction. The District Court also certified the *McRae* case as a class action on behalf of all pregnant or potentially pregnant women in the State of

New York eligible for Medicaid and who decide to have an abortion within the first 24 weeks of pregnancy, and of all authorized providers of abortion services to such women. *Id.,* at 543.

The Secretary then brought an appeal to this Court. After deciding *Beal v. Doe,* 432 U. S. 438, 97 S.Ct. 2366, 53 L.Ed.2d 464, and *Maher v. Roe,* 432 U. S. 464, 97 S.Ct. 2474, 53 L.Ed.2d 534, we vacated the injunction of the District Court and remanded the case for reconsideration in light of those decisions. *Califano v. McRae,* 433 U. S. 916, 97 S.Ct. 2993, 53 L.Ed.2d 1103.

On remand, the District Court permitted the intervention of several additional plaintiffs, including (1) four individual Medicaid recipients who wished to have abortions that allegedly were medically necessary but did not qualify for federal funds under the versions of the Hyde Amendment applicable in fiscal year 1977 and 1978, (2) several physicians who perform abortions for Medicaid recipients, (3) the Women's Division of the Board of Global Ministries of the United Methodist Church (Women's Division), and (4) two individual officers of the Women's Division.

An amended complaint was then filed, challenging the various versions of the Hyde Amendment on several grounds. At the outset, the plaintiffs asserted that the District Court need not address the constitutionality of the Hyde Amendment because, in their view, a participating State remains obligated under Title XIX to fund all medically necessary abortions, even if federal reimbursement is unavailable. With regard to the constitutionality of the Hyde Amendment, the plaintiffs asserted, among other things, that the funding restrictions violate the Religion Clauses of the First Amendment and the Due Process Clause of the Fifth Amendment.

After a lengthy trial, which inquired into the medical reasons for abortions and the diverse religious views on the subject,[6] the District Court filed an opinion and entered a judgment invalidating all versions of the Hyde Amendment on constitutional grounds.[7] The District Court rejected the plaintiffs' statutory argument, concluding that even though Title XIX would otherwise have required a participating State to fund medically necessary abortions, the Hyde Amendment had substantively amended Title XIX to relieve a State of that funding obligation. Turning then to the constitutional issues, the District Court concluded that the Hyde Amendment, though valid under the Establishment Clause,[8] violates the equal protection component of the Fifth Amendment's Due Process Clause and the Free Exercise Clause of the First Amendment. With regard to the Fifth Amendment, the District Court noted that when an abortion is "medically necessary to safeguard the pregnant woman's health, . . . the disentitlement to [M]edicaid assistance impinges directly on the woman's right to decide, in consultation with her physician and in reliance on his judgment, to terminate her pregnancy in order to preserve her health."[9] The Court concluded that the Hyde Amendment violates the equal protection guarantee because, in its view, the decision of Congress to fund medically necessary services generally but only certain medically necessary abortions serves no legitimate governmental interest. As to the Free Exercise Clause of the First Amendment, the Court held that insofar as a woman's decision to seek a medically necessary abortion may be a product of her religious beliefs under certain Protestant and Jewish tenets, the funding restrictions of the Hyde Amendment violate that constitutional guarantee as well.

Accordingly, the District Court ordered the Secretary to "[c]ease to give effect" to the various versions of the Hyde Amendment insofar as they forbid payments for medically necessary abortions. It further directed the Secretary to "continue to authorize the expenditure of federal matching funds [for such abortions]." In addition, the Court recertified the *McRae* case as a nationwide class action on behalf of all pregnant and potentially pregnant women eligible for Medicaid who wish to have medically necessary abortions, and of all authorized providers of abortions for such women.[10]

The Secretary then applied to this Court for a stay of the judgment pending direct appeal of the District Court's decision. We denied the stay, but noted probable jurisdiction of this appeal. 444 U. S._____, 100 S.Ct. 1010, 62 L.Ed.2d 749.

II

[1] It is well settled that if a case may be decided on either statutory or constitutional grounds, this Court, for sound jurisprudential reasons, will inquire first into the statutory question. This practice reflects the deeply rooted doctrine "that we ought not to pass on questions of constitutionality . . . unless such adjudication is unavoidable." *Spector Motor Co. v. McLaughlin,* 323 U. S. 101, 105, 65 S.Ct. 152, 154, 89 L.Ed. 101. Accordingly, we turn first to the question whether Title XIX requires a State that participates in the Medicaid program to continue to fund those medically necessary abortions for which federal reimbursement is unavailable under the Hyde Amendment. If a participating State is under such an obligation, the constitutionality of the Hyde Amendment need not be drawn into question in the present case, for the availability of medically necessary abortions under Medicaid would continue, with the participating State shouldering the total cost of funding such abortions.

The appellees assert that a participating State has an independent funding obligation under Title XIX because (1) the Hyde Amendment is, by its own terms, only a limitation on federal reimbursement for certain medically necessary abortions, and (2) Title XIX does not permit a participating State to exclude from its Medicaid plan any medically necessary service solely on the basis of diagnosis or condition, even if federal reimbursement is unavailable for that service.[11] It is thus the appellees' view that the effect of the Hyde Amendment is to withhold federal reimbursement for certain medically necessary abortions, but not to relieve a participating State of its duty under Title XIX to provide for such abortions in its Medicaid plan.

The District Court rejected this argument. It concluded that although Title XIX would otherwise have required a participating State to include medically necessary abortions in its Medicaid program, the Hyde Amendment substantively amended Title XIX so as to relieve a State of that obligation. This construction of the Hyde Amendment was said to find support in the decisions of two Courts of

Appeals, *Preterm, Inc. v. Dukakis,* 591 F.2d 121 (CA1 1979), and *Zbaraz v. Quern,* 596 F.2d 196 (CA7 1979), and to be consistent with the understanding of the effect of the Hyde Amendment by the Department of Health, Education, and Welfare in the administration of the Medicaid program.

[2–4] We agree with the District Court, but for somewhat different reasons. The Medicaid program created by Title XIX is a cooperative endeavor in which the Federal Government provides financial assistance to participating States to aid them in furnishing health care to needy persons. Under this system of "cooperative federalism," *King v. Smith,* 392 U. S. 309, 316, 88 S.Ct. 2128, 2132, 20 L.Ed.2d 1118, if a State agrees to establish a Medicaid plan that satisfies the requirements of Title XIX, which include several mandatory categories of health services, the Federal Government agrees to pay a specified percentage of "the total amount expended . . . as medical assistance under the State plan. . . ." 42 U. S. C. § 1396b(a)(1). The cornerstone of Medicaid is financial contribution by both the Federal Government and the participating State. Nothing in Title XIX as originally enacted, or in its legislative history, suggests that Congress intended to require a participating State to assume the full costs of providing any health services in its Medicaid plan. Quite the contrary, the purpose of Congress in enacting Title XIX was to provide federal financial assistance for all legitimate state expenditures under an approved Medicaid plan. See S.Rep.No.404, 89th Cong., 1st Sess., 83–85 (1965); H.R. Rep.No.213, 89th Cong., 1st Sess., 72–74 (1965), U. S. Code Cong. & Admin. News 1965, p. 1943.

[5–7] Since the Congress that enacted Title XIX did not intend a participating State to assume a unilateral funding obligation for any health service in an approved Medicaid plan, it follows that Title XIX does not require a participating State to include in its plan any services for which a subsequent Congress has withheld federal funding.[12] Title XIX was designed as a cooperative program of shared financial responsibility, not as a device for the Federal Government to compel a State to provide services that Congress itself is unwilling to fund. Thus, if Congress chooses to withdraw federal funding for a particular service, a State is not obliged to continue to pay for that service as a condition of continued federal financial support of other services. This is not to say that Congress may not now depart from the original design of Title XIX under which the Federal Government shares the financial responsibility for expenses incurred under an approved Medicaid plan. It is only to say that, absent an indication of contrary legislative intent by a subsequent Congress, Title XIX does not obligate a participating State to pay for those medical services for which federal reimbursement is unavailable.[13]

[8–10] Thus, by the normal operation of Title XIX, even if a State were otherwise required to include medically necessary abortions in its Medicaid plan, the withdrawal of federal funding under the Hyde Amendment would operate to relieve the State of that obligation for those abortions for which federal reimbursement is unavailable.[14] The legislative history of the Hyde Amendment contains no indication whatsoever that Congress intended to shift the entire cost of such services to the participating States. See *Zbaraz v. Quern, supra,* 596 F.2d, at 200 ("no one, whether supporting or opposing the Hyde Amendment, ever suggested that State funding would be required"). Rather, the legislative history suggests that

Congress has always assumed that a participating State would not be required to fund medically necessary abortions once federal funding was withdrawn pursuant to the Hyde Amendment.[15] See *Preterm, Inc. v. Dukakis, supra,* 591 F.2d, at 130 ("[t]he universal assumption in debate was that if the Amendment passed there would be no requirement that states carry on the service"). Accord, *Zbaraz v. Quern, supra,* 596 F.2d, at 200; *Hodgson v. Board of County Commissioners,* 614 F.2d 601, at 613 (CA8 1980); *Roe v. Casey,*_____ F.2d_____, at_____(CA3 1980). Accordingly, we conclude that Title XIX does not require a participating State to pay for those medically necessary abortions for which federal reimbursement is unavailable under the Hyde Amendment.[16]

III

[11] Having determined that Title XIX does not obligate a participating State to pay for those medically necessary abortions for which Congress has withheld federal funding, we must consider the constitutional validity of the Hyde Amendment. The appellees assert that the funding restrictions of the Hyde Amendment violate several rights secured by the Constitution—(1) the right of a woman, implicit in the Due Process Clause of the Fifth Amendment, to decide whether to terminate a pregnancy, (2) the prohibition under the Establishment Clause of the First Amendment against any "law respecting an establishment of religion," and (3) the right to freedom of religion protected by the Free Exercise Clause of the First Amendment. The appellees also contend that, quite apart from substantive constitutional rights, the Hyde Amendment violates the equal protection component of the Fifth Amendment.[17]

[12] It is well settled that, quite apart from the guarantee of equal protection, if a law "impinges upon a fundamental right explicitly or implicitly secured by the Constitution [it] is presumptively unconstitutional." *Mobile v. Bolden,* 446 U. S. _____, 100 S.Ct. 1490, 1504, 64 L.Ed.2d 47 (plurality opinion). Accordingly, before turning to the equal protection issue in this case, we examine whether the Hyde Amendment violates any substantive rights secured by the Constitution.

A

We address first the appellees' argument that the Hyde Amendment, by restricting the availability of certain medically necessary abortions under Medicaid, impinges on the "liberty" protected by the Due Process Clause as recognized in *Roe v. Wade,* 410 U. S. 113, 93 S.Ct. 705, 35 L.Ed.2d 147, and its progeny.

[13] In the *Wade* case, this Court held unconstitutional a Texas statute making it a crime to procure or attempt an abortion except on medical advice for the purpose of saving the mother's life. The constitutional underpinning of *Wade* was a recognition that the "liberty" protected by the Due Process Clause of the Fourteenth Amendment includes not only the freedoms explicitly mentioned in the Bill of Rights, but also a freedom of personal choice in certain matters of marriage and family life.[18] This implicit constitutional liberty, the Court in *Wade* held, includes the freedom of a woman to decide whether to terminate a pregnancy.

[14] But the Court in *Wade* also recognized that a State has legitimate interests during a pregnancy in both ensuring the health of the mother and protecting potential human life. These state interests, which were found to be "separate and distinct" and to "grow" in substantiality as the woman approaches term," *id.,* at 162–163, 93 S.Ct., at 731, pose a conflict with a woman's untrammeled freedom of choice. In resolving this conflict, the Court held that before the end of the first trimester of pregnancy, neither state interest is sufficiently substantial to justify any intrusion on the woman's freedom of choice. In the second trimester, the state interest in maternal health was found to be sufficiently substantial to justify regulation reasonably related to that concern. And, at viability, usually in the third trimester, the state interest in protecting the potential life of the fetus was found to justify a criminal prohibition against abortions, except where necessary for the preservation of the life or health of the mother. Thus, inasmuch as the Texas criminal statute allowed abortions only where necessary to save the life of the mother and without regard to the stage of the pregnancy, the Court held in *Wade* that the statute violated the Due Process Clause of the Fourteenth Amendment.

In *Maher v. Roe,* 432 U. S. 464, 97 S.Ct. 2376, 53 L.Ed.2d 484, the Court was presented with the question whether the scope of personal constitutional freedom recognized in *Roe v. Wade* included an entitlement to Medicaid payments for abortions that are not medically necessary. At issue in *Maher* was a Connecticut welfare regulation under which Medicaid recipients received payments for medical services incident to childbirth, but not for medical services incident to nontherapeutic abortions. The District Court held that the regulation violated the Equal Protection Clause of the Fourteenth Amendment because the unequal subsidization of childbirth and abortion impinged on the "fundamental right to abortion" recognized in *Wade* and its progeny.

It was the view of this Court that "the District Court misconceived the nature and scope of the fundamental right recognized in *Roe.*" 432 U. S., at 471, 97 S.Ct., at 2381. The doctrine of *Roe v. Wade,* the Court held in *Maher,* "protects the woman from unduly burdensome interference with her freedom to decide whether to terminate her pregnancy," *id.,* at 473–474, 97 S.Ct., at 2382, such as the severe criminal sanctions at issue in *Roe v. Wade, supra,* or the absolute requirement of spousal consent for an abortion challenged in *Planned Parenthood of Central Missouri v. Danforth,* 428 U. S. 52, 96 S.Ct. 2831, 49 L.Ed.2d 788.

But the constitutional freedom recognized in *Wade* and its progeny, the *Maher* Court explained, did not prevent Connecticut from making "a value judgment favoring childbirth over abortion, and . . . implement[ing] that judgment by the allocation of public funds." *Id.,* 432 U. S. at 474, 97 S.Ct., at 2832. As the Court elaborated:

> "The Connecticut regulation before us is different in kind from the laws invalidated in our previous abortion decisions. The Connecticut regulation places no obstacles—absolute or otherwise—in the pregnant woman's path to an abortion. An indigent woman who desires an abortion suffers no disadvantage as a consequence of Connecticut's decision to fund childbirth; she continues as before to be dependent on private sources for the service

she desires. The State may have made childbirth a more attractive alternative, thereby influencing the woman's decision, but it has imposed no restriction on access to abortions that was not already there. The indigency that may make it difficult—and in some cases, perhaps, impossible—for some women to have abortions is neither created nor in any way affected by the Connecticut regulation." *Id.,* at 474, 97 S.Ct., at 2382–83.

The Court in *Maher* noted that its description of the doctrine recognized in *Wade* and its progeny signaled "no retreat" from those decisions. In explaining why the constitutional principle recognized in *Wade* and later cases—protecting a woman's freedom of choice—did not translate into a constitutional obligation of Connecticut to subsidize abortions, the Court cited the "basic difference between direct state interference with a protected activity and state encouragement of an alternative activity consonant with legislative policy. Constitutional concerns are greatest when the State attempts to impose its will by force of law; the State's power to encourage actions deemed to be in the public interest is necessarily far broader." *Id.,* at 475–476, 97 S.Ct., at 2383. Thus, even though the Connecticut regulation favored childbirth over abortion by means of subsidization of one and not the other, the Court in *Maher* concluded that the regulation did not impinge on the constitutional freedom recognized in *Wade* because it imposed no governmental restriction on access to abortions.

[15] The Hyde Amendment, like the Connecticut welfare regulation at issue in *Maher,* places no governmental obstacle in the path of a woman who chooses to terminate her pregnancy, but rather, by means of unequal subsidization of abortion and other medical services, encourages alternative activity deemed in the public interest. The present case does differ factually from *Maher* insofar as that case involved a failure to fund nontherapeutic abortions, whereas the Hyde Amendment withholds funding of certain medically necessary abortions. Accordingly, the appellees argue that because the Hyde Amendment affects a significant interest not present or asserted in *Maher*—the interest of a woman in protecting her health during pregnancy—and because that interest lies at the core of the personal constitutional freedom recognized in *Wade*, the present case is constitutionally different from *Maher.* It is the appellees' view that to the extent that the Hyde Amendment withholds funding for certain medically necessary abortions, it clearly impinges on the constitutional principle recognized in *Wade.*

It is evident that a woman's interest in protecting her health was an important theme in *Wade.* In concluding that the freedom of a woman to decide whether to terminate her pregnancy falls within the personal liberty protected by the Due Process Clause, the Court in *Wade* emphasized the fact that the woman's decision carries with it significant personal health implications—both physical and psychological. 410 U. S., at 153, 93 S.Ct., at 726. In fact, although the Court in *Wade* recognized that the state interest in protecting potential life becomes sufficiently compelling in the period after fetal viability to justify an absolute criminal prohibition of nontherapeutic abortions, the Court held that even after fetal viability a State may not prohibit abortions "necessary to preserve the life or health of the mother." *Id.,* at 164, 93 S.Ct., at 732. Because even the compelling interest of the

State in protecting potential life after fetal viability was held to be insufficient to outweigh a woman's decision to protect her life or health, it could be argued that the freedom of a woman to decide whether to terminate her pregnancy for health reasons does in fact lie at the core of the constitutional liberty identified in *Wade.*

[16–21] But, regardless of whether the freedom of a woman to choose to terminate her pregnancy for health reasons lies at the core or the periphery of the due process liberty recognized in *Wade,* it simply does not follow that a woman's freedom of choice carries with it a constitutional entitlement to the financial resources to avail herself of the full range of protected choices. The reason why was explained in *Maher:* although government may not place obstacles in the path of a woman's exercise of her freedom of choice, it need not remove those not of its own creation. Indigency falls in the latter category. The financial constraints that restrict an indigent woman's ability to enjoy the full range of constitutionally protected freedom of choice are the product not of governmental restrictions on access to abortions, but rather of her indigency. Although Congress has opted to subsidize medically necessary services generally, but not certain medically necessary abortions, the fact remains that the Hyde Amendment leaves an indigent woman with at least the same range of choice in deciding whether to obtain a medically necessary abortion as she would have had if Congress had chosen to subsidize no health care costs at all. We are thus not persuaded that the Hyde Amendment impinges on the constitutionally protected freedom of choice recognized in *Wade.*[19]

[22–26] Although the liberty protected by the Due Process Clause affords protection against unwarranted government interference with freedom of choice in the context of certain personal decisions, it does not confer an entitlement to such funds as may be necessary to realize all the advantages of that freedom. To hold otherwise would mark a drastic change in our understanding of the Constitution. It cannot be that because government may not prohibit the use of contraceptives, *Griswold v. Connecticut,* 381 U. S. 479, 85 S.Ct. 1678, 14 L.Ed.2d 510, or prevent parents from sending their child to a private school, *Pierce v. Society of Sisters,* 268 U. S. 510, 45 S.Ct. 571, 69 L.Ed. 1070, government, therefore, has an affirmative constitutional obligation to ensure that all persons have the financial resources to obtain contraceptives or send their children to private schools. To translate the limitation on governmental power implicit in the Due Process Clause into an affirmative funding obligation would require Congress to subsidize the medically necessary abortion of an indigent woman even if Congress had not enacted a Medicaid program to subsidize other medically necessary services. Nothing in the Due Process Clause supports such an extraordinary result.[20] Whether freedom of choice that is constitutionally protected warrants federal subsidization is a question for Congress to answer, not a matter of constitutional entitlement. Accordingly, we conclude that the Hyde Amendment does not impinge on the due process liberty recognized in *Wade.*[21]

B

The appellees also argue that the Hyde Amendment contravenes rights secured by the Religion Clauses of the First Amendment. It is the appellees' view that the Hyde Amendment violates the Establishment Clause because it incorporates into law the doctrines of the Roman Catholic Church concerning the sinfulness of abortion and the time at which life commences. Moreover, insofar as a woman's decision to seek a medically necessary abortion may be a product of her religious beliefs under certain Protestant and Jewish tenets, the appellees assert that the funding limitations of the Hyde Amendment impinge on the freedom of religion guaranteed by the Free Exercise Clause.

1

[27–30] It is well settled that "a legislative enactment does not contravene the Establishment Clause if it has a secular legislative purpose, if its principal or primary effect neither advances nor inhibits religion, and if it does not foster an excessive governmental entanglement with religion." *Committee for Pub. Ed. & Rel. Lib. v. Regan,* 444 U. S. _____, _____, 100 S.Ct. 840, 846, 63 L.Ed.2d 94. Applying this standard, the District Court properly concluded that the Hyde Amendment does not run afoul of the Establishment Clause. Although neither a State nor the Federal Government can constitutionally "pass laws which aid one religion, aid all religions, or prefer one religion over another," *Everson v. Board of Education,* 330 U. S. 1, 15, 67 S.Ct. 504, 511, 91 L.Ed. 711, it does not follow that a statute violates the Establishment Clause because it "happens to coincide or harmonize with the tenets of some or all religions." *McGowan v. Maryland,* 366 U. S. 420, 442, 81 S.Ct. 1101, 1113, 6 L.Ed.2d 393. That the Judaeo-Christian religions oppose stealing does not mean that a State or the Federal Government may not, consistent with the Establishment Clause, enact laws prohibiting larceny. *Ibid.* The Hyde Amendment, as the District Court noted, is as much a reflection of "traditionalist" values towards abortion, as it is an embodiment of the views of any particular religion. See also *Roe v. Wade, supra,* 410 U. S., at 138–141, 93 S.Ct., at 719–721. In sum, we are convinced that the fact that the funding restrictions in the Hyde Amendment may coincide with the religious tenets of the Roman Catholic Church does not, without more, contravene the Establishment Clause.

2

[31,32] We need not address the merits of the appellees' arguments concerning the Free Exercise Clause, because the appellees lack standing to raise a free exercise challenge to the Hyde Amendment. The named appellees fall into three categories: (1) the indigent pregnant women who sued on behalf of other women similarly situated, (2) the two officers of the Women's Division of the Board of Global Ministries of the United Methodist Church (Women's Division), and (3) the Women's Division itself.[22] The named appellees in the first category lack standing to challenge the Hyde Amendment on free exercise grounds because none alleged, much less proved, that she sought an abortion under compulsion of religious belief.[23] See *McGowan v. Maryland, supra,* 366 U.S., at 429, 81 S.Ct., at 1106. Although the named appellees in the second category did provide a detailed description of their religious beliefs, they failed to allege either that they are or expect to

be pregnant or that they are eligible to receive Medicaid. These named appellees, therefore, lack the personal stake in the controversy needed to confer standing to raise such a challenge to the Hyde Amendment. See *Warth v. Seldin,* 422 U. S. 490, 498–499, 95 S.Ct. 2197, 2204–2205, 45 L.Ed.2d 343.

[33] Finally, although the Women's Division alleged that its membership includes "pregnant Medicaid eligible women who, as a matter of religious practice and in accordance with their conscientious beliefs, would choose but are precluded or discouraged from obtaining abortions reimbursed by Medicaid because of the Hyde Amendment," the Women's Division does not satisfy the standing requirements for an organization to assert the rights of its membership. One of those requirements is that "neither the claim asserted nor the relief requested requires the participation of individual members in the lawsuit." *Hunt v. Washington Apple Advertising Comm'n,* 432 U. S. 333, 343, 97 S.Ct. 2434, 2441, 53 L.Ed.2d 383. Since "it is necessary in a free exercise case for one to show the coercive effect of the enactment as it operates against him in the practice of his religion," *Abington School Dist. v. Schempp,* 374 U. S. 203, 223, 83 S.Ct. 1560, 1572, 10 L.Ed.2d 844, the claim asserted here is one that ordinarily requires individual participation.[24] In the present case, the Women's Division concedes that "the permissibility, advisability and/or necessity of abortion according to circumstance is a matter about which there is diversity of view within . . . our membership, and is a determination which must be ultimately and absolutely entrusted to the conscience of the individual before God." It is thus clear that the participation of individual members of the Women's Division is essential to a proper understanding and resolution of their free exercise claims. Accordingly, we conclude that the Women's Division, along with the other named appellees, lacks standing to challenge the Hyde Amendment under the Free Exercise Clause.

C

It remains to be determined whether the Hyde Amendment violates the equal protection component of the Fifth Amendment. This challenge is premised on the fact that, although federal reimbursement is available under Medicaid for medically necessary services generally, the Hyde Amendment does not permit federal reimbursement of all medically necessary abortions. The District Court held, and the appellees argue here, that this selective subsidization violates the constitutional guarantee of equal protection.

[34,35] The guarantee of equal protection under the Fifth Amendment is not a source of substantive rights or liberties,[25] but rather a right to be free from invidious discrimination in statutory classifications and other governmental activity. It is well settled that where a statutory classification does not itself impinge on a right or liberty protected by the Constitution, the validity of classification must be sustained unless "the classification rests on grounds wholly irrelevant to the achievement of [any legitimate governmental] objective." *McGowan v. Maryland, supra,* 366 U. S., at 425, 81 S.Ct., at 1105. This presumption of constitutional validity, however, disappears if a statutory classification is predicated on criteria that are, in a constitutional sense, "suspect," the principal example of which is a classification

based on race, *e.g., Brown v. Board of Education,* 347 U. S. 483, 74 S.Ct. 686, 98 L.Ed. 873.

1

[36–38] For the reasons stated above, we have already concluded that the Hyde Amendment violates no constitutionally protected substantive rights. We now conclude as well that it is not predicated on a constitutionally suspect classification. In reaching this conclusion, we again draw guidance from the Court's decision in *Maher v. Roe.* As to whether the Connecticut welfare regulation providing funds for childbirth but not for nontherapeutic abortions discriminated against a suspect class, the Court in *Maher* observed:

> "An indigent woman desiring an abortion does not come within the limited category of disadvantaged classes so recognized by our cases. Nor does the fact that the impact of the regulation falls upon those who cannot pay lead to a different conclusion. In a sense, every denial of welfare to an indigent creates a wealth classification as compared to nonindigents who are able to pay for the desired goods or services. But this Court has never held that financial need alone identifies a suspect class for purposes of equal protection analysis." 432 U. S., at 471, 97 S.Ct., at 2381, citing *San Antonio School Dist. v. Rodriguez,* 411 U. S. 1, 29, 93 S.Ct. 1278, 1294, 36 L.Ed.2d 16; *Dandridge v. Williams,* 397 U. S. 471, 90 S.Ct. 1153, 25 L.Ed.2d 491.

Thus, the Court in *Maher* found no basis for concluding that the Connecticut regulation was predicated on a suspect classification.

It is our view that the present case is indistinguishable from *Maher* in this respect. Here, as in *Maher,* the principal impact of the Hyde Amendment falls on the indigent. But that fact does not itself render the funding restriction constitutionally invalid, for this Court has held repeatedly that poverty, standing alone is not a suspect classification. See, *e.g. James v. Valtierra,* 402 U. S. 137, 91 S.Ct. 1331, 28 L.Ed.2d 678. That *Maher* involved the refusal to fund nontherapeutic abortions, whereas the present case involves the refusal to fund medically necessary abortions, has no bearing on the factors that render a classification "suspect" within the meaning of the constitutional guarantee of equal protection.[26]

2

[39] The remaining question then is whether the Hyde Amendment is rationally related to a legitimate governmental objective. It is the Government's position that the Hyde Amendment bears a rational relationship to its legitimate interest in protecting the potential life of the fetus. We agree.

In *Wade,* the Court recognized that the State has "[an] important and legitimate interest in protecting the potentiality of human life." 410 U. S., at 162, 93

S.Ct., at 731. That interest was found to exist throughout a pregnancy, "grow[ing] in substantiality as the woman approaches term." *Id.,* at 162–163, 93 S.Ct., at 731. See also *Beal v. Doe,* 432 U. S. 438, 445–446, 97 S.Ct. 2366, 2371, 53 L.Ed.2d 464. Moreover, in *Maher,* the Court held that Connecticut's decision to fund the costs associated with childbirth but not those associated with nontherapeutic abortions was a rational means of advancing the legitimate state interest in protecting potential life by encouraging childbirth. 432 U. S., at 478–479, 97 S.Ct., at 2385. See also *Poelker v. Doe,* 432 U. S. 519, 520–521, 97 S.Ct. 2391, 2392, 53 L.Ed.2d 528.

[40] It follows that the Hyde Amendment, by encouraging childbirth except in the most urgent circumstances, is rationally related to the legitimate governmental objective of protecting potential life. By subsidizing the medical expenses of indigent women who carry their pregnancies to term while not subsidizing the comparable expenses of women who undergo abortions (except those whose lives are threatened),[27] Congress has established incentives that make childbirth a more attractive alternative than abortion for persons eligible for Medicaid. These incentives bear a direct relationship to the legitimate congressional interest in protecting potential life. Nor is it irrational that Congress has authorized federal reimbursement for medically necessary services generally, but not for certain medically necessary abortions.[28] Abortion is inherently different from other medical procedures, because no other procedure involves the purposeful termination of a potential life.

[41] After conducting an extensive evidentiary hearing into issues surrounding the public funding of abortions, the District Court concluded that "[t]he interests of . . . the federal government . . . in the fetus and in preserving it are not sufficient, weighed in the balance with the woman's threatened health, to justify withdrawing medical assistance unless the woman consents . . . to carry the fetus to term." In making an independent appraisal of the competing interests involved here, the District Court went beyond the judicial function. Such decisions are entrusted under the Constitution to Congress, not the courts. It is the role of the courts only to ensure that congressional decisions comport with the Constitution.

[42] Where, as here, the Congress has neither invaded a substantive constitutional right or freedom, nor enacted legislation that purposefully operates to the detriment of a suspect class, the only requirement of equal protection is that congressional action be rationally related to a legitimate governmental interest. The Hyde Amendment satisfies that standard. It is not the mission of this Court or any other to decide whether the balance of competing interests reflected in the Hyde Amendment is wise social policy. If that were our mission, not every Justice who has subscribed to the judgment of the Court today could have done so. But we cannot, in the name of the Constitution, overturn duly enacted statutes simply "because they may be unwise, improvident, or out of harmony with a particular school of thought." *Williamson v. Lee Optical Co.,* 348 U. S. 483, 488, 75 S.Ct. 461, 464, 99 L.Ed. 563, quoted in *Dandridge v. Williams,* 397 U. S. 471, 484, 90 S.Ct. 1153, 1161, 25 L.Ed.2d 491. Rather, "when an issue involves policy choices as sensitive as those implicated [here] . . . , the appropriate forum for their resolution in a democracy is the legislature." *Maher v. Roe, supra,* 432 U. S., at 479, 97 S.Ct., at 2385.

IV

For the reasons stated in this opinion, we hold that a State that participates in the Medicaid program is not obligated under Title XIX to continue to fund those medically necessary abortions for which federal reimbursement is unavailable under the Hyde Amendment. We further hold that the funding restrictions of the Hyde Amendment violate neither the Fifth Amendment nor the Establishment Clause of the First Amendment. It is also our view that the appellees lack standing to raise a challenge to the Hyde Amendment under the Free Exercise Clause of the First Amendment. Accordingly, the judgment of the District Court is reversed, and the case is remanded to that court for further proceedings consistent with this opinion.

It is so ordered.

MR. JUSTICE WHITE, concurring.

I join the Court's opinion and judgment with these additional remarks.

Roe v. Wade, 410 U. S. 113, 93 S.Ct. 705, 35 L.Ed.2d 147 (1973), held that prior to viability of the fetus, the governmental interest in potential life was insufficient to justify overriding the due process right of a pregnant woman to terminate her pregnancy by abortion. In the last trimester, however, the State's interest in fetal life was deemed sufficiently strong to warrant a ban on abortions, but only if continuing the pregnancy did not threaten the life or health of the mother. In the latter event, the State was required to respect the choice of the mother to terminate the pregnancy and protect her health.

Drawing upon *Roe v. Wade* and the cases that followed it, the dissent extrapolates the general proposition that the governmental interest in potential life may in no event be pursued at the expense of the mother's health. It then notes that under the Hyde Amendment, Medicaid refuses to fund abortions where carrying to term threatens maternal health but finances other medically indicated procedures, including childbirth. The dissent submits that the Hyde Amendment therefore fails the first requirement imposed by the Fifth Amendment and recognized by the Court's opinion today—that the challenged official action must serve a legitimate governmental goal, *ante,* pp. 2691–2692.

The argument has a certain internal logic, but it is not legally sound. The constitutional right recognized in *Roe v. Wade* was the right to choose to undergo an abortion without coercive interference by the government. As the Court points out, *Roe v. Wade* did not purport to adjudicate a right to have abortions funded by the government, but only to be free from unreasonable official interference with private choice. At an appropriate stage in a pregnancy, for example, abortions could be prohibited to implement the governmental interest in potential life, but in no case to the damage of the health of the mother, whose choice to suffer an abortion rather than risk her health the government was forced to respect.

Roe v. Wade thus dealt with the circumstances in which the governmental interest in potential life would justify official interference with the abortion choices of pregnant women. There is no such calculus involved here. The government does not seek to interfere with or to impose any coercive restraint on the choice of any woman to have an abortion. The woman's choice remains unfettered, the government is not attempting to use its interest in life to justify a coercive restraint, and hence in disbursing its Medicaid funds it is free to implement rationally what *Roe v. Wade* recognized to be its legitimate interest in a potential life by covering the medical costs of childbirth but denying funds for abortions. Neither *Roe v. Wade* nor any of the cases decided in its wake invalidates this legislative preference. We decided as much in *Maher v. Roe*, 432 U. S. 464, 97 S.Ct. 2376, 53 L.Ed.2d 484 (1977), when we rejected the claims that refusing funds for nontherapeutic abortions while defraying the medical costs of childbirth, although not an outright prohibition, nevertheless infringed the fundamental right to choose to terminate a pregnancy by abortion and also violated the equal protection component of the Fifth Amendment. I would not abandon *Maher* and extend *Roe v. Wade* to forbid the legislative policy expressed in the Hyde Amendment.

Nor can *Maher* be successfully distinguished on the ground that it involved only nontherapeutic abortions that the government was free to place outside the ambit of its Medicaid program. That is not the ground on which *Maher* proceeded. *Maher* held that the government need not fund elective abortions because withholding funds rationally furthered the State's legitimate interest in normal childbirth. We sustained this policy even though under *Roe v. Wade*, the government's interest in fetal life is an inadequate justification for coercive interference with the pregnant woman's right to choose an abortion, whether or not such a procedure is medically indicated. We have already held, therefore, that the interest balancing involved in *Roe v. Wade* is not controlling in resolving the present constitutional issue. Accordingly, I am satisfied that the straightforward analysis followed in Mr. Justice STEWART's opinion for the Court is sound.

NOTES

1. The "categorically needy" include families with dependent children eligible for public assistance under the Aid to Families with Dependent Children program, 42 U. S. C. § 601 *et seq.*, and the aged, blind, and disabled eligible for benefits under the Supplemental Security Income Program, 42 U. S. C. § 1381 *et seq.* See 42 U. S. C. § 1396a(a)(10)(A). Title XIX also permits a State to extend Medicaid benefits to other needy persons, termed "medically needy." See 42 U. S. C. § 1396a(a)(10)(C). If a State elects to include the medically needy in its Medicaid plan, it has the option of providing somewhat different coverage from that required for the categorically needy. See 42 U. S. C. § 1396a(a)(13)(C).

2. The Department of Health, Education and Welfare was recently renamed the Department of Health and Human Services. The original designation is retained for purposes of this opinion.

3. The appropriations for HEW during October and November 1977, the first two months of fiscal year 1978, were provided by joint resolutions that continued in effect the version of the Hyde Amendment applicable during fiscal year 1977. Pub.L.No.95–130, 91 Stat. 1153; Pub.L.No.95–165, 91 Stat. 1323.

4. In this opinion, the term, "Hyde Amendment," is used generically to refer to all three versions of the Hyde Amendment, except where indicated otherwise.

5. Although the intervenor-defendants are appellees in the Secretary's direct appeal to this Court, see Sup.Ct. Rule 10(4), the term "appellees" is used in this opinion to refer only to the parties who were the plaintiffs in the District Court.

6. The trial, which was conducted between August of 1977 and September of 1978, produced a record containing more than 400 documentary and film exhibits and a transcript exceeding 5,000 pages.

7. The opinion of the District Court is as yet unreported.

8. The District Court found no Establishment Clause infirmity because, in its view, the Hyde Amendment has a secular legislative purpose, its principal effect neither advances nor inhibits religion, and it does not foster an excessive governmental entanglement with religion.

9. The District Court also apparently concluded that the Hyde Amendment operates to the disadvantage of a "suspect class," namely, teenage women desiring medically necessary abortions. See n. 26, *infra.*

10. Although the original class included only those pregnant women in the first two trimesters of their pregnancy, the recertified class included all pregnant women regardless of the stage of their pregnancy.

11. The appellees argue that their interpretation of Title XIX finds support in *Beal v. Doe,* 432 U. S. 438, 97 S.Ct. 2366, 53 L.Ed.2d 464. There the Court considered the question whether Title XIX permits a participating State to exclude *non*-therapeutic abortions from its Medicaid plan. Although concluding that Title XIX does not preclude a State's refusal "to fund *unnecessary*—though perhaps desirable—medical services," the Court observed that "serious statutory questions might be presented if a state Medicaid plan excluded necessary medical treatment from its coverage." *Id.,* at 444–445, 97 S.Ct., at 2371 (emphasis in original). The court in *Beal,* however, did not address the possible effect of the Hyde Amendment upon the operation of Title XIX.

12. In *Preterm, Inc. v. Dukakis, supra,* 591 F.2d, at 132, the opinion of the Court by Judge Coffin noted:

"The Medicaid program is one of federal and state cooperation in funding medical assistance; a complete withdrawal of the federal prop in the system with the intent to drop the total cost of providing the service upon the states, runs directly counter to the basic structure of the program and could seriously cripple a state's attempts to provide other necessary medical services embraced by its plan." (Footnote omitted.)

13. When subsequent Congresses have deviated from the original structure of Title XIX by obligating a participating State to assume the full costs of a service as a prerequisite for continued federal funding of other services, they have always expressed their intent to do so in unambiguous terms. See *Zbaraz v. Quern, supra,* 596 F.2d, at 200, n. 12.

14. Since Title XIX itself provides for variations in the required coverage of state Medicaid plans depending on changes in the availability of federal reimbursement, we need not inquire, as the District Court did, whether the Hyde Amendment is a substantive amendment to Title XIX. The present case is thus different from *TVA v. Hill,* 437 U. S. 153, 189–193, 98 S.Ct. 2279, 2299–2301, 57 L.Ed.2d 117, where the issue was whether continued appropriations for the Tellico Dam impliedly repealed the substantive requirements of the Endangered Species Act prohibiting the continued construction of the Dam because it threatened the natural habitat of an endangered species.

15. Our conclusion that the Congress that enacted Title XIX did not intend a participating State to assume a unilateral funding obligation for any health service in an approved Medicaid plan is corroborated by the fact that subsequent Congresses simply assumed that the withdrawal of federal funding under the Hyde Amendment for certain medically necessary abortions would relieve a participating State of any obligation to provide for such services in its Medicaid plan. See the cases cited in the text, *supra.*

16. A participating State is free, if it so chooses, to include in its Medicaid plan those medically necessary abortions for which federal reimbursement is unavailable. See *Beal v. Doe, supra,* 432 U. S., at 447, 97 S.Ct., at 2372; *Preterm, Inc. v. Dukakis, supra,* 591 F.2d, at 134. We hold only that a State need not include such abortions in its Medicaid plan.

17. The appellees also argue that the Hyde Amendment is unconstitutionally vague insofar as physicians are unable to understand or implement the exceptions to the Hyde Amendment under which abortions are reimbursable. It is our conclusion, however, that the Hyde Amendment is not void for vagueness because (1) the sanction provision in the Medic-

aid Act contains a clear scienter requirement under which good-faith errors are not penalized, see *Colautti v. Franklin,* 439 U. S. 379, 395, 99 S.Ct. 675, 685, 58 L.Ed.2d 596; and, (2), in any event, the exceptions to the Hyde Amendment "are set out in terms that the ordinary person exercising ordinary common sense can sufficiently understand and comply with, without sacrifice to the public interest." *Broadrick v. Oklahoma,* 413 U. S. 601, 608, 93 S.Ct. 2908, 2914, 37 L.Ed.2d 830.

18. The Court in *Wade* observed that previous decisions of this Court had recognized that the liberty protected by the Due Process Clause "has some extension to activities relating to marriage, *Loving v. Virginia,* 338 U. S. 1, 12 [87 S.Ct. 1817, 1823, 18 L.Ed.2d 1010] (1967); procreation, *Skinner v. Oklahoma,* 316 U. S. 535, 541–542 [62 S.Ct. 1110, 1113–1114, 86 L.Ed. 1655] (1942); contraception, *Eisenstadt v. Baird,* 405 U. S., [438] at 453–454 [92 S.Ct. 1029, at 1038, 1039, 31 L.Ed.2d 349]; *id.,* at 460, 463–465 [92 S.Ct., at 1042, 1043–1044] (WHITE, J., concurring in result); family relationships, *Prince v. Massachusetts,* 321 U. S. 158, 166 [64 S.Ct. 438, 442, 88 L.Ed. 645] (1944); and child rearing and education, *Pierce v. Society of Sisters,* 268 U. S. 510, 535 [45 S.Ct. 571, 573, 69 L.Ed. 1070] (1925); *Meyer v. Nebraska* [262 U. S. 390, 399, 43 S. Ct. 625, 626, 67 L.Ed. 1042 (1923).]" 410 U. S., at 152–153, 93 S.Ct., at 726–727.

19. The appellees argue that the Hyde Amendment is unconstitutional because it "penalizes" the exercise of a woman's choice to terminate a pregnancy by abortion. See *Memorial Hospital v. Maricopa County,* 415 U. S. 250, 94 S.Ct. 1076, 39 L.Ed.2d 306; *Shapiro v. Thompson,* 394 U. S. 618, 89 S.Ct. 1322, 22 L.Ed.2d 600. This argument falls short of the mark. In *Maher,* the Court found only a "semantic difference" between the argument that Connecticut's refusal to subsidize nontherapeutic abortions "unduly interfere[d]" with the exercise of the constitutional liberty recognized in *Wade* and the argument that it "penalized" the exercise of that liberty. 432 U. S., at 474 n. 8, 97 S. Ct., at 2382 n. 8. And, regardless of how the claim was characterized, the *Maher* Court rejected the argument that Connecticut's refusal to subsidize protected conduct, without more, impinged on the constitutional freedom of choice. This reasoning is equally applicable in the present case. A substantial constitutional question would arise if Congress had attempted to withhold all Medicaid benefits from an otherwise eligible candidate simply because that candidate had exercised her constitutionally protected freedom to terminate her pregnancy by abortion. This would be analogous to *Sherbert v. Verner,* 374 U. S. 398, 83 S.Ct. 1790, 10 L.Ed.2d 965, where this Court held that a State may not, consistent with the First and Fourteenth Amendments, withhold *all* unemployment compensation benefits from a claimant who would otherwise be eligible for such benefits but for the fact that she is unwilling to work one day per week on her Sabbath. But the Hyde Amendment, unlike the statute at issue in *Sherbert,* does not provide for such a broad disqualification from receipt of public benefits. Rather, the Hyde Amendment, like the Connecticut welfare provision at issue in *Maher,* represents simply a refusal to subsidize certain protected conduct. A refusal to fund protected activity, without more, cannot be equated with the imposition of a "penalty" on that activity.

20. As this Court in *Maher* observed: "The Constitution imposes no obligation on the [Government] to pay the pregnancy-related medical expenses of indigent women, or indeed to pay any of the medical expense of indigents." 432 U. S., at 469, 97 S.Ct., at 2380.

21. Since the constitutional entitlement of a physician who administers medical care to an indigent woman is no broader than that of his patient, see *Whalen v. Roe,* 429 U. S. 589, 604, and n. 33, 97 S.Ct. 869, 878, and n. 33, 51 L.Ed.2d 64, we also reject the appellees' claim that the funding restrictions of the Hyde Amendment violate the due process rights of the physician who advises a Medicaid recipient to obtain a medically necessary abortion.

22. The remaining named appellees, including the individual physicians and the New York City Health and Hospitals Corp., did not attack the Hyde Amendment on the basis of the Free Exercise Clause of the First Amendment.

23. These named appellees sued on behalf of the class of "women of all religious and nonreligious persuasions and beliefs who have, in accordance with the teaching of their religion and/or the dictates of their conscience determined that an abortion is necessary." But since we conclude below that the named appellees have not established their own standing to sue, "[t]hey cannot represent a class of whom they are not a part." *Bailey v. Patterson,* 369

U. S. 31, 32–33, 82 S.Ct. 549, 550, 7 L.Ed.2d 512. See also *O'Shea v. Littleton,* 414 U. S. 488, 494–495, 94 S.Ct. 669, 675, 38 L.Ed.2d 674.

24. For example, in *Board of Education v. Allen,* 392 U. S. 236, 249, 88 S.Ct. 1923, 1929, 20 L.Ed.2d 1060, the Court found no free exercise violation since the plaintiffs had "not contended that the [statute in question] coerce[d] them as *individuals* in the practice of their religion." (Emphasis added.)

25. An exception to this statement is to be found in *Reynolds v. Sims,* 377 U. S. 533, 84 S.Ct. 1362, 12 L.Ed.2d 506, and its progeny. Although the Constitution of the United States does not confer the right to vote in state elections, see *Minor v. Happersett,* 21 Wall. 162, 178, 22 L.Ed. 627, *Reynolds* held that if a State adopts an electoral system, the Equal Protection Clause of the Fourteenth Amendment confers upon a qualified voter a substantive right to participate in the electoral process equally with other qualified voters. See, *e.g., Dunn v. Blumstein,* 405 U. S. 330, 336, 92 S.Ct. 995, 999, 31 L.Ed.2d 274.

26. Although the matter is not free from doubt, the District Court seems to have concluded that teenage women desiring medically necessary abortions constitute a "suspect class" for purposes of triggering a heightened level of equal protection scrutiny. In this regard, the District Court observed that the Hyde Amendment "clearly operate[s] to the disadvantage of one suspect class, that is, to the disadvantage of the statutory class of adolescents at a high risk of pregnancy . . . and particularly those seventeen and under." The "statutory" class to which the District Court was referring is derived from the Adolescent Health Services and Pregnancy Prevention and Care Act, 42 U. S. C. § 300a–21 *et seq.* (Supp. II 1979). It was apparently the view of the District Court that since statistics indicate that women under 21 years of age are disproportionately represented among those for whom an abortion is medically necessary, the Hyde Amendment invidiously discriminates against teenage women.

But the Hyde Amendment is facially neutral as to age, restricting funding for abortions for women of all ages. The District Court erred, therefore, in relying solely on the disparate impact of the Hyde Amendment in concluding that it discriminated on the basis of age. The equal protection component of the Fifth Amendment prohibits only purposeful discrimination, *Washington v. Davis,* 426 U. S. 229, 96 S.Ct. 2040, 48 L.Ed.2d 597, and when a facially neutral federal statute is challenged on equal protection grounds, it is incumbent upon the challenger to prove that Congress "selected or reaffirmed a particular course of action at least in part 'because of,' not merely 'in spite of,' its adverse effects upon an identifiable group." *Personnel Administrator of Mass. v. Feeney,* 442 U. S. 256, 279, 99 S.Ct. 2282, 2296, 60 L.Ed.2d 870. There is no evidence to support such a finding of intent in the present case.

27. We address here the constitutionality of the most restrictive version of the Hyde Amendment, namely, that applicable in fiscal year 1976 under which federal funds were unavailable for abortions, "except where the life of the mother would be endangered if the fetus were carried to term." Three versions of the Hyde Amendment are at issue in this case. If the most restrictive version is constitutionally valid, so too are the others.

28. In fact, abortion is not the only "medically necessary" service for which federal funds under Medicaid are sometimes unavailable to otherwise eligible claimants. See 42 U. S. C. § 1396(a)(17)(B) (inpatient hospital care of patients between 21 and 65 in institutions for tuberculosis or mental disease not covered by Title XIX).

II. DEATH AND DYING

1. THE ETHICAL ISSUES

For centuries humanity has been cursed by illnesses that could not be controlled. Disease frequently decimated the human species. But gradually relief came. Public health measures and more adequate diets became factors in developing greater resistance to diseases. Science and medicine identified a variety of viruses and developed drugs to respond to them. Now, because of these revolutionary developments, we find ourselves in a peculiar position: medical science can prolong the dying process beyond its "natural" conclusion. And, paradoxically, it can maintain a patient's vital signs but not be able to cure his or her disease or even marginally improve his or her condition. Such a situation has given rise to a new problem: the refusal of treatment.

The tradition of Roman Catholic medical ethics has affirmed a person's moral right to refuse extraordinary forms of medical treatment, since they can be too expensive, too inconvenient, too painful, or useless in effecting a cure. Thus the tradition developed a strong position that some forms of medical treatment are, morally speaking, merely optional.

The Jehovah's Witnesses also have a position on treatment refusal, although much more narrowly drawn, but with vaster implications. This tradition demands a refusal of blood transfusions—an ordinary medical procedure and a typically life-saving one—because of the Biblical injunction against eating blood, the theological penalty for accepting a blood transfusion being the loss of salvation. Although this religious injunction is taken very seriously by Jehovah's Witnesses, physicians and hospital administrators are often reluctant to allow the individual to refuse such an ordinary procedure and such situations often end up in court. Many reasons have been put forward to justify overriding this religious belief: the procedure is lifesaving, the medical profession has an obligation to practice medicine in conformity with its standards, and life is more important than a seemingly irrational belief. When the individual is a minor and the parents have refused permission for a blood transfusion, the ethical problem becomes even more complex. A typical justification for countermanding the parental wishes is that no one can be allowed to make a martyr of one's child. Standard arguments of public welfare, state interests, the protection of third parties, and the *parens patriae* power of the state, therefore, are used to justify overriding individual beliefs. Occasionally the suggestion is made that such a refusal is simply a sign of incompetence and implies that another person should make the decision.

Such a case addresses two issues: religious freedom and freedom of choice.

The First Amendment guarantees freedom of religion, but this has typically been interpreted to refer only to one's beliefs; freedom of action based on religious beliefs has not been given such protection. Any such neat distinction, however, fails to take the nature of religion into account. Religion is a belief system—but a belief system that is practiced. Since one's beliefs inform one's practice, to interfere with the practice is to interfere with the beliefs. This is especially true when one believes that violation of a clearly taught dogma guarantees damnation. Religious freedom must include the freedom to practice one's religion.

Freedom of choice, expressed in autonomy or self-determination, is another important value. When the exercise of such a value is limited, the arguments for so doing must address real issues and be extremely compelling.

Complications multiply when those incompetent to make their own decisions refuse treatment. The major problem is who shall make the decision. One candidate is the physician, selected because of his or her medical expertise. Medical expertise, however, may have nothing to do with the patient's value system or interests, which must be the basis of the decision. The physician, while providing a necessary service, is not the best decision-maker. A second candidate is the next of kin, because they might best know the patient's values and might make decisions quite similar to those the incompetent would make. In the absence of next of kin, a legal guardian is a third alternative. He or she can identify interests appropriate to incompetents as a class and can solicit the views of others. Ultimately, however, the guardian must make the decision on a perception of the best interests of the incompetent as he or she understands them. A committee is the fourth alternative. This committee can do one of two things. It can make, or confirm, a prognosis on the basis of which treatment will or will not be terminated, or it can draw up criteria by which such a decision would be made. If the committee makes or confirms a prognosis, someone must still make the actual decision to terminate treatment. If the committee establishes criteria, it must first demonstrate its authority to do this and then justify these criteria as appropriate, since they may have no necessary relation to a patient's values and may be countermanded, indeed, by a guardian or next of kin. Such consequences are less than optimal. A fifth option is the court. The advantage of a court is that it provides a forum for discussing relevant arguments by all involved parties. But a problem with the court is that it is unclear why it should perform the function of the next of kin or guardian, even when a standard therapy is being discontinued. The resolution of such cases by the court seems to remove authority from a defined role of guardian and to weaken unnecessarily that role. It also creates a practical difficulty in that a decision may be delayed to the point that what is decided is moot. It may also turn what is essentially a family or private decision into a public issue. Thus the delegation of such decision-making authority to the court is not immediately apparent, nor is it clear how such a delegation would be an improvement over decisions made by the next of kin or guardian.

2. THE LEGAL ISSUES

Defining the constitutionally protected rights of the individual, and establishing standards and procedures for asserting those rights, are the major legal issues in death and dying, as they were in abortion. In the death and dying cases, however, there are jurisdictional differences, since, unlike the major abortion decisions, these cases were not decided by the United States Supreme Court. For example, the Massachusetts and New Jersey courts differ over the procedures necessary for establishing consent where an incompetent individual is involved. Agreeing that a guardian may, with some exceptions, assert the constitutional rights of his ward, the two courts look to different approaches for asserting those rights. The New Jersey Court in *Quinlan* accepts the objective or "reasonable person" test; it entrusts the decision on continuing artificial life support for Karen Quinlan to her guardian, her family, the attending doctors, and a hospital ethics committee. Rejecting this approach, the Massachusetts Court in *Saikewicz* favors a subjective test and applies the substituted judgment standard, in which the Court substitutes itself "as nearly as possible for the incompetent, and [acts] on the same motives and considerations as would have moved him." In *Osborne* the District of Columbia Court of Appeals decides that the patient is indeed competent; it accepts his decision to refuse a blood transfusion. If, however, the Court had relied on an objective test, Osborne's consent might have been viewed as incompetent, since in a similar situation a reasonable person presumably would have accepted treatment.

Nevertheless, similarities in these cases appear to outweigh the differences, especially respecting consititutional law. Aside from *Osborne*, which turned on the First Amendment right of religious freedom and came down before *Roe*, the decisive constitutional issue in death and dying is that of privacy, suggesting the significance of *Roe* in different medico-legal circumstances. In language much like that used by the New Jersey Court, the Massachusetts Court asserts that just as the constitutional guaranty of privacy "reaches out to protect the freedom of a woman to terminate pregnancy under certain conditions . . . , so it encompasses the right of a patient to preserve his or her right to privacy against unwanted infringements of bodily integrity in appropriate circumstances." Both courts locate the unwritten constitutional right of privacy in the penumbra of specific guarantees of the Bill of Rights "formed by emanations from those guarantees that help give them life and substance," not in the Due Process Clause of the Fourteenth Amendment as was the case in *Roe*.

The *Quinlan* and *Saikewicz* courts next examine the question of when the circumstances are appropriate for the exercise of this privacy right. Here, as in *Roe*, the discussion turns to state interests. Both courts weigh the right of an individual to refuse medical intervention or treatment against countervailing state interests—the preservation of life, the protection of the interests of innocent third parties, the prevention of suicide, and the maintenance of the ethical integrity of the medical profession. No state interest sufficient to counterbalance the patient's right to privacy and self-determination is found in the circumstances of either case. Having decided that Karen Quinlan's and Joseph Saikewicz's rights to privacy are entitled to enforcement, both courts thereby recognize that the right extends to the case of an incompetent, as well as a competent, subject.

Each court next addresses the problem of how the right to privacy of an incompetent person can be exercised, as discussed above. In the death and dying cases we learn that, under the law, consent must be "informed" in order to protect the "individual's interest in preserving the inviolability of his person" or his or her right to privacy.

In Re Osborne

District of Columbia Court of Appeals, 1972.
294 A.2d 372.

Before GALLAGHER, NEBEKER and YEAGLEY, Associate Judges.

NEBEKER, Associate Judge:

This is an appeal, expedited of necessity, from an order of Judge Bacon of the Superior Court refusing to appoint a guardian to give consent for the administration of a blood transfusion to a patient, a member of the Jehovah's Witnesses faith, who was receiving emergency treatment at a hospital. The case originated by the hospital's petition which was accompanied by an affidavit. After two hasty hearings, ably conducted by Judge Bacon—one in her home the night of the accident and the other the following day on a request for reconsideration—the case came on for emergency consideration by this court. We directed a third hearing at the bedside of the patient. Judge Bacon asked Lawrence Speiser, Esquire, to attend and represent the patient and his family. In the meantime, we listened to a tape recording of the second hearing. Immediately upon completion of the bedside hearing, we had portions of the transcript read to us over the telephone from the hospital. Counsel then returned to the court house and we heard argument on behalf of the hospital and the patient. We then affirmed Judge Bacon's order and indicated an opinion would follow.

The 34-year-old patient was admitted to the hospital with injuries and internal bleeding caused when a tree fell on him. As the need for whole blood became apparent, the patient refused to give his consent for the necessary transfusion. The patient's wife also refused the required consent. Both gave as reasons their religious beliefs which forbid infusion of whole blood into the body.

When the petition was brought to Judge Bacon's home the night of the accident, the patient's wife, brother, and grandfather were present. They stated the views of the patient and agreed with them, explaining that those views are based on strong religious convictions. The grandfather explained that the patient "wants to live very much. . . . He wants to live in the Bible's promised new world where life will never end. A few hours here would nowhere compare to everlasting life." His wife stated, "He told me he did not want blood—he did not care if he had to die."

Judge Bacon then correctly became concerned with the patient's capacity to make such a decision in light of his serious condition. She also recognized the possibility that the use of drugs might have impaired his judgment and ability for

143

choice. Counsel for the hospital advised that the patient, though receiving fluid by vein, was conscious when spoken to by a staff physician, knew what the doctor was saying, understood the consequences of his decision, and had with full understanding executed a statement refusing the recommended transfusion and releasing the hospital from liability.

Judge Bacon took note of a possible overriding state interest based on the fact that the patient had two young children. It was concluded, however, that the maturity of this lucid patient, his long-standing beliefs[1] and those of his family did not justify state intervention. At the hearing on the motion for reconsideration, it was revealed that a close family relationship existed which went beyond the immediate members, that the children would be well cared for, and that the family business would continue to supply material needs.

When the case was first presented to this court, we viewed it as unclear whether the patient would desire to continue his present physical life. We therefore directed the bedside hearing to develop that point without the exclusive use of what might be called hearsay statements. We also directed Judge Bacon to ask the patient whether he believed that he would be deprived of the opportunity for "everlasting life" if transfusion were ordered by the court. His response was, "Yes. In other words, it is between me and Jehovah; not the courts. . . . I'm willing to take my chances. My faith is that strong." He also stated, "I wish to live, but with no blood transfusions. Now, get that straight."

Judge Bacon was careful also to determine the extent, if any, of impairment of judgment or capacity for choice resulting from the use of drugs. She was informed that the patient was not then under the influence of any medication having such possible or usual side effects.

Further inquiry was then made of the patient's wife concerning the material and filial welfare of the two children. She responded:

> "My husband has a business and it will be turned over to me. And his brothers work for him, so it will be carried on. That is no problem. In fact, they are working on it right now. Business goes on.
> "As far as money-wise, everybody is all right. We have money saved up. Everything will be all right. If anything ever happens, I have a big enough family and the family is prepared to care for the children."

[1–3] In the past a few courts have considered whether to compel religiously rejected medical care. *See generally* Annot., 9 A.L.R.3d 1391 *et seq.* (1966). The issue is always whether there is sufficient state interest to override individual desires based on religious beliefs.[2] The degree of state interest justifying intrusion by court order has been viewed as "compelling". John F. Kennedy Memorial Hospital v. Heston, 58 N.J. 576, 279 A.2d 670, 674 (1971). As is most often the case, factual situations vary with the result reached. In some cases the patient is comatose and his religious views must be expressed by family members or friends. In other cases, like this one, the patient is fully capable of making the choice. That is one reason why we directed the bedside hearing. Whenever possible it is better for the judge to make a first-hand appraisal of the patient's personal desires and ability for rational choice. In this way the court can always know, to the extent possible, that the judgment is that of the individual concerned and not that of those who believe, however well-intentioned, that they speak for the person whose life is in the balance. Thus, where the patient is comatose, or suffering impairment of capacity for choice, it may be better to give weight to the known instinct for survival which can, in a critical situation, alter previously held convictions. In such cases it cannot be determined with certainty that a deliberate and intelligent choice has been made.

Another circumstance which is often present in cases like this is the existence of children, whose lives, if yet unborn, are also at stake,[3] or whose welfare, as survivors, may be unclear. In those cases, it seems less difficult for courts to find sufficient state interest to intervene and circumvent religious convictions. But even then, it is important to note that courts may be more controlled by the interest of the surviving children when there is lack of clarity respecting first-hand knowledge that the patient's current choice is competently maintained.[4]

An additional consideration which impelled us to order the bedside hearing was doubt on the initial record whether the patient, if forced to undergo the blood transfusion, would consider himself blameless to the extent that his religious life would be unaffected. We therefore obtained knowledge of the patient's beliefs respecting his view of accountability to God should he have no choice in the matter. In United States v. George, 239 F.Supp. 752 (D. Conn.1965), the court was faced with a patient who took the view that if forced "[h]is 'conscience was clear', and the responsibility for the act was 'upon the court's conscience'. . . ." Id. at 753. The patient in George stated he would not resist a court-ordered blood transfusion. It seemed possible that the same view would be taken by this patient if he were questioned in the same way. However, he expressed the belief that he was accountable to God, in the sense of a loss of everlasting life, if he unwillingly received whole blood through transfusion.

[4] Thus Judge Bacon and this court were faced with a man who did not wish to live if to do so required a blood transfusion, who viewed himself as deprived of life everlasting even if he involuntarily received the transfusion, and who had, through material provision and family and spiritual bonds, provided for the future well-being of his two children. In reaching her decision, Judge Bacon necessarily resolved the two critical questions presented—(1) has the patient validly and knowingly chosen this course for his life, and (2) is there compelling state interest which justifies overriding that decision?[5] Based on this unique record, we have been unable to conclude that judicial intervention respecting the wishes and religious beliefs of the patient was warranted under our law. Judge Bacon's decision is supported by available evidence to the degree of certainty respecting the two basic questions.

[5] A further point is worthy of mention since cases of this nature are very apt to arise in the future. Counsel for the hospital ably and commendably represented the hospital in insuring that it and the hospital staff did all they reasonably could do within their power to save the patient's life by acceptable medical procedures. Such was not only a duty, but a laudatory goal. Judge Bacon, however, appeared to recognize a need for experienced and able counsel to make independent inquiry of the patient and to represent his interests before the court. This procedure should,

when possible, be followed in future cases of this nature. It is recognized that a proceeding like this lacks many of the characteristics of the usual adversary litigation. However, such counsel can, as is often done in criminal cases, make independent threshold observations respecting competence. He can also assist in determining facts respecting the welfare of survivors.

It was with commendable insight that Judge Bacon sought for the patient and his family the very able assistance of Mr. Speiser. We express to both counsel our appreciation for a most difficult and well-done job.[6]

The judgment previously entered shall stand as our judgment on mandate.

YEAGLEY, Associate Judge (concurring):

Although I concur in the court's opinion, I would add that the thrust of the opinion in my view, while based on the First Amendment, is not, despite footnote two, based solely on religious freedom, but also on the broader based freedom of choice whether founded on religious beliefs or otherwise.

NOTES

1. His father had died a few months before and the family had stood by the father's decision to refuse blood then. The wife said, "[W]e all made a decision similar to this."

2. No case has come to light where refusal of medical care was based on individual choice absent religious convictions.

3. That was the situation of John F. Kennedy Memorial Hosp. v. Heston, 58 N.J. 576, 279 A.2d 670 (1971).

4. Lack of current capacity to make a valid choice was a decisive factor for Judge Wright in Application of President & Directors of Georgetown College, Inc., 118 U.S.App.D.C. 80, 87, 331 F.2d 1000, 1007 (1964). It would seem to follow from Judge Wright's approach that those in a position to monitor a patient and authorize previously rejected medical care may be required to continuously update the patient's desires. But we are not here dealing with a case where deterioration of capacity for choice reaches a point where previous rejection of medical procedures may be deemed reasonably altered at a time when the life can still be saved.

5. It would be unnecessary to consider the first question if we were to take the view discussed by Judge Weintraub in John F. Kennedy Memorial Hosp. v. Heston, *supra* note 3, that the state must have a compelling interest in sustaining life. The notion that the individual exists for the good of the state is, of course, quite antithetical to our fundamental thesis that the role of the state is to ensure a maximum of individual freedom of choice and conduct.

6. We are also advised that the patient has recovered though his chances were very slim and that he has been discharged from the hospital.

IN RE QUINLAN

Supreme Court of New Jersey, 1976.
70 N.J. 10, 355 A.2d 647.

HUGHES, C. J.

THE LITIGATION

The central figure in this tragic case is Karen Ann Quinlan, a New Jersey resident. At the age of 22, she lies in a debilitated and allegedly moribund state at Saint Clare's Hospital in Denville, New Jersey. The litigation has to do, in final analysis, with her life—its continuance or cessation—and the responsibilities, rights and duties, with regard to any fateful decision concerning it, of her family, her guardian, her doctors, the hospital, the State through its law enforcement authorities, and finally the courts of justice.

The issues are before this Court following its direct certification of the action under the rule, R. 2:12–1, prior to hearing in the Superior Court, Appellate Division, to which the appellant (hereafter "plaintiff") Joseph Quinlan, Karen's father, had appealed the adverse judgment of the Chancery Division.

Due to extensive physical damage fully described in the able opinion of the trial judge, Judge Muir, supporting that judgment, Karen allegedly was incompetent. Joseph Quinlan sought the adjudication of that incompetency. He wished to be appointed guardian of the person and property of his daughter. It was proposed by him that such letters of guardianship, if granted, should contain an express power to him as guardian to authorize the discontinuance of all extraordinary medical procedures now allegedly sustaining Karen's vital processes and hence her life, since these measures, he asserted, present no hope of her eventual recovery. A guardian *ad litem* was appointed by Judge Muir to represent the interest of the alleged incompetent.

By a supplemental complaint, in view of the extraordinary nature of the relief sought by plaintiff and the involvement therein of their several rights and responsibilities, other parties were added. These included the treating physicians and the hospital, the relief sought being that they be restrained from interfering with the carrying out of any such extraordinary authorization in the event it were to be granted by the court. Joined, as well, was the Prosecutor of Morris County (he being charged with responsibility for enforcement of the criminal law), to enjoin him from interfering with, or projecting a criminal prosecution which otherwise might ensue in the event of, cessation of life in Karen resulting from the exercise of such extraordinary authorization were it to be granted to the guardian.

The Attorney General of New Jersey intervened as of right pursuant to R. 4:33–1 on behalf of the State of New Jersey, such intervention being recognized by the court in the pretrial conference order (R. 4:25–1 *et seq.*) of September 22, 1975. Its basis, of course, was the interest of the State in the preservation of life, which has an undoubted constitutional foundation.[1]

The matter is of transcendent importance, involving questions related to the definition and existence of death, the prolongation of life through artificial means developed by medical technology undreamed of in past generations of the practice of the healing arts;[2] the impact of such durationally indeterminate and artificial life prolongation on the rights of the incompetent, her family and society in general; the bearing of constitutional right and the scope of judicial responsibility, as to the appropriate response of an equity court of justice to the extraordinary prayer for relief of the plaintiff. Involved as well is the right of the plaintiff, Joseph Quinlan, to guardianship of the person of his daughter.

Among his "factual and legal contentions" under such Pretrial Order was the following:

I. Legal and Medical Death
    a. Under the existing legal and medical definitions of death recognized by the State of New Jersey, Karen Ann Quinlan is dead.

This contention, made in the context of Karen's profound and allegedly irreversible coma and physical debility, was discarded during trial by the following stipulated amendment to the Pretrial Order:

Under any legal standard recognized by the State of New Jersey and also under standard medical practice, Karen Ann Quinlan is presently alive.

Other amendments to the Pretrial Order made at the time of trial expanded the issues before the court. The Prosecutor of Morris County sought a declaratory judgment as to the effect any affirmation by the court of a right in a guardian to terminate life-sustaining procedures would have with regard to enforcement of the criminal laws of New Jersey with reference to homicide. Saint Clare's Hospital, in the face of trial testimony on the subject of "brain death," sought declaratory judgment as to:

Whether the use of the criteria developed and enunciated by the Ad Hoc Committee of the Harvard Medical School on or about August 5, 1968, as well as similar criteria, by a physician to assist in determination of the death of a patient whose cardiopulmonary functions are being artificially sustained, is in accordance with ordinary and standard medical practice.[3]

It was further stipulated during trial that Karen was indeed incompetent and guardianship was necessary, although there exists a dispute as to the determination later reached by the court that such guardianship should be bifurcated, and that

Mr. Quinlan should be appointed as guardian of the trivial property but not the person of his daughter.

After certification the Attorney General filed as of right (R. 2:3–4) a cross-appeal[3.1] challenging the action of the trial court in admitting evidence of prior statements made by Karen while competent as to her distaste for continuance of life by extraordinary medical procedures, under circumstances not unlike those of the present case. These quoted statements were made in the context of several conversations with regard to others terminally ill and being subjected to like heroic measures. The statements were advanced as evidence of what she would want done in such a contingency as now exists. She was said to have firmly evinced her wish, in like circumstances, not to have her life prolonged by the otherwise futile use of extraordinary means. Because we agree with the conception of the trial court that such statements, since they were remote and impersonal, lacked significant probative weight, it is not of consequence to our opinion that we decide whether or not they were admissible hearsay. Again, after certification, the guardian of the person of the incompetent (who had been appointed as a part of the judgment appealed from) resigned and was succeeded by another, but that too seems irrelevant to decision. It is, however, of interest to note the trial court's delineation (in its supplemental opinion of November 12, 1975) of the extent of the personal guardian's authority with respect to medical care of his ward:

> Mr. Coburn's appointment is designed to deal with those instances wherein Dr. Morse,[4] in the process of administering care and treatment to Karen Quinlan, feels there should be concurrence on the extent or nature of the care or treatment. If Mr. and Mrs. Quinlan are unable to give concurrence, then Mr. Coburn will be consulted for his concurrence.

Essentially then, appealing to the power of equity, and relying on claimed constitutional rights of free exercise of religion, of privacy and of protection against cruel and unusual punishment, Karen Quinlan's father sought judicial authority to withdraw the life-sustaining mechanisms temporarily preserving his daughter's life, and his appointment as guardian of her person to that end. His request was opposed by her doctors, the hospital, the Morris County Prosecutor, the State of New Jersey, and her guardian *ad litem.*

THE FACTUAL BASE

An understanding of the issues in their basic perspective suggests a brief review of the factual base developed in the testimony and documented in greater detail in the opinion of the trial judge. *In re Quinlan,* 137 N.J.Super. 227, 348 A.2d 801 (Ch.Div.1975).

On the night of April 15, 1975, for reasons still unclear, Karen Quinlan ceased breathing for at least two 15 minute periods. She received some ineffectual mouth-to-mouth resuscitation from friends. She was taken by ambulance to Newton Memorial Hospital. There she had a temperature of 100 degrees, her pupils were unreactive and she was unresponsive even to deep pain. The history at the time of her admission to that hospital was essentially incomplete and uninformative.

Three days later, Dr. Morse examined Karen at the request of the Newton admitting physician, Dr. McGee. He found her comatose with evidence of decortication, a condition relating to derangement of the cortex of the brain causing a physical posture in which the upper extremities are flexed and the lower extremities are extended. She required a respirator to assist her breathing. Dr. Morse was unable to obtain an adequate account of the circumstances and events leading up to Karen's admission to the Newton Hospital. Such initial history or etiology is crucial in neurological diagnosis. Relying as he did upon the Newton Memorial records and his own examination, he concluded that prolonged lack of oxygen in the bloodstream, anoxia, was identified with her condition as he saw it upon first observation. When she was later transferred to Saint Clare's Hospital she was still unconscious, still on a respirator and a tracheotomy had been performed. On her arrival Dr. Morse conducted extensive and detailed examinations. An electroencephalogram (EEG) measuring electrical rhythm of the brain was performed and Dr. Morse characterized the result as "abnormal but it showed some activity and was consistent with her clinical state." Other significant neurological tests, including a brain scan, an angiogram, and a lumbar puncture were normal in result. Dr. Morse testified that Karen has been in a state of coma, lack of consciousness, since he began treating her. He explained that there are basically two types of coma, sleep-like unresponsiveness and awake unresponsiveness. Karen was originally in a sleep-like unresponsive condition but soon developed "sleep-wake" cycles, apparently a normal improvement for comatose patients occurring within three to four weeks. In the awake cycle she blinks, cries out and does things of that sort but is still totally unaware of anyone or anything around her.

Dr. Morse and other expert physicians who examined her characterized Karen as being in a "chronic persistent vegetative state." Dr. Fred Plum, one of such expert witnesses, defined this as a "subject who remains with the capacity to maintain the vegetative parts of neurological function but who * * * no longer has any cognitive function."

Dr. Morse, as well as the several other medical and neurological experts who testified in this case, believed with certainty that Karen Quinlan is not "brain dead." They identified the Ad Hoc Committee of Harvard Medical School report (*infra*) as the ordinary medical standard for determining brain death, and all of them were satisfied that Karen met none of the criteria specified in that report and was therefore not "brain dead" within its contemplation.

In this respect it was indicated by Dr. Plum that the brain works in essentially two ways, the vegetative and the sapient. He testified:

> We have an internal vegetative regulation which controls body temperature which controls breathing, which controls to a considerable degree blood pressure, which controls to some degree heart rate, which controls chewing, swallowing and which controls sleeping and waking. We have a more highly developed brain which is uniquely human which controls our relation to the outside world, our capacity to talk, to see, to feel, to sing, to think.

Brain death necessarily must mean the death of both of these functions of the brain, vegetative and the sapient. Therefore, the presence of any function which is regulated or governed or controlled by the deeper parts of the brain which in laymen's terms might be considered purely vegetative would mean that the brain is not biologically dead.

Because Karen's neurological condition affects her respiratory ability (the respiratory system being a brain stem function) she requires a respirator to assist her breathing. From the time of her admission to Saint Clare's Hospital Karen has been assisted by an MA–1 respirator, a sophisticated machine which delivers a given volume of air at a certain rate and periodically provides a "sigh" volume, a relatively large measured volume of air designed to purge the lungs of excretions. Attempts to "wean" her from the respirator were unsuccessful and have been abandoned.

The experts believe that Karen cannot now survive without the assistance of the respirator; that exactly how long she would live without it is unknown; that the strong likelihood is that death would follow soon after its removal, and that removal would also risk further brain damage and would curtail the assistance the respirator presently provides in warding off infection.

It seemed to be the consensus not only of the treating physicians but also of the several qualified experts who testified in the case, that removal from the respirator would not conform to medical practices, standards and traditions.

The further medical consensus was that Karen in addition to being comatose is in a chronic and persistent "vegetative" state, having no awareness of anything or anyone around her and existing at a primitive reflex level. Although she does have some brain stem function (ineffective for respiration) and has other reactions one normally associates with being alive, such as moving, reacting to light, sound and noxious stimuli, blinking her eyes, and the like, the quality of her feeling impulses is unknown. She grimaces, makes stereotyped cries and sounds and has chewing motions. Her blood pressure is normal.

Karen remains in the intensive care unit at Saint Clare's Hospital, receiving 24-hour care by a team of four nurses characterized, as was the medical attention, as "excellent." She is nourished by feeding by way of a nasal-gastro tube and is routinely examined for infection, which under these circumstances is a serious life threat. The result is that her condition is considered remarkable under the unhappy circumstances involved.

Karen is described as emaciated, having suffered a weight loss of at least 40 pounds, and undergoing a continuing deteriorative process. Her posture is described as fetal-like and grotesque; there is extreme flexion-rigidity of the arms, legs and related muscles and her joints are severely rigid and deformed.

From all of this evidence, and including the whole testimonial record, several basic findings in the physical area are mandated. Severe brain and associated damage, albeit of uncertain etiology, has left Karen in a chronic and persistent vegetative state. No form of treatment which can cure or improve that condition is known or available. As nearly as may be determined, considering the guarded area of remote uncertainties characteristic of most medical science predictions, she can *never* be restored to cognitive or sapient life. Even with regard to the vegetative level and improvement therein (if such it may be called) the prognosis is extremely poor and the extent unknown if it should in fact occur.

She is debilitated and moribund and although fairly stable at the time of argument before us (no new information having been filed in the meanwhile in expansion of the record), no physician risked the opinion that she could live more than a year and indeed she may die much earlier. Excellent medical and nursing care so far has been able to ward off the constant threat of infection, to which she is peculiarly susceptible because of the respirator, the tracheal tube and other incidents of care in her vulnerable condition. Her life accordingly is sustained by the respirator and tubal feeding, and removal from the respirator would cause her death soon, although the time cannot be stated with more precision.

The determination of the fact and time of death in past years of medical science was keyed to the action of the heart and blood circulation, in turn dependent upon pulmonary activity, and hence cessation of these functions spelled out the reality of death.[5]

Developments in medical technology have obfuscated the use of the traditional definition of death. Efforts have been made to define irreversible coma as a new criterion for death, such as by the 1968 report of the Ad Hoc Committee of the Harvard Medical School (the Committee comprising ten physicians, an historian, a lawyer and a theologian), which asserted that:

> From ancient times down to the recent past it was clear that, when the respiration and heart stopped, the brain would die in a few minutes; so the obvious criterion of no heart beat as synonymous with death was sufficiently accurate. In those times the heart was considered to be the central organ of the body; it is not suprising that its failure marked the onset of death. This is no longer valid when modern resuscitative and supportive measures are used. These improved activities can now restore "life" as judged by the ancient standards of persistent respiration and continuing heart beat. This can be the case even when there is not the remotest possibility of an individual recovering consciousness following massive brain damage. ["A Definition of Irreversible Coma," 205 J.A.M.A. 337,339 (1968)]

The Ad Hoc standards, carefully delineated, included absence of response to pain or other stimuli, pupilary reflexes, corneal, pharyngeal and other reflexes, blood pressure, spontaneous respiration, as well as "flat" or isoelectric electroencephalograms and the like, with all tests repeated "at least 24 hours later with no change." In such circumstances, where all of such criteria have been met as showing "brain death," the Committee recommends with regard to the respirator:

> The patient's condition can be determined only by a physician. When the patient is hopelessly damaged as defined above, the family and all colleagues who have participated in major decisions concerning the patient, and all nurses involved, should be so informed. Death is to be declared and *then* the respirator turned off. The decision to do this and the responsibility

for it are to be taken by the physician-in-charge, in consultation with one or more physicians who have been directly involved in the case. It is unsound and undesirable to force the family to make the decision. [205 J.A.M.A., *supra* at 338 (emphasis in original)].

But, as indicated, it was the consensus of medical testimony in the instant case that Karen, for all her disability, met none of these criteria, nor indeed any comparable criteria extant in the medical world and representing, as does the Ad Hoc Committee report, according to the testimony in this case, prevailing and accepted medical standards.

We have adverted to the "brain death" concept and Karen's diassociation with any of its criteria, to emphasize the basis of the medical decision made by Dr. Morse. When plaintiff and his family, finally reconciled to the certainty of Karen's impending death, requested the withdrawal of life support mechanisms, he demurred. His refusal was based upon his conception of medical standards, practice and ethics described in the medical testimony, such as in the evidence given by another neurologist, Dr. Sidney Diamond, a witness for the State. Dr. Diamond asserted that no physician would have failed to provide respirator support at the outset, and none would interrupt its life-saving course thereafter, except in the case of cerebral death. In the latter case, he thought the respirator would in effect be disconnected from one already dead, entitling the physician under medical standards and, he thought, legal concepts, to terminate the supportive measures. We note Dr. Diamond's distinction of major surgical or transfusion procedures in a terminal case not involving cerebral death, such as here:

> The subject has lost human qualities. It would be incredible, and I think unlikely, that any physician would respond to a sudden hemorrhage, massive hemorrhage or a loss of all her defensive blood cells, by giving her large quantities of blood. I think that * * * major surgical procedures would be out of the question even if they were known to be essential for continued physical existence.

This distinction is adverted to also in the testimony of Dr. Julius Korein, a neurologist called by plaintiff. Dr. Korein described a medical practice concept of "judicious neglect" under which the physician will say:

> Don't treat this patient anymore, * * * it does not serve either the patient, the family, or society in any meaningful way to continue treatment with this patient.

Dr. Korein also told of the unwritten and unspoken standard of medical practice implied in the foreboding initials DNR (do not resuscitate), as applied to the extraordinary terminal case:

> Cancer, metastatic cancer, involving the lungs, the liver, the brain, multiple involvements, the physician may or may not write: Do not resuscitate. * * *

[I]t could be said to the nurse: if this man stops breathing don't resuscitate him. * * * No physician that I know personally is going to try and resuscitate a man riddled with cancer and in agony and he stops breathing. They are not going to put him on a respirator. * * * I think that would be the height of misuse of technology.

While the thread of logic in such distinctions may be elusive to the non-medical lay mind, in relation to the supposed imperative to sustain life at all costs, they nevertheless relate to medical decisions, such as the decision of Dr. Morse in the present case. We agree with the trial court that that decision was in accord with Dr. Morse's conception of medical standards and practice.

We turn to that branch of the factual case pertaining to the application for guardianship, as distinguished from the nature of the authorization sought by the applicant. The character and general suitability of Joseph Quinlan as guardian for his daughter, in ordinary circumstances, could not be doubted. The record bespeaks the high degree of familial love which pervaded the home of Joseph Quinlan and reached out fully to embrace Karen, although she was living elsewhere at the time of her collapse. The proofs showed him to be deeply religious, imbued with a morality so sensitive that months of tortured indecision preceded his belated conclusion (despite earlier moral judgments reached by the other family members, but unexpressed to him in order not to influence him) to seek the termination of life-supportive measures sustaining Karen. A communicant of the Roman Catholic Church, as were other family members, he first sought solace in private prayer looking with confidence, as he says, to the Creator, first for the recovery of Karen and then, if that were not possible, for guidance with respect to the awesome decision confronting him.

[1] To confirm the moral rightness of the decision he was about to make he consulted with his parish priest and later with the Catholic chaplain of Saint Clare's Hospital. He would not, he testified, have sought termination if that act were to be morally wrong or in conflict with the tenets of the religion he so profoundly respects. He was disabused of doubt, however, when the position of the Roman Catholic Church was made known to him as it is reflected in the record in this case. While it is not usual for matters of religious dogma or concepts to enter a civil litigation (except as they may bear upon constitutional right, or sometimes, familial matters; cf. In re Adoption of E, 59 N.J. 36, 279 A.2d 785 [1971]), they were rightly admitted in evidence here. The judge was bound to measure the character and motivations in all respects of Joseph Quinlan as prospective guardian; and insofar as these religious matters bore upon them, they were properly scrutinized and considered by the court.

Thus germane, we note the position of that Church as illuminated by the record before us. We have no reason to believe that it would be at all discordant with the whole of Judeo-Christian tradition, considering its central respect and reverence for the sanctity of human life. It was in this sense of relevance that we admitted as amicus curiae the New Jersey Catholic Conference, essentially the spokesman for the various Catholic bishops of New Jersey, organized to give witness to spiritual values in public affairs in the statewide community. The position statement of Bishop Lawrence B. Casey, reproduced in the *amicus* brief, projects these views:

(a) The verification of the fact of death in a particular case cannot be deduced from any religious or moral principle and, under this aspect, does not fall within the competence of the Church—that dependence must be had upon traditional and medical standards, and by these standards Karen Ann Quinlan is assumed to be alive.

(b) The request of plaintiff for authority to terminate a medical procedure characterized as "an extraordinary means of treatment" would not involve euthanasia. This upon the reasoning expressed by Pope Pius XII in his "allocutio" (address) to anesthesiologists on November 24, 1957, when he dealt with the question:

Does the anesthesiologist have the right, or is he bound, in all cases of deep unconsciousness, even in those that are completely hopeless in the opinion of the competent doctor, to use modern artificial respiration apparatus, even against the will of the family?

His answer made the following points:

1. In ordinary cases the doctor has the right to act in this manner, but is not bound to do so unless this is the only way of fulfilling another certain moral duty.

2. The doctor, however, has no right independent of the patient. He can act only if the patient explicitly or implicitly, directly or indirectly gives him the permission.

3. The treatment as described in the question constitutes extraordinary means of preserving life and so there is no obligation to use them nor to give the doctor permission to use them.

4. The rights and the duties of the family depend on the presumed will of the unconscious patient if he or she is of legal age, and the family, too, is bound to use only ordinary means.

5. This case is not to be considered euthanasia in any way; that would never be licit. The interruption of attempts at resuscitation, even when it causes the arrest of circulation, is not more than an indirect cause of the cessation of life, and we must apply in this case the principle of double effect.

So it was that the Bishop Casey statement validated the decision of Joseph Quinlan:

Competent medical testimony has established that Karen Ann Quinlan has no reasonable hope of recovery from her comatose state by the use of any available medical procedures. The continuance of mechanical (cardiorespiratory) supportive measures to sustain continuation of her body functions and her life constitute extraordinary means of treatment. *Therefore, the decision of Joseph * * * Quinlan to request the discontinuance of this treatment* *is, according to the teachings of the Catholic Church, a morally correct decision.* (emphasis in original)

And the mind and purpose of the intending guardian were undoubtedly influenced by factors included in the following reference to the interrelationship of the three disciplines of theology, law and medicine as exposed in the Casey statement:

> The right to a natural death is one outstanding area in which the disciplines of theology, medicine and law overlap; or, to put it another way, it is an area in which these three disciplines convene.
>
> Medicine with its combination of advanced technology and professional ethics is both able and inclined to prolong biological life. Law with its felt obligation to protect the life and freedom of the individual seeks to assure each person's right to live out his human life until its natural and inevitable conclusion. Theology with its acknowlegement of man's dissatisfaction with biological life as the ultimate source of joy * * * defends the sacredness of human life and defends it from all direct attacks.
>
> These disciplines do not conflict with one another, but are necessarily conjoined in the application of their principles in a particular instance such as that of Karen Ann Quinlan. Each must in some way acknowledge the other without denying its own competence. The civil law is not expected to assert a belief in eternal life; nor, on the other hand, is it expected to ignore the right of the individual to profess it, and to form and pursue his conscience in accord with that belief. Medical science is not authorized to directly cause natural death; nor, however, is it expected to prevent it when it is inevitable and all hope of a return to an even partial exercise of human life is irreparably lost. Religion is not expected to define biological death; nor, on its part, is it expected to relinquish its responsibility to assist man in the formation and pursuit of a correct conscience as to the acceptance of natural death when science has confirmed its inevitability beyond any hope other than that of preserving biological life in a merely vegetative state.

And the gap in the law is aptly described in the Bishop Casey statement:

> In the present public discussion of the case of Karen Ann Quinlan it has been brought out that responsible people involved in medical care, patients and families have exercised the freedom to terminate or withhold certain treatments as extraordinary means in cases judged to be terminal, i.e., cases which hold no realistic hope for some recovery, in accord with the expressed or implied intentions of the patients themselves. To whatever extent this has been happening it has been without sanction in civil law. Those involved in such actions, however, have ethical and theological literature to guide them in their judgments and actions. Furthermore, such actions have not in themselves undermined society's reverence for the lives of sick and dying people.

It is both possible and necessary for society to have laws and ethical standards which provide freedom for decisions, in accord with the expressed or implied intentions of the patient, to terminate or withhold extraordinary treatment in cases which are judged to be hopeless by competent medical authorities, without at the same time leaving an opening for euthanasia. Indeed, to accomplish this, it may simply be required that courts and legislative bodies recognize the present standards and practices of many people engaged in medical care who have been doing what the parents of Karen Ann Quinlan are requesting authorization to have done for their beloved daughter.

Before turning to the legal and constitutional issues involved, we feel it essential to reiterate that the "Catholic view" of religious neutrality in the circumstances of this case is considered by the Court only in the aspect of its impact upon the conscience, motivation and purpose of the intending guardian, Joseph Quinlan, and not as a precedent in terms of the civil law.

If Joseph Quinlan, for instance, were a follower and strongly influenced by the teachings of Buddha, or if, as an agnostic or atheist, his moral judgments were formed without reference to religious feelings, but were nevertheless formed and viable, we would with equal attention and high respect consider these elements, as bearing upon his character, motivations and purposes as relevant to his qualification and suitability as guardian.

It is from this factual base that the Court confronts and responds to three basic issues:

1. Was the trial court correct in denying the specific relief requested by plaintiff, *i.e.,* authorization for termination of the life-supporting apparatus, on the case presented to him? Our determination on that question is in the affirmative.

2. Was the court correct in withholding letters of guardianship from the plaintiff and appointing in his stead a stranger? On that issue our determination is in the negative.

3. Should this Court, in the light of the foregoing conclusions, grant declaratory relief to the plaintiff? On that question our Court's determination is in the affirmative.

This brings us to a consideration of the constitutional and legal issues underlying the foregoing determinations.

CONSTITUTIONAL AND LEGAL ISSUES

At the outset we note the dual role in which plaintiff comes before the Court. He not only raises, derivatively, what he perceives to be the constitutional and legal rights of his daughter Karen, but he also claims certain rights independently as per parent.

[2, 3] Although generally litigant may assert only his own constitutional rights, we have no doubt that plaintiff has sufficient standing to advance both positions.

[4, 5] While no express constitutional language limits judicial activity to cases and controversies, New Jersey courts will not render advisory opinions or entertain proceedings by plaintiffs who do not have sufficient legal standing to maintain their actions. *Walker v. Stanhope*, 23 N.J. 657, 660, 130 A.2d 372 (1957). However, as in this case, New Jersey courts commonly grant declaratory relief. Declaratory Judgments Act, N.J.S.A. 2A:16–50 *et seq.* And our courts hold that where the plaintiff is not simply an interloper and the proceeding serves the public interest, standing will be found. *Walker v. Stanhope, supra,* 23 N.J. at 661–66, 130 A.2d 372; *Koons v. Atlantic City Bd. of Comm'rs,* 134 N.J.L. 329, 338–39, 47 A.2d 589 (Sup.Ct.1946), *aff'd,* 135 N.J.L. 204, 50 A.2d 869 (E. & A. 1947). In *Crescent Park Tenants Ass'n v. Realty Equities Corp.,* 58 N.J. 98, 275 A.2d 433 (1971), Justice Jacobs said:

> * * * [W]e have appropriately confined litigation to those situations where the litigant's concern with the subject matter evidenced a sufficient stake and real adverseness. In the overall we have given due weight to the interests of individual justice, along with the public interest, always bearing in mind that throughout our law we have been sweepingly rejecting procedural frustrations in favor of "just and expeditious determinations on the ultimate merits." [58 N.J. at 107–08, 275 A.2d at 438 (quoting from *Tumarkin v. Friedman,* 17 N.J.Super. 20, 21, 85 A.2d 304 (App.Div.1951), certif. den., 9 N.J. 287, 88 A.2d 39 (1952))].

The father of Karen Quinlan is certainly no stranger to the present controversy. His interests are real and adverse and he raises questions of surpassing importance. Manifestly, he has standing to assert his daughter's constitutional rights, she being incompetent to do so.

I. THE FREE EXERCISE OF RELIGION

We think the contention as to interference with religious beliefs or rights may be considered and dealt with without extended discussion, given the acceptance of distinctions so clear and simple in their precedential definition as to be dispositive on their face.

[6] Simply stated, the right to religious beliefs is absolute but conduct in pursuance thereof is not wholly immune from governmental restraint. *John F. Kennedy Memorial Hosp. v. Heston,* 58 N.J. 576, 580–81, 279 A.2d 670 (1971). So it is that, for the sake of life, courts sometimes (but not always) order blood transfusions for Jehovah's Witnesses (whose religious beliefs abhor such procedure), *Application of President & Directors of Georgetown College, Inc.* 118 U.S.App.D.C. 80, 331 F.2d 1000 (D.C.Cir.), *cert.* den., 377 U.S. 978, 84 S.Ct. 1883, 12 L.Ed.2d 746 (1964); *United States v. George,* 239 F.Supp. 752 (D. Conn.1965); *John F. Kennedy Memorial Hosp. v. Heston, supra; Powell v. Columbian Presbyterian Medical Cen-*

ter, 49 Misc.2d, 215, 267 N.Y.S.2d 450 (Sup.Ct. 1965); *but see In re Osborne,* 294 A.2d 372 (D.C.Ct.App.1972); *In re Estate of Brooks,* 32 Ill.2d 361, 205 N.E.2d 435 (Sup.Ct.1965); *Erickson v. Dilgard,* 44 Misc.2d 27, 252 N.Y.S.2d 705 (Sup.Ct. 1962); *see generally* Annot., "Power Of Courts Or Other Public Agencies, In the Absence of Statutory Authority, To Order Compulsory Medical Care for Adult," 9 A.L.R.3d 1391 (1966); forbid exposure to death from handling virulent snakes or ingesting poison (interfering with deeply held religious sentiments in such regard), *e.g., Hill v. State,* 38 Aa.App. 404, 88 So.2d 880 (Ct.App.), *cert.* den., 264 Ala. 697, 88 So. 2d 887 (Sup.Ct.1956); *State v. Massey,* 229 N.C. 734, 51 S.E.2d 179 (Sup. Ct.), appeal dismissed *sub nom., Bunn v. North Carolina,* 336 U.S. 942, 69 S.Ct. 813, 93 L.Ed. 1099 (1949); *State ex rel. Swann v. Pack,* Tenn., 527 S.W.2d 99 (Sup.Ct. 1975), *cert.* den., _____ U.S. _____, 96 S.Ct. 1429, 46 L.Ed.2d 360, 44 U.S.L.W. 3498, No. 75–956 (March 8, 1976); and protect the public health as in the case of compulsory vaccination (over the strongest of religious objections), *e.g., Wright v. DeWitt School Dist. 1,* 238 Ark. 906, 385 S.W.2d 644 (Sup.Ct.1965); *Mountain Lakes Bd. of Educ. v. Maas,* 56 N.J. Super. 245, 152 A.2d 394 (App. Div. 1959), *aff'd* o. b., 31 N.J. 537, 158 A.2d 330 (1960), *cert.* den., 363 U.S. 843, 80 S.Ct. 1613, 4 L.Ed.2d 1727 (1960); *McCartney v. Austin,* 57 Misc.2d 525, 293 N.Y.S.2d 188 (Sup.Ct.1968). The public interest is thus considered paramount, without essential dissolution of respect for religious beliefs.

[7,8] We think, without further examples, that, ranged against the State's interest in the preservation of life, the impingement of religious belief, much less religious "neutrality" as here, does not reflect a constitutional question, in the circumstances at least of the case presently before the Court. Moreover, like the trial court, we do not recognize an independent parental right of religious freedom to support the relief requested. 137 N.J.Super. at 267–68, 348 A.2d 801.

II. CRUEL AND UNUSUAL PUNISHMENT

[9] Similarly inapplicable to the case before us is the Constitution's Eighth Amendment protection against cruel and unusual punishment which, as held by the trial court, is not relevant to situations other than the imposition of penal sanctions. Historic in nature, it stemmed from punitive excesses in the infliction of criminal penalties.[6] We find no precedent in law which would justify its extension to the correction of social injustice or hardship, such as, for instance, in the case of poverty. The latter often condemns the poor and deprived to horrendous living conditions which could certainly be described in the abstract as "cruel and unusual punishment." Yet the constitutional base of protection from "cruel and unusual punishment" is plainly irrelevant to such societal ills which must be remedied, if at all, under other concepts of constitutional and civil right.

[10] So it is in the case of the unfortunate Karen Quinlan. Neither the State, nor the law, but the accident of fate and nature, has inflicted upon her conditions which though in essence cruel and most unusual, yet do not amount to "punishment" in any constitutional sense.

Neither the judgment of the court below, nor the medical decision which confronted it, nor the law and equity perceptions which impelled its action, nor the whole factual base upon which it was predicated, inflicted "cruel and unusual pun-ishment" in the constitutional sense.

III. THE RIGHT OF PRIVACY[7]

It is the issue of the constitutional right of privacy that has given us most concern, in the exceptional circumstances of this case. Here a loving parent, *qua* parent and raising the rights of his incompetent and profoundly damaged daughter, probably irreversibly doomed to no more than a biologically vegetative remnant of life, is before the court. He seeks authorization to abandon specialized technological procedures which can only maintain for a time a body having no potential for resumption or continuance of other than a "vegetative" existence.

We have no doubt, in these unhappy circumstances, that if Karen were herself miraculously lucid for an interval (not altering the existing prognosis of the condition to which she would soon return) and perceptive of her irreversible condition, she could effectively decide upon discontinuance of the life-support apparatus, even if it meant the prospect of natural death. To this extent we may distinguish *Heston, supra,* which concerned a severely injured young woman (Delores Heston), whose life depended on surgery and blood transfusion; and who was in such extreme shock that she was unable to express an informed choice (although the Court apparently considered the case as if the patient's own religious decision to resist transfusion were at stake), but most importantly a patient apparently salvable to long life and vibrant health—a situation not at all like the present case.

We have no hesitancy in deciding, in the instant diametrically opposite case, that no external compelling interest of the State could compel Karen to endure the unendurable, only to vegetate a few measurable months with no realistic possibility of returning to any semblance of cognitive or sapient life. We perceive no thread of logic distinguishing between such a choice on Karen's part and a similar choice which, under the evidence in this case, could be made by a competent patient terminally ill, riddled by cancer and suffering great pain; such a patient would not be resuscitated or put on a respirator in the example described by Dr. Korein, and *a fortiori* would not be kept *against his will* on a respirator.

Although the Constitution does not explicitly mention a right of privacy, Supreme Court decisions have recognized that a right of personal privacy exists and that certain areas of privacy are guaranteed under the Constitution. *Eisenstadt v. Baird,* 405 U.S. 438, 92 S. Ct. 1029, 31 L. Ed.2d 349 (1972); *Stanley v. Georgia,* 394 U.S. 557, 89 S. Ct. 1243, 22 L.Ed.2d 542 (1969). The Court has interdicted judicial intrusion into many aspects of personal decision, sometimes basing this restraint upon the conception of a limitation of judicial interest and responsibility, such as with regard to contraception and its relationship to family life and decision. *Griswold v. Connecticut,* 381 U.S. 479, 85 S.Ct. 1678, 14 L.Ed.2d 510 (1965).

[11] The Court in *Griswold* found the unwritten constitutional right of privacy to exist in the penumbra of specific guarantees of the Bill of Rights "formed by emanations from those guarantees that help give them life and substance." 381 U.S. at 484, 85 S.Ct. at 1681, 14 L.Ed.2d at 514. Presumably this right is broad

enough to encompass a patient's decision to decline medical treatment under certain circumstances, in much the same way as it is broad enough to encompass a woman's decision to terminate pregnancy under certain conditions. *Roe v. Wade,* 410 U.S. 113, 153, 93 S.Ct. 705, 727, 35 L.Ed.2d 147, 177 (1973).

Nor is such right of privacy forgotten in the New Jersey Constitution. N.J.Const. (1947), Art. I, par. 1.

[12] The claimed interests of the State in this case are essentially the preservation and sanctity of human life and defense of the right of the physician to administer medical treatment according to his best judgment. In this case the doctors say that removing Karen from the respirator will conflict with their professional judgment. The plaintiff answers that Karen's present treatment serves only a maintenance function; that the respirator cannot cure or improve her condition but at best can only prolong her inevitable slow deterioration and death; and that the interests of the patient, as seen by her surrogate, the guardian, must be evaluated by the court as predominant, even in the face of an opinion *contra* by the present attending physicians. Plaintiff's distinction is significant. The nature of Karen's care and the realistic chances of her recovery are quite unlike those of the patients discussed in many of the cases where treatments were ordered. In many of those cases the medical procedure required (usually a transfusion) constituted a minimal bodily invasion and the chances of recovery and return to functioning life were very good. We think that the State's interest *contra* weakens and the individual's right to privacy grows as the degree of bodily invasion increases and the prognosis dims. Ultimately there comes a point at which the individual's rights overcome the State's interest. It is for that reason that we believe Karen's choice, if she were competent to make it, would be vindicated by the law. Her prognosis is extremely poor—she will never resume cognitive life. And the bodily invasion is very great—she requires 24 hour intensive nursing care, antibiotics, the assistance of a respirator, a catheter and feeding tube.

[13] Our affirmation of Karen's independent right of choice, however, would ordinarily be based upon her competency to assert it. The sad truth, however, is that she is grossly incompetent and we cannot discern her supposed choice based on the testimony of her previous conversations with friends, where such testimony is without sufficient probative weight. 137 N.J. Super. at 260, 348 A.2d 801. Nevertheless we have concluded that Karen's right of privacy may be asserted on her behalf by her guardian under the peculiar circumstances here present.

If a putative decision by Karen to permit this non-cognitive, vegetative existence to terminate by natural forces is regarded as a valuable incident of her right of privacy, as we believe it to be, then it should not be discarded solely on the basis that her condition prevents her conscious exercise of the choice. The only practical way to prevent destruction of the right is to permit the guardian and family of Karen to render their best judgment, subject to the qualifications hereinafter stated, as to whether she would exercise it in these circumstances. If their conclusion is in the affirmative this decision should be accepted by a society the overwhelming majority of whose members would, we think, in similar circumstances, exercise such a choice in the same way for themselves or for those closest to them. It is for this reason that we determine that Karen's right of privacy may be asserted in her behalf, in this respect, by her guardian and family under the particular circumstances presented by this record.

[14] Regarding Mr. Quinlan's right of privacy, we agree with Judge Muir's conclusion that there is no parental constitutional right that would entitle him to a grant of relief *in propria persona. Id.* at 266, 348 A2d 801. Insofar as a parental right of privacy has been recognized, it has been in the context of determining the rearing of infants and, as Judge Muir put it, involved "continuing life styles." *See Wisconsin v. Yoder,* 406 U.S. 205, 92 S.Ct.1526, 32 L.Ed.2d 15 (1972); *Pierce v. Society of Sisters,* 268 U.S. 510, 45 S.Ct. 571, 69 L.Ed. 1070 (1925); *Meyer v. Nebraska,* 262 U.S. 390, 43 S.Ct. 625, 67 L.Ed. 1042 (1923). Karen Quinlan is a 22 year old adult. Her right of privacy in respect of the matter before the Court is to be vindicated by Mr. Quinlan as guardian, as hereinabove determined.

IV. THE MEDICAL FACTOR

Having declared the substantive legal basis upon which plaintiff's rights as representative of Karen must be deemed predicated, we face and respond to the assertion on behalf of defendants that our premise unwarrantably offends prevailing medical standards. We thus turn to consideration of the medical decision supporting the determination made below, conscious of the paucity of pre-existing legislative and judicial guidance as to the rights and liabilities therein involved.

> A significant problem in any discussion of sensitive medical-legal issues is the marked, perhaps unconscious, tendency of many to distort what the law is, in pursuit of an exposition of what they would like the law to be. Nowhere is this barrier to the intelligent resolution of legal controversies more obstructive than in the debate over patient rights at the end of life. Judicial refusals to order lifesaving treatment in the face of contrary claims of bodily self-determination or free religious exercise are too often cited in support of a preconceived "right to die," even though the patients, wanting to live, have claimed no such right. Conversely, the assertion of a religious or other objection to lifesaving treatment is at times condemned as attempted suicide, even though suicide means something quite different in the law. [Byrn, "Compulsory Lifesaving Treatment For The Competent Adult," 44 Fordham L. Rev. 1 (1975)]

Perhaps the confusion there adverted to stems from mention by some courts of statutory or common law condemnation of suicide as demonstrating the state's interest in the preservation of life. We would see, however, a real distinction between the self-infliction of deadly harm and a self-determination against artificial life support or radical surgery, for instance, in the face of irreversible, painful and certain imminent death. The contrasting situations mentioned are analogous to those continually faced by the medical profession. When does the institution of life-sustaining procedures, ordinarily mandatory, become the subject of medical discretion in the context of administration to persons *in extremis?* And when does the withdrawal of such procedures, from such persons already supported by them, come within the orbit of medical discretion? When does a determination as to either of the foregoing contingencies court the hazard of civil or criminal liability on the part of the physician or institution involved?

The existence and nature of the medical dilemma need hardly be discussed at length, portrayed as it is in the present case and complicated as it has recently come to be in view of the dramatic advance of medical technology. The dilemma is there, it is real, it is constantly resolved in accepted medical practice without attention in the courts, it pervades the issues in the very case we here examine. The branch of the dilemma involving the doctor's responsibility and the relationship of the court's duty was thus conceived by Judge Muir:

> Doctors * * * to treat a patient, must deal with medical tradition and past case histories. They must be guided by what they do know. The extent of their training, their experience, consultation with other physicians, must guide their decision-making processes in providing care to their patient. The nature, extent and duration of care by societal standards is the responsibility of a physician. The morality and conscience of our society places this responsibility in the hands of the physician. What justification is there to remove it from the control of the medical profession and place it in the hands of the courts? [137 N.J.Super. at 259, 348 A.2d at 818].

[15] Such notions as to the distribution of responsibility, heretofore generally entertained, should however neither impede this Court in deciding matters clearly justiciable nor preclude a re-examination by the Court as to underlying human values and rights. Determinations as to these must, in the ultimate, be responsive not only to the concepts of medicine but also the the common moral judgment of the community at large. In the latter respect the Court has a nondelegable judicial responsibility.

Put in another way, the law, equity and justice must not themselves quail and be helpless in the face of modern technological marvels presenting questions hitherto unthought of. Where a Karen Quinlan, or a parent, or a doctor, or a hospital, or a State seeks the process and response of a court, it must answer with its most informed conception of justice in the previously unexplored circumstances presented to it. That is its obligation and we are here fulfilling it, for the actors and those having an interest in the matter should not go without remedy.

Courts in the exercise of their *parens patriae* responsibility to protect those under disability have sometimes implemented medical decisions and authorized their carrying out under the doctrine of "substituted judgment." *Hart v. Brown,* 29 Conn.Sup. 368, 289 A.2d 386, 387–88 (Super.Ct.1972); *Strunk v. Strunk,* 445 S.W. 2d 145, 147–48 (Ky.1969). For as Judge Muir pointed out:

> "As part of the inherent power of equity, a Court of Equity has full and complete jurisdiction over the persons of those who labor under any legal disability. * * * The Court's action in such a case is not limited by any narrow bounds, but it is empowered to stretch forth its arm in whatever direc-

tion its aid and protection may be needed. While this is indeed a special exercise of equity jurisdiction, it is beyond question that by virtue thereof the Court may pass upon purely personal rights." [137 N.J.Super. at 254, 348 A. 2d at 816 (quoting from *Am.Jur.*2d, Equity § 69 (1966))].

But insofar as a court, having no inherent medical expertise, is called upon to overrule a professional decision made according to prevailing medical practice and standards, a different question is presented. As mentioned below, a doctor is required

"to exercise in the treatment of his patient the degree of care, knowledge and skill ordinarily possessed and exercised in similar situations by the average member of the profession practicing in his field." *Schueler v. Strelinger,* 43 N.J. 330, 344, 204 A.2d 577, 584 (1964). If he is a specialist he "must employ not merely the skill of a general practitioner but also that special degree of skill normally possessed by the average physician who devotes special study and attention to the particular organ or disease or injury involved, having regard to the present state of scientific knowledge". *Clark v. Wichman,* 72 N.J.Super. 486, 493, 179 A.2d 38, 42 (App.Div.1962). This is the duty that establishes his legal obligations to his patients. [137 N.J.Super. at 257–58, 348 A.2d at 818].

The medical obligation is related to standards and practice prevailing in the profession. The physicians in charge of the case, as noted above, declined to withdraw the respirator. That decision was consistent with the proofs below as to the then existing medical standards and practices.

Under the law as it then stood, Judge Muir was correct in declining to authorize withdrawal of the respirator.

However, in relation to the matter of the declaratory relief sought by plaintiff as representative of Karen's interests, we are required to reevaluate the applicability of the medical standards projected in the court below. The question is whether there is such internal consistency and rationality in the application of such standards as should warrant their constituting an ineluctable bar to the effectuation of substantive relief for plaintiff at the hands of the court. We have concluded not.

In regard to the foregoing it is pertinent that we consider the impact on the standards both of the civil and criminal law as to medical liability and the new technological means of sustaining life irreversibly damaged.

The modern proliferation of substantial malpractice litigation and the less frequent but even more unnerving possibility of criminal sanctions would seem, for it is beyond human nature to suppose otherwise, to have bearing on the practice and standards as they exist. The brooding presence of such possible liability, it was testified here, had no part in the decision of the treating physicians. As did Judge Muir, we afford this testimony full credence. But we cannot believe that the stated factor has not had a strong influence on the standards, as the literature on the subject plainly reveals. (See footnote 8, *infra*.) Moreover our attention is drawn not so much to the recognition by Drs. Morse and Javed of the extant practice and standards but to the widening ambiguity of those standards themselves in their application to the medical problems we are discussing.

The agitation of the medical community in the face of modern life prolongation technology and its search for definitive policy are demonstrated in the large volume of relevant professional commentary.[8]

The wide debate thus reflected contrasts with the relative paucity of legislative and judicial guides and standards in the same field. The medical profession has sought to devise guidelines such as the "brain death" concept of the Harvard Ad Hoc Committee mentioned above. But it is perfectly apparent from the testimony we have quoted of Dr. Korein, and indeed so clear as almost to be judicially noticeable, that humane decisions against resuscitative or maintenance therapy are frequently a recognized *de facto* response in the medical world to the irreversible, terminal, pain-ridden patient, especially with familial consent. And these cases, of course, are far short of "brain death."

We glean from the record here that physicians distinguish between curing the ill and comforting and easing the dying; that they refuse to treat the curable as if they were dying or ought to die, and that they have sometimes refused to treat the hopeless and dying as if they were curable. In this sense, as we were reminded by the testimony of Drs. Korein and Diamond, many of them have refused to inflict an undesired prolongation of the process of dying on a patient in irreversible condition when it is clear that such "therapy" offers neither human nor humane benefit. We think these attitudes represent a balanced implementation of a profoundly realistic perspective on the meaning of life and death and that they respect the whole Judeo-Christian tradition of regard for human life. No less would they seem consistent with the moral matrix of medicine, "to heal," very much in the sense of the endless mission of the law, "to do justice."

Yet this balance, we feel, is particularly difficult to perceive and apply in the context of the development by advanced technology of sophisticated and artificial life sustaining devices. For those possibly curable, such devices are of great value, and, as ordinary medical procedures, are essential. Consequently, as pointed out by Dr. Diamond, they are necessary because of the ethic of medical practice. But in light of the situation in the present case (while the record here is somewhat hazy in distinguishing between "ordinary" and "extraordinary" measures), one would have to think that the use of the same respirator or like support could be considered "ordinary" in the context of the possibly curable patient but "extraordinary" in the context of the forced sustaining by cardio-respiratory processes of an irreversibly doomed patient. And this dilemma is sharpened in the face of the malpractice and criminal action threat which we have mentioned.

We would hesitate, in this imperfect world, to propose as to physicians that type of immunity which from the early common law has surrounded judges and grand jurors, *see e.g., Grove v. Van Duyn,* 44 N.J.L. 654, 656–57 (E & A.1882); *O'Regan v. Schermerhorn,* 25 N.J.Misc. 1, 19–20, 50A.2d 10 (Sup.Ct.1940), so that they might without fear of personal retaliation perform their judicial duties with independent objectivity. In *Bradley v. Fisher,* 80 U.S. (13 Wall.) 335, 347, 20 L.Ed. 646, 649 (1872), the Supreme Court held:

> [I]t is a general principle of the highest importance to the proper adminis-tration of justice that a judicial officer, in exercising the authority vested in him, shall be free to act upon his own convictions, without apprehension of personal consequences to himself.

Lord Coke said of judges that "they are only to make an account to God and the King [the State]." 12 Coke Rep. 23, 25, 77 Eng.Rep. 1305, 1307 (S.C. 1608).

Nevertheless, there must be a way to free physicians, in the pursuit of their healing vocation, from possible contamination by self-interest or self-protection concerns which would inhibit their independent medical judgments for the well-being of their dying patients. We would hope that this opinion might be serviceable to some degree in ameliorating the professional problems under discussion.

A technique aimed at the underlying difficulty (though in a somewhat broader context) is described by Dr. Karen Teel, a pediatrician and a director of Pediatric Education, who writes in the *Baylor Law Review* under the title "The Physician's Dilemma: A Doctor's View: What The Law Should Be." Dr. Teel recalls:

> Physicians, by virtue of their responsibility for medical judgments are, partly by choice and partly by default, charged with the responsibility of making ethical judgments which we are sometimes ill-equipped to make. We are not always morally and legally authorized to make them. The physi-cian is thereby assuming a civil and criminal liability that, as often as not, he does not even realize as a factor in his decision. There is little or no dia-logue in this whole process. The physician assumes that his judgment is called for and, in good faith, he acts. Someone must and it has been the phy-sician who has assumed the responsibility and the risk.
>
> I suggest that it would be more appropriate to provide a regular fo-rum for more input and dialogue in individual situations and to allow the responsibility of these judgments to be shared. Many hospitals have estab-lished an Ethics Committee composed of physicians, social workers, attor-neys, and theologians, * * * which serves to review the individual circumstances of ethical dilemma and which has provided much in the way of assistance and safeguards for patients and their medical caretakers. Gen-erally, the authority of these committees is primarily restricted to the hospi-tal setting and their official status is more that of an advisory body than of an enforcing body.
>
> The concept of an Ethics Committee which has this kind of organi-zation and is readily accessible to those persons rendering medical care to patients, would be, I think, the most promising direction for further study at this point. * * *

* * * [This would allow] some much needed dialogue regarding these issues and [force] the point of exploring all of the options for a particular patient. It diffuses the responsibility for making these judgments. Many physicians, in many circumstances, would welcome this sharing of responsibility. I believe that such an entity could lend itself well to an assumption of a legal status which would allow courses of action not now undertaken because of the concern for liability. [27 Baylor L.Rev. 6, 8–9 (1975)].

The most appealing factor in the technique suggested by Dr. Teel seems to us to be the diffusion of professional responsibility for decision, comparable in a way to the value of multi-judge courts in finally resolving on appeal difficult questions of law. Moreover, such a system would be protective to the hospital as well as the doctor in screening out, so to speak, a case which might be contaminated by less than worthy motivations of family or physician. In the real world and in relationship to the momentous decision contemplated, the value of additional views and diverse knowledge is apparent.

[16] We consider that a practice of applying to a court to confirm such decisions would generally be inappropriate, not only because that would be a gratuitous encroachment upon the medical profession's field of competence, but because it would be impossibly cumbersome. Such a requirement is distinguishable from the judicial overview traditionally required in other matters such as the adjudication and commitment of mental incompetents. This is not to say that in the case of an otherwise justiciable controversy access to the courts would be foreclosed; we speak rather of a general practice and procedure.

And although the deliberations and decisions which we describe would be professional in nature they should obviously include at some state the feelings of the family of an incompetent relative. Decision-making within health care if it is considered as an expression of a primary obligation of the physician, *primum non nocere,* should be controlled primarily within the patient-doctor-family relationship, as indeed was recognized by Judge Muir in his supplemental opinion of November 12, 1975.

If there could be created not necessarily this particular system but some reasonable counterpart, we would have no doubt that such decisions, thus determined to be in accordance with medical practice and prevailing standards, would be accepted by society and by the courts, at least in cases comparable to that of Karen Quinlan.

The evidence in this case convinces us that the focal point of decision should be the prognosis as to the reasonable possibility of return to cognitive and sapient life, as distinguished from the forced continuance of that biological vegetative existence to which Karen seems to be doomed.

[17] In summary of the present Point of this opinion, we conclude that the state of the pertinent medical standards and practices which guided the attending physicians in this matter is not such as would justify this Court in deeming itself bound or controlled thereby in responding to the case for declaratory relief established by the parties on the record before us.

V. ALLEGED CRIMINAL LIABILITY

[18] Having concluded that there is a right of privacy that might permit termination of treatment in the circumstances of this case, we turn to consider the relationship of the exercise of that right to the criminal law. We are aware that such termination of treatment would accelerate Karen's death. The County Prosecutor and the Attorney General maintain that there would be criminal liability for such acceleration. Under the statutes of this State, the unlawful killing of another human being is criminal homicide. N.J.S.A. 2A:113–1, 2, 5. We conclude that there would be no criminal homicide in the circumstances of this case. We believe, first, that the ensuing death would not be homicide but rather expiration from existing natural causes. Secondly, even if it were to be regarded as homicide, it would not be unlawful.

These conclusions rest upon definitional and constitutional bases. The termination of treatment pursuant to the right of privacy is, within the limitations of this case, *ipso facto* lawful. Thus, a death resulting from such an act would not come within the scope of the homicide statutes proscribing only the unlawful killing of another. There is a real and in this case determinative distinction between the unlawful taking of the life of another and the ending of artificial life-support systems as a matter of self-determination.

[19–21] Furthermore, the exercise of a constitutional right such as we have here found is protected from criminal prosecution. *See Stanley v. Georgia, supra,* 394 U.S. at 559, 89 S.Ct. at 1245, 22 L.Ed.2d at 546. We do not question the State's undoubted power to punish the taking of human life, but that power does not encompass individuals terminating medical treatment pursuant to their right of privacy. *See id.* at 568, 89 S.Ct. at 1250, 22 L.Ed.2d at 551. The constitutional protection extends to third parties whose action is necessary to effectuate the exercise of that right where the individuals themselves would not be subject to prosecution or the third parties are charged as accessories to an act which could not be a crime. *Eisenstadt v. Baird, supra,* 405 U.S. at 445–46, 92 S.Ct. at 1034–35, 31 L.Ed.2d at 357–58; *Griswold v. Connecticut, supra,* 381 U.S. at 481, 85 S.Ct. at 1679–80, 14 L.Ed.2d at 512–13. And, under the circumstances of this case, these same principles would apply to and negate a valid prosecution for attempted suicide were there still such a crime in this State.[9]

VI. THE GUARDIANSHIP OF THE PERSON

[22] The trial judge bifurcated the guardianship, as we have noted, refusing to appoint Joseph Quinlan to be guardian of the person and limiting his guardianship to that of the property of his daughter. Such occasional division of guardianship, as between responsibility for the person and the property of an incompetent person, has roots deep in the common law and was well within the jurisdictional capacity of the trial judge. *In re Rollins,* 65 A.2d 667, 679–82 (N.J.Cty.Ct.1949).

The statute creates an initial presumption of entitlement to guardianship in the next of kin, for it provides:

> In any case where a guardian is to be appointed, letters of guardianship shall be granted * * * to the next of kin, or if * * * it is proven to the court that no appointment from among them will be to the best interest of the incompetent or his estate, then to such other proper person as will accept the same. [N.J.S.A. 3A:6–36, See In re Roll, 117 N.J.Super. 122, 124, 283 A.2d 764, 765 (App.Div.1971)].

[23] The trial court was apparently convinced of the high character of Joseph Quinlan and his general suitability as guardian under other circumstances, describing him as "very sincere, moral, ethical and religious." The court felt, however, that the obligation to concur in the medical care and treatment of his daughter would be a source of anguish to him and would distort his "decision-making processes." We disagree, for we sense from the whole record before us that while Mr. Quinlan feels a natural grief, and understandably sorrows because of the tragedy which has befallen his daughter, his strength of purpose and character far outweighs these sentiments and qualifies him eminently for guardianship of the person as well as the property of his daughter. Hence we discern no valid reason to overrule the statutory intendment of perference to the next of kin.

DECLARATORY RELIEF

[24] We thus arrive at the formulation of the declaratory relief which we have concluded is appropriate to this case. Some time has passed since Karen's physical and mental condition was described to the Court. At that time her continuing deterioration was plainly projected. Since the record has not been expanded we assume that she is now even more fragile and nearer to death than she was then. Since her present treating physicians may give reconsideration to her present posture in the light of this opinion, and since we are transferring to the plaintiff as guardian the choice of the attending physician and therefore other physicians may be in charge of the case who may take a different view from that of the present attending physicians, we herewith declare the following affirmative relief on behalf of the plaintiff. Upon the concurrence of the guardian and family of Karen, should the responsible attending physicians conclude that there is no reasonable possibility of Karen's ever emerging from her present comatose condition to a cognitive, sapient state and that the life-support apparatus now being administered to Karen should be discontinued, they shall consult with the hospital "Ethics Committee" or like body of the institution in which Karen is then hospitalized. If that consultative body agrees that there is no reasonable possibility of Karen's ever emerging from her present comatose condition to a cognitive, sapient state, the present life-support system may be withdrawn and said action shall be without any civil or criminal liability

therefor on the part of any participant, whether guardian, physician, hospital or others.[10] We herewith specifically so hold.

CONCLUSION

We therefore remand this record to the trial court to implement (without further testimonial hearing) the following decisions:

> 1. To discharge, with the thanks of the Court for his service, the present guardian of the person of Karen Quinlan, Thomas R. Curtin, Esquire, a member of the Bar and an officer of the court.
> 2. To appoint Joseph Quinlan as guardian of the person of Karen Quinlan with full power to make decisions with regard to the identity of her treatment physicians.

We repeat for the sake of emphasis and clarity that upon the concurrence of the guardian and family of Karen, should the responsible attending physicians conclude that there is no reasonable possibility of Karen's ever emerging from her present comatose condition to a cognitive, sapient state and that the life-support apparatus now being administered to Karen should be discontinued, they shall consult with the hospital "Ethics Committee" or like body of the institution in which Karen is then hospitalized. If that consultative body agrees that there is no reasonable possibility of Karen's ever emerging from her present comatose condition to a cognitive, sapient state, the present life-support system may be withdrawn and said action shall be without any civil or criminal liability therefore on the part of any participant, whether guardian, physician, hospital or others.

By the above ruling we do not intend to be understood as implying that a proceeding for judicial declaratory relief is necessarily required for the implementation of comparable decisions in the field of medical practice.

Modified and remanded.

For modification and remandment: CHIEF JUSTICE HUGHES, JUSTICES MOUNTAIN, SULLIVAN, PASHMAN, CLIFFORD and SCHREIBER and JUDGE CONFORD——7.

Opposed: None.

NOTES

1. The importance of the preservation of life is memorialized in various organic documents. The Declaration of Independence states as self-evident truths "that all men * * * are endowed by their Creator with certain unalienable Rights, that among these are Life, Liberty and the pursuit of Happiness." This ideal is inherent in the Constitution of the United States. It is explicit recognized in our Constitution of 1947 which provides for "certain natural and unalienable rights, among which are those of enjoying and defending life * * *." N.J. Const.

(1947), Art. I, par. 1. Our State government is established to protect such rights, N.J. Const. (1947), Art. I, par. 2, and, acting through the Attorney General (N.J.S.A. 52:17A–4 (h), it enforces them.

2. Dr. Julius Korein, a neurologist, testified:

A. * * * Y]ou've got a set of possible lesions that prior to the era of advanced technology and advances in medicine were no problem inasmuch as the patient would expire. They could do nothing for themselves and even external care was limited. It was—I don't know how many years ago they couldn't keep a person alive with intravenous feedings because they couldn't give enough calories. Now they have these high caloric tube feedings that can keep people in excellent nutrition for years so what's happened is these things have occurred all along but the technology has now reached a point where you can in fact start to replace anything outside of the brain to maintain something that is irreversibly damaged.

Q. Doctor, can the art of medicine repair the cerebral damage that was sustained by Karen?

A. In my opinion, no. * * *

Q. Doctor, in your opinion is there any course of treatment that will lead to the improvement of Karen's condition?

A. No.

3. The Harvard Ad Hoc standards, with reference to "brain death," will be discussed *infra.*

3.1. This cross-appeal was later informally withdrawn but in view of the importance of the matter we nevertheless deal with it.

4. Dr. Robert J. Morse, a neurologist, and Karen's treating physician from the time of her admission to Saint Clare's Hospital on April 24, 1975 (reference was made *supra* to "treating physicians" named as defendants; this term included Dr. Arshad Javed, a highly qualified pulmonary internist, who considers that he manages that phase of Karen's care with primary responsibility to the "attending physician," Dr. Morse).

5. Death. The cessation of life; the ceasing to exist; defined by physicians as a total stoppage of the circulation of the blood, and a cessation of the animal and vital functions consequent thereon, such as respiration, pulsation, etc. *Black's Law Dictionary* 488 (rev. 4th ed. 1968).

6. It is generally agreed that the Eighth Amendment's provision of "[n]or cruel and unusual punishments inflicted" is drawn verbatim from the English Declaration of Rights. *See* 1 Wm. & M., sess. 2, c. 2 (1689). The prohibition arose in the context of excessive punishments for crimes, punishments that were barbarous and savage as well as disproportionate to the offense committed. *See generally* Granucci " 'Nor Cruel and Unusual Punishments Inflicted:' The Original Meaning," 57 Calif.L.Rev. 839, 844–60 (1969)); Note, "The Cruel and Unusual Punishment Clause and the Substantive Criminal Law," 79 Harv.L. Rev. 635, 636–39 (1966). The principle against excessiveness in criminal punishments can be traced back to Chapters 20–22 of the *Magna Carta* (1215). The historical background of the Eighth Amendment was examined at some length in various opinions in *Furman v. Georgia,* 408 U.S. 238, 92 S.Ct. 2726, 33 L.Ed.2d 346 (1972).

The Constitution itself is silent as to the meaning of the word "punishment." Whether it refers to the variety of legal and nonlegal penalties that human beings endure or whether it must be in connection with a criminal rather than a civil proceeding is not stated in the document. But the origins of the clause are clear. And the cases construing it have consistently held that the "punishment" contemplated by the Eighth Amendment is the penalty inflicted by a court for the commission of a crime or in the enforcement of what is a criminal law. *See, e.g., Trop v. Dulles,* 356 U.S. 86, 94–99, 78 S.Ct. 590, 594–97, 2 L.Ed.2d 630, 638–41 (1957). *See generally* Note, "The Effectiveness of the Eighth Amendment: An Appraisal of Cruel and Unusual Punishment," 36 N.Y.U.L. Rev. 846, 854–57 (1961). A deprivation, forfeiture or penalty arising out of a civil proceeding or otherwise cannot be "cruel and unusual punishment" within the meaning of the constitutional clause.

7. The right we here discuss is included within the class of what have been called rights of "personality." *See* Pound, "Equitable Relief against Defamation and Injuries to Personality," 29 Harv.L.Rev. 640, 668–76 (1916). Equitable jurisdiction with respect to the rec-

ognition and enforcement of such rights has long been recognized in New Jersey. *See, e.g., Vanderbilt v. Mitchell,* 72 N.J.Eq. 910, 919–20, 67 A. 97 (E. & A. 1907).

8. *See, e.g., Downing, Euthanasia and the Right to Death* (1969); *St. John-Stevas, Life, Death and the Law* (1961); *Williams, The Sanctity of Human Life and the Criminal Law* (1957); Appel, "Ethical and Legal Questions Posed by Recent Advances in Medicine," 205 J.A.M.A. 513 (1968); Cantor, "A Patient's Decision To Decline Life-Saving Medical Treatment: Bodily Integrity Versus The Preservation Of Life," 26 Rutgers L. Rev. 228 (1973); Claypool, "The Family Deals with Death," 27 Baylor L.Rev. 34 (1975); Elkington, "The Dying Patient, The Doctor and The Law," 13 Vill.L.Rev. 740 (1968); Fletcher, "Legal Aspects of the Decision Not to Prolong Life," 203 J.A.M.A. 65 (1968); Foreman, "The Physician's Criminal Liability for the Practice of Euthanasia," 27 Baylor L.Rev. 54 (1975); Gurney, "Is There A Right To Die?—A Study of the Law of Euthanasia," 3 Cumb.-Sam.L.Rev. 235 (1972); Mannes, "Euthanasia vs. The Right to Life," 27 Baylor L.Rev. 68 (1975); Sharp & Crofts, "Death with Dignity and The Physician's Civil Liability," 27 Baylor L.Rev. 86 (1975); Sharpe & Hargest, "Lifesaving Treatment for Unwilling Patients," 36 Fordham L.Rev. 695 (1968); Skegg, "Irreversibly Comatose Individuals: 'Alive' or 'Dead'?," 33 Camb.L.J. 130 (1974); Comment, "The Right to Die," 7 Houston L.Rev. 654 (1970); Note, "The Time Of Death—A Legal, Ethical and Medical Dilemma," 18 Catholic Law. 243 (1972); Note, "Compulsory Medical Treatment: The State's Interest Re-evaluated," 51 Minn.L.Rev. 293 (1966).

9. An attempt to commit suicide was an indictable offense at common law and as such was indictable in this State as a common law misdemeanor. 1 *Schlosser, Criminal Laws of New Jersey* § 12.5 (3d ed. 1970); *see* N.J.S.A. 2A:85–1. The legislature downgraded the offense in 1957 to the status of a disorderly persons offense, which is not a "crime" under our law. N.J.S.A. 2A:170–25.6. And in 1971, the legislature repealed all criminal sanctions for attempted suicide. N.J.S.A. 2A:85–5.1. Provision is now made for temporary hospitalization of persons making such an attempt. N.J.S.A. 30:4–26.3a. We note that under the proposed New Jersey Penal Code (Oct. 1971) there is no provision for criminal punishment of attempted suicide. *See* Commentary, § 2C:11–6. There is, however, an independent offense of "aiding suicide." § 2C:11–6b. This provision, if enacted, would not be incriminatory in circumstances similar to those presented in this case.

10. The declaratory relief we here award is not intended to imply that the principles enunciated in this case might not be applicable in divers other types of terminal medical situations such as those described by Drs. Korein and Diamond, *supra,* not necessarily involving the hopeless loss of cognitive or sapient life.

SUPERINTENDENT of BELCHERTOWN STATE SCHOOL v. SAIKEWICZ

Supreme Judicial Court of Massachusetts, 1977.
373 Mass. 728, 370 N.E.2d 417.

Before HENNESSEY, C. J. and BRAUCHER, KAPLAN, WILKINS and LIACOS, JJ

LIACOS, Justice

On April 26, 1976, William E. Jones, superintendent of the Belchertown State School (a facility of the Massachusetts Department of Mental Health), and Paul R. Rogers, a staff attorney at the school, petitioned the Probate Court for Hampshire County for the appointment of a guardian of Joseph Saikewicz, a resident of the State school. Simultaneously they filed a motion for the immediate appointment of a guardian ad litem, with authority to make the necessary decisions concerning the care and treatment of Saikewicz, who was suffering with acute myeloblastic monocytic leukemia. The petition alleged that Saikewicz was a mentally retarded person in urgent need of medical treatment and that he was a person with disability incapable of giving informed consent for such treatment.

On May 5, 1976, the probate judge appointed a guardian ad litem. On May 6, 1976, the guardian ad litem filed a report with the court. The guardian ad litem's report indicated that Saikewicz's illness was an incurable one, and that although chemotherapy was the medically indicated course of treatment it would cause Saikewicz significant adverse side effects and discomfort. The guardian ad litem concluded that these factors, as well as the inability of the ward to understand the treatment to which he would be subjected and the fear and pain he would suffer as a result, outweighed the limited prospect of any benefit from such treatment, namely, the possibility of some uncertain but limited extension of life. He therefore recommended "that not treating Mr. Saikewicz would be in his best interests."

A hearing on the report was held on May 13, 1976. Present were the petitioners and the guardian ad litem.[1] The record before us does not indicate whether a guardian for Saikewicz was ever appointed. After hearing the evidence, the judge entered findings of fact and an order that in essence agreed with the recommendation of the guardian ad litem. The decision of the judge appears to be based in part on the testimony of Saikewicz's two attending physicians who recommended against chemotherapy. The judge then reported to the Appeals Court the two questions set forth in the margin.[2] An application for direct appellate review was allowed by this court. On July 9, 1976, this court issued an order answering the questions reported in the affirmative with the notation "rescript and opinion . . . will follow."[3] We now issue that opinion.

I

The judge below found that Joseph Saikewicz, at the time the matter arose, was sixty-seven years old, with an I.Q. of ten and a mental age of approximately two years and eight months. He was profoundly mentally retarded. The record discloses that, apart from his leukemic condition, Saikewicz enjoyed generally good health. He was physically strong and well built, nutritionally nourished, and ambulatory. He was not, however, able to communicate verbally—resorting to gestures and grunts to make his wishes known to others and responding only to gestures or physical contacts. In the course of treatment for various medical conditions arising during Saikewicz's residency at the school, he had been unable to respond intelligibly to inquiries such as whether he was experiencing pain. It was the opinion of a consulting psychologist, not contested by the other experts relied on by the judge below, that Saikewicz was not aware of dangers and was disoriented outside his immediate environment. As a result of his condition, Saikewicz had lived in State institutions since 1923 and had resided at the Belchertown State School since 1928. Two of his sisters, the only members of his family who could be located, were notified of his condition and of the hearing, but they preferred not to attend or otherwise become involved.

On April 19, 1976, Saikewicz was diagnosed as suffering from acute myeloblastic monocytic leukemia. Leukemia is a disease of the blood. It arises when organs of the body produce an excessive number of white blood cells as well as other abnormal cellular structures, in particular undeveloped and immature white cells. Along with these symptoms in the composition of the blood the disease is accompanied by enlargement of the organs which produce the cells, e.g., the spleen, lymph glands, and bone marrow. The disease tends to cause internal bleeding and weakness, and, in the acute form, severe anemia and high susceptibility to infection. Attorneys' Dictionary of Medicine L–37–38 (1977). The particular form of the disease present in this case, acute myeloblastic monocytic leukemia is so defined because the particular cells which increase are the myeloblasts, the youngest form of a cell which at maturity is known as the granulocytes. *Id.* at M-138. The disease is invariably fatal.

Chemotherapy, as was testified to at the hearing in the Probate Court, involves the administration of drugs over several weeks, the purpose of which is to kill the leukemia cells. This treatment unfortunately affects normal cells as well. One expert testified that the end result, in effect, is to destroy the living vitality of the bone marrow. Because of this effect, the patient becomes very anemic and may bleed or suffer infections—a condition which requires a number of blood transfusions. In this sense, the patient immediately becomes much "sicker" with the commencement of chemotherapy, and there is a possibility that infections during the initial period of severe anemia will prove fatal. Moreover, while most patients survive chemotherapy, remission of the leukemia is achieved in only thirty to fifty percent of the cases. Remission is meant here as a temporary return to normal as measured by clinical and laboratory means. If remission does occur, it typically lasts for between two and thirteen months although longer periods of remission are possible. Estimates of the effectiveness of chemotherapy are complicated in cases, such as the one presented here, in which the patient's age becomes a factor. According to the medical testimony before the court below, persons over age sixty have more difficulty tolerating chemotherapy and the treatment is likely to be less successful than in younger patients.[4] This prognosis may be compared with the doctors' estimates that, left untreated, a patient in Saikewicz's condition would live for a matter of weeks or, perhaps, several months. According to the testimony, a decision to allow the disease to run its natural course would not result in pain for the patient, and death would probably come without discomfort.

An important facet of the chemotherapy process, to which the judge below directed careful attention, is the problem of serious adverse side effects caused by the treating drugs. Among these side effects are severe nausea, bladder irritation, numbness and tingling of the extremities, and loss of hair. The bladder irritation can be avoided, however, if the patient drinks fluids, and the nausea can be treated by drugs. It was the opinion of the guardian ad litem, as well as the doctors who testified before the probate judge, that most people elect to suffer the side effects of chemotherapy rather than to allow their leukemia to run its natural course.

Drawing on the evidence before him including the testimony of the medical experts, and the report of the guardian ad litem, the probate judge issued detailed findings with regard to the costs and benefits of allowing Saikewicz to undergo chemotherapy. The judge's findings are reproduced in part here because of the importance of clearly delimiting the issues presented in this case. The judge below found:

"5. That the majority of persons suffering from leukemia who are faced with a choice of receiving or foregoing such chemotherapy, and who are able to make an informed judgment thereon, choose to receive treatment in spite of its toxic side effects and risks of failure.

"6. That such toxic side effects of chemotherapy include pain and discomfort, depressed bone marrow, pronounced anemia, increased chance of infection, possible bladder irritation, and possible loss of hair.

"7. That administration of such chemotherapy requires cooperation from the patient over several weeks of time, which cooperation said JOSEPH SAIKEWICZ is unable to give due to his profound retardation.[5]

"8. That, considering the age and general state of health of said JOSEPH SAIKEWICZ, there is only a 30–40 percent chance that chemotherapy will produce a remission of said leukemia, which remission would probably be for a period of time of from 2 to 13 months, but that said chemotherapy will certainly not completely cure such leukemia.

"9. That if such chemotherapy is to be administered at all, it should be administered immediately, inasmuch as the risks involved will increase and the chances of successfully bringing about remission will decrease as time goes by.

"10. That, at present, said JOSEPH SAIKEWICZ's leukemia condition is stable and is not deteriorating.

"11. That said JOSEPH SAIKEWICZ is not now in pain and will probably die within a matter of weeks or months a relatively painless death due to the leukemia unless other factors should intervene to themselves cause death.

"12. That it is impossible to predict how long said JOSEPH SAIKEWICZ will probably live without chemotherapy or how long he will probably live with chemotherapy, but it is to a very high degree medically likely that he will die sooner without treatment than with it."

Balancing these various factors, the judge concluded that the following considerations weighed *against* administering chemotherapy to Saikewicz: "(1) his age, (2) his inability to cooperate with the treatment, (3) probably adverse side effects of treatment, (4) low chance of producing remission, (5) the certainty that treatment will cause immediate suffering, and (6) the quality of life possible for him even if the treatment does bring about remission."

The following considerations were determined to weigh in *favor* of chemotherapy: "(1) the chance that his life may be lengthened thereby, and (2) the fact that most people in his situation when given a chance to do so elect to take the gamble of treatment."

Concluding that, in this case, the negative factors of treatment exceeded the benefits, the probate judge ordered on May 13, 1976, that no treatment be administered to Saikewicz for his condition of acute myeloblastic monocytic leukemia except by further order of the court. The judge further ordered that all reasonable and necessary supportive measures be taken, medical or otherwise, to safeguard the well-being of Saikewicz in all other respects and to reduce as far as possible any suffering or discomfort which he might experience.

It is within this factual context that we issued our order of July 9, 1976.

Saikewicz died on September 4, 1976 at the Belchertown State School hospital. Death was due to bronchial pneumonia, a complication of the leukemia. Saikewicz died without pain or discomfort.[6]

II

We recognize at the outset that this case presents novel issues of fundamental importance that should not be resolved by mechanical reliance on legal doctrine. Our task of establishing a framework in the law on which the activities of health care personnel and other persons can find support is furthered by seeking the collective guidance of those in health care, moral ethics, philosophy, and other disciplines. Our attempt to bring such insights to bear in the legal context has been advanced by the diligent efforts of the guardian ad litem and the probate judge, as well as the excellent briefs of the parties and amici curiae.[7] As thus illuminated, the principal areas of determination are:

A. The nature of the right of any person, competent or incompetent, to decline potentially life-prolonging treatment.

B. The legal standards that control the course of decision whether or not potentially life-prolonging, but not life-saving, treatment should be administered to a person who is not competent to make the choice.

C. The procedures that must be followed in arriving at that decision.

For reasons we develop in the body of this opinion, it becomes apparent that the questions to be discussed in the first two areas are closely interrelated. We take the view that the substantive rights of the competent and the incompetent person are the same in regard to the right to decline protentially life-prolonging treatment. The factors which distinguish the two types of persons are found only in the area of how the State should approach the preservation and implementation of the rights of an incompetent person and in the procedures necessary to that process of preservation and implementation. We treat the matter in the sequence above stated because we think it helpful to set forth our views on (A) what the rights of all persons in this area are and (B) the issue of how an incompetent person is to be afforded the status in law of a competent person with respect to such rights. Only then can we proceed to (C) the particular procedures to be followed to ensure the rights of the incompetent person.

A

1. It has been said that "[t]he law always lags behind the most advanced thinking in every area. It must wait until the theologians and the moral leaders and events have created some common ground, some consensus." Burger, The Law and Medical Advances, 67 Annals Internal Med. Supp. 7, 15, 17 (1967), quoted in Elkinton, The Dying Patient, the Doctor, and the Law, 13 Vill.L.Rev. 740 (1968). We therefore think it advisable to consider the framework of medical ethics which influences a doctor's decision as to how to deal with the terminally ill patient. While these considerations are not controlling, they ought to be considered for the insights they give us.

Advances in medical science have given doctors greater control over the time and nature of death. Chemotherapy is, as evident from our previous discussion, one of these advances. Prior to the development of such new techniques the physician perceived his duty as that of making every conceivable effort to prolong life. On the other hand, the context in which such an ethos prevailed did not provide the range of options available to the physician today in terms of taking steps to postpone death irrespective of the effect on the patient. With the development of the new techniques, serious questions as to what may constitute acting in the best interests of the patient have arisen.

The nature of the choice has become more difficult because physicians have begun to realize that in many cases the effect of using extraordinary measures to prolong life is to "only prolong suffering, isolate the family from their loved one at a time when they may be close at hand or result in economic ruin for the family." Lewis, Machine Medicine and Its Relation to the Fatally Ill, 206 J.A.M.A. 387 (1968).

Recognition of these factors led the Supreme Court of New Jersey to observe "that physicians distinguish between curing the ill and comforting and easing the dying; that they refuse to treat the curable as if they were dying or ought to die, and that they have sometimes refused to treat the hopeless and dying as if they were curable." *In re Quinlan,* 70 N.J. 10, 47, 355 A.2d 647, 667 (1976).

The essence of this distinction in defining the medical role is to draw the sometimes subtle distinction between those situations in which the withholding of extraordinary measures may be viewed as allowing the disease to take its natural course and those in which the same actions may be deemed to have been the cause of death. See Elkinton, *supra* at 743. Recent literature suggests that health care institutions are drawing such a distinction, at least with regard to respecting the decision of competent patients to refuse such measures. Rabkin, Gillerman & Rice, Orders Not to Resuscitate, 293 N.E.J. of Med. 364 (1976). Cf. Beecher, Ethical Problems Created by the Hopelessly Unconscious Patient, 278 N.E.J. of Med. 1425 (1968).

The current state of medical ethics in this area is expressed by one commentator who states that: "we should not use *extraordinary* means of prolonging life or its semblance when, after careful consideration, consultation and the application of the most well conceived therapy it becomes apparent that there is no hope for the recovery of the patient. Recovery should not be defined simply as the ability to remain alive; it should mean life without intolerable suffering." *Lewis, supra.* See Collins, Limits of Medical Responsibility in Prolonging Life, 206 J.A.M.A. 389 (1968); Williamson, Life or Death—Whose Decision? 197 J.A.M.A. 793 (1966).

Our decision in this case is consistent with the current medical ethos in this area.

[1] 2. There is implicit recognition in the law of the Commonwealth, as elsewhere, that a person has a strong interest in being free from nonconsensual invasion of his bodily integrity. *Thiabault v. Lalumiere,* 318 Mass. 72, 60 N.E.2d 349 (1945). *Commonwealth v. Clark,* 2 Metc. 23 (1840). *Union Pac. Ry. v. Botsford,* 141 U.S. 250, 251, 11 S.Ct. 1000, 35 L.Ed. 734 (1891). In short, the law recognizes the individual interest in preserving "the inviolability of his person." *Pratt v. Davis,* 118 Ill.App. 161, 166 (1905), aff'd, 224 Ill. 300, 79 N.E. 562 (1906). One means by which the law has developed in a manner consistent with the protection of this interest is through the development of the doctrine of informed consent. While the doctrine to the extent it may justify recovery in tort for the breach of a physician's duty has not been formally recognized by this court, *Schroeder v. Lawrence,* _____ Mass _____[a], 359 N.E.2d 1301 (1977); see *Baird v. Attorney Gen.,* _____ Mass. _____[b], 360 N.E.2d 288 (1977); *Reddington v. Clayman,* 334 Mass.244, 134 N.E.2d 9210 (1956); G.L. c 112, § 12F, it is one of widespread recognition. Capron, Informed Consent in Catastrophic Disease Research and Treatment, 123 U.Pa.L.Rev. 340, 365 (1975); Cantor, A Patient's Decision to Decline Life-Saving Medical Treatment: Bodily Integrity Versus the Preservation of Life, 26 Rutgers L.Rev. 228–238 (1973). W. Prosser, Torts § 18 (4th ed. 1971). As previously suggested, one of the foundations of the doctrine is that it protects the patient's status as a human being. Capron, *supra* at 366–367.

[2] Of even broader import, but arising from the same regard for human dignity and self-determination, is the unwritten constitutional right of privacy found in the penumbra of specific guaranties of the Bill of Rights. *Griswold v. Connecticut,* 381 U.S. 479, 484, 85 S.Ct. 328, 13 L.Ed.2d 339 (1965). As this constitutional guaranty reaches out to protect the freedom of a woman to terminate pregnancy under certain conditions, *Roe v. Wade,* 410 U.S. 113, 153, 93 S.Ct. 705, 35 L.Ed.2d 147 (1973), so it encompasses the right of a patient to preserve his or her right to

privacy against unwanted infringements of bodily integrity in appropriate circumstances. *In re Quinlan, supra* 70 N.J. at 38–39, 355 A.2d 647. In the case of a person incompetent to assert this constitutional right of privacy, it may be asserted by that person's guardian in conformance with the standards and procedures set forth in sections II (B) and II(C) of this opinion. See *Quinlan* at 39, 355 A.2d 647.

3. The question when the circumstances are appropriate for the exercise of this privacy right depends on the proper identification of State interests. It is not surprising that courts have, in the course of investigating State interests in various medical contexts and under various formulations of the individual rights involved, reached differing views on the nature and the extent of State interests. We have undertaken a survey of some of the leading cases to help in identifying the range of State interests potentially applicable to cases of medical intervention.

In a number of cases, no applicable State interest, or combination of such interests, was found sufficient to outweigh the individual's interests in exercising the choice of refusing medical treatment. To this effect are *Erickson v. Dilgard,* 44 Misc. 2d 27, 252 N.Y.S.2d 705 (N.Y.Sup.Ct.1962) (scheme of liberty puts highest priority on free individual choice); *In re Estate of Brooks,* 32 Ill.2d 361, 205 N.E.2d 435 (1965) (patient may elect to pursue religious beliefs by refusing life-saving blood transfusion provided the decision did not endanger public health, safety or morals); see *In re Osborne,* 294 A.2d 372 (D.C. App.1972); *Holmes v. Silver Cross Hosp. of Joliet, Ill.,* 340 F.Supp. 125 (D.Ill.1972); Byrn, Compulsory Lifesaving Treatment for the Competent Adult, 44 Fordham L. Rev. 1 (1975). See also *In re Guardianship of Pescinski,* 67 Wis.2d. 4, 226 N.W.2d 180 (1975).

Subordination of State interests to individual interests has not been universal, however. In a leading case, *Application of the President & Directors of Georgetown College, Inc.* 118 U.S. App.D.C. 80, 331 F.2d 1000, cert. denied, 377 U.S. 978, 84 S.Ct. 1883, 12 L.Ed.2d 746 (1964), a hospital sought permission to perform a blood transfusion necessary to save the patient's life where the person was unwilling to consent due to religious beliefs. The court held that it had the power to allow the action to be taken despite the previously expressed contrary sentiments of the patient. The court justified its decision by reasoning that its purpose was to protect three State interests, the protection of which was viewed as having greater import than the individual right: (1) the State interest in preventing suicide, (2) a parens patriae interest in protecting the patient's minor children from "abandonment" by their parent, and (3) the protection of the medical profession's desire to act affirmatively to save life without fear of civil liability. In *John F. Kennedy Memorial Hosp. v. Heston,* 58 N.J. 576, 279 A.2d. 670 (1971), a case involving a fact situation similar to *Georgetown,* the New Jersey Supreme Court also allowed a transfusion. It based its decision on *Georgetown,* well as its prior decisions. See *Raleigh Fitkin-Pal Morgan Memorial Hosp. v. Anderson,* 42 N.J. 421, 201 A.2d 537, cert. denied 377 U.S. 985, 84 S.Ct. 1894, 12 L.Ed.2d 1032 (1964);[8] *State v. Perricone,* 37 N.J. 463, 181 A.2d 751, cert. denied, 371 U.S. 890, 83 S.Ct. 189, 9 L.Ed.2d 124 (1962). The New Jersey court held that the State's paramount interest in preserving life and the hospital's interest in fully caring for a patient under its custody and control outweighed the individual decision to decline the necessary measures. See *United States v. George,* 239 F. Supp. 752 (D. Conn.1965); *Long Island Jewish-Hillside*

Medical Center v. Levitt, 73 Misc.2d 395, 342 N.Y.S.2d 356 (N.Y.Sup.Ct. 1973); *In re Sampson,* 65 Misc.2d 658, 317 N.Y.S.2d 641 (Fam.Ct. 1970); aff'd 37 App. Div.2d 668, 323 N.Y.S.2d 253 (1971), aff'd per curiam, 29 N.Y.2d 900, 328 N.Y.S.2d 686, 278 N.E.2d 915 (1972); *In re Weberlist,* 79 Misc.2d 753, 360 N.Y.S.2d 783 (N.Y.Sup.Ct.1974); *In re Karwath,* 199 N.W.2d 147 (Iowa 1972).

This survey of recent decisions involving the difficult question of the right of an individual to refuse medical intervention or treatment indicates that a relatively concise statement of countervailing State interests may be made. As distilled from the cases, the State has claimed interest in: (1) the preservation of life; (2) the protection of the interests of innocent third parties; (3) the prevention of suicide; and (4) maintaining the ethical integrity of the medical profession.

[3,4] It is clear that the most significant of the asserted State interests is that of the preservation of human life. Recognition of such an interest, however, does not necessarily resolve the problem where the affliction or disease clearly indicates that life will soon, and inevitably, be extinguished. The interest of the State in prolonging a life must be reconciled with the interest of an individual to reject the traumatic cost of that prolongation. There is a substantial distinction in the State's insistence that human life be saved where the affliction is curable, as opposed to the State interest where, as here, the issue is not whether but when, for how long, and at what cost to the individual that life may be briefly extended. Even if we assume that the State has an additional interest in seeing to it that individual decisions on the prolongation of life do not in any way tend to "cheapen" the value which is placed in the concept of living, see *Roe v. Wade, supra* we believe it is not inconsistent to recognize a right to decline medical treatment in a situation of incurable illness. The consitituional right to privacy, as we conceive it, is an expression of the sanctity of individual free choice and self-determination as fundamental constituents of life. The value of life as so perceived is lessened not by a decision to refuse treatment, but by the failure to allow a competent human being the right of choice.[9]

A second interest of considerable magnitude, which the State may have some interest in asserting, is that of protecting third parties, particularly minor children, from the emotional and financial damage which may occur as a result of the decision of a competent adult to refuse life-saving or life-prolonging treatment. Thus, in *Holmes v. Silver Cross Hosp. of Joliet, Ill.,* 340 F. Supp. 125 (D.Ill.1972), the court held that, while the State's interest in preserving an individual's life was not sufficient, by itself, to outweigh the individual's interest in the exercise of free choice, the possible impact on minor children would be a factor which might have a critical effect on the outcome of the balancing process. Similarly, in the *Georgetown* case the court held that one of the interests requiring protection was that of the minor child in order to avoid the effect of "abandonment" on that child as a result of the parent's decision to refuse the necessary medical measures. See Byrn, *supra* at 33; *United States v. George, supra.*[10] We need not reach this aspect of claimed State interest as it is not in issue on the facts of this case.

The last State interest requiring discussion[11] is that of the maintenance of the ethical integrity of the medical profession as well as allowing hospitals the full opportunity to care for people under their control. See *Georgetown, supra; United*

States v. George, supra; John F. Kennedy Memorial Hosp. v. Heston, supra. The force and impact of this interest is lessened by the prevailing medical ethical standards, see Byrn, *supra* at 31. Prevailing medical ethical practice does not, without exception, demand that all efforts toward life prolongation be made in all circumstances. Rather, as indicated in *Quinlan,* the prevailing ethical practice seems to be to recognize that the dying are more often in need of comfort than treatment. Recognition of the right to refuse necessary treatment in appropriate circumstances is consistent with existing medical mores; such a doctrine does not threaten either the integrity of the medical profession, the proper role of hospitals in caring for such patients or the State's interest in protecting the same. It is not necessary to deny a right of self-determination to a patient in order to recognize the interests of doctors, hospitals, and medical personnel in attendance on the patient. Also, if the doctrines of informed consent and right of privacy have as their foundations the right to bodily integrity, see *Union Pac. Ry. v. Botsford,* 141 U.S. 250,11 S.Ct. 1000, 35 L.Ed. 734 (1891), and control of one's own fate, then those rights are superior to the institutional considerations.[12]

Applying the considerations discussed in this subsection to the decision made by the probate judge in the circumstances of the case before us, we are satisfied that his decision was consistent with a proper balancing of applicable State and individual interests. Two of the four categories of State interests that we have identified, the protection of third parties and the prevention of suicide, are inapplicable to this case. The third, involving the protection of the ethical integrity of the medical profession was satisfied on two grounds. The probate judge's decision was in accord with the testimony of the attending physicians of the patient. The decision is in accord with the generally accepted views of the medical profession, as set forth in this opinion. The fourth State interest—the preservation of life—has been viewed with proper regard for the heavy physical and emotional burdens on the patient if a vigorous regimen of drug therapy were to be imposed to effect a brief and uncertain delay in the natural process of death. To be balanced against these State interests was the individual's interest in the freedom to choose to reject, to refuse to consent to, intrusions of his bodily integrity and privacy. We cannot say that the facts of this case required a result contrary to that reached by the probate judge with regard to the right of any person, competent or incompetent, to be spared the deleterious consequences of life-prolonging treatment. We therefore turn to consider the unique considerations arising in this case by virtue of the patient's inability to appreciate his predicament and articulate his desires.

B

[5] The question what legal standards govern the decision whether to administer potentially life-prolonging treatment to an incompetent person encompasses two distinct and important subissues. First, does a choice exist? That is, is it the unvarying responsibility of the State to order medical treatment in all circumstances involving the care of an incompetent person? Second, if a choice does exist under certain conditions, what considerations enter into the decision-making process?

We think that principles of equality and respect for all individuals require the conclusion that a choice exists. For reasons discussed at some length in subsection A, *supra,* we recognize a general right in all persons to refuse medical treatment in appropriate circumstances. The recognition of that right must extend to the case of an incompetent, as well as a competent, patient because the value of human dignity extends to both.

This is not to deny that the State has a traditional power and responsibility, under the doctine of parens patriae, to care for and protect the "best interests" of the incompetent person. Indeed, the existence of this power and responsibility has impelled a number of courts to hold that the "best interests" of such a person mandate an unvarying responsibility by the courts to order necessary medical treatment for an incompetent person facing an immediate and severe danger to life. *Application of the President & Directors of Georgetown College, Inc.,* 118 U.S. App.D.C. 80, 331 F.2d 1000, cert. denied, 377 U. S. 978, 84 S.Ct. 1883, 12 L.Ed.2d 746 (1964). *Long Island Jewish-Hillside Medical Center v. Levitt,* 73 Misc.2d 395, 342 N.Y.S.2d 356 (N.Y.Sup.Ct. 1973). Cf. *In re Weberlist,* 79 Misc. 2d 753, 360 N.Y.S.2d 783 (N.Y.Sup.Ct.1974). Whatever the merits of such a policy where life-saving treatment is available—a situation unfortunately not presented by this case—a more flexible view of the "best interests" of the incompetent patient is not precluded under other conditions. For example, other courts have refused to take it on themselves to order certain forms of treatment or therapy which are not immediately required although concededly beneficial to the innocent person. *In re CFB,* 497 S.W.2d 831 (Mo.App.1973). *Green's Appeal,* 448 Pa. 338, 292 A.2d 387 (1972). *In re Frank,* 41 Wash.2d 294, 248 P.2d 553 (1952). Cf. *In re Rotkowitz,* 175 Misc. 948, 25 N.Y.S.2d 624 (N.Y.Dom.Rel.Ct.1941); *Mitchell v. Davis,* 205 S.W.2d 812 (Tex.App.1947). While some of these cases involved children who might eventually be competent to make the necessary decisions without judicial interference, it is also clear that the additional period of waiting might make the task of correction more difficult. See e.g., *In re Frank, supra.* These cases stand for the proposition that, even in the exercise of the parens patriae power, there must be respect for the bodily integrity of the child or respect for the rational decision of those parties, usually the parents, who for one reason or another are seeking to protect the bodily integrity or other personal interest of the child. See *In re Hudson,* 13 Wash. 2d 673, 126 P.2d 765 (1942).

[6] The "best interests" of an incompetent person are not necessarily served by imposing on such persons results not mandated as to competent persons similarly situated. It does not advance the interest of the State or the ward to treat the ward as a person of lesser status or dignity than others. To protect the incompetent person within its power, the State must recognize the dignity and worth of such a person and afford to that person the same panoply of rights and choices it recognizes in competent persons. If a competent person faced with death may choose to decline treatment which not only will not cure the person but which substantially may increase suffering in exchange for a possible yet brief prolongation of life, then it cannot be said that it is always in the "best interests" of the ward to require submission to such treatment. Nor do statistical factors indicating that a majority of competent persons similarly situated choose treatment resolve the issue. The sig-

nificant dicisions of life are more complex than statistical determinations. Individual choice is determined not by the vote of the majority but by the complexities of the singular situation viewed from the unique perspective of the person called on to make the decision. To presume that the incompetent person must always be subjected to what many rational and intelligent persons may decline is to downgrade the status of the incompetent person by placing a lesser value on his intrinsic human worth and vitality.

The trend in the law has been to give incompetent persons the same rights as other individuals. *Boyd v. Registrars of Voters of Belchertown*, 368 Mass. _____[c], 334 N.E.2d 629 (1975). Recognition of this principle of equality requires understanding that in certain circumstances it may be appropriate for a court to consent to the withholding of treatment from an incompetent individual. This leads us to the question of how the right of an incompetent person to decline treatment might best be exercised so as to give the fullest possible expression to the character and circumstances of that individual.

The problem of decision-making presented in this case is one of first impression before this court, and we know of no decision in other jurisdictions squarely on point. The well publicized decision of the New Jersey Supreme Court in *In re Quinlan*, 70 N.J. 10, 355 A.2d 647 (1976), provides a helpful starting point for analysis, however.

Karen Ann Quinlan, then age twenty-one, stopped breathing for reasons not clearly identified for at least two fifteen-minute periods on the night of April 15, 1975. As a result, this formerly healthy individual suffered severe brain damage to the extent that medical experts characterized her as being in a "chronic persistent vegetative state." *Id.* at 24, 355 A.2d 647. Although her brain was capable of a certain degree of primitive reflex-level functioning, she had no cognitive function or awareness of her surroundings. Karen Quinlan did not, however, exhibit any of the signs of "brain death" as identified by the Ad Hoc Committee of the Harvard Medical School.[13] She was thus "alive" under controlling legal and medical standards. *Id.* at 25, 355 A.2d 647. Nonetheless, it was the opinion of the experts and conclusion of the court that there was no reasonable possibility that she would ever be restored to cognitive or sapient life. *Id.* at 26, 355 A.2d 647. Her breathing was assisted by a respirator, without which the experts believed she could not survive. It was for the purpose of getting authority to order the disconnection of the respirator that Quinlan's father petitioned the lower New Jersey court.

The Supreme Court of New Jersey, in a unanimous opinion authored by Chief Justice Hughes, held that the father, as guardian, could, subject to certain qualifications,[14] exercise his daughter's right to privacy by authorizing removal of the artificial life-support systems. *Id.* at 55, 355 A.2d 647. The court thus recognized that the preservation of the personal right to privacy against bodily intrusions, not exercisable directly due to the incompetence of the rightholder, depended on its indirect exercise by one acting on behalf of the incompetent person. The exposition by the New Jersey court of the principle of substituted judgment, and of the legal standards that were to be applied by the guardian in making this decision, bears repetition here.

"If a putative decision by Karen to permit this non-cognitive, vegetative existence to terminate by natural forces is regarded as a valuable incident of her right of privacy, as we believe it to be, then it should not be discarded solely on the basis that her condition prevents her conscious exercise of the choice. The only practical way to prevent destruction of the right is to *permit the guardian and family of Karen to render their best judgment,* subject to the qualifications [regarding consultation with attending physicians and hospital 'Ethics Committee'] hereinafter stated, *as to whether she would exercise it in these circumstances.* If their conclusion is in the affirmative this decision should be accepted by a society the overwhelming majority of whose members would, we think, in similar circumstances, exercise such a choice in the same way for themselves or for those closest to them. It is for this reason that we determine that Karen's right of privacy may be asserted in her behalf, in this respect, by her guardian and family under the particular circumstances presented by this record" (emphasis supplied). *Id.* at 41–42, 355 A.2d 647.

The court's observation that most people in like circumstances would choose a natural death does not, we believe, detract from or modify the central concern that the guardian's decision conform, to the extent possible, to the decision that would have been made by Karen Quinlan herself. Evidence that most people would or would not act in a certain way is certainly an important consideration in attempting to ascertain the predilections of any individual, but care must be taken, as in any analogy, to ensure that operative factors are similar or at least to take notice of the dissimilarities. With this in mind, it is profitable to compare the situations presented in the *Quinlan* case and the case presently before us. Karen Quinlan, subsequent to her accident, was totally incapable of knowing or appreciating life, was physically debilitated, and was pathetically reliant on sophisticated machinery to nourish and clean her body. Any other person suffering from similar massive brain damage would be in a similar state of total incapacity, and thus it is not unreasonable to give weight to a supposed general, and widespread, response to the situation.

Karen Quinlan's situation, however, must be distinguished from that of Joseph Saikewicz. Saikewicz was profoundly mentally retarded. His mental state was a cognitive one but limited in his capacity to comprehend and communicate. Evidence that most people choose to accept the rigors of chemotherapy has no direct bearing on the likely choice that Joseph Saikewicz would have made. Unlike most people, Saikewicz had no capacity to understand his present situation or his prognosis. The guardian ad litem gave expression to this important distinction in coming to grips with this "most troubling aspect" of withholding treatment from Saikewicz: "If he is treated with toxic drugs he will be involuntarily immersed in a state of painful suffering, the reason for which he will never understand. Patients who request treatment know the risks involved and can appreciate the painful side effects when they arrive. They know the reason for the pain and their hope makes it tolerable." To make a worthwhile comparison, one would have to ask whether a majority of people would choose chemotherapy if they were told merely that something outside of their previous experience was going to be done to them, that this something would cause them pain and discomfort, that they would be removed to strange surroundings and possibly restrained for extended periods of time, and that the advantages of this course of action were measured by concepts of time and mortality beyond their ability to comprehend.

[7] To put the above discussion in proper perspective, we realize that an inquiry into what a majority of people would do in circumstances that truly were similar assumes an objective viewpoint not far removed from a "reasonable person" inquiry. While we recognize the value of this kind of indirect evidence, we should make it plain that the primary test is subjective in nature—that is, the goal is to determine with as much accuracy as possible the wants and needs of the individual involved.[15] This may or may not conform to what is thought wise or prudent by most people. The problems of arriving at an accurate substituted judgment in matters of life and death vary greatly in degree, if not in kind, in different circumstances. For example, the responsibility of Karen Quinlan's father to act as she would have wanted could be discharged by drawing on many years of what was apparently an affectionate and close relationship. In contrast, Joseph Saikewicz was profoundly retarded and noncommunicative his entire life, which was spent largely in the highly restrictive atmosphere of an institution. While it may thus be necessary to rely to a greater degree on objective criteria, such as the supposed inability of profoundly retarded persons to conceptualize or fear death, the effort to bring the substituted judgment into step with the values and desires of the affected individual must not, and need not, be abandoned.

The "substituted judgment" standard which we have described commends itself simply because of its straightforward respect for the integrity and autonomy of the individual. We need not, however, ignore the substantial pedigree that accompanies this phrase. The doctrine of substituted judgment had its origin over 150 years ago in the area of the administration of the estate of an incompetent person. *Ex parte Whitbread in re Hinde, a Lunatic,* 35 Eng. Rep. 878 (1816). The doctrine was utilized to authorize a gift from the estate of an incompetent person to an individual when the incompetent owed no duty of support. The English court accomplished this purpose by substituting itself as nearly as possible for the incompetent, and acting on the same motives and considerations as would have moved him. *City Bank Farmers Trust Co. v. McGowan,* 323 U. S. 594, 599, 65 S.Ct. 496, 89 L.Ed. 483 (1945). In essence, the doctrine in its original inception called on the court to "don the mental mantle of the incompetent." *In re Carson,* 39 Misc.2d 544, 545, 241 N.Y.S.2d 288, 289 (N.Y.Sup.Ct. 1962). Cf. *Strange v. Powers,* 358 Mass. 126, 260 N.E.2d 704 (1970).

In modern times the doctrine of substituted judgment has been applied as a vehicle of decision in cases more analogous to the situation presented in this case. In a leading decision on this point, *Strunk v. Strunk,* 445 S.W.2d 145 (Ky.Ct. App.1969), the court held that a court of equity had the power to permit removal of a kidney from an incompetent donor for purposes of effectuating a transplant. The court concluded that, due to the nature of their relationship, both parties would benefit from the completion of the procedure, and hence the court could presume that the prospective donor would, if competent, assent to the procedure. Accord, *Hart v. Brown,* 29 Conn.Supp. 368, 289 A.2d 386 (1972). But see *In re Guardianship of Pescinski,* 67 Wis.2d 4, 226 N.W.2d 180 (1975). See generally Baron and others, Life Organ and Tissue Transplants from Minor Donors in Massachusetts, 55 B.U.L.Rev. 159 (1975).[16]

[8,9] With this historical perspective, we now reiterate the substituted judgment doctrine as we apply it in the instant case. We believe that both the guardian ad litem in his recommendation and the judge in his decision should have attempted (as they did) to ascertain the incompetent person's actual interests and preferences. In short, the decision in cases such as this should be that which would be made by the incompetent person, if that person were competent, but taking into account the present and future incompetency of the individual as one of the factors which would necessarily enter into the decision-making process of the competent person. Having recognized the right of a competent person to make for himself the same decision as the court made in this case, the question is, do the facts on the record support the proposition that Saikewicz himself would have made the decision under the standard set forth? We believe they do.

The two factors considered by the probate judge to weigh in favor of administering chemotherapy were: (1) the fact that most people elect chemotherapy and (2) the chance of a longer life. Both are appropriate indicators of what Saikewicz himself would have wanted, provided that due allowance is taken for this individual's present and future incompetency. We have already discussed the perspective this brings to the fact that most people choose to undergo chemotherapy. With regard to the second factor, the chance of a longer life carries the same weight for Saikewicz as for any other person, the value of life under the law having no relation to intelligence or social position. Intertwined with this consideration is the hope that a cure, temporary or permanent, will be discovered during the period of extra weeks or months potentially made available by chemotherapy. The guardian ad litem investigated this possibility and found no reason to hope for a dramatic breakthrough in the time frame relevant to the decision.

[10] The probate judge identified six factors weighing against administration of chemotherapy. Four of these—Saikewicz's age,[17] the probable side effects of treatment, the low chance of producing remission, and the certainty that treatment will cause immediate suffering—were clearly established by the medical testimony to be considerations that any individual would weigh carefully. A fifth factor—Saikewicz's inability to cooperate with the treatment—introduces those considerations that are unique to this individual and which therefore are essential to the proper exercise of substituted judgment. The judge heard testimony that Saikewicz would have no comprehension of the reasons for the severe disruption of his formerly secure and stable environment occasioned by the chemotherapy. He therefore would experience fear without the understanding from which other patients draw strength. The inability to anticipate and prepare for the severe side effects of the drugs leaves room only for confusion and disorientation. The possibility that such a naturally uncooperative patient would have to be physically restrained to allow the slow intravenous administration of drugs could only compound his pain and fear, as well as possibly jeopardize the ability of his body to withstand the toxic effects of the drugs.

[11] The sixth factor identified by the judge as weighing against chemotherapy was "the quality of life possible for him even if the treatment does bring about

remission." To the extent that this formulation equates the value of life with any measure of the quality of life, we firmly reject it. A reading of the entire record clearly reveals, however, the judge's concern that special care be taken to respect the dignity and worth of Saikewicz's life precisely because of his vulnerable position. The judge, as well as all the parties, were keenly aware that the supposed inability of Saikewicz, by virtue of his mental retardation, to appreciate or experience life had no place in the decision before them. Rather than reading the judge's formulation in a manner that demeans the value of the life of one who is mentally retarded, the vague, and perhaps ill-chosen, term "quality of life" should be understood as a reference to the continuing state of pain and disorientation precipitated by the chemotherapy treatment. Viewing the term in this manner, together with the other factors properly considered by the judge, we are satisfied that the decision to withhold treatment from Saikewicz was based on a regard for his actual interests and preferences and that the facts supported this decision.

C

We turn now to a consideration of the procedures appropriate for reaching a decision where a person allegedly incompetent is in a position in which a decision as to the giving or withholding of life-prolonging treatment must be made.[18] As a preliminary matter, we briefly inquire into the powers of the Probate Court in this context.

[12] The Probate Court is a court of superior and general jurisdiction. G.L. c. 215, § 2. *Wilder v. Orcutt,* 257 Mass. 100, 153 N.E. 332 (1926). The Probate Court is given equity jurisdiction by statute. G.L. c. 215, § 6. It has been given the specific grant of equitable powers to act in all matters relating to guardianship. G.L. c. 215, § 6. *Buckingham v. Alden,* 315 Mass. 383, 387, 53 N.E.2d 101 (1944). The Probate Court has the power to appoint a guardian for a retarded person. G.L.c.201, § 6A. It may also appoint a temporary guardian of such a person where immediate action is required. G.L. c. 201, § 14. Additionally, the Probate Court may appoint a guardian ad litem whenever the court believes it necessary to protect the interests of a person in a proceeding before it. *Buckingham v. Alden, supra.* This power is inherent in the court even apart from statutory authorization, and its exercise at times becomes necessary for the proper function of the court. *Lynde v. Vose,* 326 Mass. 621, 96 N.E.2d 172 (1951). *Buckingham v. Alden, supra.*

[13] In dealing with matters concerning a person properly under the court's protective jurisdiction, "[t]he court's action . . . is not limited by any narrow bounds, but it is empowered to stretch forth its arm in whatever direction its aid and protection may be needed. . . ." *In re Quinlan,* 70 N.J. 10, 45, 355 A.2d 647, 666 (1976), quoting from 27 Am.Jur.2d Equity § 69 (1966). In essence the powers of the court to act in the best interests of a person under its jurisdiction, *Petition of the Dep't of Pub. Welfare to Dispense with Consent to Adoption,* _____ Mass. _____[d], 358 N.E.2d 794 (1976), must be broad and flexible enough "to afford whatever relief may be necessary to protect his interests." *Strunk v. Strunk,* 445 S.W.2d 145, 147 (Ky.Ct.App. 1969), quoting from 27 Am.Jr.2d Equity § 69, at 592 (1966). The Probate Court is the proper forum in which to determine the need for

the appointment of a guardian or a guardian ad litem. It is also the proper tribunal to determine the best interests of a ward.

In this case, a ward of a State institution was discovered to have an invariably fatal illness, the only effective—in the sense of life-prolonging—treatment for which involved serious and painful intrusions on the patient's body. While an emergency existed with regard to taking action to begin treatment, it was not a case in which immediate action was required. Nor was this a case in which life-saving, as distinguished from life-prolonging, procedures were available. Because the individual involved was thought to be incompetent to make the necessary decisions, the officials of the State institutions properly initiated proceedings in the Probate Court.

The course of proceedings in such a case is readily determined by reference to the applicable statutes. The first step is to petition the court for the appointment of a guardian. (G.L. c. 201, § 6A) or a temporary guardian (G.L. c.201, § 14). The decision under which of these two provisions to proceed will be determined by the circumstances of the case, that is, whether the exigencies of the situation allow time to comply with the seven-day notice requirement prior to the hearing on the appointment of a guardian. G.L. c. 201, §§ 6A, 7. If appointment of a temporary guardian is sought, the probate judge will make such orders regarding notice as he deems appropriate. G.L. c. 201, § 14. At the hearing on the appointment of a guardian or temporary guardian, the issues before the court are (1) whether the person involved is mentally retarded within the meaning of the statute (G.L. c. 201, § 6A) and (2), if the person is mentally retarded, who shall be appointed guardian. *Id.* As an aid to the judge in reaching these two decisions, it will often be desirable to appoint a guardian ad litem, sua sponte or on motion, to represent the interests of the person. Moreover, we think it appropriate, and highly desirable, in cases such as the one before us to charge the guardian ad litem with an additional responsibility to be discharged if there is a finding of incompetency. This will be the responsibility of presenting to the judge, after as thorough an investigation as time will permit, all reasonable arguments in favor of administering treatment to prolong the life of the individual involved. This will ensure that all viewpoints and alternatives will be aggressively pursued and examined at the subsequent hearing where it will be determined whether treatment should or should not be allowed. The report of the guardian or temporary guardian will, of course, also be available to the judge at this hearing on the ultimate issue of treatment.[19] Should the probate judge then be satisfied that the incompetent individual would, as determined by the standards previously set forth, have chosen to forego potentially life-prolonging treatment, the judge shall issue the appropriate order. If the judge is not so persuaded, or finds that the interests of the State require it, then treatment shall be ordered.

[14] Commensurate with the powers of the Probate Court already described, the probate judge may, at any step in these proceedings, avail himself or herself of the additional advice or knowledge of any person or group. We note here that many health care institutions have developed medical ethics committees or panels to consider many of the issues touched on here. Consideration of the findings and advice of such groups as well as the testimony of the attending physicians and oth-

er medical experts ordinarily would be of great assistance to a probate judge faced with such a difficult decision. We believe it desirable for a judge to consider such views wherever available and useful to the court. We do not believe, however, that this option should be transformed by us into a required procedure. We take a dim view of any attempt to shift the ultimate decision-making responsibility away from the duly established courts of proper jurisdiction to any committee, panel or group, ad hoc or permanent. Thus, we reject the approach adopted by the New Jersey Supreme Court in the *Quinlan* case of entrusting the decision whether to continue artificial life support to the patient's guardian, family, attending doctors, and hospital "ethics committee."[20] 70 N.J. at 55, 355 A.2d 647, 671. One rationale for such a delegation was expressed by the lower court judge in the *Quinlan* case, and quoted by the New Jersey Supreme Court: "The nature, extent and duration of care by societal standards is the responsibility of a physician. The morality and conscience of our society places this responsibility in the hands of the physician. What justification is there to remove it from the control of the medical profession and place it in the hands of the courts?" *Id.* at 44, 355 A.2d at 665. For its part, the New Jersey Supreme Court concluded that "a practice of applying to a court to confirm such decisions would generally be inappropriate, not only because that would be a gratuitous encroachment upon the medical profession's field of competence, but because it would be impossibly cumbersome. Such a requirement is distinguishable from the judicial overview traditionally required in other matters such as the adjudication and commitment of mental incompetents. This is not to say that in the case of an otherwise justiciable controversy access to the courts would be foreclosed; we speak rather of a general practice and procedure." *Id.* at 50, 355 A.2d at 669.

We do not view the judicial resolution of this most difficult and awesome question—whether potentially life-prolonging treatment should be withheld from a person incapable of making his own decision—as constituting a "gratuitous encroachment" on the domain of medical expertise. Rather, such questions of life and death seem to us to require the process of detached but passionate investigation and decision that forms the ideal on which the judicial branch of government was created. Achieving this ideal is our responsibility and that of the lower court, and is not to be entrusted to any other group purporting to represent the "morality and conscience of our society," no matter how highly motivated or impressively constituted.

III

Finding no State interest sufficient to counterbalance a patient's decision to decline life-prolonging medical treatment in the circumstances of this case, we conclude that the patient's right to privacy and self-determination is entitled to enforcement. Because of this conclusion, and in view of the position of equality of an incompetent person in Joseph Saikewicz's position, we conclude that the probate judge acted appropriately in this case. For these reasons we issued our order of July 9, 1976, and responded as we did to the questions of the probate judge.

NOTES

1. In addition to the report of the guardian ad litem, the probate judge had before him the clinical team reports of a physician, a psychologist, and a social worker, as required by G.L.c. 201, § 6A. Expert testimony was taken from a staff physician of the Belchertown State School and two consulting physicians from the Baystate Medical Center, formerly Springfield Hospital.

2. "(1) Does the Probate Court under its general or any special jurisdiction have the authority to order, in circumstances it deems appropriate, the withholding of medical treatment from a person even though such withholding of treatment might contribute to a shortening of the life of such person?

"(2) On the facts reported in this case, is the Court correct in ordering that no treatment be administered to said JOSEPH SAIKEWICZ now or at any time for his condition of acute myeloblastic monocetic leukemia except by further order of the Court?"

3. After briefly reviewing the facts of the case, we stated in that order: "Upon consideration, based upon the findings of the probate judge, we answer the first question in the affirmative, and a majority of the Court answer the second question in the affirmative. However, we emphasize that upon receiving evidence of a significant change either in the medical condition of Saikewicz or in the medical treatment available to him for successful treatment of his condition, the probate judge may issue a further order."

4. On appeal, the petitioners have collected in their brief a number of recent empirical studies which cast doubt on the view that patients over sixty are less successfully treated by chemotherapy. E.g., Bloomfield & Theologides, Acute Granulocytic Leukemia in Elderly Patients, 226 J.A.M.A. 1190, 1192 (1973); Grann and others, The Therapy of Acute Granulocytic Leukemia in Patients More Than Fifty Years Old, 80 Annals Internal Med. 15, 16 (1974). (Acute myeloblastic monocytic leukemia is a subcategory of acute granulocytic leukemia.) Other experts maintain that older patients have lower remission rates and are more vulnerable to the toxic effects of the administered drugs. E.g., Crosby, Grounds for Optimism in Treating Acute Granulocytic Leukemia, 134 Archives Internal Med. 177 (1974). None of these authorities was brought to the consideration of the probate judge. We accept the judge's conclusion, based on the expert testimony before him and in accordance with substantial medical evidence, that the patient's age weighed against the successful administration of chemotherapy. See note 17 *infra*.

5. There was testimony as to the importance of having the full cooperation of the patient during the initial weeks of the chemotherapy process as well as during follow-up visits. For example, the evidence was that it would be necessary to administer drugs intravenously for extended periods of time—twelve or twenty-four hours a day for up to five days. The inability of Saikewicz to comprehend the purpose of the treatment, combined with his physical strength, led the doctors to testify that Saikewicz would probably have to be restrained to prevent him from tampering with the intravenous devices. Such forcible restraint could, in addition to increasing the patient's discomfort, lead to complications such as pneumonia.

6. This information comes to us from the supplemental briefs of the parties.

7. Submitting the brief for the defendant was the guardian ad litem, Patrick J. Melnik. The Attorney General submitted the brief for the plaintiffs. The Civil Rights and Liberties Division of the Department of the Attorney General prepared a brief amicus curiae on behalf of the defendant. Briefs amicus curiae were also submitted by the Mental Health Legal Advisors Committee, the Massachusetts Association for Retarded Citizens, Inc., and the Developmental Disabilities Law Project of the University of Maryland Law School.

   a. Mass.Adv.Sh. (1977) 286.

   b. Mass.Adv.Sh. (1977) 96.

8. While *Quinlan* would seem to limit the effect of these decisions, the opinion therein does not make clear the extent to which this is so.

9. *Commonwealth v. O'Neal,* 367 Mass. 440, 327 N.E.2d 662 (1975), does not compel a different result. That case considered the magnitude of the State interest in preserving life in the context of an intentional State deprivation. It does not apply to a situation where an indi-

vidual, without State involvement, may make a decision resulting in the shortening of life by natural causes.

10. The nature of the third party interest discussed here is not one where the decision has clear, immediate, and adverse effects on the third party such as in *Raleigh Fitkin-Paul Morgan Memorial Hosp., supra,* where a blood transfusion was necessary to preserve the life of a child in utero, as well as the mother. Clearly, different considerations are presented in such a case.

11. The interest in protecting against suicide seems to require little if any discussion. In the case of the competent adult's refusing medical treatment such an act does not necessarily constitute suicide since (1) in refusing treatment the patient may not have the specific intent to die, and (2) even if he did, to the extent that the cause of death was from natural causes the patient did not set the death producing agent in motion with the intent of causing his own death. Byrn, *supra* at 17–18. Cantor, *supra* at 255. Furthermore, the underlying State interest in this area lies in the prevention of irrational self-destruction. What we consider here is a competent, rational decision to refuse treatment when death is inevitable and the treatment offers no hope of cure or preservation of life. There is no connection between the conduct here in issue and any State concern to prevent suicide. Cantor, *supra* at 258.

12. Any threats of civil liability may be removed by a valid giving or withholding of consent by an informed patient. See generally Note, Statutory Recognition of the Right to Die: The California Natural Death Act, 57 B.U.L. Rev.148 (1977), for a comprehensive discussion of the common law foundations of physicians' duties and patients' rights, one legislative attempt to modernize the law, and an analysis of the ramifications for doctors and patients of recognizing the option of withholding life-sustaining procedures from a patient incapable of indicating his or her wishes.

c. Mass.Adv.Sh. (1975) 2853.

13. The brain death criteria developed by the Ad Hoc Committee was recently recognized by this court as a medically and legally acceptable definition of death. *Commonwealth v. Golston,* _____ Mass. _____, _____ _____ (Mass. Adv.Sh. [1977] 1778, 1779–1783), 336 N.E.2d 744 (1977).

14. The mandatory involvement of the family, attending doctors, and the hospital "ethics committee" was also provided for by the court. See note 20 *infra.*

15. In arriving at a philosophical rationale in support of a theory of substituted judgment in the context of organ transplants from incompetent persons, Professor Robertson of the University of Wisconsin Law School argued that "maintaining the integrity of the person means that we act toward him 'as we have reason to believe [he] would choose for [himself] if [he] were [capable] of reason and deciding rationally.' It does not provide a license to impute to him preferences he never had or to ignore previous preferences. . . . If preferences are unknown, we must act with respect to the preferences a reasonable, competent person in the incompetent's situation would have." Robertson, Organ Donations by Incompetents and the Substituted Judgment Doctrine, 76 Colum. L.Rev. 48, 63 (1976), quoting J. Rawls, A Theory of Justice 209 (1971). In this way, the "free choice and moral dignity" of the incompetent person would be recognized. "Even if we were mistaken in ascertaining his preferences, the person [if he somehow became competent] could still agree that he had been fairly treated, if we had a good reason for thinking he would have made the choices imputed to him." Robertson, *supra* at 63.

16. In a similar matter before a single justice of this court, *Nathan v. Farinelli,* Suffolk Eq. 74–87, use of the doctrine was rejected, but primarily because the facts of the case involved potential conflicts of interest and made it inapplicable.

17. This factor is relevant because of the medical evidence in the record that people of Saikewicz's age do not tolerate the chemotherapy as well as younger people and that the chance of a remission is decreased. Age is irrelevant, of course, to the question of the value or quality of life.

18. We decline the invitation of several of the amicus and party briefs to formulate a comprehensive set of guidelines applicable generally to emergency medical situations involving incompetent persons. Such a wide-ranging effort is better left to the legislative branch after appropriate study.

d. Mass.Adv.Sh. (1976) d981.

19. We note that the probate judge in the instant case would more appropriately have appointed a temporary guardian under G.L. c. 201, § 14, subsequent to an initial determination that Saikewicz was incompetent to make his own decision regarding treatment. Instead the judge appointed a guardian ad litem to discharge the duties of a general guardian. In view of the facts, however, we are of the view that nothing of substance turns on this distinction in this case. We also note the existence of some confusion and doubt concerning the power of a probate judge to appoint a temporary guardian for a mentally retarded person prior to the amendment in 1976 of G.L. c. 201, § 14, by St.1976, c. 277.

20. Specifically, the court held that "upon the concurrence of the guardian and family of Karen, should the responsible attending physicians conclude that there is no reasonable possibility of Karen's ever emerging from her present comatose condition to a cognitive, sapient state and that the life-support apparatus now being administered to Karen should be discontinued, they shall consult with the hospital 'Ethics Committee' or like body of the institution in which Karen is then hospitalized. If that consultative body agrees that there is no reasonable possibility of Karen's ever emerging from her present comatose condition to a cognitive, sapient state, the present life-support system may be withdrawn and said action shall be without any civil or criminal liability therefor on the part of any participant, whether guardian, physician, hospital or others."

"By the above ruling we do not intend to be understood as implying that a proceeding for judicial declaratory relief is necessarily required for the implementation of comparable decisions in the field of medical practice." *In re Quinlan,* 70 N.J. at 55, 355 A.2d at 672.

III. MEDICAL TREATMENT AND THE INVOLUNTARILY INSTITUTIONALIZED

1. THE ETHICAL ISSUES

The major element in obtaining consent is the determination of whether the individual is capable of giving consent. With respect to mental illness, this problem is of particular importance because, in the words of Willard Gaylin, "the organ that gives consent is the organ that is ill." In addition, the situations of all persons involuntarily institutionalized can reduce their self-determination and thereby diminish their autonomy as personal decision-makers.

A decision to refuse treatment illustrates a dimension of the problem. Such a refusal often may appear irrational, foolishly impulsive, and not in a patient's own medical interest. This perception is intensified when the individual is also judged to be mentally ill, for the refusal of treatment is seen as a further sign of mental illness and a demonstration of incompetence. This creates a trap from which the individual cannot escape. If one perceives treatment refusals as expressions of values, then the situation can be evaluated differently. For it is not apparent that all individuals have the same values. Nor is it clear that all individuals will view a particular therapy to be in their best interests. Such decisions are exercises of autonomy or self-determination; while treatment refusals may seem foolish to some, they may be quite consistent with the values of others. The critical determination is whether or not the individual is capable of assuming the responsibility of making these critical decisions. The issue, then, is the exercise of self-determination, not its expression. Mental illness *per se* does not constitute incompetence and decisions perceived by some as foolish are not necessarily signs of incompetence. Great care must therefore be taken in evaluating and testing the decisions of those judged to be mentally ill.

A second ethical problem has to do with the conducting of experiments on the institutionalized. This becomes even more complex when experimental procedure is invasive and/or irreversible, as in the case of brain surgery. Other dilemmas arise from uncertainty of the benefits to be obtained and the risks to be undertaken. A complication arises in the *Kaimowitz* decision in that the Court determines that an involuntarily institutionalized mental patient might be able to consent to a validated neurological procedure, but it forbids, in effect, the research that could lead to a practice's being validated.

193

Finally, the problem of proxy consent must be considered. First, the situation of those institutionalized as mentally ill must be carefully evaluated. Institutions have corrosive effects. Paternalistic behavior on the part of professionals and staff is the norm rather than the exception. We must also be wary of state paternalism that refuses to allow individuals to make choices that they may be capable of making and may wish to make. Self-determination and self-respect can be fostered by allowing individuals opportunities to develop these essential qualities. Extreme care, therefore, must be taken in determining whether or not to exclude a certain population from a research protocol.

Studies have indicated that much shoddy, unprofessional, and unethical experimentation has been conducted on captive populations. Those in mental hospitals are particularly vulnerable. Yet they, too, need the benefits of research. Thus, if they are *a priori* excluded from research and experimentation, they may be further disadvantaged. Institutional Review Boards or other committees for the protection of human subjects are well-accepted means of protecting the rights of subjects and reflect an institutional and federally mandated commitment to higher standards of ethical and scientific research. Thus, irresponsibility in research is less likely to occur than before.

A standard function of the guardian is to provide substitute consent, thereby providing for an incompetent person what he or she cannot do for himself or herself. This may include a determination that it is legitimate for an individual to participate in a research protocol or an experimental procedure. Such a determination must be made on the grounds of the likelihood of success and a risk-benefit evaluation. It must also include consultation with the patient. If the patient does not object, the guardian may exercise proxy consent and the protocol can receive final review and approval by an Institutional Review Board. If the patient refuses to participate, it would seem proper for the guardian to prohibit the person from participating in the protocol. Similarly, patients who can neither consent nor refuse consent ought not to be included. The patient's bodily integrity is an important value and should not be violated unless a medical emergency exists.

A final ethical problem has to do with the issue of commitment itself. There is a widespread impression that one of the major functions of mental hospitals is simply to warehouse individuals with whom society seems unable to deal in any other way. When this is coupled with inadequate staff and minimum therapy, such commitment more resembles punishment than care. This practice strikes at the heart of an individual's liberty and thereby at his or her autonomy and self-determination. When an individual is harmless, or at least not dangerous, the traditional principle of the protection of third parties from harm does not apply. And when this individual is capable of caring for his or her person—or with the assistance of family, friends, or an outpatient service—the exercise of state paternalism is difficult to justify. Therefore, the person's capacity for self-determination and the possibility of harm to others must be examined on a case-by-case basis.

A person, however, may not be dangerous and may be capable of survival, but may really have no place to go. Family or friends may be willing to assist, but they may not be able to provide living quarters or job. Thus, while the individual may be capable of survival, he or she actually may be unable to survive because of the social context to which he or she must return. In such an instance, de-institutional-ization in the name of liberty or self-determination may be highly unethical or so-cially irresponsible, though properly legal. In this or similar situations, an investigation must evaluate the situation to which the person will be returning. Only then will self-determination be genuinely protected.

2. THE LEGAL ISSUES

Whether or not there exists a constitutional right to medical treatment ap-pears as a question for the first time in *O'Connor,* with by now familiar medico-legal issues—such as privacy, consent, and competing interests—presented in *Yetter* and *Kaimowitz.* Equally familiar is the way in which the courts approach these issues: analyzing the constitutional rights involved and establishing the legal standards and procedures necessary for asserting them. In addition to unique ques-tions raised in *O'Connor,* it is the status of the person seeking relief in each case that adds a distinctive flavor to this material. All were involuntarily confined to state mental-health institutions under either civil or criminal commitment proce-dures.

In *Yetter* the Court recognizes that the right to privacy protects an "involun-tarily civilly committed" person's decision to refuse treatment that may prolong life: "In short . . . , the right of privacy includes a right to die with which the State should not interfere" when there are no overriding competing interests. An invol-untarily committed person asserts this right in the same way as a voluntarily com-mitted—or, for that matter, any other person—through personal or proxy consent, depending on whether he or she is competent or incompetent. Employing a subjec-tive test, the Court allows that if at the time Maida Yetter refused treatment she was conscious of the consequences, then her decision was competent even though it "might be considered unwise, foolish or ridiculous."

Kaimowitz differs from *Yetter* in that John Doe had been criminally commit-ted and had allegedly consented to treatment. The outcome of this case seems to turn on the nature of the particular treatment—experimental psychosurgery that is held to be scientifically unacceptable in this type of nontherapeutic treatment. In a lengthy discussion, the Court comes down heavily on the voluntary dimension of informed consent, maintaining that involuntary circumstances had precluded Doe from giving voluntary—and therefore legally adequate—consent to nontherapeutic psychosurgery. As the Court says, "psychosurgery should never be undertaken upon involuntarily committed populations, when there is a high-risk low-benefit ratio as demonstrated in this case. This is because of the impossibility of obtaining truly informed consent from such populations." The Court then discusses the con-stitutional considerations that preclude the involuntarily detained mentally ill per-son from giving effective consent to such treatment. Once again the right of privacy is extended, this time to include a person's "thoughts, behavior, personality and identity." Here the right is located in the constitutional protection of freedom of speech and expression, since experimental psychosurgery "can impinge upon the right of the individual to be free from interference with his mental processes." Fi-nally, the Court holds that under these circumstances the State of Michigan's interest in the use of experimental psychosurgery is insufficient "to overcome its proscription by the First Amendment of the United States Constitution."

In *O'Connor* what the United States Supreme Court refuses to speak to is perhaps as significant as its holding that "a finding of 'mental illness' alone cannot justify a state's locking up a person against his will and keeping him indefinitely in simple custodial confinement; there is no constitutional basis for confining such persons involuntarily if they are dangerous to no one and can live safely in freedom." The Supreme Court maintains that the Court of Appeals had raised difficult issues of constitutional law, not present in the facts of this case, by affirming the judgment of a lower court that the "Fourteenth Amendment guarantees a right to treatment to persons involuntarily civilly committed to state mental hospitals." Holding that the only constitutional issue in *O'Connor* is "every man's . . . right to liberty," the Court sees no reason to decide whether "mentally ill persons dangerous to themselves or to others have a right to treatment upon compulsory confinement by the State, or whether the State may compulsorily confine a nondangerous, mentally ill individual for the purpose of treatment." Chief Justice Burger, however, clearly rejects the Court of Appeals' position in his separate concurring opinion.

IN RE YETTER

Court of Common Pleas of Northampton County, Pennsylvania, Orphans' Court Division, 1973. 62 Pa. D. & C.2nd 619.

This matter involves the appointment of a guardian of the person for Maida Yetter, an alleged incompetent, under the Incompetent Estates Act of 1955, 50 P.S. § 3101 et seq. The petition was filed by Russell C. Stauffer, her brother, and a citation issued on May 10, 1973. The citation was served on the alleged incompetent by a deputy sheriff of Lehigh County at Allentown State Hospital, Lehigh County, Pennsylvania, on May 15, 1973. A hearing was held on May 30, 1973, as specified in the petition. Present at the hearing were the petitioner and his counsel; Dr. Ellen Bischoff, a psychiatrist on the staff of the hospital; Mrs. Marilou Perhac, a caseworker at the hospital assigned to Mrs. Yetter's ward; the alleged incompetent and her counsel. Mrs. Yetter is married, although she has been separated from and has had no contact with her husband since 1947.

From the petition and the testimony it appears that the primary purpose of the appointment of a guardian of the person is to give consent to the performance of diagnostic and corrective surgery.

Mrs. Yetter was committed to Allentown State Hospital in June 1971, by the Courts of Northampton County after hearings held pursuant to Section 406 of the Mental Health and Mental Retardation Act of 1966. Her diagnosis at that time was schizophrenia, chronic undifferentiated. It appears that late in 1972, in connection with a routine physical examination, Mrs. Yetter was discovered to have a breast discharge indicating the possible presence of carcinoma. The doctors recommended that a surgical biopsy be performed together with any additional corrective surgery that would be indicated by the pathology of the biopsy. When this recommendation was first discussed with Mrs. Yetter in December of 1972 by her caseworker, Mrs. Perhac, who has had weekly counseling sessions with Mrs. Yetter for more than a year, Mrs. Yetter indicated that she would not give her consent to the surgery. Her stated reasons were that she was afraid because of the death of her aunt which followed such surgery and that it was her own body and she did not desire the operation. The caseworker indicated that at this time Mrs. Yetter was lucid, rational and appeared to understand that the possible consequences of her refusal included death.

Mr. Stauffer, who indicated that he visits his sister regularly, and Dr. Bischoff, whose direct contacts with Mrs. Yetter have been since March 1973, testified that in the last three or four months it has been impossible to discuss the proposed surgery with Mrs. Yetter in that, in addition to expressing fear of the operation, she has become delusional in her reasons for not consenting to surgery. Her tendency to become delusional concerning this problem, although no others, was confirmed by Mrs. Perhac. The present delusional nature of Mrs. Yetter's reasoning concerning the problem was demonstrated at the hearing when Mrs. Yetter, in response to questions by the Court and counsel, indicated that the operation would interfere with her genital system, affecting her ability to have babies, and would prohibit a movie career. Mrs. Yetter is 60 years of age and without children.

Dr. Bischoff testified that Mrs. Yetter is oriented as to time, place and her personal environment, and that her present delusions are consistent with the diagnosis and evaluation of her mental illness upon admission to the hospital in 1971. The doctor indicated that, in her opinion, at the present time Mrs. Yetter is unable, by reason of her mental illness, to arrive at a considered judgment as to whether to undergo surgery.

Mr. Stauffer testified that the aunt referred to by Mrs. Yetter, although she underwent a similar operation, died of unrelated causes some 15 years after surgery. He further indicated that he has been apprised by the physicians of the nature of the proposed procedures and their probable consequences as well as the probable consequences if the procedures are not performed. He indicated that if he is appointed guardian of the person for his sister, he would consent to the surgical procedures recommended.

At the hearing Mrs. Yetter was alert, interested, and obviously meticulous about her personal appearance. She stated that she was afraid of surgery, that the best course of action for her would be to leave her body alone, that surgery might hasten the spread of the disease and do further harm, and she reiterated her fears due to the death of her aunt. On several occasions during the hearing she interjected the statements that she would die if surgery were performed.

It is clear that mere commitment to a state hospital for treatment of mental illness does not destroy a person's competency or require the appointment of a guardian of the estate or person. *In re Ryman,* 139 Pa. Super. 212. Mental capacity must be examined on a case by case basis.

In our opinion the constitutional right of privacy[1] includes the right of a mature competent adult to refuse to accept medical recommendations that may prolong one's life and which, to a third person at least, appear to be in his best interests; in short, that the right of privacy includes a right to die with which the State should not interfere where there are no minor or unborn children and no clear and present danger to public health, welfare or morals. If the person was competent while being presented with the decision and in making the decision which she did, the Court should not interfere even though her decision might be considered unwise, foolish or ridiculous.

While many philosophical articles have been published relating to this subject, there are few appellate court decisions and none in Pennsylvania to our knowledge. The cases are collected in an annotation in 9 A.L.R. 3d 1391. Considering other factors which have influenced the various courts, the present case does not involve a patient who sought medical attention from a hospital and then attempted to restrict the institution and physicians from rendering proper medical care. The state hospital as Mrs. Yetter's custodian certainly has acted properly in initiating the present proceeding through the patient's brother and cannot be said to have either overridden the patient's wishes or merely allowed her to die for lack of treatment.

The testimony of the caseworker with respect to her conversations with Mrs. Yetter in December 1972, convinces us that at that time her refusal was informed, conscious of the consequences and would not have been superseded by this Court. The ordinary person's refusal to accept medical advice based upon fear is commonly known and while the refusal may be irrational and foolish to an outside observer it cannot be said to be incompetent in order to permit the State to override the decision.

The obvious difficulty in this proceeding is that in recent months Mrs. Yetter's steadfast refusal has been accompanied by delusions which create doubt that her decision is the product of competent, reasoned judgment. However, she has been consistent in expressing the fear that she would die if surgery were performed. The delusions do not appear to us to be her primary reason for rejecting surgery. Are we then to force her to submit to medical treatment because some of her present reasons for refusal are delusional and the result of mental illness? Should we now overrule her original understanding but irrational decision?

There is no indication that Mrs. Yetter's condition is critical or that she is in the waning hours of life, although we recognize the advice of medical experts as to the need for early detection and treatment of cancer symptoms. Upon reflection, balancing the risk involved in our refusal to act in favor of compulsory treatment against giving the greatest possible protection to the individual in furtherance of his own desires, we are unwilling now to overrule Mrs. Yetter's original irrational but competent decision.

Since no additional reasons for the appointment of a guardian of the person are presented, we enter the following.

ORDER OF COURT

And now, this sixth day of June, 1973, the petition for the appointment of a guardian of the person for Maida Yetter, an alleged incompetent, is refused.

By the Court.

NOTE

1. *Roe v. Wade, 410* U. S. *113,* 35 L.Ed.2d 147 (1973).

KAIMOWITZ V. DEPARTMENT OF MENTAL HEALTH FOR THE STATE OF MICHIGAN

Circuit Court for the County of Wayne,
Michigan, July 10, 1973.
Civil Action No.73–19434–AW.

OPINION

This case came to this Court originally on a complaint for a Writ of Habeas Corpus brought by Plaintiff Kaimowitz on behalf of John Doe and the Medical Committee for Human Rights, alleging that John Doe was being illegally detained in the Lafayette Clinic for the purpose of experimental psychosurgery.[1]

John Doe had been committed by the Kalamazoo County Circuit Court on January 11, 1955, to the Ionia State Hospital as a Criminal Sexual Psychopath, without a trial of criminal charges, under the terms of the then existing Criminal Sexual Psychopathic law.[2] He had been charged with the murder and subsequent rape of a student nurse at the Kalamazoo State Hospital while he was confined there as a mental patient.

In 1972, Drs. Ernst Rodin and Jacques Gottlieb of the Lafayette Clinic, a facility of the Michigan Department of Mental Health, had filed a proposal "For the Study of Treatment of Uncontrollable Aggression."[3]

This was funded by the Legislature of the State of Michigan for the fiscal year 1972. After more than 17 years at the Ionia State Hospital, John Doe was transferred to the Lafayette Clinic in November of 1972 as a suitable research subject for the Clinic's study of uncontrollable aggression.

Under the terms of the study, 24 criminal sexual psychopaths in the State's mental health system were to be subjects of experiment. The experiment was to compare the effects of surgery on the amygdaloid portion of the limbic system of the brain with the effect of the drug cyproterone acetate on the male hormone flow. The comparison was intended to show which, if either, could be used in controlling aggression of males in an institutional setting, and to afford lasting permanent relief from such aggression to the patient.

Substantial difficulties were encountered in locating a suitable patient population for the surgical procedures and a matched controlled group for the treatment by the anti-androgen drug.[4] As a matter of fact, it was concluded that John Doe was the only known appropriate candidate available within the state mental health system for the surgical experiment.

John Doe signed an "informed consent" form to become an experimental subject prior to his transfer from the Ionia State Hospital.[5] He had obtained signatures from his parents giving consent for the experimental and innovative surgical procedures to be performed on his brain,[6] and two separate three-man review committees were established by Dr. Rodin to review the scientific worthiness of the study and the validity of the consent obtained from Doe.

The Scientific Review Committee, headed by Dr. Elliot Luby, approved of the procedure, and the Human Rights Review Committee, consisting of Ralph Slovenko, a Professor of Law and Psychiatry at Wayne State Universtiy, Monsignor Clifford Sawher, and Frank Moran, a Certified Public Accountant, gave their approval to the procedure.

Even though no experimental subjects were found to be available in the state mental health system other than John Doe, Dr. Rodin prepared to proceed with the experiment on Doe, and depth electrodes were to be inserted into his brain on or about January 15, 1973.

Early in January 1973, Plaintiff Kaimowitz became aware of the work being contemplated on John Doe and made his concern known to the *Detroit Free Press.* Considerable newspaper publicity ensued and this action was filed shortly thereafter.

With the rush of publicity on the filing of the original suit, funds for the research project were stopped by Dr. Gordon Yudashkin, Director of the Department of Mental Health, and the investigators, Drs. Gottlieb and Rodin, dropped their plans to pursue the research set out in the proposal. They reaffirmed at trial, however, their belief in the scientific, medical and ethical soundness of the proposal.

Upon the request of counsel, a Three-Judge Court was empanelled, Judges John D. O'Hair and George E. Bowles joining Judge Horace W. Gilmore. Dean Francis A. Allen and Prof. Robert A. Burt of the University of Michigan Law School were appointed as counsel for John Doe.

Approximately the same time Amicus Curiae, the American Orthopsychiatric Society, sought to enter the case with the right to offer testimony. This was granted by the Court.

Three ultimate issues were framed for consideration by the Court. The first related to the constitutionality of the detention of Doe. The full statement of the second and third questions, to which this Opinion is addressed, are set forth in the text below.

The first issue relating to the constitutionality of the detention of John Doe was considered by the Court, and on March 23, 1973, an Opinion was rendered by the Court holding the detention unconstitutional. Subsequently, after hearing testimony of John Doe's present condition, the Court directed his release.[7]

In the meantime, since it appeared unlikely that any project would go forward because of the withdrawal of approval by Dr. Yudashkin, the Court raised the question as to whether the rest of the case had become moot. All counsel, except counsel representing the Department of Mental Health, stated the matter was not moot, and that the basic issues involved were ripe for declaratory judgment. Counsel for the Department of Mental Health contended the matter was moot.

Full argument was had and the Court on March 15, 1973, rendered an oral Opinion, holding that the matter was not moot and that the case should proceed as to the two framed issues for declaratory judgment. The Court held that even though the original experimental program was terminated, there was nothing that would prevent it from being instituted again in the near future, and therefore the matter was ripe for declaratory judgment.[8]

The facts concerning the original experiment and the involvement of John Doe were to be considered by the Court as illustrative in determining whether legally adequate consent could be obtained from adults involuntarily confined in the state mental health system for experimental or innovative procedures on the brain to ameliorate behavior, and, if it could be, whether the State should allow such experimentation on human subjects to proceed.[9]

The two issues framed for decision in this declaratory judgment action are as follows:

1. After failure of established therapies, may an adult or a legally appointed guardian, if the adult is involuntarily detained, at a facility within the jurisdiction of the State Department of Mental Health give legally adequate consent to an innovative or experimental surgical procedure on the brain, if there is demonstrable physical abnormality of the brain, and the procedure is designed to ameliorate behavior, which is either personally tormenting to the patient, or so profoundly disruptive that the patient cannot safely live, or live with others?

2. If the answer to the above is yes, then is it legal in this State to undertake an innovative or experimental surgical procedure on the brain of an adult who is involuntarily detained at a facility within the jurisdiction of the State Department of Mental Health, if there is demonstrable physical abnormality of the brain, and the procedure is designed to ameliorate behavior, which is either personally tormenting to the patient, or so profoundly disruptive that the patient cannot safely live, or live with others?

Throughout this Opinion, the Court will use the term psychosurgery to describe the proposed innovative or experimental surgical procedure defined in the questions for consideration by the Court.

At least two definitions of psychosurgery have been furnished the Court. Dr. Bertram S. Brown, Director of the National Institute of Mental Health, defined the term as follows in his prepared statement before the United States Senate Subcommittee on Health of the Committee on Labor and Public Welfare on February 23, 1973:

> "Psychosurgery can best be defined as a surgical removal or destruction of brain tissue or the cutting of brain tissue to disconnect one part of the brain from another, with the intent of altering the behavior, even though there may be no direct evidence of structural disease or damage to the brain."

Dr. Peter Breggin, a witness at the trial, defined psychosurgery as the destruction of normal brain tissue for the control of emotions or behavior; or the destruction of abnormal brain tissue for the control of emotions or behavior, where the abnormal tissue has not been shown to be the cause of the emotions or behavior in question.

The psychosurgery involved in this litigation is a subclass, narrower than that defined by Dr. Brown. The proposed psychosurgery we are concerned with encompasses only experimental psychosurgery where there are demonstrable physical abnormalities in the brain.[10] Therefore, temporal lobectomy, an established therapy for relief of clearly diagnosed epilepsy is not involved, nor are accepted neurological surgical procedures, for example, operations for Parkinsonism, or operations for the removal of tumors or the relief of stroke.

We start with the indisputable medical fact that no significant activity in the brain occurs in isolation without correlated activity in other parts of the brain. As the level of complexity of human behavior increases, so does the degree of interaction and integration. Dr. Ayub Ommaya, a witness in the case, illustrated this through the phenomenon of vision. Pure visual sensation is one of the functions highly localized in the occipital lobe in the back of the brain. However, vision in its broader sense, such as the ability to recognize a face, does not depend upon this area of the brain alone. It requires the integration of that small part of the brain with the rest of the brain. Memory mechanisms interact with the visual sensation to permit the recognition of the face. Dr. Ommaya pointed out that the more we know about brain function, the more we realize with certainty that many functions are highly integrated, even for relatively simple activity.

It is clear from the record in this case that the understanding of the limbic system of the brain and its function is very limited. Practically every witness and exhibit established how little is known of the relationship of the limbic system to human behavior, in the absence of some clearly defined clinical disease such as epilepsy. Drs. Mark, Sweet and Ervin have noted repeatedly the primitive state of our understanding of the amygdala, for example, remarking that it is an area made up of nine to fourteen different nuclear structures, with many functions, some of which are competitive with others. They state that there are not even reliable guesses as to the functional location of some of the nuclei.[11]

The testimony showed that any physical intervention in the brain must always be approached with extreme caution. Brain surgery is always irreversible in the sense that any intrusion into the brain destroys the brain cells and such cells do not regenerate. Dr. Ommaya testified that in the absence of well-defined pathological signs, such as blood clots pressing on the brain due to trauma, or tumor in the brain, brain surgery is viewed as a treatment of last resort.

The record in this case demonstrates that animal experimentation and non-intrusive human experimentation have not been exhausted in determining and studying brain function. Any experimentation on the human brain, especially when it involves an intrusive, irreversible procedure in a non-life-threatening situation, should be undertaken with extreme caution, and then only when answers cannot be obtained from animal experimentation and from non-intrusive human experimentation.

Psychosurgery should never be undertaken upon involuntarily committed populations, when there is a high-risk low-benefit ratio as demonstrated in this case. This is because of the impossibility of obtaining truly informed consent from such populations. The reasons such informed consent cannot be obtained are set forth in detail subsequently in this Opinion.

There is widespread concern about violence. Personal violence, whether in a domestic setting or reflected in street violence, tends to increase. Violence in group confrontations appears to have culminated in the late 60's but still invites study and suggested solutions. Violence, personal and group, has engaged the criminal law courts and the correctional systems, and has inspired the appointment of national commissions. The late President Lyndon B. Johnson convened a commission on violence under the chairmanship of Dr. Milton Eisenhower. It was a commission that had fifty consultants representing various fields of law, sociology, criminology, history, government, social psychiatry, and social psychology. Conspicuous by their absence were any professionals concerned with the human brain. It is not surprising, then, that of recent date, there has been theorizing as to violence and the brain, and just over two years ago, Frank Ervin, a psychiatrist, and Vernon H. Mark, a neurosurgeon, wrote *Violence and the Brain*[12] detailing the application of brain surgery to problems of violent behavior.

Problems of violence are not strangers to this Court. Over many years we have studied personal group violence in a court context. Nor are we unconcerned about the tragedies growing out of personal or group confrontations. Deep-seated public concern begets an impatient desire for miracle solutions. And necessarily, we deal here not only with legal and medical issues, but with ethical and social issues as well.

Is brain function related to abnormal aggressive behavior? This, fundamentally, is what the case is about. But, one cannot segment or simplify that which is inherently complex. As Vernon H. Mark has written, "Moral values are social concerns, not medical ones, in any presently recognized sense."[13]

Violent behavior not associated with brain disease should not be dealt with surgically. At best, neurosurgery rightfully should concern itself with medical problems and not the behavior problems of a social etiology.

The Court does not in any way desire to impede medical progress. We are much concerned with violence and the possible effect of brain disease on violence. Much research on the brain is necessary and must be carried on, but when it takes the form of psychosurgery, it cannot be undertaken on involuntarily detained populations. Other avenues of research must be utilized and developed.

Although extensive pyschosurgery has been performed in the United States and throughout the world in recent years to attempt change of objectionable behavior, there is no medically recognized syndrome for aggression and objectionable behavior associated with nonorganic brain abnormality.

The psychosurgery that has been done has in varying degrees blunted emotions and reduced spontaneous behavior. Dr. V. Balasubramaniam, a leading psychosurgeon, has characterized psychosurgery as "sedative neurosurgery," a procedure by which patients are made quiet and manageable.[14] The amygdalotomy, for example, has been used to calm hyperactive children, to make retarded children more manageable in institutions, to blunt the emotions of people with depression, and to attempt to make schizophrenics more manageable.[15]

The dangers of such surgery are undisputed. Though it may be urged, as did some of the witnesses in this case, that the incidents of morbidity and mortality are low from the procedures, all agree dangers are involved, and the benefits to the patient are uncertain.

Absent a clearly defined medical syndrome, nothing pinpoints the exact location in the brain of the cause of undesirable behavior so as to enable a surgeon to make a lesion, remove that portion of the brain, and thus affect undesirable behavior.

Psychosurgery flattens emotional responses, leads to lack of abstract reasoning ability, leads to a loss of capacity for new learning and causes general sedation and apathy. It can lead to impairment of memory, and in some instances unexpected responses to psychosurgery are observed. It has been found, for example, that heightened rage reaction can follow surgical intervention on the amygdala, just as placidity can.[16]

It was unanimously agreed by all witnesses that psychosurgery does not, given the present state of the art, provide any assurance that a dangerously violent person can be restored to the community.[17]

Simply stated, on this record there is no scientific basis for establishing that the removal or destruction of an area of the limbic brain would have any direct therapeutic effect in controlling aggressivity or improving tormenting personal behavior, absent the showing of a well-defined clinical syndrome such as epilepsy.

To advance scientific knowledge, it is true that doctors may desire to experiment on human beings, but the need for scientific inquiry must be reconciled with the inviolability which our society provides for a person's mind and body. Under a free government, one of a person's greatest rights is the right to inviolability of his person, and it is axiomatic that this right necessarily forbids the physician or surgeon from violating, without permission, the bodily integrity of his patient.[18]

Generally, individuals are allowed free choice about whether to undergo experimental medical procedures. But the State has the power to modify this free choice concerning experimental medical procedures when it cannot be freely given, or when the result would be contrary to public policy. For example, it is obvious that a person may not consent to acts that will constitute murder, manslaughter, or mayhem upon himself.[19] In short, there are times when the State for good reason should withhold a person's ability to consent to certain medical procedures.

It is elementary tort law that consent is the mechanism by which the patient grants the physician the power to act, and which protects the patient against unauthorized invasions of his person. This requirement protects one of society's most fundamental values, the inviolability of the individual. An operation performed upon a patient without his informed consent is the tort of battery, and a doctor and a hospital have no right to impose compulsory medical treatment against the patient's will. These elementary statements of tort law need no citation.

Jay Katz, in his outstanding book *Experimentation with Human Beings* (Russell Sage Foundation, N.Y., 1972) points out on page 523 that the concept of informed consent has been accepted as a cardinal principle for judging the propriety of research with human beings.

He points out that in the experimental setting, informed consent serves multiple purposes. He states (pages 523 and 524):

> ". . . Most clearly, requiring informed consent serves society's desire to respect each individual's autonomy, and his right to make choices concerning his own life.
>
> "Second, providing a subject with information about an experiment will encourage him to be an active partner and the process may also increase the rationality of the experimentation process.
>
> "Third, securing informed consent protects the experimentation process by encouraging the investigator to question the value of the proposed project and the adequacy of the measures he has taken to protect subjects, by reducing civil and criminal liability for nonnegligent injury to the subjects, and by diminishing adverse public reaction to an experiment.
>
> "Finally, informed consent may serve the function of increasing society's awareness about human research. . . ."

It is obvious that there must be close scrutiny of the adequacy of the consent when an experiment, as in this case, is dangerous, intrusive, irreversible, and of uncertain benefit to the patient and society.[20]

Counsel for Drs. Rodin and Gottlieb argues that anyone who has ever been treated by a doctor for any relatively serious illness is likely to acknowledge that a competent doctor can get almost any patient to consent to almost anything. Counsel claims this is true because patients do not want to make decisions about complex medical matters and because there is the general problem of avoiding decision making in stress situations, characteristic of all human beings.

He further argues that a patient is always under duress when hospitalized and that in a hospital or institutional setting there is no such thing as a volunteer. Dr. Ingelfinger in Volume 287, page 466, of the *New England Journal of Medicine* (August 31, 1972) states:

> ". . .The process of obtaining 'informed consent' with all its regulations and conditions, is no more than an elaborate ritual, a device that when the subject is uneducated and uncomprehending, confers no more than the semblance of propriety on human experimentation. The subject's only real protection, the public as well as the medical profession must recognize, depends on the conscience and compassion of the investigator and his peers."

Everything defendants' counsel argues militates against the obtaining of informed consent from involuntarily detained mental patients. If, as he argues, truly informed consent cannot be given for regular surgical procedures by noninstitutionalized persons, then certainly an adequate informed consent cannot be given by the involuntarily detained mental patient.

We do not agree that a truly informed consent cannot be given for a regular surgical procedure by a patient, institutionalized or not. The law has long recognized that such valid consent can be given. But we do hold that informed consent cannot be given by an involuntarily detained mental patient for experimental psychosurgery for the reasons set forth below.

The Michigan Supreme Court has considered in a tort case the problems of experimentation with humans. In *Hortner* v. *Koch,* 272 Mich. 273, 261 N. W. 762 (1935), the issue turned on whether the doctor had taken proper diagnostic steps before prescribing an experimental treatment for cancer. Discussing medical experimentation, the Court said at page 282:

> "We recognize the fact that if the general practice of medicine and surgery is to progress, there must be a certain amount of experimentation carried on; but such experiments must be done with the knowledge and consent of the patient or those responsible for him, and *must not vary too radically from the accepted method of procedure.*" (Emphasis added).

This means that the physician cannot experiment without restraint or restriction. He must consider first of all the welfare of his patient. This concept is universally accepted by the medical profession, the legal profession, and responsible persons who have thought and written on the matter.

Furthermore, he must weigh the risk to the patient against the benefit to be obtained by trying something new. The risk-benefit ratio is an important ratio in considering any experimental surgery upon a human being. The risk must always be relatively low, in the non-life-threatening situation to justify human experimentation.

Informed consent is a requirement of variable demands. Being certain that a patient has consented adequately to an operation, for example, is much more important when doctors are going to undertake an experimental, dangerous, and intrusive procedure than, for example, when they are going to remove an appendix. When a procedure is experimental, dangerous, and intrusive, special safeguards are necessary. The risk-benefit ratio must be carefully considered, and the question of consent thoroughly explored.

To be legally adequate, a subject's informed consent must be competent, knowing and voluntary.

In considering consent for experimentation, the ten principles known as the Nuremberg Code give guidance. They are found in the Judgment of the Court in *United States* v. *Karl Brandt.*[21]

There the Court said:

> ". . .Certain basic principles must be observed in order to satisfy moral, ethical and legal concepts:
> "1. The voluntary consent of the human subject is absolutely essential.
> "This means that the person involved should have legal capacity to

give consent; should be so situated as to be able to exercise free power of choice, without the intervention of any element of force, fraud, deceit, duress, overreaching, or other ulterior form of constraint or coercion; and should have sufficient knowledge and comprehension of the elements of the subject matter involved as to enable him to make an understanding and enlightened decision. This latter element requires that before the acceptance of an affirmative decision by the experimental subject, there should be made known to him the nature, duration and purpose of the experiment; the methods and means by which it is to be conducted; all inconveniences and hazards reasonably to be expected; and the effects upon his health or person which may possibly come from his participation in the experiment.

"The duty and responsibility for ascertaining the quality of the consent rests upon each individual who initiates, directs, or engages in the experiment. It is a personal duty and responsibility which may not be delegated to another with impunity.

"2. The experiment should be such as to yield fruitful results for the good of society, unprocurable by other methods or means of study, and not random and unnecessary in nature.

"3. The experiment should be so designed and based on the results of animal experimentation and a knowledge of the natural history of the disease or other problem under study that the anticipated results will justify the performance of the experiment.

"4. The experiment should be so conducted as to avoid all unnecessary physical and mental suffering and injury.

"5. No experiment should be conducted where there is an a priori reason to believe that death or disabling injury will occur; except, perhaps, in those experiments where the experimental physicians also serve as subjects.

"6. The degree of risk to be taken should never exceed that determined by the humanitarian importance of the problem to be solved by the experiment.

"7. Proper preparations should be made and adequate facilities provided to protect the experimental subject against even remote possibilities of injury, disability, or death.

"8. The experiment should be conducted only by scientifically qualified persons. The highest degree of skill and care should be required through all stages of the experiment of those who conduct or engage in the experiment.

"9. During the course of the experiment the human subject should be at liberty to bring the experiment to an end if he has reached the physical or mental stage where continuation of the experiment seems to him to be impossible.

"10. During the course of the experiment the scientist in charge must be prepared to terminate the experiment at any stage, if he has probable cause to believe, in the exercise of the good faith, superior skill, and careful judgment required of him that a continuation of the experiment is likely to result in injury, disability, or death to the experimental subject."

In the Nuremberg Judgment, the elements of what must guide us in decision are found. The involuntarily detained mental patient must have legal capacity to give consent. He must be so situated as to be able to exercise free power of choice without any element of force, fraud, deceit, duress, overreaching, or other ulterior form of restraint or coercion. He must have sufficient knowledge and comprehension of the subject matter to enable him to make an understanding decision. The decision must be a totally voluntary one on his part.

We must first look to the competency of the involuntarily detained mental patient to consent. Competency requires the ability of the subject to understand rationally the nature of the procedure, its risks, and other relevant information. The standard governing required disclosure by a doctor is what a reasonable patient needs to know in order to make an intelligent decision. See Waltz and Scheunenman, "Informed Consent Therapy," 64 *Northwestern Law Review* 628 (1969).[22]

Although an involuntarily detained mental patient may have a sufficient I. Q. to intellectually comprehend his circumstances (in Dr. Rodin's experiment, a person was required to have at least an I. Q. of 80), the very nature of his incarceration diminishes the capacity to consent to psychosurgery. He is particularly vulnerable as a result of his mental condition, the deprivation stemming from involuntary confinement, and the effects of the phenomenon of "institutionalization."

The very moving testimony of John Doe in the instant case establishes this beyond any doubt. The fact of institutional confinement has special force in undermining the capacity of the mental patient to make a competent decision on this issue, even though he be intellectually competent to do so. In the routine of institutional life, most decisions are made for patients. For example, John Doe testified how extraordinary it was for him to be approached by Dr. Yudashkin about the possible submission to psychosurgery, and how unusual it was to be consulted by a physician about his preference.

Institutionalization tends to strip the individual of the supports which permit him to maintain his sense of self-worth and the value of his own physical and mental integrity. An involuntarily confined mental patient clearly has diminished capacity for making a decision about irreversible experimental psychosurgery.

Equally great problems are found when the involuntarily detained mental patient is incompetent, and consent is sought from a guardian or parent. Although guardian or parental consent may be legally adequate when arising out of traditional circumstances, it is legally ineffective in the psychosurgery situation. The guardian or parent cannot do that which the patient, absent a guardian, would be legally unable to do.

The second element of an informed consent is knowledge of the risk involved and the procedures to be undertaken. It was obvious from the record made in this case that the facts surrounding experimental brain surgery are profoundly uncertain, and the lack of knowledge on the subject makes a knowledgeable consent to psychosurgery literally impossible.

We turn now to the third element of an informed consent, that of voluntariness. It is obvious that the most important thing to a large number of involuntarily detained mental patients incarcerated for an unknown length of time, is freedom.

The Nuremberg standards require that the experimental subjects be so situated as to exercise free power of choice without the intervention of any element of force, fraud, deceit, duress, overreaching, or other *ulterior form of constraint or coercion*. It is impossible for an involuntarily detained mental patient to be free of ulterior forms of restraint or coercion when his very release from the institution may depend upon his cooperating with the institutional authorities and giving consent to experimental surgery.

The privileges of an involuntarily detained patient and the rights he exercises in the institution are within the control of the institutional authorities. As was pointed out in the testimony of John Doe, such minor things as the right to have a lamp in his room, or the right to have ground privileges to go for a picnic with his family assumed major proportions. For 17 years he lived completely under the control of the hospital. Nearly every important aspect of his life was decided without any opportunity on his part to participate in the decision-making process.

The involuntarily detained mental patient is in an inherently coercive atmosphere even though no direct pressures may be placed upon him. He finds himself stripped of customary amenities and defenses. Free movement is restricted. He becomes a part of communal living subject to the control of the institutional authorities.

As pointed out in the testimony in this case, John Doe consented to this psychosurgery partly because of his effort to show the doctors in the hospital that he was a cooperative patient. Even Dr. Yudashkin, in his testimony, pointed out that involuntarily confined patients tend to tell their doctors what the patient thinks these people want to hear.

The inherently coercive atmosphere to which the involuntarily detained mental patient is subjected has bearing upon the voluntariness of his consent. This was pointed up graphically by Dr. Watson in his testimony (page 67, April 4). There he was asked if there was any significant difference between the kinds of coercion that exist in an open hospital setting and the kinds of coercion that exist on involuntarily detained patients in a state mental institution.

Dr. Watson answered in this way:

"There is an enormous difference. My perception of the patients at Ionia is that they are willing almost to try anything to somehow or other improve their lot, which is—you know—not bad. It is just plain normal—you know—that kind of desire. Again, that pressure— again—I don't like to use the word 'coercion' because it implies a kind of deliberateness and that is not what we are talking about—the pressure to accede is perhaps the more accurate way, I think—the pressure is perhaps so severe that it probably ought to cause us to not be willing to permit experimentation that has questionable gain and high risk from the standpoint of the patient's posture, which is, you see, the formula that I mentioned we hashed out in our Human Use Committee."

Involuntarily confined mental patients live in an inherently coercive institutional environment. Indirect and subtle psychological coercion has profound effect upon the patient population. Involuntarily confined patients cannot reason as equals with the doctors and administrators over whether they should undergo psychosurgery. They are not able to voluntarily give informed consent because of the inherent inequality in their position.[23]

It has been argued by defendants that because 13 criminal sexual psychopaths in the Ionia State Hospital wrote a letter indicating they did not want to be subjects of psychosurgery, that consent can be obtained and that the arguments about coercive pressure are not valid.

The Court does not feel that this necessarily follows. There is no showing of the circumstances under which the refusal of these thirteen patients was obtained, and there is no showing whatever that any effort was made to obtain the consent of these patients for such experimentation.

The fact that thirteen patients unilaterally wrote a letter saying they did not want to be subjects of psychosurgery is irrelevant to the question of whether they can consent to that which they are legally precluded from doing.

The law has always been meticulous in scrutinizing inequality in bargaining power and the possibility of undue influence in commercial fields and in the law of wills. It also has been most careful in excluding from criminal cases confessions where there was no clear showing of their completely voluntary nature after full understanding of the consequences.[24] No lesser standard can apply to involuntarily detained mental patients.

The keystone to any intrusion upon the body of a person must be full, adequate and informed consent. The integrity of the individual must be protected from invasion into his body and personality not voluntarily agreed to. Consent is not an idle or symbolic act; it is a fundamental requirement for the protection of the individual's integrity.

We therefore conclude that involuntarily detained mental patients cannot give informed and adequate consent to experimental psychosurgical procedures on the brain.

The three basic elements of informed consent—competency, knowledge, and voluntariness—cannot be ascertained with a degree of reliability warranting resort to use of such an invasive procedure.[25]

To this point, the Court's central concern has primarily been the ability of an involuntarily detained mental patient to give a factually informed, legally adequate consent to psychosurgery. However, there are also compelling constitutional considerations that preclude the involuntarily detained mental patient from giving effective consent to this type of surgery.

We deal here with State action in view of the fact the question relates to involuntarily detained mental patients who are confined because of the action of the State.

Initially, we consider the application of the First Amendment to the problem before the Court, recognizing that when the State's interest is in conflict with the Federal Constitution, the State's interest, even though declared by statute or court rule, must give way. See *NAACP* v. *Button,* 371 U. S. 415 (1963) and *United Transportation Workers' Union* v. *State Bar of Michigan,* 401 U. S. 576 (1971).

A person's mental processes, the communication of ideas, and the generation of ideas, come within the ambit of the First Amendment. To the extent that the First Amendment protects the dissemination of ideas and the expression of thoughts, it equally must protect the individual's right to generate ideas.

As Justice Cardozo pointed out:

> "We are free only if we know, and so in proportion to our knowledge. There is no freedom without choice, and there is no choice without knowledge— or none that is illusory. Implicit, therefore, in the very notion of liberty is the liberty of the mind to absorb and to beget. . . .The mind is in chains when it is without the opportunity to choose. One may argue, if one please, that opportunity to choose is more an evil than a good. One is guilty of a contradiction if one says that the opportunity can be denied, and liberty subsist. At the root of all liberty is the liberty to know. . . .
>
> "Experimentation there may be in many things of deep concern, but not in setting boundaries to thought, for thought freely communicated is the indispensable condition of intelligent experimentation, the one test of its validity."[26]

Justice Holmes expressed the basic theory of the First Amendment in *Abrams* v. *United States,* 250 U. S. 616, 630 (1919), when he said:

> ". . . The ultimate good desired is better reached by free trade in ideas—that the best test of truth is the power of the thought to get itself accepted in the competition of the market, and that truth is the only ground upon which their wishes safely can be carried out. That at any rate is the theory of our Constitution. . . .We should be eternally vigilant against attempts to check expressions of opinions that we loathe and believe to be fraught with death, unless they so imminently threaten immediate interference with the lawful and pressing purposes of the law that an immediate check is required to save the country. . . ."

Justice Brandeis in *Whitney* v. *Cal.,* 274 U. S. 357, 375 (1927), put it this way:

> "Those who won our independence believed that the final end of the State was to make men free to value their faculties; and that in its government the deliberate force should prevail over the arbitrary. . . .They believed that freedom to think as you will and to speak as you think are means indispensable to the discovery and spread of political truth; that without free speech and assembly discussion would be futile; that with them, discussion affords ordinarily adequate protection against the dissemination of noxious doctrine; that the greatest menace to freedom is an inert people; that public discussion is a political duty; and that this should be a fundamental principle of the American government. . . ."

Thomas Emerson, a distinguished writer on the First Amendment, stated this in "Toward a General Theory of the First Amendment," 72 *Yale Law Journal* 877, 895 (1963):

"The function of the legal process is not only to provide a means whereby a society shapes and controls the behavior of its individual members in the interests of the whole. It also supplies one of the principal methods by which a society controls itself, limiting its own powers in the interests of the individual. The role of the law here is to mark the guide and line between the sphere of social power, organized in the form of the state, and the area of private right. The legal problems involved in maintaining a system of free expression fall largely into this realm. In essence, legal support for such a society involves the protection of individual rights against interference or unwarranted control by the government. More specifically, the legal structure must provide:

"1. Protection of the individual's right to freedom of expression against interference by the government in its efforts to achieve other social objectives or to advance its own interests. . . ."

"3. Restriction of the government in so far as the government itself participates in the system of expression."

"All these requirements involve control over the state. The use of law to achieve this kind of control has been one of the central concerns of freedom-seeking societies over the ages. Legal recognition of individual rights, enforced through the legal processes, has become the core of free society."

In *Stanley* v. *Georgia,* 397 U. S. 557 (1969), the Supreme Court once again addressed the free dissemination of ideas. It said at page 565–66:

"Our whole constitutional heritage rebels at the thought of giving government the power to control men's minds. . . .Whatever the power of the state to control dissemination of ideas inimical to public morality, it cannot constitutionally premise legislation on the desirability of controlling a person's private thoughts."

Freedom of speech and expression, and the right of all men to disseminate ideas, popular or unpopular, are fundamental to ordered liberty. Government has no power or right to control men's minds, thoughts, and expressions. This is the command of the First Amendment. And we adhere to it in holding an involuntarily detained mental patient may not consent to experimental psychosurgery.

For, if the First Amendment protects the freedom to express ideas, it necessarily follows that it must protect the freedom to generate ideas. Without the latter protection, the former is meaningless.

Experimental psychosurgery, which is irreversible and intrusive, often leads to the blunting of emotions, the deadening of memory, the reduction of affect, and limits the ability to generate new ideas. Its potential for injury to the creativity of the individual is great, and can impinge upon the right of the individual to be free from interference with his mental processes.

The State's interest in performing psychosurgery and the legal ability of the involuntarily detained mental patient to give consent must bow to the First Amendment, which protects the generation and free flow of ideas from unwarranted interference with one's mental processes.

To allow an involuntarily detained mental patient to consent to the type of psychosurgery proposed in this case, and to permit the State to perform it, would be to condone State action in violation of basic First Amendment rights of such patients, because impairing the power to generate ideas inhibits the full dissemination of ideas.

There is no showing in this case that the State has met its burden of demonstrating such a compelling State interest in the use of experimental psychosurgery on involuntarily detained mental patients to overcome its proscription by the First Amendment of the United States Constitution.

In recent years, the Supreme Court of the United States has developed a constitutional concept of right of privacy, relying upon the First, Fifth and Fourteenth Amendments. It was found in the marital bed in *Griswold* v. *Conn.,* 381 U. S. 479 (1962); in the right to view obscenity in the privacy of one's home in *Stanley* v. *Georgia,* 395 U. S. 557 (1969); and in the right of a woman to control her own body by determining whether she wishes to terminate a pregnancy in *Roe* v. *Wade,* 41 L W 4213 (1973).

The concept was also recognized in the case of a prison inmate subjected to shock treatment and an experimental drug without his consent in *Mackey* v. *Procunier,* _____F 2d _____ 71–3062 (9th Circuit, April 16, 1973).

In that case, the 9th Circuit noted that the District Court had treated the action as a malpractice claim and had dismissed it. The 9th Circuit reversed, saying, inter alia:

> "It is asserted in memoranda that the staff at Vacaville is engaged in medical and psychiatric experimentation with 'aversion treatment' of criminal offenders, including the use of succinycholine on fully conscious patients. It is emphasized the plaintiff was subject to experimentation without consent.
>
> "Proof of such matters could, in our judgment, raise serious constitutional questions respecting cruel and unusual punishment or *impermissible tinkering with the mental processes.* (Citing *Stanley* among other cases.) In our judgment it was error to dismiss the case without ascertaining at least the extent to which such charges can be substantiated. . . ."(Emphasis added)

Much of the rationale for the developing constitutional concept of right to privacy is found in Justice Brandeis' famous dissent in *Olmstead* v. *United States,* 277 U. S. 438 (1928), at 478, where he said:

> "The makers of our Constitution undertook to secure conditions favorable to the pursuit of happiness. They recognized the significance of man's spiri-

tual nature, of his feelings and of his intellect. They knew that only a part of the pain, pleasure, and satisfaction of life are to be found in material things. They sought to protect Americans in their beliefs, their thoughts, their emotions and their sensations. They conferred, as against the Government, the right to be let alone— the most comprehensive of rights and the right most valued by civilized men."

There is no privacy more deserving of constitutional protection than that of one's mind. As pointed out by the Court in *Huguez* v. *United States,* 406 F 2d 366 (1968), at page 382, footnote 84:

". . . Nor are the intimate internal areas of the physical habitation of mind and soul any less deserving of precious preservation from unwarranted and forcible intrusions than are the intimate internal areas of the physical habitation of wife and family. Is not the sanctity of the body even more important, and therefore, more to be honored in its protection than the sanctity of the home? . . ."

Intrusion into one's intellect, when one is involuntarily detained and subject to the control of institutional authorities, is an intrusion into one's constitutionally protected right of privacy. If one is not protected in his thoughts, behavior, personality and identity, then the right of privacy becomes meaningless.[27]

Before a State can violate one's constitutionally protected right of privacy and obtain a valid consent for experimental psychosurgery on involuntarily detained mental patients, a compelling State interest must be shown. None has been shown here.

To hold that the right of privacy prevents laws against dissemination of contraceptive material as in *Griswold* v. *Conn.* (supra), or the right to view obscenity in the privacy of one's home as in *Stanley* v. *Georgia* (supra), but that it does not extend to the physical intrusion in an experimental manner upon the brain of an involuntarily detained mental patient is to denigrate the right. In the hierarchy of values, it is more important to protect one's mental processes than to protect even the privacy of the marital bed. To authorize an involuntarily detained mental patient to consent to experimental psychosurgery would be to fail to recognize and follow the mandates of the Supreme Court of the United States, which has constitutionally protected the privacy of body and mind.

Counsel for John Doe has argued persuasively that the use of the psychosurgery proposed in the instant case would constitute cruel and unusual punishment and should be barred under the Eighth Amendment. A determination of this issue is not necessary to decision, because of the many other legal and constitutional reasons for holding that the involuntarily detained mental patient may not give an informed and valid consent to experimental psychosurgery. We therefore do not pass on the issue of whether the psychosurgery proposed in this case constitutes cruel and unusual punishment within the meaning of the Eighth Amendment.

For the reasons given, we conclude that the answer to question number one posed for decision is no.

In reaching this conclusion, we emphasize two things.

First, the conclusion is based upon the state of the knowledge as of the time of the writing of this Opinion. When the state of medical knowledge develops to the extent that the type of psychosurgical intervention proposed here becomes an accepted neurosurgical procedure and is no longer experimental, it is possible, with appropriate review mechanisms,[28] that involuntarily detained mental patients could consent to such an operation.

Second, we specifically hold that an involuntarily detained mental patient today can give adequate consent to accepted neurosurgical procedures.

In view of the fact we have answered the first question in the negative, it is not necessary to proceed to a consideration of the second question, although we cannot refrain from noting that had the answer to the first question been yes, serious constitutional problems would have arisen with reference to the second question.

One final word. The Court thanks all counsel for the excellent, lawyer-like manner in which they have conducted themselves. Seldom, if ever, has any member of this panel presided over a case where the lawyers were so well-prepared and so helpful to the Court.

The findings in this Opinion shall constitute the findings of fact and conclusions of law upon the issues framed pursuant to the provisions of G.C.R. (1963) 517.1

A judgment embodying the findings of the Court in this Opinion may be presented.

Horace W. Gilmore
Circuit Judge

George E. Bowles
Circuit Judge

John D. O'Hair
Circuit Judge

Detroit, Michigan
July 10, 1973

NOTES

1. The name John Doe has been used through the proceedings to protect the true identity of the subject involved. After the institution of this action and during proceedings his true identity was revealed. His true name is Louis Smith. For the purpose of the Opinion, however, he will be referred to throughout as John Doe.

2. C.L. 780.501 et seq. The statute under which he was committed was repealed by Public Act 143 of the Public Acts of 1968, effective August 1, 1968. He was detained thereafter under C.L. 330.35 (b), which provided for further detention and release of criminal sexual psychopaths under the repealed statute. The Supreme Court also adopted an Administrative Order of October 20, 1969 (382 Mich. xxix) relating to criminal sexual psy-

chopaths. A full discussion of these statutes is found in the Court's earlier Opinion relating to the legality of detention of John Doe, filed in this cause on March 23, 1973.

3. See Appendix to Opinion, Item 1.

4. For criteria, see Appendix, Item 2.

5. The complete "Informed Consent" form signed by John Doe is as follows:

"Since conventional treatment efforts over a period of several years have not enabled me to control my outbursts of rage and anti-social behavior, I submit an application to be a subject in a research project which may offer me a form of effective therapy. This therapy is based upon the idea that episodes of anti-social rage and sexuality might be triggered by a disturbance in certain portions of my brain. I understand that in order to be certain that a significant brain disturbance exists, which might relate to my anti-social behavior, an initial operation will have to be performed. This procedure consists of placing fine wires into my brain, which will record the electrical activity from these structures which play a part in anger and sexuality. These electrical waves can then be studied to determine the presence of an abnormality.

"In addition electrical stimulation with weak currents passed through these wires will be done in order to find out if one or several points in the brain can trigger my episodes of violence or unlawful sexuality. In other words this stimulation may cause me to want to commit an aggressive or sexual act, but every effort will be made to have a sufficient number of people present to control me. If the brain disturbance is limited to a small area, I understand that the investigators will destroy this part of my brain with an electrical current. If the abnormality comes from a larger part of my brain, I agree that it should be surgically removed, if the doctors determine that it can be done so, without risk of side effects. Should the electrical activity from the parts of my brain into which the wires have been placed reveal that there is no significant abnormality, the wires will simply be withdrawn.

"I realize that any operation on the brain carries a number of risks which may be slight, but could be potentially serious. These risks include infection, bleeding, temporary or permanent weakness or paralysis of one or more of my legs or arms, difficulties with speech and thinking, as well as the ability to feel, touch, pain and temperature. Under extraordinary circumstances, it is also possible that I might not survive the operation.

"Fully aware of the risks detailed in the paragraphs above, I authorize the physicians of Lafayette Clinic and Providence Hospital to perform the procedures as outlined above."

October 27, 1972	/S/ Louis M. Smith
Date	Signature
Calvin Vanee	/S/Emily T. Smith/Harry L. Smith
Witness	Signature of responsible relative or guardian

6. There is some dispute in the record as to whether his parents gave consent for the innovative surgical procedures. They testified they gave consent only to the insertion of depth electrodes.

7. The release was directed after the testimony of John Doe in open court and the testimony of Dr. Andrew S. Watson, who felt that John Doe could be safely released to society.

8. On Thursday, March 15, 1973, after full argument, the Court held in an Opinion rendered from the bench that the matter was not moot, relying upon *United States v. Phosphate Export Association,* 393 U. S. 199. There the United States Supreme Court said:

"The test for mootness . . . is a stringent one. Mere voluntary cessation of allegedly illegal conduct does not moot a case; if it did, the courts would be compelled to 'leave the defendant . . . free to return to his old ways.' A case might become moot if subsequent events made it absolutely clear that the allegedly wrongful behavior could not reasonably be expected to recur."

The Court also relied upon *Milford v. Peoples Community Hospital Authority,* 380 Mich. 49, where the Court said on page 55:

> "The nature of the case is such that we are unlikely to again receive the question in the near future, and doctors and other people dealing with public hospital corporations cannot hope to have an answer to the questions raised unless we proceed to decision. For these reasons, we conclude the case is of sufficient importance to warrant our decision."

It should also be noted that Defendant Department of Mental Health sought an Order of Superintending Control for a Stay of Proceedings in the Court of Appeals on the ground the case was moot. On March 26, 1973, the Court of Appeals denied the Stay.

9. As the trial proceeded, it was learned that John Doe himself withdrew his consent to such experimentation. This still did not render the proceeding moot because of the questions framed for declaratory judgment.

10. On this point, Amicus Curiae Exhibit 4 is of great interest. This exhibit is a memo to Dr. Gottlieb from Dr. Rodin, dated August 9, 1972, reporting on a visit Dr. Rodin made to Dr. Vernon H. Mark of the Neurological Research Foundation in Boston, one of the country's leading proponents of psychosurgery on noninstitutionalized patients. Dr. Rodin, in his Memo, stated:

> "When I informed Dr. Mark of our project, namely, doing amygdalotomies on patients who do not have epilepsy, he became extremely concerned and stated we had no ethical right in so doing. This, of course, opened Pandora's box, because then I retorted that he was misleading us with his previously cited book and he had no right at all from a scientific point of view to state that in the human, aggression is accompanied by seizure discharges in the amygdala, because he is dealing with only patients who have susceptible brains, namely, temporal lobe epilepsy. . . .
> "He stated categorically that as far as present evidence is concerned, one has no right to make lesions in a 'healthy brain' when the individual suffers from rage attacks only."

11. Mark, Sweet and Ervin, "The Affect of Amygdalotomy on Violent Behavior in Patients with Temporal Lobe Epilepsy," in Hitchcock, Ed. *Psycho-Surgery: Second International Conference* (Thomas Pub. 1972), 135 at 153.

12. Mark and Ervin, *Violence and the Brain* (Harper & Row, 1970).

13. Mark, "Brain Surgery in Aggressive Epileptics," the *Hastings Center Report,* Vol. 3, No. 1 (February 1973).

14. See Defendant's Exhibit 38, "Sedative Neurosurgery" by V. Balasubramaniam, T. S. Kanaka, P. V. Ramanuman, and B. Ramaurthi, 53 *Journal of the Indian Medical Association,* No. 8, page 377 (1969). In the conclusion, page 381, the writer said:

> "The main purpose of this communication is to show that this new form of surgery called sedative neurosurgery is available for the treatment of certain groups of disorders. These disorders are primarily characterized by restlessness, low threshold for anger and violent or destructive tendencies.
> "This operation aims at destruction of certain areas in the brain. These targets include the amygdaloid nuclei, the posteroventral nuclear group of the hypothalamus and the periaqueductal grey substance. . . .
> "By operating on the areas one can make these patients quiet and manageable."

15. The classical lobotomy of which thousands were performed in the 1940s and 1950s is very rarely used these days. The development of drug therapy pretty well did away with the classical lobotomy. Follow-up studies show that the lobotomy procedure was overused and caused a great deal of damage to the persons who were subjected to it. A general bleaching of the personality occurred and the operations were associated with loss of drive and concentra-

tion. Dr. Brown in his testimony before the United States Senate, supra, page 9, stated: "No responsible scientist today would condone a classical lobotomy operation."

16. Sweet, Mark & Ervin found this to be true in experiments with monkeys. Other evidence indicated it is possible in human beings.

17. Testimony in the case from Dr. Rodin, Dr. Lowinger, Dr. Breggin, and Dr. Walter, all pointed up that it is very difficult to find the risks, deficits and benefits from psychosurgery because of the failure of the literature to provide adequate research information about research subjects before and after surgery.

18. See the language of the late Justice Cardozo in *Schloendorff v. Society of New York Hospitals,* 211 N. Y. 125, 105 N. E. 92, 93 (1914) where he said, "Every human being of adult years or sound mind has a right to determine what shall be done with his own body. . . ."

19. See "Experimentation on Human Beings," 22 *Stanford Law Review* 99 (1967); Kidd, "Limits of the Right of a Person to Consent to Experimentation Upon Himself," 117 *Science* 211 (1953).

20. The principle is reflected in numerous statements of medical ethics. See the American Medical Association, "Principles of Medical Ethics," 132 *JAMA* 1090 (1946); American Medical Association, "Ethical Guidelines for Clinical Investigation" (1966); National Institute of World Medical Association, "Code of Ethics" (Declaration of Helsinki) reprinted in 2 *British Medical Journal,* 177 (1964). It is manifested in the code adopted by the United States Military Tribunal at Nuremberg which, at the time, was considered the most carefully developed precept specifically drawn to meet the problems of human experimentation. See Ladimer, I. "Ethical and Legal Aspects of Medical Research in Human Beings," 3 J. Pub. L. 467, 487 (1954).

21. Trial of War Criminals before the Nuremberg Military Tribunals. Volume 1 and 2, "The Medical Case," Washington, D. C.; U. S. Government Printing Office (1948) reprinted in Experimentation with Human Beings, by Katz (Russell Sage Foundation, 1972) page 305.

22. In *Ballentine's Law Dictionary* (Second Edition) (1948), competency is equated with capacity and capacity is defined as "a person's ability to understand the nature and effect of the act in which he is engaged and the business in which he is transacting."

23. It should be emphasized that once John Doe was released in this case and returned to the community he withdrew all consent to the performance of the proposed experiment. His withdrawal of consent under these circumstances should be compared with his response on January 12, 1973, to questions placed to him by Prof. Slovenko, one of the members of the Human Rights Committee. These answers are part of exhibit 22 and were given after extensive publicity about this case, and while John Doe was in Lafayette Clinic awaiting the implantation of depth electrodes. The significant questions and answers are as follows:

1. Would you seek psychosurgery if you were not confined in an institution?
A. Yes, if after testing this showed it would be of help.
2. Do you believe that psychosurgery is a way to obtain your release from the institution?
A. No, but it would be a step in obtaining my release. It is like any other therapy or program to help persons to function again.
3. Would you seek psychosurgery if there were other ways to obtain your release?
A. Yes. If psychosurgery were the only means of helping my physical problem after a period of testing.

24. See, for example, *Miranda v. Arizona,* 384 U. S. 436 (1966) and *Escobedo v. Illinois,* 378 U. S. 478 (1964).

Prof. Paul Freund of the Harvard Law School has expressed the following opinion:
"I suggest . . . that [prison] experiments should not involve any promise of parole or of commutation of sentence; this would be what is called in the law of confessions undue influence or duress through promise of reward, which can be as effective in overbearing the will as threats of harm. Nor should there be a pressure to conform within the prison generated by the pattern of rejecting parole applications of those who do not participate. . . ." P.A. Freund,

"Ethical Problems in Human Experimentation," *New England Journal of Medicine,* Volume 273 (1965) pages 687–92.

25. It should be noted that Dr. Vernon H. Mark, a leading psychosurgeon, states that psychosurgery should not be performed on prisoners who are epileptic because of the problem of obtaining adequate consent. He states in "Brain Surgery in Aggressive Epileptics," the *Hastings Center Report,* Vol. 3, No. 1 (February 1973): "Prison inmates suffering from epilepsy should receive only medical treatment; surgical therapy should not be carried out because of the difficulty in obtaining truly informed consent."

26. Cardozo, *The Paradoxes of Legal Science,* Columbia University Lectures, reprinted in *Selected Writings of Benjamin Nathan Cardozo.*" (Fallon Publications, 1947), pages 317 and 318.

27. See Note: 45 *So. Cal. L R* 616, 663 (1972).

28. For example, see Guidelines of the Department of Health, Education and Welfare, A C. Exhibit 17.

O'CONNOR V. DONALDSON

Supreme Court of the United States, 1975.
422 U.S. 563, 95 S.Ct. 2486, 45 L.Ed.2d 396.

MR. JUSTICE STEWART delivered the opinion of the Court.

The respondent, Kenneth Donaldson, was civilly committed to confinement as a mental patient in the Florida State Hospital at Chattahoochee in January 1957. He was kept in custody there against his will for nearly 15 years. The petitioner, Dr. J. B. O'Connor, was the hospital's superintendent during most of this period. Throughout his confinement Donaldson repeatedly, but unsuccessfully, demanded his release, claiming that he was dangerous to no one, that he was not mentally ill, and that, at any rate, the hospital was not providing treatment for his supposed illness. Finally, in February 1971, Donaldson brought this lawsuit under 42 U. S. C. § 1983, in the United States District Court for the Northern District of Florida, alleging that O'Connor, and other members of the hospital staff named as defendants, had intentionally and maliciously deprived him of his constitutional right to liberty.[1] After a four-day trial, the jury returned a verdict assessing both compensatory and punitive damages against O'Connor and a codefendant. The Court of Appeals for the Fifth Circuit affirmed the judgment, 493 F. 2d 507. We granted O'Connor's petition for certiorari, 419 U. S. 894, because of the important constitutional questions seemingly presented.

I

Donaldson's commitment was initiated by his father, who thought that his son was suffering from "delusions." After hearings before a county judge of Pinellas County, Fla., Donaldson was found to be suffering from "paranoid schizophrenia" and was committed for "care, maintenance, and treatment" pursuant to Florida statutory provisions that have since been repealed.[2] The state law was less than clear in specifying the grounds necessary for commitment, and the record is scanty as to Donaldson's condition at the time of the judicial hearing. These matters are, however, irrelevant, for this case involves no challenge to the initial commitment, but is focused, instead, upon the nearly 15 years of confinement that followed.

The evidence at the trial showed that the hospital staff had the power to release a patient, not dangerous to himself or others, even if he remained mentally ill and had been lawfully committed.[3] Despite many requests, O'Connor refused to allow that power to be exercised in Donaldson's case. At the trial, O'Connor indicated that he had believed that Donaldson would have been unable to make a "successful adjustment outside the institution," but could not recall the basis for that conclusion. O'Connor retired as superintendent shortly before this suit was filed. A few months thereafter, and before the trial, Donaldson secured his release and a judicial restoration of competency, with the support of the hospital staff.

The testimony at the trial demonstrated, without contradiction, that Donaldson had posed no danger to others during his long confinement, or indeed at any point in his life. O'Connor himself conceded that he had no personal or second-hand knowledge that Donaldson had ever committed a dangerous act. There was no evidence that Donaldson had ever been suicidal or been thought likely to inflict injury upon himself. One of O'Connor's codefendants acknowledged that Donaldson could have earned his own living outside the hospital. He had done so for some 14 years before his commitment, and immediately upon his release he secured a responsible job in hotel administration.

Furthermore, Donaldson's frequent requests for release had been supported by responsible persons willing to provide him any care he might need on release. In 1963, for example, a representative of Helping Hands, Inc., a halfway house for mental patients, wrote O'Connor asking him to release Donaldson to its care. The request was accompanied by a supporting letter from the Minneapolis Clinic of Psychiatry and Neurology, which a codefendant conceded was a "good clinic." O'Connor rejected the offer, replying that Donaldson could be released only to his parents. That rule was apparently of O'Connor's own making. At the time, Donaldson was 55 years old, and, as O'Connor knew, Donaldson's parents were too elderly and infirm to take responsibility for him. Moreover, in his continuing correspondence with Donaldson's parents, O'Connor never informed them of the Helping Hands offer. In addition, on four separate occasions between 1964 and 1968, John Lembcke, a college classmate of Donaldson's and a longtime family friend, asked O'Connor to release Donaldson to his care. On each occasion O'Connor refused. The record shows that Lembcke was a serious and responsible person, who was willing and able to assume responsibility for Donaldson's welfare.

The evidence showed that Donaldson's confinement was a simple regime of enforced custodial care, not a program designed to alleviate or cure his supposed illness. Numerous witnesses, including one of O'Connor's codefendants, testified that Donaldson had received nothing but custodial care while at the hospital. O'Connor described Donaldson's treatment as "milieu therapy." But witnesses from the hospital staff conceded that, in the context of this case, "milieu therapy" was a euphemism for confinement in the "milieu" of a mental hospital.[4] For substantial periods, Donaldson was simply kept in a large room that housed 60 patients, many of whom were under criminal commitment. Donaldson's requests for ground privileges, occupational training, and an opportunity to discuss his case with O'Connor or other staff members were repeatedly denied.

At the trial, O'Connor's principal defense was that he had acted in good faith and was therefore immune from any liability for monetary damages. His position, in short, was that state law, which he had believed valid, had authorized indefinite custodial confinement of the "sick," even if they were not given treatment and their release could harm no one.[5]

The trial judge instructed the members of the jury that they should find that O'Connor had violated Donaldson's constitutional right to liberty if they found that he had

> "confined [Donaldson] against his will, knowing that he was not mentally ill or dangerous or knowing that if mentally ill he was not receiving treatment for his alleged mental illness.
>
> "Now, the purpose of involuntary hospitalization is treatment and not mere custodial care or punishment if a patient is not a danger to himself or others. Without such treatment there is no justification from a constitutional standpoint for continued confinement unless you should also find that [Donaldson] was dangerous to either himself or others."[6]

The trial judge further instructed the jury that O'Connor was immune from damages if he

> "reasonably believed in good faith that detention of [Donaldson] was proper for the length of time he was so confined. . . .
>
> "However, mere good intentions which do not give rise to a reasonable belief that detention is lawfully required cannot justify [Donaldson's] confinement in the Florida State Hospital."

The jury returned a verdict for Donaldson against O'Connor and a codefendant, and awarded damages of $38,500, including $1,000 in punitive damages.[7]

The Court of Appeals affirmed the judgment of the District Court in a broad opinion dealing with "the far-reaching question whether the Fourteenth Amendment guarantees a right to treatment to persons involuntarily civilly committed to state mental hospitals." 493 F. 2d, at 509. The appellate court held that when, as in Donaldson's case, the rationale for confinement is that the patient is in need of treatment, the Constitution requires that minimally adequate treatment in fact be provided. *Id.,* at 521. The court further expressed the view that, regardless of the grounds for involuntary civil commitment, a person confined against his will at a state mental institution has "a consitutional right to receive such individual treatment as will give him a reasonable opportunity to be cured or to improve his mental condition." *Id.,* at 520. Conversely, the court's opinion implied that it is constitutionally permissible for a State to confine a mentally ill person against his will in order to treat his illness, regardless of whether his illness renders him dangerous to himself or others. See *id.,* at 522–527.

II

We have concluded that the difficult issues of constitutional law dealt with by the Court of Appeals are not presented by this case in its present posture. Specifically, there is no reason now to decide whether mentally ill persons dangerous to themselves or to others have a right to treatment upon compulsory confinement by the State, or whether the State may compulsorily confine a nondangerous, mentally ill individual for the purpose of treatment. As we view it, this case raises a single, relatively simple, but nonetheless important question concerning every man's constitutional right to liberty.

The jury found that Donaldson was neither dangerous to himself nor dangerous to others, and also found that, if mentally ill, Donaldson had not received treatment.[8] That verdict, based on abundant evidence, makes the issue before the Court a narrow one. We need not decide whether, when, or by what procedures, a mentally ill person may be confined by the State on any of the grounds which, under contemporary statutes, are generally advanced to justify involuntary confinement of such a person—to prevent injury to the public, to ensure his own survival or safety,[9] or to alleviate or cure his illness. See *Jackson* v. *Indiana,* 406 U. S. 715, 736–737; *Humphrey* v. *Cady,* 405 U. S. 504, 509. For the jury found that none of the above grounds for continued confinement was present in Donaldson's case.[10]

Given the jury's findings, what was left as justification for keeping Donaldson in continued confinement? The fact that state law may have authorized confinement of the harmless mentally ill does not itself establish a constitutionally adequate purpose for the confinement. See *Jackson* v. *Indiana, supra,* at 720–723; *McNeil* v. *Director, Patuxent Institution,* 407 U. S. 245, 248–250. Nor is it enough that Donaldson's original confinement was founded upon a constitutionally adequate basis, if in fact it was, because even if his involuntary confinement was initially permissible, it could not constitutionally continue after that basis no longer existed. *Jackson* v. *Indiana, supra,* at 738; *McNeil* v. *Director, Patuxent Institution, supra.*

A finding of "mental illness" alone cannot justify a State's locking a person up against his will and keeping him indefinitely in simple custodial confinement. Assuming that that term can be given a reasonably precise content and that the "mentally ill" can be identified with reasonable accuracy, there is still no constitutional basis for confining such persons involuntarily if they are dangerous to no one and can live safely in freedom.

May the State confine the mentally ill merely to ensure them a living standard superior to that they enjoy in the private community? That the State has a proper interest in providing care and assistance to the unfortunate goes without saying. But the mere presence of mental illness does not disqualify a person from preferring his home to the comforts of an institution. Moreover, while the State may arguably confine a person to save him from harm, incarceration is rarely if ever a necessary condition for raising the living standards of those capable of surviving safely in freedom, on their own or with the help of family or friends. See *Shelton* v. *Tucker,* 364 U. S. 479, 488–490.

May the State fence in the harmless mentally ill solely to save its citizens from exposure to those whose ways are different? One might as well ask if the State, to avoid public unease, could incarcerate all who are physically unattractive or socially eccentric. Mere public intolerance or animosity cannot constitutionally justify the deprivation of a person's physical liberty. See, *e.g., Cohen* v. *California,* 403 U. S. 15, 24–26; *Coates* v. *City of Cincinnati,* 402 U. S. 611, 615; *Street* v. *New*

York, 394 U. S. 576, 592; cf. *U. S. Dept. of Agriculture* v. *Moreno,* 413 U. S. 528, 534.

In short, a State cannot constitutionally confine without more a nondangerous individual who is capable of surviving safely in freedom by himself or with the help of willing and responsible family members or friends. Since the jury found, upon ample evidence, that O'Connor, as an agent of the State, knowingly did so confine Donaldson, it properly concluded that O'Connor violated Donaldson's constitutional right to freedom.

III

O'Connor contends that in any event he should not be held personally liable for monetary damages because his decisions were made in "good faith." Specifically, O'Connor argues that he was acting pursuant to state law which, he believed, authorized confinement of the mentally ill even when their release would not compromise their safety or constitute a danger to others, and that he could not reasonably have been expected to know that the state law as he understood it was constitutionally invalid. A proposed instruction to this effect was rejected by the District Court.[11]

The District Court did instruct the jury, without objection, that monetary damages could not be assessed against O'Connor if he believed reasonably and in good faith that Donaldson's continued confinement was "proper," and that punitive damages could be awarded only if O'Connor had acted "maliciously or wantonly or oppressively." The Court of Appeals approved those instructions. But that court did not consider whether it was error for the trial judge to refuse the additional instruction concerning O'Connor's claimed reliance on state law as authorization for Donaldson's continued confinement. Further, neither the District Court nor the Court of Appeals acted with the benefit of this Court's most recent decision on the scope of the qualified immunity possessed by state officials under 42 U. S. C. § 1983. *Wood* v. *Strickland,* 420 U. S. 308.

Under that decision, the relevant question for the jury is whether O'Connor "knew or reasonably should have known that the action he took within his sphere of official responsibility would violate the constitutional rights of [Donaldson], or if he took the action with the malicious intention to cause a deprivation of constitutional rights or other injury to [Donaldson]." *Id.,* at 322. See also *Scheuer* v. *Rhodes,* 416 U. S. 232, 247–248; *Wood* v. *Strickland, supra,* at 330 (opinion of Powell, J.). For purposes of this question, an official has, of course, no duty to anticipate unforeseeable constitutional developments. *Wood* v. *Strickland, supra,* at 322.

Accordingly, we vacate the judgment of the Court of Appeals and remand the case to enable that court to consider, in light of *Wood* v. *Strickland,* whether the District Judge's failure to instruct with regard to the effect of O'Connor's claimed reliance on state law rendered inadequate the instructions as to O'Connor's liability for compensatory and punitive damages.[12]

It is so ordered.

MR. CHIEF JUSTICE BURGER, concurring.

Although I join the Court's opinion and judgment in this case, it seems to me that several factors merit more emphasis than it gives them. I therefore add the following remarks.

I

With respect to the remand to the Court of Appeals on the issue of official immunity from liability for monetary damages,[13] it seems to me not entirely irrelevant that there was substantial evidence that Donaldson consistently refused treatment that was offered to him, claiming that he was not mentally ill and needed no treatment.[14] The Court appropriately takes notice of the uncertainties of psychiatric diagnosis and therapy, and the reported cases are replete with evidence of the divergence of medical opinion in this vexing area. *E.g., Greenwood v. United States,* 350 U. S. 366, 375 (1956). See also *Drope v. Missouri,* 420 U. S. 162 (1975). Nonetheless, one of the few areas of agreement among behavioral specialists is that an uncooperative patient cannot benefit from therapy and that the first step in effective treatment is acknowledgment by the patient that he is suffering from an abnormal condition. See, *e.g.,* Katz, The Right to Treatment—An Enchanting Legal Fiction? 36 U. Chi. L. Rev. 755, 768–769 (1969). Donaldson's adamant refusal to do so should be taken into account in considering petitioner's good-faith defense.

Perhaps more important to the issue of immunity is a factor referred to only obliquely in the Court's opinion. On numerous occasions during the period of his confinement Donaldson unsuccessfully sought release in the Florida courts; indeed, the last of these proceedings was terminated only a few months prior to the bringing of this action. See 234 So. 2d 114 (1969). cert. denied, 400 U. S. 869 (1970). Whatever the reasons for the state courts' repeated denials of relief, and regardless of whether they correctly resolved the issue tendered to them, petitioner and the other members of the medical staff at Florida State Hospital would surely have been justified in considering each such judicial decision as an approval of continued confinement and an independent intervening reason for continuing Donaldson's custody. Thus, this fact is inescapably related to the issue of immunity and must be considered by the Court of Appeals on remand and, if a new trial on this issue is ordered, by the District Court.[15]

II

As the Court points out, *ante,* at 570 n. 6, the District Court instructed the jury in part that "a person who is involuntarily civilly committed to a mental hospital does have a *constitutional* right to receive such treatment *as will give him a realistic opportunity to be cured*" (emphasis added), and the Court of Appeals unequivocally approved this phrase, standing alone, as a correct statement of the law. 493 F. 2d 507, 520 (CA5 1974). The Court's opinion plainly gives no approval to that holding and makes clear that it binds neither the parties to this case nor the courts of the Fifth Circuit. See *ante,* at 577–578, n. 12. Moreover, in light of its importance for future litigation in this area, it should be emphasized that the Court of Appeals' analysis has no basis in the decisions of this Court.

A

There can be no doubt that involuntary commitment to a mental hospital, like involuntary confinement of an individual for any reason, is a deprivation of liberty which the State cannot accomplish without due process of law. *Specht v. Patterson,* 386 U. S. 605, 608 (1967). Cf. *In re Gault,* 387 U. S. 1, 12–13 (1967). Commitment must be justified on the basis of a legitimate state interest, and the reasons for committing a particular individual must be established in an appropriate proceeding. Equally important, confinement must cease when those reasons no longer exist. See *McNeil v. Director, Patuxent Institution,* 407 U. S. 245, 249–250 (1972); *Jackson v. Indiana,* 406 U. S. 715, 738 (1972).

The Court of Appeals purported to be applying these principles in developing the first of its theories supporting a constitutional right to treatment. It first identified what it perceived to be the traditional bases for civil commitment—physical dangerousness to oneself or others, or a need for treatment—and stated:

> "[W]here, as in Donaldson's case, the rationale for confinement is the *'parens patriae'* rationale that the patient is in need of treatment, the due process clause requires that minimally adequate treatment be in fact provided. . . . 'To deprive any citizen of his or her liberty on the altruistic theory that the confinement is for humane therapeutic reasons and then fail to provide adequate treatment violates the very fundamentals of due process.'" 493 F. 2d, at 521.

The Court of Appeals did not explain its conclusion that the rationale for respondent's commitment was that he needed treatment. The Florida statutes in effect during the period of his confinement did not require that a person who had been adjudicated incompetent and ordered committed either be provided with psychiatric treatment or released, and there was no such condition in respondent's order of commitment. Cf. *Rouse v. Cameron,* 125 U. S. App. D. C. 366, 373 F. 2d 451 (1967). More important, the instructions which the Court of Appeals read as establishing an absolute constitutional right to treatment did not require the jury to make any findings regarding the specific reasons for respondent's confinement or to focus upon any rights he may have had under state law. Thus, the premise of the Court of Appeals' first theory must have been that, at least with respect to persons who are not physically dangerous, a State has no power to confine the mentally ill except for the purpose of providing them with treatment.

That proposition is surely not descriptive of the power traditionally exercised by the States in this area. Historically, and for a considerable period of time, subsidized custodial care in private foster homes or boarding houses was the most benign form of care provided incompetent or mentally ill persons for whom the States assumed responsibility. Until well into the 19th century the vast majority of such persons were simply restrained in poorhouses, almshouses, or jails. See A. Deutsch, The Mentally Ill in America 38–54, 1–131 (2d ed. 1949). The few States that established institutions for the mentally ill during this early period were concerned primarily with providing a more humane place of confinement and only secondarily with "curing" the persons sent there. See *id.*, at 98–113.

As the trend toward state care of the mentally ill expanded, eventually leading to the present statutory schemes for protecting such persons, the dual functions of institutionalization continued to be recognized. While one of the goals of this movement was to provide medical treatment to those who could benefit from it, it was acknowledged that this could not be done in all cases and that there was a large range of mental illness for which no known "cure" existed. In time, providing places for the custodial confinement of the so-called "dependent insane" again emerged as the major goal of the States' programs in this area and remained so well into this century. See *id.*, at 228–271; D. Rothman, The Discovery of the Asylum 264–295 (1971).

In short, the idea that States may not confine the mentally ill except for the purpose of providing them with treatment is of very recent origin,[16] and there is no historical basis for imposing such a limitation on state power. Analysis of the sources of the civil commitment power likewise lends no support to that notion. There can be little doubt that in the exercise of its police power a State may confine individuals solely to protect society from the dangers of significant antisocial acts or communicable disease. Cf. *Minnesota ex rel. Pearson v. Probate Court,* 309 U. S. 270 (1940); *Jacobson v. Massachusetts,* 197 U. S. 11, 25–29 (1905). Additionally, the States are vested with the historic *parens patriae* power, including the duty to protect "persons under legal disabilities to act for themselves." *Hawaii v. Standard Oil Co.,* 405 U. S. 251, 257 (1972). See also *Mormon Church v. United States,* 136 U. S. 1, 56–58 (1890). The classic example of this role is when a State undertakes to act as " 'the general guardian of all infants, idiots, and lunatics.' " *Hawaii v. Standard Oil Co., supra,* at 257, quoting 3 W. Blackstone, Commentaries *47.

Of course, an inevitable consequence of exercising the *parens patriae* power is that the ward's personal freedom will be substantially restrained, whether a guardian is appointed to control his property, he is placed in the custody of a private third party, or committed to an institution. Thus, however the power is implemented, due process requires that it not be invoked indiscriminately. At a minimum, a particular scheme for protection of the mentally ill must rest upon a legislative determination that it is compatible with the best interests of the affected class and that its members are unable to act for themselves. Cf. *Mormon Church v. United States, supra.* Moreover, the use of alternative forms of protection may be motivated by different considerations, and the justifications for one may not be invoked to rationalize another. Cf. *Jackson v. Indiana.* 406 U. S., at 737–738. See also American Bar Foundation, The Mentally Disabled and the Law 254–255 (S. Brakel & R. Rock ed. 1971).

However, the existence of some due process limitations on the *parens patriae* power does not justify the further conclusion that it may be exercised to confine a mentally ill person only if the purpose of the confinement is treatment. Despite many recent advances in medical knowledge, it remains a stubborn fact that there are many forms of mental illness which are not understood, some of which are untreatable in the sense that no effective therapy has yet been discovered for them, and that rates of "cure" are generally low. See Schwitzgebel, The Right to Effective Mental Treatment, 62 Calif. L. Rev. 936, 941–948 (1974). There can be little responsible debate regarding "the uncertainty of diagnosis in this field and the tentativeness of professional judgment." *Greenwood v. United States,* 350 U. S., at 375. See also Ennis & Litwack, Psychiatry and the Presumption of Expertise: Flipping Coins in the Courtroom, 62 Calif. L. Rev. 693, 697–719 (1974).[17] Similarly, as previously observed, it is universally recognized as fundamental to effective therapy that the patient acknowledge his illness and cooperate with those attempting to give treatment; yet the failure of a large proportion of mentally ill persons to do so is a common phenomenon. See Katz, *supra,* 36 U. Chi. L. Rev., at 768–769. It may be that some persons in either of these categories,[18] and there may be others, are unable to function in society and will suffer real harm to themselves unless provided with care in a sheltered environment. See, *e.g., Lake v. Cameron,* 124 U. S. App. D. C. 264, 270–271, 364 F. 2d 657, 663–664 (1966) (dissenting opinion). At the very least, I am not able to say that a state legislature is powerless to make that kind of judgment. See *Greenwood v. United States, supra.*

B

Alternatively, it has been argued that a Fourteenth Amendment right to treatment for involuntarily confined mental patients derives from the fact that many of the safeguards of the criminal process are not present in civil commitment. The Court of Appeals described this theory as follows:

"[A] due process right to treatment is based on the principle that when the three central limitations on the government's power to detain—that detention be in retribution for a specific offense; that it be limited to a fixed term; and that it be permitted after a proceeding where the fundamental procedural safeguards are observed—are absent, there must be a *quid pro quo* extended by the government to justify confinement. And the *quid pro quo* most commonly recognized is the provision of rehabilitative treatment." 493 F. 2d, at 522.

To the extent that this theory may be read to permit a State to confine an individual simply because it is willing to provide treatment, regardless of the subject's ability to function in society, it raises the gravest of constitutional problems, and I have no doubt the Court of Appeals would agree on this score. As a justification for a constitutional right to such treatment, the *quid pro quo* theory suffers from equally serious defects.

It is too well established to require extended discussion that due process is not an inflexible concept. Rather, its requirements are determined in particular instances by identifying and accommodating the interests of the individual and society. See, *e.g., Morrissey v. Brewer,* 408 U. S. 471, 480–484 (1972); *McNeil v. Director, Patuxent Institution,* 407 U. S., at 249–250; *McKeiver v. Pennsylvania,* 403

U. S. 528, 545–555 (1971) (plurality opinion). Where claims that the State is acting in the best interests of an individual are said to justify reduced procedural and substantive safeguards, this Court's decisions require that they be "candidly appraised." *In re Gault,* 387 U. S., at 21, 27–29. However, in so doing judges are not free to read their private notions of public policy or public health into the Constitution. *Olsen v. Nebraska,* 313 U. S. 236, 246–247 (1941).

The *quid pro quo* theory is a sharp departure from, and cannot coexist with, due process principles. As an initial matter, the theory presupposes that essentially the same interests are involved in every situation where a State seeks to confine an individual; that assumption, however, is incorrect. It is elementary that the justification for the criminal process and the unique deprivation of liberty which it can impose requires that it be invoked only for commission of a specific offense prohibited by legislative enactment. See *Powell v. Texas,* 392 U. S. 514, 541–544 (1968) (opinion of Black, J.).[19] But it would be incongruous, for example, to apply the same limitation when quarantine is imposed by the State to protect the public from a highly communicable disease. See *Jacobson v. Massachusetts,* 197 U. S., at 29–30.

A more troublesome feature of the *quid pro quo* theory is that it would elevate a concern for essentially procedural safeguards into a new substantive constitutional right.[20] Rather than inquiring whether strict standards of proof or periodic redetermination of a patient's condition are required in civil confinement, the theory accepts the absence of such safeguards but insists that the State provide benefits which, in the view of a court, are adequate "compensation" for confinement. In light of the wide divergence of medical opinion regarding the diagnosis of and proper therapy for mental abnormalities, that prospect is especially troubling in this area and cannot be squared with the principle that "courts may not substitute for the judgments of legislators their own understanding of the public welfare, but must instead concern themselves with the validity under the Constitution of the methods which the legislature has selected." *In re Gault,* 387 U. S., at 71 (Harlan, J., concurring and dissenting). Of course, questions regarding the adequacy of procedure and the power of a State to continue particular confinements are ultimately for the courts, aided by expert opinion to the extent that is found helpful. But I am not persuaded that we should abandon the traditional limitations on the scope of judicial review.

C

In sum, I cannot accept the reasoning of the Court of Appeals and can discern no basis for equating an involuntarily committed mental patient's unquestioned constitutional right not to be confined without due process of law with a constitutional right to *treatment.*[21] Given the present state of medical knowledge regarding abnormal human behavior and its treatment, few things would be more fraught with peril than to irrevocably condition a State's power to protect the mentally ill upon the providing of "such treatment as will give [them] a realistic opportunity to be cured." Nor can I accept the theory that a State may lawfully confine an individual thought to need treatment and justify that deprivation of liberty solely by providing some treatment. Our concepts of due process would not tolerate such a "tradeoff." Because the Court of Appeals' analysis could be read as authorizing those results, it should not be followed.

NOTES

1. Donaldson's original complaint was filed as a class action on behalf of himself and all of his fellow patients in an entire department of the Florida State Hospital at Chattahoochee. In addition to a damages claim, Donaldson's complaint also asked for habeas corpus relief ordering his release, as well as the release of all members of the class. Donaldson further sought declaratory and injunctive relief requiring the hospital to provide adequate psychiatric treatment.

After Donaldson's release and after the District Court dismissed the action as a class suit, Donaldson filed an amended complaint, repeating his claim for compensatory and punitive damages. Although the amended complaint retained the prayer for declaratory and injunctive relief, that request was eliminated from the case prior to trial. See 493 F. 2d 507, 512–513.

2. The judicial commitment proceedings were pursuant to § 394.22 (11) of the State Public Health Code, which provided:

"Whenever any person who has been adjudged mentally incompetent requires confinement or restraint to prevent self-injury or violence to others, the said judge shall direct that such person be forthwith delivered to a superintendent of a Florida state hospital, for the mentally ill, after admission has been authorized under regulations approved by the board of commissioners of state institutions, for care, maintenance, and treatment, as provided in sections 394.09, 394.24, 394.25, 394.26 and 394.27, or make such other disposition of him as he may be permitted by law. . . ." Fla. Laws 1955–1956 Extra. Sess., c. 31403, § 1, p. 62.

Donaldson had been adjudged "incompetent" several days earlier under §394.22 (1), which provided for such a finding as to any person who was "incompetent by reason of mental illness, sickness, drunkenness, excessive use of drugs, insanity, or other mental or physical condition, so that he is incapable of caring for himself or managing his property, or is likely to dissipate or lose his property or become the victim of designing persons, or inflict harm on himself or others. . . ." Fla. Gen. Laws 1955, c. 29909, § 3, p. 831.

It would appear that §394.22 (11) (a) contemplated that involuntary commitment would be imposed only on those "incompetent" persons who "require[d] confinement or restraint to prevent self-injury or violence to others." But this is not certain, for §394.22 (11) (c) provided that the judge could adjudicate the person a "harmless incompetent" and release him to a guardian upon a finding that he did "not require confinement or restraint to prevent self-injury or violence to others *and* that treatment in the Florida State Hospital is unnecessary or would be without benefit to such person. . . ." Fla. Gen. Laws 1955, c. 29909, §3, p. 835 (emphasis added). In this regard, it is noteworthy that Donaldson's "Order for Delivery of Mentally Incompetent" to the Florida State Hospital provided that he required "confinement or restraint to prevent self-injury or violence to others, *or* to insure proper treatment." (Emphasis added.) At any rate, the Florida commitment statute provided no judicial procedure whereby one still incompetent could secure his release on the ground that he was no longer dangerous to himself or others.

Whether the Florida statute provided a "right to treatment" for involuntarily committed patients is also open to dispute. Under §394.22 (11) (a), commitment "to prevent self-injury or violence to others" was "for care, maintenance, and treatment." Recently Florida has totally revamped its civil commitment law and now provides a statutory right to receive individual medical treatment. Fla. Stat. Ann. §394.459 (1973).

3. The sole *statutory* procedure for release required a judicial reinstatement of a patient's "mental competency." Public Health Code §§394.22 (15) and (16), Fla. Gen. Laws 1955, c. 29909, §3, pp. 838–841. But this procedure could be initiated by the hospital staff. Indeed, it was at the staff's initiative that Donaldson was finally restored to competency, and liberty, almost immediately after O'Connor retired from the superintendency.

In addition, witnesses testified that the hospital had always had its own procedure for releasing patients—for "trial visits," "home visits," "furloughs," or "out of state discharges"—even though the patients had not been judicially restored to competency. Those conditional releases often became permanent, and the hospital merely closed its books on the patient. O'Connor did not deny at trial that he had the power to release patients; he conceded that it was his "duty" as superintendent of the hospital "to determine whether that patient having once reached the hospital was in such condition as to request that he be considered for release from the hospital."

4. There was some evidence that Donaldson, who is a Christian Scientist, on occasion refused to take medication. The trial judge instructed the jury not to award damages for any period of confinement during which Donaldson had declined treatment.

5. At the close of Donaldson's case in chief, O'Connor moved for a directed verdict on the ground that state law at the time of Donaldson's confinement authorized institutionalization of the mentally ill even if they posed no danger to themselves or others. This motion was denied. At the close of all the evidence, O'Connor asked that the jury be instructed that "if defendants acted pursuant to a statute which was not declared unconstitutional at the time, they cannot be held accountable for such action." The District Court declined to give this requested instruction.

6. The District Court defined treatment as follows:

"You are instructed that a person who is involuntarily civilly committed to a mental hospital does have a constitutional right to receive such treatment *as will give him a realistic opportunity to be cured or to improve his mental condition.*" (Emphasis added.) O'Connor argues that this statement suggests that a mental patient has a right to treatment even if confined by reason of dangerousness to himself or others. But this is to take the above paragraph out of context, for it is bracketed by paragraphs making clear the trial judge's theory that treatment is constitutionally required only if mental illness alone, rather than danger to self or others, is the reason for confinement. If O'Connor had thought the instructions ambiguous on this point, he could have objected to them and requested a clarification. He did not do so. We accordingly have no occasion here to decide whether persons committed on grounds of dangerousness enjoy a "right to treatment."

In pertinent part, the instructions read as follows:

"The Plaintiff claims in brief that throughout the period of his hospitalization he was not mentally ill or dangerous to himself or others, and claims further that if he was mentally ill, or if Defendants believed he was mentally ill, Defendants withheld from him the treatment necessary to improve his mental condition.

"The Defendants claim, in brief, that Plaintiff's detention was legal and proper, or if his detention was not legal and proper, it was the result of mistake, without malicious intent.

"In order to prove his claim under the Civil Rights Act, the burden is upon the Plaintiff in this case to establish by a preponderance of the evidence in this case the following facts:

"That the Defendants confined Plaintiff against his will, knowing that he was not mentally ill or dangerous or knowing that if mentally ill he was not receiving treatment for his alleged mental illness.

"[T]hat the Defendants' acts and conduct deprived the Plaintiff of his Federal Constitutional right not to be denied or deprived of his liberty without due process of law as that phrase is defined and explained in these instructions. . . .

"You are instructed that a person who is involuntarily civilly committed to a mental hospital does have a constitutional right to receive such treatment as will give him a realistic opportunity to be cured or to improve his mental condition.

"Now, the purpose of involuntary hospitalization is treatment and not mere custodial care or punishment if a patient is not a danger to himself or others. Without such treatment there is no justification from a constitutional standpoint for continued confinement unless you should also find that the Plaintiff was dangerous either to himself or others."

7. The trial judge had instructed that punitive damages should be awarded only if "the act or omission of the Defendant or Defendants which proximately caused injury to the Plaintiff was maliciously or wantonly or oppressively done."

8. Given the jury instructions, see n. 6 *supra,* it is possible that the jury went so far as

to find that O'Connor knew not only that Donaldson was harmless to himself and others but also that he was not mentally ill at all. If it so found, the jury was permitted by the instructions to rule against O'Connor regardless of the nature of the "treatment" provided. If we were to construe the jury's verdict in that fashion, there would remain no substantial issue in this case: That a wholly sane and innocent person has a constitutional right not to be physically confined by the State when his freedom will pose a danger neither to himself nor to others cannot be seriously doubted.

9. The judge's instructions used the phrase "dangerous to himself." Of course, even if there is no foreseeable risk of self-injury or suicide, a person is literally "dangerous to himself" if for physical or other reasons he is helpless to avoid the hazards of freedom either through his own efforts or with the aid of willing family members or friends. While it might be argued that the judge's instructions could have been more detailed on this point, O'Connor raised no objection to them, presumably because the evidence clearly showed that Donaldson was not "dangerous to himself" however broadly that phrase might be defined.

10. O'Connor argues that, despite the jury's verdict, the Court must assume that Donaldson was receiving treatment sufficient to justify his confinement, because the adequacy of treatment is a "nonjusticiable" question that must be left to the discretion of the psychiatric profession. That argument is unpersuasive. Where "treatment" is the sole asserted ground for depriving a person of liberty, it is plainly unacceptable to suggest that the courts are powerless to determine whether the asserted ground is present. See *Jackson v. Indiana,* 406 U. S. 715. Neither party objected to the jury instruction defining treatment. There is, accordingly, no occasion in this case to decide whether the provision of treatment, standing alone, can ever constitutionally justify involuntary confinement or, if it can, how much or what kind of treatment would suffice for that purpose. In its present posture this case involves not involuntary treatment but simply involuntary custodial confinement.

11. See no. 5, *supra.* During his years of confinement, Donaldson unsuccessfully petitioned the state and federal courts for release from the Florida State Hospital on a number of occasions. None of these claims was ever resolved on its merits, and no evidentiary hearings were ever held. O'Connor has not contended that he relied on these unsuccessful court actions as an independent intervening reason for continuing Donaldson's confinement, and no instructions on this score were requested.

12. Upon remand, the Court of Appeals is to consider only the question whether O'Connor is to be held liable for monetary damages for violating Donaldson's constitutional right to liberty. The jury found, on substantial evidence and under adequate instructions, that O'Connor deprived Donaldson, who was dangerous neither to himself nor to others and was provided no treatment, of the constitutional right to liberty. Cf. n. 8, *supra.* That finding needs no further consideration. If the Court of Appeals holds that a remand to the District Court is necessary, the only issue to be determined in that court will be whether O'Connor is immune from liability for monetary damages.

Of necessity our decision vacating the judgment of the Court of Appeals deprives that court's opinion of precedential effect, leaving this Court's opinion and judgment as the sole law of the case. See *United States v. Munsingwear,* 340 U. S. 36.

13. I have difficulty understanding how the issue of immunity can be resolved on this record and hence it is very likely a new trial on this issue may be required; if that is the case I would hope these sensitive and important issues would have the benefit of more effective presentation and articulation on behalf of petitioner.

14. The Court's reference to "milieu therapy," *ante,* at 569, may be construed as disparaging that concept. True, it is capable of being used simply to cloak official indifference, but the reality is that some mental abnormalities respond to no known treatment. Also, some mental patients respond, as do persons suffering from a variety of physiological ailments, to what is loosely called "milieu treatment," *i. e.,* keeping them comfortable, well nourished, and in a protected environment. It is not for us to say in the baffling field of psychiatry that "milieu therapy" is always a pretense.

15. That petitioner's counsel failed to raise this issue is not a reason why it should not be considered with respect to immunity in light of the Court's holding that the defense was preserved for appellate review.

16. See Editorial, A New Right, 46 A. B. A. J. 516 (1960).

17. Indeed, there is considerable debate concerning the threshold questions of what constitutes "mental disease" and "treatment." See Szasz, The Right to Health, 57 Geo. L. J. 734 (1969).

18. Indeed, respondent may have shared both of these characteristics. His illness, paranoid schizophrenia, is notoriously unsusceptible to treatment, see Livermore, Malmquist, & Meehl, On the Justifications for Civil Commitment, 117 U. Pa. L. Rev. 75, 93, and n. 52 (1968), and the reports of the Florida State Hospital staff which were introduced into evidence expressed the view that he was unwilling to acknowledge his illness and was generally uncooperative.

19. This is not to imply that I accept all of the Court of Appeals' conclusions regarding the limitations upon the States' power to detain persons who commit crimes. For example, the notion that confinement must be "for a fixed term" is difficult to square with the widespread practice of indeterminate sentencing, at least where the upper limit is a life sentence.

20. Even advocates of a right to treatment have criticized the *quid pro quo* theory on this ground. *E.g.,* Developments in the Law—Civil Commitment of the Mentally Ill, 87 Harv. L. Rev. 1190, 1325 n. 39 (1974).

21. It should be pointed out that several issues which the Court has touched upon in other contexts are not involved here. As the Court's opinion makes plain, this is not a case of a person's seeking release because he has been confined "without ever obtaining a judicial determination that such confinement is warranted." *McNeil v. Director, Patuxent Institution,* 407 U. S. 245, 249 (1972). Although respondent's amended complaint alleged that his 1956 hearing before the Pinellas County Court was procedurally defective and ignored various factors relating to the necessity for commitment, the persons to whom those allegations applied were either not served with process or dismissed by the District Court prior to trial. Respondent has not sought review of the latter rulings, and this case does not involve the rights of a person in an initial competency or commitment proceeding. Cf. *Jackson v. Indiana,* 406 U. S. 715, 738 (1972); *Specht v. Patterson,* 386 U. S. 605 (1967); *Minnesota ex rel. Pearson v. Probate Court,* 309 U. S. 270 (1940).

Further, it was not alleged that respondent was singled out for discriminatory treatment by the staff of Florida State Hospital or that patients at that institution were denied privileges generally available to other persons under commitment in Florida. Thus, the question whether different bases for commitment justify differences in conditions of confinement is not involved in this litigation. Cf. *Jackson v. Indiana, supra,* at 723–730; *Baxstrom v. Herold,* 383 U. S. 107 (1966).

Finally, there was no evidence whatever that respondent was abused or mistreated at Florida State Hospital or that the failure to provide him with treatment aggravated his condition. There was testimony regarding the general quality of life at the hospital, but the jury was not asked to consider whether respondent's confinement was in effect "punishment" for being mentally ill. The record provides no basis for concluding, therefore, that respondent was denied rights secured by the Eighth and Fourteenth Amendments. Cf. *Robinson v. California,* 370 U. S. 660 (1962).

IV. DISCLOSURE AND INFORMED CONSENT

1. THE ETHICAL ISSUES

Probably the most vigorously debated topic in medicine and ethics is informed consent. Medically, informed consent is a sign of the patient's acceptance of the regimen prescribed by the physician. Ethically, informed consent affirms the patient's autonomy and self-determination. Even though it is a central concept, however, not all agree on a basic standard for imparting the knowledge on which consent is based.

One dimension concerns the role of the physician. Because of training and expertise, the physician is the one who diagnoses the illness and prescribes the regimen to be followed. How much, if anything, should the physician tell the patient? The typical professional standard is to disclose information that a reasonable medical practitioner would provide in a same or similar situation. The amount of information disclosed is based on a medical judgment and in the light of what the physician perceives to be the patient's best interest. This practice is to protect the patient, to shield him or her from any needless anxiety, and to help the patient be at ease in following the directions of the physician. The objective is to let the physician do the worrying so that the patient can concentrate on getting well.

Such an orientation, standard though it is, has several defects. First, it is paternalistic in that it assumes individuals cannot make decisions for themselves. Second, the rule is described as a medical judgment, but a decision to withhold information, some would argue, actually has nothing to do with the practice of medicine. Third, it is not clear whether or how the physician knows the "real" best interests of the patient. Certainly the patient may tell the physician what his or her interests are and may even tell the physician to do what the physician thinks best. But one should generalize only with great care from opinions about patients' best interests, in the abstract, toward the formulation of a standard policy of withholding information.

These problems, as well as other ethical considerations, suggest a different orientation to informed consent. The key figure is the patient, who has an ethical right to self-determination. For this right to be exercised, the information to be revealed by the physician is measured by the patient's need to know. This patient-centered position argues that all information a reasonable person would need to make an informed decision should be disclosed.

Such a standard has several foundations. First, the patient's own dignity as a person implies a right to self-determination. While not all will agree with individual expressions of self-determination, nonetheless this right is a most critical dimension of human dignity and must be respected. Second, this right is the primary means whereby individuals express their autonomy and implement their own values. Third, individual responsibility is enhanced because the patient will make the critical decisions. This position locates responsibility for the decision-making with the one whose health and values are at stake: the patient.

2. THE LEGAL ISSUES

Adequate disclosure and the doctrine of informed consent are "two sides of the same coin—the former a *sine qua non* of the latter," says the United States Court of Appeals, District of Columbia Circuit, in *Canterbury*. Within this context, the following cases represent two distinct legal positions on the issue of disclosure—that is, the duty of a physician to inform a patient as to what is at stake in contemplated treatment.

In *Canterbury* the Court clearly locates both the source and the scope of the "duty to disclose" in the basic premise that "every human being of adult years and sound mind has a right to determine what shall be done with his body." In almost identical language the Kansas Supreme Court in *Natanson* also seems to locate the source of disclosure in the legal premise of "thorough-going self-determination." But in addressing the scope of disclosure it forthrightly accepts the medical-usage standard, thus effectively rejecting or at least ignoring the self-determination premise. According to the Court, "the duty of the physician to disclose . . . is limited to those disclosures which a reasonable medical practitioner would make under the same or similar circumstances." Furthermore, "how the physician may best discharge his obligation to the patient" remains "primarily a question of medical judgment." If the physician is "motivated only by the patient's best therapeutic interests" and acts "as competent medical men would . . . in a similar situation," whatever he chooses to disclose is sufficient.

Agreeing with the *Natanson* Court that there is no duty to disclose risks about which a patient is already aware, the *Canterbury* Court elaborately rejects the medical-usage position. The *Canterbury* Court begins with the assumption that both the source and scope of the duty to disclose arise from individual self-determination, not from medical custom and practice. It follows, therefore, that the law and not medical usage must set the standard of that duty, which is ordinary reasonable care. And the scope of that standard to both physician and patient is objective, not subjective. It "remains objective with due regard for the patient's informational needs and with suitable leeway for the physician's situation," asserts the *Canterbury* Court. "In broad outline, we agree 'that a risk is thus material when a reasonable person, in what the physician knows or should know to be the patient's position, would be likely to attach significance to the risk or cluster of risks in deciding whether or not to forego the proposed therapy.' "

That settled, the only remaining legal question is: Given the circumstances, is the duty to disclose reasonably met or excused by either of the two exceptions or privileges the *Canterbury* Court discusses and most carefully circumscribes?

NATANSON V. KLINE

Supreme Court of Kansas, 1960.
186 Kan. 393, 350 P.2d 1093.

SCHROEDER, Justice.

This is an action for malpractice against a hospital and the physician in charge of its radiology department to recover for injuries sustained as the result of radiation therapy with radioactive cobalt, alleged to have been given in an excessive amount.

The plaintiff (appellant), Irma Natanson, suffering from a cancer of the breast, had a radical left mastectomy performed on May 29, 1955. At the direction of Dr. Crumpacker, the surgeon who performed that operation, the plaintiff engaged Dr. John R. Kline, a radiologist, for radiation therapy to the site of the mastectomy and the surrounding areas.

Dr. Kline, a licensed physician and specialist in radiation therapy, was head of the radiology department at St. Francis Hospital at Wichita, Kansas. The plaintiff seeks damages for injuries claimed to have been sustained as a result of alleged acts of negligence in the administration of the cobalt radiation treatment. Dr. Kline and the hospital were named as defendants (appellees).

The case was tried to a jury which returned a verdict in favor of both defendants. The plaintiff's motion for a new trial having been denied, this appeal followed specifying various trial errors.

The questions controlling the decision herein relate to the giving of instructions by the trial court.

It will be unnecessary to relate in detail all the facts presented by the evidence as abstracted, consisting of more than three hundred pages, to dispose of the issues on appeal.

The jury was submitted two special questions. In the first it found that the defendants were not guilty of any act or acts of negligence which were the proximate cause of plaintiff's injury. The jury having found in the negative on the first, the second question required no answer.

[1] It must be conceded, insofar as the evidence is concerned, that all presumptions are, and must be, in favor of the verdict. All issues of fact have been resolved in favor of the defendants. Lord v. Hercules Powder Co., 161 Kan. 268, 167 P.2d 299; and Beye v. Andres, 179 Kan. 502, 296 P.2d 1049.

The appellant contends, however, the uncontradicted evidence shows the defendants negligent as a matter of law.

Dr. Kline was called by the plaintiff to testify in the trial court and in great detail counsel examined Dr. Kline to educate the court and jury concerning cobalt radiation therapy in the treatment of cancer. A short summary in rough will serve as a basis for further discussion.

The purpose of any irradiation therapy is to destroy tissue. The theory of destruction of cancer by irradiation therapy is that when treatment is given in a series of doses (fractionation in medical terms), the greater ability of normal tissue to recover from irradiation effects enables it to survive while the cancerous tissue is destroyed.

Dosages of irradiation are expressed in roentgen. All forms of irradiation have some point of maximum, or one hundred per cent, dosage and diminish as they penetrate deeper into the body. In the case of X-rays the point of maximum dosage is in the skin. In the case of cobalt irradiation the maximum dosage is received at a point about five millimeters beneath the outer surface of the skin. The primary advantages of cobalt irradiation over X-ray irradiation are deeper penetration and less skin injury. The amount of X-ray which can be administered is governed in a large measure by the amount which the skin can tolerate. The amount of cobalt irradiation which can be administered is governed by the tolerance of the tissues lying five millimeters below the outer surface of the skin.

By "equilibrium" dose in relation to radioactive cobalt is meant the maximum dose, which occurs about five millimeters below the outer surface of the skin. "Tumor" dose means the quantity received at the known or assumed depth of the tumor.

Dr. Kline ordered the administration of cobalt irradiation for the appellant in "routine fashion". To him and to his assistant, Dr. Somers, this meant a tumor dose of 4,400 roentgen delivered to the supraclavicular area in a period of sixteen days. For this purpose the tumor was assumed to extend from outer surface in front to outer surface behind. "Routine fashion" also meant a dosage of 4,800 roentgen delivered over the outer two centimeters of the remainder of the left chest from a point at the rear portion of the left side of the patient's body around past the breast bone in a period of twenty-three days. It also meant an approximately equal dosage to the outer two centimeters over the breast bone including the chain of lymph nodes running longitudinally along each side of the breast bone.

Material to further discussion is the fact that the prescription or outline of treatment called for 4,800 roentgen to be delivered to the outer two centimeters of the chest wall. It also directed that this treatment be delivered by means of a rotating beam. According to the testimony of the appellant's husband the rotational equipment had not been installed and ready for use at the time of the appellant's first treatment. It was installed and ready for use soon thereafter.

A radiologist, who administers cobalt irradiation treatment with rotational equipment, must have the assistance of a specialist in physics. Dr. Kline's assistant was a hospital employee by the name of Darter who determined by necessary computations how to administer the desired quantity of radiation, ordered by Dr. Kline, by means of a moving beam. Darter had graduated from Wichita University with a B.S. degree the preceding spring and had a six months' special course on irradiation therapy at Massachusetts Institute of Technology. His actual experience with radioactive cobalt therapy began with the installation of the unit at the

St. Francis Hospital on Jaunary 29, 1955, some four months before the appellant's treatment began.

Highly summarized, the evidence upon which the appellant relies is that the radioactive cobalt beam was delivered at an angle to the chest wall in an effort to avoid injury to the lungs. In making the calculations to achieve the tumor doses (one and one-half to two centimeters deep), the equilibrium doses (five millimeters deep) were not calculated by Darter.

Dr. Paul A. Roys, an assistant professor of physics at Wichita University, who was a specialist in the field of nuclear physics of which radiation physics is a part, was called to testify concerning his calculations of the roentgen delivered to various parts of the appellant's chest wall in accordance with the time chart and dosages administered to the appellant as a result of Darter's calculations. From Dr. Roys' calculations the equilibrium doses administered at several segments of the chest wall were from 5,670 roentgen to 6,260 roentgen at a depth of five millimeters. It was in these segments where the appellant's injuries were sustained.

Dr. Kline had previously testified that the soft tissues of the chest wall could tolerate about 5,000 roentgen in twenty-four or twenty-five days; that the cartilage could tolerate about 5,500 roentgen over a period of twenty-eight days, and ordinarily bone would stand a larger amount. The appellant argues the effect upon her of the administration of amounts ranging from 5,670 roentgen to 6,280 roentgen certainly corroborates Dr. Kline's testimony. The entire chest, skin, cartilage and bone were completely destroyed in those areas.

There was other evidence which contradicted the appellant's theory, however. When Dr. Kline was called as a witness on his own behalf, he stated the prescribed dosage of 4,400 roentgen was intended as a minimum dosage, and was the smallest dosage which would be effective and had to be given, even though he knew that portions of the chest would receive a much higher dosage. He testified that a doctor has to take a chance in the treatment of cancer, that he knew there was danger of injury from such treatment, but that he took a calculated risk. This risk is determined to a large extent by the tolerance of the individual concerned. Some patients have a much higher tolerance than others. He further testified that he had treated approximately seventy-five breast and cancer cases since the treatment of the appellant, all of which were treated in the same manner with the same number of roentgens directed to be given.

Dr. Hare, a radiologist from Los Angeles, was called to testify for the appelees. He said that for five years he had been using 6,000 roentgen up to 9,000 roentgen on the treatment of cancer cases.

At the time treatment started the appellant had an ulcer about the size of a quarter under her left arm which remained from the mastectomy. It had not stopped draining. After treatment started the drainage increased and, according to the appellant, she understood the treatment was to shrink the area but instead it seemed to be growing larger.

There is no issue presented by the record as to the relationship between Dr. Kline and the St. Francis Hospital. The petition pleaded that the defendants were engaged in a joint adventure or in the alternative that the defendant physician was acting within the scope of his employment as agent, servant and employee of the defendant hospital. The answer of the defendant hospital admitted that the defendant physician "was in charge of its radiology department". Moreover, the pleadings raised no issues between the defendants.

[2] Upon the foregoing evidence on the state of the record presented herein, it cannot be said the appellees were guilty of negligence as a matter of law. At best it may be said, upon all the facts and circumstances presented by the record, there was evidence from which a jury could find that the proximate cause of the appellant's injury was the negligence of the defendants. On the other hand a jury, *properly instructed,* would be justified in finding for the appellees.

We shall next consider whether the jury was properly instructed.

[3] The code of civil procedure requires the court to give general instructions to the jury, with or without request having been made for the same. (G.S. 1949, 60–2909, *Fifth.*) This provision has frequently been interpreted to require the court to define the issues and state at least generally the law applicable thereto. Bushey v. Coffman, 109 Kan. 652, 201 P. 1103; Knox v. Barnard, 181 Kan. 943, 317 P.2d 452; and Schmid v. Eslick, 181 Kan. 997, 317 P.2d 459. The trial court in summarizing the pleadings for the jury in its instructions was quite brief. Aside from general factual recitations the material portions of this summarization given in instruction No. 1 are as follows:

> "In this case the plaintiff Irma Natanson * * * alleges * * * *that Dr. Kline and personnel of St. Francis Hospital administered to the plaintiff a series of cobalt radiation treatments in such a negligent manner* that the skin, flesh and muscles beneath her left arm sloughed away and ribs of her left chest were so burned that they became necrotic, or dead; * * *."

"The defendants then filed their answers in the case in which they allege that the treatments were properly administered and that they were not guilty of any negligence toward the plaintiff." (Emphasis added.)

Then followed the usual instruction (No. 2) that the foregoing statement taken from the pleadings set forth the various claims and contentions of the parties against each other, and that such claims and contentions are to be considered only as they may have been proved by evidence presented during the trial of the case.

Instruction No. 3 reads in part:

> "This is a lawsuit based upon negligence. In the conduct of human affairs, the law imposes upon us the obligation to use due and proper care to avoid hurt or injury to others. Thus, negligence may be defined as a violation of the duty to use due and proper care. The term, 'due and proper care' means, in this case, such care as medical specialists in radiology in this community would ordinarily and reasonably use under the same or similar circumstances."

The court then instructed that negligence is never presumed—it must be proved by a preponderance or greater weight of the evidence; it defined preponderance or greater weight of the evidence and instructed that negligence may be established by circumstantial evidence.

Instruction No. 4 given by the court reads:

> "The law does not require that treatments given by a physician to a patient shall attain nearly perfect results. He is not responsible in damages for lack of success or honest mistakes or errors of judgment unless it be shown that he did not possess that degree of learning and skill ordinarily possessed by radiologists of good standing in his community, or that he was not exercising reasonable and ordinary care in applying such skill and learning to the treatment of the patient. And if among radiologists more than one method of treatment is recognized, it would not be negligence for the physician to have adopted any of such methods if the method he did adopt was a recognized and approved method in the profession at the time and place of treatment."

On this appeal the court is not concerned with the general instructions on negligence or instruction No. 4, which correctly states the law. The cases upon which the appellees rely to substantiate these instructions are sound law. Tefft v. Wilcox, 6 Kan. 46; Sly v. Powell, 87 Kan. 142, 123 P. 881; Paulich v. Nipple, 104 Kan. 801, 180 P. 771; James v. Grigsby, 114 Kan. 627, 220 P. 267; Riggs v. Gouldner, 150 Kan. 727, 96 P.2d 694; Cummins v. Donley, 173 Kan. 463, 249 P.2d 695; and Goheen v. Graber, 181 Kan. 107, 309 P.2d 636.

[4] The amended petition pleaded negligence in eight specific particulars, one or more of which presented issues which the jury was required to determine on the basis of the evidence presented. It was proper for the trial court to exclude those specific allegations of negligence enumerated in the amended petition concerning which there was no evidence, but it should have set forth those specific allegations of negligence concerning which there was evidence. The general summarization, consisting of the italicized portion of instruction No. 1 heretofore quoted, was insufficient to meet this obligation of the trial court.

The answers filed by both of the defendants in the lower court denied the specific allegations of negligence alleged in the amended petition and pleaded "the plaintiff assumed the risk and hazard of said treatment."

One of the alleged grounds of negligence, concerning which there was evidence before the jury, was that Dr. Kline failed to warn the appellant the course of treatment which he undertook to administer involved great risk of bodily injury or death.

The appellant requested and the trial court refused to give the following instruction:

> "You are instructed that the relationship between physician and patient is a fiduciary one. The relationship requires the physician to make a full disclosure to the patient of all matters within his knowledge affecting the interests of the patient. Included within the matters which the physician must advise

the patient are the nature of the proposed treatment and any hazards of the proposed treatment which are known to the physician. Every adult person has the right to determine for himself or herself whether or not he will subject his body to hazards of any particular medical treatment.

"You are instructed that if you find from the evidence that defendant Kline knew that the treatment he proposed to administer to plaintiff involved hazard or danger he was under a duty to advise plaintiff of that fact and if you further find that defendant Kline did not advise plaintiff of such hazards then defendant Kline was guilty of negligence."

There was evidence from which the jury could have found that the appellant fully appreciated the danger and the risk of the radiation treatment. The appellant's husband testified:

"Q. Yes, how did it happen you went there for the conference with Dr. Kline? A. We, of course, made a periodic visit to Dr. Crumpacker after the operation, and he told us that as a precautionary measure Mrs. Natanson should go to the St. Francis Hospital and take the cobalt treatment. He explained to us that the cobalt was a new therapy; that it was much more powerful than the x-ray they had used previously. He suggested we see Dr. Kline."

On cross examination he testified:

"Q. Just a question or two. Mr. Natanson, when you and your wife went to see Dr. Crumpacker, did you have a discussion with him about the purpose of the irradiation? A. Yes.

"Q. And, was the general objection of irradiation explained to you? A. Yes.

"Q. And, that was when Mrs. Natanson was with you? A. Yes.

"Q. Now, did you consult any radiologist other than Dr. Kline in determining anything about this irradiation? A. No, sir.

"Q. Now, I take it that it was Dr. Crumpacker's thought or suggestion at least to you that Dr. Kline be consulted? A. Yes.

"Q. And, up to the time you engaged Dr. Kline, Dr. Crumpacker had been the doctor on the case? A. Yes."

There was also testimony from the appellant and her husband that Dr. Kline did not inform the appellant the treatment involved any danger whatever. The testimony of Dr. Kline, a radiologist with special training in cobalt irradiation, was that he knew he was "taking a chance" with the treatment he proposed to administer and that such treatment involved a "calculated risk". He testified there was always a danger of injury in the treatment of cancer. Insofar as the record discloses

Dr. Kline did not testify that he informed the appellant the treatment involved any danger. His only testimony relevant thereto was the following:

"Q. Now, tell us what transpired when you first met with the Natansons? A. I could not completely recall that meeting. It was such a long time ago.

"Q. Just tell us what you can recall of it? A. I remember Mr. and Mrs. Natanson coming in to see me. I can't remember if I met them in my office or whether we were downstairs. I remember in a very vague way. I remember in a vague way that we discussed the treatment, about how long it took, the number of areas we would irradiate. I have a recollection of that. I remember we took her into the treatment room. She was marked out, measured. I believe the marking out and measurement was done by Mr. Darter. Her first treatment occurred the first day she came. I am not sure of that but I think so.

"Q. Have you told us everything you recall? A. Yes."

No other evidence appears in the record concerning the subject.

The appellees argue that we are here concerned with a case where the patient consented to the treatment, but afterwards alleges that the nature and consequences of the risks of the treatment were not properly explained to her. They point out this is not an action for assault and battery, where a patient has given no consent to the treatment.

What appears to distinguish the case of the unauthorized surgery or treatment from traditional assault and battery cases is the fact that in almost all of the cases the physician is acting in relatively good faith for the benefit of the patient. While it is true that in some cases the results are not in fact beneficial to a patient, the courts have repeatedly stated that doctors are not insurers. The traditional assault and battery involves a defendant who is acting for the most part out of malice or in a manner generally considered as "anti-social". One who commits an assault and battery is not seeking to confer any benefit upon the one assaulted.

The fundamental distinction between assault and battery on the one hand, and negligence such as would constitute malpractice, on the other, is that the former is intentional and the latter unintentional. Hershey v. Peake, 115 Kan. 562, 223 P. 1113; and Maddox v. Neptune, 175 Kan. 465, 264 P.2d 1073.

We are here concerned with a case where the patient consented to the treatment, but alleges in a malpractice action that the nature and consequences of the risks of the treatment were not properly explained to her. This relates directly to the question whether the physician has obtained the informed consent of the patient to render the treatment administered.

The treatment of a cancer patient with radioactive cobalt is relatively new. Until the use of atomic energy appeared in this country, X ray was the type of radiation treatment used for such patients. Radioactive cobalt is manufactured by the Atomic Energy Commission in a neutron pill by bombarding the stable element of cobalt in its pure state. This makes the cobalt unstable and by reason thereof it is radioactive. The radioactive cobalt emits two homogeneous beams of pure energy called gamma rays, very close in character, which are far more powerful than the ordinary X rays. It produces no other rays to be filtered out. This makes it desirable for use in the treatment of cancer patients. The cobalt machine may be compared to a three million volt X ray machine.

Radioactive cobalt is so powerful that the Atomic Energy Commission specifies the construction of the room in which the cobalt unit is to be placed. The walls of the room are made of concrete forty inches thick and the ceiling, also concrete, is twenty-four inches thick. The room is sunken down in a courtyard outside the hospital. A passageway off the control room about ten feet long leads to the treatment room. All controls are placed in the outer control room and, when the radiation treatment is administered to a patient, the operator in the outer room looks through a specially designed thick lead quartz glass which gives a telescopic view. A periodic report of radiation outside the room must be made to the Atomic Energy Commission in accordance with regulations. These facts were given by Dr. Kline in his testimony.

These facts are not commonly known and a patient cannot be expected to know the hazards or the danger of radiation from radioactive cobalt unless the patient is informed by a radiologist who knows the dangers of injury from cobalt irradiation. While Dr. Kline did not testify that the radiation he gave the appellant caused her injury, he did state cobalt irradiation could cause the injury which the appellant did sustain.

What is the extent of a physician's duty to confide in his patient where the physician suggests or recommends a particular method of treatment? What duty is there upon him to explain the nature and probable consequences of that treatment to the patient? To what extent should he disclose the existence and nature of the risks inherent in the treatment?

We have been cited to no Kansas cases, nor has our research disclosed any, dealing directly with the foregoing questions. A recent article by William A. Kelly published in the Kansas Law Review entitled "The Physician, The Patient, And The Consent" (8 Kan.L.Rev. 405), reviews many malpractice cases dealing with the consent of the patient, but the article fails to deal with the problem of disclosure involving on one hand the right of the patient to decide for himself and on the other a possible therapeutic ground for withholding information which may create tension by depressing or exciting the patient. This subject has been touched upon in an article by Charles C. Lund, M. D.; "The Doctor, The Patient, And The Truth", (19 Tenn.L.Rev. 344 [1946]), and in an article by Hubert Winston Smith, LL.B.; M.D.; "Therapeutic Privilege To Withhold Specific Diagnosis From Patient Sick With Serious Or Fatal Illness", (19 Tenn.L.Rev. 349 [1946]). Allan H. McCoid, Associate Professor of Law, University of Minnesota, has written two recent articles, one "A Reappraisal Of Liability For Unauthorized Medical Treatment" (41 Minn.L.Rev. 381), published in March 1957, and the other "The Care Required Of Medical Practitioners" (12 Vanderbilt L.Rev. 549, 586), published in June 1959.

The courts frequently state that the relation between the physician and his patient is a fiduciary one, and therefore the physician has an obligation to make a full and frank disclosure to the patient of all pertinent facts related to his illness. We are here concerned with a case where the physician is charged with treating the patient without consent on the ground the patient was not fully informed of the nature of the treatment or its consequences, and, therefore, any "consent" obtained was ineffective. An effort will be made to review the cases from foreign jurisdictions most nearly in point with the question presently at hand, although none may be said to be directly in point.

In 1958 the Supreme Court of Minnesota in Bang v. Charles T. Miller Hospital, 251 Minn. 427, 88 N.W.2d 186, had an assault case before it, and though not alleged as a malpractice action for negligence, a new trial was granted on the ground that a fact issue was presented for the jury to determine whether the patient consented to the performance of the operation. There the patient went to a urologist because of urinary trouble and apparently consented to a cystoscopic examination and a prostate operation. He was not informed that part of the procedure of a transurethral prostatic resection would be the tying off of his sperm ducts. In the opinion the court said:

> "While we have no desire to hamper the medical profession in the outstanding progress it has made and continues to make in connection with the study and solution of health and disease problems, it is our opinion that a reasonable rule is that, where a physician or surgeon can ascertain in advance of an operation alternative situations and no immediate emergency exists, a patient should be informed of the alternative possibilities and given a chance to decide before the doctor proceeds with the operation. By that we mean that, in a situation such as the case before us where no immediate emergency exists, a patient should be informed before the operation that if his spermatic cords were severed it would result in his sterilization, but on the other hand if this were not done there would be a possibility of an infection which could result in serious consequences. Under such conditions the patient would at least have the opportunity of deciding whether he wanted to take the chance of a possible infection if the operation was performed in one manner or to become sterile if performed in another." 251 Minn. at pages 434, 435, 88 N.W.2d at page 190.

A malpractice action was before the Fifth Circuit Court in Lester v. Aetna Casualty & Surety Company, 240 F.2d 676. The patient was given electro-shock treatments prescribed by a psychiatrist and suffered a bad result. In affirming the jury's finding the court held the patient's wife gave sufficient legal consent, and said:

> "The basic, the fundamental, difficulty which confronts plaintiff on this appeal is that he presents his case as though it were one of a person being deprived by another of due process of law, instead of grounding it upon the well settled principles that a physician must, except in real and serious emergencies, acquaint the patient or, when the circumstances require it, some one properly acting for him, of the diagnosis and the treatment proposed, and obtain consent, thereto expressed or implied, and consent obtained must proceed in accordance with proper reasonable medical

standards *and in the exercise of due care* * * *" 240 F.2d at page 679. (Emphasis added.)

The appellees rely upon the Canadian case of Kenny v. Lockwood [1932], 1 D.L.R. 507, where a patient alleged the defendants falsely and recklessly, without caring whether it was true or false, and without reasonable ground for believing it to be true, represented the operation to be "simple", and that her hand "would be all right in three weeks." No evidence was presented to suggest fraud or recklessness and the plaintiff's argument proceeded mainly upon the duty which it was said the defendants owed to the plaintiff, due to the peculiar relation set up between a surgeon and his patient. The Ontario trial judge concluded that it was the duty of the defendant doctors to "enlighten the patient's mind in a plain and reasonable way as to what her ailment was, as to what were the risks of operating promptly, what were the risks of delaying the operation, and what the risks of not operating at all. Having discharged that duty, it was their further duty to secure from the patient a decision or consent as to what course is to be followed, and if that decision or consent is not had and the surgeons operate and the operation turns out badly the surgeons are liable. Such a relationship is established between a person of special skill and knowledge and a person of no skill or knowledge upon the facts required for the making of a decision that, unless the person with the special skill and knowledge discharges the duty which he owes of placing the patient in a position to make a decision, that person, when he is employed and paid because of his special skill and knowledge, has failed to perform his duty, and that breach of duty makes him liable in damages for untoward results." (Kenny v. Lockwood Clinic Ltd. [1931], 4 D.L.R. 906, 907.)

The trial court found for the plaintiff but on appeal the judgment was reversed, the appellate court saying there was some testimony that the doctors had explained all details to the plaintiff, although the extracts contained in the opinion indicate that the doctor admitted to having said that the operation was not a very serious one and that he had not clearly presented the alternatives to the plaintiff. In the court's opinion it was said:

> " * * * the duty cast upon the surgeon was to deal honestly with the patient as to the necessity, character and importance of the operation and its probable consequences and whether success might reasonably be expected to ameliorate or remove the trouble, but that such duty does not extend to warning the patient of the dangers incident to, or possible in, any operation, nor to details calculated to frighten or distress the patient." (p. 525.)

The court concluded upon the evidence presented:

> "That the defendant Stoddart reasonably fulfilled the duty laid upon him arising out of the relationship of surgeon and patient, not being guilty of 'negligence in word' or 'economy of truth' nor of misleading the plaintiff, and so is not liable for breach of the duty * * * " (p. 526.)

In the opinion it was said the duty of a surgeon is to be honest in fact and to express his honest belief, and if he does so he ought not to be judged as if he had warranted a perfect cure nor to be found derelict in his duty on any meticulous criticism of his language.

[5] The conclusion to be drawn from the foregoing cases is that where the physician or surgeon has affirmatively misrepresented the nature of the operation or has failed to point out the probable consequences of the course of treatment, he may be subjected to a claim of unauthorized treatment. But this does not mean that a doctor is under an obligation to describe in detail all of the possible consequences of treatment. It might be argued, as indicated by the authors of the various law review articles heretofore cited, that to make a complete disclosure of all facts, diagnoses and alternatives or possibilities which may occur to the doctor could so alarm the patient that it would, in fact, constitute bad medical practice. There is probably a privilege, on therapeutic grounds, to withhold the specific diagnosis where the disclosure of cancer or some other dread disease would seriously jeopardize the recovery of an unstable, temperamental or severely depressed patient. But in the ordinary case there would appear to be no such warrant for suppressing facts and the physician should make a substantial disclosure to the patient prior to the treatment or risk liability in tort.

Anglo-American law starts with the premise of thoroughgoing self-determination. It follows that each man is considered to be master of his own body, and he may, if he be of sound mind, expressly prohibit the performance of life-saving surgery, or other medical treatment. A doctor might well believe that an operation or form of treatment is desirable or necessary but the law does not permit him to substitute his own judgment for that of the patient by any form of artifice or deception.

The mean between the two extremes of absolute silence on the part of the physician relative to the treatment of a patient and exhaustive discussion by the physician explaining in detail all possible risks and dangers was well stated by the California District Court of Appeals in Salgo v. Leland Stanford, Etc. Bd. Trustees, 1957, 154 Cal.App.2d 560, 317 P.2d 170. There the court had before it a malpractice action wherein the defendants were charged with *negligence.* The patient, his wife and son testified that the patient was not informed anything in the nature of an aortography was to be performed. Two of the doctors contradicted this, although admitting that the details of the procedure involving injection of a radio-opaque substance into the aorta and the possible dangers therefrom were not explained. As a result of the aortography the patient was paralyzed from the waist down. The trial court gave a rather broad instruction on the duty of the physician to disclose to the patient "all the facts which mutually affect his rights and interests and of the surgical risk, hazard and danger, if any." 154 Cal.App. 2d at page 578, 317 P.2d at page 181. On appeal, the instruction was held to be overly broad, the court stating:

" * * * A physician violates his duty to his patient and subjects himself to liability if he withholds any facts which are necessary to form the basis of an intelligent consent by the patient to the proposed treatment. Likewise the physician may not minimize the known dangers of a procedure or operation in order to induce his patient's consent. At the same time, the physician must place the welfare of his patient above all else and this very fact places him in a position in which he sometimes must choose between two alternative courses of action. One is to explain to the patient every risk attendant upon any surgical procedure or operation, no matter how remote; this may well result in alarming a patient who is already unduly apprehensive and who may as a result refuse to undertake surgery in which there is in fact minimal risk; it may also result in actually increasing the risks by reason of the physiological results of the apprehension itself. The other is to recognize that each patient presents a separate problem, that the patient's mental and emotional condition is important and in certain cases may be crucial, and that in discussing the element of risk a certain amount of discretion must be employed consistent with the full disclosure of facts necessary to an informed consent * * *.

"The instruction given should be modified to inform the jury that the physician has such discretion consistent, of course, with the full disclosure of facts necessary to an informed consent." 154 Cal.App.2d at page 578, 317 P.2d at page 181.

The appellees rely upon Hunt v. Bradshaw, 1955, 242 N.C. 517, 88 S.E.2d 762, a North Carolina case. This was a malpractice action against a physician wherein the patient sought damages alleged to have resulted from the negligent failure of the defendant (1) to use reasonable care and diligence in the application of his knowledge and skill as a physician and surgeon, and (2) to exercise his best judgment in attempting to remove a small piece of steel from plaintiff's body. On these allegations of negligence the plaintiff contended, among other things, that the defendant advised the plaintiff the operation was simple, whereas it was serious and involved undisclosed risks. The plaintiff's evidence was sufficient to justify a finding the operation was of a very serious nature. The court after reviewing the evidence said:

" * * * Upon Dr. Bradshaw's advice the operation was decided upon. It is understandable the surgeon wanted to reassure the patient so that he would not go to the operating room unduly apprehensive. Failure to explain the risks involved, therefore, may be considered a mistake on the part of the surgeon, *but under the facts* cannot be deemed such want of ordinary care as to import liability.

"Proof of what is in accord with approved surgical procedure and what constitutes the standard of care required of the surgeon in performing an operation, like the advisability of the operation itself, are matters not within the knowledge of lay witnesses but must be established by the testimony of qualified experts * * *

"Plaintiff's expert testimony is sufficient to justify the finding the injury and damage to plaintiff's hand and arm resulted from the operation. But, as in cases of ordinary negligence, the fact that injury results is not proof the act which caused it was a negligent act. The doctrine *res ipsa loquitur* does not apply in cases of this character * * *.

"Of course, it seems hard to the patient in apparent good health that he should be advised to undergo an operation, and upon regaining consciousness finds that he has lost the use of an arm for the remainder of his life. Infallibility in human beings is not attainable. The law recognizes, and we think properly so, that the surgeon's hand, with its skill and training, is, after all, a human hand, guided by a human brain in a procedure in which the margin between safety and danger sometimes measures little more than the thickness of a sheet of paper.

"The plaintiff's case fails because of lack of expert testimony that the defendant failed, either to exercise due care in the operation, or to use his best judgment in advising it * * * " 242 N.C. at pages 523, 524, 88 S.E.2d at page 766. (Emphasis added.)

Under *the facts* presented by the case it does not appear the allegations of negligence were sufficient to encompass the failure of the physician to inform the patient of the risks.

An X-ray case upon which the appellees rely is Costa v. Regents of Univ. of California, 116 Cal.App.2d 445, 254 P.2d 85. This was a malpractice action against a hospital and certain doctors for alleged negligence in the X-ray treatment of cancer to the area of the lower jaw which resulted in necrosis of tissue. It was alleged the X-ray treatment was too drastic and extensive. While the circumstances were in many respects similar to the case at bar, it did not involve any failure of the physicians to disclose the risks. It was claimed a less drastic and extensive treatment should have been undertaken by the doctors. The court said:

" * * * The expert evidence showed clearly that the exact extent of the cancer under the surface and the absence of hidden involvements cannot in a case like appellant's be decided with such certainty that it can be safely relied on for the purpose of restricting the treatment within narrow limits. There was no expert evidence whatever that on the data available to defendants they ought in good practice to have restricted the X-ray treatment to a less drastic procedure or that the diagnostic methods now indicated by appellant if used would have yielded certainty and should have led to restriction to less dangerous treatment. Several experts testified that said methods (X-ray pictures and biopsy) could not be relied on for the purpose. In fighting so dangerous a condition as here involved, physicians may take serious risks and in doing so must rely on their judgment in deciding how far to go. See Callahan v. Hahnemann Hospital, 1 Cal.2d 447, 35 P.2d 536. To hold them responsible in the cases where the bad chance unfortunately materializes would be evidently unjust and most dangerous if physicians were deterred from going to the extent which gives their patient the best chance of survival." 116 Cal.App.2d at page 457, 254 P.2d at page 92.

The Costa case has nothing to do with the duty to inform the patient of the hazardous character of proposed treatment. The more recent case of the same court in Salgo v. Leland Stanford, Etc. Bd. Trustees, supra, covers the subject specifically.

[6] In our opinion the proper rule of law to determine whether a patient has given an intelligent consent to a proposed form of treatment by a physician was stated and applied in Salgo v. Leland Stanford, Etc. Bd. Trustees, supra. This rule in effect compels disclosure by the physician in order to assure that an informed consent of the patient is obtained. The duty of the physician to disclose, however, is limited to those disclosures which a reasonable medical practitioner would make under the same or similar circumstances. How the physician may best discharge his obligation to the patient in this difficult situation involves primarily a question of medical judgment. So long as the disclosure is sufficient to assure an informed consent, the physician's choice of plausible courses should not be called into question if it appears, all circumstances considered, that the physician was motivated only by the patient's best therapeutic interests and he proceeded as competent medical men would have done in a similar situation.

[7] Turning now to the facts in the instant case, the appellant knew she had a cancerous tumor in her left breast which was removed by a radical mastectomy. Pathological examination of the tissue removed did not disclose any spread of the cancer cells into the lymphatics beyond the cancerous tumor itself. As a precautionary measure the appellant's ovaries and fallopian tubes were removed, which likewise upon pathological examination indicated no spread of the cancer to these organs. At the time the appellant went to Dr. Kline as a patient there was no immediate emergency concerning the administration of cobalt irradiation treatment such as would excuse the physician from making a reasonable disclosure to the patient. We think upon all the facts and circumstances here presented Dr. Kline was obligated to make a reasonable disclosure to the appellant of the nature and probable consequences of the suggested or recommended cobalt irradiation treatment, and he was also obligated to make a reasonable disclosure of the dangers within his knowledge which were incident to, or possible in, the treatment he proposed to administer.

[8] Upon the record here presented Dr. Kline made no disclosures to the appellant whatever. He was silent. This is not to say that the facts compel a verdict for the appellant. Under the rule heretofore stated, where the patient fully appreciates the danger involved, the failure of a physician in his duty to make a reasonable disclosure to the patient would have no causal relation to the injury. In such event the consent of the patient to the proposed treatment is an informed consent. The burden of proof rests throughout the trial of the case upon the patient who seeks to recover in a malpractice action for her injury.

In considering the obligation of a physician to disclose and explain to the patient in language as simple as necessary the nature of the ailment, the nature of the proposed treatment, the probability of success or of alternatives, and perhaps the risks of unfortunate results and unforeseen conditions within the body, we do not think the administration of such an obligation, by imposing liability for malpractice if the treatment were administered without such explanation where explanation could reasonably be made, presents any insurmountable obstacles.

[9] The appellant's requested instruction on the duty of a physician to make a disclosure to his patient was too broad. But this did not relieve the trial court of its obligation to instruct on such issue under the circumstances here presented, since the issue was raised by the pleadings. On retrial the instruction should be modified to inform the jury that a physician has such discretion, as heretofore indicated, consistent with the full disclosure of facts necessary to assure an informed consent by the patient.

[10] On retrial of this case the first issue for the jury to determine should be whether the administration of cobalt irradiation treatment was given with the informed consent of the patient, and if it was not, the physician who failed in his legal obligation is guilty of malpractice no matter how skillfully the treatment may have been administered, and the jury should determine the damages arising from the cobalt irradiation treatment. If the jury should find an informed consent was given by the patient for such treatment, the jury should next determine whether proper skill was used in administering the treatment.

[11] The primary basis of liability in a malpractice action is the deviation from the standard of conduct of a reasonable and prudent medical doctor of the same school of practice as the defendant under similar circumstances. Under such standard the patient is properly protected by the medical profession's own recognition of its obligations to maintain its standards.

The appellant requested and the trial court refused to give the following instruction:

> "You are instructed that under the terms of the contract between defendant Kline and defendant Hospital it was the duty of defendant Kline to supervise the work of all of the personnel in the radiology department. If you find that plantiff's injury was the result of the negligence of personnel in the department your verdict shall be in favor of plaintiff and against both defendants."

Nowhere in the written instructions was there anything to indicate that either defendant could be chargeable with the negligence of anyone other than the negligence of Dr. Kline personally, unless it is to be construed from the generalization of the pleadings contained in the court's instruction No. 1. This generalization at best would be confusing to a jury on this point.

> "A physician is responsible for an injury done to a patient through the want of proper skill and care in his assistant, and through the want of proper skill and care in his apprentice, agent, or employee. The fact that a physician's assistant is a member of the same or a similar profession does not make the rule of respondeat superior inapplicable, and a physician is liable not only for negligence of laymen employed by him, but also for the negligence of nurses or other physicians in his employ.

"Corporations, or persons other than physicians, who treat patients for hire with the expectation of profit are liable for negligence or malpractice on the part of the physicians or nurses employed by them." (70 C.J.S. Physicians and Surgeons §54e, pp. 978, 979, and see cases cited therein.)

Although the court did not think it necessary to go into the doctrine of *respondeat superior,* see the facts in Rule v. Cheeseman, 181 Kan. 957, 317 P.2d 472.

In Gray v. McLaughlin, 207 Ark. 191, 179 S.W.2d 686, an X-ray specialist or roentgenologist was held liable for injuries caused by the X-ray technician employed by him.

In an action for damages founded on malpractice it is the duty of the trial court to instruct the jury with respect to the law governing the case, explaining the precise questions at issue. This includes, under the evidence presented by the record in the instant case, the responsibility of the physician for the acts or omissions of others under his supervision. (See, 70 C.J.S. Physicians and Surgeons §64, p. 1016, and cases cited.)

[12] A party is entitled to have the trial court give an instruction to the jury which is essential to his theory of the case when there is sufficient evidence to support such theory. Kreh v. Trinkle, 185 Kan. 329, 343 P.2d 213.

[13,14] In our opinion the refusal of the trial court to give the requested instruction was prejudicial and constituted reversible error. It was Dr. Somers, not Dr. Kline, who prescribed use of rotational therapy. Dr. Somers was an assistant to Dr. Kline. It was the hospital's employee, Darter, referred to by Dr. Kline as his physicist, who made the computations which resulted in administration of a dosage in excess of tolerance limits, if the jury were to give credence to the appellant's theory of the evidence, and Dr. Kline was chargeable with knowledge of the quantity and effect of the irradiation he caused to be administered to the appellant. Agnew v. Larson, 82 Cal.App.2d 176, 185 P.2d 851.

While counsel for the appellees made no objection to the testimony of Dr. Roys, they set forth in detail his testimony in a counter abstract to show he was not a physician but was testifying by virtue of an academic degree. Inferentially this may suggest Dr. Roys, not being a physician of the same school of practice as Dr. Kline, was incompetent to establish negligence concerning medical practice and treatment. Goheen v. Graber, 181 Kan. 107, 309 P.2d 636.

It is the customary practice, however, for a radiologist to have a physicist make his calculations where cobalt irradiation therapy treatments are given by a rotational beam to patients. This was confirmed not only by Dr. Kline but also by Dr. Hare. In fact, Dr. Kline testified that he did not know how to make the calculations necessary to make the irradiation administered meet the requirements for the radiation prescribed. He said he could not even understand the calculations when they had been made by others. It must be observed this is not unusual because the radiologist is not trained in nuclear physics, a specialty in itself. Dr. Roys was a technician of the same type as Darter, and, in fact, was the professor at Wichita University under whom Darter studied. Thus, there could be no legitimate objection to the competency of Dr. Roys to testify relative to the calculations made.

The appellees contend that no issue was raised in the pleadings or in the evidence at the trial, so far as the jury was concerned, which would exempt the hospital from liability for the acts of Dr. Kline under the doctrine of *respondeat superior* and that by reason thereof no instruction was required. The simple answer is that the appellees are privileged to make this admission, but the jury is entitled by an appropriate instruction to know about it. The appellees argue the appellant does not claim that Darter made any error in computation. While this is true, Darter did not, under the appellant's theory, make enough calculations to know that an excessive equilibrium dosage was administered five millimeters beneath the skin. Under these circumstances, the appellees' argument has no merit.

[15,16] The appellant contends the trial court erred in failing to instruct that the jury might consider the fact of injury as evidence of negligence, citing George v. Shannon, 92 Kan. 801, 142 P. 967. On the facts presently before the court this point is not well taken. The appellant alleges injury as a result of burns from cobalt irradiation therapy. This is not a *res ipsa loquitur* case and no presumption of negligence of a physician is to be indulged from the fact of injury or adverse result of his treatment of the patient. Cummins v. Donley, 173 Kan. 463, 249 P.2d 695, and cases cited therein.

In Costa v. Regents of Univ. of California, supra, it was contended, among other things, that necrosis did not ordinarily follow treatment from cancer X-ray and that this circumstance amounted to proof of negligence. In rejecting the contention the California court said:

> " * * * The result of the same treatment is not always the same in all cases and on all patients. When the result of a treatment is less favorable or more prejudicial than in the great majority of cases such need not indicate that the treatment was negligently performed, but may as well be the result of individual differences in reaction or the less favorable circumstances of the case * * * " 116 Cal. App.2d at page 461, 254 P.2d at page 95.

The expert testimony in the instant case confirms the correctness of the above statement. But see, King v. Ditto, 142 Or. 207, 19 P.2d 1110.

[17] Upon the record presented it is apparent the appellees were united in interest; therefore, pursuant to G.S.1949, 60–2907, the appellees were obligated in the exercise of their peremptory challenges in empaneling the jury to challenge jointly.

In conclusion we hold the trial court committed reversible error in the matter of instructing the jury. It has been held when the instructions to the jury define the issues and state the pertinent law with accuracy, the failure of the court to emphasize some particular point of law deemed important by a party litigant does not constitute error, especially when such party does not object to the instructions as given nor ask for a further instruction to supplement them. Kiser v. Skelly Oil Co. 136 Kan. 812, 18 P.2d 181. In the instant case the instructions given to the jury did not define the issues and state the pertinent law with accuracy, and further instructions were requested. By reason of the errors heretofore noted the appellant should be granted a new trial.

The judgment of the lower court is reversed with directions to grant a new trial.

PARKER, C. J., and PRICE, J., dissent.

[Editors' note: See 187 Kan. 186, 354 P.2d 670 for the opinion denying rehearing.]

CANTERBURY V. SPENCE

United States Court of Appeals, District of Columbia Circuit, 1972.
464 F.2d 772, 150 U.S.App.D.C. 263.

Before WRIGHT, LEVENTHAL and ROBINSON, Circuit Judges.

SPOTTSWOOD W. ROBINSON, III, Circuit Judge:

This appeal is from a judgment entered in the District Court on verdicts directed for the two appellees at the conclusion of plaintiff-appellant Canterbury's case in chief. His action sought damages for personal injuries allegedly sustained as a result of an operation negligently performed by appellee Spence, a negligent failure by Dr. Spence to disclose a risk of serious disability inherent in the operation, and negligent post-operative care by appellee Washington Hospital Center. On close examination of the record, we find evidence which required submission of these issues to the jury. We accordingly reverse the judgment as to each appellee and remand the case to the District Court for a new trial.

I

The record we review tells a depressing tale. A youth troubled only by back pain submitted to an operation without being informed of a risk of paralysis incidental thereto. A day after the operation he fell from his hospital bed after having been left without assistance while voiding. A few hours after the fall, the lower half of his body was paralyzed, and he had to be operated on again. Despite extensive medical care, he has never been what he was before. Instead of the back pain, even years later, he hobbled about on crutches, a victim of paralysis of the bowels and urinary incontinence. In a very real sense this lawsuit is an understandable search for reasons.

At the time of the events which gave rise to this litigation, appellant was nineteen years of age, a clerk-typist employed by the Federal Bureau of Investigation. In December, 1958, he began to experience severe pain between his shoulder blades.[1] He consulted two general practitioners, but the medications they prescribed failed to eliminate the pain. Thereafter, appellant secured an appointment with Dr. Spence, who is a neurosurgeon.

Dr. Spence examined appellant in his office at some length but found nothing amiss. On Dr. Spence's advice appellant was x-rayed, but the films did not identify any abnormality. Dr. Spence then recommended that appellant undergo a myelogram—a procedure in which dye is injected into the spinal column and traced to find evidence of disease or other disorder—at the Washington Hospital Center.

Appellant entered the hospital on February 4, 1959.[2] The myelogram revealed a "filling defect" in the region of the fourth thoracic vertebra. Since a myelogram often does no more than pinpoint the location of an aberration, surgery may be necessary to discover the cause. Dr. Spence told appellant that he would have to undergo a laminectomy—the excision of the posterior arch of the vertebra—to correct what he suspected was a ruptured disc. Appellant did not raise any objection to the proposed operation nor did he probe into its exact nature.

Appellant explained to Dr. Spence that his mother was a widow of slender financial means living in Cyclone, West Virginia, and that she could be reached through a neighbor's telephone. Appellant called his mother the day after the myelogram was performed and, failing to contact her, left Dr. Spence's telephone number with the neighbor. When Mrs. Canterbury returned the call, Dr. Spence told her that the surgery was occasioned by a suspected ruptured disc. Mrs. Canterbury then asked if the recommended operation was serious and Dr. Spence replied "not anymore than any other operation." He added that he knew Mrs. Canterbury was not well off and that her presence in Washington would not be necessary. The testimony is contradictory as to whether during the course of the conversation Mrs. Canterbury expressed her consent to the operation. Appellant himself apparently did not converse again with Dr. Spence prior to the operation.

Dr. Spence performed the laminectomy on February 11[3] at the Washington Hospital Center. Mrs. Canterbury traveled to Washington, arriving on that date but after the operation was over, and signed a consent form at the hospital. The laminectomy revealed several anomalies: a spinal cord that was swollen and unable to pulsate, an accumulation of large tortuous and dilated veins, and a complete absence of epidural fat which normally surrounds the spine. A thin hypodermic needle was inserted into the spinal cord to aspirate any cysts which might have been present, but no fluid emerged. In suturing the wound, Dr. Spence attempted to relieve the pressure on the spinal cord by enlarging the dura—the outer protective wall of the spinal cord—at the area of swelling.

[1] For approximately the first day after the operation appellant recuperated normally, but then suffered a fall and an almost immediate setback. Since there is some conflict as to precisely when or why appellant fell,[4] we reconstruct the events from the evidence most favorable to him.[5] Dr. Spence left orders that appellant was to remain in bed during the process of voiding. These orders were changed to direct that voiding be done out of bed, and the jury could find that the change was made by hospital personnel. Just prior to the fall, appellant summoned a nurse and was given a receptacle for use in voiding, but was then left unattended. Appellant testified that during the course of the endeavor he slipped off the side of the bed, and that there was no one to assist him, or side rail to prevent the fall.

Several hours later, appellant began to complain that he could not move his legs and that he was having trouble breathing; paralysis seems to have been virtually total from the waist down. Dr. Spence was notified on the night of February 12, and he rushed to the hospital. Mrs. Canterbury signed another consent form and appellant was again taken into the operating room. The surgical wound was reopened and Dr. Spence created a gusset to allow the spinal cord greater room in which to pulsate.

Appellant's control over his muscles improved somewhat after the second operation but he was unable to void properly. As a result of this condition, he came under the care of a urologist while still in the hospital. In April, following a cystoscopic examination, appellant was operated on for removal of bladder stones, and in May was released from the hospital. He reentered the hospital the following August for a 10-day period, apparently because of his urologic problems. For several years after his discharge he was under the care of several specialists, and at all times was under the care of a urologist. At the time of the trial in April, 1968, appellant required crutches to walk, still suffered from urinal incontinence and paralysis of the bowels, and wore a penile clamp.

In November, 1959 on Dr. Spence's recommendation, appellant was transferred by the F.B.I. to Miami where he could get more swimming and exercise. Appellant worked three years for the F.B.I. in Miami, Los Angeles and Houston, resigning finally in June, 1962. From then until the time of the trial, he held a number of jobs, but had constant trouble finding work because he needed to remain seated and close to a bathroom. The damages appellant claims include extensive pain and suffering, medical expenses, and loss of earnings.

II

Appellant filed suit in the District Court on March 7, 1963, four years after the laminectomy and approximately two years after he attained his majority. The complaint stated several causes of action against each defendant. Against Dr. Spence it alleged, among other things, negligence in the performance of the laminectomy and failure to inform him beforehand of the risk involved. Against the hospital the complaint charged negligent post-operative care in permitting appellant to remain unattended after the laminectomy, in failing to provide a nurse or orderly to assist him at the time of his fall, and in failing to maintain a side rail on his bed. The answers denied the allegations of negligence and defended on the ground that the suit was barred by the statute of limitations.

Pretrial discovery—including depositions by appellant, his mother and Dr. Spence—continuances and other delays consumed five years. At trial, disposition of the threshold question whether the statute of limitations had run out was held in abeyance until the relevant facts developed. Appellant introduced no evidence to show medical and hospital practices, if any, customarily pursued in regard to the critical aspects of the case, and only Dr. Spence, called as an adverse witness, testified on the issue of causality. Dr. Spence described the surgical procedures he utilized in the two operations and expressed his opinion that appellant's disabilities stemmed from his pre-operative condition as symptomized by the swollen, nonpulsating spinal cord. He stated, however, that neither he nor any of the other physicians with whom he consulted was certain as to what that condition was, and he admitted that trauma can be a cause of paralysis. Dr. Spence further testified that even without trauma paralysis can be anticipated "somewhere in the nature of one percent" of the laminectomies performed, a risk he termed "a very slight possibility." He felt that communication of that risk to the patient is not good medical practice because it might deter patients from undergoing needed surgery and might produce adverse psychological reactions which could preclude the success of the operation.

At the close of appellant's case in chief, each defendant moved for a directed verdict and the trial judge granted both motions. The basis of the ruling, he explained, was that appellant had failed to produce any medical evidence indicating negligence on Dr. Spence's part in diagnosing appellant's malady or in performing the laminectomy; that there was no proof that Dr. Spence's treatment was responsible for appellant's disabilities; and that notwithstanding some evidence to show negligent post-operative care, an absence of medical testimony to show causality precluded submission of the case against the hospital to the jury. The judge did not allude specifically to the alleged breach of duty by Dr. Spence to divulge the possible consequences of the laminectomy.

We reverse. The testimony of appellant and his mother that Dr. Spence did not reveal the risk of paralysis from the laminectomy made out a prima facie case of violation of the physician's duty to disclose which Dr. Spence's explanation did not negate as a matter of law. There was also testimony from which the jury could have found that the laminectomy was negligently performed by Dr. Spence, and that appellant's fall was the consequence of negligence on the part of the hospital. The record, moreover, contains evidence of sufficient quantity and quality to tender jury issues as to whether and to what extent any such negligence was causally related to appellant's post-laminectomy condition. These considerations entitled appellant to a new trial.

Elucidation of our reasoning necessitates elaboration on a number of points. In Parts III and IV we explore the origins and rationale of the physician's duty to reasonably inform an ailing patient as to the treatment alternatives available and the risks incidental to them. In Part V we investigate the scope of the disclosure requirement and in Part VI the physician's privileges not to disclose. In Part VII we examine the role of causality, and in Part VIII the need for expert testimony in non-disclosure litigation. In Part IX we deal with appellees' statute of limitations defense and in Part X we apply the principles discussed to the case at bar.

III

Suits charging failure by a physician[6] adequately to disclose the risks and alternatives of proposed treatment are not innovations in American law. They date back a good half-century,[7] and in the last decade they have multiplied rapidly.[8] There is, nonetheless, disagreement among the courts and the commentators[9] on many major questions, and there is no precedent of our own directly in point.[10] For the tools enabling resolution of the issues on this appeal, we are forced to begin at first principles.[11]

[2,3] The root premise is the concept, fundamental in American jurisprudence, that "[e]very human being of adult years and sound mind has a right to determine what shall be done with his own body...."[12] True consent to what happens to one's self is the informed exercise of a choice, and that entails an opportunity to evaluate knowledgeably the options available and the risks attendant upon each.[13] The average patient has little or no understanding of the medical arts, and ordinarily has only his physician to whom he can look for enlightenment with which to reach an intelligent decision.[14] From these almost axiomatic considerations springs the need, and in turn the requirement, of a reasonable divulgence by physician to patient to make such a decision possible.[15]

[4-7] A physician is under a duty to treat his patient skillfully[16] but proficiency in diagnosis and therapy is not the full measure of his responsibility. The cases demonstrate that the physician is under an obligation to communicate specific information to the patient when the exigencies of reasonable care call for it.[17] Due care may require a physician perceiving symptoms of bodily abnormality to alert the patient to the condition.[18] It may call upon the physician confronting an ailment which does not respond to his ministrations to inform the patient thereof.[19] It may command the physician to instruct the patient as to any limitations to be presently observed for his own welfare,[20] and as to any precautionary therapy he should seek in the future.[21] It may oblige the physician to advise the patient of the need for or desirability of any alternative treatment promising greater benefit than that being pursued.[22] Just as plainly, due care normally demands that the physician warn the patient of any risks to his well-being which contemplated therapy may involve.[23]

[8,9] The context in which the duty of risk-disclosure arises is invariably the occasion for decision as to whether a particular treatment procedure is to be undertaken. To the physician, whose training enables a self-satisfying evaluation, the answer may seem clear, but it is the prerogative of the patient, not the physician, to determine for himself the direction in which his interests seem to lie.[24] To enable the patient to chart his course understandably, some familiarity with the therapeutic alternatives and their hazards becomes essential.[25]

[10] A reasonable revelation in these respects is not only a necessity but, as we see it, is as much a matter of the physician's duty. It is a duty to warn of the dangers lurking in the proposed treatment, and that is surely a facet of due care.[26] It is, too, a duty to impart information which the patient has every right to expect.[27] The patient's reliance upon the physician is a trust of the kind which traditionally has exacted obligations beyond those associated with arm's-length transactions.[28] His dependence upon the physician for information affecting his well-being, in terms of contemplated treatment, is well-nigh abject. As earlier noted, long before the instant litigation arose, courts had recognized that the physician had the responsibility of satisfying the vital informational needs of the patient.[29] More recently, we ourselves have found "in the fiducial qualities of [the physician-patient] relationship the physician's duty to reveal to the patient that which in his best interests it is

important that he should know."[30] We now find, as a part of the physician's overall obligation to the patient, a similar duty of reasonable disclosure of the choices with respect to proposed therapy and the dangers inherently and potentially involved.[31]

[11,12] This disclosure requirement, on analysis, reflects much more of a change in doctrinal emphasis than a substantive addition to malpractice law. It is well established that the physician must seek and secure his patient's consent before commencing an operation or other course of treatment.[32] It is also clear that the consent, to be efficacious, must be free from imposition upon the patient.[33] It is the settled rule that therapy not authorized by the patient may amount to a tort—a common law battery—by the physician.[34] And it is evident that it is normally impossible to obtain a consent worthy of the name unless the physician first elucidates the options and the perils for the patient's edification.[35] Thus the physician has long borne a duty, on pain of liability for unauthorized treatment, to make adequate disclosure to the patient.[36] The evolution of the obligation to communicate for the patient's benefit as well as the physician's protection has hardly involved an extraordinary restructuring of the law.

IV

[13,14] Duty to disclose has gained recognition in a large number of American jurisdictions,[37] but more largely on a different rationale. The majority of courts dealing with the problem have made the duty depend on whether it was the custom of physicians practicing in the community to make the particular disclosure to the patient.[38] If so, the physician may be held liable for an unreasonable and injurious failure to divulge, but there can be no recovery unless the omission forsakes a practice prevalent in the profession.[39] We agree that the physician's noncompliance with a professional custom to reveal, like any other departure from prevailing medical practice,[40] may give rise to liability to the patient. We do not agree that the patient's cause of action is dependent upon the existence and nonperformance of a relevant professional tradition.

[15] There are, in our view, formidable obstacles to acceptance of the notion that the physician's obligation to disclose is either germinated or limited by medical practice. To begin with, the reality of any discernible custom reflecting a professional consensus on communication of option and risk information to patients is open to serious doubt.[41] We sense the danger that what in fact is no custom at all may be taken as an affirmative custom to maintain silence, and that physician-witnesses to the so-called custom may state merely their personal opinions as to what they or others would do under given conditions.[42] We cannot gloss over the inconsistency between reliance on a general practice respecting divulgence and, on the other hand, realization that the myriad of variables among patients[43] makes each case so different that its omission can rationally be justified only by the effect of its individual circumstances.[44] Nor can we ignore the fact that to bind the disclosure obligation to medical usage is to arrogate the decision on revelation to the physician alone.[45] Respect for the patient's right of self-determination on particular therapy[46] demands a standard set by law for physicians rather than one which physicians may or may not impose upon themselves.[47]

More fundamentally, the majority rule overlooks the graduation of reasonable-care demands in Anglo-American jurisprudence and the position of professional custom in the hierarchy. The caliber of the performance exacted by the reasonable-care standard varies between the professional and non-professional worlds, and so also the role of professional custom. "With but few exceptions," we recently declared, "society demands that everyone under a duty to use care observe minimally a general standard."[48] "Familiarly expressed judicially," we added, "the yardstick is that degree of care which a reasonably prudent person would have exercised under the same or similar circumstances."[49] "Beyond this," however, we emphasized, "the law requires those engaging in activities requiring unique knowledge and ability to give a performance commensurate with the undertaking."[50] Thus physicians treating the sick must perform at higher levels than non-physicians in order to meet the reasonable care standard in its special application to physicians[51]—"that degree of care and skill ordinarily exercised by the profession in [the physician's] own or similar localities."[52] And practices adopted by the profession have indispensable value as evidence tending to establish just what that degree of care and skill is.[53]

[16] We have admonished, however, that "[t]he special medical standards[54] are but adaptions of the general standard to a group who are required to act as reasonable men possessing their medical talents presumably would."[55] There is, by the same token, no basis for operation of the special medical standard where the physician's activity does not bring his medical knowledge and skills peculiarly into play.[56] And where the challenge to the physician's conduct is not to be gauged by the special standard, it follows that medical custom cannot furnish the test of its propriety, whatever its relevance under the proper test may be.[57] The decision to unveil the patient's condition and the chances as to remediation, as we shall see, is ofttimes a non-medical judgment[58] and, if so, is a decision outside the ambit of the special standard. Where that is the situation, professional custom hardly furnishes the legal criterion for measuring the physician's responsibility to reasonably inform his patient of the options and the hazards as to treatment.

[17] The majority rule, moreover, is at war with our prior holdings that a showing of medical practice, however probative, does not fix the standard governing recovery for medical malpractice.[59] Prevailing medical practice, we have maintained, has evidentiary value in determinations as to what the specific criteria measuring challenged professional conduct are and whether they have been met,[60] but does not itself define the standard.[61] That has been our position in treatment cases, where the physician's performance is ordinarily to be adjudicated by the special medical standard of due care.[62] We see no logic in a different rule for nondisclosure cases, where the governing standard is much more largely divorced from professional considerations.[63] And surely in nondisclosure cases the factfinder is not invariably functioning in an area of such technical complexity that it must be bound to medical custom as an inexorable application of the community standard of reasonable care.[64]

[18,19] Thus we distinguished, for purposes of duty to disclose, the special- and general-standard aspects of the physician-patient relationship. When medical judgment enters the picture and for that reason the special standard controls, pre-

vailing medical practice must be given its just due. In all other instances, however, the general standard exacting ordinary care applies, and that standard is set by law. In sum, the physician's duty to disclose is governed by the same legal principles applicable to others in comparable situations, with modifications only to the extent that medical judgment enters the picture.[65] We hold that the standard measuring performance of that duty by physicians, as by others, is conduct which is reasonable under the circumstances.[66]

V

Once the circumstances give rise to a duty on the physician's part to inform his patient, the next inquiry is the scope of the disclosure the physician is legally obliged to make. The courts have frequently confronted this problem but no uniform standard defining the adequacy of the divulgence emerges from the decisions. Some have said "full" disclosure,[67] a norm we are unwilling to adopt literally. It seems obviously prohibitive and unrealistic to expect physicians to discuss with their patients every risk of proposed treatment—no matter how small or remote[68]—and generally unnecessary from the patient's viewpoint as well. Indeed, the cases speaking in terms of "full" disclosure appear to envision something less than total disclosure,[69] leaving unanswered the question of just how much.

The larger number of courts, as might be expected, have applied tests framed with reference to prevailing fashion within the medical profession.[70] Some have measured the disclosure by "good medical practice,"[71] others by what a reasonable practitioner would have bared under the circumstances,[72] and still others by what medical custom in the community would demand.[73] We have explored this rather considerable body of law but are unprepared to follow it. The duty to disclose, we have reasoned, arises from phenomena apart from medical custom and practice.[74] The latter, we think, should no more establish the scope of the duty than its existence. Any definition of scope in terms purely of a professional standard is at odds with the patient's prerogative to decide on projected therapy himself.[75] That prerogative, we have said, is at the very foundation of the duty to disclose,[76] and both the patient's right to know and the physician's correlative obligation to tell him are diluted to the extent that its compass is dictated by the medical profession.[77]

[20] In our view, the patient's right of self-decision shapes the boundaries of the duty to reveal. That right can be effectively exercised only if the patient possesses enough information to enable an intelligent choice. The scope of the physician's communications to the patient, then, must be measured by the patient's need,[78] and that need is the information material to the decision. Thus the test for determining whether a particular peril must be divulged is its materiality to the patient's decision: all risks potentially affecting the decision must be unmasked.[79] And to safeguard the patient's interest in achieving his own determination on treatment, the law must itself set the standard for adequate disclosure.[80]

[21] Optimally for the patient, exposure of a risk would be mandatory whenever the patient would deem it significant to his decision, either singly or in combination with other risks. Such a requirement, however, would summon the

physician to second-guess the patient, whose ideas on materiality could hardly be known to the physician. That would make an undue demand upon medical practitioners, whose conduct, like that of others, is to be measured in terms of reasonableness. Consonantly with orthodox negligence doctrine, the physician's liability for nondisclosure is to be determined on the basis of foresight, not hindsight; no less than any other aspect of negligence, the issue on nondisclosure must be approached from the viewpoint of the reasonableness of the physician's divulgence in terms of what he knows or should know to be the patient's informational needs. If, but only if, the factfinder can say that the physician's communication was unreasonably inadequate is an imposition of liability legally or morally justified.[81]

Of necessity, the content of the disclosure rests in the first instance with the physician. Ordinarily it is only he who is in position to identify particular dangers; always he must make a judgment, in terms of materiality, as to whether and to what extent revelation to the patient is called for. He cannot know with complete exactitude what the patient would consider important to his decision, but on the basis of his medical training and experience he can sense how the average, reasonable patient expectably would react.[82] Indeed, with knowledge of, or ability to learn, his patient's background and current condition, he is in a position superior to that of most others—attorneys, for example—who are called upon to make judgments on pain of liability in damages for unreasonable miscalculation.[83]

[22] From these considerations we derive the breadth of the disclosure of risks legally to be required. The scope of the standard is not subjective as to either the physician or the patient; it remains objective with due regard for the patient's informational needs and with suitable leeway for the physician's situation. In broad outline, we agree that "[a] risk is thus material when a reasonable person, in what the physician knows or should know to be the patient's position, would be likely to attach signficance to the risk or cluster of risks in deciding whether or not to forego the proposed therapy."[84]

[23] The topics importantly demanding a communication of information are the inherent and potential hazards of the proposed treatment, the alternatives to that treatment, if any, and the results likely if the patient remains untreated. The factors contributing significance to the dangerousness of a medical technique are, of course, the incidence of injury and the degree of the harm threatened.[85] A very small chance of death or serious disablement may well be significant; a potential disability which dramatically outweighs the potential benefit of the therapy or the detriments of the existing malady may summon discussion with the patient.[86]

[24,25] There is no bright line separating the significant from the insignificant; the answer in any case must abide a rule of reason. Some dangers—infection, for example—are inherent in any operation; there is no obligation to communicate those of which persons of average sophistication are aware.[87] Even more clearly, the physician bears no responsibility for discussion of hazards the patient has already discovered,[88] or those having no apparent materiality to patient's decision on therapy.[89] The disclosure doctrine, like others marking lines between permissible and impermissible behavior in medical practice, is in essence a requirement of conduct prudent under the circumstances. Whenever nondisclosure of particular risk

information is open to debate by reasonable-minded men, the issue is for the finder of the facts.[90]

VI

[26] Two exceptions to the general rule of disclosure have been noted by the courts. Each is in the nature of a physician's privilege not to disclose, and the reasoning underlying them is appealing. Each, indeed, is but a recognition that, as important as is the patient's right to know, it is greatly outweighed by the magnitudinous circumstances giving rise to the privilege. The first comes into play when the patient is unconscious or otherwise incapable of consenting, and harm from a failure to treat is imminent and outweighs any harm threatened by the proposed treatment. When a genuine emergency of that sort arises, it is settled that the impracticality of conferring with the patient dispenses with need for it.[91] Even in situations of that character the physician should, as current law requires, attempt to secure a relative's consent if possible.[92] But if time is too short to accommodate discussion, obviously the physician should proceed with the treatment.[93]

[27] The second exception obtains when risk-disclosure poses such a threat of detriment to the patient as to become unfeasible or contraindicated from a medical point of view. It is recognized that patients occasionally become so ill or emotionally distraught on disclosure as to foreclose a rational decision, or complicate or hinder the treatment, or perhaps even pose psychological damage to the patient.[94] Where that is so, the cases have generally held that the physician is armed with a privilege to keep the information from the patient,[95] and we think it clear that portents of that type may justify the physician in action he deems medically warranted. The critical inquiry is whether the physician responded to a sound medical judgment that communication of the risk information would present a threat to the patient's well-being.

[28,29] The physician's privilege to withhold information for therapeutic reasons must be carefully circumscribed, however, for otherwise it might devour the disclosure rule itself. The privilege does not accept the paternalistic notion that the physician may remain silent simply because divulgence might prompt the patient to forego therapy the physician feels the patient really needs.[96] That attitude presumes instability or perversity for even the normal patient, and runs counter to the foundation principle that the patient should and ordinarily can make the choice for himself.[97] Nor does the privilege contemplate operation save where the patient's reaction to risk information, as reasonably foreseen by the physician, is menacing.[98] And even in a situation of that kind, disclosure to a close relative with a view to securing consent to the proposed treatment may be the only alternative open to the physician.[99]

VII

[30] No more than breach of any other legal duty does nonfulfillment of the physician's obligation to disclose alone establish liability to the patient. An unrevealed risk that should have been made known must materialize, for otherwise the

omission, however unpardonable, is legally without consequence. Occurrence of the risk must be harmful to the patient, for negligence unrelated to injury is nonactionable.[100] And, as in malpractice actions generally,[101] there must be a causal relationship between the physician's failure to adequately divulge and damage to the patient.[102]

[31] A causal connection exists when, but only when, disclosure of significant risks incidental to treatment would have resulted in a decision against it.[103] The patient obviously has no complaint if he would have submitted to the therapy notwithstanding awareness that the risk was one of its perils. On the other hand, the very purpose of the disclosure rule is to protect the patient against consequences which, if known, he would have avoided by foregoing the treatment.[104] The more difficult question is whether the factual issue on causality calls for an objective or a subjective determination.

It has been assumed that the issue is to be resolved according to whether the factfinder believes the patient's testimony that he would not have agreed to the treatment if he had known of the danger which later ripened into injury.[105] We think a technique which ties the factual conclusion on causation simply to the assessment of the patient's credibility is unsatisfactory. To be sure, the objective of risk-disclosure is preservation of the patient's interest in intelligent self-choice on proposed treatment, a matter the patient is free to decide for any reason that appeals to him.[106] When, prior to commencement of therapy, the patient is sufficiently informed on risks and he exercises his choice, it may truly be said that he did exactly what he wanted to do. But when causality is explored at a post-injury trial with a professedly uninformed patient, the question whether he actually would have turned the treatment down if he had known the risks is purely hypothetical: "Viewed from the point at which he had to decide, would the patient have decided differently had he known something he did not know?"[107] And the answer which the patient supplies hardly represents more than a guess, perhaps tinged by the circumstance that the uncommunicated hazard has in fact materialized.[108]

In our view, this method of dealing with the issue on causation comes in second-best. It places the physician in jeopardy of the patient's hindsight and bitterness. It places the factfinder in the position of deciding whether a speculative answer to a hypothetical question is to be credited. It calls for a subjective determination solely on testimony of a patient-witness shadowed by the occurrence of the undisclosed risk.[109]

[32] Better it is, we believe, to resolve the causality issue on an objective basis: in terms of what a prudent person in the patient's position would have decided if suitably informed of all perils bearing significance.[110] If adequate disclosure could reasonably be expected to have caused that person to decline the treatment because of the revelation of the kind of risk or danger that resulted in harm, causation is shown, but otherwise not.[111] The patient's testimony is relevant on that score of course but it would not threaten to dominate the findings. And since that testimony would probably be appraised congruently with the factfinder's belief in its reasonableness, the case for a wholly objective standard for passing on causation is strengthened. Such a standard would in any event ease the fact-finding process and better assure the truth as its product.

VIII

[33] In the context of trial of a suit claiming inadequate disclosure of risk information by a physician, the patient has the burden of going forward with evidence tending to establish prima facie the essential elements of the cause of action, and ultimately the burden of proof—the risk of nonpersuasion[112]—on those elements.[113] These are normal impositions upon moving litigants, and no reason why they should not attach in nondisclosure cases is apparent. The burden of going forward with evidence pertaining to a privilege not to disclose,[114] however, rests properly upon the physician. This is not only because the patient has made out a prima facie case before an issue on privilege is reached, but also because any evidence bearing on the privilege is usually in the hands of the physician alone. Requiring him to open the proof on privilege is consistent with judicial policy laying such a burden on the party who seeks shelter from an exception to a general rule and who is more likely to have possession of the facts.[115]

As in much malpractice litigation,[116] recovery in nondisclosure lawsuits has hinged upon the patient's ability to prove through expert testimony that the physician's performance departed from medical custom. This is not surprising since, as we have pointed out, the majority of American jurisdictions have limited the patient's right to know to whatever boon can be found in medical practice.[117] We have already discussed our disagreement with the majority rationale.[118] We now delineate our view on the need for expert testimony in nondisclosure cases.

[34] There are obviously important roles for medical testimony in such cases, and some roles which only medical evidence can fill. Experts are ordinarily indispensable to identify and elucidate for the factfinder the risks of therapy and the consequences of leaving existing maladies untreated. They are normally needed on issues as to the cause of any injury or disability suffered by the patient and, where privileges are asserted, as to the existence of any emergency claimed and the nature and seriousness of any impact upon the patient from risk-disclosure. Save for relatively infrequent instances where questions of this type are resolvable wholly within the realm of ordinary human knowledge and experience, the need for the expert is clear.[119]

The guiding consideration our decisions distill, however, is that medical facts are for medical experts[120] and other facts are for any witnesses—expert or not—having sufficient knowledge and capacity to testify to them.[121] It is evident that many of the issues typically involved in nondisclosure cases do not reside peculiarly within the medical domain. Lay witness testimony can competently establish a physician's failure to disclose particular risk information, the patient's lack of knowledge of the risk, and the adverse consequences following the treatment.[122] Experts are unnecessary to a showing of the materiality of a risk to a patient's decision on treatment, or to the reasonably expectable effect of risk disclosure on the decision.[123] These conspicuous examples of permissible uses of nonexpert testimony illustrate the relative freedom of broad areas of the legal problem of risk nondisclosure from the demands for expert testimony that shackle plaintiffs' other types of medical malpractice litigation.[124]

IX

[35,36] We now confront the question whether appellant's suit was barred, wholly or partly, by the statute of limitations. The statutory periods relevant to this inquiry are one year for battery actions[125] and three years for those charging negligence.[126] For one, a minor, when his cause of action accrues, they do not begin to run until he has attained his majority.[127] Appellant was nineteen years old when the laminectomy and related events occurred, and he filed his complaint roughly two years after he reached twenty-one. Consequently, any claim in suit subject to the one-year limitation came too late.

[37] Appellant's causes of action for the allegedly faulty laminectomy by Dr. Spence and allegedly careless post-operative care by the hospital present no problem. Quite obviously, each was grounded in negligence and so was governed by the three-year provision.[128] The duty-to-disclose claim appellant asserted against Dr. Spence, however, draws another consideration into the picture. We have previously observed that an unauthorized operation constitutes a battery, and that an uninformed consent to an operation does not confer the necessary authority.[129] If, therefore, appellant had at stake no more than a recovery of damages on account of a laminectomy intentionally done without intelligent permission, the statute would have interposed a bar.

[38] It is evident, however, that appellant had much more at stake.[130] His interest in bodily integrity commanded protection, not only against an intentional invasion by an unauthorized operation[131] but also against a negligent invasion by his physician's dereliction of duty to adequately disclose.[132] Appellant has asserted and litigated a violation of that duty throughout the case.[133] That claim, like the others, was governed by the three-year period of limitation applicable to negligence actions[134] and was unaffected by the fact that its alternative was barred by the one-year period pertaining to batteries.[135]

X

[39] This brings us to the remaining question, common to all three causes of action: whether appellant's evidence was of such caliber as to require a submission to the jury. On the first, the evidence was clearly sufficient to raise an issue as to whether Dr. Spence's obligation to disclose information on risks was reasonably met or was excused by the surrounding circumstances. Appellant testified that Dr. Spence revealed to him nothing suggesting a hazard associated with the laminectomy. His mother testified that, in response to her specific inquiry, Dr. Spence informed her that the laminectomy was no more serious than any other operation. When, at trial, it developed from Dr. Spence's testimony that paralysis can be expected in one percent of laminectomies, it became the jury's responsibility to decide whether that peril was of sufficient magnitude to bring the disclosure duty into play.[136] There was no emergency to frustrate an opportunity to disclose,[137] and Dr. Spence's expressed opinion that disclosure would have been unwise did not foreclose a contrary conclusion by the jury. There was no evidence that appellant's

emotional makeup was such that concealment of the risk of paralysis was medically sound.[138] Even if disclosure to appellant himself might have bred ill consequences, no reason appears for the omission to communicate the information to his mother, particularly in view of his minority.[139] The jury, not Dr. Spence, was the final arbiter of whether nondisclosure was reasonable under the circumstances.[140]

Proceeding to the next cause of action, we find evidence generating issues as to whether Dr. Spence performed the laminectomy negligently and, if so, whether that negligence contributed causally to appellant's subsequent disabilities. A report Dr. Spence prepared after the second operation indicated that at the time he felt that too-tight sutures at the laminectomy site might have caused the paralysis. While at trial Dr. Spence voiced the opinion that the sutures were not responsible, there were circumstances lending support to his original view. Prior to the laminectomy, appellant had none of the disabilities of which he now complains. The disabilities appeared almost immediately after the laminectomy. The gusset Dr. Spence made on the second operation left greater room for the spinal cord to pulsate, and this alleviated appellant's condition somewhat. That Dr. Spence's in-trial opinion was hardly the last word is manifest from the fact that the team of specialists consulting on appellant was unable to settle on the origin of the paralysis.

[40] We are advertent to Dr. Spence's attribution of appellant's disabilities to his condition preexisting the laminectomy, but that was a matter for the jury. And even if the jury had found that theory acceptable, there would have remained the question whether Dr. Spence aggravated the preexisting condition. A tortfeasor takes his victim as he finds him, and negligence intensifying an old condition creates liability just as surely as negligence precipitating a new one.[141] It was for the jury to say, on the whole evidence, just what contributions appellant's preexisting condition and Dr. Spence's medical treatment respectively made to the disabilities.

In sum, judged by legal standards, the proof militated against a directed verdict in Dr. Spence's favor. True it is that the evidence did not furnish ready answers on the dispositive factual issues, but the important consideration is that appellant showed enough to call for resolution of those issues by the jury. As in Sentilles v. Inter-Carribbean Shipping Corporation,[142] a case resembling this one, the Supreme Court stated,

> The jury's power to draw the inference that the aggravation of petitioner's tubercular condition, evident so shortly after the accident, was in fact caused by that accident, was not impaired by the failure of any medical witness to testify that it was in fact the cause. Neither can it be impaired by the lack of medical unanimity as to the respective likelihood of the potential causes of the aggravation, or by the fact that other potential causes of aggravation existed and were not conclusively negated by the proofs. The matter does not turn on the use of a particular form of words by the physicians in giving their testimony. The members of the jury, not the medical witnesses, were sworn to make a legal determination of the question of causation. They were entitled to take all the circumstances, including the medical testimony into consideration.[143]

[41] We conclude, lastly, that the case against the hospital should also have gone to the jury. The circumstances surrounding appellant's fall—the change in Dr. Spence's order that appellant be kept in bed,[144] the failure to maintain a side rail on appellant's bed, and the absence of any attendant while appellant was attempting to relieve himself—could certainly suggest to jurors a dereliction of the hospital's duty to exercise reasonable care for the safety and well-being of the patient.[145] On the issue of causality, the evidence was uncontradicted that appellant progressed after the operation until the fall but, a few hours thereafter, his condition had deteriorated, and there were complaints of paralysis and respiratory difficulty. That falls tend to cause or aggravate injuries is, of course, common knowledge, which in our view the jury was at liberty to utilize.[146] To this may be added Dr. Spence's testimony that paralysis can be brought on by trauma or shock. All told, the jury had available a store of information enabling an intelligent resolution of the issues respecting the hospital.[147]

[42–44] We realize that, when appellant rested his case in chief, the evidence scarcely served to put the blame for appellant's disabilities squarely on one appellee or the other. But this does not mean that either could escape liability at the hand of the jury simply because appellant was unable to do more. As ever so recently we ruled, "a showing of negligence by each of two (or more) defendants with uncertainty as to which caused the harm does not defeat recovery but passes the burden to the tortfeasors for each to prove, if he can, that he did not cause the harm."[148] In the case before us, appellant's evidentiary presentation on negligence survived the claims of legal insufficiency, and appellees should have been put to their proof.[149]

Reversed and remanded for a new trial.

NOTES

1. Two months earlier, appellant was hospitalized for diagnostic tests following complaints of weight loss and lassitude. He was discharged with a final diagnosis of neurosis and thereafter given supportive therapy by his then attending physician.

2. The dates stated herein are taken from the hsopital records. At trial, appellant and his mother contended that the records were inaccurate, but the one-day difference over which they argued is without significance.

3. The operation was postponed five days because appellant was suffering from an abdominal infection.

4. The one fact clearly emerging from the otherwise murky portrayal by the record, however, is that appellant did fall while attempting to void and while completely unattended.

5. See Aylor v. Intercounty Constr. Corp., 127 U.S.App.D.C. 151, 153, 381 F.2d 930, 932 (1967), and cases cited in n. 2 thereof.

6. Since there was neither allegation nor proof that the appellee hospital failed in any duty to disclose, we have no occasion to inquire as to whether or under what circumstances such a duty might arise.

7. See, e.g., Theodore v. Ellis, 141 La. 709, 75 So. 655, 660 (1917); Wojciechowski v. Coryell, 217 S.W. 638, 644 (Mo.App. 1920); Hunter v. Burroughs, 123 Va. 113, 96 S.E. 360, 366–368 (1918).

8. See the collections in Annot., 79 A.L.R. 2d 1028 (1961); Comment, Informed Consent in Medical Malpractice, 55 Calif. L.Rev. 1396, 1397 n. 5 (1967).

9. For references to a considerable body of commentary, see Waltz & Scheuneman, Informed Consent to Therapy, 64 Nw.U. L.Rev. 628 n. 1 (1970).

10. In Stivers v. George Washington Univ., 116 U.S.App.D.C. 29, 320 F.2d 751 (1963), a charge was asserted against a physician and a hospital that a patient's written consent to a bi-lateral arteriogram was based on inadequate information, but our decision did not touch the legal aspects of that claim. The jury to which the case was tried found for the physician, and the trial judge awarded judgment for the hospital notwithstanding a jury verdict against it. The patient confined the appeal to this court to the judgment entered for the hospital, and in no way implicated the verdict for the physician. We concluded "that the verdict constitutes a jury finding that [the physician] was not guilty of withholding relevant information from [the patient] or in the alternative that he violated no duty owed her in telling her what he did tell her or in withholding what he did not tell her. . . ." 116 U.S.App.D.C. at 31, 320 F.2d at 753. The fact that no review of the verdict as to the physician was sought thus became critical. The hospital could not be held derivatively liable on the theory of a master-servant relationship with the physician since the physician himself had been exonerated. And since there was no evidence upon which the verdict against the hospital could properly have been predicated independently, we affirmed the trial judge's action in setting it aside. 116 U.S.App.D.C. at 31–32, 320 F.2d at 753–754. In these circumstances, our opinion in Stivers cannot be taken as either approving or disapproving the handling of the risk-nondisclosure issue between the patient and the physician in the trial court.

11. We undertake only a general outline of legal doctrine on the subject and, of course, a discussion and application of the principles which in our view should govern this appeal. The rest we leave for future litigation.

12. Schloendorff v. Society of New York Hospital, 211 N.Y. 125, 105 N.E. 92, 93 (1914). See also Natanson v. Kline, 186 Kan. 393, 350 P.2d 1093, 1104 (1960), clarified, 187 Kan. 186, 354 P.2d 670 (1960); W. Prosser, Torts §8 at 102 (3d ed. 1964); Restatement of Torts §49 (1934).

13. See Dunham v. Wright, 423 F.2d 940, 943–946 (3d Cir. 1970) (applying Pennsylvania law); Campbell v. Oliva, 424 F.2d 1244, 1250–1251 (6th Cir. 1970) (applying Tennessee law); Bowers v. Talmage, 159 So.2d 888 (Fla.App.1963); Woods v. Brumlop, 71 N.M.221, 377 P.2d 520, 524–525 (1962); Mason v. Ellsworth, 3 Wash.App. 298, 474 P.2d 909, 915, 918–919 (1970).

14. Patients ordinarily are persons unlearned in the medical sciences. Some few, of course, are schooled in branches of the medical profession or in related fields. But even within the latter group variations in degree of medical knowledge specifically referable to particular therapy may be broad, as for example, between a specialist and a general practitioner, or between a physician and a nurse. It may well be, then, that it is only in the unusual case that a court could safely assume that the patient's insights were on a parity with those of the treating physician.

15. The doctrine that a consent effective as authority to form therapy can arise only from the patient's understanding of alternatives to and risks of the therapy is commonly denominated "informed consent." See, e. g., Waltz & Scheuneman, Informed Consent to Therapy, 64 Nw.U.L. Rev. 628, 629 (1970). The same appellation is frequently assigned to the doctrine requiring physicians, as a matter of duty to patients, to communicate information as to such alternatives and risks. See, e.g., Comment, Informed Consent in Medical Malpractice, 55 Calif.L.Rev. 1396 (1967). While we recognize the general utility of shorthand phrases in literary expositions, we caution that uncritical use of the "informed consent" label can be misleading. See, e. g., Plante, An Analysis of "Informed Consent," 36 Ford.L.Rev. 639, 671–72 (1968).

In duty-to-disclose cases, the focus of attention is more properly upon the nature and content of the physician's divulgence than the patient's understanding or consent. Adequate disclosure and informed consent are, of course, two sides of the same coin—the former a *sine qua non* of the latter. But the vital inquiry on duty to disclose relates to the physician's performance of an obligation, while one of the difficulties with analysis in terms of "informed consent" is its tendency to imply that what is decisive is the degree of the patient's comprehension. As we later emphasize, the physician discharges the duty when he makes a reasonable effort to convey sufficient information although the patient, without fault of the physician, may not fully grasp it. See text *infra* at notes 82–89. Even though the factfinder may have occasion to draw an inference on the state of the patient's enlightenment, the fact-finding process on performance of the duty ultimately reaches back to what the physician actually said or failed to say. And while the factual conclusion on adequacy of the revelation will vary as between patients—as, for example, between a lay patient and a physician-patient—the fluctuations are attributable to the kind of divulgence which may be reasonable under the circumstances.

16. Brown v. Keaveny, 117 U.S.App.D.C. 117, 118, 326 F.2d 660, 661 (1963); Quick v. Thurston, 110 U.S.App.D.C. 169, 171, 290 F.2d 360, 362, 88 A.L.R.2d 299 (en banc 1961); Rodgers v. Lawson, 83 U.S.App.D.C. 281, 282, 170 F.2d 157, 158 (1948).

17. See discussion in McCoid, The Care Required of Medical Practitioners, 12 Vand. L.Rev. 549, 586–97 (1959).

18. See Union Carbide & Carbon Corp. v. Stapleton, 237 F.2d 229, 232 (6th Cir. 1956); Maertins v. Kaiser Foundation Hosp., 162 Cal.App.2d 661, 328 P.2d 494, 497 (1958); Doty v. Lutheran Hosp. Ass'n, 110 Neb. 467, 194 N.W. 444, 445, 447 (1923); Tvedt v. Haugen, 70 N.D. 338, 294 N.W. 183, 187 (1940). See also Dietze v. King, 184 F.Supp. 944, 948, 949 (E.D.Va. 1960); Dowling v. Mutual Life Ins. Co., 168 So.2d 107, 116 (La.App.1964), writ refused, 247 La. 248, 170 So.2d 508 (1965).

19. See Rahn v. United States, 222 F.Supp. 775, 780–781 (S.D.Ga.1963) (applying Georgia law); Baldor v. Rogers, 81 So.2d 658, 662, 55 A.L.R.2d 453 (Fla.1955); Manion v. Tweedy, 257 Minn. 59, 100 N.W.2d 124, 128, 129 (1959); Tvedt v. Haugen, *supra* note 18, 294 N.W. at 187; Ison v. McFall, 55 Tenn.App. 326, 400 S.W.2d 243, 258 (1964); Kelly v. Carroll, 36 Wash.2d 482, 219 P.2d 79, 88, 19 A.L.R.2d 1174, cert. denied, 340 U.S. 892, 71 S.Ct. 208, 95 L.Ed. 646 (1950).

20. Newman v. Anderson, 195 Wis. 200, 217 N.W. 306 (1928). See also Whitfield v. Daniel Constr. Co., 226 S.C. 37, 83 S.E. 2d 460, 463 (1954).

21. Beck v. German Klinik, 78 Iowa 696, 43 N.W. 617, 618 (1889); Pike v. Honsinger, 155 N.Y. 201, 49 N.E. 760, 762 (1898); Doan v. Griffith, 402 S.W.2d 855, 856 (Ky.1966).

22. The typical situation is where a general practitioner discovers that the patient's malady calls for specialized treatment, whereupon the duty generally arises to advise the patient to consult a specialist. See the cases collected in Annot., 35 A.L.R.3d 349 (1971). See also Baldor v. Rogers, *supra* note 19, 81 So.2d at 662; Garafola v. Maimonides Hosp., 22 A.D.2d 85, 253 N.Y.S.2d 856, 858, 28 A.L.R.3d 1357 (1964); aff'd, 19 N.Y.2d 765, 279 N.Y.S.2d 523, 226 N.E.2d 311, 28 A.L.R. 3d 1362 (1967); McCoid, The Care Required of Medical Practitioners, 12 Vand.L.Rev. 549, 597–98 (1959).

23. See, *e.g.,* Wall v. Brim, 138 F.2d 478, 480–481 (5th Cir. 1943), consent issue tried on remand and verdict for plaintiff aff'd., 145 F.2d 492 (5th Cir. 1944), cert. denied, 324 U.S. 857, 65 S.Ct. 858, 89 L.Ed. 1415 (1945); Belcher v. Carter, 13 Ohio App.2d 113, 234 N.E.2d 311, 312 (1967); Hunter v. Burroughs, *supra* note 7, 96 S.E. at 366; Plante, An Analysis of "Informed Consent," 36 Ford.L.Rev. 639, 653 (1968).

24. See text *supra* at notes 12–13.

25. See cases cited *supra* notes 14–15.

26. See text *supra* at notes 17–23.

27. Some doubt has been expressed as to ability of physicians to suitably communicate their evaluations of risks and the advantages of optional treatment, and as to the lay patient's ability to understand what the physician tells him. Karchmer, Informed Consent: A Plaintiff's Medical Malpractice "Wonder Drug," 31 Mo.L.Rev. 29, 41 (1966). We do not share these apprehensions. The discussion need not be a disquisition, and surely the physician is not compelled to give his patient a short medical education; the disclosure rule summons the physician only to a reasonable explanation. See Part V, *infra.* That means generally informing the patient in non-technical terms as to what is at stake: the therapy alternatives open to him, the goals expectably to be achieved, and the risks that may ensue from particu-

lar treatment and no treatment. See Stinnett v. Price, 446 S.W.2d 893, 894, 895 (Tex.Civ. App.1969). So informing the patient hardly taxes the physician, and it must be the exceptional patient who cannot comprehend such an explanation at least in a rough way.

28. That element comes to the fore in litigation involving contractual and property dealings between physician and patient. See, e.g., Campbell v. Oliva, supra note 13, 424 F.2d at 1250; In re Bourquin's Estate, 161 Cal.App.2d 289, 326 P.2d 604, 610 (1958); Butler v. O'Brien, 8 Ill.2d 203, 133 N.E.2d 274, 277 (1956); Woodbury v. Woodbury, 141 Mass. 329, 5 N.E. 275, 278, 279 (1886); Clinton v. Miller, 77 Okl. 173, 186 P. 932, 933 (1919); Hodge v. Shea, 252 S.C. 601, 168 S.E.2d 82, 84, 87 (1969).

29. See, e.g., Sheets v. Burman, 322 F.2d 277, 279–280 (5th Cir. 1963); Hudson v. Moore, 239 Ala. 130, 194 So. 147 149, (1940); Guy v. Schuldt, 236 Ind. 101, 138 N.E.2d 891, 895 (1956); Perrin v. Rodriguez, 153 So. 555, 556–557 (La.App. 1934); Schmucking v. Mayo, 183 Minn. 37, 235 N.W. 633 (1931); Thompson v. Barnard, 142 S.W.2d 238, 241 (Tex. Civ.App.1940), aff'd, 138 Tex. 277, 158 S.W.2d 486 (1942).

30. Emmett v. Eastern Dispensary & Cas. Hosp., 130 U.S.App.D.C. 50, 54, 396 F.2d 931, 935 (1967). See also, Swan, The California Law of Malpractice of Physicians, Surgeons, and Dentists, 33 Calif. L.Rev. 248, 251 (1945).

31. See cases cited supra notes 16–28; Berkey v. Anderson, 1 Cal.App.3d 790, 82 Cal.Rptr. 67, 78 (1970); Smith, Antecedent Grounds of Liability in the Practice of Surgery, 14 Rocky Mt.L.Rev. 233, 249–50 (1942); Swan, The California Law of Malpractice of Physicians, Surgeons, and Dentists, 33 Calif.L.Rev. 248, 251 (1945); Note, 40 Minn.L.Rev. 876, 879–80 (1956).

32. See cases collected in Annot., 56 A.L.R.2d 695 (1967). Where the patient is incapable of consenting, the physician may have to obtain consent from someone else. See, e. g., Bonner v. Moran, 75 U.S.App.D.C. 156, 157–158, 126 F.2d 121, 122–123, 139 A.L.R. 1366 (1941).

33. See Restatement (Second) of Torts §§55–58 (1965).

34. See, e. g., Bonner v. Moran, supra note 32, 75 U.S.App.D.C. at 157, 126 F.2d at 122, and cases collected in Annot., 56 A.L.R.2d 695, 697–99 (1957). See also Part IX, infra.

35. See cases cited supra note 13. See also McCoid, The Care Required of Medical Practitioners, 12 Vand.L.Rev. 549, 587–91 (1959).

36. We discard the thought that the patient should ask for information before the physician is required to disclose. Caveat emptor is not the norm for the consumer of medical services. Duty to disclose is more than a call to speak merely on the patient's request, or merely to answer the patient's questions; it is a duty to volunteer, if necessary, the information the patient needs for intelligent decision. The patient may be ignorant, confused, overawed by the physician or frightened by the hospital, or even ashamed to inquire. See generally Note, Restructuring Informed Consent: Legal Therapy for the Doctor-Patient Relationship, 79 Yale L.J. 1533, 1545–51 (1970). Perhaps relatively few patients could in any event identify the relevant questions in the absence of prior explanation by the physician. Physicians and hospitals have patients of widely divergent socio-economic backgrounds, and a rule which presumes a degree of sophistication which many members of society lack is likely to breed gross inequities. See Note, Informed Consent as a Theory of Medical Liability, 1970 Wis.L. Rev. 879, 891–97.

37. The number is reported at 22 by 1967. Comment, Informed Consent in Medical Malpractice, 55 Calif.L.Rev. 1396, 1397, and cases cited in n. 5 (1967).

38. See, e. g., DiFilippo v. Preston, 3 Storey 539, 53 Del. 539, 173 A.2d 333, 339 (1961); Haggerty v. McCarthy, 344 Mass. 136, 181 N.E.2d 562, 565, 566 (1962); Roberts v. Young, 369 Mich. 133, 119 N.W.2d 627, 630 (1963); Aiken v. Clary, 396 S.W.2d 668, 675, 676 (Mo. 1965). As these cases indicate, majority-rule courts hold that expert testimony is necessary to establish the custom.

39. See cases cited supra note 38.

40. See, e. g., W. Prosser, Torts §33 at 171 (3d ed. 1964).

41. See, e. g., Comment, Informed Consent in Medical Malpractice, 55 Calif.L.Rev. 1396, 1404–05 (1967); Comment, Valid Consent to Medical Treatment: Need the Patient Know?, 4 Duquesne L.Rev. 450, 458–59 (1966); Note, 75 Harv.L.Rev. 1445, 1447 (1962).

42. Comment, Informed Consent in Medical Malpractice, 55 Calif.L.Rev. 1396, 1404 (1967); Note, 75 Harv.L.Rev. 1445, 1447 (1962).

43. For example, the variables which may or may not give rise to the physician's privilege to withhold risk information for therapeutic reasons. See text Part VI, *infra.*

44. Note, 75 Harv.L.Rev. 1445, 1447 (1962).

45. *E. g.,* W. Prosser, Torts §32 at 168 (3d ed. 1964); Comment, Informed Consent in Medical Malpractice, 55 Calif.L.Rev. 1396, 1409 (1967).

46. See text *supra* at notes 12–13.

47. See Berkey v. Anderson, *supra* note 31, 82 Cal.Rptr. at 78; Comment, Informed Consent in Medical Malpractice, 55 Calif.L.Rev. 1396, 1409–10 (1967). Medical custom bared in the cases indicates the frequency with which the profession has not engaged in self-imposition. See, *e. g.,* cases cited *supra* note 23.

48. Washington Hosp. Center v. Butler, 127 U.S.App.D.C. 379, 383, 384 F.2d 331, 335 (1967).

49. *Id.*

50. *Id.*

51. *Id.*

52. Rodgers v. Lawson, *supra* note 16, 83 U.S.App.D.C. at 282, 170 F.2d at 158. See also Brown v. Keaveny, *supra* note 16, 117 U.S.App.D.C. at 118, 326 F.2d at 661; Quick v. Thurston, *supra* note 16, 110 U.S.App.D.C. at 171, 290 F.2d at 362.

53. *E. g.,* Washington Hosp. Center v. Butler, *supra* note 48, 127 U.S.App.D.C. at 383, 384 F.2d at 335. See also cases cited *infra* note 119.

54. *Id.* at 383 ns.10–12, 384 F.2d at 335 ns. 10–12.

55. *Id.* at 384 n. 15, 384 F.2d at 336 n. 15.

56. *E. g.,* Lucy Webb Hayes Nat. Training School v. Perotti, 136 U.S.App.D.C. 122, 127–129, 419 F.2d 704, 710–711 (1969); Monk v. Doctors Hosp., 131 U.S.App.D.C. 174, 177, 403 F.2d 580, 583 (1968); Washington Hosp. Center v. Butler, *supra* note 48.

57. Washington Hosp. Center v. Butler, *supra* note 48, 127 U.S.App.D.C. at 387–388, 384 F.2d at 336–337. See also cases cited *infra* note 59.

58. See Part V, *infra.*

59. Washington Hosp. Center v. Butler, *supra* note 48, 127 U.S.App.D.C. at 387–388, 384 F.2d at 336–337; Garfield Memorial Hosp. v. Marshall, 92 U.S.App.D.C. 234, 240, 204 F.2d 721, 726–727, 37 A.L.R.2d 1270 (1953); Byrom v. Eastern Dispensary & Cas. Hosp., 78 U.S.App.D.C. 42, 43, 136 F.2d 278, 279 (1943).

60. *E.g.,* Washington Hosp. Center v. Butler, *supra* note 48, 127 U.S.App.D.C. at 383, 384 F.2d at 335. See also cases cited *infra* note 119.

61. See cases cited *supra* note 59.

62. See cases cited *supra* note 59.

63. See Part V, *infra.*

64. Comment, Informed Consent in Medical Malpractice, 55 Calif.L.Rev. 1396, 1405 (1967).

65. See Part VI, *infra.*

66. See Note, 75 Harv.L.Rev. 1445, 1447 (1962). See also authorities cited *supra* notes 17–23.

67. *E. g.,* Salgo v. Leland Stanford Jr. Univ. Bd. of Trustees, 154 Cal.App.2d 560, 317 P.2d 170, 181 (1957); Woods v. Brumlop, *supra* note 13, 377 P.2d at 524–525.

68. See Stottlemire v. Cawood, 213 F.Supp. 897, 898 (D.D.C.), new trial denied, 215 F.Supp. 266 (1963); Yeates v. Harms, 193 Kan. 320, 393 P.2d 982, 991 (1964), on rehearing, 194 Kan. 675, 401 P.2d 659 (1965); Bell v. Umstattd, 401 S.W.2d 306, 313 (Tex. Civ.App.1966); Waltz & Scheuneman, Informed Consent to Therapy, 64 Nw.U.L.Rev. 628, 635–38 (1970).

69. See, Comment, Informed Consent in Medical Malpractice, 55 Calif.L.Rev. 1396, 1402–03 (1967).

70. *E. g.,* Shetter v. Rochelle, 2 Ariz.App. 358, 409 P.2d 74, 86 (1965), modified, 2 Ariz.App. 607, 411 P.2d 45 (1966); Ditlow v. Kaplan, 181 So.2d 226, 228 (Fla.App.1965); Williams v. Menehan, 191 Kan. 6, 379 P.2d 292, 294 (1963); Kaplan v. Haines, 96 N.J.Super.

242, 232 A.2d 840, 845 (1967) aff'd, 51 N.J. 404, 241 A.2d 235 (1968); Govin v. Hunter, 374 P.2d 421, 424 (Wyo.1962). This is not surprising since, as indicated, the majority of American jurisdictions find the source, as well as the scope, of duty to disclose in medical custom. See text *supra* at note 38.

71. Shetter v. Rochelle, *supra* note 70, 409 P.2d at 86.

72. *E. g.,* Ditlow v. Kaplan, *supra* note 70, 181 So.2d at 228; Kaplan v. Haines, *supra* note 70, 232 A.2d at 845.

73. *E. g.,* Williams v. Menehan, *supra* note 70, 379 P.2d at 294; Govin v. Hunter, *supra* note 70, 374 P.2d at 424.

74. See Part III, *supra.*

75. See text *supra* at notes 12–13.

76. See Part III, *supra.*

77. For similar reasons, we reject the suggestion that disclosure should be discretionary with the physician. See Note, 109 U.Pa.L.Rev. 768, 772–73 (1961).

78. See text *supra* at notes 12–15.

79. See Waltz & Scheuneman, Informed Consent to Therapy, 64 N.W.U.L.Rev. 628, 639–41 (1970).

80. See Comment, Informed Consent in Medical Malpractice, 55 Calif.L.Rev. 1396, 1407–10 (1967).

81. See Waltz & Scheuneman, Informed Consent to Therapy, 64 N.W.U.L.Rev. 628, 639–40 (1970).

82. *Id.*

83. *Id.*

84. *Id.* at 640.

The category of risks which the physician should communicate is, of course, no broader than the complement he could communicate. See Block v. McVay, 80 S.D. 469, 126 N.W.2d 808, 812 (1964). The duty to divulge may extend to any risk he actually knows, but he obviously cannot divulge any of which he may be unaware. Nondisclosure of an unknown risk does not, strictly speaking, present a problem in terms of the duty to disclose although it very well might pose problems in terms of the physician's duties to have known of it and to have acted accordingly. See Waltz & Scheuneman, Informed Consent to Therapy, 64 N.W.U.L. Rev. 628, 630–35 (1970). We have no occasion to explore problems of the latter type on this appeal.

85. See Comment, Informed Consent in Medical Malpractice, 55 Calif.L.Rev. 1396, 1407 n. 68 (1967).

86. See Bowers v. Talmage, *supra* note 13 (3% chance of death, paralysis or other injury, disclosure required); Scott v. Wilson, 396 S.W.2d 532 (Tex.Civ.App. 1965), aff'd, 412 S.W.2d 299 (Tex.1967) (1% chance of loss of hearing, disclosure required). Compare, where the physician was held not liable. Stottlemire v. Cawood, *supra* note 68, (1/800,000 chance of aplastic anemia); Yeates v. Harms, *supra* note 68 (1.5% chance of loss of eye); Starnes v. Taylor, 272 N.C. 386, 158 S.E.2d 339, 344 (1968) (1/250 to 1/500 chance of perforation of esophagus).

87. Roberts v. Young, *supra* note 38, 119 N.W.2d at 629–630; Starnes v. Taylor, *supra* note 86, 158 S.E.2d at 344; Comment, Informed Consent in Medical Malpractice, 55 Calif.L.Rev. 1396, 1407 n. 69 (1967); Note, 75 Harv.L.Rev. 1445, 1448 (1962).

88. Yeates v. Harms, *supra* note 68, 393 P.2d at 991; Fleishman v. Richardson-Merrell, Inc., 94 N.J.Super. 90, 226 A.2d 843, 845–846 (1967). See also Natanson v. Kline, *supra* note 12, 350 P.2d at 1106.

89. See text *supra* at note 84. And compare to the contrary, Oppenheim, Informed Consent to Medical Treatment, 11 Clev.-Mar. L.Rev. 249, 264–65 (1962); Comment, Valid Consent to Medical Treatment: Need the Patient Know?, 4 Duquesne L.Rev. 450, 457–58 (1966), a position we deem unrealistic. On the other hand, we do not subscribe to the view that only risks which would cause the patient to forego the treatment must be divulged, see Johnson, Medical Malpractice—Doctrines of Res Ipsa Loquitur and Informed Consent, 37 U.Colo.L.Rev. 182, 185–91 (1965); Comment, Informed Consent in Medical Malpractice, 55 Calif.L.Rev. 1396, 1407 n. 68 (1967); Note, 75 Harv.L.Rev. 1445, 1446–47 (1962), for such a

principle ignores the possibility that while a single risk might not have that effect, two or more might do so. Accord, Waltz & Scheuneman, Informed Consent to Therapy, 64 Nw.U.L. Rev. 628, 635–41 (1970).

90. *E. g.,* Bowers v. Talmage, *supra* note 13, 159 So.2d at 889; Aiken v. Clary, *supra* note 38, 396 S.W.2d at 676; Hastings v. Hughes, 59 Tenn.App. 98, 438 S.W.2d 349, 352 (1968).

91. *E. g.,* Dunham v. Wright, *supra* note 13, 423 F.2d at 941–942 (applying Pennsylvania law); Koury v. Follo, 272 N.C. 366, 158 S.E.2d 548, 555 (1968); Woods v. Brumlop, *supra* note 13, 377 P.2d at 525; Gravis v. Physicians & Surgeons Hosp., 415 S.W2d 674, 677, 678 (Tex.Civ.App.1967).

92. Where the complaint in suit is unauthorized treatment of a patient legally or factually incapable of giving consent, the established rule is that, absent an emergency, the physician must obtain the necessary authority from a relative. See, *e. g.,* Bonner v. Moran, *supra* note 32, 75 U.S.App.D.C. at 157–158, 126 F.2d at 122–123 (15-year old child). See also Koury v. Follo, *supra* note 91 (patient a baby).

93. Compare, *e. g.,* Application of President & Directors of Georgetown College, 118 U.S.App.D.C. 80, 331 F.2d 1000, rehearing en banc denied, 118 U.S.App.D.C. 90, 331 F.2d 1010, cert. denied, Jones v. President and Directors of Georgetown College, Inc., 377 U.S. 978, 84 S.Ct. 1883, 12 L.Ed.2d 746 (1964).

94. See, *e. g.,* Salgo v. Leland Stanford Jr. Univ. Bd. of Trustees, *supra* note 67, 317 P.2d at 181 (1957); Waltz & Scheuneman, Informed Consent to Therapy, 64 Nw.U.L.Rev. 628, 641–43 (1970).

95. *E. g.,* Roberts v. Wood, 206 F.Supp. 579, 583 (S.D.Ala.1962); Nishi v. Hartwell, 52 Haw. 188, 473 P.2d 116, 119 (1970); Woods v. Brumlop, *supra* note 13, 377 P.2d at 525; Ball v. Mallinkrodt Chem. Works, 53 Tenn.App. 218, 381 S.W.2d 563, 567–568 (1964).

96. *E. g.,* Scott v. Wilson, *supra* note 86, 396 S.W.2d at 534–535; Comment, Informed Consent in Medical Malpractice, 55 Calif.L.Rev. 1396, 1409–10 (1967); Note, 75 Harv.L.Rev. 1445, 1448 (1962).

97. See text *supra* at notes 12–13.

98. Note, 75 Harv.L.Rev. 1445, 1448 (1962).

99. See Fiorentino v. Wenger, 26 A.D.2d 693, 272 N.Y.S.2d 557, 559 (1966), appeal dismissed, 18 N.Y.2d 908, 276 N.Y.S.2d 639, 223 N.E.2d 46 (1966), reversed on other grounds, 19 N.Y.2d 407, 280 N.Y.S.2d 373, 227 N.E.2d 296 (1967). See also note 92, *supra.*

100. Becker v. Colonial Parking, Inc., 133 U.S.App.D.C. 213, 219–220, 409 F.2d 1130, 1136–1137 (1969); Richardson v. Gregory, 108 U.S.App.D.C. 263, 266–267, 281 F.2d 626, 629–630 (1960); Arthur v. Standard Eng'r. Co., 89 U.S.App.D.C. 399, 401, 193 F.2d 903, 905, 32 A.L.R.2d 408 (1951), cert. denied, 343 U.S. 964, 72 S.Ct. 1057, 96 L.Ed. 1361 (1952); Industrial Savs. Bank v. People's Funeral Serv. Corp., 54 App.D.C. 259, 260, 296 F. 1006, 1007 (1924).

101. See Morse v. Moretti, 131 U.S.App.D.C. 158, 403 F.2d 564 (1968); Kosberg v. Washington Hosp. Center, Inc., 129 U.S. App.D.C. 322, 324, 394 F.2d 947, 949 (1968); Levy v. Vaughan, 42 U.S.App. D.C. 146, 153 157 (1914).

102. Shetter v. Rochelle, *supra* note 70, 409 P.2d at 82–85; Waltz & Scheuneman, Informed Consent to Therapy, 64 Nw.U.L. Rev. 628, 646 (1970).

103. Shetter v. Rochelle, *supra* note 70, 409 P.2d at 83–84. See also Natanson v. Kline, *supra* note 12, 350 P.2d at 1106–1107; Hunter v. Burroughs, *supra* note 7, 96 S.E. at 369.

104. See text *supra* at notes 23–35, 74–79.

105. Plante, An Analysis of "Informed Consent," 36 Fordham L.Rev. 639, 666–67 (1968); Waltz & Scheuneman, Informed Consent to Therapy, 64 Nw.U.L.Rev. 628, 646–48 (1970); Comment, Informed Consent in Medical Malpractice, 55 Calif.L.Rev. 1396, 1411–14 (1967).

106. See text *supra* at notes 12–13.

107. Waltz & Scheuneman, Informed Consent to Therapy, 64 Nw.U.L.Rev. 628, 647 (1970).

108. *Id.* at 647.

109. *Id.* at 646.

110. *Id.* at 648.
111. See cases cited *supra* note 103.
112. See 9 J. Wigmore, Evidence § 2485 (3d ed. 1940).
113. See, *e. g.,* Morse v. Moretti, *supra* note 101, 131 U.S.App.D.C. at 158, 403 F.2d at 564; Kosberg v. Washington Hosp. Center, Inc., *supra* note 101, 129 U.S.App.D.C. at 324, 394 F.2d at 949; Smith v. Reitman, 128 U.S.App.D.C. 352, 353, 389 F.2d 303, 304 (1967).
114. See Part VI, *supra.*
115. See 9 J. Wigmore, Evidence § 2486, 2488, 2489 (3d ed. 1940). See also Raza v. Sullivan, 139 U.S.App.D.C. 184, 186–188, 432 F.2d 617, 619–621 (1970), cert. denied, 400 U.S. 992, 91 S.Ct. 458, 27 L.Ed.2d 440 (1971).
116. See cases cited *infra* note 119.
117. See text *supra* at notes 37–39.
118. See Part IV, *supra.*
119. Lucy Webb Hayes Nat. Training School v. Perotti, *supra* note 56, 136 U.S.App.D.C. at 126–127, 419 F.2d at 708–709 (hospital's failure to install safety glass in psychiatric ward); Alden v. Providence Hosp., 127 U.S.App.D.C. 214, 217, 382 F.2d 163, 166 (1967) (caliber of medical diagnosis); Brown v. Keaveny, *supra* note 16, 117 U.S.App.D.C. at 118, 326 F.2d at 661 (caliber of medical treatment); Quick v. Thurston, *supra* note 16, 110 U.S.App.D.C. at 171–173, 290 F.2d at 362–364 (sufficiency of medical attendance and caliber of medical treatment); Rodgers v. Lawson, *supra* note 16, 83 U.S.App.D.C. at 285–286, 170 F.2d at 161–162 (sufficiency of medical attendance, and caliber of medical diagnosis and treatment); Byrom v. Eastern Dispensary & Cas. Hosp., *supra* note 59, 78 U.S.App.D.C. at 43, 136 F.2d at 279 (caliber of medical treatment); Christie v. Callahan, 75 U.S.App.D.C. 133, 136, 124 F.2d 825, 828 (1941) (caliber of medical treatment); Carson v. Jackson, 52 App.D.C. 51, 55, 281 F. 411, 415 (1922) (caliber of medical treatment).
120. See cases cited *supra* note 119.
121. Lucy Webb Hayes Nat. Training School v. Perotti, *supra* note 56, 136 U.S. App.D.C. at 127–129, 419 F.2d at 709–711 (permitting patient to wander from closed to open section of psychiatric ward); Monk v. Doctors Hosp., *supra* note 56, 131 U.S.App.D.C. at 177, 403 F.2d at 583 (operation of electro-surgical machine); Washington Hosp. Center v. Butler, *supra* note 48 (fall by unattended x-ray patient); Young v. Fishback, 104 U.S.App.D.C. 372, 373, 262 F.2d 469, 470 (1958) (bit of gauze left at operative site); Garfield Memorial Hosp. v. Marshall, *supra* note 59, 92 U.S.App.D.C. at 240, 204 F.2d at 726 (newborn baby's head striking operating table); Goodwin v. Hertzberg, 91 U.S.App.D.C. 385, 386, 201 F.2d 204, 205 (1952) (perforation of urethra); Byrom v. Eastern Dispensary & Cas. Hosp., *supra* note 59, 78 U.S.App.D.C. at 43, 136 F.2d at 279 (failure to further diagnose and treat after unsuccessful therapy); Grubb v. Groover, 62 App.D.C. 305, 306, 67 F.2d 511, 512 (1933), cert. denied, 291 U.S. 660, 54 S.Ct. 377, 78 L.Ed. 1052 (1934) (burn while unattended during x-ray treatment). See also Furr v. Herzmark, 92 U.S.App.D.C. 350, 353–354, 206 F.2d 468, 470–471 (1953); Christie v. Callahan, *supra* note 119, 75 U.S.App.D.C. at 136, 124 F.2d at 828; Sweeney v. Erving, 35 App.D.C. 57, 62, 43 L.R.A.,N.S. 734 (1910), aff'd, 228 U.S. 233, 33 S.Ct. 416, 57 L.Ed. 815 (1913).
122. See Waltz & Scheuneman, Informed Consent to Therapy, 64 Nw.U.L.Rev. 628, 645, 647 (1970); Comment, Informed Consent in Medical Malpractice, 55 Calif. L.Rev. 1396, 1410–11 (1967).
123. See Waltz & Scheuneman, Informed Consent to Therapy, 64 Nw.U.L.Rev. 628, 639–40 (1970); Comment, Informed Consent in Medical Malpractice, 55 Calif.L.Rev. 1396, 1411 (1967).
124. One of the chief obstacles facing plaintiffs in malpractice cases has been the difficulty, and all too frequently the apparent impossibility, of securing testimony from the medical profession. See, *e. g.,* Washington Hosp. Center v. Butler, *supra* note 48, 127 U.S.App.D.C. at 386 n. 27, 384 F.2d at 338 n. 27; Brown v. Keaveny, *supra* note 16, 117 U.S.App.D.C. at 118, 326 F.2d at 661 (dissenting opinion); Huffman v. Lindquist, 37 Cal.2d 465, 234 P.2d 34, 46 (1951) (dissenting opinion); Comment, Informed Consent in Medical Malpractice, 55 Calif. L.Rev. 1396, 1405–06 (1967); Note, 75 Harv.L.Rev. 1445, 1447 (1962).
125. D.C. Code § 12-301(4) (1967).

126. D.C.Code § 12-301(8), specifying a three-year limitation for all actions not otherwise provided for. Suits seeking damages for negligent personal injury or property damage are in this category. Finegan v. Lumbermens Mut. Cas. Co., 117 U.S.App.D.C. 276, 329 F.2d 231 (1963); Keleket X-Ray Corp. v. United States, 107 U.S.App.D.C. 138, 275 F.2d 167 (1960); Hanna v. Fletcher, 97 U.S. App.D.C. 310, 313, 231 F.2d 469, 472, 58 A.L.R.2d 847, cert. denied, Gichner Iron Works, Inc. v. Hanna, 351 U.S. 989, 76 S.Ct. 1051, 100 L.Ed. 1501 (1956).

127. D.C.Code §12-302(a) (1) (1967). See also Carson v. Jackson, *supra* note 119, 52 App.D.C. at 53, 281 F. at 413.

128. See cases cited *supra* note 126.

129. See text *supra* at notes 32–36.

130. For discussions of the differences between battery and negligence actions, see, McCoid, A Reappraisal of Liability for Unauthorized Medical Treatment, 41 Minn.L.Rev. 381, 423–25 (1957); Comment, Informed Consent in Medical Malpractice, 55 Calif.L.Rev. 1396, 1399–1400 n. 18 (1967); Note 75 Harv.L.Rev. 1445, 1446 (1962).

131. See Natanson v. Kline, *supra* note 12, 350 P.2d at 1110; Restatement (Second) of Torts §§ 13, 15 (1965).

132. The obligation to disclose, as we have said, is but a part of the physician's general duty to exercise reasonable care for the benefit of his patient. See Part III, *supra*.

133. Thus we may distinguish Morfessis v. Baum, 108 U.S.App.D.C. 303, 305, 281 F. 2d 938, 940 (1960), where an action labeled one for abuse of process was, on analysis, found to be really one for malicious prosecution.

134. See Maercklein v. Smith, 129 Colo. 72, 266 P.2d 1095, 1097–1098 (*en banc* 1954); Hershey v. Peake, 115 Kan. 562, 223 P. 1113 (1924); Mayor v. Dowsett, 240 Or. 196, 400 P.2d 234, 250–251 (*en banc* 1965); McCoid, A Reappraisal of Liability for Unauthorized Medical Treatment, 41 Minn.L.Rev. 381, 424–25, 434 (1957); McCoid, The Care Required of Medical Practitioners, 12 Vand.L.Rev. 586–87 (1959); Plante, An Analysis of "Informed Consent," 36 Fordham L.Rev. 639, 669–71 (1968); Comment, Informed Consent in Medical Malpractice, 55 Calif.L.Rev. 1396, 1399–4100 n. 18 (1967); Note, 75 Harv.L.Rev. 1445, 1446 (1962).

135. See Mellon v. Seymoure, 56 App.D.C. 301, 303, 12 F.2d 836, 837 (1926); Pedesky v. Bleiberg, 251 Cal.App.2d 119, 59 Cal.Rptr. 294 (1967).

136. See text *supra* at notes 81–90.

137. See text *supra* at notes 91–92.

138. See Part VI, *supra*. With appellant's prima facie case of violation of duty to disclose, the burden of introducing evidence showing a privilege was on Dr. Spence. See text *supra* at notes 114–115. Dr. Spence's opinion—that disclosure is medically unwise—was expressed as to patients generally, and not with reference to traits possessed by appellant. His explanation was:

> I think that I always explain to patients the operations are serious, and I feel that any operation is serious. I think that I would not tell patients that they might be paralyzed because of the small percentage, one percent, that exists. There would be a tremendous percentage of people that would not have surgery and would not therefore be benefited by it, the tremendous percentage that get along very well, 99 per cent.

139. See Part VI, *supra*. Since appellant's evidence was that neither he nor his mother was informed by Dr. Spence of the risk of paralysis from the laminectomy, we need not decide whether a parent's consent to an operation on a nineteen-year-old is ordinarily required. Compare Bonner v. Moran, *supra* note 32, 75 U.S.App.D.C at 157–158, 126 F.2d at 122–123.

140. See Part V, *supra*.

141. Bourne v. Washburn, 142 U.S.App.D.C. 332, 336, 441 F.2d 1022, 1026 (1971); Clark v. Associated Retail Credit Men, 70 App.D.C. 183, 187, 105 F.2d 62, 66 (1939); Baltimore & O. R. R. v. Morgan, 35 App.D.C. 195, 200–201 (1970); Washington A. & M. V. Ry. v. Lukens, 32 App.D.C. 442, 453–454 (1909).

142. 361 U.S. 107, 80 S.Ct. 173, 4 LEd.2d 142 (1959).

143. *Id.* at 109–110, 80 S.Ct. at 173 (footnote omitted).

144. Even if Dr. Spence himself made the change, the result would not vary as to the hospital. It was or should have been known by hospital personnel that appellant had just undergone a serious operation. A jury might fairly conclude that at the time of the fall he was in no condition to be left to fend for himself. Compare Washington Hosp. Center v. Butler, *supra* note 48, 127 U.S.App.D.C. at 385, 384 F.2d at 337.

145. Compare *id.* See also cases cited *supra* note 121.

146. See *id.* at 383–385, 384 F.2d at 335–337.

147. See *id.*

148. Bowman v. Redding & Co., 145 U.S. App.D.C. 294, 305, 449 F.2d 956, 967 (1971).

149. Appellant's remaining points on appeal require no elaboration. He contends that his counsel, not the trial judge, should have conducted the voir dire examination of prospective jurors, but that matter lay within the discretion of the judge, Fed.R.Civ.P. 47(a). He argues that Mrs. Canterbury, a rebuttal witness, should not have been excluded from the courtroom during other stages of the trial. That also was within the trial judge's discretion and, in any event, no prejudice from the exclusion appears. He complains of the trial judge's refusal to admit into evidence bylaws of the hospital pertaining to written consent for surgery, and the judge's refusal to permit two physicians to testify as to medical custom and practice on the same general subject. What we have already said makes it unnecessary for us to deal further with those complaints.

V. NON-DISCLOSURE AND CONFIDENTIALITY

1. THE ETHICAL ISSUES

The assumption of the confidentiality of information passed between a professional and a client has been protected and supported in varying degrees by church, state, professional associations, and clients themselves. The prototype of confidentiality has been the seal of the confessional that forbade a priest from revealing information about his penitents.

The issue of confidentiality also plays a large role in the patient-physician relationship. It is often the case that a person must literally expose his or her whole self to the physician. Certain facts, dispositions, or life situations may be revealed to the physician that could be embarrassing to the patient or put him or her in a compromising position. Even when a disclosure would contain no "dramatic" material, nonetheless the patient still expects that the physician will maintain silence to protect the patient's privacy.

The necessity of confidentiality arises from the consequences of its not being maintained: harm to the patient through embarrassment and anxiety, the breakdown of the relationship between client and professional, and the inability of the patient to receive help because of fear of the revelation of the disclosures. Neither does gossiping about one's patients benefit anyone. Thus, the necessity of frank, full, and honest disclosure by the client to the professional is enshrined in professional codes of ethics such as the Hippocratic Oath and the American Medical Association's Code of Ethics.

Difficulties, however, can arise in which the physician may be at the center of a conflict of interest with respect to public or private interests and the duty of confidentiality. Some resolutions of this conflict are mandated, such as the requirement that physicians automatically report to the authorities all gunshot wounds, cases of infectious disease, or instances of child abuse. In these and similar situations the argument is that public safety and health are more important than the duty of confidentiality. Yet these examples do not help in all cases. Should not a physician disclose to one spouse that the other has a venereal disease? Situations such as these put the physician in an uncomfortable position, for no matter what he or she does, some harm is bound to occur.

In resolving these issues, one must begin with the presumption of the primacy of the ethical duty of confidentiality. Any other interest, therefore, must be overriding and of significant social concern to justify a breach of confidentiality. Indeed, ecclesiastical law prohibits the revealing of any information obtained in the confessional for *any* reason, even to save an innocent third party from harm. Yet, state interests can be compelling and the interests of third parties can be important. Thus a demonstration of a threat to public safety could strongly suggest that confidence be breached. But the threat must concern a serious matter, public safety must be jeopardized, and the cause of the threat to public safety or health must be clearly linked to the individual in question. These elements must be documented and justified—that is, they cannot be based on suspicion, hunch, or mere likelihood.

2. THE LEGAL ISSUES

Having examined disclosure as it related to informed consent, we shall now view the same issue from a different perspective: whether or not there is a legal duty to refrain from making unauthorized disclosures of medical information, and if so, the extent of that duty.

It can be argued that the *Horne* Court bends its collective mind to turning what it readily accepts as an ethical duty of nondisclosure into a legally enforceable mandate. After reviewing foreign case law on disclosure, the *Horne* Court recognizes, as the soundest legal position on the subject, at least a qualified duty on the part of a physician to refrain from making extra-judicial disclosures to third parties of confidences obtained through the doctor-patient relationship. The qualifications of, or exceptions to, nondisclosure are prompted by "supervening interests of society or private interests of the patient himself." With a minimum of words the Court locates the general source of this duty in a patient's right of privacy, defined here as "the right of a person to be free from unwarranted publicity or unwarranted appropriation or exploitation of one's personality, publicization of one's private affairs with which the public has no legitimate concern, or the wrongful intrusion of one's private activities in such manner as to outrage or cause mental suffering, shame or humiliation to a person of ordinary sensibilities." With a maximum of words the Court then locates the specific source of this duty in the appropriate ethical requirements of the Hippocratic Oath, the AMA's Principles of Ethics, and an Alabama statute governing the licensing of physicians.

In *Tarasoff* the Court gives definite meaning to the nondisclosure exceptions, specifically those prompted by what the *Horne* Court refers to as "supervening interests of society." The *Tarasoff* Court holds that "public policy favoring protection of the confidential character of patient-psychotherapist communications must yield to the extent to which disclosure is essential to avert danger to others."

HORNE V. PATTON

Supreme Court of Alabama, 1973.
291 Ala. 701, 287 So.2d 824.

BLOODWORTH, Justice.

Plaintiff Larry Horne comes here on a voluntary nonsuit assigning as error the trial court's ruling in sustaining defendant's demurrer to his complaint.

This case is alleged to have arisen out of the disclosure by Dr. Patton, defendant herein, to plaintiff's employer of certain information acquired in the course of a doctor-patient relationship between plaintiff Horne and defendant doctor, contrary to the expressed instructions of patient Horne. Plaintiff Horne's original complaint asserted that the alleged conduct constituted a breach of fiduciary duty and an invasion of the plaintiff's right of privacy. Demurrer to this complaint was sustained. Subsequently, three amended counts were filed and demurrer to these counts was also sustained. Plaintiff thereupon took a voluntary nonsuit and filed this appeal.

There are sixty-eight assignments of error on this appeal. Appellant has expressly waived all but twenty-two, relating to the trial court's sustaining of defendant's demurrer to the complaint as last amended.

Count I of the amended complaint alleges in substance that defendant is a medical doctor, that plaintiff was a patient of defendant doctor for valuable consideration, that plaintiff instructed defendant doctor not to release any medical information regarding plaintiff to plaintiff's employer, and that defendant doctor proceeded to release full medical information to plaintiff's employer without plaintiff's authorization. Count I further alleges that the doctor-patient relationship between plaintiff and defendant was a confidential relationship which created a fiduciary duty from the defendant-doctor to the plaintiff-patient, that the unauthorized release of said information breached said fiduciary duty, moreover that said disclosure violated the Hippocratic Oath which defendant had taken and therefore constitutes unprofessional conduct. Plaintiff avers that as a direct and proximate result of the release of said information, plaintiff was dismissed from his employment.

Count II alleges the same basic facts but avers that the release of said information was an unlawful and wrongful invasion of the plaintiff's privacy.

Count III alleges, in substance, that plaintiff entered into a physician-patient contractual relationship for a consideration with the defendant, whereby through common custom and practice, impliedly, if not expressly, defendant agreed to keep confidential personal information given to him by his patient, that plaintiff believed the defendant would adhere to such an implied contract, with the usual responsibility of the medical profession and the traditional confidentiality of patient communications expressed in the Hippocratic Oath taken by the defendant. Count III goes on to allege that defendant breached said contract by releasing full medical information regarding the plaintiff to plaintiff's employer.

It is defendant's initial contention that this court cannot review appellant's assignments of error because they are deficient, relying primarily upon Alldredge v. Alldredge, 288 Ala. 625, 264 So.2d 182. Appellant's assignments of error are in the following form:

> "47. The court erred in sustaining ground No. 1 of Defendant's demurrer to the complaint as last amended and filed June 20, 1972."

The other assignments of error are in the same form assigning as error the trial court's sustaining the remaining twenty-one grounds of defendant's demurrer.

[1] The trial court's judgment sustaining the demurrer does not give specific ground for its decision. It simply reads: " * * * demurrer * * * to the complaint as last amended * * * is hereby sustained." Clearly, the approved practice has been to simply assign as error the sustaining of the demurrer to each count of the amended complaint without enumerating the specific grounds of demurrer severally. But, this court has heretofore held that the court will look at the merits where the assignment clearly presents the question for review, even though there may have been a better way to frame the assignment. See, e.g., Alabama Electric Coop., Inc. v. Alabama Power Co., 283 Ala. 157, 214 So.2d 851 (1968).

[2] In the case at bar, plaintiff has assigned as error the sustaining of the demurrer on each of the several grounds specified by defendant in his demurrer. Every ground before the trial court is included. While the judgment does not reveal which grounds of the demurrer the trial judge considered to be valid, it is obvious it must have been one or more of those enumerated by plaintiff in his assignments. It seems clear, beyond peradventure, from the assignments when considered collectively, that plaintiff challenges the trial court's sustaining of the demurrer to each count of his amended complaint. Alldredge v. Alldredge, supra, is distinguishable in this regard, and there is no sound reason for expanding this rule to encompass the instant case. It follows then that plaintiff's assignments of error do comply with Rule 1 of the Revised Rules of Practice of the Supreme Court of Alabama, however inartfully they may be drawn.

Defendant next contends that, because plaintiff assigned as error the sustaining of defendant's demurrer to the complaint as a whole, if any one of the three counts are demurrable the judgment of the trial court should be affirmed, citing Whatley v. Alabama Dry Dock and Shipbuilding Co., 279 Ala. 403, 186 So.2d 117 (1966). While counsel for plaintiff admits that this appears to be the prevailing law at present, he urges this court to consider the merits of each of the three counts. Given the result we reach, we need not consider this contention.

And, now to consider each of the counts.

COUNT I

Whether or not there is a confidential relationship between doctor and patient which imposes a duty on the doctor not to freely disclose information obtained from his patients in the course of treatment is a question of first impression in this state. The question has received only a limited consideration in other jurisdictions, and its resolution has been varied. Those states which have enacted a doctor-patient testimonial privilege statute have been almost uniform in allowing a cause of action for unauthorized disclosure. See, e.g., Hammonds v. Aetna Casualty & Surety Co., 237 F.Supp. 96, motion for reconsideration denied, 243 F.Supp. 793 (N.D.Ohio, 1965); Berry v. Moench, 8 Utah 2d 191, 331 P.2d 814 (1958); Clark v. Geraci, 29 Misc.2d 791, 208 N.Y.S.2d 564 (1960); Felis v. Greenberg, 51 Misc.2d 441, 273 N.Y.S.2d 288 (1966); Smith v. Driscoll, 94 Wash. 441, 162 Pac. 572 (1917).

Alabama, however, has not enacted such a privilege statute. In reviewing cases from other states which also do not have a doctor-patient testimonial privilege, the jurisdictions are split about evenly on this issue. After a careful consideration of this issue, it appears that the sounder legal position recognizes at least a qualified duty on the part of a doctor not to reveal confidences obtained through the doctor-patient relationship.

In the case of Hague v. Williams, 37 N.J. 328, 181 A.2d 345 (1962), the Supreme Court of New Jersey considered the question as to whether an action will lie for unauthorized disclosure by a doctor of information obtained in the doctor-patient relationship. The case arose in the context of a disclosure by a physician of the medical history of a deceased patient to the patient's life insurers. After carefully noting that New Jersey, unlike several other states which had previously recognized such a cause of action, did not recognize a doctor-patient testimonial privilege, the New Jersey court went on to distinguish testimonial and non-testimonial disclosure. The court found a confidential relationship between doctor and patient giving rise to a general duty not to make non-testimonial disclosures of information obtained through the doctor-patient relationship. The court stated the duty as follows:

> "However, the same philosophy does not apply with equal rigor to non-testimonial disclosure. The above ethical concepts, although propounded by the medical profession under its own code, are as well expressive of the inherent legal obligation which a physician owes to his patient. The benefits which inure to the relationship of physician-patient from the denial to a physician of any right to promiscuously disclose such information are self-evident. On the other hand, it is impossible to conceive of any countervailing benefits which would arise by according a physician the right to gossip about a patient's health.
>
> "A patient should be entitled to freely disclose his symptoms and condition to his doctor in order to receive proper treatment without fear that those facts may become public property. Only thus can the purpose of the

relationship be fulfilled. So here, when the plaintiffs contracted with defendant for services to be performed for their infant child, he was under a general duty not to disclose frivolously the information received from them, or from an examination of the patient.

"This is not to say that the patient enjoys an absolute right, but rather that he possesses a limited right against such disclosure, subject to exceptions prompted by the supervening interest of society. *We conclude, therefore, that ordinarily a physician receives information relating to a patient's health in a confidential capacity and should not disclose such information without the patient's consent, except where the public interest or the private interest of the patient so demands.* Without delineating the precise outer contours of the exceptions, it may generally be said that disclosure may, under such compelling circumstances, be made to a person with a legitimate interest in the patient's health. * * * " (Emphasis added)

(The court affirmed the trial court's judgment which denied relief to the plaintiffs, holding that the particular facts in the *Hague* case fell within an exception to this general rule; the parent-plaintiffs were held to have lost their right to non-disclosure by their act of filing a claim with their insurer involving the health of their child, the patient.)

Although deciding the case on another ground, an intermediate Pennsylvania appellate court in Alexander v. Knight, 197 Pa.Super. 79, 177 A.2d 142 (1962), dealing with an unauthorized disclosure to an adverse party, went one step farther and condemned a disclosure made prior to trial, even though the information disclosed would not have been privileged at trial due to Pennsylvania's lack of a doctor-patient testimonial privilege statute. The court observed:

"* * * We are of the opinion that members of a profession, especially the medical profession, stand in a confidential or fiduciary capacity as to their patients. They owe their patients more than just medical care for which payment is exacted; there is a duty of total care; that includes and comprehends a duty to aid the patient in litigation, to render reports when necessary and to attend court when needed. That further includes a duty to refuse affirmative assistance to the patient's antagonist in litigation. The doctor, of course, owes a duty to conscience to speak the truth; he need, however, speak only at the proper time. Dr. Ezickson's role in inducing Dr. Murtagh's breach of his confidential relationship to his own patient is to be and is condemned."

[3] Furthermore, decisions from states with testimonial privilege statutes are not necessarily inapposite. Where the tort duty is based upon breach of the statute or the public policy expressed by the statute, this may be true. However, whether or not testimony may be barred at trial does not necessarily control the issue of liability for unauthorized extra-judicial disclosures by a doctor.

This was recognized by the Supreme Court of Nebraska in the case of Simonsen v. Swenson, 104 Neb. 224, 177 N.W. 831 (1920). There the court, after noting that Nebraska had a testimonial privilege statute, stated that such statute did not apply to non-testimonial disclosures and therefore had no bearing upon the case at hand involving extra-judicial disclosures. In seeking a source of a duty of secrecy on the part of the defendant doctor, the court pointed to a licensing provision that included "betrayal of a professional secret to the detriment of a patient" as unprofessional conduct. From this expression of policy the court derived a legal duty of secrecy on the part of the defendant doctor, viz:

> "By this statute, it appears to us, a positive duty is imposed upon the physician, both for the benefit and advantage of the patient as well as in the interest of general public policy. The relation of physician and patient is necessarily a highly confidential one. It is often necessary for the patient to give information about himself which would be most embarrassing or harmful to him if given general circulation. This information the physician is bound, not only upon his own professional honor and the ethics of his high profession, to keep secret, but by reason of the affirmative mandate of the statute itself. A wrongful breach of such confidence, and a betrayal of such trust, would give rise to a civil action for the damages naturally flowing from such wrong. * * * "

See also the discussions of policy in the Hammonds v. Aetna Casualty & Surety Co., Berry v. Moench and Smith v. Driscoll, supra.

It should be noted that Alabama has a very similar statute which gives the state licensing board for the healing arts the power and imposes on it the duty of suspending or revoking a doctor's license who willfully betrays a professional secret. Title 46, § 257 (21), Code of Alabama 1940, as last amended, reads as follows:

> "The state licensing board for the healing arts shall have the power and it is its duty to suspend for a specified time, to be determined in the discretion of the board, or revoke any license to practice the healing arts or any branch thereof in the state of Alabama whenever the licensee shall be found guilty of any of the following acts or offenses;" * * *

"(14) Willful betrayal of a professional secret;"

Moreoever, the established ethical code of the medical profession itself unequivocally recognizes the confidential nature of the doctor-patient relationship. Each physician upon entering the profession takes the Hippocratic Oath. One portion of that required pledge reads as follows:

> "Whatever in connection with my professional practice, or not in connection with it, I see or hear, in the life of men, which ought not be spoken of abroad, I will not divulge, as reckoning that all such should be kept secret."

This pledge has been reaffirmed in the Principles of Medical Ethics promulgated by the American Medical Association in Principle 9, viz:

> "A physician may not reveal the confidences entrusted to him in the course of medical attendance, or the deficiencies he may observe in the character of patients, unless he is required to do so by law or unless it becomes necessary in order to protect the welfare of the individual or of the community." American Medical Association, Principles of Medical Ethics, 1957, § 9 (Published by AMA).

When the wording of Alabama's state licensing statute is considered alongside the accepted precepts of the medical profession itself, it would seem to establish clearly that public policy in Alabama requires that information obtained by a physician in the course of a doctor-patient relationship be maintained in confidence, unless public interest or the private interest of the patient demands otherwise. Is it not important that patients seeking medical attention be able to freely divulge information about themselves to their attending physician without fear that the information so revealed will be frivolously disclosed? As the New Jersey Supreme Court so aptly pointed out, what policy would be served by according the physician the right to gossip about a patient's health?

Only two courts have refused to recognize any duty on the part of the physician not to disclose. They are Collins v. Howard, 156 F.Supp. 322 (S.D.Ga., 1957) and Quarles v. Sutherland, 215 Tenn. 651, 389 S.W.2d 249 (1965). Neither the reasoning nor the result of either of these two cases is impressive. Both opinions fail to adequately separate the issue of testimonial privilege and the duty of confidentiality in extra-judicial communications. This problem is further complicated in that both cases involve disclosures in the context of pending litigation, such that the plaintiffs suffered no injury by virtue of the allegedly wrongful disclosures. Moreover, both courts found that no doctor-patient relationship existed on the facts there involved.

[4,5] It is thus that it must be concluded that a medical doctor is under a general duty not to make extra-judicial disclosures of information acquired in the course of the doctor-patient relationship and that a breach of that duty will give rise to a cause of action. It is, of course, recognized that this duty is subject to exceptions prompted by the supervening interests of society, as well as the private interests of the patient himself. Whether or not the alleged disclosure by the defendant doctor in the instant case falls within such an exception, is not now an issue before this court.

The trial court erred in sustaining the demurrer to Count I.

COUNT II

The gravamen of Count II is that defendant's release to plaintiff's employer of information concerning plaintiff's health constituted an invasion of plaintiff's privacy.

[6] This court has recognized the right of a person to be free from unwarranted publicity or unwarranted appropriation or exploitation of one's personality,

publicization of one's private affairs with which the public has no legitimate concern, or the wrongful intrusion of one's private activities in such manner as to outrage or cause mental suffering, shame or humiliation to a person of ordinary sensibilities. Norris v. Moskin Stores, Inc., 272 Ala. 174, 132 So.2d 321 (1961); Abernathy v. Thornton, 263 Ala. 496, 83 So.2d 235 (1955); Smith v. Doss, 251 Ala. 250, 37 So.2d 118 (1947).

[7] Whether or not unauthorized disclosure of a person's medical record constitutes an invasion of this right of privacy is likewise a question of first impression in Alabama. Looking to other jurisdictions which have considered this question, those courts have almost uniformly recognized such disclosure as a violation of the patient's right of privacy. See cases collected at 20 A.L.R.3d 1109, 1114–15.

As a federal district court so aptly stated in Hammonds v. Aetna Casualty & Surety Co., 243 F.Supp. 793 (N.D.Ohio, 1965), involving disclosure of medical information concerning the patient to the patient's insurer:

> "When a patient seeks out a doctor and retains him, he must admit him to the most private part of the material domain of man. Nothing material is more important or more intimate to man than the health of his mind and body. Since the layman is unfamiliar with the road to recovery, he cannot sift the circumstances of his life and habits to determine what is information pertinent to his health. As a consequence, he must disclose all information in his consultations with his doctor—even that which is embarrassing, disgraceful or incriminating. To promote full disclosure, the medical profession extends the promise of secrecy referred to above. The candor which this promise elicits is necessary to the effective pursuit of health; there can be no reticence, no reservation, no reluctance when patients discuss their problems with their doctors. But the disclosure is certainly intended to be private. If a doctor should reveal any of these confidences, he surely effects an invasion of the privacy of his patient. We are of the opinion that the preservation of the patient's privacy is no mere ethical duty upon the part of the doctor; there is a legal duty as well. The unauthorized revelation of medical secrets, or *any* confidential communication given in the course of treatment, is tortious conduct which may be the basis for an action in damages."

Unauthorized disclosure of intimate details of a patient's health may amount to unwarranted publicization of one's private affairs with which the public has no legitimate concern such as to cause outrage, mental suffering, shame or humiliation to a person of ordinary sensibilities. Nor can it be said that an employer is necessarily a person who has a legitimate interest in knowing each and every detail of an employee's health. Certainly, there are many ailments about which a patient might consult his private physician which have no bearing or effect on one's employment. If the defendant doctor in the instant case had a legitimate reason for making this disclosure under the particular facts of this case, then this is a matter of defense.

The trial court erred in sustaining the demurrer to Count II.

COUNT III

The gravamen of Count III is that the alleged disclosure breached an implied contract to keep confidential all personal information given to defendant doctor by his patient. This count alleges that defendant doctor entered into a physician-patient contractual relationship wherein the plaintiff agreed to disclose to defendant all facts which would help him in his diagnosis and treatment of the plaintiff, that defendant agreed to treat the plaintiff to the best of his medical ability, and to keep confidential all personal information given to him by the plaintiff. It is alleged that this agreement is implied from the facts through common custom and practice.

[8,9] This court has often stated that an implied contract arises where there are circumstances which, according to the ordinary course of dealing and the common understanding of men, show a mutual intent to contract. See, e. g., Broyles v. Brown Engineering Company, 275 Ala. 35, 151 So.2d 767 (1963). Defendant admits in his brief that the facts and circumstances alleged are such as to show a mutual intent to contract according to the ordinary course of dealing between a physician and his patient. The point of difference between the parties appears to be whether or not there is an implied term in the ordinary course of dealing between a doctor and patient that information disclosed to the doctor will be held in confidence.

Again, this question is one of first impression in this state. Few courts have considered this question. One of the fullest discussions on this point appears in Hammonds v. Aetna Casualty & Surety Co., supra, viz:

"Any time a doctor undertakes the treatment of a patient, and the consensual relationship of physician and patient is established, two jural obligations (of significance here) are simultaneously assumed by the doctor. Doctor and patient enter into a simple contract, the patient hoping that he will be cured and the doctor optimistically assuming that he will be compensated. As an implied condition of that contract, this Court is of the opinion that the doctor warrants that any confidential information gained through the relationship will not be released without the patient's permission. Almost every member of the public is aware of the promise of discretion contained in the Hippocratic Oath, and every patient has a right to rely upon this warranty of silence. The promise of secrecy is as much an express warranty as the advertisement of a commercial entrepreneur. Consequently, when a doctor breaches his duty of secrecy, he is in violation of part of his obligations under the contract."

A Pennsylvania court in Clayman v. Bernstein, 38 PaD & C 543 (1940), appears also to have recognized an implied term of confidentiality in the doctor-patient contract as it permitted the husband of a patient to maintain suit against a doctor for threatened disclosure of medical information concerning his wife:

"It would seem, moreover, that the act of defendant directly violated the rights of the husband. He is the person who is liable for his wife's medical treatment and it is with him that the contract of employment of defendant as a physician is made. Such a contract contains many implied provisions upon the breach of which the husband has a right of action. The most common of these perhaps are actions for negligence or malpractice, although they might sound in tort independent of contract. It may very well be, however, that a breach of trust or confidence, so necessarily associated with a contract of this type, may occur. Is not the unauthorized act of taking this photograph such a breach? * * * "

Although the Tennessee Supreme Court denied there was a cause of action in tort for unauthorized disclosure of medical information concerning a patient, it admitted that there might be a breach of an implied contract. Quarles v. Sutherland, 215 Tenn. 651, 389 S.W.2d 249, 252 (1965).

We have not been cited to, nor have we found in our research, any case in which a cause of action for the breach of an implied contract of confidentiality on the part of the doctor has been rejected. Moreover, public knowledge of the ethical standards of the medical profession or widespread acquaintance with the Hippocratic Oath's secrecy provision or the AMA's Principles of Ethics or Alabama's medical licensing requirements of secrecy (which is a common provision in many states) singly or together may well be sufficient justification for reasonable expectation on a patient's part that the physician has promised to keep confidential all information given by the patient.

Again, of course, any confidentiality between patient and physician is subject to the exceptions already noted where the supervening interests of society or the private interests of the patient intervene. These are matters of defense.

The trial court erred in sustaining demurrer to Count III.

The judgment of the trial court is therefore due to be reversed and remanded.

Reversed and remanded.

HEFLIN, C. J., and HARWOOD and JONES, JJ., concur.

MERRILL, MADDOX, and FAULKNER, JJ., concur in the result.

McCALL, J., dissents.

HEFLIN, Chief Justice (concurring):

I concur in the opinion of Justice Bloodworth but I would add to it.

While the language which mentions a defense to these causes of action—"supervening interests of society" and the words from Hague v. Williams, 37 N.J. 328, 181 A.2d 345, which carves out an exception when the public interest so demands, probably include within their scope a disclosure made to a legitimate research group, I would, nevertheless, specify that such a disclosure is a defense.

MERRILL, Justice (concurring specially):

I would treat any reference in the pleadings to the Hippocratic Oath as surplusage because I do not think that it has any bearing on the cause of action. I think a cause of action is averred regardless of whether the patient had ever known that there was such an oath, or whether he was able to state a single provision of the oath.

MCCALL, Justice (dissenting).

The prime issue is whether or not the trial court erred in sustaining the demurrer. In general, the complaint charges that the defendant wrongfully disclosed to the plaintiff's employer that the plaintiff suffered from a longstanding nervous condition with feelings of anxiety and insecurity. The verity of this medical opinion is not denied. The complaint does not charge that the defendant gave general circulation to this information as mentioned in Alexander v. Knight, 197 Pa.Super, 79, 177 A.2d 142, cited in the above opinion, or that the defendant spoke it abroad (in wide circulation). Nor does the complaint charge that the defendant frivolously disclosed or gossiped about the defendant's health as the opinion intimates. We are not writing to such issues. Those circumstances alluded to in cited cases are not the averments in this case.

Counts I and II of the amended complaint attempt to charge more than a single cause of action for the recovery of damages against the defendant. In Count I, the plaintiff undertakes to aver a fiduciary duty, allegedly arising out of a doctor-patient relationship, which the plaintiff charges was breached. He also undertakes to aver, in the same count, a claim for recovery in his behalf for an alleged breach of the Hippocratic oath. In Count II, the plaintiff undertakes to aver a claim for damages for allegedly releasing medical information regarding the plaintiff to the latter's employer. The plaintiff further attempts to aver, in the same count, an unlawful and wrongful invasion of the plaintiff's privacy by reason of the release of the said information. As in Count I, the plaintiff also counts on an alleged breach of the Hippocratic oath.

Irrespective of whether the matters, if properly alleged, would state good causes of action, the fact remains that the plaintiff has misjoined in a single count separate and distinct causes of action which is not sanctioned under our system of pleading. Clikos v. Long, 231, Ala. 424, 165 So. 394; Vulcan Materials Company v. Grace, 274 Ala. 653, 658, 151 So.2d 229.

If the appellant in the case at bar did not argue in his brief that the misjoinders were permissible, it is not the duty of the appellee to argue that the misjoinders were erroneous. The court in Allen v. Axford, 285 Ala. 251, 263, 231 So.2d 122 said:

> "Counsel for the appellee has performed his full duty when he files his brief replying to the points raised in appellant's brief. If appellant's brief is deficient in form, counsel for appellee is justified in relying on this deficiency in answering the contentions of the appellant."

See also Metzger Brothers, Inc. v. Friedman, 288 Ala. 386, 400, 261 So.2d 398.

If a trial court generally sustains a demurrer to a complaint, without specifying on which grounds of demurrer it relies, an appellate court must sustain the trial court, if any one ground of demurrer be found properly sustainable. Brown v. W. R. M. A. Broadcasting Co., 286 Ala. 186, 238 So.2d 540; Crommelin v. Capitol Broadcasting Co., 280 Ala. 472, 195 So.2d 524; McKinley v. Simmons, 274 Ala. 355, 148 So.2d 648. In Brown, supra, the plaintiff sued the defendant for slander, a ground akin to the allegations in the case at bar. The trial court sustained the defendant's demurrer and entered a judgment of nonsuit, and the plaintiff appealed. The court stated:

> " 'Where defendant assigns several grounds of demurrer * * * , and the plaintiff declines to plead further and appeals from the judgment sustaining the demurrer, this court on appeal from the judgment must sustain the trial court if any one ground of the demurrer was properly sustained.' "

The court agreed that it need only to consider whether a complaint is demurrable on any one of the grounds given in a document.

In Count III, the plaintiff relies on the breach of an alleged implied contract that the defendant would not divulge his medical findings about the plaintiff to the latter's employer. If there is no legal duty not to make such a disclosure, then there can be no implied contract not to disclose the information. In my opinion there is no legal duty not to make the disclosure in this case.

Alabama is a common law state. Tit. 1, § 3, Code of Alabama, 1940; Hollis v. Crittenden, 251 Ala. 320, 37 So.2d 193. At common law no privilege between physician and patient existed as to communications between physician and patient. This is the rule in the absence of a contrary statute. 58 Am.Jr. Witnesses, § 401, notes 20 and 1 on page 232. While statutes have been enacted in most states making communications between physician and patient privileged from compulsory disclosure in courts of justice, Alabama has not enacted such a law. The common law therefore remains in effect. In 61 Am.Jr.2d Physicians, Surgeons, Etc., § 101, it is said that at common law neither the patient nor the physician has the privilege to refuse to disclose in court a communication of one to the other, nor does either have a privilege that the communication not be disclosed to a third person. Quarles v. Sutherland, 215 Tenn. 651, 389 S.W.2d 249, 20 A.L.R.2d 1103, citing 1 Morgan, Basic Problems of Evidence, Ch. 5 (1954); 8 Wigmore, Evidence § 2380 (3rd Ed. 1961). In Quarles, supra, a store physician, who treated the plaintiff, immediately after her fall in the store, sent a copy of his report of findings to her lawyer and to the store's lawyer also, although he was requested not to send any medical report to anyone until notified by the plaintiff's lawyer.

The Tennessee Supreme Court said:

> "We have made a thorough search of the statutes of this State, and have found no statute which would alter the common law rule in this regard. While the arguments for and against making doctor-patient communica-

tions privileged are many, our Legislature has not seen fit to act on the matter and, therefore, we must apply the common law rule as set forth above. For a thorough treatment of the subject see Chafee, 'Privileged Communication: Is Justice Served or Obstructed by Closing the Doctor's Mouth on the Witness Stand?' 52 Yale L.Jour. 607 (1943).

"Petitioner cites T.C.A. sec. 63–618 concerning grounds for revocation of license, and T.C.A. sec. 63–619 defining unprofessional conduct for our consideration. We have carefully studied these provisions and have concluded they are merely administrative provisions concerning the licensing of physicians. The standards set out therein are merely ethical in nature, and the nonadherence to these standards might constitute grounds for the revocation of the physician's license. Our view is that the statutes cited concern only the power of the State of Tennessee to revoke or continue a physician's license, and would have no application to the case sub judice. Henderson v. Knoxville, 157 Tenn. 477, 9 S.W.2d 697, 60 A.L.R. 652 (1928).

"We are aware that physicians and surgeons are required by the ethics of their profession to preserve the secrets of their patients which have been communicated to them or learned from symptoms or examination of other bodily conditions. However, under the common law, applicable in this case, this ethical requirement is not enforceable by law and, therefore, a demurrer to a cause of action wholly dependent upon an alleged 'patient-physician privilege' must be sustained."

It is important to observe that the information allegedly revealed by the physician in the present complaint did not constitute gossiping about his patient's health or a frivolous disclosure of information, as the court alluded to in Hague v. Williams, 37 N.J. 328, 181 A.2d 345.

In Hague v. Williams, supra, the court said:

"This is not to say that the patient enjoys an absolute right, but rather that he possesses a limited right against such disclosure, subject to exceptions prompted by the supervening interest of society. * * * "

The court held that where the public interest or the private interest of a patient so demands, disclosure may be made to a person with a legitimate interest in the patient's health, and, where in the course of examining an infant patient the physician became aware of a pathological heart condition, the physician was not barred from disclosing such condition to an insurer to whom the parents had applied for life insurance on the infant, the court holding that when the parents made a claim for insurance, they lost any rights to nondisclosure that they may have had. *Hague,* supra, p. 349. In my opinion the overriding competing interest and responsibility of an employer for the welfare of all of his employees, to the public who come to his establishment and who buy his merchandise, and to the furtherance of his own business venture, should entitle him to be free from the shackles of secrecy that would prevent a physician from disclosing to the employer critical information concerning the physical or mental condition of his employees.

TARASOFF V. REGENTS
OF UNIVERSITY OF CALIFORNIA

Supreme Court of California, In Bank, 1976.
17C.3d 425, 131 Cal.Rptr. 14, 551 P.2d 334.

OPINION

TOBRINER, J.

On October 27, 1969, Prosenjit Poddar killed Tatiana Tarasoff.[1] Plaintiffs, Tatiana's parents, allege that two months earlier Poddar confided his intention to kill Tatiana to Dr. Lawrence Moore, a psychologist employed by the Cowell Memorial Hospital at the University of California at Berkeley. They allege that on Moore's request, the campus police briefly detained Poddar, but released him when he appeared rational. They further claim that Dr. Harvey Powelson, Moore's superior, then directed that no further action be taken to detain Poddar. No one warned plaintiffs of Tatiana's peril.

Concluding that these facts set forth causes of action against neither therapists and policemen involved, nor against the Regents of the University of California as their employer, the superior court sustained defendants' demurrers to plaintiffs' second amended complaints without leave to amend.[2] This appeal ensued.

Plaintiffs' complaints predicate liability on two grounds: defendants' failure to warn plaintiffs of the impending danger and their failure to bring about Poddar's confinement pursuant to the Lanterman-Petris-Short Act (Welf. & Inst. Code, § 5000 *ff.*) Defendants, in turn, assert that they owed no duty of reasonable care to Tatiana and that they are immune from suit under the California Tort Claims Act of 1963 (Gov. Code, § 810 *ff.*).

We shall explain that defendant therapists cannot escape liability merely because Tatiana herself was not their patient. (1) When a therapist determines, or pursuant to the standards of his profession should determine, that his patient presents a serious danger of violence to another, he incurs an obligation to use reasonable care to protect the intended victim against such danger. The discharge of this duty may require the therapist to take one or more of various steps, depending upon the nature of the case. Thus it may call for him to warn the intended victim or others likely to apprise the victim of the danger, to notify the police, or to take whatever other steps are reasonably necessary under the circumstances.

In the case at bar, plaintiffs admit that defendant therapists notified the police, but argue on appeal that the therapists failed to exercise reasonable care to protect Tatiana in that they did not confine Poddar and did not warn Tatiana or others likely to apprise her of the danger. Defendant therapists, however, are public employees. Consequently, to the extent that plaintiffs seek to predicate liability upon the therapists' failure to bring about Poddar's confinement, the therapists can claim immunity under Government Code section 856. No specific statutory provision, however, shields them from liability based upon failure to warn Tatiana or others likely to apprise her of the danger, and Government Code section 820.2 does not protect such failure as an exercise of discretion.

Plaintiffs therefore can amend their complaints to allege that, regardless of the therapists' unsuccessful attempt to confine Poddar, since they knew tht Poddar was at large and dangerous, their failure to warn Tatiana or others likely to apprise her of the danger constituted a breach of the therapists' duty to exercise reasonable care to protect Tatiana.

Plaintiffs, however, plead no relationship between Poddar and the police defendants which would impose upon them any duty to Tatiana, and plaintiffs suggest no other basis for such a duty. Plaintiffs have, therefore, failed to show that the trial court erred in sustaining the demurrer of the police defendants without leave to amend.

1. PLAINTIFFS' COMPLAINTS

Plaintiffs, Tatiana's mother and father, filed separate but virtually identical second amended complaints. The issue before us on this appeal is whether those complaints now state, or can be amended to state, causes of action against defendants. We therefore begin by setting forth the pertinent allegations of the complaints.[3]

Plaintiffs' first cause of action, entitled "Failure to Detain a Dangerous Patient," alleges that on August 20, 1969, Poddar was a voluntary outpatient receiving therapy at Cowell Memorial Hospital. Poddar informed Moore, his therapist, that he was going to kill an unnamed girl, readily identifiable as Tatiana, when she returned home from spending the summer in Brazil. Moore, with the concurrence of Dr. Gold, who had initially examined Poddar, and Dr. Yandell, assistant to the director of the department of psychiatry, decided that Poddar should be committed for observation in a mental hospital. Moore orally notified Officers Atkinson and Teel of the campus police that he would request commitment. He then sent a letter to Police Chief William Beall requesting the assistance of the police department in securing Poddar's confinement.

Officers Atkinson, Brownrigg, and Halleran took Poddar into custody, but, satisfied that Poddar was rational, released him on his promise to stay away from Tatiana. Powelson, director of the department of psychiatry at Cowell Memorial Hospital, then asked the police to return Moore's letter, directed that all copies of the letter and notes that Moore had taken as therapist be destroyed, and "ordered no action to place Prosenjit Poddar in 72-hour treatment and evaluation facility."

Plaintiffs' second cause of action, entitled "Failure to Warn On a Dangerous Patient," incorporates the allegations of the first cause of action, but adds the assertion that defendants negligently permitted Poddar to be released from police custody without "notifying the parents of Tatiana Tarasoff that their daughter was in grave danger from Posenjit Poddar." Poddar persuaded Tatiana's brother to share an apartment with him near Tatiana's residence; shortly after her return from Brazil, Poddar went to her residence and killed her.

Plaintiffs' third cause of action, entitled "Abandonment of a Dangerous Patient," seeks $10,000 punitive damages against defendant Powelson. Incorporating the crucial allegations of the first cause of action, plaintiffs charge that Powelson "did the things herein alleged with intent to abandon a dangerous patient, and said acts were done maliciously and oppressively."

Plaintiffs' fourth cause of action, for "Breach of Primary Duty to Patient and the Public," states essentially the same allegations as the first cause of action, but seeks to characterize defendants' conduct as a breach of duty to safeguard their patient and the public. Since such conclusory labels add nothing to the factual allegations of the complaint, the first and fourth causes of action are legally indistinguishable.

As we explain in part 4 of this opinion, plaintiffs' first and fourth causes of action, which seek to predicate liability upon the defendants' failure to bring about Poddar's confinement, are barred by governmental immunity. Plaintiffs' third cause of action succumbs to the decisions precluding exemplary damages in a wrongful death action. (See part 6 of this opinion.) We direct our attention, therefore, to the issue of whether plaintiffs' second cause of action can be amended to state a basis for recovery.

2. (2a) PLAINTIFFS CAN STATE A CAUSE OF ACTION AGAINST DEFENDANT THERAPISTS FOR NEGLIGENT FAILURE TO PROTECT TATIANA

The second cause of action can be amended to allege that Tatiana's death proximately resulted from defendants' negligent failure to warn Tatiana or others likely to apprise her of her danger. Plaintiffs contend that as amended, such allegations of negligence and proximate causation, with resulting damages, establish a cause of action. Defendants, however, contend that in the circumstances of the present case they owed no duty of care to Tatiana or her parents and that, in the absence of such duty, they were free to act in careless disregard of Tatiana's life and safety.

In analyzing this issue, we bear in mind that legal duties are not discoverable facts of nature, but merely conclusory expressions that, in cases of a particular type, liability should be imposed for damage done. As stated in *Dillon v. Legg* (1968) 68 Cal.2d 728, 734 [69 Cal.Rptr. 72, 441 P.2d 912, 29 A.L.R.3d 1316]: "The assertion that liability must . . . be denied because defendant bears no 'duty' to plaintiff 'begs the essential question—whether the plaintiff's interests are entitled to legal protection against the defendant's conduct. . . . [Duty] is not sacrosanct in itself, but only an expression of the sum total of those considerations of policy which lead the law to say that the particular plaintiff is entitled to protection.' (Prosser, Law of Torts [3d ed. 1964] at pp. 332–333.)"

In the landmark case of *Rowland v. Christian* (1968) Cal.2d 108 [70 Cal.Rptr. 97, 443 P.2d 561, 32 A.L.R.3d 496], Justice Peters recognized that liability should be imposed "for injury occasioned to another by his want of ordinary care or skill" as expressed in section 1714 of the Civil Code. **(3)** Thus, Justice Peters, quoting from *Heaven v. Pender* (1883) 11 Q.B.D. 503, 509 stated: " 'whenever one person is by circumstances placed in such a position with regard to another . . . that if he did not use ordinary care and skill in his own conduct . . . he would cause danger of injury to the person or property of the other, a duty arises to use ordinary care and skill to avoid such danger.' "

We depart from "this fundamental principle" only upon the "balancing of a number of considerations"; major ones "are the foreseeability of harm to the plaintiff, the degree of certainty that the plaintiff suffered injury, the closeness of the connection between the defendant's conduct and the injury suffered, the moral blame attached to the defendant's conduct, the policy of preventing future harm, the extent of the burden to the defendant and consequences to the community of imposing a duty to exercise care with resulting liability for breach, and the availability, cost and prevalence of insurance for the risk involved."[4]

The most important of these considerations in establishing duty is foreseeability. **(4)** As a general principle, a "defendant owes a duty of care to all persons who are foreseeably endangered by his conduct, with respect to all risks which make the conduct unreasonably dangerous." (*Rodriguez v. Bethlehem Steel Corp.* (1974) 12 Cal.3d 382, 399 [115 Cal.Rptr. 765, 525 P.2d 669]; *Dillon v. Legg, supra,* 68 Cal.2d 728, 739; *Weirum v. RKO General, Inc.* (1975) 15 Cal.3d 40 [123 Cal.Rptr. 468, 539 P.2d 36]; see Civ. Code, § 1714.) As we shall explain, however, when the avoidance of foreseeable harm requires a defendant to control the conduct of another person, or to warn of such conduct, the common law has traditionally imposed liability only if the defendant bears some special relationship to the dangerous person or to the potential victim. Since the relationship between a therapist and his patient satisfies this requirement, we need not here decide whether foreseeability alone is sufficient to create a duty to exercise reasonable care to protect a potential victim of another's conduct.

(5) Although, as we have stated above, under the common law, as a general rule, one person owed no duty to control the conduct of another[5] (*Richards v. Stanley* (1954) 43 Cal.2d 60, 65 [271 P.2d 23]; *Wright v. Arcade School Dist.* (1964) 230 Cal.App.2d 272, 277 [40 Cal.Rptr. 812]; Rest.2d Torts (1965) § 315), nor to warn those endangered by such conduct (Rest.2d Torts, *supra,* § 314, com. c.; Prosser, Law of Torts (4th ed. 1971) § 56, p. 341), the courts have carved out an exception to this rule in cases in which the defendant stands in some special relationship to either the person whose conduct needs to be controlled or in a relationship to the foreseeable victim of that conduct (see Rest.2d Torts, *supra,* §§ 315-320). Applying this exception to the present case, we note that a relationship of defendant therapists to either Tatiana or Poddar will suffice to establish a duty of care; as explained in section 315 of the Restatement Second of Torts, a duty of care may arise from either "(a) a special relation . . . between the actor and the third person which imposes a duty upon the actor to control the third person's conduct, or (b) a special relation . . . between the actor and the other which gives to the other a right of protection."

(2b) Although plaintiffs' pleadings assert no special relation between Tatiana and defendant therapists, they establish as between Poddar and defendant therapists the special relation that arises between a patient and his doctor or psycho-therapist.[6] Such a relationship may support affirmative duties for the benefit of third persons. Thus, for example, a hospital must exercise reasonable care to control the behavior of a patient which may endanger other persons.[7] A doctor must also warn a patient if the patient's condition or medication renders certain conduct, such as driving a car, dangerous to others.[8]

Although the California decisions that recognize this duty have involved cases in which the defendant stood in a special relationship *both* to the victim and to the person whose conduct created the danger,[9] we do not think that the duty should logically be constricted to such situations. Decisions of other jurisdictions hold that the single relationship of a doctor to his patient is sufficient to support the duty to exercise reasonable care to protect others against dangers emanating from the patient's illness. The courts hold that a doctor is liable to persons infected by his patient if he negligently fails to diagnose a contagious disease (*Hoffmann v. Blackmon* (Fla.App. 1970) 241 So.2d 752), or, having diagnosed the illness, fails to warn members of the patient's family (*Wojcik v. Aluminum Co. of America* (1959) 18 Misc.2d 740 [183 N.Y.S.2d 351, 357–358]; *Davis v. Rodman* (1921) 147 Ark. 385 [227 S.W. 612, 13 A.L.R. 1459]; *Skillings v. Allen* (1919) 143 Minn. 323 [173 N.W. 663, 5 A.L.R. 922]; see also *Jones v. Stanko* (1928) 118 Ohio St. 147 [6 Ohio L.Abs. 77, 160 N.E. 456]).

Since it involved a dangerous mental patient, the decision in *Merchants Nat. Bank & Trust Co. of Fargo v. United States* (D.N.D. 1967) 272 F.Supp. 409 comes closer to the issue. The Veterans Administration arranged for the patient to work on a local farm, but did not inform the farmer of the man's background. The farmer consequently permitted the patient to come and go freely during nonworking hours; the patient borrowed a car, drove to his wife's residence and killed her. Notwithstanding the lack of any "special relationship" between the Veterans Administration and the wife, the court found the Veterans Administration liable for the wrongful death of the wife.

In their summary of the relevant rulings Fleming and Maximov conclude that the "case law should dispel any notion that to impose on the therapists a duty to take precautions for the safety of persons threatened by a patient, where due care so requires, is in any way opposed to contemporary ground rules on the duty relationship. On the contrary, there now seems to be sufficient authority to support the conclusion that by entering into a doctor-patient relationship the therapist becomes sufficiently involved to assume some responsibility for the safety, not only of the patient himself, but also of any third person whom the doctor knows to be threatened by the patient." (Fleming & Maximov, *The Patient or His Victim: The Therapist's Dilemma* (1974) 62 Cal.L.Rev. 1025, 1030.)

Defendants contend, however, that imposition of a duty to exercise reasonable care to protect third persons is unworkable because therapists cannot accurately predict whether or not a patient will resort to violence. In support of this argument amicus representing the American Psychiatric Association and other professional societies cites numerous articles which indicate that therapists, in the present state of the art, are unable reliably to predict violent acts; their forecasts, amicus claims, tend consistently to overpredict violence, and indeed are more often wrong than right.[10] Since predictions of violence are often erroneous, amicus concludes, the courts should not render rulings that predicate the liability of therapists upon the validity of such predictions.

The role of the psychiatrist, who is indeed a practitioner of medicine, and that of the psychologist who performs an allied function, are like that of the physician who must conform to the standards of the profession and who must often make diagnoses and predictions based upon such evaluations. Thus the judgment of the therapist in diagnosing emotional disorders and in predicting whether a patient presents a serious danger of violence is comparable to the judgment which doctors and professionals must regularly render under accepted rules of responsibility.

We recognize the difficulty that a therapist encounters in attempting to forecast whether a patient presents a serious danger of violence. Obviously, we do not require that the therapist, in making that determination, render a perfect performance; the therapist need only exercise "that reasonable degree of skill, knowledge, and care ordinarily possessed and exercised by members of [that professional specialty] under similar circumstances." (*Bardessono v. Michels* (1970) 3 Cal.3d 780, 788 [91 Cal.Rptr. 760, 478 P.2d 480, 45 A.L.R.3d 717]; *Quintal v. Laurel Grove Hospital* (1964) 62 Cal.2d 154, 159–160 [41 Cal.Rptr. 577, 397 P.2d 161]; see 4 Witkin, Summary of Cal. Law (8th ed. 1974) Torts, § 514 and cases cited.) Within the broad range of reasonable practice and treatment in which professional opinion and judgment may differ, the therapist is free to exercise his or her own best judgment without liability; proof, aided by hindsight, that he or she judged wrongly is insufficient to establish negligence.

In the instant case, however, the pleadings do not raise any question as to failure of defendant therapists to predict that Poddar presented a serious danger of violence. On the contrary, the present complaints allege that defendant therapists did in fact predict that Poddar would kill, but were negligent in failing to warn.

Amicus contends, however, that even when a therapist does in fact predict that a patient poses a serious danger of violence to others, the therapist should be absolved of any responsibility for failing to act to protect the potential victim. In our view, however, once a therapist does in fact determine, or under applicable professional standards reasonably should have determined, that a patient poses a serious danger of violence to others, he bears a duty to exercise reasonable care to protect the foreseeable victim of that danger. While the discharge of this duty of due care will necessarily vary with the facts of each case,[11] in each instance the adequacy of the therapist's conduct must be measured against the traditional negligence standard of the rendition of reasonable care under the circumstances. (Accord *Cobbs v. Grant* (1972) 8 Cal.3d 229, 243 [104 Cal.Rptr. 505, 502 P.2d 1].) As explained in Fleming and Maximov, *The Patient or His Victim: The Therapist's Dilemma* (1974) 62 Cal.L.Rev. 1025, 1067: ". . . the ultimate question of resolving the tension between the conflicting interests of patient and potential victim is one of social policy, not professional expertise. . . . In sum, the therapist owes a legal duty not only to his patient, but also to his patient's would-be victim and is subject in both respects to scrutiny by judge and jury."

Contrary to the assertion of amicus, this conclusion is not inconsistent with our recent decision in *People v. Burnick, supra,* 14 Cal.3d 306. Taking note of the uncertain character of therapeutic prediction, we held in *Burnick* that a person cannot be committed as a mentally disordered sex offender unless found to be such by proof beyond a reasonable doubt. (14 Cal.3d at p. 328.) The issue in the present context, however, is not whether the patient should be incarcerated, but whether the therapist should take any steps at all to protect the threatened victim; some of the alternatives open to the therapist, such as warning the victim, will not result in the drastic consequences of depriving the patient of his liberty. Weighing the uncertain and conjectural character of the alleged damage done the patient by such a warning against the peril to the victim's life, we conclude that professional inaccuracy in predicting violence cannot negate the therapist's duty to protect the threatened victim.

The risk that unnecessary warnings may be given is a reasonable price to pay for the lives of possible victims that may be saved. We would hesitate to hold that the therapist who is aware that his patient expects to attempt to assassinate the President of the United States would not be obligated to warn the authorities because the therapist cannot predict with accuracy that his patient will commit the crime.

Defendants further argue that free and open communication is essential to psychotherapy (see *In re Lifshutz* (1970) 2 Cal.3d 415, 431–434 [85 Cal.Rptr. 829, 467 P.2d 557, 44 A.L.R.3d 1]); that "Unless a patient . . . is assured that . . . information [revealed by him] can and will be held in utmost confidence, he will be reluctant to make the full disclosure upon which diagnosis and treatment . . . depends." (Sen. Com. on Judiciary, comment on Evid. Code, § 1014.) The giving of a warning, defendants contend, constitutes a breach of trust which entails the revelation of confidential communications.[12]

We recognize the public interest in supporting effective treatment of mental illness and in protecting the rights of patients to privacy (see *In re Lifschutz, supra,* 2 Cal.3d at p. 432), and the consequent public importance of safeguarding the confidential character of psychotherapeutic communication. Against this interest, however, we must weigh the public interest in safety from violent assault. The Legislature has undertaken the difficult task of balancing the countervailing concerns. In Evidence Code section 1014, it established a broad rule of privilege to protect confidential communications between patient and psychotherapist. In Evidence Code section 1024, the Legislature created a specific and limited exception to the psychotherapist-patient privilege: "There is no privilege . . . if the psychotherapist has reasonable cause to believe that the patient is in such mental or emotional condition as to be dangerous to himself or to the person or property of another and that disclosure of the communication is necessary to prevent the threatened danger."[13]

We realize that the open and confidential character of psychotherapeutic dialogue encourages patients to express threats of violence, few of which are ever executed. Certainly a therapist should not be encouraged routinely to reveal such threats; such disclosures could seriously disrupt the patient's relationship with his therapist and with the persons threatened. To the contrary, the therapist's obligations to his patient require that he not disclose a confidence unless such disclosure is necessary to avert danger to others, and even then that he do so discreetly, and in a fashion that would preserve the privacy of his patient to the fullest extent compatible with the prevention of the threatened danger. (See Fleming & Maximov, *The Patient or His Victim: The Therapist's Dilemma* (1974) 62 Cal.L.Rev. 1025, 1065–1066.)[14]

The revelation of a communication under the above circumstances is not a breach of trust or a violation of professional ethics; as stated in the Principles of Medical Ethics of the American Medical Association (1957), section 9: "A physician may not reveal the confidence entrusted to him in the course of medical attendance . . . *unless he is required to do so by law or unless it becomes necessary in order to protect the welfare of the individual or of the community.*"[15] (Italics added.) We conclude that the public policy favoring protection of the confidential character of patient-psychotherapist communications must yield to the extent to which disclosure is essential to avert danger to others. The protective privilege ends where the public peril begins.

Our current crowded and computerized society compels the interdependence of its members. In this risk-infested society we can hardly tolerate the further exposure to danger that would result from a concealed knowledge of the therapist that his patient was lethal. If the exercise of reasonable care to protect the threatened victim requires the therapist to warn the endangered party or those who can reasonably be expected to notify him, we see no sufficient societal interest that would protect and justify concealment. The containment of such risks lies in the public interest. For the foregoing reasons, we find that plaintiffs' complaints can be amended to state a cause of action against defendants Moore, Powelson, Gold, and Yandell and against the Regents as their employer, for breach of a duty to exercise reasonable care to protect Tatiana.[16]

Finally, we reject the contention of the dissent that the provisions of the Lanterman-Petris-Short Act which govern the release of confidential information (Welf. & Inst. Code, §§ 5328–5328.9) prevented defendant therapists from warning Tatiana. The dissent's contention rests on the assertion that Dr. Moore's letter to the campus police constituted an "application in writing" within the meaning of Welfare and Institutions Code section 5150, and thus initiates proceedings under the Lanterman-Petris-Short Act. A closer look at the terms of section 5150, however, will demonstrate that it is inapplicable to the present case.

Section 5150 refers to a written application only by a professional person who is "a member of the attending staff . . . of an evaluation facility designated by the county," or who is himself "designated by the county" as one authorized to take a person into custody and place him in a facility designated by the county and approved by the State Department of Mental Hygiene. The complaint fails specifically to allege that Dr. Moore was so empowered. Dr. Moore and the Regents cannot rely upon any inference to the contrary that might be drawn from plaintiff's allegation that Dr. Moore intended to "assign" a "detention" on Poddar; both Dr. Moore and the Regents have expressly conceded that neither Cowell Memorial Hospital nor any member of its staff has ever been designated by the County of Alameda to institute involuntary commitment proceedings pursuant to section 5150.

Futhermore, the provisions of the Lanterman-Petris-Short Act defining a therapist's duty to withhold confidential information are expressly limited to "information and records *obtained in the course of providing services* under Division 5 (commencing with section 5000), Division 6 (commencing with section 6000), or Division 7 (commencing with section 7000)" of the Welfare and Institutions Code (Welf. & Inst. Code, § 5328). (Italics added.) Divisions 5, 6 and 7 describe a variety of programs for treatment of the mentally ill or retarded.[17] The pleadings at issue on this appeal, however, state no facts showing that the psychotherapy provided to Poddar by the Cowell Memorial Hospital falls under any of these programs. We therefore conclude that the Lanterman-Petris-Short Act does not govern the release of information acquired by Moore during the course of rendition of those services.

Neither can we adopt the dissent's suggestion that we import wholesale the detailed provisions of the Lanterman-Petris-Short Act regulating the disclosure of confidential information and apply them to disclosure of information *not governed by the act.* Since the Legislature did not extend the act to control all disclosures of confidential matter by a therapist, we must infer that the Legislature did not relieve the courts of their obligation to define by reference to the principles of the common law the obligation of the therapist in those situations not governed by the act.

(6) Turning now to the police defendants, we conclude that they do not have any such special relationship to either Tatiana or to Poddar sufficient to impose upon such defendants a duty to warn respecting Poddar's violent intentions. (See *Hartzler v. City of San Jose* (1975) 46 Cal.App.3d 6, 9–10 [120 Cal.Rptr. 5]; *Antique Arts Corp. v. City of Torrance* (1974) 39 Cal.App.3d 588, 593 [114 Cal.Rptr. 332].) Plaintiffs suggest no theory,[18] and plead no facts that give rise to any duty to warn on the part of the police defendants absent such a special relationship. They have thus failed to demonstrate that the trial court erred in denying leave to amend as to the police defendants. (See *Cooper v. Leslie Salt Co.* (1969) 70 Cal.2d 627, 636 [75 Cal.Rptr. 766, 451 P.2d 406]; *Filice v. Boccardo* (1962) 210 Cal.App.2d 843, 847 [26 Cal.Rptr. 789].)

3. (7) DEFENDANT THERAPISTS ARE NOT IMMUNE FROM LIABILITY FOR FAILURE TO WARN

We address the issue of whether defendant therapists are protected by governmental immunity for having failed to warn Tatiana or those who reasonably could have been expected to notify her of her peril. We postulate our analysis on section 820.2 of the Government Code.[19] That provision declares, with exceptions not applicable here, that "a public employee is not liable for any injury resulting from his act or omission where the act or omission was the result of the exercise of the discretion vested in him, whether or not such discretion [was] abused."[20]

Noting that virtually every public act admits of some element of discretion, we drew the line in *Johnson v. State of California* (1968) 69 Cal.2d 782 [73 Cal.Rptr. 240, 447 P.2d 352], between discretionary policy decisions which enjoy statutory immunity and ministerial administrative acts which do not. We concluded that section 820.2 affords immunity only for "*basic* policy decisions." (Italics added.) (See also *Elton v. County of Orange* (1970) 3 Cal.App.3d 1053, 1057–1058 [84 Cal.Rptr.

27]; 4 Cal. Law Revision Com. Rep. (1963) p. 810; Van Alstyne, Supplement to Cal. Government Tort Liability (Cont. Ed. Bar 1969) § 5.54, pp. 16–17; Comment, *California Tort Claims Act: Discretionary Immunity* (1966) 39 So.Cal.L.Rev. 470, 471; cf. James, *Tort Liability of Governmental Units and Their Officers* (1955) 22 U.Chi.L.Rev. 610, 637–638, 640, 642, 651.)

We also observed that if courts did not respect this statutory immunity, they would find themselves "in the unseemly position of determining the propriety of decisions expressly entrusted to a coordinate branch of government." (*Johnson v. State of California, supra,* at p. 793.) It therefore is necessary, we concluded, to "isolate those areas of quasi-legislative policy-making which are sufficiently sensitive to justify a blanket rule that courts will not entertain a tort action alleging that careless conduct contributed to the governmental decision." (*Johnson v. State of California, supra,* at p. 794.) After careful analysis we rejected, in *Johnson,* other rationales commonly advanced to support governmental immunity[21] and concluded that the immunity's scope should be no greater than is required to give legislative and executive policymakers sufficient breathing space in which to perform their vital policymaking functions.

Relying on *Johnson,* we conclude that defendant therapists in the present case are not immune from liability for their failure to warn of Tatiana's peril. *Johnson* held that a parole officer's determination whether to warn an adult couple that their prospective foster child had a background of violence "present[ed] no . . . reasons for immunity" (*Johnson v. State of California, supra,* at p. 795), was "at the lowest, ministerial rung of official action" (*id.,* at p. 796), and indeed constituted "a classic case for the imposition of tort liability." (*Id.,* p. 797; cf. *Morgan v. County of Yuba, supra,* 230 Cal.App.2d 938, 942–943.) Although defendants in *Johnson* argued that the decision whether to inform the foster parents of the child's background required the exercise of considerable judgmental skills, we concluded that the state was not immune from liability for the parole officer's failure to warn because such a decision did not rise to the level of a "basic policy decision."

We also noted in *Johnson* that federal courts have consistently categorized failures to warn of latent dangers as falling outside the scope of discretionary omissions immunized by the Federal Tort Claims Act.[22] (See *United Air Lines, Inc. v. Wiener* (9th Cir. 1964) 335 F.2d 379, 397–398, cert. den. *sub nom. United Air Lines, Inc. v. United States,* 379 U.S. 951 [13 L.Ed.2d 549, 85 S.Ct. 452] (decision to conduct military training flights was discretionary but failure to warn commercial airline was not); *United States v. State of Washington* (9th Cir. 1965) 351 F.2d 913, 916 (decision where to place transmission lines spanning canyon was assumed to be discretionary but failure to warn pilot was not); *United States v. White* (9th Cir. 1954) 211 F.2d 79, 82 (decision not to "dedud" army firing range assumed to be discretionary but failure to warn person about to go onto range of unsafe condition was not); *Bulloch v. United States* (D.Utah 1955) 133 F.Supp. 885, 888 (decision how and when to conduct nuclear test deemed discretionary but failure to afford proper notice was not); *Hernandez v. United States* (D.Hawaii 1953) 112 F.Supp. 369, 371 (decision to erect road block characterized as discretionary but failure to warn of resultant hazard was not).

We conclude, therefore, that the therapist defendants' failure to warn Tatiana or those who reasonably could have been expected to notify her of her peril does not fall within the absolute protection afforded by section 820.2 of the Government Code. We emphasize that our conclusion does not raise the specter of therapists employed by the government indiscriminately being held liable for damage despite their exercise of sound professional judgment. We require of publicly employed therapists only that quantum of care which the common law requires of private therapists. The imposition of liability in those rare cases in which a public employee falls short of this standard does not contravene the language or purpose of Government Code section 820.2.

4. (8) DEFENDANT THERAPISTS ARE IMMUNE FROM LIABILITY FOR FAILING TO CONFINE PODDAR

We sustain defendant therapists' contention that Government Code section 856 insulates them from liability under plaintiffs' first and fourth causes of action for failing to confine Poddar. Section 856 affords public entities and their employees absolute protection from liability for "any injury resulting from determining in accordance with any applicable enactment . . . whether to confine a person for mental illness." Since this section refers to a determination to confine "in accordance with any applicable enactment," plaintiffs suggest that the immunity is limited to persons designated under Welfare and Institutions Code section 5150 as authorized finally to adjudicate a patient's confinement. Defendant therapists, plaintiffs point out, are not among the persons designated under section 5150.

The language and legislative history of section 856, however, suggest a far broader immunity. In 1963, when section 856 was enacted, the Legislature had not established the statutory structure of the Lanterman-Petris-Short Act. Former Welfare and Institutions Code section 5050.3 (renumbered as Welf. & Inst. Code, § 5880; repealed July 1, 1969) which resembled present section 5150, authorized emergency detention at the behest only of peace officers, health officers, county physicians, or assistant county physicians; former section 5047 (renumbered as Welf. & Inst. Code, § 5551; repealed July 1, 1969), however, authorized a petition seeking commitment by any person, including the "physician attending the patient." The Legislature did not refer in section 856 only to those persons authorized to institute emergency proceedings under section 5050.3; it broadly extended immunity to all employees who acted in accord with "any applicable enactment," thus granting immunity not only to persons who are empowered to confine, but also to those authorized to request or recommend confinement.

The Lanterman-Petris-Short Act, in its extensive revision of the procedures for commitment of the mentally ill, eliminated any specific statutory reference to petitions by treating physicians, but it did not limit the authority of a therapist in government employ to request, recommend or initiate actions which may lead to commitment of his patient under the act. We believe that the language of section 856, which refers to any action in the course of employment and in accordance with any applicable enactment, protects the therapist who must undertake this delicate and difficult task. (See Fleming & Maximov, *The Patient or His Victim: The Therapist's Dilemma* (1974) 62 Cal.L.Rev. 1025, 1064). Thus the scope of the immunity extends not only to the final determination to confine or not to confine the person for mental illness, but to all determinations involved in the process of commitment. (Cf. *Hernandez v. State of California* (1970) 11 Cal.App.3d 895, 899–900 [90 Cal.Rptr. 205].)

Turning first to Dr. Powelson's status with respect to section 856, we observe that the actions attributed to him by plaintiffs' complaints fall squarely within the protections furnished by that provision. Plaintiffs allege Powelson ordered that no actions leading to Poddar's detention be taken. This conduct reflected Powelson's determination not to seek Poddar's confinement and thus falls within the statutory immunity.

Section 856 also insulates Dr. Moore for his conduct respecting confinement, although the analysis in his case is a bit more subtle. Clearly, Moore's decision that Poddar *be* confined was not a proximate cause of Tatiana's death, for indeed if Moore's efforts to bring about Poddar's confinement had been successful, Tatiana might still be alive today. Rather, any confinement claim against Moore must rest upon Moore's failure to overcome Powelson's decision and actions opposing confinement.

Such a claim, based as it necessarily would be, upon a subordinate's failure to prevail over his superior, obviously would derive from a rather onerous duty. Whether to impose such a duty we need not decide, however, since we can confine our analysis to the question whether Moore's failure to overcome Powelson's decision realistically falls within the protection afforded by section 856. Based upon the allegations before us, we conclude that Moore's conduct is protected.

Plaintiffs' complaints imply that Moore acquiesced in Powelson's countermand of Moore's confinement recommendation. Such acquiescence is functionally equivalent to determining not to seek Poddar's confinement and thus merits protection under section 856. At this stage we are unaware, of course, precisely how Moore responded to Powelson's actions; he may have debated the confinement issue with Powelson, for example, or taken no initiative whatsoever, perhaps because he respected Powelson's judgment, feared for his future at the hospital, or simply recognized that the proverbial handwriting was on the wall. None of these possibilities constitutes, however, the type of careless or wrongful behavior subsequent to a decision respecting confinement which is stripped of protection by the exception in section 856.[23] Rather, each is in the nature of a decision not to continue to press for Poddar's confinement. No language in plaintiffs' original or amended complaints suggests that Moore determined to fight Powelson, but failed successfully to do so, due to negligent or otherwise wrongful acts or omissions. Under the circumstances, we conclude that plaintiffs' second amended complaints allege facts which trigger immunity for Dr. Moore under section 856.[24]

5. (9) DEFENDANT POLICE OFFICERS ARE IMMUNE FROM LIABILITY FOR FAILING TO CONFINE PODDAR IN THEIR CUSTODY

Confronting, finally, the question whether the defendant police officers are immune from liability for releasing Poddar after his brief confinement, we conclude that they are. The source of their immunity is section 5154 of the Welfare and Institutions Code, which declares that: "[t]he professional person in charge of the facility providing 72-hour treatment and evaluation, his designee, *and the peace officer responsible for the detainment of the person* shall not be held civilly or criminally liable for any action by a person released at or before the end of 72 hours. . . ." (Italics added.)

Although defendant police officers technically were not "peace officers" as contemplated by the Welfare and Institutions Code,[25] plaintiffs' assertion that the officers incurred liability by failing to continue Poddar's confinement clearly contemplates that the officers were "responsible for the detainment of [Poddar]." We could not impose a duty upon the officers to keep Poddar confined yet deny them the protection furnished by a statute immunizing those "responsible for . . . [confinement]." Because plaintiffs would have us treat defendant officers as persons who were capable of performing the functions of the "peace officers" contemplated by the Welfare and Institutions Code, we must accord defendant officers the protections which that code prescribed for such "peace officers."

6. PLAINTIFFS' COMPLAINTS STATE NO CAUSE OF ACTION FOR EXEMPLARY DAMAGES

Plaintiff's third cause of action seeks punitive damages against defendant Powelson. The California statutes and decisions, however, have been interpreted to bar the recovery of punitive damages in a wrongful death action. (See *Pease v. Beech Aircraft Corp.* (1974) 38 Cal.App.3d 450, 460–462 [113 Cal.Rptr. 416] and authorities there cited.)

7. CONCLUSION

For the reasons stated, we conclude that plaintiffs can amend their complaints to state a cause of action against defendant therapists by asserting that the therapists in fact determined that Poddar presented a serious danger of violence to Tatiana, or pursuant to the standards of their profession should have so determined, but nevertheless, failed to exercise reasonable care to protect her from that danger. To the extent, however, that plaintiffs base their claim that defendant therapists breached that duty because they failed to procure Poddar's confinement, the therapists find immunity in Government Code section 856. Further, as to the police defendants we conclude that plaintiffs have failed to show that the trial court erred in sustaining their demurrer without leave to amend.

The judgment of the superior court in favor of defendants Atkinson, Beall, Brownrigg, Hallernan, and Teel is affirmed. The judgment of the superior court in favor of defendants Gold, Moore, Powelson, Yandell, and the Regents of the University of California is reversed, and the cause remanded for further proceedings consistent with the views expressed herein.

WRIGHT, C.J., SULLIVAN, J., AND RICHARDSON, J., CONCURRED.

Mosk, J., Concurring and Dissenting

I concur in the result in this instance only because the complaints allege that defendant therapists did in fact predict that Poddar would kill and were therefore negligent in failing to warn of that danger. Thus the issue here is very narrow: we are not concerned with whether the therapists, pursuant to the standards of their profession, "should have" predicted potential violence: they allegedly did so in actuality. Under these limited circumstances I agree that a cause of action can be stated.

Whether plaintiffs can ultimately prevail is problematical at best. As the complaints admit, the therapists *did* notify the police that Poddar was planning to kill a girl identifiable as Tatiana. While I doubt that more should be required, this issue may be raised in defense and its determination is a question of fact.

I cannot concur, however, in the majority's rule that a therapist may be held liable for failing to predict his patient's tendency to violence if other practitioners, pursuant to the "standards of the profession," would have done so. The question is, what standards? Defendants and a responsible amicus curiae, supported by an impressive body of literature discussed at length in our recent opinion in *People v. Burnick* (1975) 14 Cal.3d 306 [121 Cal.Rptr. 488, 535 P.2d 352], demonstrate that psychiatric predictions of violence are inherently unreliable.

In *Burnick*, at pages 325–326, we observed: "In the light of recent studies it is no longer heresy to question the reliability of psychiatric predictions. Psychiatrists themselves would be the first to admit that however desirable an infallible crystal ball might be, it is not among the tools of their profession. It must be conceded that psychiatrists still experience considerable difficulty in confidently and accurately *diagnosing* mental illness. Yet those difficulties are multiplied manyfold when psychiatrists venture from diagnosis to prognosis and undertake to predict the consequences of such illness: ' "A diagnosis of mental illness tells us nothing about whether the person so diagnosed is or is not dangerous. Some mental patients are dangerous, some are not. Perhaps the psychiatrist is an expert at deciding whether a person is mentally ill, but is he an expert at predicting which of the persons so diagnosed are dangerous? Sane people, too, are dangerous, and it may legitimately be inquired whether there is anything in the education, training or experience of psychiatrists which renders them particularly adept at predicting dangerous behavior. Predictions of dangerous behavior, no matter who makes them, are incredibly inaccurate, and there is a growing consensus that psychiatrists are not uniquely qualified to predict dangerous behavior and are, in fact, less accurate in their predictions than other professionals." ' (*Murel v. Baltimore City Criminal Court* (1972) . . . 407 U.S. 355, 364–365, fn. 2 [32 L.Ed.2d 791, 796–797, 92 S.Ct. 2091] (Douglas, J., dissenting from dismissal of certiorari).)" (Fns. omitted.) (See also authorities cited at p. 327 & fn. 18 of 14 Cal.3d.)

The majority confidently claim their opinion is not offensive to *Burnick*, on the stated ground that *Burnick* involved proceedings to commit an alleged mentally disordered sex offender and this case does not. I am not so sanguine about the distinction. Obviously the two cases are not factually identical, but the similarity in issues is striking: in *Burnick* we were likewise called upon to appraise the ability of psychiatrists to predict dangerousness, and while we declined to bar all such testimony (*id.*, at pp. 327–328) we found it so inherently untrustworthy that we would permit confinement even in a so-called civil proceeding only upon proof beyond a reasonable doubt.

I would restructure the rule designed by the majority to eliminate all reference to conformity to standards of the profession in predicting violence. If a psychiatrist does in fact predict violence, then a duty to warn arises. The majority's expansion of that rule will take us from the world of reality into the wonderland of clairvoyance.

CLARK, J.

Until today's majority opinion, both legal and medical authorities have agreed that confidentiality is essential to effectively treat the mentally ill, and that imposing a duty on doctors to disclose patient threats to potential victims would greatly impair treatment. Further, recognizing that effective treatment and society's safety are necessarily intertwined, the Legislature has already decided effective and confidential treatment is preferred over imposition of a duty to warn.

The issue whether effective treatment for the mentally ill should be sacrificed to a system of warnings is, in my opinion, properly one for the Legislature, and we are bound by its judgment. Moreover, even in the absence of clear legislative direction, we must reach the same conclusion because imposing the majority's new duty is certain to result in a net increase in violence.

The majority rejects the balance achieved by the Legislature's Lanterman-Petris-Short Act. (Welf. & Inst. Code, § 5000 et seq., hereafter the act.)[26] In addition, the majority fails to recognize that, even absent the act, overwhelming policy considerations mandate against sacrificing fundamental patient interests without gaining a corresponding increase in public benefit.

STATUTORY PROVISIONS

Although the parties have touched only briefly on the nondisclosure provisions of the act, amici have pointed out their importance. The instant case arising after ruling on demurrer, the parties must confront the act's provisions in the trial court. In these circumstances the parties' failure to fully meet the provisions of the act would not justify this court's refusal to discuss and apply the law.

Having a grave impact on future treatment of the mentally ill in our state, the majority opinion clearly transcends the interests of the immediate parties and must discuss all applicable law. It abdicates judicial responsibility to refuse to recognize the clear legislative policy reflected in the act.

Effective 1 July 1969, the Legislature created a comprehensive statutory resolution of the rights and duties of both the mentally infirm and those charged with their care and treatment. The act's purposes include ending inappropriate commitment, providing prompt care, protecting public safety, and safeguarding personal rights. (§ 5001). The act applies to both voluntary and involuntary commitment and to both public and private institutions; it details legal procedure for commitment; it enumerates the legal and civil rights of persons committed; and it spells out the duties, liabilities and rights of the psychotherapist. Thus the act clearly evinces the Legislature's weighing of the countervailing concerns presently before us—when a patient has threatened a third person during psychiatric treatment.

Reflecting legislative recognition that disclosing confidences impairs effective treatment of the mentally ill, and thus is contrary to the best interests of society, the act establishes the therapist's duty to *not* disclose. Section 5328 provides in part that "[a]ll information and records obtained in the course of providing services . . . to either voluntary or involuntary recipients of services *shall* be confidential." (Italics added.) Further, a patient may enjoin disclosure in violation of statute and may recover the greater of $500 or three times the amount of actual damage for unlawful disclosure. (§ 5330.)

However, recognizing that some private and public interests must override the patient's, the Legislature established several limited exceptions to confidentiality.[27] The limited nature of these exceptions and the legislative concern that disclosure might impair treatment, thereby harming both patient and society, are shown by section 5328.1. The section provides that a therapist may disclose "to a member of the family of a patient the information that the patient is presently a patient in the facility or that the patient is seriously physically ill . . . if the professional person in charge of the facility determines that the release of such information is in the best interest of the patient." Thus, disclosing even the fact of treatment is severely limited.

As originally enacted the act contained no provision allowing the therapist to warn anyone of a patient's threat. In 1970, however, the act was amended to permit disclosure in two limited circumstances. Section 5328 was amended, in subdivision (g), to allow disclosure "[t]o *governmental law enforcement agencies* as needed for the protection of federal and state elective constitutional officers and their families." (Italics added.) In addition, section 5328.3 was added to provide that when "necessary for the protection of the patient or *others* due to the patient's disappearance from, without prior notice to, a designated facility and his whereabouts is unknown, notice of such disappearance *may* be made to *relatives and governmental law enforcement agencies* designated by the physician in charge of the patient or the professional person in charge of the facility or his designee." (Italics added.)

Obviously neither exception to the confidentiality requirement is applicable to the instant case.

Not only has the Legislature specifically dealt with disclosure and warning, but it also has dealt with therapist and police officer liability for acts of the patient. The Legislature has provided that the therapist and the officer shall not be liable for prematurely releasing the patient. (§§ 5151, 5154, 5173, 5278, 5305, 5306.)

Ignoring the act's detailed provisions, the majority has chosen to focus on the "dangerous patient exception" to the psychotherapist-patient privilege in Evidence Code sections 1014, 1024 as indicating that "the Legislature has undertaken the difficult task of balancing the countervailing concerns." (*Ante,* p. 440). However, this conclusion is erroneous. The majority fails to appreciate that when disclosure is permitted in an evidentiary hearing, a fourth interest comes into play—the court's concern in judicial supervision. Because they are necessary to the administration of justice, disclosures to the courts are excepted from the nondisclosure requirement by section 5328, subdivision (f). However, this case does not involve a court disclosure. Subdivision (f) and the Evidence Code sections relied on by the majority are clearly inapposite.

The provisions of the act are applicable here. Section 5328 (see fn. 2, *ante*) provides, *"All information and records obtained in the course of providing services under division 5 . . . shall be confidential."* (Italics added.) Dr. Moore's letter describing Poddar's mental condition for purposes of obtaining 72-hour commitment was undisputedly a transmittal of information designed to invoke application of division 5. As such it constituted information obtained in providing services under division 5. This is true regardless of whether Dr. Moore has been designated a professional person by the County of Alameda. Although section 5150 provides that commitment for 72 hours' evaluation shall be based on a statement by a peace officer or person designated by the county, section 5328 prohibits disclosure of *all information*, not just disclosure of the committing statement or disclosure by persons designated by the county. In addition, section 5330 gives the patient a cause of action for disclosure of confidential information by "an individual" rather than the persons enumerated in section 5150.

Moreover, it appears from the allegations of the complaint that Dr. Moore is in fact a person designated by the county under section 5150. The complaint alleges that "On or about August 20, 1969, defendant Dr. Moore notified Officers Atkinson and Teel, he would give the campus police a letter of diagnosis on Prosenjit Poddar, so the campus police could pick up Poddar and take him to Herrick Hospital in Berkeley where Dr. Moore would assign a 72-hour Emergency Psychiatric Detention on Prosenjit Poddar." Since there is no allegation that Dr. Moore was not authorized to sign the document, it must be concluded that under the allegations of the complaint he was authorized and thus a professional person designated by the county.

Whether we rely on the facts as stated in the complaint that Dr. Moore is a designated person under section 5150 or on the strict prohibitions of section 5328 prohibiting disclosure of *"all information,"* the imposition of a duty to warn by the majority flies directly in the face of the Lanterman-Petris-Short Act.

Under the act, there can be no liability for Poddar's premature release. It is likewise clear there exists no duty to warn. Under section 5328, the therapists were under a duty *to not disclose*, and no exception to that duty is applicable here. Establishing a duty to warn on the basis of general tort principles imposes a Draconian dilemma on therapists—either violate the act thereby incurring the attendant statutory penalties, or ignore the majority's duty to warn thereby incurring potential civil liability. I am unable to assent to such.

If the majority feels that it must impose such a dilemma, then it has an obligation to specifically enumerate the circumstances under which the Lanterman-Petris-Short Act applies as opposed to the circumstances when "general tort principles" will govern. The majority's failure to perform this obligation—leaving to the therapist the subtle questions as to when each opposing rule applies—is manifestly unfair.

DUTY TO DISCLOSE IN THE ABSENCE OF
CONTROLLING STATUTORY PROVISION

Even assuming the act's provisions are applicable only to conduct occurring after commitment, and not to prior conduct, the act remains applicable to the most dangerous patients—those committed. The Legislature having determined that the balance of several interests requires nondisclosure in the graver public danger commitment, it would be anomalous for this court to reweigh the interests, requiring disclosure for those less dangerous. Rather, we should follow the legislative direction by refusing to require disclosure of confidential information received by the therapist either before or in the absence of commitment. The Legislature obviously is more capable than is this court to investigate, debate and weigh potential patient harm through disclosure against the risk of public harm by nondisclosure. We should defer to its judgment.

COMMON LAW ANALYSIS

Entirely apart from the statutory provisions, the same result must be reached upon considering both general tort principles and the public policies favoring effective treatment, reduction of violence, and justified commitment.

Generally, a person owes no duty to control the conduct of another. (*Richards v. Stanley* (1954) 43 Cal.2d 60, 65 [271 P.2d 23]; *Wright v. Arcade School Dist.* (1964) 230 Cal.App.2d 272, 277 [40 Cal.Rptr. 812]; Rest.2d Torts (1965) § 315.) Exceptions are recognized only in limited situations where (1) a special relationship exists between the defendant and injured party, or (2) a special relationship exists between defendant and the active wrongdoer, imposing a duty on defendant to control the wrongdoer's conduct. The majority does not contend the first exception is appropriate to this case.

Policy generally determines duty. (*Dillon v. Legg* (1968) 68 Cal.2d 728, 734 [69 Cal.Rptr. 72, 441 P.2d 912, 29 A.L.R.3d 1316].) Principal policy considerations include foreseeability of harm, certainty of the plaintiff's injury, proximity of the defendant's conduct to the plaintiff's injury, moral blame attributable to defendant's conduct, prevention of future harm, burden on the defendant, and consequences to the community. (*Rowland v. Christian* (1968) 69 Cal.2d 108, 113 [70 Cal.Rptr. 97, 443 P.2d 561, 32 A.L.R.3d 496].)

Overwhelming policy considerations weigh against imposing a duty on psychotherapists to warn a potential victim against harm. While offering virtually no benefit to society, such a duty will frustrate psychiatric treatment, invade fundamental patient rights and increase violence.

The importance of psychiatric treatment and its need for confidentiality have been recognized by this court. (*In re Lifschutz* (1970) 2 Cal.3d 415, 421–422 [85 Cal.Rptr. 829, 467 P.2d 557, 44 A.L.R.3d 1].) "It is clearly recognized that the very practice of psychiatry vitally depends upon the reputation in the community that the psychiatrist will not tell." (Slovenko, *Psychiatry and a Second Look at the Medical Privilege* (1960) 6 Wayne L.Rev. 175, 188.)

Assurance of confidentiality is important for three reasons.

DETERRENCE FROM TREATMENT

First, without substantial assurance of confidentiality, those requiring treatment will be deterred from seeking assistance. (See Sen. Judiciary Com. comment accompanying § 1014 of Evid. Code; Slovenko, *supra*, 6 Wayne L.Rev. 175, 187–188; Goldstein & Katz, *Psychiatrist-Patient Privilege: The GAP Proposal and the Connecticut Statute* (1962) 36 Conn.Bar J. 175, 178.) It remains an unfortunate fact in our society that people seeking psychiatric guidance tend to become stigmatized. Apprehension of such stigma—apparently increased by the propensity of people considering treatment to see themselves in the worst possible light—creates a well-recognized reluctance to seek aid. (Fisher, *The Psychotherapeutic Professions and the Law of Privileged Communications* (1964) 10 Wayne L.Rev. 609, 617; Slovenko, *supra*, 6 Wayne L.Rev. 175, 188; see also Rappeport, *Psychiatrist-Patient Privilege* (1963) 23 Md.L.J. 39, 46–47.) This reluctance is alleviated by the psychiatrist's assurance of confidentiality.

FULL DISCLOSURE

Second, the guarantee of confidentiality is essential in eliciting the full disclosure necessary for effective treatment. (*In re Lifschutz, supra*, 2 Cal.3d 415, 431; *Taylor v. United States* (D.C.Cir. 1955) 222 F.2d 398, 401 [95 App.D.C. 373]; Goldstein & Katz, *supra*, 36 Conn.Bar J. 175, 178; Heller, *Some Comments to Lawyers on the Practice of Psychiatry* (1957) 30 Temp.L.Q. 401; Guttmacher & Weihofen, *Privileged Communications Between Psychiatrist and Patient* (1952) 28 Ind.L.J.32, 34.)[28] The psychiatric patient approaches treatment with conscious and unconscious inhibitions against revealing his innermost thoughts. "Every person, however well-motivated, has to overcome resistances to therapeutic exploration. These resistances seek support from every possible source and the possibility of disclosure would easily be employed in the service of resistance." (Goldstein & Katz, *supra*, 36 Conn.Bar J. 175, 179; see also, 118 Am.J.Psych. 734, 735.) Until a patient can trust his psychiatrist not to violate their confidential relationship, "the unconscious psychological control mechanism of repression will prevent the recall of past experiences." (Butler, *Psychotherapy and Griswold: Is Confidentiality a Privilege or a Right?* (1971) 3 Conn.L.Rev. 599, 604.)

SUCCESSFUL TREATMENT

Third, even if the patient fully discloses his thoughts, assurance that the confidential relationship will not be breached is necessary to maintain his trust in his psychiatrist—the very means by which treatment is effected. "[T]he essence of much psychotherapy is the contribution of trust in the external world and ultimately in the self, modelled upon the trusting relationship established during therapy." (Dawidoff, *The Malpractice of Psychiatrists*, 1966 Duke L.J. 696, 704.) Patients will be helped only if they can form a trusting relationship with the psychiatrist. (*Id.*, at p. 704, fn. 34; Burham, *Separation Anxiety* (1965) 13 Arch.Gen. Psych. 346, 356; Heller, *supra*, 30 Temp.L.Q. 401, 406.) All authorities appear to agree that if the trust relationship cannot be developed because of collusive communication between the psychiatrist and others, treatment will be frustrated. (See, e.g., Slovenko (1973) *Psychiatry and Law,* p. 61; Cross, *Privileged Communications Between Participants in Group Psychotherapy* (1970) Law & Soc. Order, 191, 199; Hollender, *The Psychiatrist and the Release of Patient Information* (1960) 116 Am.J.Psych. 828, 829.)

Given the importance of confidentiality to the practice of psychiatry, it becomes clear the duty to warn imposed by the majority will cripple the use and effectiveness of psychiatry. Many people, potentially violent—yet susceptible to treatment—will be deterred from seeking it; those seeking it will be inhibited from making revelations necessary to effective treatment; and, forcing the psychiatrist to violate the patient's trust will destroy the interpersonal relationship by which treatment is effected.

VIOLENCE AND CIVIL COMMITMENT

By imposing a duty to warn, the majority contributes to the danger to society of violence by the mentally ill and greatly increases the risk of civil commitment—the total deprivation of liberty—of those who should not be confined.[29] The impairment of treatment and risk of improper commitment resulting from the new duty to warn will not be limited to a few patients but will extend to a large number of the mentally ill. Although under existing psychiatric procedures only a relatively few receiving treatment will ever present a risk of violence, the number making threats is huge, and it is the latter group—not just the former—whose treatment will be impaired and whose risk of commitment will be increased.

Both the legal and psychiatric communities recognize that the process of determining potential violence in a patient is far from exact, being fraught with complexity and uncertainty. (E.g., *People v. Burnick* (1975) 14 Cal.3d 306, 326 [121 Cal.Rptr. 488, 535 P.2d 352], quoting from *Murel v. Baltimore City Criminal Court* (1972) 407 U.S. 355, 364–365, fn. 2 [32 L.Ed.2d 791, 796–797, 92 S.Ct. 2091] (Douglas, J., dissenting from dismissal of certiorari); Ennis & Litwack, *Psychiatry and the Presumption of Expertise: Flipping Coins in the Courtroom*, 62 Cal.L.Rev. 693, 711–716; Rector, *Who Are the Dangerous?* (July 1973) Bull.Am.Acad. Psych. & L. 186; Kozol, Boucher & Garofalo, *The Diagnosis and Treatment of Dangerousness* (1972) 18 Crime & Delinq. 371; Justice & Birkman, *An Effort to Distinguish the Violent From the Nonviolent* (1972) 65 So.Med.J. 703)[30] In fact, precision has not even been attained in predicting who of those having already committed violent acts will again become violent, a task recognized to be of much simpler proportions. (Kozol, Boucher & Garofalo, *supra*, 18 Crime & Delinq. 371, 384.)

This predictive uncertainty means that the number of disclosures will necessarily be large. As noted above, psychiatric patients are encouraged to discuss all thoughts of violence, and they often express such thoughts. However, unlike this court, the psychiatrist does not enjoy the benefit of overwhelming hindsight in seeing which few, if any, of his patients will ultimately become violent. Now, confronted by the majority's new duty, the psychiatrist must instantaneously calculate potential violence from each patient on each visit. The difficulties researchers have encountered in accurately predicting violence will be heightened for the practicing psychiatrist dealing for brief periods in his office with heretofore nonviolent patients. And, given the decision not to warn or commit must always be made at the psychiatrist's civil peril, one can expect most doubts will be resolved in favor of the psychiatrist protecting himself.

Neither alternative open to the psychiatrist seeking to protect himself is in the public interest. The warning itself is an impairment of the psychiatrist's ability to treat, depriving many patients of adequate treatment. It is to be expected that after disclosing their threats, a significant number of patients, who would not become violent if treated according to existing pratices, will engage in violent conduct as a result of unsuccessful treatment. In short, the majority's duty to warn will not only impair treatment of many who would never become violent but worse, will result in a net increase in violence.[31]

The second alternative open to the psychiatrist is to commit his patient rather than to warn. Even in the absence of threat of civil liability, the doubts of psychiatrists as to the seriousness of patient threats have led psychiatrists to overcommit to mental institutions. This overcommitment has been authoritatively documented in both legal and psychiatric studies. (Ennis & Litwack, *Psychiatry and the Presumption of Expertise: Flipping Coins in the Courtoom, supra,* 62 Cal.L.Rev. 693, 711 et seq.; Fleming & Maximov, *The Patient or His Victim: The Therapist's Dilemma,* 62 Cal.L.Rev. 1025, 1044–1046; Am. Psychiatric Assn. Task Force Rep. 8 (July 1974) Clinical Aspects of the Violent Individual, pp. 23–24; see Livermore, Malmquist & Meehl, *On the Justifications for Civil Commitment,* 117 U.Pa.L.Rev. 75, 84.) This practice is so prevalent that it has been estimated that "as many as twenty harmless persons are incarcerated for every one who will commit a violent act." (Steadman & Cocozza, *Stimulus/Response: We Can't Predict Who Is Dangerous* (Jan. 1975) 8 Psych. Today 32, 35.)

Given the incentive to commit created by the majority's duty, this already serious situation will be worsened, contrary to Chief Justice Wright's admonition "that liberty is no less precious because forfeited in a civil proceeding than when taken as a consequence of a criminal conviction." (*In re Gary W.* (1971) 5 Cal.3d 296, 307 [96 Cal.Rptr. 1, 486 P.2d 1201].)

CONCLUSION

In adopting the act, the Legislature fully recognized the concerns that must govern our decision today—adequate treatment for the mentally ill, safety of our society, and our devotion to individual liberty, making overcommitment of the mentally ill abhorrent. (§ 5001). Again, the Legislature balanced these concerns in favor of nondisclosure (§ 5328), thereby promoting effective treatment, reducing temptation for overcommitment, and ensuring greater safety for our society. Psychiatric and legal expertise on the subject requires the same judgment.

The tragedy of Tatiana Tarasoff has led the majority to disregard the clear legislative mandate of the Lanterman-Petris-Short Act. Worse, the majority impedes medical treatment, resulting in increased violence from—and deprivation of liberty to—the mentally ill.

We should accept legislative and medical judgment, relying upon effective treatment rather than on indiscriminate warning.

The judgment should be affirmed.

McComb, J., concurred.

NOTES

1. The criminal prosecution stemming from this crime is reported in *People v. Poddar* (1974) 10 Cal.3d 750 [111 Cal.Rptr. 910, 518 P.2d 342].

2. The therapist defendants include Dr. Moore, the psychologist who examined Poddar and decided that Poddar should be committed; Dr. Gold and Dr. Yandell, psychiatrists at Cowell Memorial Hospital who concurred in Moore's decision; and Dr. Powelson, chief of the department of psychiatry, who countermanded Moore's decision and directed that the staff take no action to confine Poddar. The police defendants include Officers Atkinson, Brownrigg and Halleran, who detained Poddar briefly but released him; Chief Beall, who received Moore's letter recommending that Poddar be confined; and Officer Teel, who, along with Officer Atkinson, received Moore's oral communication requesting detention of Poddar.

3. Plaintiff's complaints allege merely that defendant therapists failed to warn plaintiffs—Tatiana's parents—of the danger to Tatiana. The complaints do not allege that defendant therapists failed to warn Tatiana herself, or failed to warn persons other than her parents who would be likely to apprise Tatiana of the danger. Such omissions can properly be cured by amendment. As we stated in *Minsky v. City of Los Angeles* (1974) 11 Cal.3d 113, 118–119 [113 Cal.Rptr. 102, 520 P.2d 726]: "It is axiomatic that if there is a reasonable possibility that a defect in the complaint can be cured by amendment or that the pleading liberally construed can state a cause of action, a demurrer should not be sustained without leave to amend." (Accord, *La Sala v. American Sav. & Loan Assn.* (1971) 5 Cal.3d 864, 876 [97 Cal.Rptr. 849, 489 P.2d 1113]; *Lemoge Electric v. County of San Mateo* (1956) 46 Cal.2d 659, 664 [297 P.2d 638]; *Beckstead v. Superior Court* (1971) 21 Cal.App.3d 780, 782 [98 Cal.Rptr. 779].)

4. See *Merrill v. Buck* (1962) 58 Cal.2d 552, 562 [25 Cal.Rptr. 456, 375 P.2d 304]; *Biakanja v. Irving* (1958) 49 Cal.2d 647, 650 [320 P.2d 16, 65 A.L.R.2d 1358]; *Walnut Creek Aggregates Co. v. Testing Engineers Inc.* (1967) 248 Cal.App.2d 690, 695 [56 Cal.Rptr. 700].

5. This rule derives from the common law's distinction between misfeasance and nonfeasance, and its reluctance to impose liability for the latter. (See Harper & Kime, *The Duty to Control the Conduct of Another* (1934) 43 Yale L.J. 886, 887.) Morally questionable, the rule owes its survival to "the difficulties of setting any standards of unselfish service to fellow men, and of making any workable rule to cover possible situations where fifty people might fail to rescue. . . ." (Prosser, Torts (4th ed. 1971) § 56, p. 341.) Because of these practical difficulties, the courts have increased the number of instances in which affirmative duties are imposed not by direct rejection of the common law rule, but by expanding the list of special relationships which will justify departure from that rule. (See Prosser, *supra*, § 56, at pp. 348–350.)

6. The pleadings establish the requisite relationship between Poddar and both Dr. Moore, the therapist who treated Poddar, and Dr. Powelson, who supervised that treatment. Plaintiffs also allege that Dr. Gold personally examined Poddar, and that Dr. Yandell, as Powelson's assistant, approved the decision to arrange Poddar's commitment. These allegations are sufficient to raise the issue whether a doctor-patient or therapist-patient relationship, giving rise to a possible duty by the doctor or therapist to exercise reasonable care to protect a threatened person of danger arising from the patient's mental illness, existed between Gold or Yandell and Poddar. (See Harney, *Medical Malpractice* (1973) p. 7.)

7. When a "hospital has notice or knowledge of facts from which it might reasonably

be concluded that a patient would be likely to harm himself *or others* unless preclusive measures were taken, then the hospital must use reasonable care in the circumstances to prevent such harm." (*Vistica v. Presbyterian Hospital* (1967) 67 Cal.2d 465, 469 [62 Cal.Rptr. 577, 432 P.2d 193].) (Italics added.) A mental hospital may be liable if it negligently permits the escape or release of a dangerous patient (*Semler v. Psychiatric Institute of Washington, D.C.* (4th Cr. 1976) 44 U.S.L. Week 2439; *Underwood v. United States* (5th Cir. 1966) 356 F.2d 92; *Fair v. United States* (5th Cir. 1956) 234 F.2d 288). *Greenberg v. Barbour* (E.D.Pa. 1971) 322 F.Supp. 745, upheld a cause of action against a hospital staff doctor whose negligent failure to admit a mental patient resulted in that patient assaulting the plaintiff.

8. *Kaiser v. Suburban Transportation System* (1965) 65 Wn.2d 461 [398 P.2d 14]; see *Freese v. Lemon* (Iowa 1973) 210 N.W.2d 576 (concurring opn. of Uhlenhopp, J.).

9. *Ellis v. D'Angelo* (1953) 116 Cal.App.2d 310 [253 P.2d 675], upheld a cause of action against parents who failed to warn a babysitter of the violent proclivities of their child; *Johnson v. State of California* (1968) 69 Cal.2d 782 [73 Cal.Rptr. 240, 447 P.2d 352], upheld a suit against the state for failure to warn foster parents of the dangerous tendencies of their ward; *Morgan v. County of Yuba* (1964) 230 Cal.App.2d 938 [41 Cal.Rptr. 508], sustained a cause of action against a sheriff who had promised to warn decedent before releasing a dangerous prisoner, but failed to do so.

10. See e.g., *People v. Burnick* (1975) 14 Cal.3d 306, 325–328 [121 Cal.Rptr. 488, 535 P.2d 352]; Monahan, *The Prevention of Violence,* in Community Mental Health in the Criminal Justice System (Monahan ed. 1975); Diamond, *The Psychiatric Prediction of Dangerousness* (1975) 123 U.Pa.L.Rev. 439; Ennis & Litwack, *Psychiatry and the Presumption of Expertise: Flipping Coins in the Courtroom* (1974) 62 Cal.L.Rev. 693.

11. Defendant therapists and amicus also argue that warnings must be given only in those cases in which the therapist knows the identity of the victim. We recognize that in some cases it would be unreasonable to require the therapist to interrogate his patient to discover the victim's identity, or to conduct an independent investigation. But there may also be cases in which a moment's reflection will reveal the victim's identity. The matter thus is one which depends upon the circumstances of each case, and should not be governed by any hard and fast rule.

12. Counsel for defendant Regents and amicus American Psychiatric Association predict that a decision of this court holding that a therapist may bear a duty to warn a potential victim will deter violence-prone persons from seeking therapy, and hamper the treatment of other patients. This contention was examined in Fleming and Maximov, *The Patient or His Victim: The Therapist's Dilemma* (1974) 62 Cal.L.Rev. 1025, 1038–1044; they conclude that such predictions are entirely speculative. In *In re Lifschutz, supra,* 2 Cal.3d 415, counsel for the psychiatrist argued that if the state could compel disclosure of some psychotherapeutic communications, psychotherapy could no longer be practiced successfully. (2 Cal.3d at p. 426.) We rejected that argument, and it does not appear that our decision in fact adversely affected the practice of psychotherapy in California. Counsels' forecast of harm in the present case strikes us as equally dubious.

We note, moreover, that Evidence Code section 1024, enacted in 1965, established that psychotherapueutic communication is not privileged when disclosure is necessary to prevent threatened danger. We cannot accept without question counsels' implicit assumption that effective therapy for potentially violent patients depends upon either the patient's lack of awareness that a therapist can disclose confidential communications to avert impending danger, or upon the therapist's advance promise never to reveal nonprivileged threats of violence.

13. Fleming and Maximov note that "While [section 1024] supports the therapist's less controversial *right* to make a disclosure, it admittedly does not impose on him a *duty* to do so. But the argument does not have to be pressed that far. For if it is once conceded . . . that a duty in favor of the patient's foreseeable victims would accord with general principles of tort liability, we need no longer look to the statute for a source of duty. It is sufficient if the statute can be relied upon . . . for the purpose of countering the claim that the needs of confidentiality are paramount and must therefore defeat any such hypothetical duty. In this more modest perspective, the Evidence Code's 'dangerous patient' exception may be invoked with

some confidence as a clear expression of legislative policy concerning the balance between the confidentiality values of the patient and the safety values of his foreseeable victims." (Italics in original.) Fleming & Maximov, *The Patient or His Victim: The Therapist's Dilemma* (1974) 62 Cal.L.Rev. 1025, 1063.

14. Amicus suggests that a therapist who concludes that his patient is dangerous should not warn the potential victim, but institute proceedings for involuntary detention of the patient. The giving of a warning, however, would in many cases represent a far lesser inroad upon the patient's privacy than would involuntary commitment.

15. See also Summary Report of the Task Force Confidentiality of the Council on Professions and Associations of the American Psychiatric Association (1975).

16. Moore argues that after Powelson countermanded the decision to seek commitment for Poddar, Moore was obliged to obey the decision of his superior and that therefore he should not be held liable for any dereliction arising from his obedience to superior orders. Plaintiffs in response contend that Moore's duty to members of the public endangered by Poddar should take precedence over his duty to obey Powelson. Since plaintiffs' complaints do not set out the date of Powelson's order, the specific terms of that order, or Powelson's authority to overrule Moore's desicisions respecting patients under Moore's care, we need not adjudicate this conflict; we pass only upon the pleadings at this stage and decide if the complaints can be amended to state a cause of action.

17. Division 5 includes the Lanterman-Petris-Short Act and the Short-Doyle Act (community mental health services). Division 6 relates to programs for treatment of persons judicially committed as mentally disordered sex offenders or mentally retarded. Division 7 encompasses treatment at state and county mental hospitals, the Langley Porter Neuropsychiatric Institute and the Neuropsychiatric Institute of the U.C.L.A. Medical Center.

18. We have considered *sua sponte* whether plaintiffs' complaints could be amended to assert a cause of action against the police defendants under the principles of Restatement Second of Torts (1965) section 321, which provides that "If the actor does an act, and subsequently realizes or should realize that it has created an unreasonable risk of causing physical harm to another, he is under a duty to exercise reasonable care to prevent the risk from taking effect." (See *Hartzler v. City of San Jose, supra,* 46 Cal.App.3d 6,10.) The record, however, suggests no facts which, if inserted into the complaints, might form the foundation for such cause of action. The assertion of a cause of action against the police defendants under this theory would raise difficult problems of causation and of public policy, which should not be resolved on the basis of conjectural facts not averred in the pleadings or in any proposed amendment to those pleadings.

19. No more specific immunity provision of the Government Code appears to address the issue.

20. Section 815.2 of the Government Code declares that "[a] public entity is liable for injury proximately caused by an act or omission of an employee of the public entity within the scope of his employment if the act or omission would, apart from this section, have given rise to a cause of action against that employee or his personal representative." The section further provides, with exceptions not applicable here, that "a public entity is not liable for an injury resulting from an act or omission of an employee of the public entity where the employee is immune from liability." The Regents, therefore, are immune from liability only if all individual defendants are similarly immune.

21. We dismissed, in *Johnson,* the view that immunity continues to be necessary in order to insure that public employees will be sufficiently zealous in the performance of their official duties. The California Tort Claims Act of 1963 provides for indemnification of public employees against liability, absent bad faith, and also permits such employees to insist that their defenses be conducted at public expense. (See Gov. Code, §§ 825–825.6, 995–995.2.) Public employees thus no longer have a significant reason to fear liability as they go about their official tasks. We also, in *Johnson,* rejected the argument that a public employee's concern over the potential liability of his or her employer serves as a basis for immunity. (*Johnson v. State of California, supra,* at pp. 790–793.)

22. By analogy, section 830.8 of the Government Code furnishes additional support for our conclusion that a failure to warn does not fall within the zone of immunity created by

section 820.2. Section 830.8 provides: "Neither a public entity nor a public employee is liable . . . for an injury caused by the failure to provide traffic or warning signals, signs, markings or devices described in the Vehicle Code. Nothing in this section exonerates a public entity or public employee from liability for injury proximately caused by such failure if a signal, sign, marking or device . . . was necessary to warn of a dangerous condition which endangered the safe movement of traffic and which would not be reasonably apparent to, and would not have been anticipated by, a person exercising due care." The Legislature thus concluded at least in another context that the failure to warn of a latent danger is not an immunized discretionary omission. (See *Hilts v. County of Solano* (1968) 265 Cal.App.2d 161, 174 [71 Cal.Rptr. 275].)

23. Section 856 includes the exception to the general rule of immunity "for injury proximately caused by . . . negligent or wrongful acts or omission in carrying out or failing to carry out . . . a determination to confine or not to confine a person for mental illness. . . ."

24. Because Dr. Gold and Dr. Yandell were Dr. Powelson's subordinates, the analysis respecting whether they are immune for having failed to obtain Poddar's confinement is similar to the analysis applicable to Dr. Moore.

25. Welfare and Institutions Code section 5008, subdivision (i), defines "peace officer" for purposes of the Lanterman-Petris-Short Act as a person specified in section 830.1 and 830.2 of the Penal Code. Campus police do not fall within the coverage of section 830.1 and were not included in section 830.2 until 1971.

26. All statutory references, unless otherwise stated, are to the Welfare and Institutions Code.

27. Section 5328 provides: "All information and records obtained in the course of providing services under Division 5 (commencing with Section 5000), Division 6 (commencing with Section 6000), or Division 7 (commencing with Section 7000), to either voluntary or involuntary recipients of services shall be confidential. Information and records may be disclosed only: [¶] (a) In communications between qualified professional persons in the provision of services or appropriate referrals, or in the course of conservatorship proceedings. The consent of the patient, or his guardian or conservator must be obtained before information or records may be disclosed by a professional person employed by a facility to a professional person not employed by the facility who does not have the medical responsibility for the patient's care; [¶] (b) When the patient, with the approval of the physician in charge of the patient, designates persons to whom information or records may be released, except that nothing in this article shall be construed to compel a physician, psychologist, social worker, nurse, attorney, or other professional person to reveal information which has been given to him in confidence by members of a patient's family; [¶] (c) To the extent necessary for a recipient to make a claim, or for a claim to be made on behalf of a recipient for aid, insurance, or medical assistance to which he may be entitled; [¶] (d) If the recipient of services is a minor, ward, or conservatee, and his parent, guardian, or conservator designates, in writing, persons to whom records or information may be disclosed, except that nothing in this article shall be construed to compel a physician, psychologist, social worker, nurse, attorney, or other professional person to reveal information which has been given to him in confidence by members of a patient's family; [¶] (e) For research, provided that the Director of Health designates by regulation, rules for the conduct of research. Such rules shall include, but need not be limited to, the requirement that all researchers must sign an oath of confidentiality as follows:

....
Date

As a condition of doing research concerning persons who have received services from .... (fill in the facility, agency or person), I, ..., agree not to divulge any information obtained in the course of such research to unauthorized persons, and not to publish or otherwise make public any information regarding persons who have received services such that the person who received services is identifiable.

I recognize that unauthorized release of confidential information may make me subject to a civil action under provisions of the Welfare and Institutions Code.

....
Signed

[¶] (f) To the courts, as necessary to the administration of justice. [¶] (g) To governmental law enforcement agencies as needed for the protection of federal and state elective constitutional officers and their families. [¶] (h) To the Senate Rules Committee or the Assembly Rules Committee for the purposes of legislative investigation authorized by such committee. [¶] (i) If the recipient of services who applies for life or disability insurance designates in writing the insurer to which records or information may be disclosed. [¶] (j) To the attorney for the patient in any and all proceedings upon presentation of a release of information signed by the patient, except that when the patient is unable to sign such release, the staff of the facility, upon satisfying itself of the identity of said attorney, and of the fact that the attorney does represent the interests of the patient, may release all information and records relating to the patient except that nothing in this article shall be construed to compel a physician, psychologist, social worker, nurse, attorney, or other professional person to reveal information which has been given to him in confidence by members of a patient's family. [¶] The amendment of subdivision (d) of this section enacted at the 1970 Regular Session of the Legislature does not constitute a change in, but is declaratory of, the preexisting law."

Subdivisions (g), (h), and (i) were added by amendment in 1972. Subdivision (j) was added by amendment in 1974.

Section 5328, specifically enumerating exceptions to the confidentiality requirement, does not admit of an interpretation importing implied exceptions. (*County of Riverside v. Superior Court*, 42 Cal.App.3d 478, 481 [116 Cal.Rptr. 886].)

28. One survey indicated that five of every seven people interviewed said they would be less likely to make full disclosure to a psychiatrist in the absence of assurance of confidentiality. (See, Comment, *Functional Overlap Between the Lawyer and Other Professionals: Its Implications for the Privileged Communications Doctrine* (1962) 71 Yale L.J. 1226, 1255.)

29. The burden placed by the majority on psychiatrists may also result in the improper deprivation of two other constitutionally protected rights. First, the patient's constitutional right of privacy (*In re Lifschutz, supra*, 2 Cal.3d 415) is obviously encroached upon by requiring the psychotherapist to disclose confidential communications. Secondly, because confidentiality is essential to effective treatment, the majority's decision also threatens the constitutionally recognized right to receive treatment. (*People v. Feagley* (1975) 14 Cal.3d 338, 359 [121 Cal.Rptr. 509, 535 P.2d 373]; *Wyatt v. Stickney* (M.D.Ala. 1971) 325 F.Supp. 781, 784, affd. *sub nom. Wyatt v. Aderholt* (5th Cir. 1974) 503 F.2d 1305; *Nason v. Superintendent of Bridgewater State Hosp.* (1968) 353 Mass. 604 [233 N.E.2d 908].)

30. A shocking illustration of psychotherapists' inability to predict dangerousness, cited by this court in *People v. Burnick, supra*, 14 Cal.3d 306, 326–327, footnote 17, is cited and discussed in Ennis, *Prisoners of Psychiatry: Mental Patients, Psychiatrists, and the Law* (1972): "In a well-known study, psychiatrists predicted that 989 persons were so dangerous that they could not be kept even in civil mental hospitals, but would have to be kept in maximum security hospitals run by the Department of Corrections. Then, because of a United States Supreme Court decision, those persons were transferred to civil hospitals. After a year, the Department of Mental Hygiene reported that one-fifth of them had been discharged to the community, and over half had agreed to remain as voluntary patients. During the year, only 7 of the 989 committed or threatened any act that was sufficiently dangerous to require retransfer to the maximum security hospital. Seven correct predictions out of almost a thousand is not a very impressive record. [¶] Other studies, and there are many, have reached the same conclusion: psychiatrists simply cannot predict dangerous behavior." (*Id.*, at p. 227.) Equally illustrative studies are collected in Rosenhan. *On Being Sane in Insane Places* (1973) 13 Santa Clara Law, 379, 384; Ennis & Litwack, *Psychiatry and the Presumption of Expertise: Flipping Coins in the Courtroom, supra*, 62 Cal.L.Rev. 693, 750–751.)

31. The majority concedes that psychotherapeutic dialogue often results in the patient expressing threats of violence that are rarely executed. (*Ante*, p. 441.) The practical problem, of course, lies in ascertaining which threats from which patients will be carried out. As to this problem, the majority is silent. They do, however, caution that a therapist certainly "should not be encouraged routinely to reveal such threats; such disclosures could seriously disrupt the patient's relationship with his therapist and with the persons threatened." (*Id.*)

Thus, in effect, the majority informs the therapists that they must accurately predict dangerousness—a task recognized as extremely difficult—or face crushing civil liability. The majority's reliance on the traditional standard of care for professionals that "therapist need only exercise 'that reasonable degree of skill, knowledge, and care ordinarily possessed and exercised by members of [that professional specialty] under similar circumstances' " (*ante*, p. 438) is seriously misplaced. This standard of care assumes that, to a large extent, the subject matter of the specialty is ascertainable. One clearly ascertainable element in the psychiatric field is that the therapist cannot accurately predict dangerousness, which, in turn, means that the standard is inappropriate for lack of a relevant criterion by which to judge the therapist's decision. The inappropriateness of the standard the majority would have us use is made patent when consideration is given to studies, by several eminent authorities, indicating that "[t]he chances of a second psychiatrist agreeing with the diagnosis of a first psychiatrist 'are barely better than 50–50; or stated differently, there is about as much chance that a different expert would come to some different conclusion as there is that the other would agree.' " (Ennis & Litwack, *Psychiatry and the Presumption of Expertise: Flipping Coins in the Courtroom, supra,* 62 Cal.L.Rev. 693, 701, quoting, Ziskin, *Coping With Psychiatric and Psychological Testimony,* p. 126.) The majority's attempt to apply a normative scheme to a profession which must be concerned with problems that balk at standardization is clearly erroneous.

In any event, an ascertainable standard would not serve to limit psychiatrist disclosure of threats with the resulting impairment of treatment. However compassionate, the psychiatrist hearing the threat remains faced with potential crushing civil liability for a mistaken evaluation of his patient and will be forced to resolve even the slightest doubt in favor of disclosure or commitment.

VI. ORGAN TRANSPLANTATION

1. THE ETHICAL ISSUES

Progress in the transplantation of organs from one individual to another has been one of the most striking developments in modern medicine. Heart transplants have been the most dramatic but, unfortunately, the least successful example. Kidney transplantation has been more common and quite successful. Advances made in overcoming the body's natural rejection of a foreign object have been mainly responsible for this success. But a continuing problem is the availability of properly matched organs. The closer the biological relationship between recipient and donor, the better the chance for a successful transplantation. The ideal candidate is an identical twin, with other family members close seconds. In the absence of these two sources, other donors are sought, but the prospects for incompatibility and ultimate rejection increase.

The cases presented here examine two of the many ethical dimensions of this procedure. The first problem is the validity of substitute consent; the second is the use of incompetents as donors. The tension in these particular cases is heightened because of the terminal situation of the recipients and the fact that the proposed donors are brothers of the patients in each case and ideal donors.

Consent to any procedure is often problematic. When a proposed donor is incompetent, the complications multiply. In the cases included here the potential donors were mentally retarded and mentally ill. Though they were adults, they were assumed to be incapable of giving consent. Often retardation and mental illness do make individuals incapable of giving consent, but it is not obvious that this is always so. The first priority is to determine whether the individual is competent or incompetent and in what areas. If the individual is competent, one dimension of the problem is solved. Since the individuals in the cases that follow were judged to be incompetent, if they were to serve as donors substitute consent needed to be obtained. The question then is: Who is the appropriate decision-maker and on what ground is the decision to be made? Ethically the most proper decision-maker is the parent, next of kin, or the legal guardian. These persons have an interest in the individual and have had some responsibility for care. When the individual is a ward of the state, then ethically the state, in the person of a court-appointed guardian, would be the proper decision-maker. The process of legally designating a decision-maker has the merit of allowing room for a court to evaluate a relative's claims and to function as a mediator.

Decisions made for incompetents should be in their best interests. Based on the difficulties associated with knowing and evaluating what our own best interests are, it is easy to perceive the difficulties of knowing and evaluating the interests of one who is incompetent. Benefits to be received from kidney donation construed to be in the incompetent's interest include: the individual's psychological welfare, an increase in self-esteem from being able to help, the continued companionship of the sibling, and the avoidance of the feelings of guilt that may be associated with the death of the sibling. That these *may* be genuine benefits in the incompetent's interest should not be rejected out of hand. But assumption that these actually *are* benefits to the individual and that they are in his or her best interest does not necessarily follow. Rather, any such assumption must be tested and carefully evaluated. Presumption of benefit and interest is not a sufficient reason on which to base the removal of an organ, even if such a procedure may be of low medical risk to the donor. One should also be wary of assuming that an incompetent individual will choose the same benefits as a competent individual similarly situated. What most competent individuals would do might be an appropriate guideline, but such an assumption uncritically accepted might argue for a perception of benefits that are of interest to competents. A better course is the extrapolation of benefits and interests based on what can be gathered from the incompetent individual, difficult as this may be. Only in this way can the unwarranted imposition of possibly alien values or interests be avoided.

Incompetent individuals may not be able to speak for themselves and defend their interests; they may have to depend on others for their protection and, often enough, their sustenance. Thus vulnerability and the consequent susceptibility to misuse of these individuals suggests that as a class they ought to be considered last in determining potential donors for organ transplantation. Beyond this, their possible inability to speak for themselves and to understand the complexities of the issues can lead to the conclusion that they ought not be used as donors under any circumstances. Absolute protection removes any doubts about the value of such individuals and affirms that they are not marginal to society. The importance of protecting them might well outweigh the health needs of another, no matter how urgent these might be.

2. THE LEGAL ISSUES

Reaching opposite conclusions from rather analogous circumstances, the Kentucky and Wisconsin courts seem to agree that renal donation is essentially an altruistic act, beneficial primarily to the recipient and therefore requiring, toward the donor, a strict standard of informed consent. Neither of the proposed donors, Jerry Strunk and Richard Pescinski (brothers of the proposed recipients), was capable of meeting this requirement, since each was under a legal disability—mental retardation and mental illness, respectively. In the absence of the necessary informed consent both courts require a showing of definite benefit to the incompetent donor if the renal transplantation is to be allowed.

The Kentucky Court finds that the best interest of the incompetent donor is met, since Jerry Strunk's "well-being would be jeopardized more severely by the loss of his brother than by the removal of a kidney." In reaching this conclusion the Court apparently relies heavily on the fact that all those involved—the immediate family, the Department of Mental Health, and the lower courts—had approved transplantation on this basis. Furthermore, the Court emphasizes that throughout the legal process a guardian *ad litem* had represented Jerry Strunk and had questioned the power of the State of Kentucky to authorize this particular operation. Having settled that, the Court invokes the doctrine of substituted judgment, holding that a court of equity has "the power to permit a kidney to be removed from an incompetent ward of the state upon petition of his committee [in effect, a guardian], who is also his mother, for the purpose of being transplanted into the body of his brother who is dying of fatal kidney disease."

In contrast, the Wisconsin Court rejects the doctrine of substituted judgment, but only after failing to find any benefit to the proposed incompetent donor, Richard Pescinski. The majority holds that "in the absence of real consent on [Pescinski's] part, and in a situation where no benefit to him has been established, we fail to find any authority for the county court, or this court, to approve this operation."

STRUNK v. STRUNK

Court of Appeals of Kentucky, 1969.
445 S.W. 2d 145.

OSBORNE, Judge.

The specific question involved upon this appeal is: Does a court of equity have the power to permit a kidney to be removed from an incompetent ward of the state upon petition of his committee, who is also his mother, for the purpose of being transplanted into the body of his brother, who is dying of a fatal kidney disease? We are of the opinion it does.

The facts of the case are as follows: Arthur L. Strunk, 54 years of age, and Ava Strunk, 52 years of age, of Williamstown, Kentucky, are the parents of two sons. Tommy Strunk is 28 years of age, married, an employee of the Penn State Railroad and a part-time student at the University of Cincinnati. Tommy is now suffering from chronic glomerulus nephritis, a fatal kidney disease. He is being kept alive by frequent treatment on an artificial kidney, a procedure which cannot be continued much longer.

Jerry Strunk is 27 years of age, incompetent, and through proper legal proceedings, has been committed to the Frankfort State Hospital and School, which is a state institution maintained for the feebleminded. He has an I.Q. of approximately 35, which corresponds with the mental age of approximately six years. He is further handicapped by a speech defect, which makes it difficult for him to communicate with persons who are not well acquainted with him. When it was determined that Tommy, in order to survive, would have to have a kidney the doctors considered the possibility of using a kidney from a cadaver if and when one became available or one from a live donor if this could be made available. The entire family, his mother, father and a number of collateral relatives were tested. Because of incompatability of blood type or tissue none were medically acceptable as live donors. As a last resort, Jerry was tested and found to be highly acceptable. This immediately presented the legal problem as to what, if anything, could be done by the family, especially the mother and the father to procure a transplant from Jerry to Tommy. The mother as a committee petitioned the county court for authority to proceed with the operation. The court found that the operation was necessary, that under the peculiar circumstances of this case it would not only be beneficial to Tommy but also beneficial to Jerry because Jerry was greatly dependent upon Tommy, emotionally and psychologically, and that his well-being would be jeopardized more severely by the loss of his brother than by the removal of a kidney.

Appeal was taken to the Franklin Circuit Court where the chancellor reviewed the record, examined the testimony of the witnesses and adopted the findings of the county court.

A psychiatrist, in attendance to Jerry, who testified in the case, stated in his opinion the death of Tommy under these circumstances would have "an extremely traumatic effect upon him" (Jerry).

The Department of Mental Health of this Commonwealth has entered the case as amicus curiae and on the basis of its evaluation of the seriousness of the operation as opposed to the traumatic effect upon Jerry as a result of the loss of Tommy, recommended to the court that Jerry be permitted to undergo the surgery. Its recommendations are as follows:

> "It is difficult for the mental defective to establish a firm sense of identity with another person and the acquisition of this necessary identity is dependent upon a person whom one can conveniently accept as a model and who at the same time is sufficiently flexible to allow the defective to detach himself with reassurances of continuity. His need to be social is not so much the necessity of a formal and mechanical contact with other human beings as it is the necessity of a close intimacy with other men, the desirability of a real community of feeling, an urgent need for a unity of understanding. Purely mechanical and formal contact with other men does not offer any treatment for the behavior of a mental defective; only those who are able to communicate intimately are of value to hospital treatment in these cases. And this generally is a member of the family.
>
> "In view of this knowledge, we now have particular interest in this case. Jerry Strunk, a mental defective, has emotions and reactions on a scale comparable to that of a normal person. He identifies with his brother Tom; Tom is his model, his tie with his family. Tom's life is vital to the continuity of Jerry's improvement at Frankfort State Hospital and School. The testimony of the hospital representative reflected the importance to Jerry of his visits with his family and the constant inquiries Jerry made about Tom's coming to see him. Jerry is aware he plays a role in the relief of this tension. We the Department of Mental Health must take all possible steps to prevent the occurrence of any guilt feelings Jerry would have if Tom were to die.
>
> "The necessity of Tom's life to Jerry's treatment and eventual rehabilitation is clearer in view of the fact that Tom is his only living sibling and at the death of their parents, now in their fifties, Jerry will have no concerned, intimate communication so necessary to his stability and optimal functioning.
>
> "The evidence shows that at the present level of medical knowledge, it is quite remote that Tom would be able to survive several cadaver transplants. Tom has a much better chance of survival if the kidney transplant from Jerry takes place."

Upon this appeal we are faced with the fact that all members of the immediate family have recommended the transplant. The Department of Mental Health has likewise made its recommendation. The county court has given its approval. The circuit court has found that it would be to the best interest of the ward of the state that the procedure be carried out. Throughout the legal proceedings, Jerry has been represented by a guardian ad litem, who has continually questioned the power of the state to authorize the removal of an organ from the body of an incompetent who is a ward of the state. We are fully cognizant of the fact that the question before us is unique. Insofar as we have been able to learn, no similar set of facts has come before the highest court of any of the states of this nation or the federal courts. The English courts have apparently taken a broad view of the inherent power of the equity courts with regard to incompetents. Ex parte Whitebread (1816), 2 Mer. 99; 35 E.R. 878, L.C. holds that courts of equity have the inherent power to make provisions for a needy brother out of the estate of an incompetent. This was first followed in this country in New York, In the Matter of Willoughby, a Lunatic, 11 Paige 257 (NY 1844). The inherent rule in these cases is that the chancellor has the power to deal with the estate of the incompetent in the same manner as the incompetent would if he had his faculties. This rule has been extended to cover not only matters of property but also to cover the personal affairs of the incompetent. 27 Am.Jur.2, Equity, § 69, p. 592, as follows:

> "It is a universal rule of equity that where a person is not equal to protecting himself in a particular case, the court will protect him. As part of the inherent power of equity, a court of equity has full and complete jurisdiction over the persons of those who labor under any legal disability and also over their property. While the general control over such persons has very generally been transferred by statute to probate courts, it does not follow, unless the equity court has been definitely shorn of power, that equity jurisdiction thereover may no longer be exercised. Where legal disability of the individual is shown, the jurisdiction of the court is plenary and potent to afford whatever relief may be necessary to protect his interests and preserve his estates. The court's action in such a case is not limited by any narrow bounds, but is empowered to stretch forth its arm in whatever direction its aid and protection may be needed. While this is indeed a special exercise of equity jurisdiction, it is beyond question that by virtue thereof the court may pass upon purely personal rights.
>
> "With regard to the origin and source of equity jurisdiction, the doctrine now commonly maintained is that it represents a delegation to the chancellor of the Crown's right as parens patriae to interfere in particular cases for the benefit of such persons as are incapable of protecting themselves, that such jurisdiction belonged to the High Court of Chancery and was exercised by it from its first establishment, and that the jurisdiction exists in the United States by inheritance from the English court, and not because equitable rights or titles are involved."

The right to act for the incompetent in all cases has become recognized in this country as the doctrine of substituted judgment and is broad enough not only to cover property but also to cover all matters touching on the well-being of the ward. The doctrine has been recognized in American courts since 1844.

"The 'doctrine of substituted judgment,' which apparently found its first expression in the leading English case of Ex parte Whitebread (1816) 2 Meriv 99, 35 Eng Reprint 878 (Ch), supra § 3(a), was amplified in Re Earl of Carysfort (1840) Craig & Ph 76, 41 Eng Reprint 418, where the principle was made to apply to one who was not next of kin of the lunatic but a servant of his who was obliged to retire from his service by reason of age and infirmity. The Lord Chancellor permitted the allowance of an annuity out of the income of the estate of the lunatic earl as a retiring pension to the latter's aged personal servant, although no supporting evidence could be found, the court being 'satisfied that the Earl of Carysfort would have approved if he had been capable of acting himself.' " Annot., 24 A.L.R.3d 863 (1969).

In this state we have delegated substantial powers to committees of persons of unsound minds, see KRS 387.230 and KRS 387.060, and to county courts in their supervision. However, as pointed out in American Jurisprudence, these statutes were not intended to divest the equity courts of their inherent common law powers. These powers we have continued to exercise in spite of the jurisdiction granted to the county courts. See Pearl v. M'Dowell (1830) 26 Ky. (3JJ Marsh) 658; Dalton v. Dalton (1916) 172 Ky. 585, 189 S.W. 902; Casebier v. Casebier (1921) 193 Ky. 490, 236 S.W. 966; Polivick v. Polivick (1935) 259 Ky. 653, 83 S.W.2d 8; Arms' Committee v. Arms (1935) 260 Ky. 634, 86 S.W.2d 542; Thomasson v. Thomasson (1949) 310 Ky. 234, 219 S.W.2d 957.

The medical practice of transferring tissue from one part of the human body to another (autografting) and from one human being to another (homografting) is rapidly becoming a common clinical practice. In many cases the transplants take as well where the tissue is dead as when it is alive. This has made practicable the establishment of tissue banks where such material can be stored for future use. Vascularized grafts of lungs, kidneys and hearts are becoming increasingly common. These grafts must be of functioning, living cells with blood vessels remaining anatomically intact. The chance of success in the transfer of these organs is greatly increased when the donor and the donee are genetically related. It is recognized by all legal and medical authorities that several legal problems can arise as a result of the operative techniques of the transplant procedure. Curran, A Problem of Consent: Kidney Transplantation in Minors, 34 N.Y. University Law Review 891, (1959).

The renal transplant is becoming the most common of the organ transplants. This is because the normal body has two functioning kidneys, one of which it can reasonably do without, thereby making it possible for one person to donate a kidney to another. Testimony in this record shows that there have been over 2500 kidney transplants performed in the United States up to this date. The process can be effected under present techniques with minimal danger to both the donor and the donee. Doctors Hamburger and Crosneir describe the risk to the donor as follows:

"This discussion is limited to renal transplantation, since it is inconceivable that any vital organ other than the kidney might ever be removed from a healthy living donor for transplantation purposes. The immediate operative risk of unilateral nephrectomy in a healthy subject has been calculated as approximately 0.05 per cent. The long-term risk is more difficult to estimate, since the various types of renal disease do not appear to be more frequent or more severe in individuals with solitary kidneys than in normal subjects. On the other hand, the development of surgical problems, trauma, or neoplasms, with the possible necessity of nephrectomy, do increase the long-term risks in living donors; the long-term risk, on this basis, has been estimated at 0.07 per cent (Hamburger et al., 1964). These data must, however, be considered in the light of statistical life expectancy which, in a healthy 35 year old adult, goes from 99.3 percent to 99.1 per cent during the next five succeeding years; this is an increase in risk equal to that incurred by driving a car for 16 miles every working day (Merrill, 1964). The risks incurred by the donor are therefore very limited, but they are a reality, even if, until now, there have been no reports of complications endangering the life of a donor anywhere in the world. Unfortunately, there is no doubt that, as the number of renal transplants increase, such an incident will inevitably be recorded."[1]

Review of our case law leads us to believe that the power given to a committee under KRS 387.230 would not extend so far as to allow a committee to subject his ward to the serious surgical techniques here under consideration unless the life of his ward be in jeopardy. Nor do we believe the powers delegated to the county court by virtue of the above statutes would reach so far as to permit the procedure which we are dealing with here.

We are of the opinion that a chancery court does have sufficient inherent power to authorize the operation. The circuit court having found that the operative procedures in this instance are to the best interest of Jerry Strunk and this finding having been based upon substantial evidence, we are of the opinion the judgment should be affirmed. We do not deem it significant that this case reached the circuit court by way of appeal as opposed to a direct proceeding in that court.

Judgment affirmed.

HILL, C. J., MILLIKEN and REED, JJ., concur.

NEIKIRK, PALMORE and STEINFELD, JJ., dissent.

STEINFELD, Judge (dissenting).

Apparently because of my indelible recollection of a government which, to the everlasting shame of its citizens, embarked on a program of genocide and experimentation with human bodies I have been more troubled in reaching a decision in this case than in any other. My sympathies and emotions are torn between a compassion to aid an ailing young man and a duty to fully protect unfortunate members of society.

The opinion of the majority is predicated upon the authority of an equity court to speak for one who cannot speak for himself. However, it is my opinion that in considering such right in this instance we must first look to the power and authority vested in the committee, the appellee herein. KRS 387.060 and KRS 387.230 do nothing more than give the committee the power to take custody of the incompetent and the possession, care and management of his property. Courts have restricted the activities of the committee to that which is for the best interest of the incompetent. Harding's Adm'r v. Harding's Ex'r., 140 Ky. 277, 130 S.W. 1098 (1910); Miller v. Keown, 176 Ky. 117, 195 S.W. 430 (1912) and 3 A.L.R. 3d 18. The authority and duty have been to protect and maintain the ward, to secure that to which he is entitled and preserve that which he has. Ramsey's Ex'r v. Ramsey, 243 Ky. 202, 47 S.W.2d 1059 (1932); Aaronson v. State of New York, 34 Misc.2d 827, 229 N.Y.S.2d 550, 557 (1962) and Young v. State, 32 Misc.2d 965, 225 N.Y.S.2d 549 (1962). The wishes of the members of the family or the desires of the guardian to be helpful to the apparent objects of the ward's bounty have not been a criterion. "A curator or guardian cannot dispose of his ward's property by donation, even though authorized to do so by the court on advice of a family meeting, unless a gift by the guardian is authorized by statute." 44 C.J.S. Insane Persons § 81, p. 191.

Two Kentucky cases decided many years ago reveal judicial policy. In W. T. Sistrunk & Co. v. Navarra's Committee, 268 Ky. 753, 105 S.W.2d 1039 (1937), this court held that a committee was without right to continue a business which the incompetent had operated prior to his having been declared a person of unsound mind. More analogous is Baker v. Thomas, 272 Ky. 605, 114 S.W.2d 1113 (1938), in which a man and woman had lived together out of wedlock. Two children were born to them. After the man was adjudged incompetent, his committee, acting for him, together with his paramour, instituted proceedings to adopt the two children. In rejecting the application and refusing to speak for the incompetent the opinion stated:

> "The statute does not contemplate that the committee of a lunatic may exercise any other power than to have the possession, care, and management of the lunatic's or incompetent's estate. No authority is given by any statute to which our attention has been called, or that we have been by careful research able to locate, giving the committee of a lunatic or an incompetent authority to petition any court for the adoption of a person or persons as heirs capable of the inheritance of his or her estate."

The same result was reached in In re Bourgeois, 144 La. 501, 80 So. 673 (1919), in which the husband of an incompetent wife sought to change the beneficiary of her insurance policy so that her children would receive the proceeds. Grady v. Dashiell, 24 Wash.2d 272, 163 P.2d 922 (1945), stands for the proposition that a loan to the ward's adult insolvent son made at a time when it was thought that the ward was incurably insane constituted an improper depletion of the ward's estate.

The majority opinion is predicated upon the finding of the circuit court that there will be psychological benefits to the ward but points out that the incompetent has the mentality of a six-year-old child. It is common knowledge beyond dispute that the loss of a close relative or a friend to a six-year-old child is not of major impact. Opinions concerning psychological trauma are at best most nebulous. Furthermore, there are no guarantees that the transplant will become a surgical success, it being well known that body rejection of transplanted organs is frequent. The life of the incompetent is not in danger, but the surgical procedure advocated creates some peril.

It is written in Prince v. Massachusetts, 321 U.S. 158, 64 S.Ct. 438, 88 L.Ed. 645 (1944), that "Parents may be free to become martyrs themselves. But it does not follow they are free, in identical circumstances, to make martyrs of their children, before they have reached the age of full and legal discretion when they can make that choice for themselves." The ability to fully understand and consent is a prerequisite to the donation of a part of the human body. Cf. Bonner v. Moran, 75 U.S.App.D.C. 156, 126 F.2d 121, 139 A.L.R. 1366 (1941), in which a fifteen-year-old infant's consent to removal of a skin patch for the benefit of another was held legally ineffective.

Unquestionably the attitudes and attempts of the committee and members of the family of the two young men whose critical problems now confront us are commendable, natural and beyond reproach. However, they refer us to nothing indicating that they are privileged to authorize the removal of one of the kidneys of the incompetent for the purpose of donation, and they cite no statutory or other authority vesting such right in the courts. The proof shows that less compatible donors are available and that the kidney of a cadaver could be used, although the odds of operational success are not as great in such case as they would be with the fully compatible donor brother.

I am unwilling to hold that the gates should be open to permit the removal of an organ from an incompetent for transplant, at least until such time as it is conclusively demonstrated that it will be of significant benefit to the incompetent. The evidence here does not rise to that pinnacle. To hold that committees, guardians or courts have such awesome power even in the persuasive case before us, could establish legal precedent, the dire result of which we cannot fathom. Regretfully I must say no.

Neikirk and Palmore, JJ., join with me in this dissent.

NOTE

1. Hamburger and Crosneir, Moral and Ethical Problems in Transplantation, in HUMAN TRANSPLANTATION 37, (Rapaport and Dausset ed. 1968).

In Re Guardianship of Pescinski

Supreme Court of Wisconsin, 1975.
67 Wis.2d 4, 226 N.W.2d 180.

WILKIE, Chief Justice.

Does a county court have the power to order an operation to be performed to remove a kidney of an incompetent ward, under guardianship of the person, and transfer it to a sister where the dire need of the transfer is established but where no consent has been given by the incompetent or his guardian *ad litem,* nor has any benefit to the ward been shown?

That is the issue presented on appeal here. The trial court held that it did not have that power and we agree. The appellant, Janice Pescinski Lausier, on her own petition, was appointed guardian of the person of her brother, the respondent, Richard Pescinski. In 1958, Richard was declared incompetent and was committed to Winnebago State Hospital. He has been a committed mental patient since that date, classified as a schizophrenic, chronic, catatonic type.

On January 31, 1974, Janice Pescinski Lausier petitioned for permission to Dr. H. M. Kauffman to conduct tests to determine whether Richard Pescinski was a suitable donor for a kidney transplant for the benefit of his sister, Elaine Jeske. Elaine had both kidneys surgically removed in 1970 because she was suffering from kidney failure diagnosed as chronic glomerulonephritis. In order to sustain her life, she was put on a dialysis machine, which functions as an artificial kidney. Because of the deterioration of Elaine, the petition contended that a kidney transplant was needed. Subsequent tests were completed establishing that Richard was a suitable donor, and a hearing was then held on the subject of whether permission should be granted to perform the transplant. The guardian *ad litem* would not give consent to the transplant and the county court held that it did not have the power to give consent for the operation.

At the time of the hearing Elaine was thirty-eight and her brother Richard was thirty-nine. Evidence was produced at the hearing that the other members of the Pescinski family had been ruled out as possible donors on the basis of either age or health. The father, aged seventy, and the mother, aged sixty-seven, were eliminated as possible donors by Dr. Kauffman because, as a matter of principle, he would not perform the operation on a donor over sixty. A similar rationale was applied by Dr. Kauffman as to all of the six minor children of Elaine, the doctor concluding that he "would not personally use their kidneys" as a matter of his "own moral conviction." Mrs. Jeske's sister, Mrs. Lausier, was excluded as a donor because she had diabetes. Another brother, Ralph Pescinski, testified that he was forty-three years old, had been married twenty years and had ten children, nine of whom remained at home. He is a dairy farmer and did not care to be a donor because there would be nobody to take over his farm and he felt he had a duty to his family to refuse. He further testified that he had a stomach disorder which required a special diet and had a rupture on his left side. He had been to see Dr. Capati at the Neillsville Clinic, who told him he should not get involved and that his family should come first.

The testimony showed that Richard was suffering from schizophrenia—catatonic type—and that while he was in contact with his environment there was marked indifference in his behavior. Dr. Hoffman, the medical director at the Good Samaritan Home, West Bend, Wisconsin, testified that in layman's terms Richard's mental disease was a flight from reality. He estimated Richard's mental capacity to be age twelve. No evidence in the record indicates that Richard consented to the transplant. Absent that consent, there is no question that the trial court's conclusion that it had no power to approve the operation must be sustained.

[1] "A guardian of the person has the care of the ward's person and must look to the latter's health, education, and support."[1] The guardian must act, if at all, "loyally in the best interests of his ward."[2] There is absolutely no evidence here that any interests of the ward will be served by the transplant.

[2] As far as the court's own power to authorize the operation, we are satisfied that the law in Wisconsin is clearly to the contrary. There is no statutory authority given the county court to authorize a kidney transplant or any other surgical procedure on a living person. We decline to adopt the concept of "substituted judgment" which was specifically approved by the Kentucky Court of Appeals in Strunk v. Strunk.[3] In that case, the Kentucky court held a court of equity had the power to permit the removal of a kidney from an incompetent ward of the state upon the petition of his committee who was also his mother. Apparently a committee in Kentucky is like a guardian in this state. The Kentucky Court of Appeals authorized the operation based on the application of the doctrine of substituted judgment. However, the court also held that neither the committee nor the county court had the power to authorize the operation, in the absence of a showing that the life of the ward was in jeopardy—only the Court of Appeals had the power. In the instant case the county court had no power to authorize the procedure, and the question is whether this supreme court can by using the doctrine of substituted judgment.

[3] As the dissenting opinion in Strunk v. Strunk points out, "substituted judgment" is nothing more than an application of the maxim that equity will speak for one who cannot speak for himself. Historically, the substituted judgment doctrine was used to allow gifts of the property of an incompetent. If applied literally, it would allow a trial court, or this court, to change the designation on a life insurance policy or make an election for an incompetent widow, without the requirement of a statute authorizing these acts and contrary to prior decisions of this court.[4]

We conclude that the doctrine should not be adopted in this state.

We, therefore, must affirm the lower court's decision that it was without power to approve the operation, and we further decide that there is no such power in this court. An incompetent particularly should have his own interests protected. Certainly no advantage should be taken of him. In the absence of real consent on his part, and in a situation where no benefit to him has been established, we fail to find any authority for the county court, or this court, to approve this operation.

Order affirmed. No costs on this appeal.

DAY, Justice (dissenting).

I would reverse the decision in this case. The majority of the court holds that in the absence of a showing of "benefit" to the incompetent in this case or proof of consent on his part, the trial court and this court lack authority to authorize a kidney transplant operation to be performed on him to save the life of his sister. I disagree.

I think the court as a court of equity does have authority to permit the kidney transplant operation requested in the petition of the guardian of Richard Pescinski. I agree with the reasoning of the Court of Appeals of the state of Kentucky wherein that court said:

> "The specific question involved upon this appeal is: Does a court of equity have the power to permit a kidney to be removed from an incompetent ward of the state upon petition of his committee, who is also his mother, for the purpose of being transplanted into the body of his brother, who is dying of a fatal kidney disease? We are of the opinion it does." Strunk v. Strunk (Ky.1969), 445 S.W.2d 145, 35 A.L.R.3d 683.

That case involved the authorization of a transplant from a 27-year-old incompetent to his 28-year-old brother. The court in that case did find, based on the testimony of a psychiatrist, that while the incompetent had the mental age of six, it would be of benefit to him to keep his brother alive so that his brother could visit him on occasion; I would regard this as pretty thin soup on which to base a decision as to whether or not the donee is to be permitted to live. In the case before us, if the incompetent brother should happily recover from his mental illness, he would undoubtedly be happy to learn that the transplant of one of his kidneys to his sister saved her life. This at least would be a normal response and hence the transplant is not without benefit to him.

The guardian ad litem for the incompetent in this case has interposed strong objection to the transplant from Richard Pescinski to his sister, who at the time of the determination, was a 39-year-old mother of six minor children and who, as we were informed on February 24th at the time of oral arguments, in attempting to live on a bi-weekly "washing" of her blood through a kidney dialysis machine has now deteriorated to the point of confinement in a wheelchair. We were advised that without a kidney transplant death for her is quite imminent. The brother, on the other hand, the incompetent is in good health. The medical testimony is that the removal of one of his kidneys would be of minimal risk to him and that he would function normally on one kidney for the rest of his natural life, as do thousands of others in similar circumstances. The guardian ad litem argues strenuously that for us to permit this transplant is to bring back memories of the Dachau concentration camp in Nazi Germany and medical experiments on unwilling subjects, many of whom died or were horribly maimed. I fail to see the analogy—this is not an experiment conducted by mad doctors but a well-known and accepted surgical procedure necessitated in this case to save the life of the incompetent's sister. Such a transplant would be authorized, not by a group of doctors operating behind a barbed-wire stockade but only after a full hearing in an American court of law. To avoid the concerns expressed by the guardian ad litem, there are certain definite standards which could and should be imposed. First of all, a strong showing should be made that without the kidney transplant the proposed donee or recipient stands to suffer death. This is certainly the evidence here. Secondly, that reasonable steps have been taken to try and acquire a kidney from other sources and the record is clear that such attempt was made here. Because of the fact that the donee has had six children, she has built up certain chemical resistance to the receipt of foreign tissue into her body which can be overcome only by a transplant from one close to her by blood such as a brother or sister. The testimony showed the impracticality of acquiring a kidney from either her other brother or her sister. No suitable kidney from a cadaver has been found since her kidneys were removed in 1970. The next showing that should be made is that the incompetent proposed-donor is closely related by blood to the proposed donee, such as a brother or sister, which of course is the case here. Showing should be made that the donor, if competent, would most probably consent because of the normal ties of family. Here, the trial court specifically found "... the conclusion would appear to be inescapable that the ward [the incompetent proposed-donor] would so consent and that such authorization should be granted."[5] Another showing should be that the proposed incompetent-donor is in good health and that was shown here. And lastly, that the operation is one of minimal risk to the donor and that the donor could function normally on one kidney following such operation. The medical testimony is all to the effect that the donor would undergo minimal risk and would be able to function normally on one kidney. In fact, the testimony is that a person can function on as little as one tenth of one normal kidney.

With these guidelines the fear expressed that institutions for the mentally ill will merely become storehouses for spare parts for people on the outside is completely unjustified. I agree with the trial court that if the brother here were competent in all probability he would be willing to consent to the transplant to save his sister's life. For him it would be a short period of discomfort which would not affect his ability either to enjoy life or his longevity.

The majority opinion says there is no showing of consent by the incompetent. Dr. William C. P. Hoffman, medical director of the Good Samaritan Home where the incompetent is a patient, testified that one with the mental condition of the incompetent has no lucid intervals and that his reasoning is completely impaired in making decisions. The doctor testified the incompetent would not be aware of what the proceedings involved and testified the incompetent is "insane seven days a week." From such a record it is difficult to see how one could ever get a meaningful "consent" from the incompetent in this case.

The majority opinion would forever condemn the incompetent to be always a receiver, a taker, but never a giver. For in holding that only those things which financially or physically benefit the incompetent may be done by the court, he is forever excluded from doing the decent thing, the charitable thing. The British courts have not so held. Two British cases cited in *Strunk* permitted the estate of an incompetent to provide a pension for a faithful servant in one instance and in another to help an indigent brother—this by the device known as "substituted judgment" where the court in effect does for the incompetent what it is sure he would do himself if he had the power to act. This approach gives the incompetent the benefit of the doubt, endows him with the finest qualities of his humanity, assumes the goodness of his nature instead of assuming the opposite.

The equities in this case favor taking the action which may save this mother's life.

NOTES

1. 39 Am.Jur.2d, Guardian and Ward, p.60, sec.68.

2. Guardianship of Nelson (1963), 21 Wis.2d 24, 32, 123 N.W.2d 505, 509. *Cf* sec. 880.19(5)(b), Stats.

3. (Ky.1969), 445 S.W.2d 145.

4. Kay v. Erickson (1932), 209 Wis.147, 244 N.W. 625; Van Steenwyck v. Washburn (1884), 59 Wis. 483, 17 N.W. 289.

5. The trial court concluded, however, that such an authorization would be analogous to giving away an incompetent's property and since there was no "benefit" to him the court had no authority to act.

VII. GENETICS

1. THE ETHICAL ISSUES

The understanding of genetics has increased markedly since the dramatic discovery of the structure of DNA by Watson and Crick in 1953. The technique of recombinant DNA has opened new doors in genetic engineering. Other technologies have had dramatic impacts on human reproduction, especially amniocentesis and *in vitro,* or test-tube, fertilization. Yet many social dilemmas surround the application of this new knowledge of genetics.

The *Buck* case discusses the relation of the state and individual, especially with respect to the demands the state can make on the individual. Holmes argues that the state can demand sacrifices of its citizens, which is the basis of the state's exercising its police power or its *parens patriae* power to coerce citizens, to enforce conformity to law, and so forth. Holmes distinguishes, however, between the "best" citizens and "those who sap the strength of the state." He argues that since the state can require the "best" to sacrifice their lives in war, surely lesser sacrifices, such as giving up one's reproductive capacities, can be demanded "to prevent our being swamped with incompetents." One can wonder whether the state has really asked the "best" to sacrifice in any significant way. Draft laws, for example, have always allowed the "best" either to avoid service or to serve in safe surroundings. Some have argued that tax laws favor the wealthy, a typical index of belonging to the "best," so that often they pay few or no taxes. The conclusion that some should be sterilized to prevent our being overrun with incompetents is neither a necessary nor exclusive conclusion. It could follow that this class of citizens should be protected by the state or enrolled in special training programs.

Holmes also rejects a right for these classes of individuals to refuse treatment and bases this on references to compulsory vaccination rulings. While vaccination is a violation of one's bodily integrity, it is neither a surgical intervention with a mortality risk, many would argue, nor an irreversible procedure. Neither does mental retardation constitute a danger to public safety or welfare. Thus Holmes proceeds from a reasonable public health argument used to justify a minor bodily invasion to an irreversible surgical intervention for a problem that does not create a public health danger.

Research into specific genetic syndromes, such as the XYY that some claim is associated with lower intelligence and aggression, has caused many controversies in both the conducting of the research and in the social applications of the results. Although freedom of inquiry has wide support in our general value system, the advisability of research into topics that might prove embarrassing to specific racial groups or that might suggest doubtful public policies is questionable. If research into the XYY syndrome confirms aggressive behavior in individuals with the syndrome, these individuals might experience discrimination and be denied opportunities available to others. Even if research did not confirm such behavior, individuals with the characteristics of the syndrome could still be discriminated against because of labelling.

The protection of subjects is also important in such research. In infant screening programs, for example, it is obvious that the infants cannot consent; the parents must give proxy consent. If, however, the parents are fully informed of the nature of the study, such knowledge could influence the research results. For example, if one explained to the parents that one purpose of the study was to test for a relation between the XYY syndrome and aggressive behavior, the parents might treat the child in such a way that he or she would behave aggressively. But if the parents do not know this, do they have the information on which to base consent?

These concerns point to another dimension: the social uses to which this knowledge could be put. It is possible that new genetic research could be used to support a new eugenics movement in which those with genetic anomalies would be at a disadvantage. Pressure could be placed on individuals who are carriers of socially unacceptable genes to restrict their reproduction or to refrain from it altogether.

The growing acceptance of amniocentesis to diagnose genetic diseases *in utero* has given rise to many dilemmas. One arises when, occasionally, a mother is either not informed of the availability of such a diagnostic procedure or is not informed of all the findings. When the birth of an afflicted child follows, a number of consequences are possible. The most problematic of these are suits for wrongful birth and wrongful life. In the latter, the allegation is that nonexistence is preferable to an existence with birth anomalies. Such a suit clearly focuses on the quality-of-life argument as a basis for making decisions in a medical context.

While most will grant that quality of life is an important consideration, many will not grant that nonexistence is preferable to existence with a diminished quality. Life is such a precious good and fundamental value that it must be prized and nourished even when its particular quality may be poor. This view accepts biological life as the highest value, since it is the *sine qua non* of everything else. But others argue that while life itself is important, it has meaning only insofar as it allows other important human values to mature and flourish. Without these, life is meaningless.

Typically courts have not favored quality-of-life arguments. Many assume that most people would generally choose life with defects rather than no life at all. The hesitancy of courts in the face of such momentous decisions is understandable; yet one should be aware of the strength of the arguments of the other position. Both positions have weaknesses that will not be resolved if argued only from unexamined assumptions.

2. THE LEGAL ISSUES

The cases in this section address the issue of genetics, yet lend themselves to at least two classifications: (1) hereditary mental illness or retardation, and (2) hereditary birth defects.

In its 1927 *Buck* decision, the United States Supreme Court accepts the concept of inherited mental abnormality as scientific fact, which then becomes the basis for upholding a Virginia statute providing for sterilization of institutionalized wards of the state "who shall be found to be affected with an hereditary form of insanity or imbecility." Also without much hesitation the Court rejects the argument so persuasive in present-day medico-legal cases that the Due Process Clause of the Fourteenth Amendment includes protection of the bodily integrity or privacy of the mentally ill or retarded. *Buck* remains "good law."

In 1975 the New York Supreme Court in *Yukl* disallows the use of XYY syndrome evidence to support a criminal defense claim of hereditary insanity. Rejection is clearly grounded in the Court's conclusion that XYY scientific data fail to reach the necessary standards of acceptance and reliability in either the scientific or legal communities.

Indeed, the *Buck* and *Yukl* decisions both reflect the fact that the law is very much influenced by the degree of sophistication in scientific claims having to do with human genetics.

Respecting hereditary birth defects, the *Berman* decision reflects a refusal to recognize a tort for "wrongful life" that would allow an infant to recover damages for her mongoloid condition. The Supreme Court of New Jersey asserts that being brought into existence does not give rise to an action cognizable at law: "life—whether experienced with or without a major physical handicap—is more precious than non-life," says the Court. On the other hand, the case also gives recognition to legal action founded upon "wrongful birth" if the Court finds, as it does here, that the mother of the deformed child had been deprived of the opportunity to make a "meaningful" decision to abort. Respecting the measure of allowable damages, the Court holds that it be limited to the mental and emotional anguish the parents have suffered and will continue to suffer due to their child's condition.

BUCK V. BELL

Supreme Court of the United States, 1927.
274 U.S. 200, 47 S.Ct. 584, 71 L.Ed. 1000.

MR. JUSTICE HOLMES delivered the opinion of the Court.

This is a writ of error to review a judgment of the Supreme Court of Appeals of the State of Virginia, affirming a judgment of the Circuit Court of Amherst County, by which the defendant in error, the superintendent of the State Colony for Epileptics and Feeble Minded, was ordered to perform the operation of salpingectomy upon Carrie Buck, the plaintiff in error, for the purpose of making her sterile. 143 Va. 310. The case comes here upon the contention that the statute authorizing the judgment is void under the Fourteenth Amendment as denying to the plaintiff in error due process of law and the equal protection of the laws.

Carrie Buck is a feeble minded white woman who was committed to the State Colony above mentioned in due form. She is the daughter of a feeble minded mother in the same institution, and the mother of an illegitimate feeble minded child. She was eighteen years old at the time of the trial of her case in the Circuit Court, in the latter part of 1924. An Act of Virginia, approved March 20, 1924, recites that the health of the patient and the welfare of society may be promoted in certain cases by the sterilization of mental defectives, under careful safeguard, &c.; that the sterilization may be effected in males by vasectomy and in females by salpingectomy, without serious pain or substantial danger to life; that the Commonwealth is supporting in various institutions many defective persons who if now discharged would become a menace but if incapable of procreating might be discharged with safety and become self-supporting with benefit to themselves and society; and that experience has shown that heredity plays an important part in the transmission of insanity, imbecility, &c. The statute then enacts that whenever the superintendent of certain institutions including the above named State Colony shall be of opinion that it is for the best interests of the patients and of society that an inmate under his care should be sexually sterilized, he may have the operation performed upon any patient afflicted with hereditary forms of insanity, imbecility, &c., on complying with the very careful provisions by which the act protects the patients from possible abuse.

The superintendent first presents a petition to the special board of directors of his hospital or colony, stating the facts and the grounds for his opinion, verified by affidavit. Notice of the petition and of the time and place of the hearing in the institution is to be served upon the inmate, and also upon his guardian, and if there is no guardian the superintendent is to apply to the Circuit Court of the County to appoint one. If the inmate is a minor notice also is to be given to his parents if any with a copy of the petition. The board is to see to it that the inmate may attend the hearings if desired by him or his guardian. The evidence is all to be reduced to writing, and after the board has made its order for or against the operation, the superintendent, or the inmate, or his guardian, may appeal to the Circuit Court of the County. The Circuit Court may consider the record of the board and the evidence before it and such other admissible evidence as may be offered, and may affirm, revise, or reverse the order of the board and enter such order as it deems just. Finally any party may apply to the Supreme Court of Appeals, which, if it grants the appeal, is to hear the case upon the record of the trial in the Circuit Court and may enter such order as it thinks the Circuit Court should have entered. There can be no doubt that so far as procedure is concerned the rights of the patient are most carefully considered, and as every step in this case was taken in scrupulous compliance with the statute and after months of observation, there is no doubt that in that respect the plaintiff in error has had due process of law.

The attack is not upon the procedure but upon the substantive law. It seems to be contended that in no circumstances could such an order be justified. It certainly is contended that the order cannot be justified upon the existing grounds. The judgment finds the facts that have been recited and that Carrie Buck "is the probable potential parent of socially inadequate offspring, likewise afflicted, that she may be sexually sterilized without detriment to her general health and that her welfare and that of society will be promoted by her sterilization," and thereupon makes the order. In view of the general declarations of the legislature and the specific findings of the Court, obviously we cannot say as matter of law that the grounds do not exist, and if they exist they justify the result. We have seen more than once that the public welfare may call upon the best citizens for their lives. It would be strange if it could not call upon those who already sap the strength of the State for these lesser sacrifices, often not felt to be such by those concerned, in order to prevent our being swamped with incompetents. It is better for all the world, if instead of waiting to execute degenerate offspring for crime, or to let them starve for their imbecility, society can prevent those who are manifestly unfit from continuing their kind. The principle that sustains compulsory vaccination is broad enough to cover cutting the Fallopian tubes. Jacobson v. Massachusetts, 197 U.S. 11. Three generations of imbeciles are enough.

But, it is said, however it might be if this reasoning were applied generally, it fails when it is confined to the small number who are in the institutions named and is not applied to the multitudes outside. It is the usual last resort of constitutional arguments to point out shortcomings of this sort. But the answer is that the law does all that is needed when it does all that it can, indicates a policy, applies it to all within the lines, and seeks to bring within the lines all similarly situated so far and so fast as its means allow. Of course so far as the operations enable those who otherwise must be kept confined to be returned to the world, and thus open the asylum to others, the equality aimed at will be more nearly reached.

Judgment affirmed.

MR. JUSTICE BUTLER dissents.

PEOPLE V. YUKL

Supreme Court, Trial Term, New York County, 1975.
83 Misc.2d 364, 372 N.Y.S.2d 313.

JOSEPH A. MARTINIS, Justice:

Defendant, charged with murder, has, through his counsel, submitted an omnibus motion with several branches, all of which, with the exception of two, have already been determined.

The court reserved decision on the remaining two branches because each of them raised questions of law and considerations of policy that required an extended research and analysis of the issues presented and the arguments made.

The first of these, in order that they will be considered, requests a bifurcated trial for the defendant; and, the second, the appointment of a cytogeneticist to conduct chromosomal tests of defendant's blood.

MOTION FOR A BIFURCATED TRIAL

[1] The defendant, Charles Yukl, has been indicted and charged with the murder of twenty-three-year-old Karen Schlegel. The alleged crime is said to have occurred on the night of August 19, 1974, in the defendant's apartment while the defendant's wife was temporarily away. The body of the deceased was discovered in a state of disarray shortly thereafter on the roof of defendant's apartment house.

The defendant had been involved in a similar brutal killing in 1966, for which he was convicted, sentenced and eventually released on parole in 1973 from Walkill State Prison.

It appears that the defendant intends to interpose an insanity defense. The psychiatric testimony adduced from defense experts will, of necessity, rest heavily on the defendant's prior violent behavior, in particular the 1966 brutal killing of Susan Reynolds. In addition, there may be potentially damaging admissions made by the defendant during the course of the psychiatric examination, which the defense would seek to use solely to establish defendant's mental incapacity at the time of the crime.

The defendant has made a motion for a bifurcated trial on the issues of guilt and insanity. In order to avoid what he claims is the inherent prejudice that would result from the introduction of testimony with respect to the 1966 killing and any admissions made to the psychiatrists, the defendant has requested that the issue of insanity be tried first to a separate jury, and then, should defendant be found sane, another jury will determine if the defendant is guilty of the crime as charged.

The questions that this court must determine are whether bifurcation is a necessary procedure under these circumstances and, secondly, whether it is a proper procedure under the law.

The concept of a bifurcated trial whereby the issues of culpability and mental capacity are tried sequentially is often put forth as a curative procedure to remedy problems similar to those posed by the defendant herein. Thus with ever-increasing frequency defendants similarly situated have been challenging the traditional procedures by which an insanity defense is raised and determined.

No court has yet accepted the argument that the concept of a bifurcated trial is a constitutional right that inures to a defendant in any given case (Murphy v. Florida, 495 F.2d 553 [5th Cir., 1974]; United States v. Huff, 409 F.2d 1225 [5th Cir.], cert. den., 396 U.S. 857, 90 S.Ct. 123, 24 L.Ed.2d 108 [1969]; Simpson v. State, 275 A.2d 794 [Del., 1971]; Commonwealth v. Bumpus, 290 N.E.2d 167 [Mass., 1972]). In this jurisdiction, an appeal was urged on the ground that the defendant should have been granted a bifurcated trial. The Court of Appeals in People v. Staten, 28 N.Y.2d 904, 322 N.Y.S.2d 732, 271 N.E.2d 563, affirmed the conviction without opinion, where the People had contended there was no constitutional right to a bifurcated trial.

However, the concept of a two-staged trial where a defendant raises the defense of insanity has not been totally discarded and, indeed, some of the courts believe that there may be good cause for its adoption in given instances. Three of our states—California, Colorado and Texas—have adopted such a procedure by statute.

However, the procedure, whether prescribed by a court through its inherent powers or by statute, is not feasibly workable. To dichotomize the two issues in separate trials as urged by its proponents cannot be done under the substantive penal law.

The trial of either issue, in whatever sequence, necessitates the determination of some of the elements in the other. So that the concept itself is pregnant with notes of self-contradiction.

Examining this procedural concept which was embodied in the state statute, the highest court of Arizona, the Supreme Court of that state, analyzed and evaluated its feasibility and the history of its application in its own and in other states in State v. Shaw, 106 Ariz. 103, 471 P.2d 715.

In its well-reasoned and studied opinion, replete with citations and quotations of other cases and legal commentaries, the court sets forth the labyrinthal paths and the prestidigitation required to overcome the paradoxical conclusions to which the adoption of a bifurcated trial has led and ultimately invalidated the statute as being in violation of constitutional due process.

The basic fallacy in the concept of bifurcation is that the intent to commit the crime with which the defendant is charged is a major element in all serious criminal cases to be alleged and proven by the state. Any diminution of that intent is competent evidence which the defendant must not be precluded from presenting to the trier of facts. Thus his culpability is predicated not only upon the act that he committed, but also upon his mental state of awareness and/or responsibility at the time he committed the act. Any evidence affecting his capacity to form an intent to commit the act is indeed part of the case. So that it is patently clear that the culpability trial will necessitate the adducing of evidence bearing upon his mental responsibility in cases where an insanity defense is raised. Therefore, elements of his insanity defense will become materially relevant to determine his intent at the time he committed the act.

The adjudication of the insanity issue prior to the determination of the culpability trial would present questions of whether the defendant in fact committed the act with which he is charged. For without such a finding, the resultant adjudication of the defendant's sanity would be made without a predicate, which is the act that he committed or the corpus of the crime. And, moreover, such an adjudication, if the defendant were found insane at the time he is alleged to have committed such an act, would not be dispositive of the case. It would leave the defendant without any adjudication that he did or did not commit the act, and might very well lead to the raising of constitutional issues of due process because the effect of such adjudication might result in his being institutionalized in accordance with our proceedings. (See section 330.20 of the Criminal Procedure Law.)

Thus analyzed, such a procedure, if judicially adopted in this jurisdiction as proposed, though sounding, at first blush, as meritorious and expeditious, would not in my opinion be legally feasible under our Penal Law. It is laden with problems of due process and does not accomplish the movant's purpose of dichotomizing the stated issues in an absolute way. To duplicate the issues in a two-stage proceeding, as is done in the states that have adopted this kind of procedure by statute (California, Colorado and Texas), would only result in exacerbating the legal complexities and furthering delay in the trial of cases.

> " 'The bifurcated trial system as it now stands, still appears to be fraught with the same basic legal infirmities which accompanied it at its inception. Such infirmities cannot be cured by the application of procedural remedies' " (*State v. Shaw,* supra. 723, citing 3 Cal. West L.Rev. 159).

Accordingly, the motion for a bifurcated trial is in all respects denied.

MOTION FOR THE APPOINTMENT OF A CYTOGENETICIST

Also, as part of the insanity defense of his client, the attorney seeks the appointment of a qualified cytogeneticist to carry out the chromosomal testing of the defendant's blood at county expense. Although it is suggested that such testing is not mechanically complex and is inexpensive, the use of the results, if favorable to the insanity defense, would be offered at the trial of the action. Thus the court must determine whether or not evidence of chromosome abnormality should be admitted as a part of the defense of insanity in criminal trials.

[2] Prior to admitting evidence of a scientific nature, the court must deter-

mine the threshold question: is the scientific theory, instrument, or test sufficiently established to have gained general acceptance in the particular field to which it belongs? (*People v. Leone*, 25 N.Y.2d 511, 307 N.Y.S.2d 430, 255 N.E.2d 696, IIIA Wigmore [3d ed.] section 990, p. 992.)

The existence of the XYY genetic phenomenon was firmly established in 1961.[1] Early studies of chromosome imbalance focused almost exclusively on prison populations. The XYY male, in prison samples, appears to be a very tall, slightly retarded individual with a severely disordered personality characterized by violent, aggressive behavior.[2] However, the sampling, thus far, has been inadequate and inconclusive.[3] A built-in bias exists because samples comprised of institutionalized persons will, of course, contain more than a fair number of violent and aggressive types. The statistical significance to be attached to the results of these studies is in doubt until such time as adequate control group data can be compiled.[4] Scientists and legal commentators appear to be in agreement that further study is required to confirm the initial findings and to concretely establish a causal connection between one's genetic complement and a predisposition toward violent criminal conduct.[5]

The courts have therefore been noticeably reluctant to admit evidence of genetic abnormality as a factor to negate criminal responsibility. In Maryland, Carl Millard sought to introduce evidence of his XYY condition in his trial for armed robbery. The court excluded the evidence and held that research into the relationship between genetics, criminality, and insanity did not yet "meet reasonable medical certainty standards" necessary for its admission into evidence. The Appellate Court, affirming the order, did not find that a defense based on XYY was beyond the pale of proof, but that on the basis of the record the trial court acted properly in declining to permit the information to go to the jury (*Millard v. State*, 8 Md.App. 419, 261 A.2d 227, [1970]).

In *People v. Tanner*, 13 Cal.App.3d 596, 91 Cal.Rptr. 656, 42 A.L.R.3d. 1408 (Ct. of Apps., 2d District, Div. 3, 1970), the California intermediate appellate court upheld a lower court ruling barring admission of XYY testimony to support a defense of insanity, stating:

> "The studies of the '47 XYY individuals' undertaken to this time are few, they are rudimentary in scope, and their results are at best inconclusive." (*Supra*, 91 Cal.Rpt. p. 659, 42 A.L.R.3d p. 1412.)

Moreover, the court indicated three specific objections that precluded admission of the testimony of genetic abnormality. First, the experts merely suggested that aggressive behavior may be one manifestation of the XYY syndrome. However, they could not confirm that all XYY individuals are involuntarily aggressive; in fact, some identified XYY individuals have not exhibited such tendencies. Second, the experts could not determine whether or not the defendant's aggressive behavior even resulted from chromosome imbalance. Third, the experts were unable to state that possession of the XYY anomaly resulted in mental disease which would constitute legal insanity under California law.

The California Appellate Court considered the problem and found it an entirely proper use of discretion for the lower court to exclude evidence of an XYY condition because the evidence was "not clear and convincing." (*People v. Tanner,* 42 A.L.R.3d 1408, 1413.) The court analogized to other scientific data—i.e., voice print analysis, lie detector testing—which had likewise been denied admission because they failed to reach the necessary standards of acceptance and reliability in their field.

The objections raised in *People v. Tanner,* supra, appear to be equally valid in this jurisdiction. The Penal Law, section 30.05 states:

"1. A person is not criminally responsible for conduct if at the time of such conduct, as a result of mental disease or defect, he lacks substantial capacity to know or appreciate either:
    a. The nature and consequence of such conduct; or
    b. That such conduct was wrong."

[3] Thus, in New York an insanity defense based on chromosome abnormality should be possible only if one establishes with a high degree of medical certainty an etiological relationship between the defendant's mental capacity and the genetic syndrome. Further, the genetic imbalance must have so affected the thought processes as to interfere substantially with the defendant's cognitive capacity or with his ability to understand or appreciate the basic moral code of his society.

[4] While there is strong evidence which indicates a relationship between genetic composition and deviant behavior, the exact biological mechanism has yet to be determined. Moreover, studies have failed to indicate why only some XYY individuals appear to have propensity for violence and aggression and not others. The answers to these problems are currently being sought by scientists and their solution will assist immeasurably in providing a firmer footing for the incorporation of chromosome abnormality under the defense of insanity.

However, in New York, Judge Farrell has taken a different approach and permitted, in *People v. Farley,* Supreme Court, Queens County, Indictment Number 1827 (April 30, 1969), evidence of an XYY condition to go to the jury. The defendant's insanity defense consisted of the testimony of two witnesses. A reputable psychiatrist rendered his opinion as to the defendant's mental state at the time of the commission of the crime without regard to the chromosome imbalance of the defendant. The other witness, a medical doctor engaged in genetics research, testified that, based on recent studies in the field, inmates in penal institutions have higher incidence of chromosome imbalance and in the expert's opinion, the defendant's chromosome abnormality affected his antisocial bahavior. The jury rejected the insanity defense and found the defendant guilty of murder as charged.

Judge Farrell, writing for St. John's Law Review, indicated that "Its [the XYY syndrome] relevancy as part of an insanity defense should not be opened to serious dispute. At present, the law is geared to continuous expansion of the latitude of proof to be allowed to a defendant in such cases."[6]

In addition, a court in Australia has accepted the XYY syndrome as part of a valid insanity defense. Laurence E. Hannett was charged with murder and was acquitted after a psychiatrist testified that every cell in his body was abnormal.[7] Likewise in France, Daniel Hugon presented the XYY abnormality as a defense and the court permitted its use in mitigation of sentence.[8]

Notwithstanding the comments of and the practices followed by Judge Farrell in the trial over which he presided and the acceptance by some foreign courts of the XYY syndrome, it appears on the whole that the genetic imbalance theory of crime causation has not been satisfactorily established and accepted in either the scientific or legal communities to warrant its admission in criminal trials.

Accordingly, the motion for the appointment of a cytogeneticist is denied.

NOTES

1. Sandberg, Koepf, Ishehara and Hauschka, An XYY Human Male, 2 Lanat 488 (1961).

2. Telfer, Are Some Criminals Born That Way? N.Y.L.J., Feb. 6, 1969, p.4.

3. Note-The XYY Chromosome Defense, 57 Georgetown L.J. 892 (1968-69); Cockrell, Law Responsibility and The XYY Syndrome, 7 Houston L.Rev. 355 (1969-70); Alderman, Comment—The XYY Syndrome: Its Effects on Criminal Responsibility in New York, 21 Syracuse L.Rev. 1221 (Summer 1970); XYY Chromosomal Abnormality; Use and Misuse in the Legal Process, 9 Harv.J.Legis. 469 (March 1972).

4. See Note 3.

5. While many commentators have suggested that XYY evidence can be admitted on the limited data now available, they do agree that further study is necessary to determine how the chromosomal abnormality translates itself into aggressive conduct. See Burke, The XYY Syndrome: Genetics Behavior and the Law, 46 Denver L.J. 261 (1969); Money, Gaskin and Hull, Impulse, Aggression and Sexuality in the XYY Syndrome, 44 St. John's Law Rev. 220 (1969-70).

6. Farrell, The XYY Syndrome In Criminal Law: An Introduction, 44 St. John's L.Rev. 217, 218 (1969-70).

7. Housley, Criminal Law: The XYY Chromosome Complement and Criminal Conduct, 22 Oklahoma L.Rev. 287 (1969).

8. See note 7.

BERMAN v. ALLAN

Supreme Court of New Jersey, 1979.
80 N.J. 421, 404 A.2d 8.

The opinion of the court was delivered by

PASHMAN, J.

In *Gleitman v. Cosgrove,* 49 N.J. 22, 227 A.2d 689 (1967), decided 12 years ago, this Court refused to recognize as valid causes of action either a claim for "wrongful life" asserted on behalf of a physically deformed infant or a claim for "wrongful birth" put forth by the infant's parents. Both prayers for relief were premised upon the allegation that had the physician treating Mrs. Gleitman during her pregnancy followed standard medical practice, an abortion would have been procured and the child would never have come into existence. In this case, we are called upon to assess the continued validity of both of our holdings in *Gleitman.*

On September 11, 1975, Paul and Shirley Berman, suing both in their own names and as Guardians *ad litem* for their infant daughter Sharon, instituted the present malpractice action against Ronald Allan and Michael Attardi, medical doctors licensed by the State of New Jersey. Two causes of action were alleged. The first, a claim for damages based upon "wrongful life," was asserted by Mr. Berman on behalf of the infant Sharon. The second, a claim denominated "wrongful birth," sought compensation for injuries suffered by the parents in their own right.

The factual allegations underlying each of these prayers for relief can be briefly summarized. From February 19 until November 3, 1974, Mrs. Berman, while pregnant with Sharon, was under the care and supervision of Drs. Allan and Attardi, both of whom are specialists in gynecology and obstetrics. At the time of her pregnancy, Mrs. Berman was 38 years of age. On November 3, Sharon was born afflicted with Down's Syndrome—a genetic defect commonly referred to as mongolism.

Plaintiffs allege that defendants deviated from accepted medical standards by failing to inform Mrs. Berman during her pregnancy of the existence of a procedure known as amniocentesis. This procedure involves the insertion of a long needle into a mother's uterus and the removal therefrom of a sample of amniotic fluid containing living fetal cells. Through "karyotype analysis"—a procedure in which the number and structure of the cells' chromosomes are examined—the sex of the fetus as well as the presence of gross chromosomal defects can be detected. See W.

Fuhrmann & F. Vogel, *Genetic Counseling* 91–94 (2d Ed. 1976); A. Emery, *Elements of Medical Genetics* 54–59 (3d Ed. 1974); Note, "Father and Mother Know Best: Defining the Liability of Physicians for Inadequate Genetic Counseling," 87 *Yale L. J.* 1488, 1493 & n. 21 (1978). Prenatal diagnosis of genetic abnormalities is potentially available for approximately 60 to 90 metabolic defects, including Tay-Sachs Disease and Down's Syndrome. See Milunsky, "Prenatal Diagnosis of Genetic Disorders," 295 *NewEng.J.Med.* 377 (1976); Golbus, "The Antenatal Detection of Genetic Disorders," 48 *Obstetrics & Gynecology* 497 (1976). Recent studies indicate that amniocentesis is highly accurate in predicting the presence of chromosomal defects, and that the risk of even minor damage to mother or fetus deriving from the procedure is less than one percent. See NICHD National Registry of Amniocentesis Study Group, "Midtrimester Amniocentesis for Prenatal Diagnosis," 236 *J.Am.Med.A.* 1471 (1976) (99.4% accuracy in 1,040 cases); Simpson, Dallaire, Miller, Siminovich, Hamerton, Miller & McKeen, "Prenatal Diagnosis of Genetic Disease in Canada," 115 *Canadian Med.A.J.* 739 (1976) (99.4% accuracy in 1,223 cases).

Due to Mrs. Berman's age at the time of her conception, plaintiffs contend that the risk that her child, if born, would be afflicted with Down's Syndrome was sufficiently great that sound medical practice at the time of pregnancy required defendants to inform her both of this risk and the availability of amniocentesis as a method of determining whether in her particular case that risk would come to fruition. Had defendants so informed Mrs. Berman, the complaint continues, she would have submitted to the amniocentesis procedure, discovered that the child, if born, would suffer from Down's Syndrome, and had the fetus aborted.

As a result of defendants' alleged negligence, the infant Sharon, through her Guardian *ad litem* seeks compensation for the physical and emotional pain and suffering which she will endure throughout life because of her mongoloid condition. Mr. and Mrs. Berman, the child's parents, request damages in their own right both for the emotional anguish which they have experienced and will continue to experience on account of Sharon's birth defect, and the medical and other costs which they will incur in order to properly raise, educate and supervise the child.

On November 4, 1977, the trial judge granted summary judgment in favor of defendants on the ground that plaintiffs had failed to state any actionable claim for relief. In his view, *Gleitman v. Cosgrove, supra,* was dispositive of the issues presented. On December 22, 1977, plaintiffs filed a notice of appeal to the Appellate Division. While the matter was pending before the appellate judges, we directly certified the case to this Court on our own motion. See R. 2:12–1.

I

Before addressing the merits of the various contentions put forth by the parties, it is important to emphasize the procedural posture in which the present controversy reaches us. Plaintiffs' complaint was dismissed before trial for failure to state a valid cause of action. As such, we must accept as true each and every element of that complaint and construe all reasonable inferences flowing from plaintiffs' allegations in a light most favorable to their cause. See, *e.g., Heavner v. Uniroyal, Inc.* 63 N.J. 130, 133–134, 305 A.2d 412 (1973); *Melone v. Jersey Central Power & Light Co.*, 18 N.J. 163, 170, 113 A.2d 13 (1955).

Specifically, we must assume that at the time of pregnancy: (1) defendants failed to inform Mrs. Berman of the availability of amniocentesis; (2) this failure to inform constituted a departure from acceptable medical practice; (3) had she been informed, Mrs. Berman would have submitted to amniocentesis; (4) the results of the procedure would have indicated that the child, if born, would be afflicted with Down's Syndrome; and (5) upon being notified of this fact, she would have had the fetus aborted. Our sole inquiry is whether any or all plaintiffs would be entitled to damages should they substantiate each of the above allegations at trial.

II

The claim for damages asserted on behalf of the infant Sharon has aptly been labeled a cause of action grounded upon "wrongful life." Sharon does not contend that absent defendants' negligence she would have come into the world in a normal and healthy state. There is no suggestion in either the pleadings below or the medical literature which we have scrutinized that any therapy could have been prescribed which would have decreased the risk that, upon birth, Sharon would suffer from Down's Syndrome. Rather, the gist of the infant's complaint is that had defendants informed her mother of the availability of amniocentesis, Sharon would never have come into existence.

As such, this case presents issues different from those involved in malpractice actions where a plaintiff asserts that a defendant's deviation from sound medical practices *increased* the probability that an infant would be born with defects. See, e.g., *Sylvia v. Gobeille,* 101 R.I. 76, 220 A.2d 222 (1966). Nor are we here confronted with a situation in which an individual's negligence while a child was in gestation caused what otherwise would have been a normal and healthy child to come into the world in an impaired condition. See, e. g., *Smith v. Grennan,* 31 N.J. 353, 157 A.2d 497 (1960); W. Prosser, *Law of Torts* § 55 at 335–338 (4th Ed. 1971). Here, defendants' alleged negligence neither caused the mongoloid condition nor increased the risk that such a condition would occur. In the words of the *Gleitman* majority, "the infant plaintiff [asserts] . . . not that [she] should not have been born without defects but [rather] that [she] should not have been born at all. . . ." 49 N.J. at 28, 227 A.2d at 692. In essence, Sharon claims that her very life is "wrongful."

The *Gleitman* majority refused to recognize as valid a cause of action predicated upon wrongful life. Its main reason for so holding was that damages would be impossible to ascertain. See 49 N.J. at 28–29, 227 A.2d 689; id. at 63 (Weintraub, C. J., concurring and dissenting).

The primary purpose of tort law is that of compensating plaintiffs for the injuries that they have suffered wrongfully at the hands of others. As such, damages are ordinarily computed by "comparing the condition plaintiff would have been in, had the defendants not been negligent, with plaintiff's impaired condition as a result of the negligence." Id. at 28, 227 A.2d at 692; see generally, W. Prosser, *Supra,*

§ 55 at 335–338; Note, "Wrongful Life and A Fundamental Right to be Born Healthy," 27 *Buffalo L.Rev.* 537, 555–559 (1978). In the case of a claim predicated upon wrongful life, such a computation would require the trier of fact to measure the difference in value between life in an impaired condition and the "utter void of nonexistence." *Gleitman, supra,* 49 N.J. at 28, 227 A.2d 689. Such an endeavor, however, is literally impossible. As Chief Justice Weintraub noted, man, "who knows nothing of death or nothingness," simply cannot affix a price tag to non-life. Id. at 63 (Weintraub, C. J., concurring & dissenting). See, e.g., *Gildiner v. Thomas Jefferson Univ. Hospital,* 451 F.Supp. 692, 694 (E.D.Pa.1978); *Elliot v. Brown,* 361 So.2d 546, 547–549 (Ala.Sup.Ct. 1978); *Stills v. Gratton,* 55 Cal.App.3d 698, 127 Cal.Rptr. 652, 656–657 (Dist.Ct.App. 1976); *Becker v. Schwartz,* 46 N.Y.2d 401, 413, N.Y.S.2d 895, 386 N.E.2d 807 (Ct.App. 1978); *Dumer v. St. Michael's Hospital,* 69 Wis.2d 766, 233 N.W.2d 372, 375–376 (Sup.Ct.1975); Note, "Toward Rational Boundaries of Tort Liability for Injury to the Unborn: Prenatal Injuries, Preconception Injuries and Wrongful Life," 1978 *Duke Law Journal,* 1401, 1445. See generally, Note, *supra,* 27 *Buffalo L.Rev.* at 555–559.

Nevertheless, although relevant to our determination we would be extremely reluctant today to deny the validity of Sharon's complaint solely because damages are difficult to ascertain. The courts of this and other jurisdictions have long held that where a wrong itself is of such a nature as to preclude the computation of damages with precise exactitude, it would be a "perversion of fundamental principles of justice to deny all relief to the injured [party], and thereby relieve the wrongdoer from making any amend for his acts." *Story Parchment Co. v. Paterson Parchment Paper Co.,* 282 U.S. 555, 563, 51 S.Ct. 248, 250, 75 L.Ed. 544, 548 (1931); see, e. g., *Martin v. Bengue, Inc.,* 25 N.J. 359, 373, 136 A.2d 626 (1957); *Jenkins v. Pennsylvania R.R. Co.,* 67 N.J.L. 331, 334, 51 A. 704 (E. & A. 1902). To be sure, damages may not be determined by mere speculation or guess and, as defendants emphasize, placing value upon non-life is not simply difficult—it is humanly impossible. Nonetheless, were the measure of damages our sole concern, it is possible that some judicial remedy could be fashioned which would redress plaintiff, if only in part, for injuries suffered. See, e. g., Kashi, "The Case of the Unwanted Blessing: Wrongful Life," 31 *U.Miami L.Rev.* 1409 (1977); Note, "A Cause of Action for 'Wrongful Life,' " 55 *Minn.L.Rev.* 58 (1970).

[1] Difficulty in the measure of damages is not, however, our sole or even primary concern. Although we conclude, as did the *Gleitman* majority, that Sharon has failed to state an actionable claim for relief, we base our result upon a different premise—that Sharon has not suffered any damage cognizable at law by being brought into existence. See, e. g., *Becker v. Schwartz, supra,* 46 N.Y.2d at 411, 413 N.Y.S.2d at 900, 386, N.E.2d at 812; Note, *supra,* 87 *Yale L. J.* at 1500–1502.

One of the most deeply held beliefs of our society is that life—whether experienced with or without a major physical handicap—is more precious than non-life. See *In re Quinlan,* 70 N.J. 10, 19, & n. 1, 335 A.2d 647 (1976). Concrete manifestations of this belief are not difficult to discover. The documents which set forth the principles upon which our society is founded are replete with references to the sanctity of life. The federal constitution characterizes life as one of three fundamental rights of which no man can be deprived without due process of law. *U.S.*

Const., Amends. V and XIV. Our own state constitution proclaims that "enjoying and defending [of] life" is a natural right. *N.J. Const.* (1947), Art. I, § 1. The Declaration of Independence states that the primacy of man's "unalienable" right to life is a "self-evident truth." Nowhere in these documents is there to be found an indication that the lives of persons suffering from physical handicaps are to be less cherished than those of non-handicapped human beings.

State legislatures—and thus the people as a whole—have universally reserved the most severe criminal penalties for individuals who have unjustifiably deprived others of life. Indeed, so valued is this commodity that even one who has committed first degree murder cannot be sentenced to death unless he is accorded special procedural protections in addition to those given all criminal defendants. See, e. g., *Furman v. Georgia,* 408 U.S. 238, 92 S.Ct. 2726, 33 L.Ed.2d 346 (1972). Moreover, it appears that execution is constitutionally impermissible unless the crime which a defendant has perpetrated was one which involved the taking of another's life. See *Coker v. Georgia*, 433 U.S. 584, 592, 97 S.Ct. 2861, 2866, 53 L.Ed. 2d 982, 989 (1977). Again, these procedural protections and penalties do not vary according to the presence or absence of physical deformities in the victim or defendant. It is life itself that is jealously safeguarded, not life in a perfect state.

Finally, we would be remiss if we did not take judicial notice of the high esteem which our society accords to those involved in the medical profession. The reason for this is clear. Physicians are the preservers of life.

No man is perfect. Each of us suffers from some ailments or defects, whether major or minor, which make impossible participation in all the activities the world has to offer. But our lives are not thereby rendered less precious than those of others whose defects are less pervasive or less severe.

We recognize that as a mongoloid child, Sharon's abilities will be more circumscribed than those of normal, healthy children and that she, unlike them, will experience a great deal of physical and emotional pain and anguish. We sympathize with her plight. We cannot, however, say that she would have been better off had she never been brought into the world. Notwithstanding her affliction with Down's Syndrome, Sharon, by virtue of her birth, will be able to love and be loved and to experience happiness and pleasure—emotions which are truly the essence of life and which are far more valuable than the suffering she may endure. To rule otherwise would require us to disavow the basic assumption upon which our society is based. This we cannot do.

Accordingly, we hold that Sharon has failed to state a valid cause of action founded upon "wrongful life."

III

The validity of the parents' claim for relief calls into play considerations different from those involved in the infant's complaint. As in the case of the infant, Mr. and Mrs. Berman do not assert that defendants increased the risk that Sharon, if born, would be afflicted with Down's Syndrome. Rather, at bottom, they allege that they were tortiously injured because Mrs. Berman was deprived of the option of making a meaningful decision as to whether to abort the fetus, see *Gleitman, supra* 49 N.J. at 63–65, 227 A.2d 689 (Weintraub, C.J., concurring & dissenting)— a decision which, at least during the first trimester of pregnancy, is not subject to state interference, see *Roe v. Wade,* 410 U.S. 113, 93 S.Ct. 705, 35 L.Ed.2d 147 (1973). They thus claim that Sharon's "birth"—as opposed to her "life"—was wrongful.

Two items of damage are requested in order to redress this allegedly tortious injury: (1) the medical and other costs that will be incurred in order to properly raise, supervise and educate the child; and (2) compensation for the emotional anguish that has been and will continue to be experienced on account of Sharon's condition.

The *Gleitman* majority refused to recognize as valid a cause of action grounded upon wrongful birth. Two reasons underlay its determination. The first related to measure of damages should such a claim be allowed. In its view,

> In order to determine [the parents'] compensatory damages a court would have to evaluate the denial to them of the intangible, unmeasurable, and complex human benefits of motherhood and fatherhood and weigh these against the alleged emotional and money injuries. Such a proposed weighing is . . . impossible to perform. . . . [49 N.J. at 29, 227 A.2d at 693]

Second, even though the Court's opinion was premised upon the assumption that Mrs. Gleitman could have legally secured an abortion, the majority concluded that "substantial [public] policy reasons" precluded the judicial allowance of tort damages "for the denial of the opportunity to take an embryonic life." 49 N.J. at 30, 227A.2d at 693.

[2] In light of changes in the law which have occurred in the 12 years since *Gleitman* was decided, the second ground relied upon by the *Gleitman* majority can no longer stand in the way of judicial recognition of a cause of action founded upon wrongful birth. The Supreme Court's ruling in *Roe v. Wade, supra,* clearly establishes that a woman possesses a constitutional right to decide whether her fetus should be aborted, at least during the first trimester of pregnancy. Public policy now supports, rather than militates against, the proposition that she not be impermissibly denied a meaningful opportunity to make that decision.

As in all other cases of tortious injury, a physician whose negligence has deprived a mother of this opportunity should be required to make amends for the damage which he has proximately caused. Any other ruling would in effect immunize from liability those in the medical field providing inadequate guidance to persons who would choose to exercise their constitutional right to abort fetuses which, if born, would suffer from genetic defects. See Note, *supra* 87 *Yale L.J.* at 1504–1508; see, e. g., *Gildiner, supra,* 451 F.Supp. at 696; *Dumer, supra,* 233 N.W.2d at 376–377; *Jacobs v. Theimer,* 519 S.W.2d 846, 849 (Sup.Ct. Tex. 1975). See generally, Note, "Wrongful Conception: Who Pays for Bringing Up the Baby?," 47 *Fordham, L.Rev.* 418, 419–422 (1978). Accordingly, we hold that a cause of action founded upon wrongful birth is a legally cognizable claim.

[3] Troublesome, however, is the measure of damages. As noted earlier, the first item sought to be recompensed is the medical and other expenses that will be incurred in order to properly raise, educate and supervise the child. Although these costs were "caused" by defendants' negligence in the sense that but for the failure to inform, the child would not have come into existence, we conclude that this item of damage should not be recoverable. In essence, Mr. and Mrs. Berman desire to retain all the benefits inhering in the birth of the child—i.e., the love and joy they will experience as parents—while saddling defendants with the enormous expenses attendant upon her rearing. Under the facts and circumstances here alleged, we find that such an award would be wholly disproportionate to the culpability involved, and that allowance of such a recovery would both constitute a windfall to the parents and place too unreasonable a financial burden upon physicians. See e.g., *Rieck v. Medical Protective Co.,* 64 Wis.2d 514, 219 N.W.2d 242, 244–245 (Sup.Ct. 1974); *Coleman v. Garrison,* 349 A.2d 8 (Sup.Ct.Del. 1975).

[4] The parents' claim for emotional damages stands upon a different footing. In failing to inform Mrs. Berman of the availability of amniocentesis, defendants directly deprived her—and, derivatively, her husband—of the option to accept or reject a parental relationship with the child and thus caused them to experience mental and emotional anguish upon their realization that they had given birth to a child afflicted with Down's Syndrome. See generally, note, *supra,* 1978 *Duke Law Journal* at 1453. We feel that the monetary equivalent of this distress is an appropriate measure of the harm suffered by the parents deriving from Mrs. Berman's loss of her right to abort the fetus. See *Gleitman, supra* 49 N.J. at 64–65, 227 A.2d 689 (Weintraub, C. J., concurring & dissenting).

Unlike the *Gleitman* majority, we do not feel that placing a monetary value upon the emotional suffering that Mr. and Mrs. Berman have and will continue to experience is an impossible task for the trier of fact. In the 12 years that have elapsed since *Gleitman* was decided, courts have come to recognize that mental and emotional distress is just as "real" as physical pain, and that its valuation is no more difficult. Consequently, damages for such distress have been ruled allowable in an increasing number of contexts. See, e. g., *Zahorian v. Russell Fitt Real Estate Agency,* 62 N.J. 399, 301 A.2d 754 (1973); *Falzone v. Busch,* 45 N.J. 559, 214 A.2d 12 (1965); *Muniz v. United Hospitals Medical Center Presbyterian Hospital,* 153 N.J.Super. 79, 379 A.2d 57 (App.Div.1977); *Lemaldi v. DeTomaso of America, Inc.,* 156 N.J.Super. 441, 383, A.2d 1220 (Law Div.1978); *W. Prosser, Law of Torts* § 54 at 327–335 (4th Ed. 1971). Moreover, as discussed in Part II ante, to deny Mr. and Mrs. Berman redress for their injuries merely because damages cannot be measured with precise exactitude would constitute a perversion of fundamental principles of justice. See *supra* at 428.

Consequently, we hold that Mr. and Mrs. Berman have stated actionable claims for relief. Should their allegations be proven at trial, they are entitled to be recompensed for the mental and emotional anguish they have suffered and will continue to suffer on account of Sharon's condition.

Accordingly, the judgment of the trial court is affirmed in part and reversed in part, and this case remanded for a plenary trial.

For affirmance as to the infant and reversal and remandment as to the parents: Chief Justice HUGHES and Justices MOUNTAIN, SULLIVAN, PASHMAN, CLIFFORD and SCHREIBER—6.

For reversal as to the infant and reversal and remandment as to the parents: Justice HANDLER—1.

HANDLER, J., concurring in part and dissenting in part.

We are called upon in this medical malpractice lawsuit to revisit the sensitive and perplexing problems engendered by the birth of a congenitally defective child and the suffering of its parents, aggrieved by the medical doctors who negligently failed to forewarn them of their misfortune. The Court wrestled with these questions some years ago in *Gleitman v. Cosgrove*, 49 N.J. 22, 227 A.2d 689 (1967) and a majority ruled that neither the parents nor the handicapped child had a sustainable cause of action for injuries, there being no claim that the malpractice in any way caused the birth defects of the child. Today we overrule that decision, at least in part.

The Court now recognizes that the parents of the impaired child have a cause of action for the doctors' breach of duty to render competent medical advice and services and that they are entitled to compensation for their mental and emotional suffering over the birth of their damaged child. I agree with this. However, I hold to a somewhat broader view of mental and emotional injury in these circumstances and would also include as an element of these damages impaired parenthood or parental capacity.

The Court does not, in its opinion, recognize as sustainable a cause of action on behalf of the child. On this, I differ. The child, in my view, was owed directly, during its gestation, a duty of reasonable care from the same physicians who undertook to care for its mother—then expectant—and that duty, to render complete and competent medical advice, was seriously breached. The child, concededly, did not become defective because of the physicians' dereliction; nevertheless, it suffered a form of injury or loss in having been born of parents whose parental capacity may have been substantially diminished by the negligence of their doctors. This is a loss to the child which should be recompensed. For these reasons I concur in part and dissent in part from the opinion of the Court.

I

It is important to have a clear picture of the claims which are asserted on behalf of the respective plaintiffs. Since the matter comes before the Court on the dismissal of plaintiffs' complaint for failure to state a cause of action, R. 4:6–2(e), the allegations of the complaint are to be accepted as true. These assertions, as pointed out by the Court, are that the defendant doctors were guilty of medical malpractice in failing to advise Mrs. Berman of the availability of amniocentesis, a procedure which would have revealed the defective condition of the unborn child and the certainty of its birth with Down's Syndrome; Mrs. Berman would have had the amniocentesis test administered and, upon learning that she was bearing a mongoloid child, she would have had an abortion to terminate her pregnancy; hence, the birth of her impaired child came about as a result of her physicians' medical negligence. *Ante* at 425-26. While these allegations are to be considered as true, I would not treat them as self-limiting. It is important to remember that the record in this case became fixed on the close of the pleadings, a very early, and perhaps, premature stage of the litigation. If the case were to take a normal course, including discovery, as well it might upon remand, plaintiffs would have the opportunity to clarify or amplify their claim. R. 4:9-1 to –4. The proofs, whether on plaintiffs' or defendants' case, might show that Mrs. Berman, instead of obtaining an abortion, would have elected to give birth to her child. In either event a tortious wrong has occurred and this should not affect the plaintiffs' claim for compensation. Moreover, with respect to such claims, particularly in light of our opinions, e. g. *ante* at 430-31, plaintiffs should be able to seek to establish that mental and emotional suffering involves moral strife and includes the element of impaired parenthood and, further, that the child has a legitimate injury claim in the nature of a diminished childhood. I would approach the issues in the case from this wider perspective.

II

The Court recognizes a valid cause of action on behalf of the parents for the "wrongful birth" of their child. It does so by repudiating the sufficiency of the reasons which earlier persuaded this Court in *Gleitman* to disallow such a claim. *Ante* at 431–32. Certainly the premise of our first decision, that a woman bearing a child with a birth defect could not in the earliest stages of pregnancy legally secure an abortion, is no longer tenable. The legal barriers to early abortion have been dropped. *Roe v. Wade*, 410 U.S. 113, 93 S.Ct. 705, 35 L.Ed.2d 147, reh. den. 410 U.S. 959, 93 S.Ct. 1409, 35 L.Ed.2d 694 (1973). These matters are no longer simply the prerogative of government. Individual rights of personal autonomy in this area are now accorded full weight. Public policy and social conscience no longer dictate judicial blindness and inaction with respect to the plight of a woman who has wrongfully been denied the opportunity to determine her destiny in whether or not to give birth to a gravely handicapped infant. Tribe, "Forward: Toward a Model of Roles in the Due Process of Life and Law", 87 *Harv.L.Rev.* 1 (1973); G. Gunther, *Cases and Materials on Constitutional Law* (9th ed. 1975) ch. 9, § 3, pp. 651–652; Sneideman, "Abortion: A Public Health and Social Policy Perspective," 7 N.Y.U.Rev.L. & Soc. Change 187, 201–202 (1978).

Other sound reasons are also advanced in support of a sustainable cause of action which touch upon the corrective purposes of the law of torts. Doctors would not be discouraged from malpractice if the claims of their wronged patients were disallowed. Also, to bar a claim for this kind of serious medical negligence would be tantamount to conferring immunity upon doctors from liability for their wrongful conduct. *Ante* at 432.

We have further determined that recovery for the wrong should not be stifled because the measure of damages may be troublesome. *Ante* at 432. The Court properly holds that damages should include "the monetary equivalent" of the emotional distress the parents experienced in giving birth to the defective child, "deriving from Mrs. Berman's loss of her right to abort the fetus. See *Gleitman, supra,* 49 N.J. at 64–65, 227 A.2d 689 (Weintraub, C. J., concurring and dissenting)." *Ante* at 433. It is to be recognized, however, that the measurement of damages for nonphysical injury is at best elusive and complex. Particularly in this kind of case, where these injuries stand alone and flow from the special relationship between an afflicted child and its parents, should care be taken in identifying compensable losses.

Approaches are suggested by a generous body of precedent. Our courts have long approved the award of damages for mental or emotional suffering resulting from tortious conduct. See e. g., *Morris v. MacNab,* 25 N.J. 271, 135 A.2d 657 (1957); *Allen v. Camden and Philadelphia Ferry Co.,* 46 N.J.L. 198 (E. & A. 1884); *Muniz v. United Hsps. Med. Ctr. Pres. Hsp.* 153 N.J.Super. 79, 379 A.2d 57 (App. Div.1977); *Kuzma v. Millinery Workers, etc., Local 24,* 27 N.J.Super. 579, 99 A.2d 833 (App.Div.1953); *Spiegel v. Evergreen Cemetery Co.,* 117 N.J.L. 90, 186 A. 585 (Sup.Ct.1936); *Harris v. D., L. & W.R.R. Co.,* 77 N.J.L. 278, 72 A. 50 (Sup.Ct.1909), aff'd on appeal from remand, 82 N.J.L. 456, 82 A. 881 (E. & A. 1912). *Cf. Falzone v. Busch,* 45 N.J.L. 559, 214 A.2d 12 (1965). Such damages have also been essayed, at least on the trial level, in breach of contract warranty actions. See, *Lemaldi v. DeTomasso of America, Inc.,* 156 N.J.Super. 441, 383 A.2d 1220 (Law Div.1978), *cf. Fiore v. Sears, Roebuck & Co.,* 144 N.J.Super. 74, 364 A.2d 572 (Law Div.1976). Humiliation damages for the indignities inflicted by acts of invidious discriminaton have been approved in the civil rights area. *Zahorian v. Russell Fitt Real Estate Agency,* 62 N.J. 399, 301 A.2d 754 (1973); *Harvard v. Bushberg Bros.,* 137 *N.J.Super.* 537, 350 A.2d 65 (App.Div.1975), certif. granted 71 N.J. 493, 366 A.2d 649 (1976) (dismissed by stipulation); *Gray v. Serruto Builders, Inc.,* 110 *N.J.Super.* 297, 265 A.2d 404 (Ch.Div. 1970); cf. *Castellano v. Linden Board of Education,* 79 N.J. 407, 416, 400 A.2d 1182 (1978) (Handler, J., concurring in part and dissenting in part). Also see *W. Prosser, Law of Torts* § 12, pp. 49–62 (4th ed. 1971); 1 *J. Dooley, Modern Tort Law* § 15.01–15.13 (1977). Damages have also been allowed for the psychic injury to a mother resulting from an actual or anticipated tragic birth produced by negligent conduct. See e. g., *Graf v. Taggert,* 43 N.J. 303, 204 A.2d 140 (1964) (plaintiff could not recover for death of unborn child *en ventre sa mere* but could recover for emotional upset accompanying stillbirth); *Carter v. Public Service Coord. Transport,* 47 N.J.Super. 379, 136 A.2d 15 (App.Div.1957) (pregnant plaintiff entitled to damages for anxiety over possible loss of unborn child). A trial court has recognized the reality of pain and suffering of a mother over the welfare of a child and that this anguish can endure for a period of time after the birth of the child. E. g., *Friel v. Vineland Obst. and Gynecological Professional Assoc.,* 166 N.J.Super. 579, 400 A.2d 147 (Law Div.1979) (damages may be awarded for anxiety and shock as well as the uncertainty as to child's normality during formative years as a result of negligently caused premature birth).

Without dobut, expectant parents, kept in ignorance of severe and permanent defects affecting their unborn child, suffer greatly when the awful truth dawns upon them with the birth of the child. Human experience has told each of us, personally or vicariously, something of this anguish. Parents of such a child experience a welter of negative feelings—bewilderment, guilt, remorse and anguish—as well as anger, depression and despair. Griffin, Kavanagh & Sorenson, "Genetic Knowledge, Client Perspectives, and Genetic Counselling", 2 *Soc. Work in Health Care* 171, 174–175 (1976–77); also Faleck & Britton, "Phases in Coping: The Hypothesis and Its Implications", 21 *Soc. Biology* 1 (1974). When such a tragedy comes without warning these terrible emotions are bound to be felt even more deeply. "Novelty shock" may well exacerbate the suffering. Wolfensberger & Menolascino, "A Theoretical Framework for the Management of Parents of the Mentally Retarded", *Psychiatric Approaches to Mental Retardation* 475 (Menolascino ed. 1970); Sammons, "Ethical Issues in Genetic Intervention", 23 *Soc. Work* 237, 238 (1978). This, I believe, is the crux of the wrong done in this case. Through the failure of the doctors to advise an expectant mother, and father, of the likelihood or certainty of the birth of a mongoloid child, the parents were given no opportunity to cushion the blow, mute the hurt, or prepare themselves as parents for the birth of their seriously impaired child. Their injury is real and palpable. *Cf. Graf v. Taggert, supra.* Moreover, it is not easy to overcome these feelings or adjust to the tragedy of having a defective child. It is recognized that a mother, even in normal circumstances, may suffer depressive and negative feelings upon the birth of a healthy child. If her psychological state has been further impaired by the shock of the birth of a defective child her recovery may well be even more prolonged and dubious. Olshansky, "Chronic Sorrow: A Response to Having a Mentally Defective Child", 43 *Soc. Casework* 171, 192 (1962); Griffin, Kavanagh & Sorenson, "Genetic Knowledge, Client Perspectives, and Genetic Counselling", *supra* at 175. In any given case, the mental and emotional suffering of parents might continue for some period of time beyond the birth of a child and should be recognized as an important aspect of the parents' injury. *Cf. Friel v. Vineland Obst. and Gynecological Professional Assoc. supra.*

Because of the unique nature of the tort, involving as it does the denial of the opportunity to decide whether to become the parents of a handicapped child, the suffering of the parents assumes another, important dimension. There should be recognized in the stressful setting of this case the reality of moral injury. Such injury may be thought of as deprivation of moral initiative and ethical choice. *Cf. Gleitman v. Cosgrove, supra* 49 N.J. at 64–65, 227 A.2d 689 (Weintraub, C.J., concurring and dissenting). Persons confronted with the awesome decision of whether or not to allow the birth of a defective child, face a moral dilemma of enormous consequence. They deal with a profound moral problem. See e. g., Engelhardt, "The Ontology of Abortion", 84 *Ethics* 217 (1974); Newton, Humans and Persons. A Reply to Tristain Englehardt", 84 *Ethics* 332 (1975). To be denied the opportunity—indeed, the right— to apply one's own moral values in reaching that decision, is a serious, irreversible wrong. *Cf. In re Quinlan*, 70 N.J. 10, 355 A.2d 647 (1976). Shorn of ethical choice in bringing into the world a defective human being, some individuals will be torn by moral conflict. Moral suffering in this sense may be felt keenly by a person who, as a matter of personal conscience,